The Banquet of the Brethren

The Institute of Ismaili Studies

Ismaili Texts and Translations Series, 27

Previously published titles:

1. Ibn al-Haytham. *The Advent of the Fatimids: A Contemporary Shi'i Witness*. An edition and English translation of Ibn al-Haytham's *Kitāb al-Munāẓarāt*, by Wilferd Madelung and Paul E. Walker (2000).
2. Muḥammad b. 'Abd al-Karīm al-Shahrastānī. *Struggling with the Philosopher: A Refutation of Avicenna's Metaphysics*. A new Arabic edition and English translation of al-Shahrastānī's *Kitāb al-Muṣāra'a*, by Wilferd Madelung and Toby Mayer (2001).
3. Ja'far b. Manṣūr al-Yaman. *The Master and the Disciple: An Early Islamic Spiritual Dialogue*. Arabic edition and English translation of Ja'far b. Manṣūr al-Yaman's *Kitāb al-'Ālim wa'l-ghulām*, by James W. Morris (2001).
4. Idrīs 'Imād al-Dīn. *The Fatimids and their Successors in Yaman: The History of an Islamic Community*. Arabic edition and English summary of Idrīs 'Imād al-Dīn's *'Uyūn al-akhbār*, vol. 7, by Ayman Fu'ad Sayyid, in collaboration with Paul E. Walker and Maurice A. Pomerantz (2002).
5. Naṣīr al-Dīn Ṭūsī. *Paradise of Submission: A Medieval Treatise on Ismaili Thought*. A new Persian edition and English translation of Naṣīr al-Dīn Ṭūsī's *Rawḍa-yi taslīm*, by S. J. Badakhchani with an

introduction by Hermann Landolt and a philosophical commentary by Christian Jambet (2005).

6. al-Qāḍī al-Nuʿmān. *Founding the Fatimid State: The Rise of an Early Islamic Empire*. An annotated English translation of al-Qāḍī al-Nuʿmān's *Iftitāḥ al-daʿwa*, by Hamid Haji (2006).
7. Idrīs ʿImād al-Dīn. *ʿUyūn al-akhbār wa-funūn al-āthār*. Arabic critical edition in 7 volumes by Ahmad Chleilat, Mahmoud Fakhoury, Yousef S. Fattoum, Muhammad Kamal, Maʾmoun al-Sagherji and Ayman Fuʾad Sayyid (2007–2014).
8. Aḥmad b. Ibrāhīm al-Naysābūrī. *Degrees of Excellence: A Fatimid Treatise on Leadership in Islam*. A New Arabic Edition and English Translation of al-Naysābūrī's *Ithbāt al-imāma*, by Arzina Lalani (2009).
9. Ḥamīd al-Dīn Aḥmad b. ʿAbd Allāh al-Kirmānī. *Master of the Age: An Islamic Treatise on the Necessity of the Imamate*. A critical edition of the Arabic text and English translation of Ḥamīd al-Dīn Aḥmad b. ʿAbd Allāh al-Kirmānī's *al-Maṣābīḥ fī ithbāt al-imāma*, by Paul E. Walker (2007).
10. *Orations of the Fatimid Caliphs: Festival Sermons of the Ismaili Imams*. An edition of the Arabic texts and English translation of Fatimid *khuṭbas*, by Paul E. Walker (2009).
11. Taqī al-Dīn Aḥmad b. ʿAlī al-Maqrīzī. *Towards a Shiʿi Mediterranean Empire: Fatimid Egypt and the Founding of Cairo*. The reign of the Imam-caliph al-Muʿizz, from al-Maqrīzī's *Ittiʿāẓ al-ḥunafāʾ bi-akhbār al-aʾimma al-Fāṭimiyyīn al-khulafāʾ*, translated by Shainool Jiwa (2009).
12. Taqī al-Dīn Aḥmad b. ʿAlī al-Maqrīzī. *Ittiʿāẓ al-ḥunafāʾ bi-akhbār al-aʾimma al-Fāṭimiyyīn al-khulafāʾ*. Arabic critical edition in 4 volumes, with an introduction and notes by Ayman F. Sayyid (2010).
13. Naṣīr al-Dīn Ṭūsī. *Shiʿi Interpretations of Islam: Three Treatises on Theology and Eschatology*. A Persian edition and English

translation of Naṣīr al-Dīn Ṭūsī's *Tawallā wa tabarrā, Maṭlūb al-muʾminīn and Āghāz wa anjām*, by S. J. Badakhchani (2010).

14. al-Muʾayyad al-Shīrāzī. *Mount of Knowledge, Sword of Eloquence: Collected Poems of an Ismaili Muslim Scholar in Fatimid Egypt*. A translation from the original Arabic of al-Muʾayyad al-Shīrāzī's *Dīwān*, translated by Mohamed Adra (2011).
15. Aḥmad b. Ibrāhīm al-Naysābūrī. *A Code of Conduct: A Treatise on the Etiquette of the Fatimid Ismaili Mission*. A critical Arabic edition and English translation of Aḥmad b. Ibrāhīm al-Naysābūrī's *Risāla al-mūjaza al-kāfiya fī ādāb al-duʿāt*, by Verena Klemm and Paul E. Walker with Susanne Karam (2011).
16. Manṣūr al-ʿAzīzī al-Jawdharī. *Inside the Immaculate Portal: A History from Early Fatimid Archives*. A new edition and English translation of Manṣūr al-ʿAzīzī al-Jawdharī's biography of al-Ustādh Jawdhar, the *Sīrat al-Ustādh Jawdhar*, edited and translated by Hamid Haji (2012).
17. Nāṣir-i Khusraw. *Between Reason and Revelation: Twin Wisdoms Reconciled*. An annotated English translation of Nāṣir-i Khusraw's *Kitāb-i Jāmiʿ al-ḥikmatayn*, translated by Eric Ormsby (2012).
18. al-Qāḍī al-Nuʿmān. *The Early History of Ismaili Jurisprudence: Law and Society under the Fatimids*. An Arabic edition and English translation of al-Qāḍī al-Nuʿmān's *Kitāb minhāj al-farāʾid*, edited and translated by Agostino Cilardo (2012).
19. Ḥātim b. Ibrāhīm al-Ḥāmidī. *The Precious Gift of the Hearts and Good Cheer for Those in Distress. On the Organisation and History of the Yamanī Fatimid Daʿwa*. A critical edition of the Arabic text and summary English translation of Ḥātim b. Ibrāhīm al-Ḥāmidī's *Tuḥfat al-qulūb wa furjat al-makrūb*, by Abbas Hamdani (2012).
20. Abū Ṭāhir Ismāʿīl al-Manṣūr biʾllāh. *The Shiʿi Imamate: A Fatimid Interpretation*. An Arabic edition and English translation

of al-Manṣūr's *Tathbīt al-imāma* attributed to Abū Ṭāhir Ismāʿīl al-Manṣūr bi'llāh, edited and translated by Sami Makarem (2013).

21. Idrīs ʿImād al-Dīn. *The Founder of Cairo: The Fatimid Imam-Caliph al-Muʿizz and his Era*. An English translation of the section on al-Muʿizz from Idrīs ʿImād al-Dīn's *ʿUyūn al-akhbār*, edited and translated by Shainool Jiwa (2013).
22. Ibn al-Walīd. *Avicenna's Allegory on the Soul: An Ismaili Interpretation*. An Arabic edition and English translation of Ibn al-Walīd's *al-Risāla al-mufīda*, edited by Wilferd Madelung and translated and introduced by Toby Mayer (2015).
23. Ḥasan-i Maḥmūd-i Kātib. *Spiritual Resurrection in Shiʿi Islam: An Early Ismaili Treatise on the Doctrine of Qiyāmat*. A new Persian edition and English translation of the *Haft bāb* by Ḥasan-i Maḥmūd-i Kātib, edited and translated by S. J. Badakhchani (2017).
24. Ḥasan ʿAlī Shāh, Aga Khan I. *The First Aga Khan: Memoirs of the 46th Ismaili Imam*. A Persian edition and English translation of the *ʿIbrat-afzā* of Muḥammad Ḥasan al-Ḥusaynī, also known as Ḥasan ʿAlī Shāh, edited and translated by Daniel Beben and Daryoush Mohammad Poor (2018).
25. Muḥammad b. ʿAbd al-Karīm al-Shahrastānī. *Command and Creation: A Shiʿi Cosmological Treatise*. A Persian edition and English translation of Muḥammad al-Shahrastānī's *Majlis-i maktūb-i munʿaqid dar Khʷārazm*, edited and translated by Daryoush Mohammad Poor (2021).
26. Abū ʿAbd Allāh al-Shīʿī and his brother Abu'l-ʿAbbās (attrib.) *Affirming the Imamate: Early Fatimid Teachings in the Islamic West*. An Arabic critical edition and English translation by W. Madelung and Paul E. Walker (2021).

The Banquet of the Brethren

An Ismaili Guide to Spiritual Hermeneutics

Part 1, A Persian critical edition of Nāṣir-i Khusraw's *Khwān al-ikhwān*

by

Rahim Gholami

I.B.TAURIS
LONDON • NEW YORK • OXFORD • NEW DELHI • SYDNEY
in association with
THE INSTITUTE OF ISMAILI STUDIES
LONDON, 2024

I.B. TAURIS
Bloomsbury Publishing Plc
50 Bedford Square, London, WC1B 3DP, UK
1385 Broadway, New York, NY 10018, USA
29 Earlsfort Terrace, Dublin 2, Ireland

In association with The Institute of Ismaili Studies
Aga Khan Centre, 10 Handyside Street, London N1C 4DN
www.iis.ac.uk

First published in Great Britain 2024

Cover design: Adriana Brioso

A catalogue record for this book is available from the British Library.

A catalog record for this book is available from the Library of Congress.

ISBN: HB: 978-0-7556-5392-8
PB: 978-0-7556-5391-1
ePDF: 978-0-7556-5394-2
eBook: 978-0-7556-5393-5

Series: Ismaili Texts and Translations Series

Typeset by RefineCatch Limited, Bungay, Suffolk
Printed and bound in Great Britain

The Institute of Ismaili Studies

The Institute of Ismaili Studies, established in 1977, has an extensive programme of multilingual and interdisciplinary research and publications. Informed by rigorous scholarly research, we endeavour to make available texts relating to Islam and Muslim communities in their historical and contemporary contexts. Our focus is on Ismaili and related Shiʿi studies, Qurʾanic studies, and also Islam's diverse devotional, literary, intellectual, artistic, and esoteric traditions. Many of these publications highlight the relationship of faith and practice to broader dimensions of society, culture, and modern life.

IIS publications take the form of monographs; critical editions and translations of significant primary or secondary texts; edited volumes and conference proceedings; reference works such as bibliographies, manuscript catalogues, and encyclopaedias; occasional papers and essays; and trade non-fiction works aimed at lay audiences.

Authors of the Institute's publications hail from various parts of the world and express a range of views and ideas, which are not necessarily those of the Institute itself.

A full list of the publications of the Institute of Ismaili Studies can be found on our website at www.iis.ac.uk.

For my beloved mother, Maryam Ghaffari, whose love and wisdom illuminate my path, and in cherished memory of my late father, ʿAlishah Gholami, whose guiding spirit forever leads me. May peace be upon him.

My soul, in its felicitous serendipity, shall bask in radiant fortune,
so long as this steadfast heart is graced by thy affectionate,
loving blessings!

If the all-encompassing arms of thy guidance illuminate this
pilgrimage, Divine Providence shall be my secret sharer.

All dread shadows that haunt both realms shall dissolve, so long as
my trust, deeply rooted in the Beloved's mercy, remains unshaken.

A splendid destiny shall emerge as my intimate companion,
especially when Divine Might and Wisdom stand as my patrons.

Were it not for the propitious break of day brought by thy
enlightening gleam, words and script would lack the
strength of expression!

Rahim Gholami
13 December 2023

Contents

Acknowledgements

Here I should like to express my sincere gratitude to The Institute of Ismaili Studies, especially Dr Farhad Daftary, the Institute's Director Emeritus, and Professor Zayn Rahim Kassam, the Director of the Institute, for their support during my work on this publication. I would also like to convey my special thanks to Professor Paul E. Walker for his advice which helped me to realise the significance of studying Nāṣir-i Khusraw's *Khwān al-ikhwān* and urging me to choose this work as the topic of my PhD thesis in Spring 2013. I am also deeply obliged to the late and much missed Professor Wilferd Madelung for verifying some important Biblical passages quoted in *Khwān al-ikhwān* and keeping the door of his office open to me despite his very busy schedule. I would also like to express my sincere thanks to Dr Orkhan Mir-Kasimov for helping me locate and acquire high quality JPEG images of the oldest manuscript of *Khwān al-ikhwān* without which this project would have not progressed beyond its inception.

I am personally and intellectually indebted to Dr Jane Lewisohn and her late husband Professor Leonard Lewisohn, my initial PhD supervisor, an inspiring friend and a free soul, whose warmth of thought and conversation were always felt in the depths of the heart.

I should thank Dr István T. Kristó-Nagy, who took over the task of supervision after the untimely death of Leonard Lewisohn; also Professor Sajjad Rizvi, Professor Robert Gleave, Professor Christine Robins, and Ms Vicky Colton at the University of Exeter, as well as Professor Dominic Brookshaw at the University of Oxford, for their academic and personal support.

Here, it is most appropriate to offer my special thanks to Dr Gholam Hossein Ebrahimi Dinani and Dr Mohammad Rasekh in

Tehran and London, Rai Karamaly Bawa and his late wife, Yasmine, in Karachi, Professor Mohammad Ali Amir-Moezzi in Paris, Russell Harris, Dr Faquir Muhammad Hunzai, Dr Mohamed Keshavjee, Dr Isabel Miller and Tara Woolnough in London, and Professor Shafique Virani at the University of Toronto, and Dr Jamil Anwar Kassam in Edmonton, Canada, for their cordial support and encouragement.

I am much obliged to my colleagues in the Department of Academic Research and Publications at The Institute of the Ismaili Studies, London, as well as the staff of the Aga Khan Library, who have been generous with their time and from whose expert advice and congenial company I have benefited during all these years.

Here, I would like to offer my humblest gratitude to my siblings Allahyar, Athena and Hassan, my sister-in-law Zahra, my dearest nephew Faryan, my mother, Maryam Ghaffari, my late father, ʿAlishah Gholami, and my dearly missed maternal and paternal grandparents, Shahrbānū and ʿAlī-Ḥasan Ghaffārī, and Nāziʿa and Allahyar Gholami, whose blessings are the guiding lights of the firmament of their children's lives. I also wish to express my gratitude to my dear in-laws, Muhammad-ʿAlī and Fatimah-Sultan. I am particularly grateful to my beloved wife Zohreh for her constant support.

Rahim Gholami

12 October 2023

Abbreviations

BB	Nāṣir-i Khusraw, Ḥakīm Abū Mu'īn. *The Banquet of the Brethren*, ed. and tr. Rahim Gholami, Parts 1 and 2.
DA	—. *Dīwān-i Ash'ār-i Ḥakīm Nāṣir-i Khusraw-i Qubādyānī*, ed. Naṣrullāh Taqavī et al. Tehran, 1304–1307 Sh./1925–1928.
Jāmi'	—. *Kitāb-i Jāmi' al-ḥikmatayn*, ed. Henry Corbin and M. Mu'īn. Tehran-Paris, 1953; repr. Tehran, 1984.
JHE	—. *Kitāb-i Jāmi' al-ḥikmatayn*, English trans. Eric Ormsby as *Between Reason and Revelation: Twin Wisdoms Reconciled: An Annotated English Translation of Nāṣir-i Khusraw's Kitāb-i Jāmi' al-ḥikmatayn*. London, 2012.
Zād	—. *Zād al-musāfir*, ed. S. Isma'il Emadi Haeri. 2nd ed., Tehran, 2014.
Wellsprings	—. *Kitāb al-Yanābī'*, English trans. Paul E. Walker as *The Book of Wellsprings*, in his *The Wellsprings of Wisdom*. Salt Lake City, UT, 1994.
EI	*Encyclopaedia of Islam*, first edition, ed. M. Th. Houtsma et al. Leiden–London, 1913–1938, repr., London, 1987.
EI2	*Encyclopaedia of Islam*, New edition, ed. H.A.R. Gibb et al. Leiden–London, 1960–2004.
EI3	*Encyclopaedia of Islam Online*, ed. Kate Fleet et al. 2010—
EIs	*Encyclopaedia Islamica*, ed. W. Madelung and F. Daftary. London, 2008—
۞	Arabic/Persian punctuation mark.

Introduction

Nāṣir-i Khusraw, the Author of *Khwān al-ikhwān*

Nāṣir-i Khusraw, whose full name was Abū Muʿīn Ḥamīd al-Dīn Nāṣir b. Khusraw b. Ḥārith al-Qubādyānī al-Balkhī al-Marwazī (394–ca. post 462/1004–1070), wrote *Khwān al-ikhwān* (*The Banquet of the Brethren*) in Persian at some point during the second part of his life, the greater part of which unfolded in the eastern Islamic lands.

In his *Dīwān-i ashʿār*, Nāṣir-i Khusraw records the year of his birth as 394 AH (1004 CE) and says that he was born in Qubādyān.[1] He came from a family of government bureaucrats and, as an adult, he worked as a government official, scribe, and tax collector, in the eastern dominions of the Ghaznavids and Saljūqs until 437/1045 which was a pivotal year in his life.[2]

It was at this juncture, when he was forty-two years old that, as Nāṣir-i Khusraw declares in his *Dīwān-i ashʿār* and *Safarnāma*, his rational soul embarked upon a pilgrimage in search of wisdom.[3] His *Safarnāma* is the record of his seven-year journeyings to the Fatimid capital, Cairo, the centre of the Ismaili *daʿwa*, on this quest. It presents a unique image of the Fatimid caliphate at the height of its power

[1] *DA*, p. 173 (line 9):

بگذشت ز هجرت پس سیصد نود و چار ۔ بنهاد مرا مادر بر مرکز اغبر.

[2] See Nāṣ ir-i Khusraw, *Nasir-i Khusraw's Book of Travels: Safarnama*, tr. W. M. Thackston (Costa Mesa, CA, 2001), pp. 1–2; also see *JHE*, p. 3.

[3] *DA*, p. 173 (line 13):

پیموده شد از گنبد بر من چهل و دو ۔ جویای خرد گشت مرا نفس سخنور.

Cf. *Nasir-i Khusraw's Book of Travels*, pp. 1–2.

from the perspective of an Ismaili adherent. It was in Cairo that Nāṣir-i Khusraw studied for several years. His studies completed, he returned to the east as the *ḥujjat* of Khurasan, arriving at the end of his long journeyings in Jumādā II 444/ October 1052.

Nāṣir-i Khusraw is celebrated both as one of the great Persian poets and philosophers and as a significant figure in the Ismaili *daʿwa*, notably spearheading its spread in the region of Badakhshan,[4] nowadays split between Tajikistan and Afghanistan. His writings reflect and contributed to the intellectual work of the Ismaili *daʿwa*, particularly in the Iranian lands. Nāṣir-i Khusraw created all his enduring works, listed below, following his return from Egypt in 444/1052.[5]

Despite all the tribulations he endured as an Ismaili *dāʿī*, Nāṣir-i Khusraw's fidelity to the Ismaili Imam of the Time, the Fatimid Imam-caliph al-Mustanṣir bi'llāh[6] (r. 427–487/1036–1094), remained steadfast.[7] His literary oeuvre, consisting of his *Dīwān-i ashʿār*,[8] and his prose works, *Zād al-musāfir* (*The Wayfarer's Provisions*),[9] *Jāmiʿ al-ḥikmatayn* (*Twin Wisdom Reconciled*),[10] *Gushāyish wa Rahāyish* (*Knowledge and Liberation*),[11] and *Khwān al-ikhwān*,[12] documents his

[4] The following is a concise definition of the term *daʿwa*: 'mission or propaganda; in the religio-political sense, *daʿwa* is the invitation or call to adopt the cause of an individual or family claiming the right to the imamate; it also refers to the entire hierarchy of ranks, sometimes called *ḥ udūd*, within the particular religious organization developed for this purpose, especially amongst the Ismāʿīlīs. The Ismāʿīlīs often referred to their movement simply as *al-daʿwa*, or more formally as *al-da ʿwa al-hādiya*, "the rightly guiding mission".' Farhad Daftary, *The Ismāʿīlīs: Their History and Doctrines* (2nd ed., Cambridge, 2007), p. 515; see also Ahmad Pakatchi and Farhad Daftary, 'Daʿwa', *EIs*.

[5] See *JHE*, pp. 5–6.

[6] See H.A.R. Gibb and P. Kraus, 'al-Mustanṣ ir', *EI2*.

[7] *JHE*, pp. 5–6.

[8] *DA*, pp. 51 (lines 15–19), 148 (lines 15–25), 216 (lines 4–10), 224 (lines 7–9), 271 (lines 3–4), 283 (lines 21–24), 303 (lines 1–4), 307 (lines 13–18), 354 (lines 1–3), 409 (lines 16–18), 411 (lines 8–10), 413 (lines 3–4), and 431 (line 4).

[9] *Zād*, pp. 3 and 414.

[10] *Jāmiʿ*, pp. 16–17.

[11] Nāṣ ir-i Khusraw, *Knowledge and Liberation (Gushāyish wa Rahāyish): A Treatise on Philosophical Theology*, ed. and tr. Faquir M. Hunzai, with an introduction and commentary by Parviz Morewedge (London, 1998), para. [129] (Persian p. 50; translation p. 83).

allegiance and commitment to al-Mustanṣir bi'llāh. A particularly moving stanza from his *Dīwān-i ashʿār* vividly declares his devotion, 'Marked am I, with Mustanṣir bi'llāh's seal upon my flank and breast, and o'er my brow it rests',[13] symbolising his deep and indelible connection to his spiritual leader.

Nāṣir-i Khusraw's time as *ḥujjat* of Khurasan began during the reign of the Saljūq sultan, Ṭughril (d. 455/1063).[14] The Saljūqs, staunch advocates of Sunni Islam, were committed to curtailing the sway of Shiʿi Islam in the Islamic world, endeavouring to consolidate their own religious stance as the dominant form of the faith.[15]

A significant consequence of the Saljūq championing of Sunni Islam was the persecution of Ismailis and their *dāʿīs* throughout their empire, which covered the eastern Islamic lands and stretched as far as northern Syria and central Anatolia. As for Nāṣir-i Khusraw, at some point before the year 453/1061 his house in Balkh was ransacked and he was attacked. Fearing for his safety, he fled from Balkh and took sanctuary in Badakhshan, specifically in the secluded mountainous region of Yumgān, under the aegis of the amir of Badakhshan, ʿAlī b. al-Asad. This refuge became his permanent abode, where he devoted the rest of his life to writing and disseminating the teachings of the Ismaili *daʿwa* among the inhabitants of the Pamir mountains, continuing his scholarly and missionary calling in a more secure environment.[16]

[12] See *BB*, para. [§42:32].

[13] *DA*, p. 431 (line 4):

داغ مستنصر بالله نهادستم ـ بر بر و سینه و بر پهنهٔ پیشانی.

[14] See C.E. Bosworth, 'Ṭoghril Beg', *EI2*.

[15] Daftary, *The Ismāʿīlīs*, p. 195.

[16] See *Jāmiʿ*, pp. 15–18, and 314–16, tr. *JHE*, pp. 30–33, and 277–79.

The Significance of *Khwān al-ikhwān*

Before Nāṣir-i Khusraw, three notable Persian works of Ismaili *taʾwīl* were produced. The earliest of these is *Sharḥ-i qaṣīda-yi Abu'l-Haytham* by Muḥammad b. Surkh Nīshāpūrī, dating from the 4th to 5th/10th to 11th century, representing the only text of Ismaili *taʾwīl* originally composed in Persian prior to Nāṣir-i Khusraw's era. Following this, *Kashf al-maḥjūb* by Abū Yaʿqūb al-Sijistānī is believed to be a Persian rendition of an Arabic manuscript no longer available. The third, *Bunyād-i taʾwīl*, is attributed to al-Muʾayyad fi'l-Dīn al-Shīrāzī and is a translation of al-Qāḍī al-Nuʿmān's *Asās al-taʾwīl*. These works testify to the role of Persian in the dissemination and expansion of Ismaili esoteric wisdom, a tradition further enriched and broadened by Nāṣir-i Khusraw's writings including the seminal *Khwān al-ikhwān*.

Beyond making al-Sijistānī's Arabic *Kitāb al-Yanābīʿ* accessible to Persian readers in their native language, *Khwān al-ikhwān* distinguishes itself as the first Ismaili work in Persian to encompass a wide spectrum of esoteric topics in a single volume. Nāṣir-i Khusraw provided Persian translations for all the Qurʾanic verses and hadiths he referenced, a pioneering initiative to render these spiritual and theological resources accessible to a Persian-speaking Ismaili audience. This was not only designed to facilitate a deeper understanding of Ismaili teachings but also underscored the significance for the community of engaging with the original texts.

The Manuscripts, Previous Editions, and the Current Edition

This publication presents an annotated critical edition of the Persian text of *Khwān al-ikhwān*, segmented into clearly numbered paragraphs for ease of reference and enhanced readability, accompanied by detailed annotation. This critical edition is the first part of a two-

part publication, the second part presenting a complete English translation of the text. This two-pronged approach aims to expand the accessibility of *Khwān al-ikhwān*, previously limited to manuscripts or incomplete Persian editions, to a broader audience. By providing both Persian and English versions, this publication seeks to facilitate comprehensive access to this important work for scholars and students of Islamic studies, in particular those interested in Shiʿi and Ismaili esoteric literature and interpretation.

The edition of the Persian is based on the two surviving manuscripts. The critical edition primarily utilises Manuscript A (MS A) as its base. For those sections where MS A is incomplete, Manuscript B (MS B) has been utilised to fill in the gaps. Notably, MS A lacks all but folio [16b] of the *Kitāb-i Rawshanāʾī-nāma*, as well as paragraphs [§1] to [§9] of *Khwān al-ikhwān*, which feature Nāṣir-i Khusraw's *Orisons* immediately preceding his *Exordium*. These missing sections have been reconstructed with the aid of MS B. Additionally, MS B has provided the titles for chapters 33 to 100 from the List of the One-Hundred Courses, immediately following the *Exordium*, alongside the text from paragraphs [§1:1]–[§1:4] through to the start of paragraph [§2:2]. MS A exhibits signs of vandalism and derogatory annotations on folio no. [1a], suggesting that it was once held by individuals who were hostile to Shiʿi literature, including Nāṣir-i Khusraw's works. This antagonism could account for the absence of the introductory sections (i.e., the *Kitāb-i Rawshanāʾī-nāma* and the initial *Orisons* of *Khwān al-ikhwān*), where Nāṣir-i Khusraw fervently supports the cause of Imam ʿAlī and the Shiʿi Imams from his lineage.[17]

[17] Mīr-Bāqirī Fard and Raʾīsī make no mention of the abusive notes and defacement of folio no. [1a] from MS A.

- MS A, catalogued as Istanbul FY.1062.2 and dated 27 Ṣafar 674 (28 August 1275), which is almost 20 years after the destruction of the Nizari Ismaili state in Iran, was copied in *nastaʿlīq* script by the scribe Muḥammad b. Abī Ṭālib b. Abi'l-Qāsim al-Ḥusaynī. The manuscript consists of 139 folios,[18] averaging 19 lines per page, and is currently housed in the Istanbul University Central Library. If MS A had survived in its entirety, it would have contained the *Kitāb-i Rawshanāʾī-nāma* spanning folios [1b]–[17b] and *Khwān al-ikhwān* in folios [18a]–[138b]. However, the manuscript is missing the whole of *Kitāb-i Rawshanāʾī-nāma* except for folio [16b], which includes the concluding three pages of Chapter Six. Additionally, the initial folios of *Khwān al-ikhwān*, specifically [18a]–[18b] that would typically cover the title page and the opening *Orisons*, are absent. The final folios, [139a] and [139b], are blank, save for a notation on [139b] that dates back to a relatively recent period, approximately the year 1847–48 CE (1264 AH), which retrospectively states, 'It (MS A) was written 590 years ago,' alluding to its original completion in the year 674 AH.
- MS B, identified as Aya Sofya 1778 and dated to 19 Dhu'l-Qaʿda 862/7 October 1458, features clear *nastaʿlīq* script throughout its 149 folios,[19] with an average of 27 lines per page. The scribe of this manuscript remains anonymous. It is held in the Süleymaniye Library, Istanbul. The manuscript comprises *Khwān al-ikhwān* from folios [1b] to [130a], with an additional segment on folio no. [149b], and the *Kitāb-i Rawshanāʾī-nāma* spanning from folio [131b] to [149a]. Uniquely, in MS B, *Kitāb-i Rawshanāʾī-nāma* is

[18] Based on the images of MS A received, there is no visible evidence of measuring devices, such as rulers or colour-coded paper, being used during the scanning process. Therefore, accurately determining the manuscript's actual size has not been possible.

[19] Based on the images of MS B received, there is no visible evidence of measuring devices, such as rulers or colour-coded paper, being used during the scanning process. Therefore, accurately determining the manuscript's actual size has not been possible.

positioned just before the concluding folio of *Khwān al-ikhwān*, a sequencing choice the rationale for which is not immediately apparent.

The textual similarities and evidence present in both manuscripts suggest that MS A, or a manuscript closely resembling it that no longer exists, probably served as the prototype for the creation of MS B under the auspices of the Ottoman sultan, Mehmed the Conqueror (r. 848–50/1444–46 and 855–86/1451–81).[20] The commissioning of MS B can be attributed to Sultan Mehmed's engagement with the arts and literature. Known for his scholarly pursuits and support for both contemporary and classical works, he established an important library containing over 8000 manuscripts in various languages, including Persian, Ottoman Turkish, Arabic, Latin and Greek. This demonstrates the sultan's dedication to cultural and intellectual enrichment, positioning MS B as a product of his extensive patronage. Subsequently, in the nineteenth century the reigning sultan, Maḥmūd II, included MS B in a *waqf* or endowment.[21]

On the initial folio of MS B, folio no. [1a], there are three seals along with an endowment note, arranged as follows:

1. The seal belonging to Sultan al-Ghāzī Mahmūd Khān, specifically Maḥmūd II, who reigned from 1223 to 1255/1808 to 1839,[22] and spearheaded the endowment initiative. This seal comprises a prayer in Arabic[23] alongside the sultan's *ṭughrā*, a distinctive calligraphic emblem or signature.

[20] Vildan Serdaroğlu Coşkun, 'Avni (Mehmed II)', *EI3*.

[21] Gülru Necipoğlu, 'Visual Cosmopolitanism and Creative Translation: Artistic Conversations with Renaissance Italy in Mehmed II's Constantinople', *Muqarnas*, 29 (2012), pp. 1–81.

[22] Münir Aktepe and A. Levy, 'Maḥ mūd', *EI2*.

[23] Sultan al-Ghāzī Maḥ mūd Khān's prayer: 'Praise be to God, who guided us to this, and we would not have been guided, had it not been for God guiding us.'

الحمد لله الذي هدينا لهذا وما كنا لنهتدي لولا أن هدينا الله.

2. An endowment declaration from Aḥmad Shaykh Zādah,[24] which certifies the manuscript's donation as a legal endowment (*waqf-an ṣaḥīḥ-an sharʿiyyan*) under the directive of Sultan al-Ghāzī Maḥmūd Khān. In this note, Aḥmad Shaykh Zādah identifies himself, adding the descriptor *al-faqīr* ('the one in need'), and his role as the endowment's inspector (*mufattish*).
3. Aḥmad Shaykh Zādah's own seal, including his name with the invocation: 'O God, only from Thee, earnestly, Aḥmad prays for succour (*yā rabb zi-tu tawfīq tamannā kunad Aḥmad*).'
4. The *ṭughrā* of Mehmed the Conqueror, the original patron of the transcription of MS B, further substantiating the manuscript's historical and cultural significance in the Ottoman sultanate's patronage of literature and arts.

The presence of MS A, one of the extant manuscripts of *Khwān al-ikhwān*, exclusively in Istanbul might be attributed to the efforts of Muslim scholars to safeguard their cultural and intellectual legacy amidst the devastations wrought by the Mongol invasions. The Mongol assault on Persia between 616–654/1219–1256 prompted numerous scholars and literary figures to seek refuge in Anatolia, possibly carrying their most prized literary works to prevent their annihilation. Additionally, the Armenian historian Smbat Sparapet, who lived during the Mongol incursions, mentions the existence of

[24] Endowment note by Aḥ mad Shaykh Zādah: 'His Majesty, our greatest Sultan, the supreme Khagan, the ruler of both lands and seas, the servant of the two noble Sanctuaries, the Sultan son of Sultan, the Conqueror (al-Ghāzī) Maḥ mūd Khān, has endowed this noble copy as a valid religious endowment, for anyone who peruses and seeks guidance, turns [to God], and seeks to benefit. May God perpetuate his glorious reign. Authored by the modest (*al-faqīr*) Aḥ mad Shaykh Zādah, the Inspector of the Endowments of the Two Noble Sanctuaries, may forgiveness be granted through them.'

قَدْ وَقَفَ هَذِهِ النُّسْخَةَ الْجَلِيلَةَ سُلْطَانُنَا الأَعْظَمُ، وَالْخَاقَانُ الْمُعَظَّمُ، مَالِكُ الْبَرَّيْنِ وَالْبَحْرَيْنِ، خَادِمُ الْحَرَمَيْنِ الشَّرِيفَيْنِ، السُّلْطَانُ بْنُ السُّلْطَانِ، السُّلْطَانُ الْغَازِي مَحْمُود خَان، وَقْفًا صَحِيحًا شَرْعِيًّا لِمَنْ طَالَعَ وَاسْتَرْشَدَ وَأَنَابَ وَاسْتَسْعَدَ. خَلَّدَ اللهُ مُلْكَهُ الأَمْجَدَ. حَرَّرَهُ الْفَقِيرُ أَحْمَد شَيْخ زَادَه، الْمُفَتِّشُ بِأَوْقَافِ الْحَرَمَيْنِ الشَّرِيفَيْنِ، غُفِرَ بِهِمَا.

Here, it should be noted that the Arabic diacritics were not present in the original text and have been added for enhanced clarity.

Ismaili communities in Cappadocia, in central Anatolia. This historical detail suggests another potential avenue through which MS A could have found its way to its current location.[25]

Discrepancies observed in either manuscript are detailed in the footnotes, which also clarify the rationale behind the textual choices selected for this edition. In producing this new critical edition, a thorough comparison of both manuscripts was undertaken, with the text itself serving as a guiding reference for editorial decisions. This approach included tracing the progression of arguments to resolve ambiguities in spelling or to rectify transcription errors. Additionally, the Persian text marks the beginning and conclusion of all folios pertinent to both manuscripts in the critical apparatus accompanying the footnotes.

The critical apparatus documents all variances identified in both manuscripts. To maintain clarity and minimise footnotes, for recurring variations between MSS A and B, only the first occurrence is given, accompanied by a note detailing the editorial decision applicable to similar subsequent instances. Additionally, a specific editorial guideline was adopted regarding the Persian auxiliary verb 'to be' (specifically 'is', *ast*), whereby all contracted forms are separated from their base word. A footnote at the first occurrence explains this uniform adjustment throughout the text. For instance, when the Persian preposition *bih* (meaning 'to', 'towards', 'with', etc.) is utilised in a manner that does not alter the meaning or syntactic role of the subsequent word, it is kept distinct. Conversely, if it modifies the meaning or syntactic function of the following word, they are combined. For these and other aspects of Persian orthography, *Dehkhoda's Persian Dictionary* (*Lughatnāma-i Dihkhudā*) has been adhered to as the authoritative reference.

[25] Bayarsaikhan Dashdondog, *Mongols and Armenians 1220-1335* (Leiden, 2011), p. 125.

The overview below summarises previous Persian editions of *Khwān al-ikhwān*:

1. **Yaḥyā al-Khashshāb, ed.** (Cairo, 1940): Al-Khashshāb's edition exclusively used MS B for reasons not specified in his publication.

2. **ʿAlī Qavīm, ed.** (Tehran, 1338 Sh./1959): It seems Qavīm's edition relied on al-Khashshāb's work without making acknowledgment. This version lacks references to any manuscripts and introduces unexplained textual modifications.[26]

3. **Parvin Peerwani** (PhD, Tehran University, 1975): Peerwani's doctoral thesis, a typewritten document, is in poor condition, with many sections difficult to read.

4. **S.A.A. Mīr-Bāqirī Fard and I. Raʾīsī, ed.** (Tehran, 2015): Released for a conference marking Nāṣir-i Khusraw's millennium, this edition lacks an introduction and offers a minimal critical apparatus.

5. **S.A.A. Mīr-Bāqirī Fard and I. Raʾīsī, ed.** (Tehran, 2018): Addressing some deficits of their 2015 publication, this edition includes an introduction and revisions. The introduction presents a chapter correlation table between *Khwān al-ikhwān* and *Kitāb al-Yanābīʿ*, absent from the critical apparatus. However, it omits discussion on the transmission history and physical evidence such as the *ṭughrā* of Sultan Mehmed the Conqueror, Sultan al-Ghāzī Maḥmūd Khān's seal, and Aḥmad Shaykh Zādah's endowment documentation and personal seal.

[26] For the Russian translation of *Khwān al-ikhwān*, based on Qavīm's edition, see Насир Хусрав (Nasir Khusrav), *Трапеза Братьев (Trapeza Brat'ev)*, tr. Mukhammadsalom Makhshulov, ed. and intro. H. Elnazarov and R. Nazariev (Dushanbe, 2017), p. 16 (introduction).

Khwān al-ikhwān is composed of 100 discourses, with 38 of them closely paraphrasing discourses from al-Sijistanī's *Kitāb al-Yanābī'*, albeit not in the same sequence. This indicates the significant influence of *Kitāb al-Yanābī'* on *Khwān al-ikhwān*.[27] In this critical edition, chapters from both works have been compared to identify and correct errors in the manuscripts of *Khwān al-ikhwān*, with these corrections reflected in the critical apparatus.

The preparation of this edition has been enriched by access to the Arabic text of al-Sijistānī's *Kitāb al-Yanābī'* as edited by Henry Corbin.[28] Annotations include references to corresponding chapters in *Kitāb al-Yanābī'* or specific passages to support amendments made to the Persian text of *Khwān al-ikhwān*. Citations from Corbin's edition of *Kitāb al-Yanābī'* are provided, with occasional vocalisation of Arabic words for clarity. Definitions for obscure terms are provided from Dehkhoda's *Persian Dictionary* or Lane's *Arabic-English Lexicon*. References for traditions of the Prophet, sayings of the Imams, and other sources, are detailed in footnotes. When esoteric concepts arise without explanation in the text, interpretations are offered based on Nāṣir-i Khusraw or al-Sijistānī's other works, both in the Persian critical edition (Part 1) and the English translation (Part 2) of this current publication. Key passages in *Khwān al-ikhwān* are highlighted including any references to corresponding passages in Nāṣir-i Khusraw's other works.

The comprehensive annotation, thorough references, and methodical approach to textual amendments and exegesis in this edition are anticipated to significantly enhance the reader's comprehension of *Khwān al-ikhwān*'s profundity, alongside its historical and scholarly context. Applying modern scholarly standards, this edition aims to serve as a valuable resource for scholars

27 *Wellsprings*, p. 33.
28 *Yanābī'*, pp. 1–97.

and students of Islamic studies, with a keen interest in Shiʿi esoteric literature and Ismaili esoteric interpretation. By developing this annotated critical edition in Persian, along with an annotated English translation to be published subsequently, the goal is to enrich the understanding of Nāṣir-i Khusraw's intellectual contributions to Islam's broader intellectual history as well as to the Ismaili intellectual tradition, in particular.

Khwān al-Ikhwān

(*The Banquet of the Brethren*)

By

Nāṣir-i Khusraw

خوان الاخوان

کتاب
خوان الاخوان

تألیف

حکیم ابومعین حمیدالدین ناصرِ خسرو قبادیانی

جلد ۱ از ۲

تصحیح انتقادی متن فارسی بر اساس دو نسخه کهن

به اهتمام

رحیم غلامی

مؤسسه مطالعات اسماعیلی

۱۴۰۲ش/۱۴۴۴ق

با قدردانی
از مادر عزیزم مریم غفّاری
و برای شادی روح پدرم علیشاه غلامی

اَللّهُمَّ یا مَوْلانا

جانِ خوش اقبالْ مرا بختِ گهربار بُوَد تا که نظرگاهِ شما این دلِ رهوار بُوَد
چون نوک پرگارِ شما بر سرِ این کار بود بختِ خداسازْ مرا محرمِ اسرار بود
هول و ولا در دو جهان بی خود و بیکار بود تا که امید دلِ من بخششِ دلدار بود
بختِ سرافرازْ مرا شاهدِ غم خوار بود خاصه که تقدیر و قضا هردو مددکار بود
طالعِ خوش وقتِ شما مطلعِ انوار بود ورنه کی این حرف و صدا درخورِ گفتار بود

رحیم غلامی

فهرست نمودارها

علائم اختصاری بکار رفته

اس	نسخهٔ استانبول	+ \ -	دارد \ ندارد
ایا	نسخهٔ ایاصوفیا	←¦	شروع یا ابتدای متن در برگ جدید
ج	جلد یا مجلد، یا جمع	[کذا]	به اشتباه [چنین] نوشته شده است
ح	حدود	[ ]	افزوده یا توضیح مصحّح داخل کروشه
س	سطر	*	نشانهٔ آخر آیت قرآن
ش	شمسی	=	هم معنی یا مترادف
ص	صفحه یا صفحات	§	نشانهٔ بند (قسمت) به همراه شماره بند درون [ ]
ق	قمری، یا قبل	\	یا، و یا آخر بیت
م	میلادی	/	همچنین، و یا آخر سطر یا مصرع
نك:	مراجعه کنید به:			همانجا (همان نسخه)
قس:	مقایسه کنید با:	||	مطلب یا توضیح دیگر

فهرست کتاب

صف هشتم

صف نهم

صف دهم

صف یازدهم

صف دوازدهم

صف سیزدهم

صف چهاردهم

صف پانزدهم

صف شانزدهم

صف هفدهم

صف بیست و هفتم

صف بیست و هشتم

صف بیست و نهم

صف سی‌ام

صف سی و یکم

صف سی و دوّم

صف سی و سِیُم

صف سی و چهارم

صف سی و پنجم

صف سی و ششم

صف سی و هفتم

صف سی و هشتم

صف سی و نهم

صف چهلم

صف چهل و یکم

صف چهل و دوم

صف چهل و سِیُم

صف چهل و چهارم

صف چهل و پنجم

صف چهل و ششم

صف هفتاد و هفتم

صف هفتاد و هشتم

صف هفتاد و نهم

صف هشتادم

صف هشتاد و یکم

صف هشتاد و دوم

صف هشتاد و سِیُّم

صف هشتاد و چهارم

صف هشتاد و پنجم

صف هشتاد و ششم

صف نود و هفتم

صف نود و هشتم

صف نود و نهم

صف صدم

بِسْمِ اللّٰهِ تَيَمُّناً[۱] بذکرِهِ

[§۱] سپاس مر پدیدآرندهٔ چیز را نه از چیز پیش از مکان و زمان، و آفریننده از آن چیز مر مایهٔ[۲] چیزها را، که او است[۳] خداوند زمان و مکان.

[§۲] و صنعت اوّل است مر او را عالم جرمانی[۴] [و نورانی][۵] که پدید آمدن او بِهَم است با زمان و مکان، و دوم که از کارکردِ او است عالم افزونی‌پذیر از عنصر و ارکان[۶] که اندر حصار مکان است و زیر زمان.

[§۳] سپاس خویشتن‌شناسان به بندگی اندر سیُم حصار از حصارهای آفرینش. و سپاس رهایش‌جویان ازین زندان تاریك و گذشتن بر این[۷] راه بلند و باریك به متابعت دانایانِ راه‌دان.

---

۱ دهخدا: تیمناً. [تَ یَ مْ مُ نَنْ] بطور میمنت و برکت. برای تیمن.

۲ نك: دهخدا: مایه. [یَ/ یِ] بنیاد هرچیز را گویند...اصل و مادهٔ هرچیز را گویند...اصل و ریشه و بنیاد و مصدر و اساس و جوهر...: پرنور و صور شد ز شما خاك ازیرا / مایهٔ صور وروشنی و کان ضیائید. ناصرخسرو. (دیوان اشعار، [ص ۱۲۴، س ۳، به‌اهتمام: نصرالله تقوی]). || قس: همین کتاب بند [§۵۸:۲]: و نفس کلّ مایه است مر طبیعت را، و بجنباند مر پدیدآورده‌های خویش را، و از کردارهای خویش بعضی را نُمُو داد اعنی افزودن چون رستنیها و بعضی را حس داد اعنی شناختن چون جانوران. و مر فعل او را بدین کی کرد طبع خواندند. و آنچ نفس جزوی کرد مر آن را صنع خواندند.

۳ در این کتاب، فعل «است» همه جا از کلمه ماقبل جدا شده است. هرجا این فعل راجع به صرف زمان حال کامل (ماضی نقلی) بوده است، «ه/ە» آخر، که نشانه صفت مفعولی مشتق از مصدر فعل است، به آخر کلمه قبل اضافه شده است.

۴ ایا: روحانی [کذا]. || تصحیح قیاسی. نك: همین کتاب، بند [§۲۱:۵]: دیگر قسمت آن است کی مع‌الزّمان است چون عالم جرمانی و نورانی که روزگار را با او پیشی و پسی نیست.

۵ تصحیح قیاسی. نك: یادداشت قبل.

۶ نك: دهخدا: اسطقس. [اُ طُ قُ س س/ اِ طُ قِ]...(از یونانی اوستوقس، عنصر) ماده. مایه. مادهٔ از هرچیزی...اصل هر شئ:...اسطقس کلمه‌ای است یونانی، و معنی آن اصل هرچیز باشد. و عناصر اربعه را هم که عبارت از آب و خاك و هوا و آتش باشد به اسطقسات تعبیر کنند...[و هریك از] آنرا رکن گویند.

۷ ایا: [حروف «ب» و «ر» در کلمه «برین» (یعنی: بر این) مخدوش است.]

[§۴] و شکر مر آفریدگارِ مایهٔ وهمها[۸] را، که جزوهای او گردگرفته است مر کُلّ جسمها را، تا از یك روی اوهام اندر اجسام است، و از دیگر روی اجسام اندر اوهام است.[۹]

[§۵] پاکا خدایا که مُبدَعِ[۱۰] او پادشاىِ بندگان است[۱۱] و مخلوقِ[۱۲] او خازن مکان و زمان است.

[§۶] شکر مر او را، شکرِ افزونی جویندگان از نعمتِ گروندگانِ به بندگیِ پیوستگانِ به نورِ وحدت از دریاىِ دهشت و بیابانِ شكّ و شبهت.

[§۷] و درود بر صبح روشنِ عالمِ دین، و روزِ رحمتِ ربّ‌العالمین، و بازوىِ جسدِ حکمت، و بار درخت نعمت، و در گشادهٔ جنّت، و پوشیده صورتِ حکمت زیر چادرِ شریعت، محمّد مصطفیٰ. دریای رحمتِ رحمان و راهبانْ[۱۳] بر اهل طاعت و عصیان، خداوند حوض و شفاعت، و پشت و پناه اهل طاعت. درودی که در همسایگی او ما را جای دهد، جایی که جای‌گیرِ او بدان از بند جسد و زندان طبیعت برهد.

۸ نك: وجه دین، گفتار ۱۲، ص ۱۱۷: و نیست مر هیچ وهم را طاقت آن کز مایهٔ وهمها که آن عقل است بگذرد تا به پدیدآرندهٔ عقل چه رسد.

۹ قس: وجه دین، گفتار ۴، ص ۴۱ تا ۴۲؛ قس: زادالمسافر: قول ۴، ص ۲۵ تا ۲۷؛ نیز قول ۵، ص ۳۱ تا ۴۰.

۱۰ مُبدَع اشارت است به «عقل کلّ». || نك: همین کتاب بند [§۷:۱۰۰]: و مُبْدَعْ که او عقل است چیزی پدیدآورده نه از چیزی [است]. و او محیط است بر جملگی هر چه او را هستی است.

۱۱ ایا: بنده آنست.

۱۲ مخلوق اشارت است به «نفس کلّ». || نك: همین کتاب بند [§۸:۱۰۰]: و مخلوق اوّل نفس کلّی است کی او نخستین چیز است پدیدآمده از چیزی، اعنی کی پدید آمدن او به میانجی عقل است از امر باری سبحانه.

۱۳ ایا: راه بان.

[۸§] و پس ازو[۱۴] درودی پاك از غشّ و خیانت، اندر لباسِ دیانت و حلیَتِ صیانت، بر مغربِ[۱۵] نور یزدان و بخشش کُنِ درکات نیران و درجات جِنان، [علی مرتضی].[۱۶] خداوند بیان و برهان و دستگیر راهجوی[۱۷] و کتاب سخنگوی، مر حکما را حکیم، و مطیعان را نعیم و عاصیان را جحیم. و او خود مسکین[۱۸] ایستاده اندر دین بجای یتیم.[۱۹]

۱۴ ¦⟵برگ [ایا:۲-الف].

۱۵ نك: وجه دین، گفتار ۱۱، ص ۱۰۳: و همی حدود را یاد کند خدایتعالی، قوله: رَبُّ الْمَشْرِقَيْنِ وَ رَبُّ الْمَغْرِبَيْنِ [سورة الرحمٰن (۵۵)، آیت ۱۷]، همی گوید پروردگار دو مشرق و بدان مر عقل و نفس را میخواهد که نور وحدت از ایشان پدید آمد؛ و پروردگار دو مغرب و بدان مر ناطق و اساس را میخواهد که آن نور کز آن دو مشرق برآید و بدین دو مغرب فرو شود.

۱۶ نك: ابن عقدة الکوفي، احمد بن محمد، فضائل أمیر المؤمنین (ع)، به‌اهتمام: عبدالرزاق محمد حسین حرزالدین (قم، ۱۴۲۴ق/۱۳۸۲ش)، ص ۱۰۲؛ الصفّار، محمد بن الحسن، بصائر الدرجات في فضائل آل محمد(ص)، التحقیق والتصحیح: محسن کوچه باغي التبریزی (قم، مکتبة آیة اللّٰه المرعشي النجفي، ۱۴۰۴ق)، الجزء الثامن، باب ۱۸: في امیرالمؤمنین(ع) أنّه قسیم الجنة والنار، ص ۴۱۴ تا ۴۱۸.

۱۷ ایا: راه جوی.

۱۸ نك: وجه دین، گفتار ۲۸، ص ۲۱۱ تا ۲۱۲: قوله تعالی: إِنَّمَا الصَّدَقٰاتُ لِلْفُقَرٰاءِ وَ الْمَسٰاكِینِ وَ الْعٰامِلِینَ عَلَيْهٰا ... [سورة التوبة ۹، آیت ۶۰] گفت صدقات مر درویشان راست یعنی حدود مر ناطقانراست و ایشان را فقرا [یعنی درویشان] بدان گفت که اندرین عالم کسی نیست که ایشان ازو فایده گیرند و درویش اند سوی حدود علوی..../ صدقات از پس فقیران مر مسکینان راست، و بدان مر اساسان را خواست اندر هرزمانی که سکون امت بر تأویل ایشانست، و گفت <وَ الْعٰامِلِینَ عَلَيْهٰا> یعنی کارکنان را بر صدقات و بدان مر امامان را خواست از بهر آنکه ناطق کتاب شریعت تألیف کرد و اساس مر آنرا تأویل گفت بفرمان رسول و هر دو را بامام سپردند تا بدان کار کند و ایشان کار کنند بدان تا بقیامت.

۱۹ نك: وجه دین، گفتار ۳۱، ص ۲۳۵: و به یتیمان مر امامان را خواهد که ایشان را اندر عالم جسمانی مادر و پدر نفسانی نباشد و پرورش ایشان به تأیید است از عالم علوی.

[۹§] و بر فرزندان او بارخدایانِ خلق هر یك اندر روزگار خویش، و عالم را از ایشان خالی نه از پس و پیش. و درودِ امیددار به رحمتِ هر یك از ایشان پس یکدیگر تا روز محشر[۲۰] بر میعاد ایزد دادگر.[۲۱]

۲۰ اس: - بسم الله تَیَمُّناً بذکرِه...تا روز محشر. || ¦⟵برگ [اس:۱۹-الف]. || در نسخهٔ تصویریِ نسخهٔ خطی استانبول (اس)، از ۳۶ صفحهٔ اول این نسخه، بجز تصویر برگهای [اس:۱-الف] و [اس:۱۶-ب]، تصویر برگ های [اس:۱-ب] تا [اس:۱۸- ب] — که حاوی متن کتاب روشنائی نامه، و دعای افتتاح کتاب در ابتدای خوان الاخوان بوده است — در دست نیست. || برگ [اس:۱-الف]، صفحهٔ اول، به ترتیب حاوی عنوان: «کتاب روشنائی نامه، و خوان الاخوان صد صف / من تألیف ملك الحکما سلطان المحققین حجّة الحق علی الخلق وارث علوم الأنبیاء والمرسلین ابومعین ناصر بن خسرو قدس الله روحه العزیز» است. بر این برگ، در میان دیگر یادداشتها، یك امضاء بچشم میخورد که مانند امضاء حاشیهٔ سمتِ چپِ پایینِ برگ [اس:۱۳۸-ب] است. مضافاً، بر این صفحه یادداشتهای پراکنده و گاه ناسزا و خط خوردگی هائی مشاهده میشود که نشانهٔ غفلت در نگهداری از این نسخه، ولو زمانی اندك، بوده است. || برگ [اس:۱۶-ب] تنها بخش باقی مانده از ابتدای نسخهٔ استانبول است که حاوی صفحات ماقبل آخر از فصل ششم — «اندر ثواب و عقاب و شرح آن»، از کتاب روشنائی نامه است. دستخط این قسمتِ باقیمانده از کتاب روشنائی نامه با خط کاتب این نسخه، مطابقت می کند؛ همچنین، محتوای آن با مبحث بند [۱۴:۷§] و نیز عنوان همین صف، و بند [۱۷:۳۳§]، از این کتاب، یعنی خوان الاخوان، شباهت نزدیك دارد. || در ظهریّهٔ برگ اول از نسخه ایاصوفیا (ایا)، یعنی برگ [ایا:۱-الف]، سه مهر و تحریرِ وقفِ نسخه به ترتیب و عبارت ذیل آمده است: (۱) مهر اول: متعلق به سلطان محمود الثانی (ح۱۲۲۳-۱۲۵۵ق/۱۸۰۸-۱۸۳۹م) است که شامل «طغرای» او و جمله دعایی ذیل است: «الْحَمْدُ لِلَّهِ الَّذِي هَدَينَا لِهَذَا وَمَا كُنَّا لِنَهْتَدِيَ لَوْلَا أَنْ هَدَينَا اللَّهُ». (۲) تحریر وقف نسخه: «قَدْ وَقَفَ هَذِهِ النُّسْخَةَ الْجَلِيلَةَ سُلْطَانُنَا الْأَعْظَمُ، وَالْخَاقَانُ الْمُعَظَّمُ، مَالِكُ الْبَرَّيْنِ وَالْبَحْرَيْنِ، خَادِمُ الْحَرَمَيْنِ الشَّرِيفَيْنِ، السُّلْطَانُ بْنُ السُّلْطَانِ، السُّلْطَانُ الْغَازِي مَحْمُود خَان، وَقْفًا صَحِيحًا شَرْعِيًّا، لِمَنْ طَالَعَ وَاسْتَرْشَدَ وَأَنَابَ وَاسْتَسْعَدَ. خَلَّدَ اللَّهُ مُلْكَهُ الْأَمْجَدَ. حَرَّرَهُ الْفَقِيرُ أَحْمَد شَيْخ زَادَه، الْمُفَتِّشُ بِأَوْقَافِ الْحَرَمَيْنِ الشَّرِيفَيْنِ، غُفِرَ بِهِمَا» [اصل اعراب ندارد]. (۳) مهر دوم: متعلق به احمد شیخ زاده که جمله دعایی ذیل را شامل است: «یا رب ز تو توفیق تمنّا کند احمد». (۴) مهر سوم: طغرای سلطان محمد الثانی (ح۸۴۸-۸۵۰ق/۱۴۴۴-۱۴۴۶م، و ۸۵۵-۸۸۶ق/۱۴۵۱-۱۴۸۱م).

۲۱ اس: [«بر میعاد» مخدوش است].

آغاز[1] کتاب

[§۱۰] ای خداوندان گوشهای شنوا، داد شنوایی که شما را داده‌اند بدهید به شنودن سخن حقّ! و ای نگرندگان به چشم روشن، بنگرید سوی آفرینشِ خویش و سوی ترکیبِ عالم! و ای هوشیاران، اندریابید معنی پادشائی[2] خویش بر دیگر جانوران! و بدانید کی[3] هر که دادِ گوش به شنودن و دادِ چشم به نگرستن و دادِ دل به دانستن ندهد ستمکار باشد! قوله: وَ اللّٰهُ لاٰ يَهْدِي الْقَوْمَ الظّٰالِمِينَ.[4]

[§۱۱] و چون مر خویشتن را از شنوایی اندر پادشائی همی‌یابید، که شما را اندر بدست آوردن آن توانایی نبود، بدانید که شما را این پادشائی ازبهر آن دادند که شما را بدان حاجت بود. و چون مر جانوری را که شنوا نیست اندر این زندگانی گذرنده با خویشتن انباز[5] همی‌یابید، بدانید که این پادشائی شما را ازبهر این زندگانی ندادند. پس ضایع مکنید مر این هدیهٔ عظیم را، و فایدهٔ خویش ازو بگیرید به شنودنِ آنچ شما آن ندانید.

[§۱۲] و چون از بینایی شما را بهره‌مند کردند، بی‌خواستِ شما، تا بدین بینایی، به میانجی نور آفتاب جسمانی، از جایهای هلاك دنیاوی حذر کردید، از آنچ اندر زیر دیدنیها پوشیده است، به میانجی آفتاب روحانی، از عذاب جاویدی حذر کنید. و گوش و چشم به سخن و اشارت آن کس دارید که آفریدگار شما مر او را گفت،

---

۱ اس: [«آ» در ابتدای کلمه «آغاز» محو شده است.]

۲ پادشائی =بهره‌مندی، فرمانروایی، برخورداری از نعمت و قدرت.

۳ در هرجا از نسخهٔ اس «کی» و «که» آمده است صورت آن حفظ شده است. || نك: دهخدا: کی. (حرف ربط) به معنی که.

۴ نك: آیت ۲۵۸ از سورة البقرة (۲)؛ آیت ۸۶ از سورة آل عمران (۳)؛ آیات ۱۹ و ۱۰۹ از سورة التوبة (۹)؛ آیت ۷ از سورة الصف (۶۱)؛ و آیت ۵ از سورة الجمعة (۶۲). این آیت شش بار در قرآن آمده است. همچنین آیت: «إِنَّ اللّٰهَ لاٰ يَهْدِي الْقَوْمَ الظّٰالِمِينَ» در چهار آیت دیگر آمده است: آیت ۵۱ از سورة الماعدة (۵)؛ آیت ۱۴۴ از سورة الأنعام (۶)؛ آیت ۵۰ از سورة القصص (۲۸)؛ و آیت ۱۰ از سورة الأحقاف (۴۶). (در کتابت آیات قرآنی، همه جا از رسم الخط نیریزی پیروی شده است).

۵ انباز = شريك.

قوله:[6] أَسْمِعْ بِهِمْ وَ أَبْصِرْ يَوْمَ يَأْتُونَنا لٰكِنِ الظّٰالِمُونَ الْيَوْمَ فِي ضَلٰالٍ مُبِينٍ.[7] گفت: «بشنوان[8] و بنمای ایشان را آن روز که سوی ما آیند، و لکن ستمکاران امروز اندر گُم‌بودگی[9] پیدا اند».

[§۱۳] و بیاموزید دانش چون همی‌دانید که آلتِ آموختن یافته‌اید از دلِ پذیرا و آموزگار دانا که هردو پیش شما است بقول خدای تعالی که همی‌گوید، قوله: فَسْئَلُوا[10] أَهْلَ الذِّكْرِ إِنْ كُنْتُمْ لاٰ تَعْلَمُونَ * بِالْبَيِّنٰاتِ وَ الزُّبُرِ.[11] همی‌گوید: «بپرسید از اهل قرآن اگر همی‌ندانید [به][12] پیدائیها و کتابها».[13]

[§۱۴] و این آیت همی‌آواز دهد که کتاب و پیدائی شما را[14] دانا نکند بی‌خداوندِ

---

۶ ¦⟵برگ [ایا:۱-ب].

۷ سورة مریم (۱۹)، آیت ۳۸.

۸ نك: دهخدا: شنواندن. [شَ / شِ نَ وا دَ] شنوانیدن. به گوش رسانیدن. مطلبی را به سمع کسی رساندن.

۹ گُم بودَگی = گمراهی و هراس. نك: دهخدا: گم بودگی. [گُ دَ / دِ] هراسان شدن.

۱۰ اس، ایا: فسألوا.

۱۱ آیات ۴۳ تا ۴۴ از سورة النحل (۱۶)؛ آیت ۴۳ از آن، در آیت ۷ از سورة الأنبياء (۲۱)، و آیت ۴۴ از آن، در آیت ۱۸۴ از سورة آل عمران (۳) نیز آمده اند.

۱۲ تصحیح قیاسی. نك: همین کتاب، بند [§۱۸].

۱۳ قس: جامع‌الحکمتین، ص ۵۳، بند (۴۸): بگوی مر خلق را که بنگرید که چیست اندر آسمانها و زمین یعنی از نشانیهاء حکمت. آنگاه گفت: و سود ندارد نشانیها راندن پیغامبران مر گروهی را که نگرویدند بدین آیت: قوله: «قُلِ انْظُرُوا مٰاذٰا فِي السَّمٰاوٰاتِ وَ الْأَرْضِ وَ مٰا تُغْنِي الْآيٰاتُ وَ النُّذُرُ عَنْ قَوْمٍ لاٰ يُؤْمِنُونَ».

۱۴ ¦⟵برگ [اس:۱۹-ب].

کتاب، و بر پاشنهٔ[۱۵] خویش بازمگردید که آن رفتن دیوان است؛[۱۶] و بر آن سو[۱۷] روید که راه و دلیل یزدان است، و روی سوی روی خدای دارید که روی او میرنده نیست.[۱۸]

[§۱۵] چنانك فرمود، قوله: كُلُّ شَيْءٍ هٰالِكٌ إِلاّٰ وَجْهَهُ لَهُ الْحُكْمُ وَ إِلَيْهِ تُرْجَعُونَ.[۱۹] همی‌گوید: «هرچیزی هلاك شونده است مگر روی او، او را است حکم، و شما را بازگشت سوی او است». این آیت همی‌دلیل کند که حکم اندر خلق مر امام را است، از فرزندان رسول، و بازگشت خلق بدو است.

[§۱۶] ازبهرآنك بدیگر جای گفته است که مردمان مؤمن نگردند تا مر رسول را خداوند مُحَكِّم[۲۰] ندارند اندر داوریهای خویش، قوله: فَلاٰ وَ رَبِّكَ لاٰ يُؤْمِنُونَ حَتّٰى يُحَكِّمُوكَ فِيمٰا شَجَرَ بَيْنَهُمْ.[۲۱] «سوگند است از خدای تعالی که مؤمن نباشند مؤمنان تا ترا ای محمّد حاکم نکنند اندر آنچ میان ایشان باشد از داوری».

---

۱۵ اس: بابسته؛ ایا: باپـــــتهٔ [کذا]. || تصحیح قیاسی. نك: دهخدا: پایشنه. [یِ نَ / نِ] ... پاشنه. [«بر پاشنهٔ خویش بازگردیدن» = پشت کردن، بازگشتِ به، و پیروی کورکورانه از عادات و رسوم گذشتگان]. || نك: جامع‌الحکمتین، ص ۱۰۰، بند (۹۵): چنانك گفت «محمّد جز رسول نبود که پیش ازو رسولان گذشته‌اند، پس اگر او بمیرد یا بکشندش، شما از دین همی بازخواهید گشتن» بدین آیت: قوله «وَ مٰا مُحَمَّدٌ إِلاّٰ رَسُولٌ قَدْ خَلَتْ مِنْ قَبْلِهِ الرُّسُلُ أَ فَإِنْ مٰاتَ أَوْ قُتِلَ انْقَلَبْتُمْ عَلىٰ أَعْقٰابِكُمْ...». (آل‌عمران (۳)، آیت ۱۴۴) || قس: «... وَ مٰا جَعَلْنَا الْقِبْلَةَ الَّتِي كُنْتَ عَلَيْهٰا إِلاّٰ لِنَعْلَمَ مَنْ يَتَّبِعُ الرَّسُولَ مِمَّنْ يَنْقَلِبُ عَلىٰ عَقِبَيْهِ وَ إِنْ كٰانَتْ لَكَبِيرَةً إِلاّٰ عَلَى الَّذِينَ هَدَى اللّٰهُ وَ مٰا كٰانَ اللّٰهُ لِيُضِيعَ إِيمٰانَكُمْ إِنَّ اللّٰهَ بِالنّٰاسِ لَرَؤُفٌ رَحِيمٌ». (البقرة (۲)، آیت ۱۴۳)

۱۶ نك: جامع‌الحکمتین، ص ۱۴۰، بند (۱۴۲): ابلیس پیش از آنك مر او را طاعت آدم فرمود، از پریان بود. پس آفریده بدو قسم بود: یکی مردم و دیگر پری. و پری بدو قسم شد: یکی فرشته و دیگر دیو، اعنی آنچ از پری بطاعت بماند فرشته شد، و آنچ بی‌طاعت شد دیو گشت.

۱۷ اس: [«سو» مخدوش است].

۱۸ اس: [«میرنده نیست» مخدوش است].

۱۹ سورة القصص (۲۸)، آیت ۸۸.

۲۰ نك: دهخدا: محکم. [مُ حَ كْ كِ] استوارکننده. || بازدارنده. منع کننده... || پیر کارآزمودهٔ باحکمت و خود انصاف دهنده.

۲۱ سورة النساء (۴)، آیت ۶۵.

[§۱۷] و دیگر جای[22] همی‌گوید: [يَوْمَ نَدْعُوا كُلَّ أُنَاسٍ بِإِمَامِهِمْ]. «آن روز که بخوانیم [هر] مردمانی را به امام ایشان».[23] این آیت همی‌دلیل کند که بازگشت هر گروهی به امام ایشان باشد، تا چون امام را بخوانند، ایشان همه خوانده شوند.

[§۱۸] و بجویید آن کس را که بازگشت شما بدو است، که او نایافته نیست؛ چه اگر آن کس، که ما را ازو همی‌بباید پرسیدن آنچ ندانیم نایافته بودی، ایزد تعالی نفرمودی که: «از اهل ذکر بپرسید اگر همی‌ندانید به پیدائیها و کتابها».[24]

[§۱۹] و بدانید، ای مسکینان که شما اندر زندانی سخت ژرفید، و شادی مکنید بدین جای تاریك و خورش[25] پلید و بدین پوشش کهن شوندهٔ ریزنده که یافته‌اید.

[§۲۰] و بدانید که من چون خویشتن را پادشا یافتم بر جانوران و به سالاری من زندگانی یافتند، و فایده از آفرینش ایشان ضایع نشد به تباه کردن ددگان درنده مر ایشان را، دانستم که آفریدگار بر من کسی گماشته است که اگر من اندر نگاه داشت او شوم، فایده از آفرینش من ضایع نشود. و طلب کردم مر آن پادشای خویش را، و بدو رهایش جستم از رنج نادانی و هلاك جاویدی، برمثال ستوری کز رنج سرما و گرما[26] و بیم درندگان سوی خانهٔ خداوند خویش گریزد.

[§۲۱] و یافتم آن کس را کزو من به درجهٔ ستور بودم از مردم؛ و او مرا از زمهریر نادانی بپوشانید، و از سموم گفتارهای فریبندگان به نسیم بهاری رسانید. و جان مرا از زهر دندان اهل تقلید و تعطیل و تشبیه برهانید. و به طعام و شراب جان‌افزای، جانِ مرا سیر و سیراب گردانید.[27]

---

۲۲ ایا: [«جای» بالای سطر نوشته شده است].

۲۳ سورة الإسراء (۱۷)، آیت ۷۱.

۲۴ سورة النحل (۱۶)، آیات ۴۳ تا ۴۴.

۲۵ ¦←برگ [ایا:۳-الف].

۲۶ ¦←برگ [اس:۲۰-الف]. || اس: [«و گرما» در ابتدای برگ [اس:۲۰-الف] تکرار شده است]. همچنین رقم «۱۹»، که بعداً برای شماره گذاری بر حواشی برگهای نسخه خطی اضافه شده، سهواً دوبار درج شده است.

۲۷ در سخن ناصرخسرو «طعام» و «شراب» به ترتیب برابر تنزیل و تأویل هستند.

[§۲۲] و من از حال شما، ای همجنسان، بدین قامت، الفی[۲۸] بازنمودم.[۲۹]

[§۲۳] و او خداوند بَرِ شما به نظرِ خویش سوی شما رحمت خدای بارانید. و زان طعام و شراب، که من بدان از خطر مرگ رسته شدم، سوی شما فرستاد برِ دست من بنده.[۳۰]

[§۲۴] و اکنون من از آن طعام و شراب این خوان را بیاراستم به گونه‌گونه خورشهای پاك و میوه‌های با لذت و بوی‌ناك، و پیش متابعان خداوند سخنگویان آوردم.

[§۲۵] و آن خوان این کتاب است که مر او را خوان‌الاخوان نام نهادم؛ بدانچ برو مر طلبکاران حکمت را خوردنیهای جان‌پرور است و شرابهای ساقیِ کوثر.

---

۲۸ اس: [«الفی» مخدوش است].

۲۹ برای تأویل ناصرخسرو از مفهوم «قامت»، یعنی «اقامة»، که پس از اذان (بانگِ نماز) و جهت برپای داشتن نماز خوانده میشود، نك: وجه دین، گفتار ۱۸، ص ۱۴۷: بانگ نماز که جفتگان جفتگان است و جز آن روا نیست از بهر آنکه آن دلیل است بر دعوت ناطق که مرو را دو قوّت بود یکی ظاهر و یکی باطن، یکی قوّت تنزیل و دیگر قوّت تأویل. || نیز نك: وجه دین، گفتار ۱۸، ص ۱۴۹ تا ۱۵۰: و بانگ نماز و قامت نکنند مگر اندر پنج نماز که آنرا خدای تعالی موقت و مکتوب گفته است یعنی وقت پیدا کرده به نوشته؛ یعنی که طاعت نیست مگر ناطقان را و اساسان را و دعوت نیست جز مر ایشان را که یکی را بانگ نماز دلیل است و یکی را قامت. و اندر هرزمانی امام به جای ناطق است و حجّت به جای اساس تا همیشه که ناطق است بانگ نماز است. ... چون بانگ نماز بگویند مردمان اندر مسجد یگان یگان آیند و پیش از قامت هر کسی جدا جدا نماز همی گزارد؛ معنیش آنست که خلق از دینهای پراگنده سوی دعوت ناطق آیند و هر که ناطق را اجابت کند تا اساس را اجابت نکند به هوای خویش رونده باشد چنانکه هر کسی که پیش از قامت نماز همی گزارد گوناگون، آن طاعت هواداران مخالف باشد. و قامت دلیل است بر دعوت وصیّ بسوی تأویل شریعت. || نیز نك: وجه دین، گفتار ۱۹، ص ۱۵۴: و آن سه سنّت بانگ نماز است و قامت و جماعت — بانگ نماز دلیل است بر متم که بخواند خلق را بظاهر، و قامت دلیل است بر حجّت که او بپای دارد باطن را، و جماعت دلیل است بر داعی که جمع شدن مؤمنان بروست. || نك: دهخدا: قامت. [مَ] (عربی اسم)...|| اقامه.... اذان خفیف که پس از اذان گویند.

۳۰ ایا: – بنده.

[۲۶§] و راست کردم بر این خوان از طعام و شراب صد صَفّ[۳۱] بر این ترتیب، همچنانك بر خوان جسمی سرکه و حلوا به یکجای باشد.

[۲۷§] تا هرکه دست نفس خویش از آلایش خمر شریعت و چربه و گوشت خوکان دین شسته است، و معدهٔ فکرت را به گوارش پرهیزکاری از اخلاط بی‌باکی پاك گردانیده است، ازین خوان بردارد بهرهٔ خویش، به زایش دوم،[۳۲] براندازه‌ای[۳۳] که تواند بخورد حلال و گوارنده باد او را.

[۲۸§] و ایزد تعالی دستهای ناشسته و معده‌های آلوده را ازین خوان حکمت بی‌بهره گرداناد به فضل خویش.[۳۴]

۳۱ صفّ به مفهوم رتبه، درجه، و شأن بوده، و در اینجا به معنی «سفره و خوان آراسته از خوراکی و نوشیدنی» است. همچنین، مؤلف به شکل ضمنی به تأویل آیات ذیل اشاره دارد: سورة النور (۲۴): آیت ۴۱؛ سورة الصافات (۳۷): آیات ۱، و ۱۶۵؛ سورة الطور (۵۲): آیت ۲۰؛ سورة الصف (۶۱): آیت ۴؛ سورة النّبأ (۷۸): آیت ۳۸؛ سورة الغاشية (۸۸): آیت ۱۵؛ و سورة الفجر (۸۹): آیت ۲۲.

۳۲ مؤلف بهره مندی از این خوان حکمت را همچون زایش دوم، پس از تولد جسمانی، معرفی میکند. زیرا با آن انسان از عالم طبیعت بدرآمده و به عالم نفس و عقل درمی آید.

۳۳ اس، ایا: براندازهٔ.

۳۴ ¦⟵برگ [ایا:۳-ب]. || دعای مؤلف الهام یافته از آیات ۷۷ تا ۸۰، در سورة الواقعة (۵۶)، است: إِنَّهُ لَقُرْآنٌ كَرِيمٌ * فِي كِتَابٍ مَكْنُونٍ * لَا يَمَسُّهُ إِلَّا الْمُطَهَّرُونَ * تَنْزِيلٌ مِنْ رَبِّ الْعَالَمِينَ.

فهرست صد صف که اندر این کتاب است[1]

۱. صف نخستین: سخن اندر راه پذیرفتن علم

۲. صف دوم: سخن اندر دلیل و مدلول[2]

۳. صف سوم: سخن اندر نام و نامدار

۴. صف چهارم: سخن اندر اثبات حقیقت

۵. صف پنجم: سخن اندر راست و دروغ و [علّت] بسیاری دروغ اندر سخن مردمان

۶. صف ششم: سخن اندر معاد (انسان)

۷. صف هفتم: سخن اندر چگونگی درجات ثواب

۸. صف هشتم: سخن اندر اثبات نفس مجرّد و اثبات ثواب و عقاب مر نفس بی‌جسم

۹. صف نهم: سخن اندر آنك هر که بدکردار است دشمن خدای است و دلایل عقلی بر آن

۱۰. صف دهم: سخن اندر عقل کلّی که او را جز بذات خود نگریدن نیست

۱۱. صف یازدهم: سخن اندر مُزد و بَزَه

۱۲. صف دوازدهم: سخن اندر آنك مر هستیها را کرانه است[3]

---

۱ عنوان صفوف در فهرست ذیل از لحاظ نحوه بیان در انتخاب کلمات مترادف و ترتیب عبارات گاهی اندکی با متن اصلی تفاوت دارد؛ اما، مفهوم عناوین صفوف تغییر خاصّ نمی‌کند. هر جا در این فهرست کلمه یا عبارتی داخل کروشه، []، گذاشته شده است یعنی در فهرست نیست اما در متن اصلی آمده است. و هر جا که کلمه یا عبارتی داخل هلالین، ()، گذاشته شده است یعنی در فهرست هست، اما در متن اصلی به قرینه معنوی، یا به هر علّت دیگری، حذف شده است.

۲ ¦⟵برگ [اس:۲۰-ب].

۳ ¦⟵برگ [اس:۲۱-الف].

۱۳. صف سیزدهم: سخن اندر چگونگی پیدا شدن مردم[۴]

۱۴. صف چهاردهم: سخن اندر عالم عقلانی

۱۵. صف پانزدهم: سخن اندر چرائی پیوستن فایدهٔ نفس کلّی به مردم بیرون از دیگر حیوان

۱۶. صف شانزدهم: سخن اندر چرائی لازم کردن پیامبران بر خلق اقرارِ به توحید (باری)

۱۷. صف هفدهم: سخن اندر آنچ هر چه پیغامبر،[۵] [علیه السّلام،] فرمود [و خود بکرد] بعقل نیکو است و هر چه [از آن مر خلق را] بازداشت [و خود نکرد] [سوی عقل] زشت است

۱۸. صف هجدهم: سخن اندر چرائی بهشتی [ماندن] اندر نعمت [همیشه] و ماندن دوزخی [در عذاب همیشه] (اندر شدّت)؟

۱۹. صف نوزدهم: اندر باقی گشتن کارهای مردم و ضایع ناشدن بد و نیك سوی خدای

۲۰. صف بیستم: سخن اندر نفس کی چون پاکیزه شود دیدار اوفتدش اندر [لطایف و اندر] بودنیها

۲۱. صف بیست و یکم: سخن اندر آفرینش عالم و بخشهای آنچ موجود است از لطایف و کثایف

۲۲. صف بیست و دوم: سخن اندر واجبی عمل شریعت و حجّت بر آنك دست [از آن] بازداشتن روا نیست[۶]

۲۳. صف بیست و سیّم:[۷] سخن اندر هویّت مُبدِع [حقّ] (سبحانه وتعالی)

۲۴. صف بیست و چهارم: سخن اندر (معنی) الله که بزرگ تر نام خدای است

---

۴ ¦⟵برگ [ایا:۴-الف].

۵ اس: پیامبر؛ ایا: پیمبر.

۶ ¦⟵برگ [اس:۲۱-ب].

۷ اس: صف بیست و دوم [کذا].

۸ ¦⟵برگ [ایا:۴-ب].

۹ اینجا پایان برگ [اس:۲۱-ب] است. بعلاوه، در نسخه استانبول یادداشتی ناخوانا در پایان این برگ پس از عنوان صف سی‌ودوم آمده است. فهرست بقیه صفها تا پایان فهرست صف صدم، و ابتدای صف دوم، در نسخه استانبول مفقود شده است. و ابتدای برگ [اس:۲۲-الف] از میانهٔ جمله چهارم در صف دوم آغاز میشود.

---

۱۰ ¦←برگ [ایا:۵-الف].

۵۵. صف پنجاه و پنجم:[۱۱] سخن اندرآنك ثواب و عقاب علمی است نه حسّی[۱۲]

۵۶. صف پنجاه و ششم: سخن اندر بهشت و دوزخ و وصف (آن)

۵۷. صف پنجاه و هفتم: سخن اندرآنك صورت عالم پیش از آفرینش نزدیك باری نبود[۱۳]

۵۸. صف پنجاه و هشتم: سخن اندر چیزهای طبیعی و صنیعی

۵۹. صف پنجاه و نهم: (سخن) اندرآن کی نفس تأییدی تواند که شرف خویشتن بنماید مر آن [نفس] را که فرود او است

۶۰. صف شستم: سخن اندر هستیها کی با عقل پدید آمد

۶۱. صف شست و یکم: سخن اندر شش جهت عالم

۶۲. صف شست و دوم: سخن اندرآنك بدی را در آفرینش مایه نیست

۶۳. صف شست و سیم: سخن اندر فضل اهل ثواب بر یکدیگر

۶۴. صف شست و چهارم: سخن اندرآنك نفس به مرتبت عقل نرسد

۶۵. صف شست و پنجم: سخن اندر چگونگی بسیار[ی] (چیزها اندر) عالم از یك امر

۶۶. صف شست و ششم: سخن اندر معنیِ نام کلمه مُبدِع حقّ [سبحانه]

۶۷. صف شست و هفتم: سخن اندر اثبات سه فرع [روحانی]: جدّ و فتح و خیال

۶۸. صف شست و هشتم: سخن اندر آنك ازو توهّم نتوان کردن

۶۹. صف شست و نهم: سخن اندر شرح «کن» کی امر خدای است[۱۴]

---

۱۱ ایا: صف پنجاه و ششم [کذا].

۱۲ ¦⟵برگ [ایا:۵-ب].

۱۳ ایا: بود [کذا].

۱۴ ¦⟵برگ [ایا:۶-الف].

۱۵ ایا: این عالم [کذا]. || تصحیح قیاسی.

۱۶ ¦⟵برگ [ایا:۶-ب].

---

۱۷ ایا: پیمبری.

۱۸ ایا: نباشد.

۱۹ ↓←برگ [ایا:۷-الف].

صَفِّ نخستین

سخن اندر راه پذیرفتن علم

[§۱:۱] بدانید که نفس را سوی اندر یافتن آنچ نداند دو راه است: یکی گوش و دیگر چشم. و گوش به دلالت زبان یابد مر علم را کز گوینده بشنود. و چشم به دلالت دست یابد مر علم را که نبشته ببیند.[۱] و خداوندانِ حواس درست شنوندگان یا بینندگان اندر آنچ گوینده بگوید[۲] انبازانند. و شناسندگان نبشته مخصوص‌اند از شنودگان اندر آنچ از نبشته برخوانند.

[§۱:۲] و بدین فصل که بگفتیم پیدا شد که گوش ماده است که فایده‌پذیر است از زفان[۳] که نر است و فایده دهنده است. و هر دو جفتان یکدیگراند. و چشم ماده است که فایده‌پذیر است از دست که نر است و فایده‌دهنده است. و هر دو جفتان یکدیگراند. و نیز پیدا شد که شناسندگان نبشته شریفتراند از شنوندگان، ازبهر آنك همه نویسندگان مردم‌اند و همه مردم نویسنده نیستند.

[§۱:۳] و نیز همه شنوندگان مردم نیستند چنانك همه نویسندگان مردم‌اند. و کتابت مردم را صنعتی است که هیچ جانور با او اندر آن انباز نیست. وگر نویسنده را از عالم برگیری به وهم، مردم برگرفته نشود؛ وگر مردم را به وهم از عالم برگیری، نویسنده برگرفته شود. و همچنانك اگر مردم را به وهم از عالم برگیری، حیوان برگرفته نشود؛ وگر حیوان را به وهم برگیری، مردم برگرفته شود. ازبهر آنك هر مردمی حیوان است و هر حیوانی مردم نیست.

[§۱:۴] و هردو چیزی که به برگرفتن یکی از ایشان آن دیگر برگرفته شود، آن دیگر که برگرفته شود بازپس‌تر از آن یار خویش پدید آمده باشد. چنانك نویسنده که

---

۱ ایا: به بیند.

۲ ایا: بگویند.

۳ زفان = زبان.

به برگرفتن مردم همی‌برگرفته شود،[۴] سپس از پدیدآمدنِ مردم پدید آمده است؛ و هر چه اندر بودش بازپس‌تر است، ازو به شرف بیشتر است. پس درست شد که نویسندگان را بر نانویسندگان آن شرف است که مردم را بر دیگر حیوان همان شرف است.

۴ ¦←برگ [ایا:۷-ب].

صف دوم

سخن اندر دلیل و مدلول

[§۱:۲] چیزها بر دو روی است. یکی ازو آن است که مر او را بذات او اندر توان یافتن و به دلیلی حاجتمند نشود جویندهٔ او. و دیگری آن است که مر او را بذات او اندر نتوان یافتن، آن چیزها است که او را به جدا ازو توان یافتن.

[§۲:۲] اما آنچ مر او را بذات او بتوان یافتن[1] آن چیزها است که خداوندِ حواسِ درست مر او را بیابد، و او نیز دلیل باشد بر یافتن آنچ مر او را بذات او بتوان یافتن. چون درخت که او دیدنی است بذات خود، و حاجتمند نیست به چیزی دیگر که بر یافتن او دلیلی کند.

[§۳:۲] و دیگر جنبش است اندر درخت که مر او را نتوان یافتن مگر به گشتن حال درخت چون مر جنبش را بپذیرد، و جنبش آن است که [از] حسّ پنهان است.

[§۴:۲] و حاجتمندی به دلیل ازبهر نزدیکی چیزها است و دوری دیگر چیزها، و ازبهر پیدائی چیزها و پوشیدگی دیگر چیزها، و آن بر چهار بخش است:

[§۵:۲] یك[2] بخش ازو آن است که از چیزی ظاهر بر چیزی ظاهر دلیل گیری. و این محال است ازبهرآنك هر ظاهری خود بر خویشتن دلیل است، و از دلالتِ دیگر بی‌نیاز است.

[§۶:۲] دیگر بخش آن است که باطنی بر باطنی دیگر دلیل گیری. و این نیز محال است ازبهرآنك[3] این باطن نایافته و نادانسته است، بدیگر نادانسته‌ای[4] بر وی دلیل چگونه شاید گرفتن، که هر یکی از ایشان خود حاجتمند است به دلیلی دیگر.

---

۱ اس: - صف سی و سوم [(از فهرست فصول)] ... بتوان یافتن. || ¦⟵برگ [اس:۲۲-الف].

۲ ایا: یکی.

۳ اس: [«آنك» بالای سطر نوشته شده است].

۴ اس، ایا: نادانسته‌ء.

[§۷:۲] و سدیگر بخش آن است که باطنی بر ظاهری دلیل گیری. و این نیز محال است از بهر آنك آنچ باطن است خود بذات خویش ناپیداست، پس چگونه دلیلی کند بر دیگری.

[§۸:۲] و چهارم بخش که حقّ است آن است کی به ظاهرِ پیدا[۵] دلیل گیری بر باطنِ پوشیده، و باطن و ظاهر که یکی دلیل است و دیگر مدلول، و هر دو آفریدگانند، و بر یکدیگر به هم‌جنسی دلالت کنند. و بدین شرح که بکردیم پیدا شد که آفریده بر آفریدگار دلیلی کند.

[§۹:۲] معارضه اگر کسی گوید: پس ما[۶] مر خدای را تعالی جز بدین عالم، که آفریدهٔ او است، بچه دانیم؟ که چون کارکرد همی‌بینیم ازین عالم، و او را دانش نیست،[۷] و اندر آن چیزها که همی‌عالم پدید آرد آثار حکمت است، و اندر نهاد عالم آثار حکمت است، بدانستیم که این عالم کار بفرمان خدای همی‌کند.

[§۱۰:۲] جواب او را گوییم که هر نادانی که[۸] کار بحکمت کند، ناچاره کار بفرمان کاربندی کند حکیم. و کار مر نفس را است به یاری عقل. و هر نفسی کز عقل بهره بیش دارد کار او نیکوتر است.

[§۱۱:۲] و چون اندر عالم هر کارکنی، که هست، کار بفرمان نفس همی‌کند،

---

۵ |←برگ [ایا:۸-الف].

۶ ایا: – پس ما.

۷ قس: گشایش و رهایش، مسئله بیست و دوم، جواب، بند [۱۲۶]: بدان ای برادر که ما عالم را کارکن می بینیم که او را دانش نیست، پس دانستیم که این کار بذات خویش نکند ناچار بفرمان دیگری کند، پس اینجا درست شد که عالم و آنچ دروست کار بفرمان کسی میکند و کارکردن نادان بفرمان دانا بود و آن بر دو روی باشد یا بگفتار بود یا بکردار و کردار فرود گفتار است از بهر آنك کردار ستور راست و گفتار مردم راست.

۸ ایا: + او.

چنانك دست‌افزارهای پیشه‌وران و اندامهای ایشان[۹] همه بفرمان نفسهای ایشان همی‌کارکند.[۱۰]

[§۱۲:۲] و آسیاها و دولابها، که همی‌کارکند، بدان حکمت همی‌کارکند که نفس مردم اندر ایشان نهاده است، دانستیم که این آسیای عظیم که این عالم است بفرمان نفس همی‌کارکند.

[§۱۳:۲] و مر نفس را و مر این عالم را هر دو را خداوندی دیگر است که او از کارکن و ناکارکن، که ضدّ یکدیگراند،[۱۱] برتر است.

[§۱۴:۲] و دلیل بر درستی این قول آن است که ما هر صانعی را که اندر عالم همی‌یابیم، که به رویی از رویها به مصنوع خویش ماند، و مر ایشان هردو را صانعی دیگر یابیم. چنانك درودگر که صانع است و تخت مصنوع او است، و تخت همچون درودگر جسم است. و به جسمی صانع مانند مصنوع است، هردو را مصنوع طبایع یافتیم، بدانچ چوب نبات است، و درودگر از نبات بحاصل آمده است. و نبات مصنوع طبایع است چون درودگر، و طبایع همه جسم بودند، صانع و مصنوع نیز مانند یکدیگر بودند.

[§۱۵:۲] پس گوییم که ایشان را صانعی است بر افراز ایشان. پس گوییم که نفس‌کلّی صانع ایشان است.[۱۲] باز چون درودگر را و طبایع را و نفس را جوهر یافتیم، گفتیم که صانع به مصنوع مانندە‌تر است، باید که صانع حقیقت پدیدآورندۀ جوهر باشد نه از چیزی.

[§۱۶:۲] و از دیگر روی، چون مر عالم را از نفس اثرپذیر یافتیم، دانستیم که

۹ ¦←برگ [اس:۲۲-ب].
۱۰ ایا: [«کند» مخدوش است].
۱۱ اس: یکدیگرند.
۱۲ ¦←برگ [ایا:۸-ب].

اگر میان نفس و میان عالم هم‌گوشگی[۱۳] نیستی، عالم از نفس صورت و صنعت نپذیردی. و مر آن هم‌گوشگی را میان ایشان به جوهریّت یافتیم، و از جوهر برتر چیزی نشناختیم.

[§۱۷:۲] پس دانستیم که مُبدِع حقّ آن است که جوهر را او جوهر گردانیده است[۱۴] نه از چیزی، بل به وحدت خویش که فراز جوهر است. و فراز جوهر نه مر وهم را راه است، و نه مر سخن را جای گشتن است. و آن برتر از صفت و ناصفت است.

۱۳ نك: دهخدا: هم‌گوشه. [هَ شَ / شِ] هم جنس و همسایه.

۱۴ نك: زادالمسافر، قول ۲۳، ص ۳۶۴، س ۹: ... پس باری — سبحانه و تعالی — جوهر نیست بل مُجَوهِر الجواهر است. قس: زادالمسافرین، قول ۲۳، ص ۳۵۳.

صف سوم

سخن اندر نام و نامدار

[§۱:۳] بدانید کی نام دلیل است بر نامدار، و نامدار از نام بی‌نیاز است. و نام حرفهای ترکیب کرده است که راه برد مردم را سوی مقصود او. و نام بر پانزده روی[۱] است: یکی را ازو موضوع خوانند، یعنی نهاده، چون آب و آتش و خاك، و جز آن که معروف است میان اهل لغت پارسی. و نه ازبهر معنی را[۲] مر آب را آب خوانند، و مر آتش را آتش، بل که نام نهاده چُنین باشد. و دیگر نام صورت است اعنی چهره[۳] چنانك گویی ستور، و نبات و میوه و جز آن. و این نامها است که بر صورتها اُفتَد.

[§۲:۳] سدیگر نام فاعل است، اعنی کننده، چنانك گویی گوینده و خورنده و بخشنده و جز آن که ازبهر آن[۴] کار که کرد او را این نام نهادند. چهارم نام فعل است چون خوردن و بخشیدن و گفتار و جز آن که نام آن کار است که کارکنی کند. پنجم نام کرده است، و آن را مفعول گویند. چنانك گویی خورده و بخشیده و گفته و جز آن.

[§۳:۳] ششم نام را مشتق گویند اعنی شکافته، چون گرمابه که شکافته از آبْ گرم است، و چون گردون کی شکافته از گشتن است که فعل او است. هفتم نام را موصول گویند اعنی[۵] پیوسته چون عبداللّه، و پسرِ احمد، و برادر محمّد، و جز آن که دو نام بهم پیوسته است. هشتم نام آن است که کسی را بخوانی[۶] که ای فلان به مخاطبه، اگر نامش آن باشد که تو گویی یا نباشد.

---

۱ ایا: [«روی» مخدوش است].

۲ ¦⟵برگ [اس:۲۳-الف].

۳ ایا: [«چهره» مخدوش است].

۴ ایا: این.

۵ ¦⟵برگ [ایا:۹-الف].

۶ ایا: خوانی.

[§۳:۴] نهم نام سوگند است چنانك گویی والله و بقبله و بمسلمانی و جز آن از سوگندها.[۷] دهم نام فرمان است چنانك گویی برو و بیای و بخور و جز آن.

[§۳:۵] یازدهم نام صفت است، و آن بسیار گونها است؛ ازو بعضی آن است که نام خویش از ذات خویش یافته است. چون سپیدی که نام خود از ذات خویش یافته است. و چون سیاهی و جز آن. و دیگر نام از صفتی است که نام از جهت نوع خویش یافت. چنانك گویی[۸] چوب و گوشت نام از جهت چوبی و گوشتی یافتند که هر یکی نوعی است از جسم. دیگرگونه از نام صفات آن است که نام نه از جهت خویش یافته است بل که از چیزی دیگر یافته است. چون دراز و کوتاه که نام از جهت درازی و کوتاهی یافتند، و درازی و کوتاهی دیگر است، و دراز و کوتاه دیگر.

[§۳:۶] دوازدهم نام را مضاف گویند اعنی بازبسته. چون کهن و نو و بنده و آزاد و جز آن، که هر یکی ازین چیزها این نام بسبب بازبستن او یابد به مخالف او. چنانك کهن را به نو توان شناختن، و بسیار را به اندك توان شناختن که بسیار بیش ازو است. چنانك اندك را به بسیار توان شناختن، از بهر آنك چون اندك را به بسیار بازبسته شود آن وقت اندك اندك[۹] توان خواندن.[۱۰]

[§۳:۷] سیزدهم نام را اشارت خوانند. چنانك گویی من و تو و این و آن و ایشان و ما و جز آن. چهاردهم نام را ادوات گویند اعنی دست افزارها چون کاغذ و دوات و قلم و جز آن. پانزدهم نام را مصادر[۱۱] گویند چون بریدن، و دوختن، و نبشتن، و جز آن. این است حدّ نام و نامدار که بازنموده شد، و زین مر جویندهٔ توحید را راه گشاید.

---

۷ ایا: – از سوگندها.

۸ ایا: – گویی.

۹ اس: [«اندك» دوم در حاشیه اضافه شده است].

۱۰ ¦⟵برگ [اس:۲۳-ب].

۱۱ ایا: مصادت.

صف چهارم

سخن اندر اثبات حقیقت

[§۴:۱] مذهب سوفسطای این است که گویند[1] هیچ چیز را حقیقت نیست. و عالم برمثال خواب است و چیزها همه خیال است. و دلیل آرند بدین قول کی هیچ چیز اندر عالم بر یك حال نیست. نه آنچ یافتنی است از چیزها، و نه آنچ یابنده است از مردم و حیوان. و خواب چنین است کی ساعتی اندر او چیزی یابی و ساعتی نیابی.

[§۴:۲] و فیثاغورس[2] حکیم گوید: ‹من جز به هندسه مر قول سوفسطای را ردّ نتوانستم کردن›.

[§۴:۳] و ما گوییم اندر ردّ قول سوفسطای و اثبات حقیقت به گفتارهای کوتاه، با برهان کی سوفسطای همی‌گوید که چیزها را حقیقت نیست. و این حکم که ایشان کردند از چیزها است و از دو بیرون نیست: یا مر چیزها را حقیقت نیست یا حقیقت است مر چیزها را. اگر چیزها را حقیقت نیست، و قول ایشان را حقیقت است، پس درست شد که قول ایشان باطل است، چون قول ایشان حقیقت آمد. و اگر قول ایشان خود حقیقت نیست، پس مر چیزها را حقیقت است. و به هر دو روی قول سوفسطای باطل است.

[§۴:۴] و این قضیّت را که ایشان گفتند قضیّت سلب گویند. و چون قضیّت سلب دروغ‌زن شود آنچ قضیّت برو باشد نه چنان باشد که گوینده گفته باشد. چنانك

---

۱ ¦⟵برگ [ایا:۹-ب].

۲ نك: دهخدا: فیثاغورس. [رِ] پیثاگوراس. پیتاگر. از فلاسفهٔ بزرگ یونان است که میان سالهای ۵۸۳ تا ۵۷۲ ق. م. در شهر سامس تولد یافت ... فیثاغورس به ریاضیات عشق و عقیدهٔ بسیار داشت، چنانکه اصل فلسفی اعداد و تطبیق آنها با علوم طبیعی و الهی و معرفةالروح واخلاق، زادهٔ فکر اوست.

چون گوید: 'امیر بدین شهر نیست'، اگر او دروغ همی‌گوید پس چنان نیست که او گفت، و امیر بدین شهر است.

[§۵:۴] و قضیّت ایجاب چون راست آید آن چیز که قضیّت برو باشد چنان باشد که گوینده گفته باشد. چنانك چون گوید: 'امیر بدین شهر است' اگر راست همی‌گوید امیر به شهر است.

[§۶:۴] وگر قضیّت ایجاب دروغ آید آن سخن نیز دروغ آید. و لکن قضیّت سلب بخلاف این باشد. ازبهرآنك چون گوید 'امیر بدین شهر نیست' اگر چنین کی او گفت[۳] هست، امیر بدین شهر نیست. و اگر امیر بدین شهر هست چنین که او گفت نیست.

[§۷:۴] و چون چیزها را حقیقت هست و حواسّ بر آن گوایی همی‌دهد، پس قول سوفسطای را حقیقت نیست. و هرکه مر حس را منکر شود با او سخن نشاید گفتن.

۳ ¦⟵برگ [اس:۲۴-الف].

صف پنجم

سخن اندر راست و دروغ و علّت بسیاری دروغ اندر سخن مردمان[1]

[§۵:۱] از سخن آنچ در او راست و دروغ بیاید خبر است. و خبر بر دو روی است: ابتدا است و جواب. و فرق میان راست و دروغ آن است کی راست سخنی باشد که مردمان آن را بدانند اندر چیزی که آن چیز یافته باشد. چنانك کسی گوید کی آتش گرم است.

[§۵:۲] و دروغ سخنی باشد که مردمان مر آن را ندانند اندر چیزی که آن چیز نایافته باشد و نادانسته. چنانك کسی گوید ’آتش سخنگوی است‘. و آتش نامی است کی مردمان آن را بدانند، و سخن گفتن نیز معلوم است؛ و لکن آتش نیز بدین صفت نایافته است از آنچ آتش سخنگوی نیست.

[§۵:۳] و دروغ بر دو بخش است: یك بخش ازو ممکن است. و دیگر بخش محال است. و ممکن چنان است که گوید ’فلان چنین گفت‘. شاید بودن که گفت، و شاید بودن که نگفت. و ناممکن و محال آن است کی گوید ’سنگ بپرید‘.

[§۵:۴] و اما خبر دادن حکایت کردن است از گفتار و کردار. و قضا و قضیّت مر آن را گویند: که گویی که ’چنین است‘ و آن را ایجاب گویند، یا گویی که ’چنین نیست‘ و آن را سلب گویند.

[§۵:۵] و چون قضیّت ایجاب از یك روی راست آید بسیار رویها دروغ آید، چنانك چون[2] گویی ’آتش گرم است‘، این قضیّت بدین یك روی راست باشد. و لکن چون گویی ’آتش سرد است یا تر است یا خاك است و جز این‘، هر چه همی‌توان گفتن همه دروغ باشد.

---

۱ |←برگ [ایا:۱۰-الف].

۲ ایا: - چون.

[§۶:۵] و چون قضیّت سلب از یك روی دروغ آید، از بسیار رویهای دیگر راست آید، چنانك اگر گوید ‹آتش گرم نیست›، این یکی قضیّت دروغ باشد. و لکن اگر گوید ‹سخنگوی و پرنده و نویسنده و تر و سرد نیست و جز آن›، هرچه گوید همه راست باشد،[۳] چون لفظ ‹نه› اندر میان باشد.

[§۷:۵] پس بدین بیان که بکردیم پیدا شد[۴] کی چون سخنِ راست بر وجهِ اثبات گفته شود، چنانك گویی ‹چنین است›، آن سخن را اندازه پدید باشد.

[§۸:۵] و چون دروغ بر وجه اثبات گفته شود، مر آن را اندازه پدید نباشد. چنانك چون گوید ‹آتش گرم است و خشك است و روشن است›، این همه راست است.[۵] و لکن ازین بسیار نتوان گفتن. و چون گویی ‹آتش سرد است و پرنده است و سیاه است و جز آن›، بی‌اندازه صفت توان گفتن کی همه دروغ باشد.

[§۹:۵] و بر عین این حال، چون سخن بر وجه نفی و سلب گفته شود، دروغ اندر او براندازه[۶] آید، و راست نه[۷] براندازه[۸] آید. چنانك گوید ‹آتش گرم نیست و خشك و روشن نیست› این همه دروغ باشد؛ و لکن، ازین راستْ دروغ، نتوان بسیار گفتن. و چون گویی آتش سیاه نیست و استر و اسب و خاك نیست همه راست باشد؛[۹] و لکن، اندازه نیست کزین راست چند توان گفتن.

[§۱۰:۵] پس سخن مردمان بیشتر دروغ ازبهر آن همی‌آید کی آنچ همی‌گویند اندر اثبات همی‌گویند. ازبهرآنك ممکن نیست اندر سلب سخن گفتن. چنان کی[۱۰]

---

۳ اس، ایا: + و.

۴ ¦←برگ [اس:۲۴-ب].

۵ ¦←برگ [ایا:۱۰-ب].

۶ ایا: بی اندازه. || اس: [ذیل «بر» در زیر سطر، به دلیلی نامعلوم، خطی منحنی کشیده شده که اگر دقت نشود خواننده ممکن است به اشتباه «براندازه» را «بی اندازه» بخواند].

۷ ایا: - نه.

۸ اس: نبراندازه؛ ایا: براندازه.

۹ ایا: - باشد.

۱۰ ایا: چنانك.

کسی که آب خورده باشد بوجه اثبات گوید کی 'آب خوردم'. این آسان‌تر از آن تواند گفتن کی بوجه سلب گوید 'نان نخورده‌ام[۱۱] و گوشت و انگور و خربزه نخورده‌ام'.[۱۲] و همه خوردنیهای جهان را بگوید که نخورده‌ام[۱۳] جز آب را تا گفته شود که 'آب[۱۴] خورده‌ام'.[۱۵]

[§۵:۱۱] و لکن[۱۶] اگر سخن مردمان بوجه نفی و سلب بودی راست اندر او بیشترِ دروغ بودی بدین روی که بیان آن نمودیم. بازنموده شد حدّ دروغ و راست، و شرح کرده آمد علّت بسیاری دروغ اندر سخن مردمان. خدای تعالی ما را بر راست گفتن بداراد.

۱۱ اس: نه خورده ام؛ ایا: نخوردم.

۱۲ اس: نه خورده ام؛ ایا: نه خوردم.

۱۳ ایا: بخورده‌ام.

۱۴ ایا: + و.

۱۵ ایا: [حرف «خ» در «خورده‌ام» مخدوش است].

۱۶ ایا: و و لکن [حرف «و» دوبار نوشته شده است].

صف ششم

سخن اندر معاد [۱]

[§۶:۱] بدانید که عالم بذات خویش صورتی است بر هیولی پیدا شده. و زایشهای او از نبات و حیوان همه صورتها است که بر هیولیها پیدا همی‌آید. و امروز اندر عالم هیولی پیدا است و صورت پنهان کی پیدا همی‌آید.

[§۶:۲] و این حال همی دلیل کند که ترکیب کنندهٔ عالم برتر از هیولی و صورت است و نخست هیولی بحاصل کرده است، آن وقت این صورت را که ما همی‌بینیم ازین گنبد عظیم و روشنایی‌ها که اندر او است بر آن هیولیها پدید آورده است.

[§۶:۳] و چون مصنوعات به چهار علّت بوده شود چون [۲] علّت هیولانی، و علّت فاعله، و علّت [۳] آلتی و علّت تمامی، دانیم که این عالم را همین علّتها هست.

[§۶:۴] و علّت هیولانیش طبایع است که صورتها همی‌پذیرد. و علّت فاعلهٔ او نفس‌کلّی است کی آثار خویش اندر عالم پیدا همی‌آرد به نفسهای جزوی. و علّت آلتیش این افلاك و ستارگان است کی چون دست افزارند مر نفس‌کلّی را.

[§۶:۵] پس دانستیم کی این علّت چهارمش است کی آن از خلق پنهان [۴] است کز بهر چه کردستش. و چون آن مراد حاصل آید بازگشت عالم باشد بدانچ ازو پدید آمده است.

[§۶:۶] و چون مردم که غایت زایشهای عالم است اندر این عالم مر صورتها را اندر نفس خویش همی‌تواند آوردن و لطیف گردانیدن، و باز مر آن لطیف را بر

---

۱ قس: کتاب الینابیع، الینبوع الثامن والثلاثون (۳۸): في أنّ للبشر عودًا إلى ثواب أبديّ، ص۸۷ تا ۹۰.

۲ ¦⟵برگ [اس:۲۵-الف].

۳ ¦⟵برگ [ایا:۱۱-الف].

۴ ایا: نهان.

هیولیءِ کثیف همی‌تواند بیرون آوردن، و مر حکمتها را کی دانسته است به گفتار و نبشتن همی مجسّم تواند گردانیدن، دانیم که مردم را بازگشت بدان کس است کی مر حکمتها را بر هیولی او ترکیب کرده است اندر آفرینش عالم.

[۶§:۷] دیگر دلیل بر معاد مردم آن است که اندر حیوان دو قوّت است: چون شهوانی، و آن قوّت آرزوکننده است؛ و چون قوّت غضبی، و آن قوّت خشم گیرنده است.

[۶§:۸] و مراد این هردو قوّت بر جسم بحاصل آید. چنانك چون گرسنه یا تشنه شود یا مجامعت آرزو کند آن وقت خشنود شود کی نان یا آب بخورد یا با جفتی قرار گیرد. و چون از کسی خشم آیدش آن وقت خشنود شود که او را بزند، یا بکشد. و این حال همی دلیل کند بر آنك بازگشت حیوان بدین عالم جسمانی است.

[۶§:۹] و حیوان را ایزد تعالی ازبهر منفعت مردم آفریده است، چنانك گفت، قوله: وَ الْأَنْعَامَ خَلَقَهَا لَكُمْ فِيهَا دِفْءٌ وَ مَنَافِعُ وَ مِنْهَا تَأْكُلُونَ.[۵] گفت: «بیافریدم آفرینش مر ستوران را که مر شما را اندر آن نگاه‌داشت است از سرما، و منفعتها است مردم را، و زو بخورد».

[۶§:۱۰] و مردم را با این قوّتها که حیوان را است قوّت عاقله هست و ناطقه که مردم را به دانستن چیزها و گفتن آنچ داند به جسمی حاجت نیست مر بحاصل کردن مراد این دو قوّت را. پس این دلیل است بر آنك بازگشت او نه به عالم جسمانی است. و چون مردم جسم است و نفس[۶] و درست شد که بازگشت مردم بدین سرای جسمانی نیست، بضرورت پیدا آمد که بازگشت او به سرای نفس است. وَ اللّٰهُ أَعْلَمُ وَ أَحْكَمُ.[۷]

۵ سورة النحل (۱۶)، آیت ۵.

۶ ¦⟵برگ [ایا:۱۱-ب].

۷ ¦⟵برگ [اس:۲۵-ب]. || نك: یادداشت ۱۳، ص ۱۴۵.

صف هفتم

سخن اندر چگونگی درجات ثواب[۱]

[§۱:۷] بباید دانستن که غایت درجات اندر شرف و نور و نعمت و رحمت مر رسول را است. ازبهرآنك او اندر عالم دین به مرتبت هفتم است.

[§۲:۷] و چیزها به هفتم مرتبه تمام شود. چنانك آفرینش مردم از سلاله[۲] و نطفه و عَلَقَه و مُضْغَه و عِظام و لحم که ششم است به هفتم تمام شود که خلق آخر است.

[§۳:۷] و اندر دین همچنین مرتبت هفت است از مستجیب و مأذون و داعی و حجّت و امام و اساس. و این شش مرتبت را تمامی ناطق است کی هفتم ایشان است.

[§۴:۷] و گوایی دهد بر درستی این منزلتها قول رسول مصطفی، صلی الله علیه وآله، کی فرمود: أَخَذْتُ مِنَ الخَمْسِ و أعْطَيْتُ إلى الخَمْسِ. گفت: «بستدم حکمت آلهی را از پنج میانجی، و دادم به پنج میانجی».[۳]

[§۵:۷] و آن پنج میانجی اساس بود و امام و حجّت و داعی و مأذون. هریکی از

۱ قس: كتاب الينابيع، الينبوع التاسع والعشرون (۲۹): في كيفيّة التفاضل بين المثابين، ص ۶۹ تا ۷۰. || نیز قس: الملیجی، ابوالقاسم عبد الحاكم بن وهب، المجالس المستَنصِريَّة، المجلس الرابع: تأويل 'لاَ إِلَهَ إلاّ اللّهُ'، تأويل جزء من سورة الحمد، ص ۳۶ تا ۴۰.

۲ نك: دهخدا: سلالة. [سُ لَ] آنچه بیرون کشیده شود از چیزی... برگزیده. خلاصهٔ هرچیز... || گِل نرم که چون آن را بفشارند آب از آن برآید. || قس: جامع الحکمتین، ص ۵۳، بند (۴۹)؛ نیز نك: سورة المؤمنون (۲۳)، آیات ۱۲ تا ۱۴.

۳ النعمان بن محمّد، القاضي ابوحنیفه، اساس التأويل، تصحیح: عارف تامر (بیروت، ۱۹۶۰)، ص ۷۰: قال رسول الله (صلّى الله عليه و سلم): انني آخذ الوحي عن جبريل، و جبريل يأخذه عن ميكائيل، و ميكائيل يأخذه عن اسرافيل، و اسرافيل يأخذه عن اللوح، و اللوح يأخذه عن القلم، فصار التأييد يتصل بالنطقاء من خمسة حدود علوية، و يتصل عنهم للمستجيبين بواسطة خمسة حدود سفلية، فالحدود العُلويَّة هم الذين ذكرناهم، و الحدود السُّفْلِيَّة هُمُ الْأُسُس و الْأَئِمَّة و الْحُجَج و النُّقَباء أصحاب الجزائر، و الْأَجْنِحَة و هم الدُّعاة.

برتر خویش بستد و به فروتر خویش بداد. و خود اندر میان ستاننده و دهنده ایستاده بود.

[§۷:۶] و هریکی ازین میانجیان اندر مرتبت خویش همان کنند کی رسول اندر مرتبت خویش کند.

[§۷:۷] و مستجیب میانجی نبود. ازبهر آنك او ستانندهٔ نادهنده بود[۴] به طرف فرودین، چنانك ناطق ستانندهٔ نادهنده[۵] بود به طرف زبرین.

[§۷:۸] پس گوییم که ازین شش مرتبت کی فرود از ناطق است هرکه بناطق نزدیکتر است ثواب او تمامتر و با راحت‌تر است.

[§۷:۹] و مثل ثواب رسول اندر سرای معاد، چون مثل کسی است کی چیزی خواهد خریدن که جملگی آن چیز به هفت درم فروشند، و او هفت درم دارد که جملگی آن را بخرد.

[§۷:۱۰] و اساس او خداوند شش درم است. و امام خداوند پنج درم است. و حجّت خداوند چهار درم است. و داعی خداوند سه درم است. و مأذون خداوند دو درم است. و مستجیب خداوند یك درم است.

[§۷:۱۱] و هریکی از ایشان براندازهٔ ملك خویش[۶] از آن چیز بیابند. و بر قدر کار و علم خویش به رحمت و نعمت آخرتی برسند. چنانك خدای تعالی همی‌گوید، قوله: وَ لِكُلٍّ دَرَجٰاتٌ مِمّٰا عَمِلُوا وَ لِيُوَفِّيَهُمْ أَعْمٰالَهُمْ وَ هُمْ لاٰ يُظْلَمُونَ.[۷] همی‌گوید: «و مر هرکسی را درجات است از آنچ کرده‌اند. و بدیشان رساند[۸] مزد کارشان و بر ایشان ستم نکنند».

---

۴ ایا: +و

۵ اس، ایا: دهندهٔ ناستاننده [کذا]. || تصحیح قیاسی.

۶ ←¦ برگ [ایا:۱۲-الف].

۷ سورة الأحقاف (۴۶)، آیت ۱۹.

۸ ←¦ برگ [اس:۲۶-الف].

[§۱۲:۷] امّا رحمت عظیم بر آن کسها که به درجت کمتر باشند، از ایزد تعالی آن است که هیچ کس را اندر بهشت از مرتبت آن کس کی برتر ازو است خبر ندارد تا حسدش نیاید. و مرتبت هر کسی مانند مرتبت خویش داند.

[§۱۳:۷] هم بر این مثال که اندر این عالم است کی هر کسی بدان مقدار کی علم او است شادان است. و نمیداند بدانك برتر ازو است از علم چه می‌داند. و چون نداند چیزی را ازو آرزو نیایدش. و چون آرزو نباشد نیاز نباشد.[۹]

[§۱۴:۷] و هر کسی آن آرزو کند اندر بهشت کی یافته باشد. چنانك خدای تعالی همی‌گوید، قوله: وَ فِيهٰا[۱۰] مٰا تَشْتَهِيهِ[۱۱] الْأَنْفُسُ وَ تَلَذُّ الْأَعْيُنُ وَ أَنْتُمْ فِيهٰا خٰالِدُونَ.[۱۲] گفت: «اندر بهشت آن است کی نفسها آن آرزو کند و چشمها بدان خوشی یابد و شما اندر او جاودانه مانید».

[§۱۵:۷] این آیت[۱۳] همی دلیل کند که بهشتی را آن نعمت آرزو کند که یافته باشد و بیش از آن خبر ندارد. ازبهرآنك ما دانیم که ثواب ناطق برتر است و شریفتر است از ثواب امّت، ازبهرآنك علم و عمل او بغایت کمال است. پس آرزوی نفس او بغایت کمال باشد و مر او را از ثواب آن باشد که نفس او آرزو کند نه آنك نفس مستجیب آرزو کند با کوتهیِ پایگه[۱۴] او.

[§۱۶:۷] و از بزرگی علم او و شرف نفس او بود کی خدای تعالی مر او را، علیه السلام، گفت، قوله:[۱۵] وَ لَسَوْفَ يُعْطِيكَ رَبُّكَ فَتَرْضىٰ.[۱۶] گفت: «و باشد کی بدهد

---

۹ قس: زاد المسافر: قول ۱۸: اندر لذّات و اثبات آن، ص ۲۳۳ تا ۲۵۹.

۱۰ ایا: فی.

۱۱ اس، ایا: تشتهی.

۱۲ سورة الزخرف (۴۳)، آیت ۷۱.

۱۳ ایا: آیة.

۱۴ ایا: بانکه.

۱۵ ایا: – قوله.

۱۶ سورة الضحی (۹۳)، آیت ۵.

ترا کردگار تو تا تو خشنود شوی». این آیت همی دلیل کند کی رسول را خشنودی نبود بدان ثواب کی مر امّت را دانست کی خواهندشان دادن.

[§۱۷:۷] و معاد جای بازگشتن باشد. و هر شاگردی را بازگشت آن جهانی به دانا و آموزگار خویش بود. اگر علم حقّ آموزد و راست باشد و عمل بکند به ثواب آموزگار خویش برسد. و اندر شفاعت او باشد چون جفت او باشد که شفاعت از شفع[۱۷] گرفته اند.

[§۱۸:۷] و شفع به لغت عرب جفت باشد. و مستجیب جفت داعی باشد. و ثواب اندر شفاعت او یابد. اگر جفتش نیك است به ثواب نیکی رسد. وگر جفتش بد است به پاداش بدی رسد.

[§۱۹:۷] چنانك رسول مصطفی، صلی الله علیه وآله، گفت: اَلْمَرْءُ مَعَ مَنْ أَحَبَّ.[۱۸] گفت: «مرد با آن کس است کی او را دوست دارد». اگر دوستار[۱۹] اولیای خدای باشد،[۲۰] او دوست خدای باشد.

[§۲۰:۷] چنانك خدای تعالی همی‌گوید، قوله: قُلْ إِنْ كُنْتُمْ تُحِبُّونَ اللّٰهَ فَاتَّبِعُونِي يُحْبِبْكُمُ اللّٰهُ.[۲۱] گفت: «بگو ای محمّد که اگر خدای را همی دوست دارید، از پس من روید تا خدای شما را دوست دارد».

---

۱۷ ¦⟵برگ [ایا:۱۲-ب].

۱۸ نك: مصباح الشريعة المنسوب للإمام الصادق (ع) (بیروت: اعلمی، ۱۴۰۰ق)، ج ۱، باب الثالث والتسعون في الحب لله، ص ۱۹۴: قَالَ الصَّادِقُ (ع) الْمُحِبُّ فِي اللّٰهِ مُحِبُّ اللّٰهِ وَ الْمَحْبُوبُ فِي اللّٰهِ حَبِيبُ اللّٰهِ لِأَنَّهُمَا لَايَتَحَابَّانِ إِلَّا فِي اللّٰهِ قَالَ رَسُولُ اللّٰهِ (ص) الْمَرْءُ مَعَ مَنْ أَحَبَّ فَمَنْ أَحَبَّ عَبْداً فِي اللّٰهِ فَإِنَّمَا أَحَبَّ اللّٰهَ تَعَالَى وَ لَايُحِبُّ اللّٰهَ تَعَالَى إِلَّا مَنْ أَحَبَّهُ اللّٰهُ...؛ نیز نك: البرقي، احمد بن محمد، المحاسن، تصحیح: جلال الدین الحسینی المحدث (قم: دار الكتب الإسلامية، ۱۳۷۱ق)، ج ۱، باب (۳۴): الحب والبغض في الله، ص ۲۶۳؛ الشیخ المفید، محمد بن محمد بن النعمان، الأمالي، تصحیح: علی اکبر غفاری (قم، ۱۴۰۳ق/۱۳۶۲ش)، المجلس التاسع عشر، ص ۱۵۱ تا ۱۵۲.

۱۹ ایا: دوستدار.

۲۰ ¦⟵برگ [اس:۲۶-ب].

۲۱ سورة آل عمران (۳)، آیت ۳۱.

[§۲۱:۷] و هرکه پس رو دشمنان اولیآءِ خدای باشد اندر تاریکی اوفتد. و به عذاب آتش جاویدی رسد چنانك خدای تعالی همی‌گوید، قوله: وَ الَّذِينَ كَفَرُوا أَوْلِيٰاؤُهُمُ الطّٰاغُوتُ يُخْرِجُونَهُمْ مِنَ النُّورِ إِلَى الظُّلُمٰاتِ أُولٰئِكَ أَصْحٰابُ النّٰارِ هُمْ فِيهٰا خٰالِدُونَ.[۲۲] همی‌گوید: «و آنها که حقّ را بپوشانیدند دوستان ایشان دیوان‌اند،[۲۳] بیرون آرندشان از روشنایی سوی تاریکیها. ایشان اهل آتش‌اند، و ایشان اندر او جاودانه‌اند».

[§۲۲:۷] و مثل عالِم و متعلّم چون مثل علّت و معلول است. ازبهرآنك هرکجا عالِم است متعلّم آنجا است، و هریکی نام خویش به اضافت یار خویش یافته‌اند. همچنانك علّت از معلول جدا نیست و هستی هردو بیك وقت بوده است، بی‌زمان اندر میان ایشان.

[§۲۳:۷] چنانك آفتاب کی علّت روز است برآمد، معلول او که روز است هم در آن وقت حاصل آمد بی هیچ زمانی به میان ایشان. و لکن هرچند که میان علّت و معلول جدایی نیست، شرف و نهاد پیشی و بهتری و کمال مر علّت را است. و ضعیفی و بیچارگی[۲۴] و بازپس‌ماندگی و نیاز مر معلول را است.

[§۲۴:۷] و همچنین است حال میان عالِم و متعلّم که پیشی و شرف و بهتری و کمال مر عالِم را است. و سپسی و کهتری و نقصان مر متعلّم را است.

[§۲۵:۷] امّا باید که مؤمن مستجیب مطیع و خاضع عالِم باشد. وگر عالِم نباشد متابع خداوند حقّ باشد. و بداند که حقّ آن کس را است که خدای تعالی مر او را بگزیده است و آن ناطق است. وز پس او حقّ آن کس را است که ناطق مر او را بگزیده است.

۲۲ سورة البقرة (۲)، آیت ۲۵۷.

۲۳ ایا: دیوانند.

۲۴ ایا: + مر معلول.

[§۷:۲۶] و آن کس که گزیدهٔ ناطق است گزیدهٔ خدای است.[۲۵] و هر که با گزیدهٔ خدای دیگری گزیند او با خدای انبازی جسته باشد.

[§۷:۲۷] و هر که با خدای انبازی جوید مر این گناه را از خدای عفو نیابد؛ چنانك میفرماید، قوله: إِنَّ اللّٰهَ لاٰ يَغْفِرُ أَنْ يُشْرَكَ بِهِ وَ يَغْفِرُ مٰا دُونَ ذٰلِكَ لِمَنْ يَشٰاءُ وَ مَنْ يُشْرِكْ بِاللّٰهِ فَقَدْ ضَلَّ ضَلاٰلاً بَعِيداً.[۲۶] همی‌گوید: «که خدای نیامرزد مر آن را کی با او انباز گیرد. و بیامرزد هر چه فرود از آن است از گناهان هر که را خواهد. و هر که با خدای انباز گیرد گم‌بوده شود گم‌بودگی دور».[۲۷]

[§۷:۲۸] امام زمانه[۲۸] رضای خدای است ازبهرآنك اندر خشنودی او خشنودی خدای است. و دشمن امام زمانه خشم[۲۹] خدای[۳۰] است، ازبهرآنك به متابعت او[۳۱] بنده به خشم خدای و عذاب دوزخ رسد.

[§۷:۲۹] و هر که پس دشمن امام رود نماز و روزهٔ او ناچیز کنند. چنانك خدای تعالی همی‌گوید، قوله: ذٰلِكَ بِأَنَّهُمُ اتَّبَعُوا مٰا أَسْخَطَ اللّٰهَ وَ كَرِهُوا رِضْوٰانَهُ فَأَحْبَطَ

---

۲۵ ¦⟵ برگ [ایا:۱۳-الف].

۲۶ سورة النساء (۴)، آیت ۱۱۶.

۲۷ ¦⟵ برگ [اس:۲۷-الف].

۲۸ نك: دهخدا: زمانه. [زَ نَ/ نِ] (اسم) روزگار. دهر. (یادداشت بخط مرحوم دهخدا) (فرهنگ فارسی معین). روزگار. ... پورداود در ذیل «زروان، زمانه» آرد: ... چنانکه در فروردین یشت فقرات ۵۳ و ۵۵ و زامیاد یشت فقرهٔ ۲۶ و یسنا ۶۲ فقرهٔ ۳... و چندین بار زروان در ردیف ایزدان دیگر شمرده شده و از آن فرشتهٔ زمانهٔ بی کرانه اراده گردیده است ... و در رسالهٔ فارسی علمای اسلام «زمان درنگ خدای» شده است از این دو صفت بخوبی پیداست که از برای زمانه آغاز و انجامی شمرده نشده و آن را همیشه پایدار یا به عبارت دیگر جاودانی و فناناپذیر دانسته اند.

۲۹ اس: خسم.

۳۰ ایا: خدا.

۳۱ ایا: + ازبهرآنك بمتابعت او [روی این عبارت، که تکرار شده، با جوهر شَنگرف خط کشیده شده است].

أَعْمٰالَهُمْ.[۳۲] گفت: «ازبهر آنك ایشان پس آن رفتند که خدای را به خشم آورد. و دشوار داشتند مر خشنودی او را. پس ناچیز کرد کردارهاشان را».

[§۷:۳۰] طاعت فرمان‌برداری باشد؛ و معصیت بگذاشتنِ فرمان باشد. و هرکه فرمان رسول را دست بازداشت،[۳۳] و به مراد خویش امام اختیار کرد، اندر رسول عاصی شد. و هرکه اندر رسول عاصی شد، اندر خدای عاصی شد، و گُم‌بوده گشت. بقول خدای که همی‌گوید، قوله: وَ مٰا كٰانَ لِمُؤْمِنٍ وَ لاٰ مُؤْمِنَةٍ إِذٰا قَضَى اللّٰهُ وَ رَسُولُهُ أَمْراً أَنْ يَكُونَ لَهُمُ الْخِيَرَةُ[۳۴] مِنْ أَمْرِهِمْ وَ مَنْ يَعْصِ اللّٰهَ وَ رَسُولَهُ فَقَدْ ضَلَّ ضَلاٰلاً مُبِيناً.[۳۵] همی‌گوید: «و نبود[۳۶] مر مؤمنی را نه مرد و نه زن چون بداند خدای و پیامبر[۳۷] او کاری کی ایشان اختیار کنند اندر کار خویش. و هرکه فرمان خدای و رسول او را بگذارد گم‌بوده شود گم‌بودنی پیدا».

[§۷:۳۱] این آیت همی ندا کند بر گم‌بودگی آن کسها که به اختیار خویش امام بپای کردند. و آن کس را که خدای و رسول بپای کرده بود دست بازداشتند.

[§۷:۳۲] و هرکه با گماشتهٔ خدای انباز گیرد او با خدای انباز گرفته[۳۸] باشد، و سزاوار عقوبت جاودانگی باشد.

[§۷:۳۳] این است چگونگی درجات ثواب اندر معاد. و این است تأویل انباز گرفتن با خدای تعالی.

---

۳۲ سورة محمّد (۴۷)، آیت ۲۸.

۳۳ نك: دهخدا: دست بازداشتن. [دَ تَ] رها کردن. ترك گفتن. دست کشیدن.

۳۴ ایا: الخیر.

۳۵ سورة الأحزاب (۳۳)، آیت ۳۶.

۳۶ اس، ایا: نه بود.

۳۷ ایا: پیمبر.

۳۸ ¦⟵برگ [ایا:۱۳-ب].

صف هشتم

سخن[1] اندر اثبات نفس مجرّد: واجب کردن ثواب و عقاب مر او را نه جسم را با نفس[2]

[§۸:۱] بدانید که ایزد تعالی مر این عالم پیدای را دلیل عالم پنهانی کرده است. و مر آفرینش جسمی را دلیل آفرینش نفسی گردانیده است.

[§۸:۲] و ما همی دانیم مر نفس جزوی[3] را که به کالبد پیوسته است که مر این کالبد را[4] به خانهٔ خویش همی‌دارد، و خورش که مر او را باید، ازبهر عمارت این خانه را، مر آن را نخست به آلات جسدانی پاك کند. و هر چه ازو ناشایسته است بیَوکَنَد[5] چون افکندن کاه و کفه و سبوس از گندم.

[§۸:۳] و چون نیز به آلت جسدانی ممکن نشود مر آن را پاك کردن از بیرون، آن وقت مر آن را به دندان همی[6] کند[7] و بدین خانهٔ خویش کی کالبد است اندر کشدش، و مر او را به آلاتهای[8] اندرونی بپزد و نرم کند، و هر چه ازو لطافت است جدا کند. وزان لطافت بر قدر حاجت خویش بازگیرد. و دیگر که بماند مر آن را به آنچ او را نشاید بیرون افکند، و بدان ننگرد که اگر آن پوست و کاه و گوشت و گندم نبودی آن لطافت بدو نرسیدی بل که به غرض خویش نگرد.

[§۸:۴] پس بدین فعل کز نفس جزوی پدید آمد اندر عمارت این خانهٔ او، که کالبد است، همی دلیل کند که او مر این خانه را دست باز خواهد داشتن، و نیز بدو

---

۱ اس: – سخن.

۲ ایا: – واجب کردن ... نفس. | + و اثبات ثواب و عقاب مر نفس را بی جسم.

۳ ایا: جزئی.

۴ ¦←برگ [اس:۲۷-ب].

۵ نك: دهخدا: بیوکندن. [یَ / یُو کَ دَ] بیوگندن. اوکندن. افکندن. بیفکندن.

۶ ایا: – همی.

۷ ایا: بکند.

۸ ایا: آلتهای.

بازنگردد. و چون مراد خویش به تمام شدن خویش اندر او بحاصل کرد، از بازگشتن بدو ننگ دارد، و بدان ننگرد که اگر کالبد نبودی او تمام نشدی. بل که آمدن او اندر این خانه بسبب تمام شدن بود.

[§۸:۵] و این کالبد مر نفس را پس از آنك ازو تمام گشته[۹] جدا شود هم بر آن منزلت باشد که آن طعام پیشی آمده ناشایسته باشد که آن را از خانهٔ خویش که کالبد است بیرون کرده باشد برابر، نه کم و نه بیش.

[§۸:۶] و نفس مردم سزاوار ثواب و عقاب به کارهای خویش شود که اندر این عالم کرده باشد. و چون بدان عالم خویش رسد و ناتمام باشد، بداند[۱۰] که ناتمام[۱۱] شدن، او را ازیجا[۱۲] روی[۱۳] نیست. و جز بدین عالم جسمانی چیزی نتواند بدست آوردن که او را به عالم روحانی از آن راحت باشد. و آن نعمتها را که آنجا است بدان بتواند[۱۴] یافتن.

[§۸:۷] و بر درستی این حال دو دلیل است. یکی از قول خدای تعالی، و دیگر از آفرینش خلق. امّا قول خدای تعالی آن است که همی‌گوید، از قول دوزخیان، قوله: أَوْ نُرَدُّ فَنَعْمَلَ غَيْرَ الَّذِي كُنَّا نَعْمَلُ.[۱۵] گفت: «ایدون گویند که ما را بازبرندی تا بکنیمی جز آن که کرده بودیم».

[§۸:۸] و دلیل از آفرینش آن است که هر که از مادر نابینا یا کر زاید هیچ کس را امید نیوفتد که او را بینا یا شنوا تواند کردن. ازبهر آنك آن آلت اندر شکم مادر همی‌بایست که[۱۶] راست شدی و این جهان مر نفس را ازبهر راست کردن صورت

۹ اس: کشسه؛ ایا: کشته.
۱۰ |⟵برگ [ایا:۱۴-الف].
۱۱ ایا: تمام؛ اس: بابمام [«با» در «بابمام» کمرنگ شده است].
۱۲ اس: ازبحا؛ ایا: ازانجا. || تصحیح قیاسی: [«ازیجا» شکل مخفف «از این جا» است].
۱۳ نك: دهخدا: روی. چاره. ... علاج...صلاح. مصلحت.
۱۴ ایا: بتوان.
۱۵ سورة الأعراف (۷)، آیت ۵۳.
۱۶ |⟵برگ [اس:۲۸-الف].

نفسانی، برمثال شکم مادر است، مر راست کردن صورت جسمانی را برابر، نه کم و نه بیش.

[§۸:۹] و هر که طاعت دارد و علم آموزد و کار کند هم اندر این جهان نیك بخت شود. و هر که سر بکشد و نادانی گزیند و شریعت را دست بازدارد، هم اینجا بدبخت شود. و دلیل بر درستی این دعوی قول رسول مصطفی، صلی[۱۷] اللّٰه علیه وآله، است کی گفت: اَلسَّعِيدُ مَنْ سَعِدَ فِي بَطْنِ أُمِّهِ، وَ الشَّقِيُّ مَنْ شَقِيَ فِي بَطْنِ أُمِّهِ.[۱۸] گفت: «نیك بخت آن است کی اندر شکم مادر نیك بخت است؛ و بدبخت آن است که اندر شکم مادر بدبخت شود».

[§۸:۱۰] پس این عالم مر نفس را چون شکم مادر است مر جسم را. و این کالبد مر نفس را همچنان پوست است کی کودك اندر او باشد کز شکم مادر بیرون آید. و ما همی‌بینیم که آن پوست را کی آن کودك اندر او تمام شده باشد بخاك اندر کنند و کس نیز نام او نبرد و مادر کودك بر حال خویش بماند.

[§۸:۱۱] همچنین دانیم که این کالبد را[۱۹] چون بخاك اندر کردند نیز بکار نیاید، و بدو حاجتی نباشد. و این عالم که برمثال شکم مادر است برجای بماند.

[§۸:۱۲] وگر ثواب و عقاب مر کالبد را بودی بایستی که کالبد رسول مصطفی، صلی اللّٰه علیه وآله، بزرگتر بودی از کالبد همهٔ خلایق. ازبهرآنك ثواب او[۲۰] بیش از ثواب همه امّت است.

[§۸:۱۳] و همچنین بایستی که کالبدهای عاصیان سخت بزرگ بودی، ازبهرآنك عقوبت ایشان سخت بزرگ است. و چون رسول مصطفی به کالبد همچند[۲۱] دیگر

---

۱۷ اس: صل.

۱۸ نك: القمی، علی ابن ابراهیم، تفسیر القمی، تصحیح: السید طیب الموسوی الجزائری (قم، ۱۴۰۴ق)، ج ۱، تفسیر سورة الأعراف، آیات ۲۶ تا ۳۰، رَدُّ الجَبَرِيَّة والقَدَرِيَّة، ص ۲۲۶ تا ۲۲۷.

۱۹ ایا: + که.

۲۰ ¦⟵برگ [ایا:۱۴-ب].

۲۱ نك: دهخدا: هم چند. [هَ چَ] برابر. به اندازه . به مقدار.

مردمان بود و همچنان کالبد او را بخاك اندر بایست کردن، دانستیم که ثواب مر نفس را است نه مر جسم را.

[§۸:۱۴] و دلیل دیگر بر آنك ثواب و عقاب مر نفس را است، نه مر جسم را، که این نفس سخنگوی که مردم را است ازین عالم نیست؛ بل‌کی[۲۲] عالم او هَمچُنو[۲۳] لطیف است، و اینجا از بهر آموختن آورده‌اندش. و دلیل بر درستی این دعوی قول خدای است کی همی‌گوید، قوله: لَقَدْ جِئْتُمُونٰا كَمٰا خَلَقْنٰاكُمْ أَوَّلَ مَرَّةٍ بَلْ زَعَمْتُمْ أَلَّنْ[۲۴] نَجْعَلَ لَكُمْ مَوْعِداً.[۲۵] گفت: «بیامدید سوی ما همچنانك بیافریدیم‌تان[۲۶] نخستین بار. بل کی چنان دانستید که ما مر شما را وعده‌گاهی[۲۷] نکنیم». و مردم که نخست اندر آفرینش آید نادان باشد. پس این آیت همی‌آواز دهد[۲۸] کی نادان نباید رفتن ازینجا. و همی ندا کند کی اینجا مر نفس را از بهر آموختن آورده‌اند اندر این سرای. درست شد که او ازینجا نیست.

[§۸:۱۵] و چون نفس اینجایی نیست لازم نیاید که خدای تعالی او را جاودانی اینجا بدارد. از بهر آنك ستم باشد چیزی نه بجای او جاوید گردانیدن. و خدای تعالی همی‌گوید: من ستمکار نیستم. قوله: وَ مٰا رَبُّكَ بِظَلّٰامٍ لِلْعَبِيدِ.[۲۹] همی‌گوید: «ای محمّد پروردگار تو ستمکار نیست بر بندگان». و بدین شرح که بکردیم درست شد خردمند را که مرگ حقّ است. و جاوید زیستن اگر بودی ستم بودی.

[§۸:۱۶] پس گوییم که همچنان که نفس را که ایدری[۳۰] نیست ایدر جاوید

---

۲۲ ایا: بلك.

۲۳ دهخدا: همچنو. [هَ چُ] (حرف اضافه + ضمیر) هم چنو. هم چون او. مانند او.

۲۴ ایا: ان لن.

۲۵ سورة الکهف (۱۸)، آیت ۴۸. همچنین نك: سورة الأنعام(۶)، آیت ۹۴. || نیز نك: گشایش و رهایش، ص ۶۲ تا ۶۳، بند [۱۵۸].

۲۶ ایا: + بار [روی «بار» با جوهر شنگرف کمرنگ خط کشیده شده است].

۲۷ ایا: وعدکاهی؛ اس: [جوهرِ حروف «گ» و «ا» در کلمه «وعده گاهی» محو شده است].

۲۸ ¦⟵برگ [اس:۲۸-ب].

۲۹ سورة فصّلت (۴۱)، آیت ۴۶.

۳۰ نك: دهخدا: ایدری. [دَ] اینجایی... || اینجهانی. دنیوی.

گردانیدن ستم باشد، بجای خویش بازبردن داد باشد. همچنین نیز کالبد گران تاریك را به عالم لطیف روشن بردن نیز ستم باشد، و مر او را جاوید گردانیدن ستم بر ستم باشد.

[۱۷:۸§] پس درست کردیم، چون آفتاب سوی خردمند، که ثواب مر نفس را است نه مر کالبد را. و نیز گوییم که چون نفس از کالبد به عالم خویش بازرسد با صورت تمام، بی‌نیاز باشد از جسد که بدان فایده پذیرد. بل‌که[۳۱] او آنجا از علّت خویش بی‌میانجی فایده[۳۲] پذیرد. و آن مر او را ثواب باشد.

[۱۸:۸§] برمثال کودك که چون آلت غذا پذیرفتن اندر جسد خویش اندر شکم مادر تمام کند، نیز به میانجی مادر حاجتمند نشود، و بیرون آید تا غذا کز پستان مادر کز بیرون است بستاند. و چون نیز قوی‌تر شود خود آن طعام و شراب که مادرش همی‌خورد بخورد. و مادر را از میان خویش و میان طعام و شراب برگیرد.

[۱۹:۸§] و لذّتها که اندر طعام و شراب همی‌آید از عالم نفس همی‌آید. و چون نفس جزوی اندر عالم جسمانی باشد، به میانجی طبایع و میانجی جسد خویش تواند مر آن لذّتها را یافتن، و چون به عالم خویش رسد از میانجی بی‌نیاز شود. برمثال کسی که علم آموزد، و چون عالم گشت آلت آموختن همه بیَوگَنَد: از دفتر، و قلم و مَحبَرَه[۳۳] و جز آن. و خود از ذات خویش تألیف کند، بی هیچ آلت دیگر، و فایده‌های دیگر نفسها از نفس خویش بیرون آرد چون تمام شد.

---

۳۱ ایا: بلك.

۳۲ ↤برگ [ایا:۱۵-الف].

۳۳ نك: دهخدا: محبره. [مَ بَ رَ / رِ] جعبه که در آن اسباب تحریر و قلم و دوات و کاغذ و جز آن گذارند.

صف نهم

سخن اندر آنك هر که بدکردار است دشمن خدای است و دلایل عقلی بر آن

[§۱:۹] بباید دانستن[۱] که تمامی دانش و توانایی و حکمت مر آفریدگار را است. و دلیل بر راستی این دعوی از دو روی است. یکی از کتاب خدای. و دیگر از روی عقل.

[§۲:۹] اما دلیل از کتاب خدای آن است کی بسیار جای همی‌گوید، قوله: وَ اللّٰهُ عَلِيمٌ حَكِيمٌ.[۲] و بسیار جای همی‌گوید: وَ اللّٰهُ عَلىٰ كُلِّ شَيْءٍ قَدِيرٌ.[۳] گوید: «خدای بر هر چیزی قادر است».

[§۳:۹] و دلیل از روی عقل آن است کی ما مر خویشتن را دانا و توانا و با حکمت همی‌یابیم براندازه‌ای،[۴] و اندر مردم این فضیلتها را به مرتبت همی‌بینیم. و یکی از ما از دیگری دانا و تواناتر است، دانیم کی این جزوها است از آن کل کی تمامی دانش و توانایی و حکمت او را است.

[§۴:۹] پس گفتیم که کل این جزوهاءِ علم و قدرت و حکمت مر پدیدآرندهٔ این جزوها را است اندر این عالم. و چون مر این جزوها را اندر این عالم یافتیم، دانستیم که کل علم و قدرت و حکمت مر آفریدگار این عالم را است.

[§۵:۹] چون درست شد کی دانش[۵] و توانایی و حکمت مر آفریدگار را است

---

۱ ¦⟵برگ [اس:۲۹-الف].

۲ اس، ایا: حَكِيمٌ عَلِيمٌ. || نك: النساء (۴)، آیت ۲۶؛ الأنفال (۸)، آیت ۷۱؛ التوبة (۹)، آیات ۱۵، ۶۰، ۹۷، ۱۰۶، و ۱۱۰؛ الحج (۲۲)، آیت ۵۲؛ النور (۲۴)، آیات ۱۸، ۵۸، و ۵۹؛ الحُجُرات (۴۹)، آیت ۸؛ المُمتَحَنَة (۶۰)، آیت ۱۰.

۳ البقرة (۲)، آیت ۲۸۴؛ آل عمران (۳)، آیات ۲۹، ۱۸۹؛ المائدة (۵)، آیات ۱۷، ۱۹، ۴۰؛ الأنفال (۸)، آیت ۴۱؛ التوبة (۹)، آیت ۳۹؛ الحشر (۵۹)، آیت ۶.

۴ اس، ایا: براندازهء.

۵ ¦⟵برگ [ایا:۱۵-ب].

بتمامی، لازم آید که مراد او اندر آفرینش عالم همه نیکی و صلاح و راستی است بغایت‌الغایات. از بهر آنك بدی و زشتی و فساد و کژی از نادانی و عاجزی آید و این چیزها از آفریدگار دور است.

[§۹:۶] و اتفاق همه دانایان از اهل[۶] علمِ شریعت و گویندگانِ به علم آلهی غرض آفریدگار عالم از آفرینش این عالم مردم است. و چون مردم این صورت جسمی است با نفس سخنگوی بهم، و باز به مرگ ایشان از یکدیگر جدا شوند، دلیل همی‌کند که غرض آفریدگار ازین عالم نه این صورت جسمی بود که ویران شد، بل صورتی دیگر بود، که به میانجی آن صورتِ[۷] جسمی، تمام شد و بحاصل آمد.

[§۹:۷] وگر نه چنین بود آفرینش صورت مردم باطل بودی. و آفرینشی[۸] کی باطل شد، وز او چیز بحاصل نیاید، بازی باشد. و بازی از آفریدگار دور است. چنانك همی‌گوید، قوله: أَ فَحَسِبْتُمْ أَنَّمٰا خَلَقْنٰاكُمْ عَبَثاً وَ أَنَّكُمْ إِلَيْنٰا لاٰ تُرْجَعُونَ.[۹] همی‌گوید، بر روی زِلیفَن:[۱۰] «کی[۱۱] پنداشتید که شما را به بازی آفریدیم، و شما را بسوی ما بازنگردانند؟». پس گوییم که مراد آفریدگار اندر آفرینش مردم همه نیکویی و خیر است.

[§۹:۸] و دلیل بر درستی این دعوی آن است که مر جسد مردم را پذیرای نیك و بد آفرید[۱۲] چون درستی، و بیماری، و راحت، و رنج، و خوشی، و درد و پدید آمدن و نیست شدن. و عقل داد مر او را تا این مخالفان را بشناسد، و بهتر را از بدتر بداند، و راحت را بر رنج بگزینند.

---

۶ ایا: [کلمهٔ «اهل» در بالای خط نوشته شده است].

۷ ایا: [کلمهٔ «صورت» در بالای خط نوشته شده است].

۸ اس: افرىىش.

۹ سورة المؤمنون (۲۳)، آیت ۱۱۵.

۱۰ نك: دهخدا: زلیفن. [زِ / زَ فَ] تهدید بود یعنی ترسانیدن.

۱۱ ایا: که.

۱۲ ¦⟵برگ [اس:۲۹-ب].

[۹:۹§] و چون مر جسد مردم را چنان آفرید که مر این مخالفان را که یاد کرده شد تواند پذیرفتن، و اندر نفس او عقل نهاد که مر این مخالفان را بشناسد، این یك حکمت بزرگ بود که اندر آفرینش مردم نهاد.

[۱۰:۹§] و دیگر حکمت آن بود که نفس مردم را حواس داد. و توانایی داد بر کاربستن خیر و شر مر او را. و این نیز پذیرای مخالفان آمد همچون جسد. ازبهر آنك جسد گوهری کثیف بود و نفس گوهری لطیف است، و بحکم گوهری با یکدیگر سازوار آمدند، و بحکم لطافت و کثافت[۱۳] یکدیگر را مخالف آمدند تا غرض از آفرینش پدید آمد.

[۱۱:۹§] برمثال پدید آمدن فرزند از نر و ماده، که به روی جسد ظاهر نر و ماده مر یکدیگر را مخالفند، و بباطن مر یکدیگر را موافقند. چنانك شرح آن اندر کتاب مصباح[۱۴] که پیش ازین کتاب مر آن را تألیف کردیم گفته شده است.

[۱۲:۹§] و نفس را پذیرای علم و عمل آفرید و شناسای خیر و شر تا نیکی و صلاح بیلفنجد،[۱۵] و بدی و فساد را دست بازدارد، تا بدین روی مر نفس را صورت ابدی پیدا آید؛ بل‌که[۱۶] بودش او از آن باشد. و آن را خدای اندر قرآن 'النَّشْأَةَ الْآخِرَةَ'[۱۷] خوانده است.

[۱۳:۹§] و بباید دانستن کی چون مر جسم را صورت پیدا آید بدان صورت بشناسندش. و چون مر نفس را صورت پیدا آرد، بدان صورت بشناسد مر چیزها را. و صورت نیکو مر جسد را آن باشد که سوی بینندگان به چشم سر نیکو نماید.

---

۱۳ ¦⟵برگ [ایا:۱۶-الف].

۱۴ این کتاب نایافته و مفقود شده است.

۱۵ نك: دهخدا: بیلفنجیدن. [یَ فَ دَ] الفغدن. الفختن. الفنجیدن. کسب کردن و بهم رسانیدن و جمع کردن و اندوختن باشد.

۱۶ ایا: بلك.

۱۷ اس: نشاط لاخره [کذا]. || ایا: نشاط الاخره [کذا]. || سورة العنکبوت (۲۹)، آیت ۲۰؛ قس: جامع الحکمتین، ص ۵۳ تا ۵۴، بند (۴۹).

و صورت نیکو مر نفس را آن باشد که چیزهای نیکو داند و نیکی گزیند و سوی دانایان نیکو باشد. و چون نفس از همه بدیها دور شود بغایت نیکُوی[۱۸] رسد، چنانك چون جسم از همه عیبها دور باشد بغایت خوبی باشد.[۱۹]

[§۱۴:۹] و چون جسم فانی است نیکویی او فانی شود، و نفس که باقی است نیکویی[۲۰] او باقی باشد. پس صورت نفس که دوم آفرینش است، غایت مراد آفریدگار است، از بهر آنك مر او را فساد نیست. و چون صورت نفس ‹به راستی و بخیر›[۲۱] افتد، بغایت شرف رسد؛ و چون به ناراستی و شرّ افتد، بغایت فرومایگی باشد.[۲۲]

[§۱۵:۹] پس ازین روی لازم آید که امید دادن آفریدگار مر نفسها را، و طاعت داشتن ایشان بغایت امیدها باشد؛ و آن بهشت است، کی غایت آرزوی نفوس است. و همچنین باید که بیم کردن آفریدگار مر نفسها را و معصیت که زیشان

۱۸ ایا: نیکویی. || نك: دهخدا: نیکوی. [كُ وی] نیکویی. نیکوئی. نکویی.

۱۹ نك: زاد المسافر: قول ۲۱: اندر چگونگی پیوستن نفس به جسم، ص ۲۹۹ تا ۳۰۱: نخست موجودی مر جوینده را جسم است که ایزد تعالی مر او را با نفس ‹مجانست› داده است اندر جوهریّت تا مر یکدیگر را نفی نکنند به سبب این مجانست، پس از آنکه به صفت از یکدیگر جدااند بدانچه جسم جوهری ‹منفعل است› و نفس جوهری فاعل است، تا بدان مشاکلت که با یکدیگر دارند اندر جوهریّت، با یکدیگر بیامیزند و بدان مخالفت ‹که میان› ایشان است اندر صفت، یک چیز نشوند و چو غرض از آمیختن ایشان حاصل آید، از یکدیگر جدا شوند. و وجود ‹نفس و شناختن› مر جسم را به حواس ظاهر، دلیل است مر او را بر شناختن ذات خویش و دیگر چیزهای نامحسوس تا چو مر خویشتن ‹را و› دیگر معقولات را بشناسد، آفریدگار این دو جوهر را — کز او یکی دلیل است و دیگر مدلولٌ علیه — بشناسد که رسول مصطفی صلّی اللّه علیه وآله گفت: اَعرَفُکُم بِنَفسِهِ اَعرَفُکُم بِرَبِّه. پس [بدین شرح] ظاهر کردیم که وجود جسم علّت شناخت نفس است مر باری را ‹—سبحانه—› و آنچه او علّت شناختن خدای باشد، مر او را شناختن واجب است؛ و هر که مر دلیل را نداند به مدلولٌ علیه نرسد. و این فصل بدان یاد کردیم اندر فضل جسم، وا† دونی او اندر مرتبت از موجودات، تا عقلا بکوشند و [مر] چیزها ‹را› به حق بشناسند. || † یعنی: با.

۲۰ اس: نکوی. || نك: دهخدا: نکوی. [نِ] ... نکو. رجوع به نکو شود.

۲۱ ایا: بخیر و براستی.

۲۲ |⟵برگ [اس:۳۰-الف].

آید،[۲۳] بغایت دشواری و رنج باشد و آن دوزخ فرودین است،[۲۴] که گسسته شدن راحتها و شادیها است.

[§۹:۱۶] و این دو آفرینش را خدای تعالی اندر قرآن یاد کرد، تا خردمندان بدانند که بودشِ دوم مراد آفریدگار است، نه بودش نخستین. چنانك فرمود، قوله: قُلْ سِيرُوا فِي الْأَرْضِ فَانْظُرُوا كَيْفَ[۲۵] بَدَأَ الْخَلْقَ ثُمَّ اللَّهُ يُنْشِئُ النَّشْأَةَ الْآخِرَةَ.[۲۶] گفت: «بگوی که بروید اندر زمین، پس بنگرید که چگونه آغاز کرد خدای آفرینش را؛ پس خدای بیافرید آفرینشی دیگر بازپسین».

[§۹:۱۷] و تأویلِ «رفتن اندر زمین» طلب کردن علم دعوت است که قرارهایِ[۲۷] نفوس بر علم دعوت است، چنانك قرار جسم را بر زمین است. و تأویل «نگرستن به آفرینش نخستین چگونه بود تا دیگر آفرینش را ازو بدانی»، آن است که از زمین هرچه پدیدار آید از نبات — که آغاز نفسها از[۲۸] او است — آنچ ازو به اوّل پیدا آید، نه آن باشد، بل که آنچ بازپس پدید آید، مراد از آن نبات آن باشد.[۲۹]

[§۹:۱۸] ازبهرآنك از هر نباتی نخست برگ و شاخ پدید آید، و به آخِر بار پدید آید. و غرض از درخت نه برگ و شاخ باشد، بل کی[۳۰] بار باشد. پس ما را همی‌فرماید ایزد تعالی نگرستن اندر حال آنچ از زمین پدید آید تا بدانیم کی مراد از آفرینش نه جسد است، بل‌که[۳۱] نفس است.

[§۹:۱۹] و جسد مر نفس را برمثال پولی است که نفس برو ازین عالم بگذرد.

---

۲۳ ایا: [«آید» روی کلمه «زیشان» بالای سطر نوشته شده است].
۲۴ ایا: [«است» روی کلمه «فرودین» بالای سطر نوشته شده است].
۲۵ |⟵برگ [ایا:۱۶-ب].
۲۶ سورة العنكبوت (۲۹)، آیت ۲۰. || قس: جامع الحکمتین، ص ۵۳ تا ۵۴، بند (۴۹) تا (۵۰).
۲۷ اس: قرارها.
۲۸ ایا: – از.
۲۹ قس: زادالمسافر، ص ۴۱۱ تا ۴۱۲.
۳۰ ایا: بلك.
۳۱ ایا: بلك.

برمثال کسی کز آبی بر پولی بگذرد. و گوایی دهد بر درستی این قول آنچ رسول مصطفی، صلی الله علیه وآله، فرمود: اَلدُّنْیَا قَنْطَرَةٌ فَاعْبُرُوهَا وَ لاَ تَعْمُرُوهَا.[۳۲] گفت: «این جهان پلی است بگذرید برو، و آبادان مکنیدش».

[§۹:۲۰] و هر کجا اندر قرآن دنیا را یاد کند، بدان مر این جهان را خواهد و جسد مردم را و ظاهر شریعت را. و هر کجا مر آخرت را یاد کند، بدان مر آن جهان را خواهد،[۳۳] و مر نفس مردم را و تأویل را.

[§۹:۲۱] پس ایزد تعالی صلاح جسد مردم را طعام و شراب و پوشش و برنشست[۳۴] و دیگر منافع پدید آورد. و صلاح نفس مردم را[۳۵] دین و علم و عمل فرمود و به هر رویی حجّت بر مردم لازم کرد.

[§۹:۲۲] اما حجّت به جسد بر مردم آن لازم کرد که او را اندامهای تمام داد، ذی بهانه گردانیدش اندر حاصل کردن آنچ جسد او را بدان حاجت است، از بهر آنک نعمتها از خوردنی و آشامیدنی و پوشیدنی و برنشستنی و خانه[۳۶] و جز آن مر او را یافته کرد اندر این عالم و روی آن پیدا کرد کی چگونه باید بدست آوردن تا حلال باشد.

[§۹:۲۳] و اما حجّت به نفس بر مردم آن لازم کرد که او را عقل دریابنده داد که گوهر او آن است که اختیار نیکو کند،[۳۷] و از زشتی دور باشد، و نیکوکار را دوست دارد، و از بدکردار بگریزد، و او را دشمن دارد.

---

۳۲ نك: الشيخ المفيد، الأمالي، المجلس السادس، ص ۴۳؛ نیز نك: ابن بابويه، محمد بن علی، الخصال، تصحیح: علی اکبر غفاری (قم، ۱۴۰۳ق/۱۳۶۲ش)، ج ۱، باب الإِثْنَيْن، اَلدُّنْيَا وَ اَلْآخِرَةُ إِلاَّ كَكَفَّتَيِ الْمِيزَانِ: ص ۶۴ تا ۶۵.

۳۳ ¦⟵برگ [اس:۳۰-ب].

۳۴ نك: دهخدا: برنشست. [بَ نِ شَ] سوار شدن... سواری کردن....|| مَرکب.

۳۵ اس: – را [جوهر حروف «ر» و «ا» محو شده است]؛ ایا: [«را» با جوهر شنگرف کم رنگ، بین «مردم» و «دین»، بالای سطر اضافه شده است].

۳۶ ایا: + و خانه [روی «و خانه» با جوهر شنگرفِ کمرنگ خط گرفته شده است].

۳۷ ¦⟵برگ [ایا:۱۷-الف].

[§۹:۲۴] و بدین هر دو روی حجّت خدای بر مردم لازم شد. و عقل حجّت خدای است بر خلق اندر آفرینش. و حجّت دوم از خدای رسول او است سوی مردم که بیاید و عقل که اندر آفرینش مردم بقوّت است بپروراند و سوی فعل بیرون آرد. و بازنماید که بدین دو روی شکر آفریدگار بر مردم واجب است و از ناسپاسی کردن دور بودن بر مردم لازم است.

[§۹:۲۵] چنانك خدای تعالی همی‌گوید، قوله: لَئِنْ شَكَرْتُمْ لَأَزِيدَنَّكُمْ وَ لَئِنْ كَفَرْتُمْ إِنَّ عَذَابِي لَشَدِيدٌ.[۳۸] گفت: «اگر شکر کنید در نعمت شما زیادت کنم، وگر کفران آرید، یعنی که ناسپاسی کنید، عذاب من سخت است».

[§۹:۲۶] و اندر گوهر[۳۹] عقل بی تعلیم خود شکر کردن مر دهندهٔ نعمت را موجود است؛ و لکن چگونگی شکر آفریدگار اندر گوهر عقل غریزی موجود نیست. پس رسولان ازبهر بازنمودن چگونگی شکر آفریدگار بایستند ازو سوی آفریدگان او.

[§۹:۲۷] و مثل این حال چنان است که مهتری باشد نیکوکار و بخشنده و کهتران بسیار دارد. و آن کهتران هر کسی براندازهٔ خویش دانند که شکر آن مهتر بر ایشان فریضه است؛ و لکن ندانند کی چگونه شکر باید کردن تا مر آن مهتر را پسند اُفتد. پس از جملهٔ کهترانِ آن مهتر یکی باشد که بدو نزدیك باشد، و بداند کی خشنودی آن مهتر اندر چیست،[۴۰] اندر گفتار است یا اندر کردار یا اندر هر دو؟ و مر آن کهتران را بازنماید که خشنودی مهتر از شما[۴۱] اندر چیست که شما چاکران بر این دو شکر توانائی دارید. و چون آن کهتر خاص مر دیگر کهتران را بیآگاهاند که شکر مهتر خویش چگونه کنید، آن وقت شکر از حدّ جواز اعنی روا بودن به حدّ واجبی آمده باشد.

---

۳۸ سورة ابراهیم (۱۴)، آیت ۷.

۳۹ اس: [کلمه «گوهر» در بالای خط نوشته شده است].

۴۰ |⟵برگ [اس:۳۱-الف].

۴۱ ایا: – از شما.

[۲۸:۹§] و تا رسول نیامده بود اندر عقل روا همی‌بود شکر آفریدگار کردن، و چون چگونگی شکر پدید آمد به گفتار رسول، آن وقت واجب گشت شکر کردن.

[۲۹:۹§] پس دست بازنداشتن شکر آفریدگار، سپس از واجب شدن، از عبادت و صلاح و خیر است. و دست بازداشتن شکر ناسپاسی و فساد و شر است،[۴۲] و باطل کردن آفرینش است هم به جسم و هم به نفس. ازبهرآنك جسم مردم چنانك گفتیم پذیرای رنج و راحت و خوشی و درد ازبهر آن باشد تا بهتری گزیند، و از بدی باز باشد.

[۳۰:۹§] و نفس مردم توانا بر بدی و نیکی باشد، و شناسای هردو ازبهر آن آمد تا خویشتن را بهتر اختیار کند. و چون مردم با این دو حجّت که برو لازم گشته است سوی فساد و شر و بدی میل کند، مر آفریدگار خویش را مخالف شده باشد، و مر حاکمی را که خدای برو گماشته است، و آن عقل است، دروغزن[۴۳] کرده باشد.

[۳۱:۹§] و چون از خیر و صلاح روی بگرداند و سوی شر و فساد آید، مراد آفریدگار که غایت مرادها است باطل کرده باشد، و از بهشت که نعمت او بی‌نهایت است سوی دوزخ آمده باشد که رنج او بغایت غایت است.

[۳۲:۹§] هرکه خیر و صلاح را گرفت، از شر و فساد دور ماند. همچنانك هرکه خوشی و آسانی یافت، از درد و رنج رسته شد.

[۳۳:۹§] و نیز مر این را قسم سدیگر نیست، چنانك رسول مصطفی، صلّی اللّٰه علیه وآله، گفت: فَوَ الَّذِي نَفْسُ مُحَمَّدٍ بِيَدِهِ مَا بَعْدَ الْمَوْتِ غَيْرُ الْجَنَّةِ أَوِ[۴۴] النَّارِ.[۴۵]

۴۲ |←برگ [ایا:۱۷-ب].

۴۳ اس، ایا: دروغ‌زن.

۴۴ اس، ایا: و.

۴۵ نك: الکلینی، محمد بن یعقوب، الکافي، تصحیح: علی اکبر غفاری و محمد آخوندی (تهران، ۱۴۰۷ق)، ج ۲، (۳۴) بَابُ الْخَوْفِ وَ الرَّجَاءِ، ص ۷۰: ۹- ... فَوَ الَّذِي نَفْسُ مُحَمَّدٍ بِيَدِهِ مَا بَعْدَ الدُّنْيَا مِنْ مُسْتَعْتَبٍ وَمَا بَعْدَهَا مِنْ دَارٍ إِلَّا الْجَنَّةُ أَوِ النَّارُ. نیز نك: الطوسی، نصیرالدین، اخلاق محتشمی، با دیباچه و تصحیح محمّد تقی دانش‌پژوه (تهران: انتشارات و چاپ دانشگاه تهران،

گفت: «و سوگند خورد بدان کس که نفس محمد به دست او است که نیست پس از مرگ جز بهشت یا آتش».

[§۹:۳۴] و نیز گوییم که چون غرض آفریدگار، به آفرینش عالم جسمانی نازِندَه، مردم بود که زندهٔ گویندهٔ میرنده است، غرض او به آفرینش عالم روحانی پدیدآوردن صورت زندهٔ داناءِ نامیرنده[۴۶] بود.

[§۹:۳۵] و به نخستین آفرینش[۴۷] ازین عالم صورت ابدی بحاصل نیامد چنانك از خاك خرمای رسیده برنیاید. بل که نخست درخت برآید که خرما است اندر حدّ قوّت، آن وقت از آن درخت خرما بیرون آید. پس گوییم که زین عالم مرده مردم زندهٔ مردنی پدید آمد[۴۸] و از مردم صورت نفسانی زندهٔ نامیرنده پدید آید.

[§۹:۳۶] آن نخستین آفرینش به میانجی لطایف جسمانی بود از افلاك[۴۹] و ستارگان. و این دیگر آفرینش به میانجی لطایف نفسانی بود، که ناطقان و اساسان و امامان‌اند. پس جسد اینجهانی است، محسوس و فانی؛ و نفس آنجهانی است، معقول و باقی. و ایزد تعالی مردم را پذیرای خوشی و درد گردانید هم به جسم و هم به نفس.

[§۹:۳۷] و درد و خوشی جسمانی بیماری و تندرستی است. و بیماری به دو بخش است: یکی بخش آن است کز اندرون جسد خیزد، چون غلبه کردن طبیعتی بر دیگری، یا فساد اندامی از اندامهاء درونی. و دیگر بخشش آن است که بیرون

۱۳۷۷ ش)، چاپ ۳، الجزء ۱، ص ۱۲۸: «وَالَّذِي نَفْسُ مُحَمَّدٍ بِيَدِهِ: مَا بَعْدَ الْمَوْتِ مِنْ مُسْتَعْتِبٍ، وَمَا بَعْدَ الدُّنْيَا مِنْ دَارٍ إِلَّا الْجَنَّةُ أَوِ النَّارُ. ...بدان خدای که جان محمد بفرمان [(بدست)] او است که پس از مرگ جای عذر خواستن نباشد، و بعد از دنیا جز بهشت یا دوزخ سرایی دیگر نبود».

۴۶ ایا: نامیرندهء دانا.

۴۷ ¦⟵برگ [اس:۳۱-ب].

۴۸ ایا: آید.

۴۹ ¦⟵برگ [ایا:۱۸-الف].

جسد افتد. چون سرما و گرما و ریش و زخم. و برابر هر دردی آسانی[۵۰] هست. و برابر هر بیماری درستی هست.

[§۹:۳۸] و درد و خوشی نفسانی نیز به دو بخش است چون اندوه و شادی و خشم و خشنودی و پشیمانی و خرّمی و کام و ناکام. و این درد و خوشی مر نفس را نیز همچنان است که مر جسم را از بیرون و اندرون. آنچ از بیرون است چون اندوه است کز نادانستن عملی[۵۱] رسدش، و آنچ از اندرون است چون اندوه است کز نادانستن علمی رسدش. و راحتش نیز هم به دو بخش است بر این قیاس.

[§۹:۳۹] و مردم را از راحت و درد جسدانی [...][۵۲] کز حد درگذشته افتد مرگ جسدانی افتد. چنانك اگر به جسد دردی سخت یابد، از زخمی یا از دردی کز غلبۀ اخلاط باشد، روح او از کالبد جدا شود. همچنین اگر راحتی سخت رسدش از خوردن خوش یا از آشامیدن بافراط یا از جماع بی روی[۵۳] نیز مرگِ فِجا[۵۴] باشدش. و آن بدان سبب باشد که گرمی طبیعتی که مردم بدان زنده است بفسرد، یا سخت بگدازد، تا مردم هلاك شود.

[§۹:۴۰] همچنین به درد و آسانی نفسانی نیز مردم را هلاك باشد. و چون کسی کی او را غمی سخت رسد ناگاه و حرارت غریزی او همه به مرکز دل فراز آید، و بسبب جمله گشتن حرارت سوخته شود، و تن را فسردن حرارت خوانند. و اگر کسی را شادی بی اندازه بیکبار بی هیچ مقدمه فراز رسد[۵۵] وزان گشاده گشتن حرارت باشد و پراکندن از جای خویش تا مردم بمیرد، و آن را تحلیل خوانند.[۵۶]

---

۵۰ ایا: آسانیی.
۵۱ اس، ایا: علمی [کذا]. || تصحیح قیاسی.
۵۲ اس: [پس از کلمه «جسدانی» به اندازه فاصله دوکلمه خط پاك شده است، اما به معنی جمله لطمه ای نمیزند].
۵۳ ایا: [کلمه «بی روی» بالای خط نوشته شده است].
۵۴ ایا: - فجا. || نك: دهخدا: فجا. [فِ] ناگهان.
۵۵ ¦⟵برگ [اس:۳۲-الف].
۵۶ ¦⟵برگ [ایا:۱۸-ب].

[§۹:۴۱] پس درد و راحت جسمانی همچون جسم گذرنده و عارضی است؛ و درد و راحت نفسانی چون نفس باقی است، و جوهری و بی زوال. و نیز مردم را به جسد سوختن افتد به آتش طبیعی. همچنین نفس را نیز سوختن افتد به غم و حسرت. وگر کسی را به جسد اندر آتش طبیعی افکنند گوید:[۵۷] 'مرا در آتش افکندی و بسوختی'. وگر سخنی گویندش که او را از آن غمی سخت آید گوید: 'مرا بر آتش نهادی و بسوختی بدین سخن که گفتی، یا بدین کار که کردی'. پس آتش اندیشه مر نفس را بسوزد، و آتش طبیعی مر جسم را بسوزد. و سوختن آتشِ اندیشه باقی است چنانك نفس باقی است[۵۸] کی هرگز نمیرد.

[§۹:۴۲] و گوا است بر این قول خدای تعالی که گفت، قوله: كَلَّا لَيُنْبَذَنَّ فِي الْحُطَمَةِ * وَ مٰا أَدْرٰاكَ مَا الْحُطَمَةُ * نٰارُ اللّٰهِ الْمُوقَدَةُ * الَّتِي تَطَّلِعُ عَلَى الْأَفْئِدَةِ.[۵۹] گفت: «اندر افکندش به دوزخ و تو چه دانی ای محمد که دوزخ چیست، آتش خدای است افروخته، آنك او بر دلها جاکول شود».

[§۹:۴۳] تأویلش آن است که آتش که بر دل جاکول است مر دل را بسوزد، و آتش کی مر دل را بسوزد جز اندیشه و حسرت نیست. و دل بدین جای مر نفس عاقله را خواهد که او از نفسهای روینده و خورنده و گوینده هم بدان منزلت است که دل مردم از تن مردم است. و نفس عاقله سالار و پاسبان این نفسها است، همچنانك دل پاسبان و سالار تن است.

[§۹:۴۴] و خدای تعالی همی‌گوید بر درستی آنك مر نفس عاقله را همی‌خواهد، قوله: نَزَلَ بِهِ الرُّوحُ الْأَمِينُ * عَلىٰ قَلْبِكَ لِتَكُونَ مِنَ الْمُنْذِرِينَ * بِلِسٰانٍ عَرَبِيٍّ مُبِينٍ.[۶۰] گفت: «فرو فرستادیم جبرئیل را به قرآن بر دل تو ای محمد، تا تو از ترسانندگان

---

۵۷ اس، ایا: گویند.
۵۸ ایا: [عبارت «چنانك نفس باقیست» در بین خطوط نوشته شده است].
۵۹ سورة الهُمَزَة (۱۰۴)، آیات ۴ تا ۷.
۶۰ سورة الشُّعَراء (۲۶)، آیات ۱۹۳ تا ۱۹۵.

باشی، به زفان تازی پیدا». و قلب دل باشد؛ و به دل نه آن پاره گوشت همی‌خواهد، بل‌که[۶۱] مر آن نفس عاقله را همی‌خواهد که به مرکز دل پیوسته است.

[§۹:۴۵] و اندر سخن عرب چنین بسیار است که مر چیزی را بسبب همسایگی او با چیزی دیگر به نام آن همسایه‌اش بازخوانند. چنانك مر اشتر را به تازی[۶۲] راویه گویند[۶۳] و باز مر آن مَزادَة[۶۴] را که آب اندر او کنند بر پشت اشتر نیز راویه خوانند. بسبب آنك بر[۶۵] پشت آن شتر باشد که نام او راویه است.[۶۶]

[§۹:۴۶] پس هر نفسی کز[۶۷] بدکرداریِ خویش ازین[۶۸] عالم با بیم و به پشیمانی بیرون شود، آن درد و پشیمانی و بدکرداری جاودان با او بماند، و آن عقوبت او باشد. و هر نفسی کز نیکوکرداری خویش با خرّمی و شادی ازین عالم بیرون شود، آن خرمی و راحت با او جاودان بماند، و آن ثواب او باشد.

[§۹:۴۷] پس گوییم که رسولان خدای تعالی بدانچ گفتند آتش دوزخ هرگز نمیرد، آتش روحانی عقلی را خواستند که مردم به دست بازداشتن از علم و عمل اندر این جهان، پَسِ مرگ جسمانی اندر آن افتد، و جاوید معذب بماند. از بهر آنك نفس او مر عالم عقل را مخالف باشد به نادانی خویش و مخالف ضعیف از مخالف قوی به عذاب رسد ناچاره.

---

۶۱ ایا: بلك.

۶۲ ایا: – به تازی.

۶۳ ایا: خوانند.

۶۴ اس، ایا: مراده. || نك: دهخدا: مزادة. [مَ دَ] توشه دان فراخ... آبدست دان... آفتابه. خیك... مشك بزرگ... || نیز نك: لغتنامه عربی-به-انگلیسی ادوارد ویلیام لِیْن، ج ۳ (د-ز)، ص ۱۲۶۸.

۶۵ اس: [«بر» مخدوش است].

۶۶ قس: السجستاني، ابویعقوب إسحاق، کتاب الإفتخار، باب الثاني عشر: في معرفة مأخذ التأویل من القرآن، به‌اهتمام: اسماعیل ق. ح. پوناوالا (بیروت: دار الغرب الإسلامي، ۲۰۰۰)، ص ۲۱۸.

۶۷ ¦⟵برگ [ایا:۱۹-الف].

۶۸ ¦⟵برگ [اس:۳۲-ب].

[۴۸:۹§] و به نعیم و لذّت بهشت جاویدی که هرگز فنا نپذیرد، لذّات عقلانی را خواستند که مردم بدان رسد، چون اندر این جهان به علم و عمل بکوشد، و مر شناخت معاد را و نفس خویش را بخیر و صلاح بپرورد تا چون بدان عالم رسد نفس او را با عالم عقلانی موافقت باشد، و موافق ضعیف از موافق قوی به راحتی عظیم رسد.

[۴۹:۹§] برمثال کوزهٔ آب که اندر دریای بزرگ ریزی، و آن آب اندك به یاری آن آب بسیار قوی گردد، و همان کار کردن گیرد که آن دریای بزرگ میکرد.

[۵۰:۹§] و لکن مردم علم از آن راه تواند پذیرفتن کی عادت او بر آن بوده باشد. و چون مردم جسدانی و طبیعی بود بفعل آمده، و عقلانی و نفسانی بود اندر حدّ قوّت، پیغامبران، علیهم السّلام، دانستند که ایشان علم آن عالم را که برتر از طبیعت است نتوانند اندریافتن مگر از راهنمون[۶۹] کردن مر ایشان را بدانچ زیر طبیعت اندر است، تا اندك اندك به دانستن آن، و دلیل گرفتن از آن بر چیزی که برتر از آن است به علم عالم روحانی عقلانی رسند.

[۵۱:۹§] پس هریکی از رسولان مر خلق را از آن راه سخن گفتند کی مردم آن روزگارِ او دست در آن داشتند، تا بر ایشان پذیرفتن آن آسان‌تر بود. و گوایی[۷۰] دهد بر درستی این دعوی قول خدای تعالی که همی‌گوید، قوله: وَ مٰا أَرْسَلْنٰا مِنْ رَسُولٍ إِلاّٰ بِلِسٰانِ قَوْمِهِ لِيُبَيِّنَ لَهُمْ.[۷۱] گفت: «و نفرستادیم[۷۲] هیچ رسولی مگر به زفان آن قومِ او».

[۵۲:۹§] و تأویل زفان بدین جای علم است، ازبهر آنك گذرگاه علم بر زفان است. و این نام علم بر زفان هم بدان[۷۳] سبب همسایگی را است کز پیش یاد کردیم.

---

۶۹ اس، ایا: راه نمون.

۷۰ ¦⟵ برگ [ایا:۱۹-ب].

۷۱ سورهٔ ابراهیم (۱۴)، آیت ۴.

۷۲ اس، ایا: نه فرستادیم.

۷۳ ¦⟵ برگ [اس:۳۳-الف].

[۵۳:۹§] و فرستادن رسول سوی خلق تا از آن علم کی خلق اندر آن باشند ایشان را سخن گوید، حکمت آن بود تا علم ایشان اندر علم رسول ضعیف شود، و عاجزی خلق پیدا آید، و نگویند: 'کی او آن علم همی‌گوید که ما را اندر آن دست نیست'، و حریص شوند به آموختن آن علم کی ندانند، چنین که اندر این دور خلق حریص شده است بر آموختن فصاحت کی معجز رسول مصطفی،[۷۴] صلّی الله علیه وآله، بود. و او مر فصیحان عرب را بدان عاجز کرد تا چون به ظاهر آن رغبت کنند و بیاموزند و به باطن آن اندر رسند.

[۵۴:۹§] به دلالت راهنمایانِ[۷۵] حقّ از فرزندان رسولِ دور، علیه السلام، بازنموده شد به برهانهای عقلی که خواستِ آفریدگار عالم اندر آفرینش عالم همه خیر است و هر که بدکردار است مخالف خدای است.

---

۷۴ ایا: مصطفا.

۷۵ اس، ایا: راه‌نمایان.

صف دهم

سخن[۱] اندر عقل کلّ کی او را جز بسوی ذات خود نگریدن[۲] نیست

[§۱:۱۰] گوییم مر برادران خویش را که بر این خوان نشینند که عقل کلّ نخست پدیدآوردهٔ باری است و تمام است بفعل و قوّت، چنانک شرح آن اندر کتاب گشایش و رهایش گفته‌ایم.[۳]

[§۲:۱۰] و دلیل بر آنك عقل نخست پدیدآورده است آن است کی هر چیزی که آن اندر پدید آوردن پیشتر بوده است بذات جاکول است بر آنچ سپس‌تر[۴] پدید آمده است؛ چنانك علّت بر معلول جاکول است، و جنس بر نوع جاکول است. برمثال حیوان که بذات جاکول است بر چارپای و پرنده و خزنده[۵] و مردم. از بهر آنك به برگرفتن حیوان این همه انواع برگرفته شود. همچنین نیز به برگرفتن عقل به وهم که داننده است همه دانشها برگرفته شود.

[§۳:۱۰] پس جاکول بودن عقل بر همه چیزها همی‌دلیل کند کی او پیشتر[۶] از همه چیزها هست شده است. و چون درست شد که نخستین هستی بود و دانا بود، پس درست شده باشد[۷] که دانستهٔ او جز ذات او نبود. و چون ذات او نخست هستی بود و تمام بود، دلیل باشد که همه محسوسات و معقولات بجملگی اندر ذات او بود و دانستهٔ او بود.

[§۴:۱۰] که اگر کسی گوید که هیچ چیز هست کی نابوده است یا خواهد بودن

۱ اس: – سخن.
۲ ایا: نگریستن.
۳ نك: گشایش و رهایش، مسئلهٔ بیست و دوم، ص ۴۹ تا ۵۲، بند [۱۲۵] تا [۱۳۴].
۴ اس: سپستر.
۵ ایا: چرنده.
۶ ¦←برگ [ایا:۲۰-الف].
۷ ایا: درست شد.

که اندر ذات عقل تخم نکشته بود[8] نخست که او به ابداع باری نه از چیزی پدید آمد، گفته باشد کی عقل نه تمام بود، و نقص به ابداع باری سبحانه بازبسته باشد، و دور است ابداع باری سبحانه از نقص و عجز.

[§۱۰:۵] و چیز ناتمام نگرنده باشد اندرآنك تمام باشد، تا بدان قوّت که اندر آن تمام باشد آن ناتمام تمام شود. و نگرستن عقل کلّ بذات خویش جوهری بود نه تکلّفی، ازبهرآنك جوهر عقل نگرستن و دانستن است. و چون خود جز عقل چیز نبود و جوهر او دانستن بود، دانندهٔ خویش بود.

[§۱۰:۶] و هرچیز که او داننده باشد از حدّ قوّت به حدّ فعل بیرون آید. برمثال شاگرد که از نگرستن اندر استاد خویش بفایده پذیرفتن از حدّ قوّت به حدّ فعل بیرون آید.

[§۱۰:۷] و چون حکم داننده مر چیزی را و نگرنده اندر چیزی آن بود کز حدّ قوّت به حدّ فعل بیرون آید، و عقل کلّ خود تمام بود بقوّت و فعل، چون ذات او مرو[9] را دانسته شد، و او جوهری باقی نورانی بود، ازو برخاست جوهری که او اندر حدّ قوّت بود و بیرون آینده بود. کز فعل همی بدان حکمی که یاد کردیم، کز دانستن و نگرستن، چیز از حدّ قوّت به حدّ فعل آید.

[§۱۰:۸] و چون همه، اندك و بسیار، از روحانی و جسمانی که هست و می‌باشد، تخم آن اندر عقل کلّ بود، واجب نیاید که عقل کلّ جز بذات خود بنگرد. برمثال کسی که سخن اندر معنی بداند و باز هم مر آن سخن را بنویسد، هرگز حاجتمند نشود که آن سخن را از نبشتهٔ خویش برخواند.

[§۱۰:۹] پس اگر کسی گوید که عقل کلّ حاجتمند است به نگرستن سوی آنچ عالم روحانی و جسمانی است از روحانیان و جسمانیان، چنان گفته باشد که مر

---

۸ ؛←برگ [اس:۳۳-ب].

۹ ایا: مر او.

نویسنده را که بر نوشتن سخت جاکول گشته باشد حاجت است به نگرستن اندر حروف ابجد تا بداند[۱۰] که هر حرفی را شکل چیست و حکم هریکی از حروف اندر پیوستن و گسستن چیست. پس اگر این محال باشد این قول ازین محال‌تر است.

۱۰ ¦⟵برگ [ایا:۲۰-ب].

صف یازدهم

سخن اندر مُزد و بَزَه

[§۱۱:۱] مزد را بتازی اجر خوانند. و بزه[۱] را بتازی اثم خوانند. و نام مزد و بزه آن است اندر میان خلق که چون کسی کاری بکند او را مکافاتِ آن بدهند، و آن مکافات را مزد خوانند.[۲] و لکن نام بزه جز اندر دین رونده نیست؛ و بحقیقت مزدِ مکافاتِ کاری باشد که ازو شر و فساد پدید آید. و مزد نیز آن باشد اندر این جهان کزو بدان جهان مزد بحاصل کنندهٔ آن را ثواب بحاصل آید. و بزه آن باشد که مر خداوندِ او را بعاقبت عقوبت واجب آید.

[§۱۱:۲] و بزه را نیز وزر خوانند بتازی. و خبر است از رسول مصطفی، صلی[۳] الله علیه وآله، کی فرمود:[۴] مَنْ سَنَّ سُنَّةً حَسَنَةً فلَهُ أَجْرُهَا وَ أَجْرِ مَنْ عَمِلَ بِهَا إِلَیٰ یَوْمِ الْقِیٰمَةِ مِنْ غَیْرِ أَنْ یَنْقُصَ مِنْ أَجرِهِمْ شَیْئًا وَ مَنْ سَنَّ سُنَّةً سَیِّئَةً فلَهُ وِزْرُهَا وَ وِزْرِ مَنْ عَمِلَ بِهَا إِلَیٰ یَوْمِ الْقِیٰمَةِ مِنْ غَیْرِ أَنْ یَنْقُصَ مِنْ وِزْرِهِمْ شَیْءٌ. گفت: «هرکه سنّتی نیکو بنهد او را باشد مزد آن و مزد آنك بدان سنّت کار کند تا روز قیامت، بی آنك از مزد آن کس‌ها چیزی کم شود. و هر که سنّتی بد نهد[۵] او را باشد بزه آن و بزه هر که بدان سنّت کار کند تا روز قیامت، بی آنك از بزه آن کس‌ها چیزی کم شود».

[§۱۱:۳] و خداوند صلاح را از آن مزد واجب شد که اندر صلاح خیر است و راستی

---

۱ نك: دهخدا: بزه. [بَ زَ/ زِ] [در تداول امروز گاه «بِزِهْ» نیز گویند] گناه و خطا باشد.

۲ ¦⟵برگ [اس:۳۴-الف].

۳ اس، ایا: صل.

۴ قس: ابن حنبل، احمد، مسند الإمام احمد بن حنبل، ۱۲ مجلد (قاهره: دار ابن الجوزی، ۱۴۳۷ق/۲۰۱۶م)، ج ۹، ص ۲۵۶ تا ۲۵۷، حدیث ۱۹۵۰۹:... و من حدیث جریر بن عبد الله البجلی عن النبی صلی الله علیه و سلم: مَنْ سَنَّ سُنَّةً حَسَنَةً كَانَ لَهُ أَجْرُهَا وَ مِثْلُ أَجْرِ مَنْ عَمِلَ بِهَا مِنْ غَیْرِ أَنْ یُنْتَقَصَ مِنْ أُجُورِهِمْ شَیْءٌ وَ مَنْ سَنَّ سُنَّةً سَیِّئَةً كَانَ عَلَیْهِ وِزْرُهَا وَ مِثْلُ وِزْرِ مَنْ عَمِلَ بِهَا مِنْ غَیْرِ أَنْ یُنْتَقَصَ مِنْ أَوْزَارِهِمْ شَیْءٌ قَالَ مَرَّةً یَعْنِی أَبَا مُعَاوِیَةَ مِنْ غَیْرِ أَنْ یَنْقُصَ.

۵ ایا: بنهد.

و آبادانی و ببودش[۶] کی خواست آفریدگار عالم آن است؛ و خداوند فساد را بزه از آن باشد که اندر فساد شرّ است و خلاف و پراکنده شدن و زشتی، و این همه خلافِ خواست آفریدگار است.

[§۴:۱۱] و سزاوار است جویندهٔ خیر و صلاح و موافق مراد آفریدگار عالم به هر نیکی. و سزاوار است طلب کنندهٔ شرّ و فساد و مخالف مراد آفریدگار عالم به هر عقوبتی. و نیکوکار و بدکردار[۷] هرکسی بدانچ کند جزای خویش بیابد چنانك خدای تعالی همی‌گوید، قوله: إِنْ أَحْسَنْتُمْ أَحْسَنْتُمْ لِأَنْفُسِكُمْ وَ إِنْ أَسَأْتُمْ فَلَهَا.[۸] گفت:[۹] «اگر نیکویی کنید[۱۰] نیکویی مر خویشتن را کنید[۱۱] وگر بد کنید[۱۲] مر نفسهای شما را است».

۶ اس، ایا: ببودش. || نك: دهخدا: بودش. [دِ] هستی و بود که بعربی کَوْنْ خوانند.

۷ ایا: + از.

۸ سورة الإسراء (۱۷)، آیت ۷. || قس: گشایش و رهایش، ص ۶۳، بند [۱۵۹].

۹ ¦⟵برگ [ایا:۲۱-الف].

۱۰ اس: کنند.

۱۱ اس: کنند.

۱۲ اس: کنند.

صف دوازدهم

سخن اندر آنك مر هستها را كرانه است[1]

[§١:١٢] هست همه بر دو گونه است. یا لطیف است یا کثیف و مر هر دو را کرانه است. از بهر آنك نخست قسمت لطیف بر کرانهٔ کثیف است. و کثیف بر کرانهٔ لطیف است، بحکم مخالفت که اندر میان ایشان است. چه هر چیزی بر نهایت مخالف[2] خویش تواند ایستادن.

[§٢:١٢] و بدین نهایت که همی‌گوییم نه مر جایگاهی مکانی را همی‌خواهیم، بل‌که[3] مر حدّ آن چیزی را خواهیم که مر او را مخالف است. چنانك گرمی مخالف سردی است. و چاره نیست کی گرمی از سردی جداست. چه اگر ازو جدا نبودی مخالف سردی نبودی.

[§٣:١٢] و چون گرمی سردی را مخالف است و ازو جدا است، بضرورت آخر حدّ گرمی به اول حدّ سردی باشد. همچنانك همیشه آخر کنارهٔ روشنائی آفتاب به اول کنارهٔ سایه باشد. پس بباید دانستن که لطافت بر کنارهٔ کثافت است، و به کثافت محدود است.

[§۴:١٢] و دیگر دلیل بر آنك[4] هستها بی‌کرانه نیست آن است کز جمله هستها یکی این عالم کثیف است و این را نهایت است.

[§۵:١٢] و دلیل بر آنك این عالم را نهایت است آن است که جزوهایش را غایت است. و هر چه مر جزوهای او را نهایت باشد، مر کل او را نهایت باشد.

---

١ قس: كتاب الينابيع، الينبوع الرابع عشر (١۴): في أنّ الأيسيّات كلّها متناهية ذوات غايات، ص ٣٨ تا ۴٠.

٢ ¦⟵برگ [اس:٣۴-ب].

٣ ایا: بلك.

۴ ایا: [عبارت «بر آنك» بالای خط نوشته شده است].

[§۱۲:۶] و زمین از جزوهای این عالم است و او را نهایت است. این روی او که ما همی‌ببینیم که به هوا پیوسته است نهایت او است. و هر چیزی که به رویی[۵] از رویهای[۶] خویش متناهی باشد[۷] به همه رویها متناهی باشد.

[§۱۲:۷] و چون مر این یك جزو عالم را نهایت است دلیل است کی همه جزوهایش را نهایت است. و چون همه جزوهای او متناهی باشد کل او متناهی باشد.

[§۱۲:۸] و چون درست کردیم که این عالم از جملهٔ هستها است و متناهی است، لازم آید که هستها متناهی باشد.

[§۱۲:۹] از بهر آنك این عالم جزوی باشد از کل هستها، و چون جزوها را نهایت پیدا شد مر کل را نهایت پیدا شد. و نیز گوییم که هر چیزی که مر او را جزو باشد او متناهی باشد از بهر آنك جزو[۸] کم از کل باشد و مر او را به روی کمتری مخالف باشد.

[§۱۲:۱۰] و هر کسی کی گوید کی کلّ عالم نامتناهی است، بضرورت گفته باشد کی جزوش متناهی است از بهر آنك صفت جزو مخالف صفت کل باشد اندر آن معنی که کل نام کلّی بدان یافته است، و آن معنی از روی کمی و بیشی است.

[§۱۲:۱۱] و چون گفت بضرورت که جزوهای[۹] عالم متناهی است، اقرار کرد که عالم متناهی است از بهر آنك از متناهی نامتناهی نیاید که ایشان هر دو مر یکدیگر را مخالف اند. و هر که گوید از متناهی نامتناهی آید گفته باشد که از گرم سرد آید و از سیاه[۱۰] سپید آید. و خردمندان با او سخن نگویند چون محسوس را منکر شود.

---

۵ اس، ایا: روی.

۶ اس: رویها.

۷ ایا: [کلمه «باشد» بالای خط نوشته شده است].

۸ ¦⟵برگ [ایا:۲۱-ب].

۹ اس: جزوها.

۱۰ ¦⟵برگ [اس:۳۵-الف].

[§١٢:١٢] و اندر مُبدَعات و هستی آن گوئیم که اگر مبدعات که لطیف است کرانه نبودی، آفریده نبودی. و ما دانیم که مبدَع به ابداع آفریده شد. و هرچه هست شد نه از هست، مر او را نهایت است.

[§١٢:١٣] ازبهرآنك اگر بی‌نهایت بودی مر او را کرانه نبودی و هست شدن او نه از هست کرانهٔ او بود، و آن ابداع است که به ابداع کرانهٔ مُبدَع باشد. اما مر ابداع را هستی[١١] نیست و دور است از نیستی[١٢] و چیزی.[١٣]

[§١٢:١٤] و هرچه اندر عقل اوّل پیدا باشد از ابداع مر او را نهایت نیست ازبهرآنك وهم را سوی پیدا شدن او راه نیست که او علّت همه علّتها است. وگر مر او را علّت لازم آمدی سخن اندر این معنی به کناره نرسیدی و هر علّتی را نیز علّتی پیش ازو بایستی.

[§١٢:١٥] وگر اوّل علّتها علّتی نبودی که پیش ازو علّت نبودی معلول پیدا نیامدی. و چون مر[١٤] عالم را معلول یافتیم دانستیم که مر علّتها را نهایت است. و مر آن نهایت علّتها را ابداع گفتیم.

[§١٢:١٦] و برهان بر درستی این قول آن است کی مرغی را بینی و او را هست دانی و نهایت او بشناسی چه از کنارهای جسم او و چه از حدّ مرغیِ او کی او[١٥] بدان از ستور و خزنده و جز آن جدا است.

[§١٢:١٧] و چون آن مرغ از تو غایب شود، پیدا شود ترا نیستی‌ای،[١٦] ‹و تو مر آن

---

١١ ایا: ســتی.

١٢ اس: سستی؛ ایا: بیــتی. || [نك: یادداشت بعد].

١٣ اس: حیزی؛ ایا: چیزی. || نك: كتاب الینابیع، الینبوع الرابع عشر (١٤): في أنّ الأیسیّات كلّها متناهیة ذوات غایات، بند (٧٠)، ص ٣٩، س ٢ تا ٣: فأمّا الإبداع نفسه، فهو اللیس بمعنی نفي الأیسیّة واللّیسیّة.

١٤ ایا: − مر.

١٥ ایا: − او.

١٦ اس: بیستیء؛ ایا: نیستیء.

نیستی کرانها نمی‌یابی،[۱۷] چنانك مر هستش را نهایت یافته بودی. ازیراك لازم شد نیستیِ آن مرغ و آن نهایت بود مر هستیِ او را.

[§۱۲:۱۸] و چون مر یکی[۱۸] هست را نیستی[۱۹] کرانه یافتیم، و مر آن نیستی را کرانه نبود، دلیل است کی نابوده شود همه هستیها[۲۰] و آن کرانهٔ همهٔ[۲۱] هستیها[۲۲] باشد. پس درست شد کی مر همه هستها را کرانه است، و نیست را کرانه نیست.

[§۱۲:۱۹] و نیز از حکم عقل لازم آید که مر همه هستها را نهایت باشد از بهر آنك هست آن است کی بدانندش، و چیزی که او را بدانند به رویی[۲۳] از رویها دانندش، و دانش داننده به رویی از رویها اندر آن هست رسد، و آن هست ناچاره از آن روی که دانش داننده بدو رسد متناهی باشد.

[§۱۲:۲۰] و هر که گوید مر هست را نهایت نیست محال گفته باشد، از بهر آنك بی‌نهایت ناشناخته باشد بذات خویش، و جز از[۲۴] ذات خویش، و نشاید که چیزی باشد که او ناشناخته باشد هم اندر ذات خویش و هم نزدیك شناسندهٔ دیگر.

---

۱۷ اس: تو و مران نستی برانها‌نتی نابی [کذا]. ایا: تو و مران نیستی ترا نهانتی یابی [کذا]. || مقابلهٔ متن فارسی با متن عربی ازکتاب الینابیع، الینبوع الرابع عشر (۱۴): في أنّ الأَيسيّات كلّها متناهية ذوات غايات، بند (۷۱)، ص ۳۹، س ۷ تا ۸: 'ثمّ لا تجد لليسيّة الذرّة نهاية وغاية تقف عليها، كما وجدتَ النهاية لأَيسيّتها'، و بندهای بعدی همین متن، نشان میدهد که کاتب نسخهٔ استانبول «و تو مر آن نیستی کرانها نمی یابی» را سهواً «تو و مران نستی برانها‌نتی نابی» نگاشته است.

۱۸ ایا: یك.

۱۹ ایا: [کلمه «نیستی» بالای خط و معکوس نوشته شده است].

۲۰ ایا: هستها.

۲۱ ¦⟵برگ [ایا:۲۲-الف].

۲۲ ایا: هستها.

۲۳ اس: [کلمه «برویی» در بالای خط نوشته شده است].

۲۴ ¦⟵برگ [اس:۳۵-ب].

[§۱۲:۲۱] و عقل کلّ که اوّل مبدعات است شناختهٔ جوهر خویش است ذات پاك او. و گرد گرفته است[۲۵] شناختهٔ او مر جوهر او را تا این نام را مستحقّ شده است.

[§۱۲:۲۲] پس درست شد که هرچه هست است مر او را نهایت است، و نیست را نهایت نیست. ازبهر آنك نیست را بهیچ روی نتوان شناختن.

۲۵ اس: [«است» مخدوش است].

صف سیزدهم

سخن اندر چگونگی پیدا شدن مردم[1]

[§۱:۱۳] خلاف نیست میان دانایان که قوّتهای عالم گسلنده و بُرَندَه نیست و شَوَندَه. و کس نبیند[2] که چیزی آشکارا شود اندر عالم مگر که همچنانی پیدا شده باشد یا پیدا شود اندر زمانی دیگر. از بهر آنك ممکن نیست ضعیف شدن و اسپری شدن قوّتهای طبیعی تا به اسپری[3] شدن آن نیز پیدا نیاید آن چیز کی یکبار پیدا آمد.

[§۲:۱۳] پس رویی نیست مر نفس جزوی را به اندریافتن آغاز پدید آمدن مردم جز بر این حال که همی پیدا شود. و چون امروز همی‌یابیم قوّتهای[4] طبایع و افلاك و انجم را به زایش مردم پیوسته، دانیم که پیدا آمدن مردم با[5] پیدا[6] آمدن عالم بیك دفعه بوده است.

[§۳:۱۳] و خردمند چون داند که پیدا آمدن عالم با طبایع و افلاك و انجم بیك دفعه بود عجب نیایدش ‹از آنك›[7] جانوران، کی اجزای این عالم‌اند، با این عالم نیز بهم پدید آمدند. و بر عاقل آن واجب است کی طلب نکند آنچ اندر یافتن آن ممکن نیست مر عقل جزوی را، و آن فعل کلیّات نفس و عقل است.

[§۴:۱۳] و نباید طلب کردن آغازها را تا پیدا شود مر خردمند را شرف عقل[8] کلّی

---

۱ قس: کتاب الینابیع، الینبوع الثاني والعشرون (۲۲): في کیفیّة ابتداء الإنسان، ص ۵۳ تا ۵۶.

۲ اس، ایا: نه بیند.

۳ ایا: [«اسپری» مخدوش است].

۴ اس: قوتها.

۵ ایا: + بتداء. [روی «بتداء» با جوهر شنگرف خط زده شده است].

۶ اس: ننداء.

۷ ایا: ازان که.

۸ ¦⟵برگ [ایا:۲۲-الف].

که محیط است به مردم، و عاجز است مردم از اندر رسیدن به قوّت[۹] و قدرت کل خویش.

[§۱۳:۵] و ایزد تعالی اندر آفرینش مردم پیدا کرده است[۱۰] نشان آن که[۱۱] مر او را راه نیست سوی اندریافتن ابتدای خویش و آن آن است که مردم نتواند دانستن[۱۲] مر حرکات نفس را اندر فعلهای[۱۳] او کز چیست. و چون بر ابتدای حرکات نفس محیط شدن سزاوار[۱۴] نیست، بر ابتدای بودش او ناسزاوارتر است محیط شدن.

[§۱۳:۶] وگر کسی گوید که این مردم بسیار از یك جفت مردم پدید آمده است و بر آن حجّت آرد بر آنك گوید ممکن است کز یك جفت مردم فرزندان پیوسته شوند و زندگانی ایشان دراز شود و نسلهای دیگر مردمان بریده شود تا همه بمیرند، چنانك جز فرزندان آن یك جفت مردم اندر عالم مردم نماند و زین روی درست شود که این همه مردم از یك جفت مردم زاده است.

[§۱۳:۷] معارضه با او آن است که گویی سبیل اندر چیزهای طبیعی بر تفاوت است و ممکن است که همه مردمان از یك جفت مردم باشند. همچنانك بسیاری از یکی پدید آید.

[§۱۳:۸] امّا نوعی که او را شخصی نباشد ممکن نیست، و نوع را همتا نیست و نه مر جنس را اندر یگانگی، ازبهر آنك شخص بعدد بیشتر از نوع باشد و نوع بعدد کمتر از شخص باشد.

---

۹ ایا: بقوّة.

۱۰ ایا: کرد است.

۱۱ ایا: آنك.

۱۲ ¦⟵برگ [اس:۳۶-الف].

۱۳ در ویرایش حاضر از متن خوان الاخوان، هرجا که در نسخهٔ استانبول یا ایاصوفیا بعد از «ها»یِ جمع، همزه (ء) آمده است، همزه حذف و حرف «ی» نوشته شده است. مثلا در اینجا «فعلهاء» با املای «فعلهای» نگاشته شده است.

۱۴ اس: [کلمه «سزاوار» بالای خط نوشته شده است].

[§۹:۱۳] پس اگر کسی گوید که نوع مردم همه[۱۵] بشود تا به یکی شخص بازآید که او را همتایی نباشد راست کرده باشد مر نوع را با شخص ازبهرآنک نوع یکی باشد و شخص یکی.

[§۱۰:۱۳] و چون چنین باشد نوع باطل باشد، ازیراك شخص بجای نوع ایستاده است. و هرچند که شخص بسیار است نوع لازم است مر او را.

[§۱۱:۱۳] وگر یك شخص علّت نوع خویش باشد روا نباشد، ازبهرآنك نوع پیش از شخص است، چنانك جنس پیش از نوع است.

[§۱۲:۱۳] پس درست شد که نوع را بر شخص پیشی هست. و چون نوع پیش از شخص باشد اندر نوع شخصهای بسیار همیشه باید[۱۶] و روا نباشد که یك شخص بیش نباشد.

[§۱۳:۱۳] و سخن بی‌خلل آن است که پدید آمدن عالم با آنچ اندر او هست و بود و باشد بیك دفعه بود، کی هیچ چیز بر دیگری پیشی نداشت. امّا اندر حدّ قوّت بود چیزها، و بفعل همی بیرون آید.

[§۱۴:۱۳] و بودن مردم بیك دفعه نه صعب‌تر از بودن عالم است.[۱۷] با این شکل عظیم بیك دفعه، چنانك خدای تعالی همی‌گوید، قوله: لَخَلْقُ السَّمٰاوٰاتِ وَ الْأَرْضِ أَكْبَرُ مِنْ خَلْقِ النّٰاسِ وَ لٰكِنَّ أَكْثَرَ النّٰاسِ لاٰ يَعْلَمُونَ.[۱۸] همی‌گوید: «آفریدن آسمانها و زمین بزرگتر است[۱۹] از آفریدن مردمان و لکن بیشتر از مردمان ندانند».[۲۰]

---

۱۵ ایا: – همه.

۱۶ اس یاند؛ ایا: یابد. || تصحیح قیاسی.

۱۷ |⟵برگ [ایا:۲۳-الف].

۱۸ سورهٔ غافر (۴۰)، آیت ۵۷.

۱۹ |⟵برگ [اس:۳۶-ب].

۲۰ نك: جامع الحکمتین، فصل ۲۱: ‹اندر پدید آمدن انواع از شخص›، ص ۲۳۹ تا ۲۴۰، بند (۲۷۰): پس هرکه بعقل خویش بازگردد و بداند که این عالم عظیم بفرمان صانعی چنین است که هست، چه بایدش عجب داشتن از آنك همان کس که این صنع بزرگ کرد بی هیچ

آلتی، آن شخص اوّلی را — کو عالم صغیر بود — هم او کرد بفرمان؟ و اگر اینك همی بینیم <انسان کبیر> — اعنی عالم — واجب است که بوده است، انسان نیز واجب است چنانك خدای گفت «لَخَلْقُ السَّمٰاوٰاتِ وَ الْأَرْضِ أَكْبَرُ مِنْ خَلْقِ النّٰاسِ وَ لٰكِنَّ أَكْثَرَ النّٰاسِ لاٰ يَعْلَمُونَ.» همی گوید بوجه تأکید که آفریدن آسمانها و زمین بزرگترست از آفریدن مردمان و لکن بیشتر از مردمان همی ندانند — یعنی همی تفکّر نکنند — که چو آفرینش عالم پیداست که بفرمان است، آفرینش مردم هم ازوست.

صف چهاردهم

سخن اندر عالم عقلانی[۱]

[§۱:۱۴] چون خردمند اندر عالم طبیعی نگاه کند و مر او را مانند طبایع نماید، و طبایع را مانند عالم نماید، و از شاهد بر غایب دلیل داند گرفتن، بداند کی عالم عقل و نفس مانده باشد به عقل و نفس. و عقل و نفس مانده باشد به عالم خویش.

[§۲:۱۴] و چون[۲] ما مر عقل و نفس جزوی را چنان همی‌یابیم که نتوانیم گفتن که اندر عالم طبیعی‌اند برمثال چیزی جای‌گیر، یا از عالم بیرون‌اند برمثال چیزی بر چیزی دیگر محیط، پس همچنین گوییم [که نتوان گفتن][۳] که عقل و نفس کلّی اندر عالم طبیعت‌اند، برمثال چیزی متمکّن اندر او، و یا ازین عالم بیرون‌اند برمثال جرمی محیط بر جرمی دیگر، بل گوییم که نفس و عقل کلّی اندر این عالم‌اند به معنی بیرون از بهر آنك جای‌گیر نیستند، و افعال و آثار ایشان اندر او است، و بیرون‌اند ازین عالم به معنی آنك اندر این عالم‌اند.

[§۳:۱۴] یعنی که[۴] تقدیر و تدبیر ایشان اندر این عالم است، یا چنان‌اند که اندرون‌اند و بذات اندر این عالم نایافته‌اند، یا[۵] چنان‌اند[۶] کز بیرون‌اند و بحقیقت

---

۱ قس: کتاب الینابیع الینبوع الرابع (۴): في بیان عالم العقل وعالم النفس وکیفیّتهما، ص ۲۰ تا ۲۲.

۲ ایا: – چون.

۳ تصحیح قیاسی: از مقایسه این قسمت با کتاب الینابیع، ص ۲۰، س ۹ تا ۱۱: 'و کذلك نقول أنّ العقل والنفس الکُلّیِّین لا یقال لهما داخلانِ في العالم ولا خارجانِ منه، بمعنی مُمَکَّن محاط أو بمعنی مکان محیط، بل هما داخلانِ فیه بمعنی الخروج، خارجان منه بمعنی الدخول.'، معلوم میشود که «پس همچنین گوییم که نتوان گفتن» درست است.

۴ ایا: – که.

۵ اس: تا.

۶ اس، ایا: چنانند.

نفس و عقل ازین عالم بیرون‌اند به شرف و جوهر خویش، ازبهرآنك این عالم کثیف تاریك مر لطیف نورانی را بکار نیاید.

[§۴:۱۴] و دلیل بر درستی این دعوی آن است که علم هرچیزی که اندر نفس مردم باشد نفس مردم از اندرون آن خبر باشد که اندر نفس او است به وقت صورت کردن مر آن را و چون از آن صورت پرداخته شود چنان باشد که گویی آن صورت از نفس بیرون است.

[§۵:۱۴] پس همچنین است حال نفس و عقل کلّی با عالم که پنداری که اندر عالم طبیعت‌اند چون بینی که صورتها[۷] بر[۸] حکمت اندر عالم پدید همی‌آید، و باز پنداری که بیرون اویند چون بینی کزان صورتها[۹] همی‌پردازند.

[§۶:۱۴] و هرکه پندارد کی بیرون این فلك چیزی هست که او را مسافت است اعنی دوری و نزدیکی غلط پندارد ازبهرآنك مسافت از اندرون فلك است، و هرچیز که او را اندرون باشد ناچاره مر او را بیرون باشد. و بیرون چیز بخلاف اندرون باشد.[۱۰]

[§۷:۱۴] و چون همی‌بینیم که این عالم را اندرون است دلیل همی‌کند کی او را بیرون است. و چون اندرونش را مسافت است دلیل می‌کند کی بیرون او را مسافت نیست بحکم خلاف کی میان اندرون و بیرون است و میان مسافت و نه مسافت.

[§۸:۱۴] پس اگر کسی گوید از بیرون این عالم مسافت است قول خویش را نقیضه کرده باشد. و گفته باشد کی بیرون این عالم هم اندرون این عالم است. و تا مسافت نفی نکند بیرون او اثبات نکرده باشد.

---

۷ اس: صورتهاء؛ ایا: صورتهای.

۸ ایا: پر.

۹ ¦⟵برگ [ایا:۲۳-ب].

۱۰ ¦⟵برگ [اس:۳۷-الف].

[§۱۴:۹] و از فضیلت و شرف جوهر روحانی آن است کی چیزهای روحانی را از حال خویش نگرداند. بدان معنی که اندر جوهر روحانی فساد را راه نیست.

[§۱۴:۱۰] و آن جوهر کز حدّ قوّت به حد فعل آید عالم روحانی مر آن را نگاه دارد. و از حال فعل باز حال قوّت نبردش ازبهر آنك اندر جوهر روحانی اضداد و مخالفت نیست.

[§۱۴:۱۱] و چیزهای طبیعی فساد پذیرد. و گوهرهای طبیعی مر چیزهائی را کز حدّ قوّت به حدّ فعل آورده باشد به حدّ قوّت بازبردش، و بر یك حال ‹نگاه نتواندش›[۱۱] داشتن.

[§۱۴:۱۲] ازبهر آنك اندر طبایع دشمنان و مخالفان‌اند، و همه اندر یك مکان‌اند،[۱۲] و مر یکدیگر را از مکانها بیرون کنند، تا حالهای ایشان گردنده همی‌باشد. و جواهر روحانی را به مکان حاجت نیست.

[§۱۴:۱۳] و بدین برهان عقلی و سخن منطقی[۱۳] درست شد که عالم طبیعت به جزویّات و کلیّات خویش اندرون عالم عقل و نفس است. بدان معنی که این طبیعیّات را مکان و زمان است، و از حال خویش گردنده است، و آن لطایف را به مکان و زمان حاجت نیست. لاجرم از حال خویش گردنده نیست.

[§۱۴:۱۴] و آنچ مر او را مکان نباشد اندر این عالم نباشد، بحکم عقل.

[§۱۴:۱۵] و دلیل بر آنك عالم جسمانی اندر عالم عقل است نه به روی مکان بل به روی احاطت علمی آن است که عقل[۱۴] کل را مُبدِع حقّ تمام آفرید. و هیچ چیز را ازو[۱۵] بیرون نگذاشت.

---

۱۱ ایا: نتواندش نگاه.

۱۲ اس، ایا: مکانند.

۱۳ ایا: مصطفی.

۱۴ |⟵برگ [ایا:۲۴-الف].

۱۵ ایا: + ن [بعد از «ازو» حرف «ن» با جوهر شنگرف خط زده شده است].

[§۱۶:۱۴] وگر چیزی از عقل بیرون بودی امروز عقل مر آن را نشناختی. و عقل ناقص بودی اگر برو چیزی پوشیده بودی.

[§۱۷:۱۴] پس چون هیچ چیز بر عقل پوشیده نیست، دلیل است که همه چیزها بیك دفعه اندر جوهر عقل پدید آورده است مُبدِع حقّ[۱۶] و هیچ چیز ازو بیرون نبوده است.

[§۱۸:۱۴] و چون عالم طبیعت از جملهٔ چیزها است، نتیجهٔ این مقدّمه آن باشد کی عالم طبیعت و عالم نفس اندر عالم عقل است.

[§۱۹:۱۴] و بباید دانستن که مر عالم طبیعت را نزدیك عالم روحانی مقداری نیست.

[§۲۰:۱۴] دلیل بر درستی این دعوی آن است کی چون میان نفسی از نفسهای جزوی و میان نفس کلّی فایده پیوسته شود، آن نفس جزوی مر کل خویش را جستن گیرد، و معلومات عقلی را از کل خویش طلب کند.

[§۲۱:۱۴] و آنچ از نفس کلّی به نفس جزوی رسد از فواید آن عالم اندکی باشد. و بدان اندك مایه فواید کزان عالم بیابد مر این عالم را فراموش کند.

[§۲۲:۱۴] و گوایی دهد بر درستی این قول دست بازداشتن پیغامبران، علیهم السّلام، و حکما از لذّات و شهوات این عالم، و کرانه گرفتن ایشان از طلب کردن این عالم.

[§۲۳:۱۴] وگر این عالم را نزدیك آن عالم مقداری بودی نفس جزوی بدان اندك مایه معرفت کزان عالم همی‌یابد مر این عالم را فراموش نکردی.

[§۲۴:۱۴] و چون درست شد که این عالم را نزدیك شناسندهٔ بعضی از آن عالم

---

۱۶ ¦⟵برگ [اس:۳۷-ب].

مقداری نیست، درست شد کی جملگی این عالم نزدیك جملگی آن عالم سخت بی‌خطر است.

[§۱۴:۲۵] وز خاصیت عالم عقلی آن است که همه مسافتها اندر او گنجیده است و او خود نقطه‌ای[۱۷] است وهمی، پس از بزرگی پنهان است از روی شرف و علم، وز خردی پنهان نیست از روی جسمی.

[§۱۴:۲۶] و عالم عقل[۱۸] پایدار است، و عالم جسمانی ناپایدار است. و هرچه بدان عالم رسید بر حال خویش بماند.

[§۱۴:۲۷] بباید کوشیدن تا نفس تو ای برادر چنان شود اندر این عالم که اگر بر آن حال بمانی ترا روا باشد. ‹و این نه این باشد›[۱۹] مگر آن وقت که تمام شوی.[۲۰] ازبهر آنك ناتمام رنجه باشد هم بدین سرای و هم بدان سرای.

۱۷ اس، ایا: نقطهء.

۱۸ ایا: عقلی.

۱۹ ایا: و این نباشد.

۲۰ ¦⟵برگ [ایا:۲۴-ب].

صف پانزدهم

سخن اندر چرائی پیوستن فایدهٔ نفس کلّی به مردم بیرون از دیگر حیوان[۱]

[§۱:۱۵] گوییم که فایدهٔ نفس به مردم از آن پیوسته شد که جوهر نفس بر حدّ اعتدال بود،[۲] و معنیش آن همی‌خواهیم که او غایت لطایف نبود چنانك عقل است کزو برتر هستی نیست.

[§۲:۱۵] و نیز به نهایت لطافت نبود چنانك هیولی است[۳] کزو فروتر لطیفی نیست. بل کز غایت لطایف فروتر بود، و از نهایت آن برتر بود.

[§۳:۱۵] و مردم اندر عالم جسمانی آفرینش بر حدّ اعتدال یافت. و پدید آمدن انواع حیوانات مر طبایع را پاکیزگی افتاده بود تا مردم از آن طبایع پاکیزه شدهٔ معتدل گشته آفرینش یافت.

[§۴:۱۵] و دلیل بر درستی این دعوی آن است که آنچ از جانوران برو طبع خاك غالب بود، خاك مر او را سوی خویش کشید تا جز به چهار پای همی‌نتواند ایستادن، چون ستوران و ددگان.

[§۵:۱۵] و بعضی را طبیعت خاکی چنان قهر کرد که خود پای نیافت، تا از خاك ‹جدا توانستی شدن›[۴] چون کرمان و ماران و جز آن.

[§۶:۱۵] و بعضی را طبیعت آتشی[۵] و هوایی غالب آمد تا بهوا برپریدند. و شرح این حال اندر[۶] کتاب دلیل المتحیّرین گفته‌ایم پیش ازین.

---

۱ ایا: حیوان ن.

۲ اس: – بود.

۳ ¦⟵برگ [اس:۳۸-الف].

۴ ایا: توانستی جدا شدن.

۵ ایا: آتش.

۶ ایا: در.

[§۷:۱۵] و مردم که بر حدّ اعتدال آمد، نه خاك مر او را سوی[7] خویش کشید تا به چهار ستون برپای باشد، و نه آتش او را سوی خویش کشید تا بپریدی. بل کی بر قامت الفی باستاد. به رویی چون خزندگان خزنده[8] و به رویی چون پرندگان به دو پای دوان.

[§۸:۱۵] و چون میان مردم و میان نفس کلّی بر حدّ اعتدال نسبت افتاد با او هم گوهر گشت. و به هم گوهری، نفس کلّی مر نفس مردم را دوست گرفت. و او را به قوّت امر باری سوی خویش خواند. و از جوهر خویش مر او را نفقات داد به علم، تا همچنو باقی و دانا و نورانی و فایده پذیر گشت.

---

۷ ایا: بسوی.

۸ ایا: - خزنده.

صف شانزدهم

سخن اندر چرائی لازم کردن پیامبران بر خلق اقرارِ به توحید[۱]

[§۱۶:۱] پیش ازین گفتیم که نخست حجّت از آفریدگار بر مردم عقل است که ایزد در آفرینش او نهاده است.

[§۱۶:۲] و آن را عقل غریزی خوانند. و آن عقلی است اندر حدّ قوّت. و چیزی که اندر حدّ قوّت باشد، مر او را به حدّ فعل نتواند آوردن مگر چیزی که هم ازو باشد و به حدّ فعل شده باشد.

[§۱۶:۳] و دلیل بر درستی این قول آن است که همه شاگردان دانایان‌اند اندر حدّ قوّت. از بهر آنك هیچ دانایی نیست که او شاگرد[۲] دیگری نبوده است. و مر شاگرد را جز دانایی که به حدّ فعل دانا باشد دانا نتواند کردن.

[§۱۶:۴] و چون این مقدّمه دانسته باشی، گوییم که مر عقل غریزی را که اندر آفرینش به حدّ قوّت است، عقلی بفعلی آمده بایست تا مر او را از حدّ قوّت به حدّ فعل بیرون آرد.

[§۱۶:۵] و هر پیغامبری اندر زمان خویش از عقل بفعل آمده ناطق شده بود، که عقلها را که اندر زمان او به حدّ قوّت بودند به حدّ فعل بیرون آورد.

[§۱۶:۶] و ایزد تعالی مردم را چنان آفریده بود اندر این عالم که حکم طبایع برو روان بود اندر حالهای او بی‌مراد او، چون تشنه و گرسنه و محنتها و بیماریهای گران را از خویش بازنتواند داشتن.

[§۱۶:۷] و اندر حال بیچارگی بدانچ اندر آن عقل غریزی او نهاده است اقرار دهد، و فریاد خواهد از پدیدآرندهٔ خویش و رهایش جوید از آنچ اندر آن افتاده باشد

---

۱ ایا: + باری. || ¦⟵برگ [ایا:۲۵-الف].

۲ ¦⟵برگ [اس:۳۸-ب].

از آفریدگار خویش چنانك خدای تعالی همی‌گوید، قوله: وَ إِذٰا مَسَّ الْإِنْسٰانَ الضُّرُّ دَعٰانٰا لِجَنْبِهِ أَوْ قٰاعِداً أَوْ[۳] قٰائِماً فَلَمّٰا كَشَفْنٰا عَنْهُ ضُرَّهُ مَرَّ كَأَنْ لَمْ يَدْعُنٰا إِلىٰ ضُرٍّ مَسَّهُ.[۴] گفت: «چون بپساود[۵] مردم را دشواری بخواند ما را بر پهلو یا نشسته یا ایستاده؛ پس چون آن دشواری ازو بازکردیم بگذرد چنانك گویی هرگز ما را نخواندستی اندر دشواری».

[§۸:۱۶] و چون این حال مردم اندر عقل غریزی بود کز آفریدگار فریاد خواهد اندر حال ضرورت، چون عقل بفعل آمده که رسول دوّم بود از کردگار سوی مردم بیامد مر او را سوی آن اقرار خواند که اندر غریزت او بود و[۶] آن را برو استوار کرد، تا پیش از آمدن شدّت و ضرورت آن اقرار بکرد.

[§۹:۱۶] تا همچنان‌که[۷] ازین دشواری دنیاوی بدان اقرار همی رهایش جوید از دشواریهای آخرتی کلّی[۸] که بدین اقرار همیشه رهایی باشد. و هرکه خدای را تعالی به اخلاص بخواند هیچ دشواری نبیند.[۹]

---

۳ اس، ایا: – أَوْ.

۴ سورة یونس (۱۰)، آیت ۱۲.

۵ نك: دهخدا: بپساویدن. [بِ دَ] ... سودن. ساویدن... ساییدن. مالیدن. نیز نك: بپسودن. [بِ دَ] ... بپسودان. لمس. لامسه کردن.

۶ ¦←برگ [ایا:۲۵-ب].

۷ ایا: همچنانك.

۸ =بتمامی، تماماً. کاملاً.

۹ اس، ایا: نه‌بیند.

صف هفدهم

سخن اندر آنك هر چه پیغامبر، علیه السّلام، فرمود و خود بکرد، بعقل نیکو است و هر چه از آن مر خلق را بازداشت و خود نکرد، سوی عقل زشت است

[۱:۱۷§] گوییم نفس شهوانی بدفرمای است. و مردم را[۱] چیزهائی فرماید که فایدهٔ آن همه مر جسد را باشد. و از پسند عقل دور باشد. چون زنا و لواطت و خواستهٔ مردمان ستدن و مردم کشتن به ناحق و جفا نمودن مر کسی را که سزاوار جفا نباشد، و فرایض خدای و سنّت رسول او بگذاشتن. و اندر این همه فعلهای بد خوشی مر نفس شهوانی را است.

[۲:۱۷§] و خدای تعالی همی‌گوید از قول یوسف، علیه السّلام، قوله: إِنَّ النَّفْسَ لَأَمّٰارَةٌ بِالسُّوءِ إِلاّٰ مٰا رَحِمَ رَبِّي[۲] إِنَّ رَبِّي غَفُورٌ رَحِيمٌ.[۳] همی‌گوید: «نفس فرماینده است به بدی. مگر آنك برو رحمت کرد پرودگار من. چه پروردگار من پوشانندهٔ[۴] مهربان است». و بدین نفس مر نفس شهوانی را همی‌خواهد. از بهر آنك اندر این گناهان که گفتیم خوشی مر نفس شهوانی را است.

[۳:۱۷§] امّا به زنا و لواطت نفس شهوانی دو لذت یابد. یکی لذّت جماع که تمامی آن مر ستور را است و دیگر لذت بی‌فرمانی که بی‌فرمانی را لذتی هست بدان سبب کی ‹مردم به بی‌فرمانی›[۵] مانند ستور شود، و نفس بهیمی چون بی‌فرمان شود خوشتر باشدش.

---

۱ ←|برگ [اس:۳۹-الف].

۲ اس، ایا: – رَبِّي.

۳ سورة یوسف (۱۲)، آیت ۵۳.

۴ ایا: پوشندهٔ [بالای «پوشندهٔ»، در فاصله بین دو سطر، با خط ریزتر «پوشانندهٔ» نوشته شده است].

۵ اس: مردم ببی فرمانی؛ ایا: ببی فرمانی مردم.

[۴:۱۷§] و اما به دست بازداشتن پرستش خدای و سنّت رسول نفس شهوانی لذت سوی جسد به بی‌فرمانی و بی‌سالاری کشد، و گریختن از کار واجب. و اما نفس شهوانی، به خواسته ستدن، لذّت توانگری یابد که جسد او بدان آسوده شود.

[۵:۱۷§] و اما به مردم کشتن، نفس شهوانی لذت کینه کشیدن یابد و کامکاری و بی‌فرمانی. و اما به جفا نمودن، نفس شهوانی لذت کاربستنِ خوی بد یابد که برو پادشا گشته باشد[۶] با لذت کینه کشیدن. و این همه کارها به نزدیك عقل زشت است.

[۶:۱۷§] و نفس عاقله آن است کی علم و دیانت و توحید او تواند پذیرفتن. و نفس سخنگوی تا علم نپذیرد نفس عاقله نباشد، اندر حدّ قوّت، و ممکن باشد که روزی عاقله شود.

[۷:۱۷§] و اکنون بازنماییم زشتی این کارها سوی عقل، و گوییم که زشتی زنا و لواطت سوی عقل آن است کی هر چیزی که مردم خردمند زشت دارد که کسی با او بکند، بعقل چنان لازم آید که او آن کار با دیگر کس نکند.

[۸:۱۷§] و هیچ خردمند روا ندارد که کسی با زن و فرزند او زنا و لواطت کند.[۷] پس روا ناداشتن[۸] عاقل زنا و لواطت را بر زن و فرزند خویش روا ناداشتن عقل است این دو کار ناستوده را. پس بعقل واجب آمد فرمان‌برداری رسول خدای کردن و دست بازداشتن از زنا و لواطت به جسمانی و روحانی. و رسول مصطفی، صلّی[۹] اللّه علیه وآله، فرمود: لا تَزنُوا فتزنُوا نساءکم.[۱۰] گفت: «زنا مکنید کی با زنان خویش

۶ ¦⟵برگ [ایا:۲۶-الف].

۷ ¦⟵برگ [اس:۳۹-ب].

۸ ایا: داناشتن. || اس: [در کلمه «ناداشتن» دو حرف اول کلمه یعنی «نا» با خط نازك و بدون نقطه در بالای حرف «د» روی سطر نوشته شده است].

۹ اس، ایا: صل.

۱۰ اس، ایا: نساکم.

زنا کرده باشید». یعنی که با زنان شما زنا کنند.[۱۱]

[§۹:۱۷] اما خواستهٔ[۱۲] مردمان ستدن، بعقل زشت است و ناپسندیده، ازبهر آنك خواسته پادشای مردم است. و هیچ خردمند روا ندارد که او را از پادشائی او بیرون کنند. و زوال پادشائی[۱۳] جسدانی به زوال خواسته است. و زوال پادشائی روحانی به زوال علم است.

[§۱۰:۱۷] و بدانك ناسزا منزلت علم از عالِم بستاند. و پادشائی تمام عقل را است که بودش دو عالَم ازو است. و درویشی تمام مر ابلیس ملعون را است که مخالف عقل است. و هر که را مال است، مر او را اندر جسمانی پایگاه عقل است. و چون از کسی مال او ستدند، او درویش گشت و حال او برابر حال ابلیس شد.

[§۱۱:۱۷] ازبهر آنك پیوستگان ابلیس را که اهل دوزخ‌اند به هیچ روی از رویها اندر آتش کام‌روایی نیست. پس مر توانگر را درویش گردانیدن ماننده است بدانك مر بهشتی را دوزخی گردانیدن، و این به روی عقل ناپسندیده است.

[§۱۲:۱۷] امّا دزدی و راهداری[۱۴] و بیداد کردن بعقل زشت است. ازبهر آنك اندر آنْ شدنِ مُلكِ مردم است، و هر که بیداد و دزدی[۱۵] روا دارد چنان باشد که روا داشته باشد که عقل نباشد. ازیراك او مخالف عقل باشد. و مخالف مر مخالف را نیست خواهد.

---

۱۱ نك: البرقي، احمد بن محمد، المحاسن، تصحیح: جلال الدین الحسینی المحدث (قم: دارالکتب الإسلامیة، ۱۳۷۱ق)، ج ۱، باب (۴۶): عقاب الزاني، ص ۱۰۷: ۹۴ - ... لَا تَزْنُوا فَتَزْنِيَ نِسَاؤُكُمْ.

۱۲ نك: دهخدا: خواسته. [خوا / خا تَ / تِ] (اِسم) زر. مال. اسباب. جمعیت. سامان. ملک. املاک. آنچه دلخواه باشد.... مال. عَرَض. ضیعت. مال جز محصولات ارضی. ... || مرغوب. مطلوب. محبوب. آنچه را که کسی خواسته است. مراد. مقصود.

۱۳ اس: پادشای.

۱۴ اس، ایا: راه داری.

۱۵ ¦⟵برگ [ایا:۲۶-ب].

[§۱۳:۱۷] و هر که عقل را نیست خواهد چنان باشد که خواهد که خلق را از خدای نفع نباشد. دیگر هر که درویشی را توانگر کند بدانچ ورا ملکی دهد برابر آن باشد که مردمی را به علم و حکمت به صورتِ معاد رساند.

[§۱۴:۱۷] و هر که صورت عقل اندر یك تن درست تواند نگاشتن همچنان باشد که همه مردم را زنده کرده باشد؛ بدان معنی که همه مردم چون یك مردم‌اند، و هر چه با یك مردم کنی اگر با همه توانستی همان کردی.

[§۱۵:۱۷] و هر که خواستهٔ کسان ستدن، به ناحق روا دارد، زوال منزلت امام روا داشته باشد، که خواسته‌دار بحقیقت امام است.[۱۶] و آن کس اندر دین و دنیا به‌غصب[۱۷] کردن با ابلیس لعین برابر باشد و انباز.

[§۱۶:۱۷] و هر که انباز ابلیس باشد فساد و هلاك همه خلق خواسته باشد. چنانك خدای تعالی از آن ملعون همی‌حکایت کند قوله: قٰالَ رَبِّ بِمٰا أَغْوَيْتَنِي لَأُزَيِّنَنَّ لَهُمْ فِي الْأَرْضِ وَ لَأُغْوِيَنَّهُمْ أَجْمَعِينَ.[۱۸] گفت: «ای خدای بَدانك مرا بفریفتی بیارایم مر امّت را اندر زمین، یعنی کی زشت را نزدیك ایشان نیکو گردانم، و بفریبمشان بجملگی».

[§۱۷:۱۷] ازبهر آن بود که خدای تعالی مر نیکوکاران را با یك تن، نیکوکردار خواند با همه خلق، و بدکردار را با یك تن، بدکردار خواند با همه خلق؛ قوله: مِنْ أَجْلِ ذٰلِكَ كَتَبْنٰا عَلىٰ بَنِي إِسْرٰائِيلَ أَنَّهُ مَنْ قَتَلَ نَفْساً بِغَيْرِ نَفْسٍ أَوْ فَسٰادٍ فِي الْأَرْضِ فَكَأَنَّمٰا قَتَلَ النّٰاسَ جَمِيعاً وَ مَنْ أَحْيٰاهٰا فَكَأَنَّمٰا أَحْيَا النّٰاسَ جَمِيعاً.[۱۹] گفت: «از بهر آن نبشتیم بر پسران[۲۰] اسرائیل که هر که یك تن را بکشد بی آنك او کسی

---

۱۶ |⟵برگ [اس:۴۰-الف].

۱۷ اس: بغصب؛ ایا: بغضب.

۱۸ سورة الحِجْر (۱۵)، آیت ۳۹.

۱۹ سورة المائدة (۵)، آیت ۳۲.

۲۰ ایا: + بنی [ظاهراً، بعداً کلمه «بنی» با جوهر شنگرف خط زده شده است].

را بکشته[۲۱] باشد یا اندر زمینی فساد کرده باشد، چنان باشد که همه مردمان را بکشت. و هرکه یك تن را زنده کند چنان باشد که همه مردمان را زنده کرد».

[§۱۸:۱۷] و تأویلش آن است کی هرکه یك تن را بجسمانی بکشد، یا[۲۲] مَرتبتِ دانایی غصب کند، که آن کشتن روحانی است، همچنان باشد که همه خلق را بکشت. و هرکه زندگی یك تن به نیکوکرداری با او بجوید، یا[۲۳] دانایی را اندر[۲۴] دین بر مرتبت او نگاه دارد، زندگی همه خلق روا داشته باشد. و خدای تعالی مر او را مزد براندازهٔ نیّت او دهد.

[§۱۹:۱۷] پس ازین روی واجب شد دست از خواستهٔ مردمان بازداشتن مگر حقّ خویش طلب کردن. اما کشتن مردم به ستم سوی عقل سخت زشت است و هیچ خردمند روا ندارد که مر کسی را بی‌گناه بکشد.

[§۲۰:۱۷] و لکن واجب است به روی عقل گناهکار[۲۵] را کشتن تا هرکه گناه خواهد کردن چون از آن بادَفَراه[۲۶] سخت بیندیشد دست از گناه بازدارد.

[§۲۱:۱۷] و اندر آن، زندگیِ خلق باشد چنانك خدای تعالی همی‌گوید، قوله: وَ لَكُمْ فِي الْقِصٰاصِ حَيٰاةٌ يٰا أُولِي الْأَلْبٰابِ.[۲۷] همی‌گوید: «‹مر شما را اندر قصاص›[۲۸]

---

۲۱ ایا: کشته.

۲۲ ایا: با.

۲۳ ایا: تا.

۲۴ ¦⟵برگ [ایا:۲۷-الف].

۲۵ اس، ایا: گناه‌کار.

۲۶ نك: دهخدا: بادفراه. [دَ فَ] مخفف بادآفراه [مخفف بادآفراه]...بمعنی...جزا و مکافات بدی باشد.

۲۷ سورة البقرة (۲)، آیت ۱۷۹.

۲۸ ایا: اندر قصاص مر شما را.

زندگی است ای خردمندان». و کشتن هم‌گوشهٔ خویش بی‌آنك او[۲۹] مر کسی را ازآنِ تو کشته باشد[۳۰] اندر عقل ناپسندیده است.

[§۲۲:۱۷] معارضه، اگر کسی به اندیشهٔ فاسد خویش چنان اندیشد که پیغامبر، علیه السّلام، بسیار مردم را بکشت، که هیچ کس، براستْ، او گناهی نداشتند، و همه همچون او مردم بودند، جواب او را گوییم که بباید دانستن که آن زشت باشد از کنندهٔ آن که مر او را اندر آن کار زشت مرادی نباشد نیکو.

[§۲۳:۱۷] و چون مردی دزد که زاهدی را بکشد شاید دانستن که مراد آن مفسد بکشتن او از دو کار است. یکی از بازداشتن آن زاهد مر او را از فساد، تا از بازداشتن او برهد، و دیگر تا خواستهٔ آن زاهد بستاند، و بدین هردو بهانه سخت زشت و ناپسندیده است بسوی عقل.

[§۲۴:۱۷] امّا چون مراد اندر فسادی ظاهر[۳۱] سخت نیکو باشد، روا باشد، بل‌که[۳۲] واجب باشد آن فساد کردن. چنانك رسول، صلی[۳۳] اللّٰه علیه وآله، به ابتدای رسالت کافران مکّه را بکشت. و آن حکمتی سخت بزرگ بود، ازبهرآنك مراد او، علیه السلام، اندر آن کشتن سوی عقل سخت ستوده بود.[۳۴]

[§۲۵:۱۷] ازبهرآنك رسول، علیه السلام، مر کافران را ازبهر امر معروف و نهی منکر کشت، و طبع و خاصیّت عقل امر معروف و نهی منکر است. و رسول، علیه السلام، مر کافران را از پرستش بتان که غایت منکر است سوی پرستش خدای خواند[۳۵] که غایت معروف است.

---

۲۹ ایا: – او.

۳۰ ¦⟵برگ [اس:۴۰-ب].

۳۱ ایا: [«ظاهر» در فاصله بین سطور نوشته شده است].

۳۲ ایا: بلك.

۳۳ اس: صل.

۳۴ قس: جامع الحکمتین، ص ۲۹۷ تا ۲۹۸، بند: ۳۴۰.

۳۵ ¦⟵برگ [ایا:۲۷-ب].

[§۲۶:۱۷] و چون ازو نصیحت نپذیرفتند، و بغایت جهل بودند، او، علیه السّلام، دانست به نور نبوت که اندر باقی عمرِ ایشان، از ایشان به پذیرفتن ایمان صلاحی نخواهد آمدن که بدان راحت ابدی یابند، و بر جهل بخواهند مردن، ایشان را بکشت تا بغایت ناستودهٔ خود برسند.

[§۲۷:۱۷] و دیگر گروه که زیشان امید صلاح بود بکشتن ایشان عبرت گرفتند، و اندر ایمان رغبت کردند. و از منکر بازگشتند و معروف را بپذیرفتند.

[§۲۸:۱۷] پس ازین نیکوتر مرادی چگونه توان بحاصل کردن، که رسول، علیه السّلام، کرد، که بکشتن جاهلان چندین خلق را کز روزگار او، علیه السّلام، تا امروز آمدند اندر این عالم، و تا قیامت خواهند آمدن، بصلاح بازآورد.

[§۲۹:۱۷] و هر روزی آن صلاح برفزون است، تا به آخر آن صلاح به آخر دهر بکمال رسد. و این همچنان بود که کسی صلاح صد هزار تن نیکوکار[۳۶] به فساد یك تن بدکردار بجوید. و این سوی عقل سخت پسندیده است.

[§۳۰:۱۷] چنانك چون حال بعکس این باشد، سوی عقل ناپسندیده باشد. و آن آن باشد که کسی صلاح یك تن مفسد به فساد صدهزار مصلح بجوید.

[§۳۱:۱۷] ازین روی بود که رسول، صلی[۳۷] اللّٰه علیه وآله، به آغاز پیغامبری بت‌پرستان را به امر خدای تعالی بکشت، چنانك خدای تعالی فرموده بود او را، قوله: یٰا أَیُّهَا النَّبِیُّ جٰاهِدِ الْکُفّٰارَ وَ الْمُنٰافِقِینَ وَ اغْلُظْ عَلَیْهِمْ.[۳۸] گفت: «ای پیامبر جهد کن با کافران و منافقان و سطبر دل باش بر ایشان».

[§۳۲:۱۷] پس از روی نگاهبانی[۳۹] او مر خلق را نهادن قصاص میان مردم تا از گناه باز باشند. و دیت فرمود و مر جراحت را مکافات فرمود. چنانك خدای تعالی

۳۶ |⟵برگ [اس:۴۱-الف].

۳۷ اس: صل.

۳۸ سورة التوبة (۹)، آیت ۷۳؛ سورة التحریم (۶۶)، آیت ۹.

۳۹ اس، ایا: نگاه‌بانی.

گفت، قوله: وَ كَتَبْنٰا عَلَيْهِمْ فِيهٰا[۴۰] أَنَّ النَّفْسَ بِالنَّفْسِ وَ الْعَيْنَ بِالْعَيْنِ وَ الْأَنْفَ بِالْأَنْفِ وَ الْأُذُنَ بِالْأُذُنِ وَ السِّنَّ بِالسِّنِّ وَ الْجُرُوحَ قِصٰاصٌ.[۴۱] گفت: «بر ایشان نوشتم اندر توریت[۴۲] کی تن را تن بدل باشد، و چشم را چشم، و بینی را بینی، و گوش را گوش، و دندان را دندان، و جراحتها را قصاص». یعنی همچنان جراحت کنند مر آن کس را که کسی را جراحت کند.[۴۳]

[§۳۳:۱۷] و مر دزد را عقوبت فرمود به دست بریدن.[۴۴] چنانك گفت، قوله: وَ السّٰارِقُ وَ السّٰارِقَةُ فَاقْطَعُوا أَيْدِيَهُمٰا جَزٰاءً بِمٰا كَسَبٰا نَكٰالاً مِنَ اللّٰهِ.[۴۵] گفت: «هرکه دزدی کند از مرد و زن دستهای ایشان ببرّید مکافات آنچ ایشان الفغدند،[۴۶] تا رسوا شوند از خدای و رسول او». و مر زناکننده را حد فرمود صد تازیانه چنانك گفت، قوله: الزّٰانِيَةُ وَ الزّٰانِي فَاجْلِدُوا كُلَّ وٰاحِدٍ مِنْهُمٰا مِائَةَ جَلْدَةٍ وَ لاٰ تَأْخُذْكُمْ بِهِمٰا رَأْفَةٌ فِي دِينِ اللّٰهِ.[۴۷] گفت: «هرکه زنا کند از مرد و زن هر یکی را صد تازیانه بزنید و بر ایشان شما را رحمت مبادا اندر دین خدای».

---

۴۰ اس، ایا: - فِيهٰا.

۴۱ سورة المائدة (۵)، آیت ۴۵.

۴۲ نك. دهخدا. توریت. [تَ] کتاب موسی (ع)...که توراة نیز گویند.

۴۳ نك: کتاب مقدس: کتب عهد عتیق و عهد جدید، ترجمه از زبانهای اصلی عبرانی و کلدانی و یونانی، بریتش و فورن بَیبَل سوسائیتئ (جماعت بریتانیایی و خارجی انجیل مقدّس) دار السّلطنهٔ لندن (لندن، ۱۸۹۵م)، توریت سِفرِ لاویان (باب ۲۴)، ص ۱۹۳، آیات ۱۹ تا ۲۱: ۱۹-و کسیکه همسایهٔ خود را عیب رسانیده باشد چنانکه او کرده باشد باو کرده خواهد شد. ۲۰-شکستگی عوض شکستگی چشم عوض چشم دندان عوض دندان چنانکه بآن شخص عیب رسانیده همچنان باو رسانیده شود. ۲۱-و کسیکه بهیمهٔ را کشت عوض آن را بدهد امّا کسیکه انسانرا کشت، کشته شود.

۴۴ |←برگ [ایا:۲۸-الف].

۴۵ سورة المائدة (۵)، آیت ۳۸.

۴۶ نك: دهخدا: الفغدن. [اَ فَ دَ] ... اندوختن. کسب کردن... جمع کردن. ذخیره کردن. گرد کردن. الفاختن. الفختن. الفخدن. الفیدن. الفنجیدن. ماضی الفغدن از خود آن و امر و نهی و مضارع آن از الفنجیدن می‌آید مانند الفغدم، بیلفنج. رجوع به الفاختن شود.

۴۷ سورة النور (۲۴)، آیت ۲.

[§۳۴:۱۷] و خدای مفسدان را و راهزنان[۴۸] را کشتن و بردار نهادن نهاد. چنانك فرمود قوله: إِنَّمَا جَزَاءُ الَّذِينَ يُحَارِبُونَ اللّٰهَ وَ رَسُولَهُ وَ يَسْعَوْنَ فِي الْأَرْضِ فَسَاداً أَنْ يُقَتَّلُوا أَوْ يُصَلَّبُوا أَوْ تُقَطَّعَ أَيْدِيهِمْ وَ أَرْجُلُهُمْ مِنْ خِلَافٍ.[۴۹] گفت: «مکافات آنها که با خدای و رسول او حرب کنند و اندر زمین فساد کنند آن است که بکشندشان یا بردارشان کنند[۵۰] یا دست و پایشان مخالف ببرند».

[§۳۵:۱۷] پس رسول این حدها و قصاصها بفرمان خدای بفرمود تا مردم را بازداشتْ باشد از بی‌فرمانی و فساد. و بجمله هر کاری که آن بظاهر زشت است و مر آن را بباطن مرادی و مقصودی نیکوست آن کار پسندیدهٔ عقل است. و بعکس هر کاری ازین که آن بظاهر نیکوست و مر آن را بباطن مرادی و مقصودی زشت است آن[۵۱] کار نزدیك عقل نکوهیده است.

[§۳۶:۱۷] مثال این چنان است که اگر مردی را فرزندی دزد و مردم‌کش و بدکردار باشد، و آن مرد فرزند خویش را بکشد، فرزند کشتن بظاهر کاری زشت است سوی عقل، و لکن چون غرض آن کس بکشتن فرزند خویش صلاح بسیار مردم باشد، چون صلاح پدرش و صلاح دیگر فرزندان و همسایگان و جز آن، او ازین همه مردمان بازداشته شود، کشتن فرزند بدین روی سوی عقل سخت نیکوست.

[§۳۷:۱۷] و بعکس این، اگر کسی مر دزدی را و مفسدی را نفقات و ستور و سلاح دهد بظاهر این نیکویی کردن نیکوست و لکن چون بدانی کز بهر آن همی‌دهد تا براه مردمان شود و مال مردمان بستاند و بی‌گناهان را بکشد بدین مقصودِ زشت[۵۲] آن نیکُوی[۵۳] سوی عقل سخت زشت باشد.

۴۸ اس، ایا: راه‌زنان.

۴۹ سورة المائدة (۵)، آیت ۳۳.

۵۰ ¦⟵برگ [اس:۴۱-ب].

۵۱ ایا: [روی حرف «ن» از کلمه «آن» اندکی جوهر پخش شده است اما کلمه هنوز خوانا است].

۵۲ ¦⟵برگ [ایا:۲۸-ب].

۵۳ ایا: نیکویی.

[۳۸:۱۷§] همچنین عفو کردن نیکوست؛ و لکن اگر امیری مر دزدی مردم‌کشی را که اندر او هیچ مصلحت نباشد عفو کند تا او دیگرباره مردم کشد و راه زند بیشتر از آن که کرده بود، آن عفو سوی عقل سخت زشت باشد، بسبب زشتی آن غرض.

[۳۹:۱۷§] پس درست کردیم که زشت داشتن و نیکو داشتن عقل مر کارها را به مقدار مقصودها است که اندر آن کارها باشد. و غرض کارهای رسولان خدای تعالی همه بغایت نیکوست، از آنچ فرازآرندهٔ صلاح و خیر و دورکنندهٔ فساد و شر، کارهای ایشان، علیهم السّلام، است. و همه پسندیدهٔ عقل کلّ است و هر چه پسندیدهٔ عقل کلّ است، پسندیدهٔ باری سبحانه است.

[۴۰:۱۷§] امّا تقصیر کردن اندر عبادت از نماز و روزه و دیگر فرایض چون طاعت ولیِّ زمانه و جز آن همه تقصیر است[۵۴] اندر شکر آفریدگار، و تقصیر شکر آفریدگار ناسپاسی است. و ناسپاسی بعقل زشت است و هر که ناسپاس است مخالف عقل است، و از خدای تعالی مستوجب عذاب است.

۵۴ |←برگ [اس:۴۲-الف].

صف هجدهم

سخن اندر چرائی بهشتی ماندن اندر نعمت همیشه و ماندن دوزخی در[۱] عذاب همیشه؟

[§۱۸:۱] گشتن از حالی به حالی مر جسم را است. از بهر آنك حقیقتِ جسم چیزی است کی مر او را جزوهای مختلف است، و پذیرندهٔ صفات مختلف است. چنانك جسم آن باشد که مر او را زیر و زبر باشد. و این دو جزو مختلف‌اند کی جز جسم را این نباشد.

[§۱۸:۲] و همچنین پیش و پس و چپ و راست همه مر جسم را باشد. و صفات مختلف نیز جسم پذیرد چون سیاهی و سپیدی، و روشنی و تاریکی، و کژی و راستی و جز آن. از بهر آنك ترکیب جسم از اجزای مختلف است. پس همچنان مر صفات مختلف را پذیرا است. و عالم جسمانی پذیرای صفات مختلف از آن است کی ترکیب او از چهار طبع مختلف است، که هر یکی از طبایع ضدّ است مر دیگری را. لاجرم هر چه اندر عالم جسمانی چیز است از حال به حال گردنده است. گاهی چیزی ضعیف است و گاهی قوی،[۲] گاهی خرد و گاهی بزرگ، و گاهی نیکو و گاهی زشت. و همچنین احوال مختلف اندر او رونده است.

[§۱۸:۳] و اندر عالم بقا که لطیف است مخالفت نیست، و واجب نیاید. از بهر آنك بودشِ او را علّت یکی بوده است، بی‌میانجی و آن کلمه باری است.

[§۱۸:۴] و هر چه اندر آن عالم تخم کشته است بقوّت اندر این عالم بفعل همی‌بیرون آید. و اندر این عالم آن اصل صورت روحانی به پرورش امامان حقّ از حال به حال همی‌گردد، تا چون از کالبد جدا شود به عالم خویش بازرسد. آن عالم

۱ ایا: اندر.

۲ |⟵برگ [ایا:۲۹-الف].

که اندر او هیچ خلاف نیست. و چنان که آنجا رسد هم بر آن حال بماند ابدالآبدین بسبب بی‌خلافی آن عالم، و یکتائی آن از اضداد و مخالفان.

[§۵:۱۸] و آن عالم که همی‌گوییم که نفسهای مردم آنجا بازگردد، بدان مر نفس کلّی را همی‌خواهیم که نیکوکاران را ثواب بی‌اندازه ازو است، و گناهکاران[۳] را عذاب بی‌کناره[۴] ازو است، بی‌آنك هیچ خلاف افتد مر آن را. از بهر آنك[۵] هم ثواب نیکوکار و هم عذاب گناهکار[۶] از یك چیز است، و آن چیز از حال خویش گردنده نیست. و نه این نفس کی آنجا رسد نیز هیچ گردش پذیرد.

[§۶:۱۸] آنجا بسبب یکتائی و بی‌خلافی آن عالم، پس مُثاب[۷] جاویدان اندر ثواب بماند، و مُعاقَب[۸] جاویدان اندر عقاب بماند. این است سبب همیشگی ثواب مر بهشتی را و عقاب مر دوزخی را.

---

۳ اس، ایا: گناه کاران.

۴ ایا: بی کرانه.

۵ ←| برگ [اس:۴۲-ب].

۶ اس، ایا: گناه کار.

۷ نك: دهخدا: مثاب. [مُ] جزا و پاداش و ثواب داده شده.

۸ نك: دهخدا: معاقب. [مُ قَ] شکنجه شده و عقوبت کرده شده و عذاب کرده شده.

صف نوزدهم

اندر باقی گشتن کارهای مردم و ضایع ناشدن ‹بد و نیک›[۱] نزدیك خدای[۲]

[§۱:۱۹] به گوایی[۳] کتاب و عقل بر دانا واجب است مر علم حقیقت را بشرح و بیان به فهم مستجیب نزدیك گردانیدن، و راه بررسیدن[۴] اندر علم بر شاگرد، به برهان عقلی و آیات قرآن، کوتاه کردن؛ تا عالم بنفس خویش مزدومند[۵] شود و رنج او مر متعلّم را برومند[۶] گردد.

[§۲:۱۹] پس ما گوییم که پیش ازین اندر این کتاب بازنمودیم کز خاصیّت عقل است اختیار نیکو کردن و از زشتی و ناپسند دور بودن. و اکنون گوییم کی نیکو داشتن مر نیکو را امر معروف باشد،[۷] و زشت داشتن مر زشتی را بازداشتن باشد از منکر، و این حال به همه عقلها اندر است. و همهٔ رسولان از خدای تعالی بر استوار کردن این دو حال آمدند به امر معروف و نهی منکر.

[§۳:۱۹] و هیچ عاقل نیست کی چون زشتی بکند لابد نداند[۸] که آنچ او کرد زشت است، ازبهرآنك عقل را به گوا حاجت نیست از بیرون خویش.

---

۱ ایا: نیك و بد.

۲ ایا: + تعالی.

۳ اس: بکوابی؛ ایا: بکوائی.

۴ ایا: پرسیدن. || نك: دهخدا: بررسیدن. [بَ رْ، رَ/رِ دَ] (مصدر مرکب) پرسیدن... سؤال کردن. ... وارسی کردن. فحص کردن. تفتیش کردن. پژوهش کردن. تحقیق کردن. تفحص و تجسس کردن... جستجو کردن: ... بررس از علم قرآن و علم تأویلش بدان / گر همی زین چَهْ بساق عرش برخواهی رسید. (ناصرخسرو، دیوان اشعار، [ص ۹۴، س ۱۵، به‌اهتمام: نصرالله تقوی])

۵ نك: دهخدا: مزدمند. [مُ مَ] دارندهٔ مزد. دارندهٔ پاداش.

۶ نك: دهخدا: برومند. [بَ مَ] (از: بر + اومند، صورت قدیم «مند»، پسوند اتصاف) برمند. دارای بر. باردار و بارور و صاحب نفع.

۷ ¦←برگ [ایا:۲۹-ب].

۸ اس: بداند؛ ایا: بداند.

[§۱۹:۴] و مثل آن چنان است که کسی که او دروغ گوید بسبب کشیدن فایده‌ای[۹] سوی خویش یا بسبب دور کردن رنجی از خویشتن یا بیدادی بکند و مردمان را چنان نماید که او راستگوی[۱۰] و حق‌جوی است و سوی مردمان چنان باشد بظاهر گفتار کی او راستگوی[۱۱] و دادگر است.

[§۱۹:۵] و لکن نزدیك خویش مر او را گوایی نباید که بدان سوی خویش راستگوی[۱۲] شود از بهر آنك عقل دروغ نگوید و او به نزدیك خویش و نزدیك خدای دروغزن[۱۳] و بیدادگر بباشد.[۱۴]

[§۱۹:۶] و آن دروغ و بیداد اندر نفس او نگاری شود که هرگز آن نگار پاك نشود و امروز دانستن او مر آن دروغ را و بیچارگی اندر ذات خویش، که سوی خویش به هیچ حیلت مر خویشتن را راستگوی[۱۵] نتواند کردن، گوایی همی‌دهد[۱۶] کی آن نگارِ دروغ و بیدادی ازو نخواهد شدن. و اگر از این عالم بی‌توبه بیرون شود آن نگارِ بیدادی اندر نفس او درد و عذاب گردد و بحسرت و پشیمانی بماند ابدالآبدین.

[§۱۹:۷] وگر بوقتی از وقتها اندر حال زندگانی این جهانی گناهان خویش را یادآرد وزان توبه کند و نیز به چنان دروغ و گناه بازنگردد و مکافات آن به کار نیکو بکند آن کار زشت از نفس او پاك شود.

[§۱۹:۸] وگر همچنان بی‌توبه ازین عالم برود اندر آن رنج جاودانه بماند؛ از بهر آنك تباه کردن آن را اندر آن عالم روی نیست. چنانك خدای تعالی همی‌گوید، قوله: وَ

---

۹ اس، ایا: فایده‌ء.

۱۰ اس، ایا: راست‌گوی.

۱۱ اس، ایا: راست‌گوی [«گوی» در «راست‌گوی» با خط ریز بالای «راست» نوشته شده است].

۱۲ اس، ایا: راست‌گوی.

۱۳ اس، ایا: دروغ‌زن.

۱۴ ایا: باشد.

۱۵ اس، ایا: راست‌گوی.

۱۶ ¦⟵برگ [اس:۴۳-الف].

حَرٰامٌ عَلیٰ قَرْيَةٍ أَهْلَكْنٰاهٰا أَنَّهُمْ لاٰيَرْجِعُونَ.[۱۷] گفت: «حرام است بر آن دیه که آن را هلاك کردیم که ایشان با این جهان آیند».

[§۱۹:۹] و نیز گوییم که هر نفسی نگارهای زشت که کرده باشد بدان جهان بیاویزد و اندامهای او بر آن کار برو گوایی دهد.

[§۱۹:۱۰] و دلیل بر درستی این دعوی آن است از روی عقل[۱۸] که مردم بدکرداری بدین اندامها تواند کردن که بر جسم مردم دست افزارهای نفس است.

[§۱۹:۱۱] و هر که چیزی بخورد دهان و کام او مر او را گوایی دهد بچگونگی مزهٔ آن طعام. وگر زنا و لواطت کند فرج او بدان لذّت که بیابد مر نفس را خبر دهد.

[§۱۹:۱۲] و همچنین چشم بدانچ ببیند[۱۹] گوای نفس است. اگر آنچ بیند زشت یا نیکو خبر آن براستی پیش نفس برد و بگوید که چه دیدم. وگر از کسی چیزی بستاند به دست ستاند و دست گوایی دهد مر ذات نفس را که من ستدم.

[§۱۹:۱۳] و هم امروز این آلتها با نفس مردم خود سخن می‌گوید و هیچ کس مر این حال را منکر نتواند شدن.

[§۱۹:۱۴] پس چرا عجب باید داشتن از آنك روز قیامت همین گوایی اندر آن نفس بدکردار نگار گشته باشد که اندر هر اندامی ازین اندامها از نفس مردم شاخی است که آن اندام آن فعل بقوّت آن شاخ کز شاخهای نفس بدو پیوسته بود [تواند کردن]؟[۲۰]

[§۱۹:۱۵] و گوییم کی هر فعلی کزین اندامها بیاید، از بد و نیك، آن فعل اندر نفس مردم نگار کرده شود. و گوا است بر درستی این قول آنچ خدای تعالی

۱۷ سورة الأنبياء (۲۱)، آیت ۹۵.

۱۸ ⟵| برگ [ایا:۳۰-الف].

۱۹ اس: به بیند.

۲۰ تصحیح قیاسی.

همی‌گوید، قوله: يَوْمَ تَشْهَدُ عَلَيْهِمْ أَلْسِنَتُهُمْ وَ أَيْدِيهِمْ وَ أَرْجُلُهُمْ بِمَا كَانُوا يَعْمَلُونَ.[۲۱] گفت: «آن روز گوایی دهند بر ایشان زفانهای ایشان و دستها و پایهای ایشان بدانچ کرده باشند».

[§۱۹:۱۶] پس گوییم که کارهای مردم اندر نفس مردم نگار شود و نفس نامه‌ای[۲۲] گردد نیك و بد نبشته چنانك هم او خود[۲۳] آن نبشته را بخواند و همه نفسها مر آن بدکردار را بشناسند.

[§۱۹:۱۷] از بهر آنك نفسها اندر آن عالم مجرّد باشد از کالبد و از تاریکی طبیعت چنانك خدای تعالی همی‌گوید، قوله: فَمَنْ يَعْمَلْ مِثْقَالَ ذَرَّةٍ خَيْراً يَرَهُ * وَ مَنْ يَعْمَلْ مِثْقَالَ ذَرَّةٍ شَرًّا يَرَهُ.[۲۴] گفت: «هرکه همسنگ ذرّهء اندر این جهان نیکی کند مر آن را ببیند و هر که همسنگ ذرّهء بدی کند مر آن را ببیند».[۲۵]

[§۱۹:۱۸] و سخن اندر نیکوکرداران هم چنین است. اگر کسی راستگوی[۲۶] و حق‌شناس و نیك‌خواه[۲۷] و نصیحت‌کار باشد و مردمان مر او را دروغزن[۲۸] و مُبْطِل و بدخواه و خاین دارند او به نزدیك خویش و نزدیك خدای راستگوی[۲۹] و محق باشد پس علم او به راستی و حق خویش صورت نفس او باشد.

[§۱۹:۱۹] و به نیکُوی[۳۰] صورت خویش مر او را لذّت و شادی‌ای[۳۱] و توانگری

۲۱ سورة النور (۲۴)، آیت ۲۴.

۲۲ اس، ایا: نامهء

۲۳ ¦⟵برگ[اس:۴۳-ب].

۲۴ سورة الزلزلة (۹۹)، آیات ۷ تا ۸.

۲۵ اس، ایا: به بیند.

۲۶ اس، ایا: راست گوی.

۲۷ ایا: نیکوخواه.

۲۸ اس، ایا: دروغ زن. || ¦⟵برگ [ایا:۳۰-ب].

۲۹ اس، ایا: راست گوی.

۳۰ ایا: نیکویی.

۳۱ اس: شادیء؛ ایا: شادیئی.

بحاصل آید که آن شادی و توانگری جاوید با او بماند. چنانك خدای تعالی گفت اندر صفت بدکرداران و نیکوکاران، قوله: إِنَّهُ مَنْ يَأْتِ رَبَّهُ مُجْرِماً فَإِنَّ لَهُ جَهَنَّمَ لٰا يَمُوتُ فِيهٰا وَ لٰا يَحْيىٰ * وَ مَنْ يَأْتِهِ مُؤْمِناً قَدْ عَمِلَ الصّٰالِحٰاتِ فَأُولٰئِكَ لَهُمُ الدَّرَجٰاتُ الْعُلىٰ * جَنّٰاتُ عَدْنٍ تَجْرِي مِنْ تَحْتِهَا الْأَنْهٰارُ خٰالِدِينَ فِيهٰا وَ ذٰلِكَ جَزٰاءُ مَنْ تَزَكّٰى.[۳۲] گفت: «هرکه گناهکار[۳۳] پیش خدای شود مر او را است دوزخ که اندر او نه میرد و نه زید؛ و هر که پیش خدای شود مؤمن، و کردارهای نیك کرده، ایشان را است درجتهای برترین؛ بهشتهای جاوید که جویها زیر او همی‌رود و جاوید ایشان اندر او باشند، آن است مکافات آن کسی که خویش را پاکیزه کند».

[§۱۹:۲۰] و دلیل بر درستی این حال ظاهرِ مردم است که هر که او بدین صورت جسدانی نکو چهره و درست‌اندام است شادمانه باشد به درستی و نیکوئی خویش. و خرّمی گذرنده است به گذشتن صورت جسدانی که همه مردم بر یقین است از مرگ خویش و ناچیز شدن جسد.

[§۱۹:۲۱] و همچنین هر مردم که داند کی چهرهٔ او زشت است و اندام او ناقص است او همیشه اندوهگن باشد و از دیگر مردمان پرهیز کند و شرم‌زده باشد.

[§۱۹:۲۲] و لکن این اندوه گذرنده است به گذشتن زندگانی این جهانی؛ و شادی و خرمی و خوشی و توانگری و نیکویی و غم و اندوه و زشتی و دشواری و درویشی نفسانی باقی ست به بقای نفس ناطقه.

[§۱۹:۲۳] همه خداوندان مُقرّاند که نفس نمیرد و باقی شود اندر عالم علوی پس از جدا شدن از جسد.

[§۱۹:۲۴] و اندر عقل چنان لازم است[۳۴] که نفس مردم پس از شناخت توحید باقی باشد، ازبهرآنك جسدها به نفس زنده است و نفس لطیف است.

۳۲ سورة طه (۲۰)، آیات ۷۴ تا ۷۶.

۳۳ اس، ایا: گناه کار. || ایا: + به.

۳۴ ¦⟵برگ [اس:۴۴-الف].

[§۲۵:۱۹] وگر نفس نیز زنده به چیزی دیگر بودی بایستی که نفس مرده یافتیمی و روح ازو جدا شده چنانك جسد بی‌روح همی‌یابیم[۳۵] و نیز اگر مر نفس لطیف را روحی[۳۶] روا بودی همچنین ارواح بی‌نهایت شدی.

[§۲۶:۱۹] پس چون حال چنین بود واجب آید کی ارواح را نهایت باشد یا یکی باشد تا هزاران بدو زنده باشند و او خود بذات خویش نامیرنده باشد.

[§۲۷:۱۹] و چون آفرینش از دوگونه یافتیم یا لطیف یا کثیف و کثیف را میرنده یافتیم و لطیف بخلاف آن بود دانستیم که لطیف نامیرنده است.

[§۲۸:۱۹] پس از هر رویی زندگی نفس لازم است. پس نفس مردمِ عاقلِ نیکوکردار، گستاخ و امّیدوار باشد که پاداش کار نیکوی[۳۷] خویش از آفریدگار بسزای کار خویش بیابد و ایمن و آرمیده باشد از بیم بادافراه که پاداش بدکرداران[۳۸] است.

[§۲۹:۱۹] چنانك خدای تعالی همی گوید، قوله: يٰا أَيَّتُهَا النَّفْسُ الْمُطْمَئِنَّةُ * ارْجِعِي إِلىٰ رَبِّكِ رٰاضِيَةً مَرْضِيَّةً * فَادْخُلِي فِي عِبٰادِي * وَادْخُلِي جَنَّتِي.[۳۹] همی‌گوید: «ای نفس آرمیده بازآی سوی پروردگارت خشنود و پسندیده و اندرآی به بندگان من و اندر بهشت من». درست کردیم خردمند را که کار مردم باقی است.

---

۳۵ ¦⟵برگ [ایا:۳۱-الف].

۳۶ اس: [حرف «و» در «روحی» مخدوش است].

۳۷ اس: نیکوء.

۳۸ ایا: بدکردار.

۳۹ سورة الفجر (۸۹)، آیات ۲۷ تا ۳۰.

صف بیستم

سخن اندر نفس که چون پاکیزه شود دیدار اوفتدش اندر لطایف و اندر بودنیها

[§۲۰:۱] گوییم که مر نفس را بذات او اندر دیداری است جز این دیدار چشم، و رفتن و ایستادن است او را و گرفتن و دست بازداشتن است او را و جز آن برابر این فعلها که اندر محسوسات می‌کند؛ و فعلهای ذاتی او شریفتر است از این عرضی.

[§۲۰:۲] پس همی‌نماید که مر نفس را اندر ذات او حواسی است که این حواس ظاهر ماننده است مر آن را ماننده‌گی‌ای[۱] دور؛ از بهر آنك بسیار کس است کز مادر نابینا زاده است و علمهای شریف آموخته است چون علم[۲] حساب و هندسه و منطق و کتاب خدای را یاد گرفته است و کتب حکما را دانسته است تا نفس او بذات خویش کتابها گشته است و او همی‌بیند اندر هر علمی آنچ مر او را بنمایند[۳] و دیگر کسان[۴] از دیدن آن چیزها که او همی‌بیند نابینااند.

[§۲۰:۳] پس این حال همی‌دلیل کند که نفس را چشمی هست از ذات او و مر آن[۵] چشم را از نفس دانای آموزگار آفتابی هست کی چیزها را بدان چشم ذاتی نفس بنماید. برمثال آفتاب و چراغ که شکل و صورت جسمانی به چشم نگرندگان اندر پدید آرد.

[§۲۰:۴] و گوایی دهد بر درستی این قول دعوی خدای تعالی که مر رسول را، علیه السّلام، گفت، قوله: یٰا أَیُّهَا النَّبِیُّ إِنّٰا أَرْسَلْنٰاكَ شٰاهِداً وَ مُبَشِّراً وَ نَذِیراً * وَ دٰاعِیاً

---

۱ اس، ایا: ماننده‌گیء.

۲ ایا: - علم.

۳ نك: زادالمسافر، قول ۲: اندر کتابت که آن در علم غایبان است، ص ۱۳ تا ۱۷.

۴ ¦⟵برگ [اس:۴۴-ب]. || اس: [عبارت «و دیگر کسان» در ابتدای برگ تکرار شده است].

۵ ¦⟵برگ [ایا:۳۱-ب].

إِلَى اللّٰهِ بِإِذْنِهِ وَ سِراجاً مُنِيراً.[۶] گفت: «ای پیامبر ما بفرستادیم ترا گوا بر خلق و مژده دهنده و بیم کننده و خواننده سوی خدای به دستوری او و چراغی روشن».

[§۲۰:۵] و گروهی از مردمان چنین گویند که چون مردم جهد کند و نفس خویش را از ناشایستها دور کند او را دیدار اوفتد اندر چیزهای بودنی و خبر یابد از عالم علوی، و وحی پیامبران آن است!

[§۲۰:۶] و ما گوییم که چنین نشاید گفتن کی پیامبری[۷] به جهد خویش یافتند پیامبران؛ چه وحی از کردار پیغامبران آن است کزان مراد کردگار عالم بحاصل آید، و مراد از خداوندِ مراد، کی توانا باشد، جز بدو و به خواست او بحاصل نشود.

[§۲۰:۷] وگر به خواستِ کسی دیگر مراد خدای بحاصل آمدی آن کس با خدای انباز بودی. و هر کس که با خدای انباز گیرد کافر باشد.

[§۲۰:۸] پس آن کسها کی گفتند پیامبری به جهد بتوان یافتن کافر شدند بقول خدای تعالی کی همی‌گوید، قوله: إِنَّ اللّٰهَ لاٰ يَغْفِرُ أَنْ يُشْرَكَ بِهِ وَ يَغْفِرُ مٰا دُونَ ذٰلِكَ لِمَنْ يَشٰاءُ.[۸] همی‌گوید: «خدای نیامرزد آن کس را که با او انباز گیرد و بیامرزد فرود از آن هر که را خواهد».

[§۲۰:۹] پس ما گوییم که نفس مردم را گرفتن است و یله کردن[۹] بذات، بیرونِ گرفتن و یله کردن به آلت، چون اعتقاد کردن چیزی و یله کردن چیزی دیگر؛ و چون یاد کردن علمی و از یاد بگذاشتن دیگری.

[§۲۰:۱۰] و او را نیز رفتن و ایستادن است بذات خویش چون رفتن اندر علمی از آغاز او تا به انجام او، و ایستادن است مر او را بجایهایی که از آن گذر بباید به

---

۶ سورة الأَحزاب (۳۳)، آیات ۴۵ تا ۴۶.

۷ ایا: پیمبری.

۸ سورة النساء (۴)، آیات ۴۸ و ۱۱۶.

۹ دهخدا: یله کردن. [یَ لَ / لِ کَ دَ] (مصدر مرکب) رها کردن و گذاشتن و سر دادن... بر جای نهادن.

دانستن آن، چنانك خدای تعالی همی‌گوید، قوله: كُلَّما أَضاءَ لَهُمْ مَشَوْا فِيهِ وَ إِذا أَظْلَمَ عَلَيْهِمْ قامُوا.[۱۰] همی‌گوید: «هر وقت که روشنایی پیدا آید بروند اندر او و چون بر ایشان تاریك شود[۱۱] بایستند».

[§۲۰:۱۱] و بدین مر کسانی را میخواهد که کتاب خدای را برای خویش معنی جویند و بعضی را معنی بتوانند یافتن و اندر آن بشتابند و چون متشابهی مشکل پیش آید برجای بایستند.

[§۲۰:۱۲] و فعلهای ذاتی مر نفس را شریفتر است از فعلهای آلتی عرضی. و چون مردم بقوّت نفس ناطقه مر نفس شهوانی را بشکند و به چیزهای دنیایی به‌لذّات[۱۲] حسّی مشغول نشود نفس ناطقهٔ او قوی شود و چیزها بی‌تعلیم ببیند.[۱۳]

[§۲۰:۱۳] از بهر آنك نفس را کارکردن طبع است و چون مر او را از چیزهای طبیعی بازداری و او از کار فرونشیند، بقوّت نفسانی چیزهایی ببیند[۱۴] از عالم خویش کی آن اندر ذات او است.

[§۲۰:۱۴] برمثال چشم که چون کار او دیدن است هر وقت کی مر او را از علّت پاك گردانی چیزهای جسمانی را بی‌تکلّف و بی‌نمونِ[۱۵] نُماینده[۱۶] ببیند.[۱۷]

[§۲۰:۱۵] و این برهانی روشن است خردمندان را از جسمانی[۱۸] به روحانی.

۱۰ سورة البقرة (۲)، آیت ۲۰. || ¦⟵برگ [اس:۴۵-الف].
۱۱ ¦⟵برگ [ایا:۳۲-الف].
۱۲ ایا: و لذات.
۱۳ اس، ایا: به بیند.
۱۴ اس، ایا: به بیند.
۱۵ نك: دهخدا: نمون. [نُ/نِ/نَ] ... نماینده... هادی. دلیل... || – رهنمون؛ هادی راه... راه‌نماینده. راهنمای. رهنما.
۱۶ نك: دهخدا: نماینده. [نُ / نِ / نَ یَ دَ / دِ]... آنکه می نماید و هویدا می کند.... نشان دهنده.... ظاهرکننده. نمایان کننده.
۱۷ اس، ایا: به بیند.
۱۸ اس: [قبل از کلمه «جسمانی»، «رو» نوشته شده، اما روی آن خط کشیده شده است].

صف بیست و یکم

سخن اندر آفرینش عالم و بخشهای آنچ[۱] موجود است از لطایف و کثایف

[§۱:۲۱] هر گروهی را از دانایان چه از حکماءِ[۲] علم دین و چه از پیش‌روان علم طبایع و چه از رئیسان علم آلهی اندر وجود عالم جسمانی سخن است و اندر جواهر عالی و صورتهای عقلی اختلاف کرده‌اند.

[§۲:۲۱] و ما از جمله آنچ محصول و مراد و مغز سخنها است بیرون کنیم و بازنماییم جویندگان حق را که بر این خوان آراستهٔ ما نشینند با دست شسته به آب پرهیز و معدهٔ گرسنهٔ طعام و شراب نفسانی.

[§۳:۲۱] گوییم که آفریدهٔ مُبدِعِ حقّ سبحانه جمله بر سه قسمت[۳] است.

[§۴:۲۱] یکی ازو فوق‌الزّمان است چون عالم آلهی و عقلانی و نفسانی کز روزگار برتر است و او را زوال نیست.

[§۵:۲۱] دیگر قسمت آن است کی مع‌الزّمان است چون عالم جرمانی و نورانی که روزگار را با او پیشی و پسی نیست.[۴]

[§۶:۲۱] سیّم قسمت آن است که تحت‌الزّمان است اعنی که زیر روزگار است و آن عالم جسمانی است.[۵]

---

۱ ایا: آنجه.

۲ اس: حکما؛ ایا: حکمای.

۳ ایا: قسم. || نك: زادالمسافر، قول ۱۰: اندر زمان، ص ۱۰۷ تا ۱۱۳؛ نیز قس: جامع الحکمتین، فصل ۹: ‹اندر دهر و حقّ و سرور و حیات روزگذار و کمال و غیبت›، ص ۱۱۲ تا ۱۲۲.

۴ نك: دهخدا: اجرام. [اَ] ... جِ جِرْم. تن ها. اجسام (و اکثر استعمال اجرام در لطیف است و اجسام درکثیف)...و گاه اجرام گویند مطلق، و از آن اجرام فلکی و ستارگان خواهند.

۵ ¦⟵برگ [ایا:۳۲-ب].

[§۲۱:۷] پس گوییم که آنچ زیر زمان است از موجودات[۶] هم کاین است و هم فاسد اعنی هست شونده است و نیست شونده ازبهرآنك اندر جایگاه بودش و نابودش است.

[§۲۱:۸] و آنچ با زمان برابر است از موجودات از کاین است و لکن فاسد نیست. و آن افلاك و انجم است که گوهر ایشان فساد و تغیّر نپذیرد ازبهرآنك صورت ایشان بر هیولی جاکول است.

[§۲۱:۹] و طبایع و موالید فساد پذیرد ازبهرآنك هیولیٰءِ[۷] ایشان جاکول است بر صورت ایشان.

[§۲۱:۱۰] و نیز گوییم که چون جرمانی میانجی آمد میان عالم عقلانی و عالم هیولانی بدان روی که زان عالم قوّت پذیرنده است و بدین عالم رساننده است، همچنان میانجی‌اند که نه برتر از زمانند و نه از زیر زمان بل کی با زمان برابراند[۸] بر میانجی.

[§۲۱:۱۱] و نیز نه چون عالم عقلانی آمد[۹] که نه کاین است و نه فاسد، و نه چون عالم هیولانی آمد[۱۰] که هم کاین است و هم فاسد، بل‌که[۱۱] بر میانجی آمد[۱۲] که کاین است و فاسد نیست.

---

۶ ¦⟵برگ [اس:۴۵-ب].

۷ اس: هیولي.

۸ اس: [روی حرف «ن» در واژهٔ «اند»، با جوهر شنگرف یك نقطه اضافه شده است]. || ایا: آمد [علامت مدّ بالای حرف «آ» مخدوش است].

۹ اس: [«آمد» بعد از اضافه نقطه و فتحه با جوهر شنگرف بصورت «آفَد» درآمده است]. || ایا: اند.

۱۰ اس: [«امد» بعد از اضافه نقطه با جوهر شنگرف بصورت «افَد» درآمده است]. || ایا: آمد.

۱۱ ایا: بلك.

۱۲ اس: [«امد» بعد از اضافه نقطه و فتحه با جوهر شنگرف بصورت «افَد» درآمده است]. || ایا: آمد. [این تلاش در نسخه ایاصوفیا برای شبیه سازی رسم الخط میتواند نشانه این باشد، و شاید بتوان گفت، که نسخه ایاصوفیا از روی نسخه استانبول — یا نسخه‌ای شبیه آن که امروزه در دست نیست — رونویسی شده است].

[§۱۲:۲۱] و آنچ برتر از روزگار است از موجودات نه کاین است و نه فاسد و آن عالم عقل است که گوهر محض است و اندر او کون و فساد نیست البته.

[§۱۳:۲۱] و چون این سخن روشن کردیم گوییم که قول حکماء[۱۳] دین و پیش‌دستان از خلق به تأیید آلهی اندر کونِ عالم هیولانی و اثبات عالم روحانی آن است که گفتند که مُبدِع حقّ محض مر عقل را پدید آورد نه از چیزی و تمام پدید آوردش بقوّت و فعل.

[§۱۴:۲۱] دلیل بر درستی این قول آن است که هر چیزی که بر چیزی دیگر باشد میان این چیز واپسین[۱۴] و میان آن چیز پیشین میانجی باشد که آن چیز بازپسین بدان میانجی از آن چیز پیشین پدید آید. آن وقت چون میانجی اندر میان آمد، میان این دو چیز تفاوت افتد و بازپسین از پیشین کمتر آید.

[§۱۵:۲۱] و چون مُبدِع حقّ تعالی مر عقل را نه از چیزی ابداع کرد لازم آید به برهان عقلی که عقل بغایت کمال و هستی باشد، به دو سبب: یکی بدین سبب که گفتیم که او را نه از چیز[۱۵] ابداع کرد تا او کمتر از آن چیز بودی[۱۶] که بودش ازو یافت، دیگر بدان سبب که مُبدِع حقّ مر او را ابداع کرد بی هیچ میانجی.

[§۱۶:۲۱] و گفتند که مُبدِع حقّ صورت همه موجودات از جسمانی و روحانی اندر گوهر عقل گرد آورد.

[§۱۷:۲۱] گفتند کز عقل گوهری دیگر به انبعاث پدید آورد بی‌زمانی[۱۷] حسّی و[۱۸] وهمی.

---

۱۳ اس: حکما؛ ایا: حکمای.

۱۴ ایا: [بین دو حرف «ا» و «پ»، در کلمه «واپسین»، حرف «ن» نوشته شده و روی آن با جوهر شنگرف خط زده شده است].

۱۵ ایا: چیزی. [روی «ی» آخر در کلمه «چیزی» با جوهر شنگرف خط زده شده است].

۱۶ ¦⟵برگ [ایا:۳۳-الف].

۱۷ ¦⟵برگ [اس:۴۶-الف].

۱۸ اس، ایا: [«و» در بالای کلمه «حسی» با جوهر شنگرف نوشته شده است].

[§۱۸:۲۱] و فرق میان ابداع و انبعاث آن است که انبعاث مر چیزی را باشد که او نه اندر مکان و زمان باشد و لکن پدید آینده باشد از چیزی دیگر، و ابداع مر چیزی را باشد که او نه اندر مکان و زمان باشد و لکن نه از چیزی پدید آمده باشد.

[§۱۹:۲۱] پس آن مُبدَع که از چیزی نبود بغایت کمال آمد و این منبعث کز چیزی بود او به درجه کمتر آمد چنانك اندر حکم عقل لازم است.

[§۲۰:۲۱] پس آن منبعث بفرمان مُبدِع حقّ، نگاه کرد اندر فضیلت و شرف عقل اوّل و رغبت کرد به تمامی که اندر او دید.

[§۲۱:۲۱] رغبتی ممکن نه ممتنع و ناممکن از بهر آنك نفس کلّی بقوّت چون عقل کلّی بود ازیراك وجودش ازو بود.

[§۲۲:۲۱] و چیزی که بقوّت چون چیزی دیگر باشد و هم از آن چیز زیادت پذیرد ممکن باشد، که به فایده گرفتن از چیزِ تمام، روزی به تمامی او برسد[۱۹] و همچُنو شود.

[§۲۳:۲۱] و گوییم که معلولات بر سه بهر است، اعنی چیزهائی که بودش او را سبب باشد. یکی ازو آن است که به همه رویها چون علّت خویش بباشد[۲۰] و دیگر آن است که به هیچ روی چون علّت خویش نشود و سدیگر آن است که به رویی چون علّت خویش باشد و به رویی نه چُنو باشد.

[§۲۴:۲۱] اما آن معلول که به همه رویها چون علّت خویش بباشد[۲۱] آن نطفهٔ حیوان است و خایهٔ مرغان که چون از اصل خویش یاری یابد به پروردن، روزی حیوان گردد، از مردم یا مرغ یا جز آن.

---

۱۹ ایا: رسد.

۲۰ اس، ایا: نباشد.

۲۱ ایا: نباشد.

[§۲۱:۲۵] و اما آن معلول که به هیچ روی چون علّت خویش نگردد[۲۲] آن آب وَذی[۲۳] و آب مَذیِ[۲۴] حیوان است که معلول حیوان است و هرگز چون حیوان نشود. و چون دَرگَهْ معلولِ درودگر است و هرگز چون درودگر نشود.

[§۲۱:۲۶] اما آن معلول که به رویی چون علّت خویش باشد و به رویی نباشد آن چون روز است که او[۲۵] معلول آفتاب است و بدانچ روشنایی دارد همچون آفتاب است و لکن ازو نور بیرون نیاید و فعلها چنانك از آفتاب بیرون آید. پس روز بیك روی چون آفتاب است و بدیگر روی چُنو نیست.

[§۲۱:۲۷] پس نفس از آن معلولات است که به همه رویها چون علّت خویش بباشد[۲۶] از راه تمامی، قول حکماء[۲۷] شرعی این است.

[§۲۱:۲۸] پس چون نفس کلّی از جملهٔ معلولات[۲۸] بدین صفت بود و نظر کرد اندر عقل، ممکن ببود[۲۹] که به فایده گرفتن ازو همچُنو تمام شود.

[§۲۱:۲۹] طلب تمامی کرد و تمامی خویش را بدید اندر پدید آمدن خداوند قیامت، علیه افضل السّلام.

[§۲۱:۳۰] و دانسته شد مر نفس را که وجود قیامت نباشد مگر آنگاه که دورهای پیامبران بگذرد.

---

۲۲ اس: نه گردد.

۲۳ نك: دهخدا: وذی. [وَ ذی ی] ... وَذْیْ. آبی که پس از انزال از کسی خارج میشود.

۲۴ نك: دهخدا: مذی. [مَ ذْیْ] ... رطوبت است که در غلبهٔ شهوت ظاهر می‌شود... آب نشاط.

۲۵ ¦⟵برگ [ایا:۳۳-ب].

۲۶ ایا: نباشد [نقطهٔ حروف «ن» و «ب» با جوهر شنگرف و کمرنگ نوشته شده است].

۲۷ أیا: حکمای.

۲۸ ¦⟵برگ [اس:۴۶-ب].

۲۹ اس، ایا: بود.

[§۳۱:۲۱] و بشناخت که دورهای پیغامبران جز به بودش خداوندان تأیید[۳۰] نباشد.

[§۳۲:۲۱] و خداوندان تأیید نباشند تا پاکیزه کردن نباشد مر نفسها را از راه تعلیم.

[§۳۳:۲۱] و پاکیزگی نباشد از راه تعلیم تا جویندگان نباشند حقایق را.

[§۳۴:۲۱] و جویندگان نباشند تا خداوندان طلب کردن حق نباشند.

[§۳۵:۲۱] و این همه درجات نباشد تا فایده‌گیرندگان مؤمن نباشند.

[§۳۶:۲۱] و مؤمنان را یقین نباشد تا مُقَدَّران نباشند که نخست حق را بقهر پذیرفته باشند.

[§۳۷:۲۱] و مُقَدَّران[۳۱] نباشند تا کسی نباشد که تکلیف پذیرد.

[§۳۸:۲۱] و تکلیف پذیرنده آن باشد کی اگر بیاموزندش بتواند آموختن، چون مردم که اگر بیاموزیش علم بیاموزد، و چون ستور که نتواند علم آموختن که مُکَلَّف نیست.

[§۳۹:۲۱] و تکلیف نباشد ‹جز آن که›[۳۲] به نخست درجه مُهمَل باشد اعنی گذاشته بی علم.

[§۴۰:۲۱] و مردم مُهمَل نباشد تا حیوان نباشد و حیوان نباشد تا نبات نباشد و نبات نباشد تا گوهرها گدازنده[۳۳] و ناگدازنده[۳۴] نباشد.

---

۳۰ نك: جامع الحکمتین، فصل ۲۰: ‹اندر ابداع›، ص ۲۱۴، بند (۲۳۴): و چهارم گروه از خاندانند که گویند: عالم مخترَع است هم بصورت و هم بهیولی. و این گروه خداوندان تأیید اند از فرزندان رسول مصطفی صلّی الله علیه وآله.

۳۱ قس: ناصرخسرو، دیوان اشعار، ص ۱۱۸، س ۲۲: تقدیرگر شدند چو تقدیر یافتند / زانسو مُقَدِّرند و زینسو مُقَدَّرند. (به‌اهتمام: نصرالله تقوی)

۳۲ ایا: جز انك.

۳۳ نك: دهخدا: گدازنده. [گُ زَ دَ /دِ] || آب شونده. ذوب شونده.- جوهر یا گوهر یا فلز گدازنده؛ جوهر یا فلز قابل گداختن.

۳۴ نك: جامع الحکمتین، فصل ۱۰: ‹اندر طبیعت کلّی›، ص ۱۲۴، بند (۱۲۰): و گوییم کز پس

[§۴۱:۲۱] و جواهر نباشد تا طبایع نباشد و طبایع نباشد تا عالم نباشد و عالم نباشد تا هیولی و صورت نباشد.

[§۴۲:۲۱] پس آغاز کرد اندر صنعت و حاصل کردن قیامت، که اوّل اندیشهٔ نفس آن بود، از هیولی و صورت که آخر اندیشهٔ او آن بود.

[§۴۳:۲۱] و این معنی قول حکما است کی گفتند: أَوَّلُ الفکرة آخِر العمل[۳۵] وأَوَّلُ العمل آخِر الفکرة. گفتند: «آغاز اندیشه[۳۶] پایان کارکرد باشد و آغاز کار پایان اندیشه باشد».

[§۴۴:۲۱] و بومحّمد قتیبی اندر کتابی که آن را ادب الکُتّاب[۳۷] خوانند، گفته است کی «کسی باشد که این نداند تا به آموختن این حاجت آیدش؛ و لکن نابینایان از روشنایی آفتاب چه آگهند»؟!

[§۴۵:۲۱] و نزدیك حکماءِ[۳۸] شریعی چنان است کی خود عالم هیولانی از سه حال بود:

اقسام این جسم کلّی-اعنی خاك و آب و هوا و آتش و افلاك و انجم-موالید است از جواهر معدنی گدازنده و ناگدازنده، وز آن اشکال بسیار است، که هریکی را از آن صورتی است، کو بدان صورت از جملگی موجودات مولوداتی و امّهاتی جداست، و هریکی را از نبات و حیوان نیز — از پشّه تا پیل و از گندنا و پیاز تا درخت گوز و ساج — صورتی دیگر است.

۳۵ نك: جامع الحکمتین، فصل ۱: اندر ذکر سبب تصنیف کتاب و نام او، ص ۷، بند (۱۱): حکمای دین حق و فلسفه را اتّفاقست بر آن که نخستین علّت معلولی علّت غائی آنست، ازبهر آنك بازبینی علّت تخت برنشستن پادشاه بِزَوَرِ† صنع از درودگر با آلت و از چوب بسبب فرمان پادشاه پدید آید، که بر تخت خواهد نشستن. پس آخر چیزی که بر مصنوع پدید آید اوّل علّتِ آن باشد، وبدین روی گویند حکما این قول معروف را «اوّل الفکر آخر العمل.» نبینی که نخست اندیشهٔ درودگر آن باشد که شاه را تختی باشد، و آخر کارش آن باشد که شاه بتخت برنشبند، و چرائی عالم بآخرْ مردم پدید کند و سپس ازو چیز پدید نیاید. گفتند قصد صانع عالم باوّلِ این صُنعْ حاصل کردن مرد[م] بود، تا از صنعش بآخر مردم پدید آمد. || † (به + زَوَرِ = به بالایِ)

۳۶ ¦⟵برگ [ایا:۳۴-الف].

۳۷ عنوان دیگر این کتاب «ادب الکاتب» است.

۳۸ ایا: حکمای.

[§۲۱:۴۶] نخست از حکمت مُبدِع حقّ کزان صورتهای مجرّد و گوهرهای عالی پدید آمد و آن فعلِ مُبدِع حقّ است[۳۹] و فعلِ مُبدِع حقّ همه کارکنانند و کار ایشان را پذیرندگان واجب نیاید و نه جایگاه و جای.

[§۲۱:۴۷] فعل ایشان طبیعت کلّی[۴۰] است که آن اصل بودش عالم هیولانی است و فرعهای آن اصل دوآند[۴۱] یکی هیولی و دیگر صورت کز ایشان این عالم هیولانی پدید آمده است.

[§۲۱:۴۸] و پذیرندهٔ فعل عالم هیولانی این صورت مردم است که پذیرای آثار عقل و نفس است تا بآخرِ کار صورتها مجرّد گردند چون فعل باری.[۴۲]

---

۳۹ ¦⟵برگ [اس:۴۷-الف].

۴۰ نك: جامع الحکمتین، فصل ۱۰: ‹اندر طبیعت کلّی›، ص ۱۲۵، ۱۲۸، ۱۳۰ تا ۱۳۱، بندهای (۱۲۱)، (۱۲۹)، (۱۳۲): (۱۲۱) و اکنون چو مر نام طبیعت را معنی ثابت کردیم، گوییم: فلاسفه و اهل طبایع اندر چه چیزی طبیعت مختلف شدند. ارسطاليس اندر کتاب «سمع الکیان» خویش گفته است که «طبیعت آغاز حرکت و سکونست» یعنی: چو جوهر جسم موجود شد، با مفردات طبایع بهم موجود شد، اندر یك وهلت بود بی‌هیچ درنگی و مدّتی. و چو این اعراض اولی با جواهر هیولی بهم شد، آغاز حرکت و سکون مکانی از آن وهلت بود، یعنی: چو این مفردات طبایع — از گرمی و سردی و تری و خشکی — بدین جوهر پذیراء این مفردات برین تقدیر که هست، متّحد شد، آغاز حرکت آن بود. [...] (۱۲۹) و امّا جواب اهل تأویل — علیهم السّلام — اندر اثبات ‹طبیعت› آنست که گفتند. طبیعت بمثل نایب نفس کلّی است، که موکّلست در نگاه داشتن مر اقسام جسم را بر صورتهاء آن. و ردّ کردند قول آنها را که گفتند که طبیعت — کو نگاه دارندهٔ مصوّرات است — رطوبت یا حرارت است، بدانچ گفتند: حرارت و رطوبت نیز صورتهااند، نه مصوّران‌اند. و رطوبت مر آب را جوهریست، و مر او را اندر جوهر آب بحافظی حاجتست، همچنانك حرارت را اندر جوهر آتش بحافظی حاجت است، از بهر آنك این هر دو — اعنی رطوبت و حرارت — اعراض‌اند، و عرض را بذات خویش قیام نیست، و آنچ مر او را بذات خویش قیام نباشد، مر او را فعل نباشد. [...] (۱۳۲) و این حکمتی عظیمست و دلیلی ظاهرست بدانك طبیعت کلّی همی عالم را از آلایشها و آمیزشهاء شوریده بشوید و پاکیزه کند از بهر صنع نفس کلّی را. || قس: زادالمسافر، قول ۵: اندر جسم و اقسام آن، ص ۳۱ تا ۴۰.

۴۱ ایا: دو نوع اند.

۴۲ نك: جامع الحکمتین، فصل ۱۰: ‹اندر طبیعت کلّی›، ص ۱۳۱ تا ۱۳۲، بند (۱۳۴): (۱۳۴) از بهر آن گفتند حکماء دین حقّ — که فلسفهٔ الهی مر ایشان راست — که طبیعت کلّی شاگرد نفس کلّی است، با آنك خاصّیّت فعل نفس کلّی ایجاد نفس ناطقه است اندر هیکل انسانی، و

[§۴۹:۲۱] پس گوییم که قسمت اول از وجود عالم هیولانی بازبست است به حکمت مُبدِع حقّ؛ و قسمت دوم وجود عالم بازبست است به تمام شدن نفس و رسیدن به درجهٔ عقل؛ و قسمت سوّم از وجود عالم بازبست است به وجود خداوند قیامت.

[§۵۰:۲۱] پس ابتدای هیولی و صورت که پدید آمد آن بود که نفس تمامی خویش طلب کرد. و از آن طلب جنبشی وهمی پدید آمد.

[§۵۱:۲۱] و چون آن جنبش از جوهری عالی بود اثر، از آن جنبش، گوهری سفلی پدید آمد.

[§۵۲:۲۱] و چون آن جنبش پدید آمد ازو حرارت پدید آمد و چون حرارت بغایت رسید غایت او برودت آمد و چون برودت اعنی سردی بغایت رسید ازو تری پدید آمد همه جدا جدا و چون تری بغایت رسید ازو خشکی پدید آمد.

[§۵۳:۲۱] و معنی آنچ گفتیم که این چیزها جداجدا پدید آمد آن است کی همی‌باید که این چهار طبع جداجدا صورت شود اندر نفس جویندهٔ علم حقیقت.

[§۵۴:۲۱] و قول حکما آن است که ‹گوهر مُبدَع لطیفتر است از اثر مُبدَع›[۴۳] اعنیٰ که نفس‌کلّ کمتر است از عقل کلّ که او اثر مُبدَع است.[۴۴]

[§۵۵:۲۱] و همچنین گوهر نفس‌کلّی شریفتر است از اثر آن که مبداء عالم هیولانی است آن هیولیءِ مطلق که او را هیولیءِ اولیٰ گویند.

[§۵۶:۲۱] و آغاز هیولی از طاعت کردن نفس‌کلّ پدید آمد از آن علّت کی گفتیم.

کار کرد بر اجسام اندر اشخاص بتصویر، و تحویل مر نبات را بصورت حیوانی اندر اشخاص، و دیگر حالتها و استحالتها، همه مر طبیعت کلّی راست، که او اندرین عالم است میان فلك قمر و میان آن نقطه که مرکز عالم آنست. و همگی اُمَّهات و افلاك را تکیه بر آنست، و عالم از طبیعت کلّی پر است، بی‌آنك هیچ جای اندرو بگرفتست، از بهر آنك او جوهری ناجای‌گیرست.

۴۳ اس، ایا: اثر ابداع لطیفتر است از گوهر مُبدَع [کذا]. || تصحیح قیاسی.

۴۴ اس، ایا: ابداعست [کذا]. || تصحیح قیاسی. || ¦⟵برگ [ایا:۳۴-ب].

و وجود صورت که مبداء دوّم است از افاضت الّهی پدید آمد که عقل به نفس رسانید بفرمان مُبدِع حقّ.

[§۵۷:۲۱] و بدین قول که گفتیم پیدا کردیم که نخست هیولی بود آنگه پس از آن صورت بود و دلیل بر درستی این قول آن است که امروز صورتها را نفسهای جزوی بر[۴۵] هیولیها همی‌پدید آرد چون نگاشتن درودگر مر صورت در را بر چوب و نشاختن[۴۶] انگشتری‌گر[۴۷] صورت انگشتری را بر سیم.

[§۵۸:۲۱] پس مر مبداء اوّل را علّت هیولانی خوانند و مبداء دوّم را علّت صوری خوانند.

[§۵۹:۲۱] پس نفس‌کلّی به افاضت عقل کلّی،[۴۸] از جود باری، از پس هیولیءِ نخست آن چهار طبع مفرد را که اندر[۴۹] اندیشهٔ نفس‌کلّی صورت شد به هشت قسمت کرد.

[§۶۰:۲۱] و هریکی را از آن به دو نیمه کرد. گرمی را به دو بخش کرد یك بخش ازو به خشکی پیوست و زو گوهر آتش آمد و دیگر بخش ازو به تری پیوست و زو گوهر هوا آمد.

[§۶۱:۲۱] و مر تری مفرد را به دو بخش کرد یك بخش ازو به سردی پیوست و زو گوهر آب آمد و دیگر بخش ازو به گرمی پیوست و زو گوهر هوا آمد.

---

۴۵ اس، ایا: و [کذا]. || تصحیح قیاسی.

۴۶ ایا: بساختن؛ اس: نشاخنن. || نك: دهخدا: نشاختن. [نِ تَ] (مصدر) نشاندن ...نشانیدن... || نشاندن. نصب کردن. تعبیه کردن. کار گذاشتن... || نشاندن. فروبردن. جای‌دادن...

۴۷ ¦⟵برگ [اس:۴۷-ب].

۴۸ اس، ایا: کوبی [کذا]. [بر اساس قرائن، این خطای کاتب در هردو نسخه است].

۴۹ اس: کاندر؛ ایا: کندر.

[§۶۲:۲۱] و مر سردی[۵۰] مفرد را به دو بخش کرد یك بخش ازو به خشکی پیوست و زو گوهر خاك آمد و دیگر بخش ازو به تری پیوست و زو گوهر آب آمد.

[§۶۳:۲۱] و مر خشکی مفرد را به دو بخش کرد یك بخش ازو به گرمی پیوست و زو گوهر آتش آمد و دیگر بخش ازو به سردی پیوست و زو گوهر خاك آمد.

[§۶۴:۲۱] و گفتند حکما کزین چهار طبایع دو کارکنانند و دو کارپذیرانند. و آن دو کارکن گرمی و سردی‌اند. و آن دو کارپذیر تری و خشکی‌اند.

[§۶۵:۲۱] و آن دو کارکن یکی کارکن مهتر است و دیگر کارکن کهتر است. وزین دو کارپذیر یکی کارپذیر مهین[۵۱] است و یکی کارپذیر کهین است.

[§۶۶:۲۱] امّا کارکن مهین گرمی است و کارکن کهین سردی است و کارپذیر مهین خشکی است و کارپذیر[۵۲] کهین تری است. و گرمی کارکن سبکی است و سردی کارکن گرانی است. و خشکی کارپذیر زودی است و تری کارپذیر دیری است.

[§۶۷:۲۱] پس گوهر آتش مرکب است از کارکن مهین که گرمی است و از کارپذیر مهین که خشکی است، وز دو فعل ایشان یکی سبکی و دیگری زودی اثر دارد. بدین سبب از دیگران لطیف‌تر و شریفتر و عالی‌تر آمد و کناره عالم گرفت.

[§۶۸:۲۱] و گوهر هوا مرکب است از کارکن مهین که گرمی است و کارپذیر کهین که تری است ازین سبب یك سرش به کارکن مهین پیوسته است که آتش است و دیگر سرش به کارپذیر کهین پیوسته است که آب است و خود اندر این دو میانه باستاد.

۵۰ اس: + سردی.
۵۱ نك: دهخدا: مهین. [مِ] (صفت تفضیلی، صفت عالی) (مه = بزرگ + ین) بزرگتر. ... بزرگترین.... مقابل کهین. اکبر. اسن. بزاد برآمده ترین. آن بزرگتر به سال.
۵۲ |⟵برگ [ایا:۳۵-الف].

[§۶۹:۲۱] و گوهر آب مرکب است از کارکن کهین که سردی است وز کارپذیر کهین که تری است، وز فعلهای ایشان که[۵۳] تری و گرانی است اثر دارد.

[§۷۰:۲۱] و گوهر زمین مرکب است از کارکن کهین که سردی است و از کارپذیر مهین که خشکی است و از فعل ایشان که گرانی و زودی است اثر دارد.

[§۷۱:۲۱] پس این رکنی[۵۴] که اندر او زودی بود که زمین است مر آن رکن سبك را که آتش بود به برتر درجتی برد و آن سبك مر آن گران را که زمین بود به فروتر حدّی آورد.

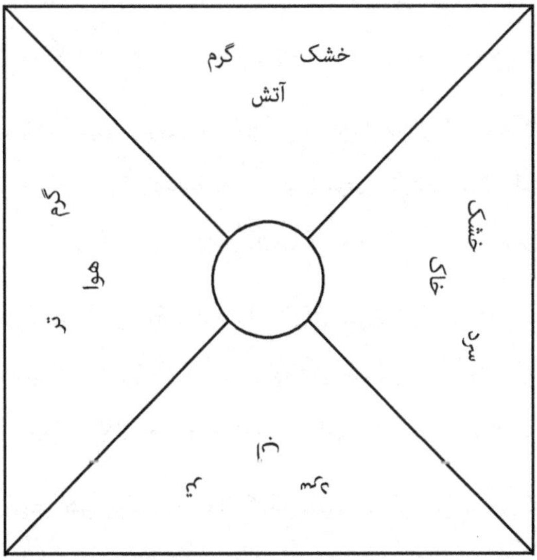

[نمودار ۱: طبایع چهار ارکان (عناصر اربعه)]

[§۷۲:۲۱] و بجمله این کارکنان و کارپذیران به‌هم‌گوشگی[۵۵] و خویشاوندی یکدیگر پیوسته‌اند، چون گرمی آتش با گرمی هوا و تری هوا با تری آب و سردی آب با سردی زمین.

۵۳ ¦←برگ [اس:۴۸-الف].

۵۴ ایا: رگن.

۵۵ نك: دهخدا: هم گوشه. [هَ شَ/شِ] (صفت مرکب) هم جنس و همسایه.

[§۲۱:۷۳] و به آخر درجتی خشکی زمین بماند، چنانك اول درجتی خشکی آتش مانده بود، پس خشکی زمین را خشکی آتش پیوست. و این بستها را به شکلْ بیرون آوردش تا آموزنده را تصورکردن آسان باشد.[۵۶]

[§۲۱:۷۴] و بباید دانستن که هر بودشی کز طبایع پدید آید از جهت هم‌گوشگی این رکنها باشد و پیوستگی ایشان به یکدیگر.

[§۲۱:۷۵] و هر فسادی و پراکندگی که اندر زایش عالم پدید آید از جهت دشمنی و نادَرخوری این رکنها است که دارند از[۵۷] یکدیگر.

[§۲۱:۷۶] وزان سبب کی علّت بودش عالم این بود که گفته شد از گفتار حکما، گوییم که اوّل زایشی کز عالم پدید آمد گوهرهای ناگدازنده بود و نهایت او به شرف یاقوت سرخ است.

[§۲۱:۷۷] پس مادّتی دیگر پدید آمد از نفس‌کلّی بر طبیعت‌کلّی و حاصل این شرف آن است که غذای مردم است و آن گندم است.

[§۲۱:۷۸] پس مادّتی دیگر پدید آمد از نفس‌کلّی بر طبیعت‌کلّی اندر عالم هیولانی و آن حیوان بود که اصل او به شرف مردم است.

[§۲۱:۷۹] و چون مردم آخِر آفرینش آمد و نور نفس به شخص مردم برسید آن نور بعکس بازگشت و پیوسته شد به کلّیت خویش.[۵۸]

[§۲۱:۸۰] این نفس جزوی به بازگشتن آن نور وز نفس‌کلّی قوّتی دیگر بپذیرفت و

---

۵۶ نك: جامع الحکمتین، فصل ۱۲: ‹اندر شرح «یکی»›، بند (۱۵۱)، ص ۱۴۹ تا ۱۵۱.

۵۷ ¦⟵برگ [ایا:۳۵-ب]. || حرف «از» در ابتدای برگِ [ایا:۳۵-ب] تکرار شده است.

۵۸ قس: وجه الدین: گفتار ۳۱، ص ۲۳۳، س ۱۵ تا ۱۸: ...مگر آن حدّ برین که او امر باریست سبحانه و تعالی دهنده است به حقیقت و ستاننده نیست و آن فرودین حدّ که مستجیب است ستانندهٔ حقیقت است و دهنده نیست تا آخر عالم دین مانند شده است به اوّل خویش و دایره گشته است.

آن قوّت نفس منطقی بود که آن از عالم روحانی اثر است و حاصل لطافت است[۵۹] و اوّل اندیشهٔ نفس کلّ است[۶۰] که به آخِرْ عملِ او پدید آمد.

[§۲۱:۸۱] و مر مبدای[۶۱] سیّم را که نورها از نفس کلّی بدو پدید آمد علّت فاعله خوانند، و نهایت این همه حاصلها به وجود خداوند قیامت باشد و آن را علّت مُتَمِّمَه خوانند که عالم بدو تمام شود.

[§۲۱:۸۲] پس نزدیك حکماءِ[۶۲] شریعی و علماءِ[۶۳] طبیعی آن کسان کی اندر علوم آلهی و اسرار پیغامبری شروع کردند سخن آن است کز مبدای[۶۴] عالم هیولانی چهار چیز واجب آید یکی هیولی و دیگر صورت و سدیگر فاعله و چهارم تمام.

[§۲۱:۸۳] و نزدیك حکماء[۶۵] شرعی و علماء[۶۶] علوم آلهی چنان است که پدید آرندهٔ بودش و گوهر و رواداشتن اثبات عالم ایزد است سبحانه.

[§۲۱:۸۴] و کارکن اندر آن نفس کلّ است و فاعلِ تدبیرِ فعلش طبیعت کلّ است.

[§۲۱:۸۵] و طبیعت کلِّ قوّتی است از قوّتهای نفس کلّ کی مُشْرِف است بر عالم هیولانی و نگاه‌دار است مر نوعها و صورتهای او اندازها را.

---

۵۹ ¦⟵برگ [اس:۴۸-ب].

۶۰ ایا: کل است.

۶۱ ایا: مبداء. || نك: دهخدا: مبدا. [مَ] ... آغاز. مبداء...: چون آخرِ عمرِ این جهان آمد / امروز ببایدش یکی مبدا. (ناصرخسرو، دیوان اشعار، ص ۱۹، [س ۳، به‌اهتمام: نصرالله تقوی]). گفتم چه چیز جنبشِ مبدای هر دُوان؟ / گفتا که هست آرامِ انجامِ هر صور. (ناصرخسرو، دیوان اشعار، ص ۱۸۸، [س ۱۶، به‌اهتمام: نصرالله تقوی]).

۶۲ اس: حکما؛ ایا: حکمای.

۶۳ اس: علما؛ ایا: علمای.

۶۴ ایا: مبداء.

۶۵ ایا: حکمای.

۶۶ اس: علما؛ ایا: علمای.

[§۲۱:۸۶] و تفاوت فعلهای[۶۷] عالم را بازبست به طبیعت است و جملگیش را بازبست به نفس کلّ است.

[§۲۱:۸۷] بدان معنی که به میانجی نفس کلّ پدید آمد عالم از فرمان مُبدِع حقّ.

[§۲۱:۸۸] مثال این چنان باشد که گویی پدیدآرندهٔ گوهرِ سیم ایزد است و فاعل انگشتری زرگر است و آنكِ انگشتری را کاربندد خداوند انگشتری است.

[§۲۱:۸۹] پس آن انگشتری‌گر نفس[۶۸] کلّ است و خداوند انگشتری طبیعت کل است.

[§۲۱:۹۰] معارضه اگر کسی گوید که عالم هیولانی خود از نفس پدید آمد و از طبیعت کلّی؛ جواب او را گوییم که نخست بباید شناختن که فعل[۶۹] بر چند روی است تا سخن بر بصیرت باشد.

[§۲۱:۹۱] و چون ما مر عالم‌هیولانی را که حاصل آفرینشِ ‹ظاهری است›[۷۰] شش جانب یافتیم، که عیْنِ عالمْ هفتمِ آن بُوَد، دانستیم که فعل بر هفت روی لازم آید:

[§۲۱:۹۲] نخست ابداعی و آن عقل اول است هستی نه از هست.

[§۲۱:۹۳] و دیگر انبعاثی چون نفس‌کلّی هستی از هستی دیگر.

[§۲۱:۹۴] و سدیگر تکوینی اعنی باشیدنی چون افلاك و ستارگان.

[§۲۱:۹۵] و چهارم طبیعی چون طبایع چهارگانه.

[§۲۱:۹۶] و پنجم زایشی چون زایشهای عالم کز طبایع پدید آمد.

---

۶۷ اس: فعلها.

۶۸ ¦⟵برگ [ایا:۳۶-الف].

۶۹ اس، ایا: علم [کذا]. || تصحیح قیاسی.

۷۰ ایا: ظاهرست.

[§۹۷:۲۱] و ششم تناسلی چون فعل کز میان نر و ماده پدید آمد.

[§۹۸:۲۱] و هفتم صناعی چون صنعتها که مردم کند.

[§۹۹:۲۱] پس فعل مُبدِع حقّ ابداعی است و انبعاثی و مُبدِع حقّ فعل زمانی نکند[۷۱] که فعل زمانی را آلت[۷۲] و مادّت باید.

[§۱۰۰:۲۱] و مر عالم را ابتدای زمانی نیست و لکن ابتدای فکری هست او را.

[§۱۰۱:۲۱] و مُبدِع حقّ دور است از اندیشه و از صفت اندیشندگان هم کلّی و هم جزوی؛ تَعٰالَی اللّٰهُ عَمّٰا یَقُولُ الظّٰالِمُونَ عُلُوًّا کَبِیراً.[۷۳]

[§۱۰۲:۲۱] ایزد تعالی مر آن مؤمن مخلص را برحق نگاه داراد که این سرهای لطیف و سخنهای شریف را که اندر کیفیّت کون عالم مرکّب و بسیط بگفتیم از اسرار حکما و محققان نگاه دارد.

۷۱ اس: [«ن» دوم و «د» اندکی مخدوش است].

۷۲ ¦⟵برگ [اس:۴۹-الف].

۷۳ اشارت به سورة الإسراء (۱۷)، آیت ۴۳: سُبْحٰانَهُ وَ تَعٰالیٰ عَمّٰا یَقُولُونَ عُلُوًّا کَبِیراً.

صف بیست و دوم

سخن اندر واجبی عمل شریعت و حجّت بر آنك روا نیست دست از آن بازداشتن

[§۱:۲۲] بباید دانستن کی ظاهر شریعت پیامبران برابر است با عالم جسمانی.

[§۲:۲۲] از بهر آنك عالم جسمانی صورتهای مخالف است، و ظاهر کتاب و شریعت مثلها وکارهای مخالف است.

[§۳:۲۲] چنانك یکی طاعت نماز است، به شکلها متفاوت، از ایستادن و خسبیدن و سر بر زمین نهادن و جز آن.

[§۴:۲۲] و یك طاعت روزه است که طعام و شراب ناخوردن است و جماع ناکردن بروز. و یك طاعت به مکّه شدن است به زیارت خانهٔ سنگین.

[§۵:۲۲] و این همه چیزهای مخالف است چنانك از عالم[1] یك چیز آفتاب است بدان روشنی و گرمی و یك چیز آب است بدان سردی و تری و یك زایش عالم درخت است پای بزمین فروبرده و استوار ایستاده و یکی زایش مرغ است که بر هوا همی‌پرّد و این اثر همه مخالف است.

[§۶:۲۲] و ترکیب عالم از چهار طبع است مخالف بظاهر و بباطن موافق. و ترکیب دین از چهار چیز مخالف است بظاهر و بباطن موافق چون کتاب و شریعت و تأویل و توحید.

[§۷:۲۲] و همچنانك از[2] آن چهار طبع عالم سه طبع همیشه پیداست و بی‌میانجی یافته است چون خاك و باد و آب و یك رکن او که آتش است نایافته است مگر به میانجی آن سه یار دیگر.

۱ ¦←برگ [ایا:۳۶-ب].

۲ اس: – از.

[§۲۲:۸] آن چهار رکن دین نیز سه یافته است چون کتاب و شریعت و تأویل و یکی نایافته است چون علم توحید مگر به میانجی این سه یار او که گفتیم.

[§۲۲:۹] پس پیغامبران، علیهم السلام، این علمهای فرودین از کتاب و شریعت و عمل ساختند تا خلق ازین راه به علم وحدانیّت رسند[۳] که نور علم وحدانیت از بزرگواری و لطافت چنان است که اندر او جز به میانجیان نتوان رسیدن.

[§۲۲:۱۰] و پیغامبران، علیهم السلام، به یافتن آن نور بر خلق پادشائی یافتند. و خلق بدان نور مر ایشان را گردن داده شد.

[§۲۲:۱۱] نبینی[۴] که خدای تعالی اندر حدیث موسی بر سبیل مثل مر رسول مصطفی را، علیه السّلام، میگوید، قوله: وَ هَلْ أَتٰاكَ حَدِيثُ مُوسىٰ * إِذْ رَأىٰ نٰاراً فَقٰالَ لِأَهْلِهِ امْكُثُوا إِنِّي آنَسْتُ نٰاراً لَعَلِّي آتِيكُمْ مِنْهٰا بِقَبَسٍ أَوْ أَجِدُ عَلَى النّٰارِ هُدىً.[۵] همی‌گوید: «چه آمد به تو ای محمّد حدیث موسی که او آتشی دید پس گفت مر اهل خویش را که باشید کی من آتشی دیدم مگر از آنجا[۶] پاره‌ای[۷] به شما آرم یا[۸] راه راست بر آن آتش بیابم».[۹]

[§۲۲:۱۲] و تأویل این آیت آن است کی موسی، علیه السّلام، آن آتش اندر

۳ ¦⟵برگ [اس:۴۹-ب].

۴ اس، ایا: نه بینی.

۵ سورة طه (۲۰)، آیات ۹-۱۰.

۶ اس: از نجا.

۷ اس، ایا: پاره‌ء.

۸ ایا: [هم «یا» خوانده میشود و هم «تا»].

۹ نك: کتاب مقدس: کتب عهد عتیق و عهد جدید، توریت سِفرِ خروج (باب ۳)، ص ۸۵ تا ۸۶، آیات ۲ تا ۶: ۲-و فرشتهٔ خداوند در شعلهٔ آتش از میان بوتهٔ بر وی ظاهر شد و چون او نگریست اینک آن بوته بآتش مشتعلست امّا سوخته نمیشود. ۳-و موسی گفت اکنون بدان طرف شوم و این امر غریب را به بینم که بوته چرا سوخته نمیشود. ۴-چون خداوند دید که برای دیدن مایل بدآنسو میشود خدا از میان بوته بوی ندا درداد و گفت ایموسی! ای موسی! گفت لبّیک. ۵-گفت بدین جا نزدیک میآ نعلین خود را از پایهایت بیرون کن زیرا مکانیکه در آن ایستادهٔ زمین مُقدَّس است. ۶-و گفت من هستم خدای پدرت خدای ابراهیم و خدای اسحاق و خدای یعقوب آنگاه موسی روی خود را پوشانید زیرا ترسید که بخدا بنگرد.

نفس مقدّس خویش دید و آن آتش نور توحید بود که مر او را بدرفشید[۱۰] و بدانچ: 'مر اهل خویش را گفت بباشید' آن خواست که هم بر این دین و این طریقت که هستید بباشید تا من از این نور که مرا درفشید خبری[۱۱] توانم یافتن که به شما رسانم و شما و من راه راست یابیم.

[۱۳:۲۲§] و این راه اندر دین گفت کی بیابیم نه اندر دنیا، اگر او آن آتش به چشم سر دیده بودی ایشان را بنمودی، چه آتش[۱۲] را به شب هر که بصر درست دارد بتواند دیدن.

[۱۴:۲۲§] و اگر او آن آتش به چشم سر دیده بودی کسی را توانستی فرمودن تا بنگرد که آن آتش چیست و لکن آن آتش نور توحید بود که موسی، علیه السلام، مر آن را به چشم بصیرت بدید و نتوانست به کسی نمودن بی‌میانجی کتاب و شریعت و عمل.

[۱۵:۲۲§] چنانك آتش دنیایی روی ننماید مگر به میانجی چیزی که از آب و خاك رسته باشد و اندر هوا پرورده شده باشد. پس هر که مر کتاب و شریعت و عمل را دست بازدارد البته مر جان او نور توحید را نتواند یافتن؛ همچنانك اگر کسی گوید که: 'من به هیچ چیز کز آب روید و از خاك یاری نخواهم بر جُستنِ آتش'، آن کس البته به آتش نرسد، و فایدهٔ آتش ازو بریده گردد.

[۱۶:۲۲§] و چون آتش طبیعی، کی او را هیچ دانش نیست، جز به میاجیان[۱۳] که با او آشنا اند همی روی ننماید، علم توحید سزاوارتر که روی ننماید جز بدان کس که سپس فرمان آشنایان او برود از پیامبران، علیهم السّلام. پس هر که کتاب خدای را و شریعت رسول را و عمل و طاعت را بیشتر کاربندد علم توحید سوی

---

۱۰ نك: دهخدا: درفشیدن. [دِ رَ دَ] (مصدر) درخشیدن که تابان و منور بودن باشد.

۱۱ اس: خیری.

۱۲ |⟵برگ [ایا:۳۷-الف].

۱۳ |⟵برگ [اس:۵۰-الف].

او روشن‌تر شود. همچنانك هر که هیزم بیشتر جمع کند روشنی و گرمی از آتش طبیعی بیشتر یابد.

صف بیست و سِیُّم[۱]

سخن اندر هویّت مُبدِع حقّ[۲]

[§۱:۲۳] گوییم براندازهٔ طاقت بندگی خویش اندر توحید و نه براندازهٔ حَقومندیِ او، که مُبدِع حقّ دور است از هویّت و ناهویّت.

[§۲:۲۳] ازبهر آنك هویّت مر عقل را است که هستی حق او را است و ناهویّت مر ابداع را است که جود[۳] مُبدِع حقّ است بر عقل اوّل.

[§۳:۲۳] و عقل اوّل بدلیلیِ هستیِ خویش، و نیستیِ ابداع، مر مُبدِع حقّ[۴] را بشناخت؛ و این هردو صفت از پدیدآورندهٔ خود دور کرد.

[§۴:۲۳] و عقل به شناختن هستیِ خویش هویّت آفریدگار را از هست و ناهست دور کرد.

[§۵:۲۳] نه بدانك آنجا هویّتی[۵] ناهویّتی ‹یا هویّتی›[۶] موجود یافت بیرون آنك عقل پیدا کرد از هستی خویش، که هویّت مُبدِع حقّ نه چون هویّت[۷] هستها است، و نه ناهویّت[۸] مُبدِع حقّ ناهویّت[۹] نیستها است.

---

۱ ایا: سوم.

۲ قس: کتاب الینابیع، الیبوع الثانی (۲): في هویّة المبدع المحضة، ص ۱۵ تا ۱۷.

۳ اس، ایا: خود [کذا]. || تصحیح قیاسی. نك: کتاب الینابیع، الینبوع الثانی، ص ۱۵، بند (۲۲)، س ۸ تا ۹: أنّ الهویّة المحضة التي تضاف إلى المُبدِع — سبحانه عن هو ولا هو — إنما هي أیسیّة السابق من أیسیّة ألإبداع المَجُود به علیه.

۴ ایا: خویش.

۵ ایا: + یا.

۶ ایا: ناهویتی. [روی «ناهویتی» به این گمان که تکرار، به اشتباه، کلمه قبل یعنی «ناهویتی» است با جوهر شنگرف خط زده شده است].

۷ ایا: هویّة.

۸ ایا: ناهویّة.

۹ ایا: با هویت. || ⟵| برگ [ایا:۳۷-ب].

[§٢٣:٦] بل‌که[١٠] شناختن مُبدِع حقّ آن است که نفی کنی هویّات را و ناهویّات را ازو. سُبْحانَهُ وَ تَعالیٰ عَمّا یَقُولُ الظّالِمُونَ عُلُوًّا کَبِیراً.[١١]

[§٢٣:٧] وگر مُبدِع حقّ را به هویّت اعتقاد کردی مر او را ماننده کرده بودی بهستی بخویش. وگر عقل مر مُبدع را به ناهویّت اعتقاد کردی ماننده کرده بودی مر او را به نیستی به ابداع.

[§٢٣:٨] وگر عقل به هستی خویش درست کردی آفریدگار خویش را و هستی مر عقل را بود پس از این قیاس مُبدِع حقّ خود عقل بودی. و نتیجهٔ این سخن آن آمد که کسی گوید آفریده خود آفریدگار است و این محال است.

[§٢٣:٩] وگر عقل هویّت مُبدِع حقّ به[١٢] نیستی ابداع درست کردی این خود چون شایستی بودن درست کردن[١٣] از جهت[١٤] نیستی و این قسمت محال‌تر است از قسمت نخستین.

[§٢٣:١٠] و آنك عقل کلّ بدان خاصه است از همه آفریده‌ها آن است که علّت او با او یکی است بی هیچ جدایی. و آنك بیرون هویّت محض است که عقل بدان یکتا است، آن افاضت عقل است بر نفس کلّی بفرمان مُبدِع حقّ؛ و مُبدِع حقّ منزّه است و پاك است از همه هویتها و ناهویتها.

[§٢٣:١١] بازنماییم بیان قول خویش که چرا هویت از مُبدِع حقّ نفی کردیم و گوییم که هر هویتی که همی‌یابیم اندر عالم مر آن را علّتی هست و هیچ چیز از عقل شریفتر و لطیف‌تر نیست و هویّت او به‌علّت او پدید آمده است که آن

١٠ ایا: بلك.

١١ اشارت به سورة الإسراء (١٧)، آیت ٤٣: سُبْحانَهُ وَ تَعالیٰ عَمّا یَقُولُونَ عُلُوًّا کَبِیراً.

١٢ ایا: – به.

١٣ ؛⟵برگ[اس:٥٠-ب].

١٤ اس، ایا: جهة.

علّتْ امرِ مُبدِع حقّ است و آفریدگار را علّت واجب نیاید، و[۱۵] چون علّت واجب نیاید[۱۶] روا نباشد که مر او را جل و تعالی هویّت گوییم.

[§۲۳:۱۲] و چون علّت هویت که معلول است ناهویت باشد که ابداع است، و بازگوییم که ناهویت را که علّت است هویتی باید، چنان باشد کی گوییم که[۱۷] مر علّت را علّت باید یا علّتْ علّتِ معلول باید، و این محال است.

[§۲۳:۱۳] پس گوییم که مر هویّت را نهایت تا به عقل است و ناهویّت را نهایت تا به امر است؛ و برتر از هویت و ناهویت لازم نیاید بدین برهانهای عقلی که گفتیم. و ایزد تعالی برتر است از علّت و معلول و از هویّت و ناهویّت. جَلَّ وَ تَعٰالیٰ عَمّٰا یَقُولُ الظّٰالِمُونَ عُلُوًّا کَبِیراً.[۱۸]

---

۱۵ ایا: – و.

۱۶ ایا: [عبارت «چون علّت واجب نیاید» بالای خط نوشته شده است].

۱۷ اس: – که.

۱۸ اشارت به سورة الإسراء (۱۷)، آیت ۴۳: سُبْحٰانَهُ وَ تَعٰالیٰ عَمّٰا یَقُولُونَ عُلُوًّا کَبِیراً. ||←برگ [ایا:۳۸-الف].

صف بیست و چهارم[۱]

سخن اندر الله که بزرگ‌تر نام خدای است[۲]

[§۱:۲۴] بدانید کی چهار حرف که اندر این نام بزرگ است دلیل است بر چهار اصل روحانی و جسمانی که پایداری همه آفریدگان از روحانی و جسمانی بدان است، از فریشتگان نزدیك گردانیده و بندگان نیك؛ و هر حرفی ازین حرفها معدن است مر خیرات دو جهانی را:

[§۲:۲۴] چون الف کزو برابر عقل است که او معدن تأیید است؛ و لام کزو برابر نفس‌کلّ است که معدن ترکیب است؛ و چون لام دیگر کزو برابر ناطق آمد که معدن[۳] تألیف است؛ و چون ها کزو برابر بیان است از اساس که معدن تأویل است؛ برابر حرفهای نام[۴] خدای با معدنهای خیر اندر دو عالم.

[§۳:۲۴] و این چهار معدن روحانی برابر است با چهار معدن جسمانی طبیعی، کز طبیعتِ کلّ پدید آمده است، و قوام جسمانیان بدان است، چون: آتش کی معدنِ گرمی است و چیزها را لطیف گرداند؛ و هوا معدنِ بیرون آوردن[۵] و ترکیب کردنِ چیزها است؛ و آب معدنِ گرد کردن و سرشتن است؛ و زمین معدنِ نگاه‌داشتن و بسیار گردانیدن است و بزرگ کردن.

[§۴:۲۴] و اگر خردمند بنگرد اندر آفرینش طبایع و چگونگی نهاد این چهار رکن عالم، مر نام الله اندر او به آفرینش نبشته بیند. چنانك ببیند مر آتش را که سوی

---

۱ قس: کتاب الینابیع، الینبوع الأول: في معني الینبوع، ص ۸ تا ۱۵.

۲ ایا: + تعالی.

۳ ¦⟵برگ [اس:۵۱-الف].

۴ ایا: [«نام» بالای «حرفهای» مابین سطور نوشته شده است].

۵ نك: دهخدا: بیرون آوردن. [وَ دَ] (مصدر مرکب) بیرون بردن. برآوردن. بدر آوردن. خارج کردن.... برون آوردن. اخراج: که آرد از شجر بیرون که بخشد لذت و بویش / که اندر شاخ چوب او را نگوئی بارور دارد. (ناصرخسرو، دیوان اشعار، ص ۱۳۴، س ۸، به‌اهتمام: نصرالله تقوی).

بالا همی‌کشد بی هیچ کژی و تَأنی چون الف آن اللّه و لام اوّل را برابر هوا بیند از بهر آنك هوا را دو کناره است یك کناره‌اش به آتش و دیگر کناره‌اش به آب است [چنانك لام را دو اندازه است از درازی و پهنی.] و همچنین لام دیگر را بیند که چون آب است میان دو اندازه از درازی و پهنی. [از بهر آنك آب را دو کناره است یك کناره‌اش به هوا و دیگر کناره‌اش به زمین است.] و ها را بیند که گرد است برابر زمین و آرام[۶] جانوران بر زمین است که او از نام اللّه به منزلتِ ها است.[۷]

[§۵:۲۴] و همچنین معدنهایِ روحانی چهارگانه که یادکردیم مانندە است به چهار رکن طبایع ازبهرآنك عقلِ کلّ ماننده‌ٔ آتش است که مر نفس را گرم کند بدانچ آرزوی تمامی [به][۸] بررسیدن به ثواب ابدی اندر نفس از عقل پدید آید. و عقل لطیف کند نفس منطقی را تا او را از حدّ قوّت به حدِّ[۹] فعل آردش و از دایرهٔ طبیعت بیرون بردش.

[§۶:۲۴] و همچنانك عقل نهایت است مر آن چهار اصل بزرگ را، آتش نهایت

---

۶ ایا: + جای.

۷ تصحیح قیاسی. نك: کتاب الینابیع، الینبوع الأول: في معنى الینبوع، ص ۹ تا ۱۰، بند (۱۱) و (۱۲): (۱۱) ... ولو أن العاقل نظر في خلقة الأمهات وهيئاتها في نفس حروف الله، لوجد كلّ حرف منها يشبه ما يقابله من أركان هذا العالم الطبيعي./ (۱۲) وذلك أنّ حرف الألف بـإزاء النار الصاعد علوّاً في الاستقامة بل ميل إلى احد الجوانب. واللام بـإزاء الهواء ذي طرفين، طرف منه إلى النار، وطرف منه إلى الماء، كذلك اللام ذو قدرين: طول وعرض. واللام الأخرى بـإزاء الماء ذي طرفين: طرف منه إلى الهواء، وطرف منه إلى الأرض. كذلك اللام الأخرى ذو قدرين: طول وعرض. والهاء المدور الكرى بـإزاء الأرض المدوّرة الكُريّة التي عليها قرار المواليد كما استقرّ اسم الله على حرف الهاء.

۸ تصحیح قیاسی. نك: همین کتاب، پایان صف ۶۳، بند ۹ تا ۱۱: و نیز تفاوت اهل ثواب بر دیگر روی آن است کی رسیدن ثواب به هر نفسی براندازهٔ آرزوی او باشد به علم. و نفس [را] آرزو به علم بر مقدار لطافت و پاکیزگی گوهر او باشد. هر که نفس او لطیف تر و صافی تر باشد آرزوی او به بررسیدن بر چیزها بیشتر باشد و به تمامیِ خویش آهنگ بیشتر کند و ثواب او عظیم تر باشد. و هر که گوهر نفس او تاریك و کثیف باشد آرزوی او به بررسیدن بر چیزها کمتر باشد و تمامیِ خویش را کمتر جوید و ثواب او کمتر باشد. این است تفاوت میان اهل ثواب.

۹ |⟵برگ [ایا:۳۸-ب].

است مر چهار رکن عالم را. و همچنانك آتش پیدا نشود مگر به گوهری فرود ازو که مر او را بپذیرد، عقل نیز پیدا نشود مگر به گوهر نفس کی فرود ازو است که مر او را بپذیرد.

[۷:۲۴§] و از آتش برتر، اندر آفرینش، فلك قمر است که بسته است از افراز او. و فلك قمر که برتر از آتش است بیرون است از صفات این چهار طبع که زیر او است.

[۸:۲۴§] همچنین برتر از جوهرِ عقلِ کلّی بسته است کلمه[۱۰] ایزد که بیرون است از صفات همه موجودات که هستها است از روحانی و جسمانی.[۱۱] و همچنانك با آتش هیچ چیز توانایی ندارد و ازو است صلاح زندگی و رسیدن چیزهای خام، همچنین به تأیید عقلِ اوّل است صلاح دین خدای و نظام دو جهان.

[۹:۲۴§] و نفس کلّ ماننده شد به همه رویها به هوا. از بهر آنك از نفس کلّ است بیرون آوردن پیامبران و اثر دادن از تأیید اندر نفوس ایشان.

[۱۰:۲۴§] و از نفس کلّ است بیرون آوردن عالم طبیعت و اثر کردن اندر عالم تا عالم صورتهای طبیعی بپذیرد.

[۱۱:۲۴§] و از چهار رکن عالم به هوا ببینند[۱۲] رکنها و صورتها را، و همچنین به نفس کلّی ببینند پیامبران[۱۳] صورتهای عالم را.

[۱۲:۲۴§] و همچنانك هوا تاریکی و روشنایی پذیرد[۱۴] نفسها از نفس کلّی بهری هدی پذیرد و بهری ضلالت.

---

۱۰ اس، ایا: کلمت. || تصحیح قیاسی. نك: همین کتاب، صف ۶۶، بند ۹. || این تصحیح همه جا در این کتاب، بدون اشاره مجدد، انجام شده است.

۱۱ ¦⟵برگ [اس:۵۱-ب].

۱۲ اس، ایا: به بیند.

۱۳ ایا: پیمبران.

۱۴ ایا: بپذیرد.

[§۱۳:۲۴] و همچنانك به هوا بود اعتدال زندگی و فساد آن، همچنان به اثر نفس کلّی بود صلاح نفس منطقی، و به زوال اثر او بود فساد نفس منطقی.

[§۱۴:۲۴] و همچنانك از هوا خلق عالم بیماری و تندرستی پذیرد، از اثر نفس کلّی نفسهای منطقی بهرهٔ ثواب پذیرد و بهرهٔ عقاب.

[§۱۵:۲۴] پس گوییم که ناطق[۱۵] ماننده شد به همه رویها به آب ازبهرآنك از ناطق[۱۶] است جمع کردن حکمتهای[۱۷] آلهی اندر عالم طبیعی، وز ناطق[۱۸] بود سرشتن علمهای[۱۹] شریعی که موافق بود مردمان دور را.

[§۱۶:۲۴] وز آب بود[۲۰] موجها که خلق بدان هلاك شوند. همچنین از ظاهر ناطق[۲۱] پدید آید موجهای اختلاف که هلاك نفسهای منطقی بدان باشد.

[§۱۷:۲۴] و صلاح آب اندر پوشیده بیشتر از آن است کی اندر ظاهر است. همچنین صلاح حکمت شریعت پیامبر[۲۲] اندر ذهن و تمییز بیشتر از آن است کی اندر ظاهر شریعت است ازبهرآنك ظاهر شریعت موافق جسدها است و باطن او به تمییز کردن موافق ارواح است.

---

۱۵ اس، ایا: نطق [کذا]. تصحیح بر اساس متن کتاب الینابیع، ص ۱۱، بند (۱۵): ثم الناطق یشبه الماء في جمیع أحواله، إذ منه جمیع الحکم والعلوم وجري الشریعة الموافقة لأهل دوره. وأنّ من الماء تلتطم الأمواج الهائلة المهلکة للخلق، کذلك في ظاهر الناطق وحیّزه تتولّد أمواج الاختلاف المؤدیّة الموبقة. وصلاح الماء في باطن الأشیاء اکثر منه في ظاهره. وأنّ الماء أبداً بین صعود ونزول من غیر فترة، کذلك الناطق بین صعود إلی مرتبة التالي — لیستفید منه حظه من الکلمة — وبین إفادة منه لمن دونه.

۱۶ اس، ایا: نطق [کذا]. تصحیح بر اساس متن کتاب الینابیع. نك: یادداشت بالا.

۱۷ اس: حکمتها.

۱۸ اس، ایا: نطق [کذا]. تصحیح بر اساس متن کتاب الینابیع. نك: یادداشت بالا.

۱۹ اس: علمها.

۲۰ ¦⟵برگ [ایا:۳۹-الف].

۲۱ اس، ایا: نطق [کذا]. تصحیح بر اساس متن کتاب الینابیع. نك: یادداشت بالا.

۲۲ ایا: پیامبران.

[§۱۸:۲۴] و آب را خاصیّت آن است که همیشه از آن کنار که لطیف باشد سوی بالا شود و آنگاه بدان معدنِ خویش آید بی‌درنگ. همچنین نفس ناطقه[۲۳] همیشه به بالا همی‌شود تا نصیب خویش از نفس‌کلّی بپذیرد و باز مر آن نصیب را کثیف کند و بدان دهد که زیر او باشد چنانك پیغامبران، علیهم السّلام، کردند.

[§۱۹:۲۴] و نفس ممیّزه[۲۴] ماننده شد به زمین از همه رویها و معنی نفس ممیّزه[۲۵] جداکننده باشد بد را از نیك. و از نفس ممیّزه بود نگاه‌داشت مر نفسهای منطقی را[۲۶] بر دین خداوند شریعت و تأویل متشابهات تا شریعت بر مردم استوار شود و صورت معادی به علم آلهی و به عمل شریعی تمام گردد. برمثال نگاه‌داشت زمین و تمام کردن او مر چیزها را.

[§۲۰:۲۴] و از نفس ممیزه بود پدید آمدن نوعهای بیان اندر دین خدای، همچنانك از زمین بود پدید آمدن صورتهای جسمانی.

[§۲۱:۲۴] و همچنانك آب و هوا و آتش اندر زمین پنهان شوند، تأیید عقل کلّی و توفیق نفس‌کلّی و تعلیم ناطق[۲۷] اندر نفس ممیّزه جمله شوند.

[§۲۲:۲۴] و آغاز این چهار حرف اللّٰه از الف است که او از حساب یکی است همچنانك آغاز چهار از یکی است و انجامش به یکی است. ازبهرآنك چون به همه چهار را چون یکی و دو و سه و چهار جمله کنی ده بود. و یکی، یکی باشد اندر ذات خویش.[۲۸]

[§۲۳:۲۴] پس چنانك آغاز و انجام چهار به یکی است آغاز و انجام این چهار حرف اللّٰه یکی است بدانچ آغازش الف است و انجامش آن الف است کی آخرِ ها

---

۲۳ در اینجا «نفس ناطقه» معادل اصطلاح «التالی»، در کتاب الینابیع، است.

۲۴ «نفس ممیّزه» را ناصرخسرو برای اصطلاح «اساس» بکار برده است.

۲۵ ¦⟵برگ [اس:۵۲-الف].

۲۶ ایا: – را.

۲۷ اس، ایا: نطق [کذا]. || تصحیح قیاسی بر اساس متن کتاب الینابیع. نك: یادداشت بالا.

۲۸ نك: کتاب الینابیع، ص ۱۲، بند (۱۷)، س ۵: وهو واحد في ذاتها.

است[۲۹] و معنی پوشیده اندر این باب آن است که علّت این چهار اصل، کی گفتیم، به وحدت ایزد است.

[§۲۴:۲۴] و همچنین آغاز چهار ارکان از طبیعت که او قوّت فاعله است اعنی کارکن، و انتهای آن اشخاص است که جزو نپذیرد.

[§۲۴:۲۵] و اندر هر شخصی دلیلِ ده موجود است که از ذات خویش پدید کند و آن گوهر آن چیز است که برگرفته است مر نه عرض را که سوی اهل[۳۰] علم منطق آن نُه عرض دانسته است.

[§۲۴:۲۶] پس هر چیزی بدین شرح که گفتیم آغاز آن یکی است و انجامش یکی است. همچنان که الله را اوّل یك است که الف است و آخرش یك است که الف است آخرِ حرفِ ها[۳۱] اندر. پس موافق آمد شمار از جهت آفرینش و نظم عالم با[۳۲] تألیف این نام بزرگ.

[§۲۴:۲۷] و لام و الف که بهم آری حاصل ازو کلمه نفی باشد، و آن لا باشد. و چون لام دیگر را با ها گرد آری، ازو کلمه اثبات آید و آن له[۳۳] باشد، و مشار[۳۴] باشد.

[§۲۴:۲۸] یعنی که روحانیان نامشارند چون لا و آن عقل است و نفس کلّی، و قوّت نُطق و تمییز چون له بود، یعنی مشار. پس ان دو نامشارند و این دو مشارند.

[§۲۴:۲۹] و ایزد تعالی، جلّ ذکره، نه مشار است و نه نامشار است. و همچنین از

۲۹ ¦⟵برگ[ایا:۳۹-ب].
۳۰ اس: [کلمه «اهل» بالای خط نوشته شده است].
۳۱ اس: حرفها.
۳۲ ایا: تا.
۳۳ اس: آله.
۳۴ نك: دهخدا: مشار. [مُ] (عربی، صفت) اشارت کرده شده. ... راهنمائی شده. ...: خیل سخن را رهی و بندهٔ من کرد / آن که ز یزدان به علم و عدل مشار است. (ناصرخسرو، دیوان اشعار، [ص ۵۱، س ۱۶، به اهتمام: نصرالله تقوی]).

چهار رکن عالم[۳۵] طبیعی، آتش و هوا نامشار است از جهت[۳۶] اندر رسیدن بدیشان از لطافت. و آب و زمین مشارند که کثیف‌اند.

[§۲۴:۳۰] و همچنین حکما صورت فلك را بخش کردند به چهار قسمت و آن را اوتاد[۳۷] خوانند یعنی میخها. و یکی را از آن میخها طالع خوانند، و آن آن خانه باشد کز مشرق برآید آن وقت کی حکم خواهند کردن، و آن را خانهٔ زندگانی خوانند.

[§۲۴:۳۱] و دیگر از آن میخها چهارم باشد از خانهٔ طالع و آن را خانهٔ عاقبت خوانند.

[§۲۴:۳۲] و سدیگر از آن میخها خانهٔ هفتم باشد از طالع و آن را خانهٔ خصومت خوانند.

[§۲۴:۳۳] و چهارم از آن میخها خانهٔ دهم باشد و آن را خانهٔ عزّ و پادشایی[۳۸] خوانند. یعنی که آغاز صورتهای روحانی از چهار اصل است.

---

۳۵ ¦⟵برگ [اس:۵۲-ب].

۳۶ ایا: جهة.

۳۷ نك: دهخدا: اوتاد. [اَ] (ع اِ) ج ِ وَتَد. میخ ها....- اوتاد ارض؛ کوههای روی زمین: وَ الْجِبٰالَ أَوْتٰاداً. (قرآن ۷۸/۷)....|| (اصطلاح صوفیه) اقطاب و بزرگان، چهار نفر مرد هستند که منزلهای آنان بر چهار منزل یعنی ارکان عالم است که مشرق و مغرب و شمال و جنوب باشد و با هریک از آنان مقام آن جهت میباشد. ... - اوتاد اربعه؛ در اصطلاح منجمین عبارتند از: طالع، غارب، وتدالسماء، وتدالارض. خانهٔ اول و چهارم و هفتم و دهم زایجه را گویند. ... - اوتاد طالع؛ بدانکه نزد منجمین اوتاد طالع مولود چهار است. اول برج طالع که خانهٔ اول است و آن تعلق دارد به تن و جان و عمر و زندگانی مولود. دوم خانهٔ چهارم و آن تعلق دارد بمعاش و روزی و ملک و مقام و پدر. سوم خانهٔ هفتم و آن تعلق داردبه تزویج و زوجه و مراد و مقصود. چهارم خانهٔ دهم و آن تعلق دارد بحکومت و شغل و عمل و دولت. || نیز نك: دهخدا: وتد. [وَ تَ] ... میخ. ...ج، اَوْتٰادْ. ... || (در اصطلاح رَمل) وتد نزد اهل رمل بر چند معنی اطلاق کرده می آید. آنکه میگویند که خانهٔ اول و چهارم و هفتم و دهم هریک وتد است. و دوم و پنجم و هشتم و یازدهم هر یک مایل وتد است. و سوم و ششم و نهم و دوازدهم هر یک زائل وتد است. و ساقط عن الوتد نیز گویند. به جهت آنکه هریک از این خانه ها نظر به طالع ندارد. ...

۳۸ ایا: پادشاهی.

[§۳۴:۲۴] و خانهٔ زندگانی که طالع است دلیل عقل است که او طالع اوّل است، بدانچ[۳۹] از کلمه باری سبحانه نخست او پیدا شد و بدو یافتند زندگانی همه روحانیات و جسمانیات.

[§۳۵:۲۴] و خانهٔ چهارم خانهٔ عاقبت است دلیل نفس‌کلّ است کی عاقبت کارها بدو باشد و از نفس‌کلّ است تمام شدن اصلها.[۴۰]

[§۳۶:۲۴] و وَتدِ سدیگر به خانهٔ هفتم است که خانهٔ خصومت است که دلیل ناطق[۴۱] است، که ناطق یکی است از جملهٔ هفت اندام مردم و آن زفان است. و خصومتها هم از جهت ناطق[۴۲] افتد.

[§۳۷:۲۴] و وَتدِ چهارم که خانهٔ دهم است و خانهٔ عزّ و پادشائی است دلیل است بر نفس ممیزه که بدو تمام شود حدود روحانی و جسمانی. و شرح حروف اللّٰه بسیار است ما بدین مقدار اقتصار کردیم.

---

۳۹ ¦⟵برگ [ایا:۴۰-الف].

۴۰ نک: کتاب الینابیع، ص ۱۴، بند (۲۰)، س ۱ تا ۲: وعنوا بالوتد الثانی — وهو الرابع الذی سموه بیت العاقبة — التالی، اذ الیه تنتهی عواقب الامور، ومنه اکمال الأُصول الاربعة.

۴۱ اس، ایا: نطق [کذا]. || تصحیح قیاسی بر اساس متن کتاب الینابیع. نک: یادداشتهای پیشین.

۴۲ اس، ایا: نطق [کذا]. || تصحیح قیاسی بر اساس متن کتاب الینابیع. نک: یادداشتهای پیشین.

صف بیست و پنجم

سخن اندر آنچ مردم بدو سزاوار پیغامبری شود[1]

[§۱:۲۵] چهار قوّت است که چون هر چهار اندر مردمی گرد آید آن مردم تأیید پذیرد: ‹به انبازی›[2] مویّدی، اعنی که چون دانایی که او علمهای پوشیده را به دلالت ظاهرها همی‌بیند مر او را چیزی بنماید او همچنان پوشیده پیش شود بدان انبازی کی نفس او را با نفس دانا اوفتد.

[§۲:۲۵] و دیگر آن است که چون به انبازی تأییدپذیر گشت مر آن را بورزد تا از ذات خویش همچنان اشارتی که دانا بدو کرده باشد بیرون آرد تا تأییدپذیر باشد به تنهایی.[3] وگر بیم دراز شدن کتاب نبودی مثالی ازین اشارت بنمودمی.

[§۳:۲۵] و سدیگر آن است که چون نفس او را اندر چیزهای لطیف دیدار اوفتاد مر نطق او را قوّت آن باشد که مر آن را بتواند گفتن پوشیده.

[§۴:۲۵] چهارم آن باید که چون بگوید مر آن پوشیده را بر چیزهای آشکارا گوید و معنی آن را بزیر آن ظاهر اندر پوشیده کند تا عامه را ظاهر آن سخن قید و بند باشد. و خاصه را معنی آن قول پند و رستگاری باشد.

[§۵:۲۵] پس هر مردمی که برو بر این چهار خصلت منّت نهاد[4] او شایسته شود مر رسولی را از خالق سوی خلق، و سالار و رئیس گردد بر دیگر[5] هم‌جنسان[6] خویش.

---

۱ قس: کتاب الینابیع، الینبوع السادس والثلاثون (۳۶): في رتبة صاحب القیامة، ص ۸۳، بند (۱۶۴).

۲ اس: با ساری؛ ایا: با بیاریء.

۳ ¦←برگ [اس:۵۳-الف].

۴ اس: نهّد؛ ایا: نهد [کذا].

۵ ¦←برگ [ایا:۴۰-ب].

۶ ایا: همجنسان.

[§۶:۲۵] و دلیل بر درستی این دعوی آن است که مردم جانوری است از جملهٔ جانوران همچنانك رسول مردمی باشد از جملهٔ مردمان. و لکن چون مردم چهار قوّت را بردارد سالار شود بر جملهٔ دیگر جانوران.

[§۷:۲۵] و آن چهار قوّت که او را است یکی از آن نمو است و آن بربالیدن است چون نبات و ستوران که همی‌بالند. و دیگر حس است و آن شناختن جنس خویش و معرفت دشمن خویش است چنانك همه جانوران شناسند. و سدیگر نطق است و آن سخن گفتن است و عبارت کردن آنچ بداند مر هم‌جنس[۷] خویش را. چهارم عقل است کی بپذیرد و دانا شود به لطافتها.

[§۸:۲۵] و به گرد آوردن این چهار قوّت مردم گردد و زیر[۸] خویش آورد مر جانوران دیگر را که با او بنمو و حس و آواز برابر بودند. و چون این قوّتها که ستوران را بود بپذیرفت و نیز بر آن عقل و نطق زیادت پذیرفت سزاوار گشت مر سالاری جانوران را.

[§۹:۲۵] آن کس کی همه قوّتهای[۹] مردمی پذیرفته باشد و چهار قوّت دیگر چنانك یاد کردیم بپذیرد خداوند هشت قوّت شود، که به چهار قوّت از آن، مردم از درجهٔ ستوری برتر آمد.

[§۱۰:۲۵] از حکم عقلی واجب آید که آن کس که آن هشت قوّت را جمله کند او بر سالار جانوران سالار شود.

۷ ایا: همجنس.

۸ ایا: و ز بر.

۹ اس: قوتها.

[§۱۱:۲۵] و[۱۰] سالار جانوران مردم است. سالار مردم پیغامبران‌اند، صلوات الله علیهم اجمعین. این برهانی روشن است[۱۱] مر خداوند بصیرت را، وَ اللّهُ[۱۲] أَعْلَمُ وَ أَحْکَمُ.[۱۳]

۱۰ ایا: – و.

۱۱ ¦⟵برگ [اس:۵۳-ب].

۱۲ ایا: + تعالی.

۱۳ عبارت برگرفته از آیات قرآنی است، از جمله، نک: آل عمران، ۳۶؛ النِّسَاء، ۲۵؛ الأَنْعَام، ۱۲۴؛ هُود، ۴۵؛ العَنْکَبُوت، ۱۰؛ التِّین، ۸.

صف بیست و ششم

سخن اندر خداوند قیامت[۱] که چرا او[۲] شریعت نو بیارد؟

[§۲۶:۱] گوییم کی چیزها را که هست اندر عالم دو کناره و میانه است و هر بوده‌ای[۳] را تمامیِ آن اندر کنارهٔ بازپسین او است. چنانك مر چیزها را کی اندر او روح است کنارهٔ نخستین او نبات است و میانه‌اش حیوان است و کنارهٔ بازپسین او مردم است که بر نبات[۴] و حیوان سالار است. و تمامی حیوان اندر او است.

[§۲۶:۲] پس حال اندر دین همچنین واجب آید ازبهرآنك آفرینش مردم ازبهر دین بوده است و تمامیِ مردم اندر دین است. و هرکه او را دین نیست او ناقص است ازبهر آن بود که پیامبران، علیهم السّلام، مر کافران را کشتن فرمودند.[۵]

[§۲۶:۳] و مثل مردم که دین [نـ]پذیرفته[۶] باشد چون مثل نطفه باشد که به حدّ قوّت مردم باشد.

[§۲۶:۴] چه اگر کسی ده بار مجامعت کند با حلال خویش کی هر مجامعتی ممکن بودی که فرزندی بودی وزان ده مجامعت او هیچ فرزند نباشد او را بدان گرفتاری نباشد هرچند که آن نطفه که او مردم بود تباه شد ازبهرآنك ناقص بود. پس کشتن مردم بی‌دین برابر است با تباه شدن نطفه و ازو بزه‌ای[۷] نباشد به کشتن او بل‌که[۸] ثواب باشد مر کشندهٔ او را.

۱ قس: کتاب الینابیع، الینبوع السادس والثلاثون (۳۶): في رتبة صاحب القیامة، ص ۸۲ تا ۸۵. || نیز قس: الملیجی، المجالس المستَنصِریَّة، المجلس الثالث: قائم القیامة — تأویل 'بِسْمِ اللّهِ الرَّحْمٰنِ الرَّحِیمِ'، الحدود الروحانیّة والجسمانیّة، ص ۳۱ تا ۳۶.

۲ ایا: او چرا.

۳ اس، ایا: بوده‌ء.

۴ ¦⟵برگ [ایا:۴۱-الف].

۵ نك: جامع الحکمتین: بند ۳۴۰.

۶ اس، ایا: پذیرفته [کذا]. || تصحیح قیاسی.

۷ اس، ایا: بزه‌ء.

۸ ایا: بلك.

[§۵:۲۶] پس گویم که مر دین را همچنین سه مرتبت است. نخست ازو مرتبهٔ ناطق[۹] است و آن پیغامبری است که شریعت آرد و تألیف کتاب و اَعمال کند و خلق را بر پذیرفتن ظاهر آن تکلیف کند.

[§۶:۲۶] و دیگر مرتبت وصایت است که بنیاد تأویل او نهد و مثلها و رمزها را معنی بگوید و خلق را از موج دریای شبهت به خشکی و ایمنی حقیقت برساند.

[§۷:۲۶] و سدیگر مرتبت امامت است که ظاهر و باطن را امام نگاه دارد و خلق را براندازهٔ طاقت ایشان از علم تأویلی بهره دهد اندر هر زمانی. و این کنارهٔ بازپسین است اندر دین و تمامیِ دین اندر امام است.

[§۸:۲۶] پس گوییم که این سه مرتبت اندر خلق از سر دور آدم، علیه السّلام، تا به آخر دور محمّد مصطفیٰ،[۱۰] صلی[۱۱] اللّه علیه وآله، بگشت هر مرتبتی اندر شش تن و هژده تن اندر عالم اندر این سه مرتبت ایستادند. چون آدم و اساس او و امام او، و نوح و اساس او و امام او،[۱۲] و ابراهیم و اساس او و امام او،[۱۳] و موسی و اساس او و امام او، و عیسی و اساس او و امام او، و محمّد مصطفیٰ و اساس او و امام او، علیهم السّلام.

[§۹:۲۶] و به هفتم ایشان کار دین تمام شود. و آن هفتم ایشان نوزدهم باشد مر این هژده را چنانك خدای تعالی فرمود، قوله: سَأُصْلِيهِ سَقَرَ * وَ مٰا أَدْرٰاكَ مٰا سَقَرُ * لاٰ تُبْقِي وَ لاٰ تَذَرُ * لَوّٰاحَةٌ لِلْبَشَرِ * عَلَيْهٰا تِسْعَةَ عَشَرَ * وَ مٰا جَعَلْنٰا أَصْحٰابَ النّٰارِ إِلاّٰ مَلاٰئِكَةً وَ مٰا جَعَلْنٰا عِدَّتَهُمْ إِلاّٰ فِتْنَةً لِلَّذِينَ كَفَرُوا لِيَسْتَيْقِنَ الَّذِينَ أُوتُوا الْكِتٰابَ وَ

۹ اس، ایا: نطق [کذا]. || تصحیح قیاسی.

۱۰ ¦⟵برگ [اس:۵۴-الف].

۱۱ اس، ایا: صل.

۱۲ ایا: + و نوح و اساس او و امام او [عبارت «و نوح و اساس او و امام او» تکرار شده است؛ اما، روی این کلمات با جوهر شنگرف خط کشیده شده است].

۱۳ ¦⟵برگ [ایا:۴۱-ب].

يَزْدٰادَ الَّذِينَ آمَنُوا إِيمٰاناً وَ لاٰ يَرْتٰابَ الَّذِينَ أُوتُوا الْكِتٰابَ[۱۴] وَ الْمُؤْمِنُونَ وَ لِيَقُولَ الَّذِينَ فِي قُلُوبِهِمْ مَرَضٌ وَ الْكٰافِرُونَ مٰاذٰا أَرٰادَ اللّٰهُ بِهٰذٰا مَثَلاً.[۱۵] همی گوید: «سرانجام اندر افکنیمش به دوزخ؛ و تو چه دانی ای محمّد که آن چه دوزخ است؛ و آن آن است کی نه بمانند و نه بگذارند؛ درفشنده است مردم را؛ و برو نوزده موکل[۱۶] است؛ و نکردیم خداوندان آتش مگر فریشتگان و نکردیم شمار ایشان مگر آزمایشی مر آنها را که کافر شدند، تا زیادت شود ایمان گروندگان و بشكّ نیوفتند آن کسها که کتاب را بپذیرفتند و گروندگان، و تا بگویند کافران و آن کسها که دلهای ایشان اندر دین بیمار است که چه خواست خدای بدین مثل کی زد».

[§۲۶:۱۰] و تأویل این آیت آن است که به دوزخ مر ظاهر شریعت را همی‌خواهد که مردم ازو نه برحق باشد و نه بر باطل. و همی‌درفشد[۱۷] مردم را ازو چیزی که بدو نتواند رسیدن بی‌میانجی.

[§۲۶:۱۱] و برو نوزده موکل است از شش ناطق و شش اساس و شش امام و یکی خداوند قیامت. و بدانچ همی‌گوید: «نکردیم خداوندان آتش مگر فریشتگان»[۱۸] بدان آتش مر عقل کلّ را همی‌خواهد که فریشتگان ازو پدید آیند اندر عالم جسمانی.

[§۲۶:۱۲] و هر که این نوزده حد را بداند ایمانش زیادت شود بقوّت خدای تعالی. و هر که مر ایشان را نداند متحیّر شود و گوید: «این چه مثل است کی خدای همی‌زند؟».[۱۹]

---

۱۴ ایا: – وَيَزْدٰادَ ... الْكِتٰابَ.

۱۵ سورة المدثر (۷۴)، آیات ۲۶ تا ۳۱.

۱۶ ایا: مؤکل.

۱۷ نك: دهخدا: درفشیدن. [دِ رَ دَ] ... درخشیدن که تابان و منور بودن باشد.

۱۸ اشارت به آیت ۳۱ از سورة المدثر (۷۴).

۱۹ نك: بند [§۲۶:۹]. اشارت می کند به انتهای آیت ۳۱ از سورة المدثر (۷۴): وَ لِيَقُولَ الَّذِينَ فِي قُلُوبِهِمْ مَرَضٌ وَ الْكٰافِرُونَ مٰاذٰا أَرٰادَ اللّٰهُ بِهٰذٰا مَثَلاً. قس: سورة المُلك (۶۷)، آیت ۳۰؛ نیز قس: مثنوی معنوی، دفتر دوم، حکایت: «انکار فلسفی بر قرائت: إِنْ أَصْبَحَ مٰاؤُكُمْ غَوْراً...»، ابیاتِ

[§۱۳:۲۶] چون مر این سه شش را[۲۰] کی آن به هفتم بازپسین رسد و این ششان همه عمل فرموده اند[۲۱] واجب آید که آخر عمل حساب بود که شمار آن عملها آن هفتم از خلق بخواهد.

[§۱۴:۲۶] و دلیل بر درستی این قول آن است که جسد کثیف کی به شش حال بگردد از سلالة تا به لحم، به هفتم مرتبت او را حالی دیگر باشد که بدان شش حال گذشته نماند، و عیب و هنر آن شش حال بدان هفتم پدید آید.

[§۱۵:۲۶] و بدان هفتم حال از راست کردنِ صورتِ او بپردازند و حواس او و اندامهای او بکار پیمودن اندر افتد از آن معنیها که او را ازبهر آن آفریده باشند.[۲۲]

[§۱۶:۲۶] پس همچنین بِبرون آمدنِ آن هفتم حد، حساب این عملهای کرده از خلق بخواهند که او خداوند بازجستن کارهای کرده باشد نه فرمایندهٔ کار باشد.

[§۱۷:۲۶] و عقل گوایی همی دهد که چندین پیامبران بیامدند و خلق را به خدای خواندند و کار شرایع فرمودند و بعضی از مردم آن بپذیرفت و کار کرد و بعضی نپذیرفت و کار نکرد و هردو گروه ازین عالم رفتند و پیدا نیامد فضل آن مطیع فرمان بردار بر آن عاصی بی فرمان. باید که روزی باشد که آن فضل پدید آید.

[§۱۸:۲۶] و این تأخیر که بوده است و همی باشد مر آمدن آن هفتم را همی باشد، و خدای تعالی همی گوید، قوله: أَمْ حَسِبَ الَّذِینَ اجْتَرَحُوا السَّیِّئَاتِ أَنْ نَجْعَلَهُمْ کَالَّذِینَ آمَنُوا وَ عَمِلُوا الصَّالِحَاتِ سَوَاءً مَحْیَاهُمْ وَ مَمَاتُهُمْ سَاءَ مَا یَحْکُمُونَ.[۲۳] همی گوید: «یا چنان همی پندارند آن کسها که بدی کردند که ما مر ایشان را چون

۱۶۳۳ تا ۱۷۱۷: مُقْریی می خوانْد از روی کتاب / مٰاؤُکُمْ غَوْرًا ز چشمه بندم آب [...] لیك هرگز مستِ تصویر و خیال / در نیابد ذاتِ ما را بی مثال. (به اهتمام: رینولد ألّین نیکُلْسون).

۲۰ ¦⟵برگ [اس:۵۴-ب].

۲۱ ¦⟵برگ [ایا:۴۲-الف].

۲۲ قس: همین کتاب: صف هفتم: سخن اندر چگونگی درجات ثواب، بندهای [§۱:۷] تا [§۱۰:۷].

۲۳ سورة الجاثیة (۴۵)، آیت ۲۱.

آن کسان کنیم که بگرویدند و کارهای نیکو کردند، برابر باشد مردگی و زندگی ایشان، بد حکمی است این که همی‌کنند». و چون اندر حال زندگی بدکردار و نیک‌کردار پدید نیامد و پس مرگ پدید نیاید بد حکمی باشد و خدای تعالی حکم بد نکند، قوله: أَلَيْسَ اللّٰهُ بِأَحْكَمِ الْحاكِمِينَ.[۲۴]

۲۴ سورة التين (۹۵)، آیت ۸.

صف بیست و هفتم

سخن اندر آنك چرا عقل و نفس به یك مرتبت نبدند[۱] اگر اصل ایشان امر بود و اندر آن عالم خلاف نبود؟[۲]

[§۱:۲۷] بباید دانستن که تفاوت میان چیزها از جهت نزدیکی گروهی از آن باشد به علّت خویش[۳] و دوری گروهی از علّت خویش.[۴] و هر چه به علّت نزدیك باشد قوی‌تر از آن باشد کز علّت خویش دورتر باشد.

[§۲:۲۷] و مثال این چنان است که مادر و پدر کودك قوی‌تر از کودك باشد بسبب آنك علّت ایشان همه نبات است و مادر و پدر به علّت خویش رسیده‌اند و از نبات همی توانند خوردن. و کودك که از نبات غذا نمی‌تواند کشیدن تا نخست مادرش از نبات بخورد و مر آن را شیر بگرداند و آن وقت به کودك برساند. پس آن کودك از علّت خویش کی نبات است دور است و مادرش میان او و میان علّت او میانجی است لاجرم ضعیف است و مادر و پدرش که به نبات رسیده‌اند قوی‌اند.

[§۳:۲۷] و چون کودك به کشیدن غذا از نبات به میانجی مادر قوی شود آن وقت میانجی از میان برخیزد و او همچون مادر و پدر خویش گردد.

[§۴:۲۷] و ما دانیم که علّت همه بودها کلمه باری سبحانه است و آن کلمه یکی است و معلول او بحقیقت بی‌هیچ میانجی یکی لازم آید تا باز به میانجی آن یكْ معلولْ دیگر معلولات پدید آیند.

---

۱ ایا: نسدند.

۲ قس: کتاب الینابیع، الینبوع الخامس والثلاثون (۳۵)، في أنّ أحداً لا یبلغ مرتبة العقل، ص ۸۱ تا ۸۲.

۳ ¦⟵برگ [اس:۵۵-الف].

۴ ¦⟵برگ [ایا:۴۲-ب].

[§۲۷:۵] برمثال درختی که [از][۵] تخمی پدید آید تا باز به میانجی آن درخت از آن تخم شاخهای[۶] بسیار و برگها و بارها پدید آید.

[§۲۷:۶] پس آن نخستین معلول عقل بود که قوّت علّت خویش بی میانجی بتمامی پذیرفت. و نفس از کلمه به میانجی عقل پدید آمد.

[§۲۷:۷] پس خلافی نیست اندر آن که آنچ پدید آمدن او از چیزی دیگر بذات او باشد شریفتر از آن چیز باشد که پدید آمدن او از چیزی دیگر به میانجی دیگر باشد.

[§۲۷:۸] و هرچند که اندر آن عالم خلافی نیست و آرام عقل و نفس بر کلمه باری است، نام دومی از بهر آن بر ایشان اوفتاده است که نفس فایده‌پذیر است و عقل فایده‌دهنده است. و اگر نه چنین بودی نام دومی[۷] بر ایشان نیوفتادی و هر دو خود یکی بودندی.

[§۲۷:۹] و اندر مردم خود این دو چیز موجود است که جز بدان نامها و معنیها مر ایشان را از یکدیگر نتوان شناختن. و آن آن است کی هر مردمی را نفسی است که همی دانشی جوید و به نگاهبانی حاجتمند است و آن نگاهبان و دانش‌آموزِ او عقل است، که چون نفس بر خویشتن[۸] سالاری کردن گیرد وز جایگاهِ مخاطرهٔ نادانی پرهیزیدن گیرد گویند عاقل شد.[۹]

[§۲۷:۱۰] و عقل را جز به نفس پدید آمدن نیست و فعل نفس جز به جسد پیدا نشود.

[§۲۷:۱۱] پس این سه مرتبت به یکدیگر پیوسته است که پیدا شدن فعل نفس

۵ تصحیح قیاسی.

۶ اس: شاخها.

۷ ایا: دوی.

۸ ¦⟵برگ [ایا:۴۳-الف].

۹ ¦⟵برگ [اس:۵۵-ب].

از راه جسد است و پیدا شدن اثر عقل بر نفس است و عقل را با جسد پیوستگی نیست بی‌میانجی نفس، همچنانك از یکی سه پدید نیاید مگر به میانجی دو.

[۱۲:۲۷§] و چون نفس مردم بی‌عقل ناتمام و خوار است دانیم که اندر عالم علوی همین حال موجود است و نفس به عقل حاجتمند است.

صف بیست و هشتم

سخن اندر عقل که او هستِ نخست است[۱]

[§۱:۲۸] دلیل بر آنك عقل نخست چیز است کز جود باری سبحانه پیدا شده است هم از کتاب خدای است و هم از خبر رسول، علیه السّلام، و هم از اتفاقِ حکماء شریعی و حکماء[۲] علم آلهی و از شهادت عقلهای[۳] جزوی.

[§۲:۲۸] اما دلیل از کتاب خدای تعالی بر آنك عقل نخستین پدیدآمده است از جود باری سبحانه آن است کی همی‌گوید، قوله: هُوَ الَّذِي خَلَقَكُمْ مِنْ تُرابٍ ثُمَّ مِنْ نُطْفَةٍ ثُمَّ مِنْ عَلَقَةٍ ثُمَّ يُخْرِجُكُمْ طِفْلاً ثُمَّ لِتَبْلُغُوا أَشُدَّكُمْ ثُمَّ لِتَكُونُوا شُيُوخاً وَ مِنْكُمْ مَنْ يُتَوَفّٰى مِنْ قَبْلُ وَ لِتَبْلُغُوا أَجَلاً مُسَمًّى وَ لَعَلَّكُمْ تَعْقِلُونَ.[۴] همی‌گوید: «خدای شما را بیافرید از خاك، پس از آب اندك، پس از خون بسته، پس بیرون آوردتان کودك خرد تا برسید به نیرویِ سخت خویش، پس تا بباشید پیران و از شما کس است کز پیش بمیرد و تا برسید به وقتی نامزد کرده مگر که عقل را بیابید».

[§۳:۲۸] این همه احوال مردم را یاد کرد و به آخر گفت مگر به عقل برسید ازبهرآنك اصل آفرینش از عقل رفته بود. و چاره نیست از بازگشتن مر چیزی را کز چیزی پدید آید به آخِر کار از آنچ ازو پدید آمده باشد. پس گفتار خدای به آخِر کار که «مگر شما مر عقل را بیابید» همی دلالت کند که نخست پدیدآمده‌ای[۵] عقل بوده است، [و] به آخر پدیدآمده‌ای،[۶] کی مردم است، به آخرِ کار خویش همی بدو خواهد رسیدن.

---

۱ قس: کتاب الینابیع، الینبوع الخامس (۵): في أنّ العقل الأوّل مُبدَع، ص ۲۲ تا ۲۴.

۲ ایا: حکمای.

۳ ایا: عقلای.

۴ سورة غافر (۴۰)، آیت ۶۷.

۵ اس، ایا: پدیدآمده‌ء.

۶ اس، ایا: پدیدآمده‌ء.

[§۴:۲۸] برمثال درختی[۷] کز خرمادانه‌ای[۸] باشد پدیدآمده[۹] و بتمامی آن درخت آن باشد که اندر خرما[۱۰] کزو پدید آید دانهٔ[۱۱] او به مغز آکنده شود تا آخر درخت به اوّل درخت بازگردد. و هرکه از عقل به میانجی حدود دین حق فایده پذیرد به آخر بدو بازگردد.

[§۵:۲۸] و اما دلیل از خبر رسول، صلی[۱۲] الله علیه وآله، بر پیشیِ هست شدنِ عقل پیش از دیگر هستها آن است که فرمود: أَوَّل ما خَلَقَ اللّهُ تعالی اَلْعَقْلُ فَقَالَ لَهُ أَقْبِلْ فَأَقْبَلَ ثُمَّ قَالَ لَهُ أَدْبِرْ فَأَدْبَرَ[۱۳] فَقَالَ وَ عِزَّتِي وَ جَلَالِي مَا خَلَقْتُ خَلْقاً أَعِزُّ عَلَيَّ مِنْكَ بِكَ أُثِيبُ وَ بِكَ أُعَاقِبُ. گفت: «نخستین چیزی که خدای بیافرید عقل بود. مر او را گفت پیش آی پیش آمد؛ پس گفت بازپس شو بازپس شد. پس خدای تعالی سوگند یاد کرد به عزّ و جلال خویش که چیزی نیافریدم گرامی‌تر بر من از تو. به تو ثواب دهم و به تو عقاب کنم».[۱۴]

[§۶:۲۸] و اندر دین حق همچنین است، هرکه عقل را کار بندد اندر پرستش خدای و عبادت بر بصیرت کند به ثواب ابدی رسد و هرکه عقل را ضایع کند و کار بی‌دانش کند به آتش جاویدی رسد.

---

۷ اس: [پس از «درختی» به اندازه یك یا دو کلمه متن محو شده است].

۸ اس، ایا: خرمادانهء.

۹ اس، ایا: پدید آید [کذا]. || تصحیح قیاسی.

۱۰ ¦←برگ [اس:۵۶-الف].

۱۱ ¦←برگ [ایا:۴۳-ب].

۱۲ اس: صل.

۱۳ اس: فاذْربر.

۱۴ نك: الکلینی، محمد بن یعقوب، الکافي، تصحیح: علی اکبر غفاری و محمد آخوندی (تهران، ۱۴۰۷ق)، ج ۱، کِتَابُ الْعَقْلِ وَ الْجَهْلِ، ص ۱۰ و ۲۰. نیز نك: المؤیَّد في الدين الشيرازی، المجالس المؤيَّديَّة، تحقیق و تقدیم: مصطفی غالب (بیروت، ۱۹۷۴)، المجلس الأوّل من المِائة الأُولی، ص ۶. قس: المجلسی، محمّد باقر، بحار الأنوار، تصحیح: س. ا. المیانجی و م. ب. البهبودی (بیروت: دار إحیاء التراث العربي، ۱۴۰۳ق/۱۹۸۳م)، ج ۱، باب ۲: حقيقة العقل وكيفيته وبدو خلقه، ص ۹۶ تا ۹۹.

[§۷:۲۸] و اما دلیل از شهادت عقلهای جزوی بر آنك عقل کلّی نخست پدیدآورده است به جود باری سبحانه آن است که موجودات بجملگی از دو گونه است یا محیط است یا محاط.

[§۸:۲۸] و محیط آن باشد که به گرد چیزی دیگر اندرآمده باشد یا بذات یا به شرف. و محاط آن چیزی باشد که زیر چیزی دیگر اندر باشد بذات یا به فرومایگی.

[§۹:۲۸] امّا محیط بذات چنان باشد که آسمان است که محیط زمین است که ذات آسمان به گرد ذات زمین اندرآمده است. و محاط بذات چنان باشد که زمین است که محاط آسمان است که زیر او اندر مانده است به همه رویها.

[§۱۰:۲۸] امّا محیط به شرف چنان باشد که نفس است محیط جسد که نفس مر جسد را پاکیزه و شریف و آبادان همی‌دارد و از پراکنده شدن نگاهبان او گشته است.

[§۱۱:۲۸] که اگر نفس عنایت خویش از جسد بازگیرد جسد بمیرد و پلید شود و خوار گردد و ویران بباشد و پراکنده شود. و همچنین مردم به شرف محیط است بر حیوان و حیوان محاط است مردم را به فرومایگی.

[§۱۲:۲۸] و هر محیطی شریفتر از محاط خویش باشد؛[۱۵] و هر چه او شریفتر باشد بودش او پیش از آن باشد کزو کمتر باشد[۱۶] به شرف.

[§۱۳:۲۸] وگر محیط را وجود پیش از محاط نبودی، محیط نگشتی بر محاط.

[§۱۴:۲۸] وگر نخست وجود مر محاط را بودی آن وقت مر محیط را، بایستی که نخست مر محاط را یافتیمی آن وقت مر محیط را.

---

۱۵ ¦←برگ [اس:۵۶-ب].

۱۶ ¦←برگ [ایا:۴۴-الف].

[§۱۵:۲۸] و ما نخست مر عقل را همی‌یابیم تا بدو مر چیزها را اندر یابیم؛ و تا عقل را نیابیم بر چیزها محیط نشویم.

[§۱۶:۲۸] دلیل همی‌کند این حال که عقل محیط است و چون محیط است وجود او پیشتر از وجود هر محاطی بوده است. و چون ما به عقل بر چیزها محیط شدیم، حکم کردیم بر پیشی هست شدن او.

[§۱۷:۲۸] و ممکن نیست توهّم کردن چیزی را از چیزها که عقل يك راه بر آن محیط شود و يك راه نه محیط باشد برو.

[§۱۸:۲۸] پس گوییم که آن توهّم یا عقلی باشد یا نباشد. اگر عقلی باشد عقل بر آن محیط باشد؛ وگر نه عقلی باشد اندر چیزی وهمی نتوان رسیدن مگر از جهت عقل.

[§۱۹:۲۸] و نیز گوییم که جوهری که به علّتش نزدیکتر باشد محیط بود بر آن جوهر که علّتش دورتر بود. و عقل نزدیکتر جوهری است به علّت همه علّتها. پس واجب آید که عقل محیط باشد بر همه گوهرهای جسمانی و روحانی.

[§۲۰:۲۸] و ایزد تعالی برتر است از محیط و محاط. تَعَالَى اللّٰهُ عَنْ ذٰلِكَ عُلُوًّا كَبِيراً.[۱۷]

[§۲۱:۲۸] و دیگر که عقل مانند است به یکی که اوّل شمار است، و هیچ چیز از عدد بر یکی پیشی ندارد، بلك هستی همه شمارها از یکی است.

[§۲۲:۲۸] همچنین عقل اوّلْ یکی است و ذات همه ‹معقولات است؛ پس معقولات›[۱۸] همه از عقل وجود یافته است، همچنانك شمارها همه از یکی پدید آمده است.

---

۱۷ اشارت به سورة الإسراء (۱۷)، آیت ۴۳: سُبْحٰانَهُ وَ تَعٰالىٰ عَمّٰا يَقُولُونَ عُلُوًّا كَبِيراً.

۱۸ اس، ایا: معلولاتست پس معلولات [كذا]. [در نسخهٔ اس حرف «ل»، در هردو کلمه، پس از حرف «ع» احتمالاً تحریف شده و به نظر میرسد ابتدا «ق» بوده و بعداً به هر دلیل پاك

[§۲۸:۲۳] و همه عددها نام یکی دارد چون یك هزار و صد هزار، و بیش و کم نام یکی بر همه افتاده است. و آغاز شمارها همه از یکی باشد و انجامش نیز به یکی باشد.

[§۲۸:۲۴] همچنین پدیدآمدن همه چیزها از عقل است و باز عقل بر همه چیزها محیط است و محیط بودن عقل بر چیزها گوایی همی‌دهد که همه چیزها ازو پدید آمده است که عقل است.

[§۲۸:۲۵] و همچنانك یکی[۱۹] بدان قوّت که اندر او است مر شمارها را مادّت دهد تا بسیار شود، شمارهای عقل نیز بقوّت خویش مادّت دهد تا معقولات بسیار شود.[۲۰]

[§۲۸:۲۶] و ایزد تعالی وصف کرد امر خویش را که بدان آفرید همه مبدعات[۲۱] و مخلوقات را به کلمه کن؛ و این خطاب خدای است و خطاب را جوهری خطاب‌پذیر واجب آید.

[§۲۸:۲۷] و محال باشد که ایزد تعالی خطاب کند با چیزی که آن چیز خطاب ایزد

شده است و روی آن «ل» نوشته شده است. همچنین مقایسه این بخش با کتاب‌الینابیع نشان میدهد که کلمه «معقولات» درست است]. نك: یادداشت [۲۰] ذیل بند [§۲۸:۲۵].

۱۹ ایا: - یکی.

۲۰ ¦⟵برگ [اس:۵۷-الف]. || قس: کتاب الینابیع، ص ۲۳ تا ۲۴، بند (۳۹). وأیضاً فانّ العقل یشبه الواحد الذی هو أوّل الأعداد، ولم یسبقه شیء من الأعداد، لا من الأفراد ولا من الأزواج، بل الأعداد کلّها انّما تتکثّر من الواحد وبالواحد. و کذالك العقل واحد، وهو الذات لجمیع المعقولات. ثمّ تتکثّر المعقولات من العقل وبالعقل. وهکذا الکثرة العددیّة ترجع کلّها الی الواحد الجامع لأجزائها، فانّها في الألف والعشرة آلاف عدد واحد. وکذالك ما بعد الألف وقبلها: کلّ عدد انّما هو عدد واحد، وان کانت الکثرة فیه موجودة. کذالك جمیع المعقولات ترجع کلّها الی معرفة واحدة عقلیّة. فاذًا کان العقل شبیه الواحد من هذه الجهات، بل الواحد العددیّ افاضته علی الأعداد. ثمّ وجدت الواحد علّة الأعداد وأوّلها، لم یسبقه شیء من الأعداد؛ والأحری والأولی أن یکون العقل أوّل المعلولات* وعلّة لم یسبقه شیء منها، فاعرفه. || [* نك: یادداشت شماره [۴] در ترجمه انگلیسی همین بند از کتاب خوان الاخوان].

۲۱ ¦⟵برگ [ایا:۴۴-ب].

نداند. و خطاب نه روا باشد مگر با جوهری که خطاب شناسد. پس گوییم که آن جوهر خطاب شناس عقل است که توانای پذیرفتن امر باری است.[۲۲]

[§۲۸:۲۸] و چون امر ایزد به پیدا کردن عالم طبیعت رسید، مضاف کرد، اعنی بازبسته کرد، آفرینش عالم طبیعی را با آفرینش تقدیری.[۲۳]

[§۲۸:۲۹] و آفرینش تقدیری به منزلت فرود از آفرینش ابداعی است.

[§۲۸:۳۰] نبینی[۲۴] که مر آفرینش آسمانها و زمین را «کن» نگفت مگر گفت، قوله: خَلَقَ السَّمٰاوٰاتِ وَ الْأَرْضَ وَ جَعَلَ الظُّلُمٰاتِ وَ النُّورَ.[۲۵] و اکنون گفت: «بیافرید آسمانها و زمین را و بکرد تاریکیها و روشنایی را».

[§۲۸:۳۱] از بهرآنك مر آسمانها و زمین را طاقت پذیرفتن فرمان نبود.

[§۲۸:۳۲] و همچنین بازبسته کرد آفرینش جسدهای ما را به آفرینش تقدیری و

۲۲ نك: جامع الحکمتین، فصل ۱: اندر ذکر سبب تصنیف کتاب و نام او، ص ۱۲، بند (۱۶): و هر که اعتقاد چنان دارد کز چرائی و چگونگی آفرینش تفحّص بباید کردن، آنکس مر نفس ناطقهٔ علم جوی را و نیز بر حیوانات زمینی مسلّطست بتسلیط الهی، تا همه را بندگان خویش کرده است و مردم نیز بدین نفسْ سزاوارِ خطابِ خدای تعالی شدست. موکّل است — اعنی نفسِ سخن گوی — بتوکیل الهی بر تجسّس از آنچ بیند و شنود از مکیّنات کآن چونست، و از مقولات* که معنی آن چیست.

|| * نك: دهخدا: - مقولات عشر: (اصطلاح فلسفی) یک جوهر و نه عرض، پس افراد جوهر پنج است یکی جسم دوم هیولی سوم صورت چهارم نفس ناطقه پنجم عقل یعنی ملائکه. و نه عرض این است: اول کیف، دوم کم، سوم اَیْن، چهارم مَتیٰ، پنجم اضافت، ششم وضع، هفتم فعل، هشتم انفعال، نهم ملک.

۲۳ نك: جامع الحکمتین، فصل ۲۰: ‹اندر اِبداع›، ص ۲۱۰ تا ۲۱۱: اگر بخواهم از تو دلیل بر اِبداع / چه آوری که عیانم بدو کنی اخبار؟! چه چیز بود نه از چیز، چون نمایی چیز؟ / چگونه دانی کرد آشکاره این اسرار؟!... ابداع گویند و اختراع گویند مر پدید آوردن چیز را نه از چیز، و خلق گویند — یعنی آفریدن — مر تقدیر چیز را از چیز، چنانك درودگر از چوب تخت کند، و او خالق تخت باشد، و مُبدِعِ صورت تخت باشد، و مردم را بر ابداع جسم قدرت نیست.

۲۴ اس، ایا: نه بینی.

۲۵ سورة الأنعام (۶)، آیت ۱: الْحَمْدُ لِلّٰهِ الَّذِي خَلَقَ السَّمٰاوٰاتِ وَ الْأَرْضَ وَ جَعَلَ الظُّلُمٰاتِ وَ النُّورَ ثُمَّ الَّذِينَ كَفَرُوا بِرَبِّهِمْ يَعْدِلُونَ.

گفت، قوله: هُوَ الَّذِي خَلَقَكُمْ مِنْ تُرَابٍ.[۲۶] گفت: «او آن است که تقدیر کرد شما را از خاك».

[§۲۸:۳۳] و چون ما طاقت پذیرفتن فرمان نداشتیم، به اوّل آفرینش ما را[۲۷] کن نگفت.

[§۲۸:۳۴] و همچنین رسول، صلی[۲۸] الله علیه وآله، خطاب نکرد با کودکان که عقل نداشتند.

[§۲۸:۳۵] و چون عقل اندر ما پیدا شد و معرفت توحید و معرفت رسالت بیافتیم سزاوار امر و نهی گشتیم.

[§۲۸:۳۶] پس این حال که شرح کرده شد، از واجب ناشدن فرمان خدای پیش از یافتن عقل، همی دلیل کند که این کن که فرمان خدای بود ازو تعالی واجب نیامد، مگر آن وقت که پذیرای آن امر موجود شده بود.

[§۲۸:۳۷] و نیز دلیل است، که این برهانها که نمودیم، که پذیرندهٔ کن از خدای تعالی جز عقل نبود و هیچ چیز از مبدعات بر عقل پیشی نداشت.

[§۲۸:۳۸] پاك است آن خدایی که عقل را ابداع کرد بدین شرف و جلالت؛ و مُبدِع حقّ یگانه است از صفات مبدعات خویش.

[§۲۸:۳۹] ازین شریفتر سخن چون توان گفتن اندر اثبات صانع که ما گفتیم اندر صفت عقل؟

[§۲۸:۴۰] و چون آفریده بدین شرف[۲۹] باشد که عقل اوّل است، و آفریدگار از

---

۲۶ سورهٔ غافر(۴۰)، آیت ۶۷.

۲۷ ایا: – را.

۲۸ اس، ایا: صل.

۲۹ ¦←برگ [ایا:۴۵-الف].

صفات[۳۰] مبدَع و ابداع منزّه کرده باشد، سخن گوینده بغایت کمال باشد اندر[۳۱] توحید.

[§۴۱:۲۸] و آن کس کی بدین علم دانا باشد توحیدش مجرّد باشد از تشبیه و تعطیل.

[§۴۲:۲۸] کجا اَند آن ملحدان و دهریان[۳۲] کی بر اهل دیانت و مذهب حقیقت دروغ گویند، و دعوی کنند بشیعت خاندان؟

[§۴۳:۲۸] باثبات صانع نگویند و وهم اندر دل ضعفاء دیانت افکنند، و اهل حقّ را بچشم نادانان زشت کنند. و آنچ اندر ما گویند ایشان خود بدان صفت اند.

[§۴۴:۲۸] و شکر خدای را و اولیای او را که ما را بر ره‌نمائی اولیاء خویش از نعمت ابدی و اسرار آلهی نصیب کرد.[۳۳]

---

۳۰ ¦⟵برگ [اس:۵۷-ب].

۳۱ اس: [حرف «ن» در کلمه «اندر» مخدوش است].

۳۲ نك: جامع الحکمتین، فصل ۳: اندر اثبات صانع و ذکر توحید او سبحانه، و در آن قولهاست، ص ۳۱، بند (۲۵): گوییم جملگی خلق با بسیاری اخلاق و اعتقادات ایشان بدو فرقت اند. یکی فرقت دهریان اند که اهل تعطیل اند و گویند: عالم قدیم است و مر او را صانع نیست بل صانع موالید از نبات و حیوان خِرَدِ افلاك و انجم است که همیشه بودست و همیشه باشد.

۳۳ ایا: + لله الحمد و المنة.

صف بیست و نهم

سخن اندر آنك پیش از عقل توهّم چیزی کردن محال است[1]

[§۱:۲۹] از طریق هندسه بازنماییم که پیش از عقل چیز نیست. و گوییم که هرکجا دو چیز برابر شوند، یا هردو به بزرگی چَندِ یکدیگر باشند یا یکی از دیگری بزرگتر باشد. و چون درست شود که یکی از آن دو چیز از یار خویش بزرگتر نیست، و نیز کهتر ازو نیست، درست شده باشد کی همچند او است.

[§۲:۲۹] و مثال کنیم مر این قول را بدین دو خط یکی خط الف و دیگر خط با. و گوییم اگر خط الف همچند خطّ با نیست و بزرگتر از خط با نیز نیست ناچاره خطّ الف کهتر از خط با باشد؛ وگر خط الف بزرگتر [یا کهتر][2] از خط با نیست، ناچاره خط الف همچند خط با باشد.

[§۳:۲۹] و چون این مقدّمه هندسی که گفتیم، گوییم که ما چیزهای بسیار همی یابیم چه از معقول و چه از محسوس و چیزها را همی‌بینیم کز یکدیگر پدید همی‌آیند چون حیوان از نبات و نبات از طبایع.

[§۴:۲۹] پس چاره نیست که یك چیز پیش از همه چیزها بوده است پدیدآمده تا دیگر چیزها ازو پدید آمده است. و چون عقل را بر چیزها جاکول همی‌یابیم بدانستیم که عقل است آنچ پیش از همه چیزها بوده است.

[§۵:۲۹] پس اگر کسی گوید که 'پیش از عقل چه بود و چرا روا نباشد که پیش از عقل چیز باشد؟' گوییم که 'هرچه[3] خواهی[4] از موجودات اختیار کن'. و آتش را بگیریم، و گوییم که 'چرا روا نباشد که آتش پیش از عقل باشد؟'

---

۱ قس: کتاب الینابیع، الینبوع السادس (۶): في أن قبل العقل الأوّل لایتوهّم شیء البتّةً، ص ۲۵.

۲ تصحیح قیاسی.

۳ ¦←برگ [ایا:۴۵-ب].

۴ ¦←برگ [اس:۵۸-الف].

[§۶:۲۹] پس گوییم که عقل موجودی است و آتش نیز موجودی است؛ اگر گوییم که آتش پیش از عقل بود، پس بایستی که به آتش عقل را کاربستیمی نه به عقل مر آتش را کار فرمودیم،[۵] چنین که همی‌فرماییم. پس درست شد که آتش پیش از عقل نبوده است.

[§۷:۲۹] پس اگر گوید با عقل برابر بوده است، گوییم چون چیزها از چیزی همی‌پدید آید روا نبود که همه چیزها از دو چیز پدید آید، کی اگر روا بودی که چیزها از دو چیز بودی، نیز روا بودی که همه چیزها بیکبار موجود بودی.

[§۸:۲۹] و چون همی‌یابیم که چیزی از چیزی همی پدید آید لازم گشت دانستن که چیز نخستین نه از چیزی پدید آمد، بضرورت که اگر جز چنین گویی موجودات روا نبودی که پدید آمدی.

[§۹:۲۹] پس گفتیم که آن چیز که نه از چیز پدید آمد یکی بود. پس درست شد که آتش با عقل برابر نبود. و چون آتش پیش از عقل نبود و با عقل برابر نبود درست شد که عقل پیش از آتش بود.

[§۱۰:۲۹] و نیز گوییم که پیش از عقل چیز چگونه اندر وهم آید و همه چیزها چیزی به عقل یافتند؟ و بتازی مر چیز را شیء گویند و مر چیزی را شیئیّت گویند، و همه چیزها بدین قول خود عقل باشد از بهر آنك چیزها چیزی از عقل یافتند.

[§۱۱:۲۹] پس چگونه پیش از چیزی چیز باشد؟ وگر[۶] پیش از چیزی که به تازی آن شیئیت است چیز روا باشد همچنان باشد که پیش از ذات خویش چیزی موجود باشد و این محال بود توهّم کردن.

[§۱۲:۲۹] و ایزد تعالی مر عقل را گفت[۷] بر همه چیزها قادر است چنانك به

۵ ایا: فرمودیمی.

۶ ایا: و اگر.

۷ اس: [«گفت» مخدوش است].

بسیار جای اندر قرآن همی‌گوید، قوله: إِنَّ اللَّهَ عَلَىٰ كُلِّ شَيْءٍ قَدِيرٌ.[۸] گوید: «خدای بر همه چیزها قادر است». و بدان مر عقل را همی‌خواهد که همه چیزها زیر او است.

[§۱۳:۲۹] و هر خردمند که معنی این قول که خدای تعالی به چند جای بازگفته است اندر کتاب خویش[۹] بداند مقدار خویش بشناسد و نفس او توهّم نکند باری را سبحانه اندر یابد، که این کفر و شرك باشد.

[§۱۴:۲۹] بل‌که[۱۰] هرکه گمان برد که او باری را، سبحانه، دانسته است[۱۱] دعوی کرده باشد که او از خدای برتر است!

[§۱۵:۲۹] پس بباید دانستن که بر[۱۲] عقل هیچ چیز را به توانایی و جاکول شدن نیست. و پدیدآرندهٔ عقل مر عقل را نه از چیزی برو پادشا است بدین صنع لطیف.

[§۱۶:۲۹] و بباید دانستن که ابداع که مُبدَع اوّل بدان پدید آورده شده است چیزی نیست.

[§۱۷:۲۹] ازبهرآنك اگر ابداع چیزی باشد، با مُبدَع چیزی دیگر برابر باشد یا پیش ازو، و آن وقت عقل نه مبدَع باشد ازبهرآنك مبدَع چیزی باشد نه از چیزی دیگر.

[§۱۸:۲۹] وگر [با][۱۳] او یا پیش ازو چیزی بودی این نام مُبدَع مر مُبدَع را دروغ بودی.

---

۸ مجموعاً در هشت آیت: سورة البقرة (۲)، آیات ۲۰، ۱۰۹، ۱۴۸؛ سورة آل عمران (۳)، آیت ۱۶۵؛ سورة النحل (۱۶)، آیت ۷۷؛ سورة النور (۲۴)، آیت ۴۵؛ سورة العنکبوت (۲۹)، آیت ۲۰؛ سورة فاطر (۳۵)، آیت ۱.

۹ ¦←برگ [ایا:۴۶-الف].

۱۰ ایا: بلك.

۱۱ ¦←برگ [اس:۵۸-ب].

۱۲ اس: [«بر» مخدوش است].

۱۳ تصحیح قیاسی.

[§۲۹:۱۹] وگر با مُبدِع چیزی بودی، مُبدَع چیزی بودی آفریده از آنچ با او پیش ازو چیزی بود که او را ازو آفریده بودند، و نیز چیزی بودی ناآفریده، بدانچ مُبدَع آن باشد که او نه از چیزی باشد.

[§۲۹:۲۰] و این چنان باشد که کسی گوید من نشستهٔ ایستاده دیدم[۱۴] و این متناقض باشد و متناقض دروغ باشد.

[§۲۹:۲۱] پس درست شد که ابداع چیزی نیست، وگر پیش از مُبدَع چیزی بودی، از دو بیرون نبودی: یا مُبدَع بودی نه از چیز پدیدآمده، یا چیزی بودی از چیزی پدیدآمده.

[§۲۹:۲۲] و این چیزی باشد کز پیشِ چیزی باشد و باز همی‌شود از چیزی به‌چیزی دیگر، تا از نهایت بشود، و این محال باشد اندر عقل. پس بدین برهان که نمودیم پیش از عقل چیزی نه روا باشد.[۱۵]

[§۲۹:۲۳] و نیز گوییم که چیز[ی][۱۶] ذاتی باشد از جملهٔ ذاتها. و ذاتها بر دو گونه است یا محسوسات است یا معقولات. و هستی محسوس به حس درست شود و هستی معقول به عقل درست شود.

[§۲۹:۲۴] و چیزی که حس مر او را نتواند یافتن مر او را به عقل یابند و موهوم باشد.[۱۷] پس چیزیِ معقولات به عقل است و چون زیر عقل اندرنیاید نه محسوس

۱۴ اس: [«دیدم» مخدوش است].

۱۵ قس: کتاب الینابیع، الینبوع السادس (۶): في أن قبل العقل الأوّل لایتوهّم شیء البتّةً، ص ۲۵، بند (۴۲)، س ۴ تا ۱۳.

۱۶ تصحیح قیاسی. نك: کتاب الینابیع، الینبوع السادس (۶): في أن قبل العقل الأوّل لایتوهّم شیء البتّةً، ص ۲۵، بند (۴۳)، س ۱۴ تا ۱۸: وأیضاً فانّ معنی الشیئیة انّما هو اثبات لذات مّا، ثم وجدت الذواتُ امّا محسوسة وامّا معقولة. فشیئیّة المحسوسات ثباتها بالحسّ، وما لم یثبته الحسّ، فثباته في العقل موهوم، فشیئیّة المعقولات اذًا بالعقل. وما جاز العقل، فلا ثبات له البتّةً لا محسوسًا ولا موهومًا. و ما لا ثبات له محسوساً و<لا> موهومًا، فشیئیّته اذًا غیر موجودة. فاعرفه.

۱۷ نك: دهخدا: موهوم. [مَ] (عربی صفت) پنداشته. ... توهم شده. خیال شده. تصورشده.

باشد[۱۸] و نه موهوم. و آنچ نه اندر حس آید و نه اندر عقل او نه چیز باشد و نه موجود.[۱۹]

گمان شده. || هرچیزی که وجود خارجی نداشته باشد.

۱۸ ¦⟵برگ [ایا:۴۶-ب].

۱۹ ¦⟵برگ [اس:۵۹-الف].

صف سی‌ام

سخن اندر آنك نفس بذات خویش مرکّب است

[§۳۰:۱] نفس تا ترکیب نپذیرد با هستی نیاید؛ و ترکیب او به مادّت عقل است.

[§۳۰:۲] و دلیل بر درستی این دعوی آن است کی نفس کلّ چون از عقل کلّ مادّت یافت اندر ذات خویش مادّت‌پذیر بود. و آنچ مادّت‌پذیر باشد مرکّب باشد. و چون از عقل مادّت یافت خداوند ترکیب آمد.

[§۳۰:۳] و نفس جزوی تا با عقل مرکّب نشد از خدای تعالی مخاطبه نیافت. نبینی[۱] کی خدای تعالی[۲] همی‌گوید، قوله: فَاعْتَبِرُوا يٰا أُولِي الْأَبْصٰارِ.[۳] همی‌گوید: «اندازه گیرید ای خداوندان چشمها».

[§۳۰:۴] یعنی خردمندان. و هر نفسی که با عقل جفت ‹بشود عَوْد›[۴] برو نیوفتد. و نفس خردمند چون به عقل مرکّب گشت از حکم قیاس لازم آید که به وزن بیش از نفسِ بیخرد است.

[§۳۰:۵] و میان مردمان رونده است که خردمند را گران‌سنگ و گرانمایه خوانند. و بیخرد را سبکسار و سبك‌مایه گویند. از بهر آنك آن یکی با خرد جفت است و این دیگر از خرد تنها است.

[§۳۰:۶] و درست کند مر این دعوی را قول خدای تعالی که میفرماید، قوله: فَأَمّٰا مَنْ ثَقُلَتْ مَوٰازِينُهُ * فَهُوَ فِي عِيشَةٍ رٰاضِيَةٍ * وَ أَمّٰا مَنْ خَفَّتْ مَوٰازِينُهُ * فَأُمُّهُ هٰاوِيَةٌ.[۵]

---

۱ اس، ایا: نه‌بینی.

۲ اس، ایا: تع.

۳ سورة الحشر (۵۹)، آیت ۲.

۴ اس: بشود عرد [کذا]؛ ایا: نشود عدد [کذا]. || مبنی بر فحواء آیت ۹۴ از سورة الأنعام(۶) که در بندهایِ بعدی متن آمده است، و همچنین سبك و سیاق رسم الخط نسخهٔ استانبول، این تصحیح انجام شد.

۵ سورة القارعة (۱۰۱) ، آیات ۶ تا ۹.

همی‌گوید: «هرکه گران شود ترازوهای او وی اندر زیستنی پسندیده است و هر که سبك شود ترازوهای او جای او دوزخ است».

[§۳۰:۷] و اندر حال ظاهر پیدا است که نفس کسی که با خرد جفت است، آهستگی و آرام که نشان گرانی و ترکیب است، اندر آن کس پدید آمده است. و نفس کسی کز خرد بهره و ترکیب ندارد بی‌آرام و بی‌ثبات مانده است.

[§۳۰:۸] پس درست شد که نفسِ تمامْ اندر ذات خویش مرکّب است به عقل، و تا به عقل ترکیب نپذیرد هستی نیابد. و هر نفسی که با عقل مرکّب‌ناشده بدان[۶] عالم بازگردد از بدبختان باشد بقول خدای تعالی، قوله: وَ لَقَدْ جِئْتُمُونٰا فُرٰادیٰ کَمٰا خَلَقْنٰاکُمْ أَوَّلَ مَرَّةٍ وَ تَرَکْتُمْ مٰا خَوَّلْنٰاکُمْ وَرٰاءَ ظُهُورِکُمْ.[۷] همی‌گوید: «اندر خطاب با بدبختان روز قیامت که بیامدید سوی ما تنها همچنانك بیافریدیم با نخستین بار و دست بازداشتید آنچ شما را داده بودیم سپس پشت خویش».

[§۳۰:۹] این آیت همی دلیل کند که جز این[۸] کی نفس را به عقل همی ترکیب باید کردن به دلالت خداوند دَور خویش و راهنمایان[۹] خلق از فرزندان او، و نفس را همچنان بی‌خرد تنها بدان عالم نباید بردن،[۱۰] خداوندان حقّ را [به][۱۱] منکر شدن به حق ایشان از پس پشت نباید داشتن.

[§۳۰:۱۰] که معنی علم ناپذیرفتن ازو آن باشد که او را از پس پشت کرده باشی؛

---

۶ ¦⟵برگ [ایا:۴۷-الف].

۷ سورة الأنعام (۶)، آیت ۹۴.

۸ ¦⟵برگ [اس:۵۹-ب].

۹ اس: راه نمایان.

۱۰ اس، ایا: + و. || تصحیح قیاسی.

۱۱ تصحیح قیاسی.

کی هر چه از پس پشت مردم باشد مردم ‹مر او را›[۱۲] نبیند[۱۳] ‹و هر چه›[۱۴] به چیزی بنگرد مر او را نبیند[۱۵] و مر آن را سپس پشت کرده باشد.

۱۲ اس: مرو را؛ ایا: ورا.

۱۳ اس، ایا: نه بیند.

۱۴ ایا: هر که جه [کلمه «که» با جوهرشنگرف نوشته شده است].

۱۵ اس، ایا: نه بیند.

صف سی و یکم

سخن اندر ریاست نفس ناطقه بر نفس حسی

[§۱:۳۱] قاعدهٔ آفرینش ای برادر اندر لطایف و کثایف چنان است کی لطایف پیش از کثایف بوده است.

[§۲:۳۱] لاجرم اندر زایشهای[1] عالم لطایف اندر آخر بودش هر زایشی پدیدآید و کثایف اندر اوّل آن پدید آید.

[§۳:۳۱] چنانك اندر زایش بودنیهای رستنیها نخست شاخ و برگ و خار پدید آید که کثیف است و به آخِرِ کار از نبات بار پدید آید که لطیف است.

[§۴:۳۱] و بار درخت را بر برگ و شاخ ریاستی پیدا است که همه فوایدها از درخت سوی او شود و پایداری و عزّ درخت به بار است.[2]

[§۳۱:۵] و همچنین است حال اندر جانوران که نخست جانوران سخن‌ناگوی بوده‌اند و آن وقت مردم آخرِ همه جانوران پدید آمده است و برهان این دعوی روشن کرده شده است اندر گشایش و رهایش که کرده‌ایم.

[§۶:۳۱] لاجرم مردم که به آخر[3] پدید آمده است رئیس و سالار همه جانوران است بفرمان خدای تعالی کی می‌فرماید، قوله: اللّٰهُ الَّذِي جَعَلَ لَكُمُ الْأَنْعَامَ لِتَرْكَبُوا مِنْهَا وَ مِنْهَا تَأْكُلُونَ * وَ لَكُمْ فِيهَا مَنَافِعُ وَ لِتَبْلُغُوا عَلَيْهَا حَاجَةً فِي صُدُورِكُمْ وَ عَلَيْهَا وَ

---

۱ اس: زایشها.

۲ نك: همین کتاب: صف ۲۸، بند [§۳:۲۸]: این همه احوال مردم را یاد کرد و به آخر گفت مگر به عقل برسید از بهر آنك اصل آفرینش از عقل رفته بود. و چاره نیست از بازگشتن مر چیزی را کز چیزی پدید آید به آخر کار از آنچ ازو پدید آمده باشد. پس گفتار خدای به آخر کار 'که مگر شما مر عقل را بیابید' همی دلالت کند که نخست پدیدآمده‌ای عقل بوده است، [و] به آخر پدیدآمده‌ای، کی مردم است، به آخرِ کار خویش همی بدو خواهد رسیدن. || قس: زادالمسافر، قول ۲۵، ص ۴۱۱ تا ۴۱۲.

۳ ¦⟵برگ [ایا:۴۷-ب].

عَلَى الْفُلْكِ تُحْمَلُونَ.[۴] همی گوید: «خدای آن است کز بهر شما ستوران آفرید تا ازو برنشینید و زو[۵] بخورید مر شما را اندر او فایده‌ها است و تا بر رسید[۶] بر ستوران به حاجتی که اندر دلهای شما است و بر ستور و بر کشتی برنشینید».[۷]

[§۷:۳۱] پس چون بدین آیت ریاست مردم بر ستوران همی پدید آید، ظاهر گشت که نفس ناطقه را، که مردم را بدان مخصوص است، بر نفس حسّی همان ریاست است کی مردم را بر ستور است.

[§۸:۳۱] و نیز چون نفس ناطقه فعل از کالبد مردم سپس از فعل نفس حسّی همی پدید کند[۸] دلیل همی‌کند که نفس ناطقه لطیف‌تر است و اندر بودش عالم وجود نفس ناطقه پیش از وجود نفس حسّی بوده است. و نفس ناطقه رئیس و مهتر است بر نفس حسّی.

[§۹:۳۱] و همچنین بدانچ نفس حسّی اندر کالبد مردم اثر خویش پیشتر از اثر نفس ناطقه همی پدید آرد، همی باید که نفس حسّی از مردم که او برمثال درختی روحانی است برمثال برگ و شاخ است کز درخت نخست او پدید آید و نفس ناطقه از مردم و درخت او به منزلت بار است که مراد نشانندهٔ درخت از درخت او است.

[§۱۰:۳۱] و گوییم که پیامبران، علیهم السّلام، اندر خلق مثال درخت خرما بوده‌اند که اندر خاك پیدا شود و هرچه خوشی و لطافت و شیرینی باشد اندر آن خاك بخویشتن کشد و جمله کند باز مر آن بار شیرین لطیف را بر زمین بباراند.

[§۳۱:۱۱] پس هر خاکی که بیخهای آن درخت مر آن را بپذیرد از درجهٔ خاکی به

---

۴ سورهٔ غافر (۴۰)، آیات ۷۹-۸۰.

۵ اس: [حرف «و» در کلمه «زو» (از او) با جوهر شنگرف اضافه شده است].

۶ اس: بر رسند.

۷ اس: بر نشیند.

۸ ¦⟵برگ [اس:۶۰-الف].

درجهٔ خرمایی رسد. و پس از آن که ستوران مر آن خاك را می‌سپردند به زیر پای، همان خاك بر طبقی زرّین به خوان پادشاهان[۹] رسد بقوّت آن درخت خرما که مر او را بپذیرفت.

[§۱۲:۳۱] چون خاك نادان بدانچ نزدیك آن درخت خرما بود و خویشتن را بدو داد از آن فرومایگی و خواری که بود بدین پرمایگی و عزیزی همی رسد، مردم سزاوارتر است که مر درخت خرمای[۱۰] خویش را که رسول دور او است و امام روزگار خویش را که درخت‌پرور است مطیع باشد.

[§۱۳:۳۱] و خویشتن به طاعت و فرمان‌برداری بدو سپارد تا از درجهٔ خاکی به درجهٔ خرمایی رسد و از خواری و ذل به عزّ و شادی رسد و شایسته شود مر خوان نفس‌کلّ را[۱۱] تا چون نفس‌کلّی مر او را از راه امام زمانه به غذای خویش کرده باشد از فنا و کثافت برهد و به بقا و لطافت رسد و جاودان[۱۲] اندر نعیم جاوید بماند.

[§۱۴:۳۱] پس گوییم که چون درست کردیم که نفس ناطقه بر نفس حسّی رئیس است، مردم آن باشد که بکوشد تا رعیت خویش را بر نفس خویش ریاست ندهد که اگر چنین کند هلاك شود.

[§۱۵:۳۱] و آن چنان باشد که مردم سپس آرزوهای نفس[۱۳] حسّی رود و نادانی و ستوری را بر آموختن علم و یُوزیدنِ[۱۴] دین بگزینند تا نفس حسّی او مر نفس ناطقهٔ

---

۹ ¦⟵برگ [ایا:۴۸-الف].

۱۰ اس، ایا: خرماء.

۱۱ ایا: + نفس.

۱۲ ایا: جاودانه.

۱۳ ایا: – نفس.

۱۴ ایا: بوزیدن [کذا]؛ اس: ـُوزیدن [با جوهر شنگرف زیر حرف «ـ» در ابتدای کلمه یک نقطه اضافه شده است و بین حروف «و» و «ز» زیر کلمه نیز با جوهر شنگرف حرف «ر» اضافه شده است. || نك: دهخدا: ورزیدن. [وَدَ] ... برزیدن. کار کردن... عمل کردن. به کار بردن...]. || تصحیح قیاسی. نك: دهخدا: یوزیدن. [دَ] (مصدر) جستن و جهیدن و برجستن. ... طلب

او[۱۵] را بخورد[۱۶] برمثال زمینی که درخت خویش را تباه کند و بیفشاند تا سزاوار سوختن شود از بهر آنك درخت چون از بار خویش بازماند جز سوختن را نشاید.

[۳۱§:۱۶] و بباید نگرستن اندر فرمان پیامبران،[۱۷] علیهم السّلام، که ایشان کُلّ نفس ناطقه بودند که چگونه نفسهای خلق کی بجملگی کُلّ نفسِ حسّی بودند مر ایشان را، علیهم السّلام، فرمانبردار شدند و هر طعام و شراب که پیامبران، علیهم السّلام، ایشان را حلال کردند بپذیرفتند، و بر آن قرارگرفتند.

[۳۱§:۱۷] و چون بر آن خوکردند، خوکردن ایشان بر آن فرمان آن بود که نفس ناطقهٔ آن پیامبر مر نفسهای حسّیِ ایشان را بخورد و با خویشتن یکی کرد.

[۳۱§:۱۸] و چون پیامبر دیگر بیامد و ایشان را[۱۸] از آن طعام و شراب بازداشت و چیزی بخلاف آن بیاورد نپذیرفتند و دشوار داشتند مر آن را و حس ایشان مر آن را نپذیرفت.

[۳۱§:۱۹] و امروز اندر میان اهل اسلام پیدا است کی نفسهای حسّی ایشان همی مر نفس ناطقه را سَپَس‌رَوی کند.[۱۹] و نشان این حال آن است کی اگر کسی از مسلمانان نادانسته گوشت خوك بخورد معدهٔ او مر آن را بپذیرد و هیچ عیب نرسدش.

[۳۱§:۲۰] پس اگر نفس ناطقه‌اش[۲۰] آگاه شود که آنچ بخورد گوشت خوك بود نپسنددش و به ناپسندِ او نفس حسّیِ او مر آن خورده را و پسندیده را رد کند و بازدهد.

نمودن و جُستن. ...جستجو کردن. تفحص کردن. طلب کردن. جُستن. طلبیدن...

۱۵ ایا: – او.

۱۶ ¦⟵برگ [اس:۶۰-ب].

۱۷ ایا: پیغامبران.

۱۸ ¦⟵برگ [ایا:۴۸-ب].

۱۹ نك: دهخدا: پسروی کردن. [پَ رَ كَ دَ] (مصدر مرکب) پیروی کردن. تابعیت کردن. متابعت.

۲۰ اس: ناطقه ش.

[§۲۱:۳۱] از بهر آنك نفس حسّی او متابع نفس ناطقهٔ او گشته است و نفس ناطقهٔ او که مر نفس پیغامبر خویش را به منزلت نفس حسّی است مر نفس ناطقه را متابع گشته است.

[§۲۲:۳۱] و چون رسول، او کی نفس ناطقه امّت خویش داشت، چیزی را نپسندد[۲۱] نفسهای ناطقهٔ امّت مر آن را نپسندد.[۲۲]

[§۲۳:۳۱] و هر چه نفس ناطقهٔ امّت رد کند نفس حسّی ایشان مر آن را نپذیرد.

[§۲۴:۳۱] و این برهانی است[۲۳] روشن‌تر از آفتاب[۲۴] مر خداوندان بصیرت را.

۲۱ اس، ایا: نه پسندد.

۲۲ اس، ایا: نه پسندد. || ایا: [عبارت «نفسهاء ناطقهٔ امّت مرانرا نپسنددد» بشکل معکوس بالای خط نوشته شده است].

۲۳ ایا: – است.

۲۴ ایا: + است.

صف سی و دوّم

سخن اندر اثبات نفس کلّی[۱]

[§۱:۳۲] هرچیزی که او را بیابند یکبار، وانگه نابوده شود، پس باز دیگربار همچنان پیدا آید، و آن نابوده‌شده جائی نبود کزان همانجای پیدا آمد، آن چیز جزوی باشد از کلی که از آن کل پیدا شود و بدان کل بازشود.[۲]

[§۲:۳۲] چنانك موجود است اندر شخص مردم گرمی و سردی[۳] و تری و خشکی اندر وقتی، و باز نابوده شود به مرگ جسمانی آن مردم، یا مر آن را بذات او نیابند البته، و باز به وقتی دیگر پیدا شود اندر شخصی دیگر همچنانك پیش از آن جای دیگر بوده بود. پس دانسته شد که این جزوهای گرمی و سردی و تری و خشکی را کلّها است که این جزوها از آن است و بدان بازشود.[۴]

[§۳:۳۲] پس گوییم که همچنین چون بازیافتیم جوهری[۵] که او را شناخته[۶] نیك و بد است و اثرکرد اندر شخص مردم، و او اندریابندۀ پوشیده‌ها بود، پس آن شخص

---

۱ قس: کتاب الینابیع، الینبوع السابع عشر (۱۷): في إثبات نفس کلّیّة منها تنبعث الجزئیّات في البشر؛ نیز قس: الینبوع الثامن عشر (۱۸): في أنّ ما في البشر أجزاؤه وجوهره من النفس الکلّیّة.

۲ قس: کتاب الینابیع، الینبوع السابع عشر (۱۷)، ص ۴۴، بند (۸۵)، س ۴ تا ۶: انّ کلّ شئ یوجد مرّة، ثمّ یعدم تارة أُخری مع ظهور مثله ممّا لاوجود له قبل الظهور، انّما هو اجزاء من کلّ منه تظهر والیه تعود.

۳ ¦⟵برگ [اس:۶۱-الف].

۴ قس: کتاب الینابیع، الینبوع السابع عشر (۱۷)، ص ۴۴، بند (۸۵)، س ۶ تا ۹: کوجودنا في شخص الانسان الحرارة والرطوبة والبرودة والیبوسة، وعدمها عنه في وقت آخر، وظهور مثلها في شخص آخر ممّا لم یمکن للشخص الآخر ظهور قبله. فیعلم أنّ لهذه الأجزاء من الحرارة والرطوبة والبرودة والیبوسّ کلّیّات هی أجزاء وجواهر منها ظهرت والیها تعود.

۵ ¦⟵برگ [ایا:۴۹-الف].

۶ یعنی که 'نیك و بدْ' او را شناخته (دانسته) است و اندر شخص مردم او را 'اثر کرد' است. || نك: دهخدا: شناخته. [شِ تَ/تِ] (نعت مفعولی) دانسته. دانسته شده. وقوف یافته. ج، شناختگان.

مردم که این گوهر از آن پیدا شده بود ناپدید شد، و باز ماننده‌ٔ آن از شخصی دیگر پیدا شد، که اندر آن شخص پیش از پیداشدنِ آن جوهر اثری [ن]بود، بدانستیم که این جزوی است که همی پیدا شود از کلی و باز بدو بازشود. پس درست شد که نفسهای جزوی را کلّ است و آن کل به عالم طبیعت محیط است.[۷]

[§۴:۳۲] و نیز اتفاق است میان اهل علم و حکمت که صورت مردم عالم صغیر است و عالم بزرگ انسان کبیر است. پس گوییم که جزوهای انسان کبیر که عالم است پراکنده است؛ و منفعتهای آن پیدا نشود مگر اندر عالم صغیر که مردم است و جزوهای او مجموع است.[۸]

[§۵:۳۲] پس درست شد که عالم صغیر که مردم است غرض آفریدگار است که انسان کبیر را آفرید که عالم است. و این جزوها است از کل خویش که منفعتهای عالم اندر او همی پدید آید. و همچنین جزوهای عالم با منفعتهای او پیدا نشود مگر به کسب کردن این نفسهای جزوی از کل خویش مر فایده‌های او را.[۹]

[§۶:۳۲] و چون مر نفسهای مردم را الفنجیده یافتیم اندر عالم، آن علم دانستیم که مر این جزوها را کلّی هست ازبهرآنك اندر عالم هیچ کلّی کسب نکند[۱۰]

---

۷ قس: کتاب الینابیع، الینبوع السابع عشر (۱۷)، ص ۴۴، بند (۸۵)، س ۱۰ تا ۱۵: وکذلك نقول: لمّا وجدنا جوهرًا ممتدًّا في شخص الانسان درّاكًا یدرك الخفیّات، ثمّ یعدم عنه مع وجود مثله في شخص آخر، لم یکن لذلك الشخص أثر قبل ظهوره فیه، فیعلم أنّه جزء من کلّ منه یظهر والیه یعود. فاذًا هذه النفوس الجزئیّة أجزاء لها کلّ، وهی النفس الکلّیّة المحیطة بالعالم الطبیعیّ، فاعرفه.

۸ قس: کتاب الینابیع، الینبوع السابع عشر (۱۷)، بند (۸۶)، ص۴۴،س ۱۶ تا ص ۴۵، س ۱ تا ۳: وأیضاً فانّ المتّفق علیه عند أهل العلم والحکمة أنّ هذه الأشخاص أجزأ من العالم الجسمانیّ الکبیر، وسُمیت العالم الصغیر بقیاسه اذا نسب الی العالم الکبیر. ولا یستقیم هذا العالم الصغیر، ولا تـثبت أجزاؤه ولا تظهر منافعه الّا بالأجزأ التی فیه من النفس الکلّیّة.

۹ قس: کتاب الینابیع، الینبوع السابع عشر (۱۷)، ص ۴۵، بند (۸۶)، س ۳ تا ۷: كذلك نقول أنّ العالم الکبیر لا تثبت أجزاؤه ولا تظهر منافعه الّا بالاکتساب من النفس الکلّیّة، کما لم تصلح أمور أجزائه التی هی العالم الصغیر الّا بالاکتساب من أجزاء النفس الکلّیّة المسمّاة بالنفس الجزئیّة؛ فقد صحّ اذًا ثبات نفس کلّیّة منها تنبعث الأجزاء، فاعرفه.

۱۰ اس: + از.

از چیزی همچون خویشتن کلّ، بلك جزو کسب کند از جزوی دیگر همچون خویشتن.[۱۱]

[§۳۲:۷] چون زمینی کلّی که زیادتی نمی‌جوید از زمینی دیگر و نه کلّ آب زیادتی همی‌جوید از آبی دیگر، کلّ همچون خویشتن، و نه کلّ هوا کسبی همی‌کند از هوایی دیگر و نه آتش کلّ زیادتی همی‌گیرد از آتشی دیگر.[۱۲]

[§۳۲:۸] بل کی جزوهای خاك را همی‌بینیم کز دیگر جزوهای خاك زیادت همی‌پذیرد و قوی همی‌شود و همچنان جزوهای دیگر او که از جزوهای کلّ خویش هریکی قوی همی‌شود و زیادت همی‌گیرد. و کلّ هریکی[۱۳] ازین چهار رکن بر حال خویشتن است بی‌هیچ زیادت و نقصان[۱۴] و بی‌نیاز است کلّها از کسب.[۱۵]

[§۳۲:۹] و چون[۱۶] این مقدمات دانسته شد و نفسها را یافتیم کی اندر شخصها فایده همی‌گیرد از دیگر[۱۷] نفسها که اندر دیگر شخصها اند دانستیم کی[۱۸] نفسها

۱۱ قس: کتاب الینابیع، الینبوع السابع عشر (۱۷)، ص ۴۵، بند (۸۷)، س ۸ تا ۹: وأیضًا فانّ الموجود في الکلّیّات انّها لا واحد منها یکتسب من شئ مثله بل من غیره، ولا جزء منها یکتسب من جزء آخر هم مثله.

۱۲ قس: کتاب الینابیع، الینبوع السابع عشر (۱۷)، ص ۴۵، بند (۸۷)، س ۱۰ تا ۱۱: ...کالأرض الکلّیّة، فانّها لا تکتسب من أرض أُخری، ولا الماء الکلّيّ من ماء آخر، ولا الهواء الکلّيّ من هواء آخر.

۱۳ ¦⟵برگ [اس:۶۱-ب].

۱۴ ¦⟵برگ [ایا:۴۹-ب].

۱۵ قس: کتاب الینابیع، الینبوع السابع عشر (۱۷)، ص ۴۵، بند (۸۷)، س ۱۱ تا ۱۳: ونری اجزاء کلّ واحد من الاُمّهات یستغنی کلّ جزء منها بالجزء الآخر من أجزائها. فأمّا کلّیّاتها، فانّها مستغنیة عن الاکتساب من أمثالها.

۱۶ اس: [حرف «ن» در «چون» کمرنگ شده است].

۱۷ اس: [حروف «ز» و «د» و «ی» در عبارت «از دیگر» کمرنگ شده اند].

۱۸ اس: [حرف «ك» در «کی» مخدوش است].

کی[۱۹] اندر حدّ جزوی‌اند کی فایده‌دهنده و فایده‌پذیرنده‌اند، و چون نشان جزو[۲۰] کی[۲۱] نفسها بدین روی کی زیادت پذیرند از مانندانِ خویش، درست پیدا آمد کی اینِ نفسها را کلّی هست کی پدید آمدن ایشانْ ازو است و بازگشتن‌شان بدو است.[۲۲]

۱۹ ایا: – کی.

۲۰ ایا: جزوئ.

۲۱ ایا: – کی.

۲۲ قس: کتاب الینابیع، الینبوع السابع عشر (۱۷)، ص ۴۵، بند (۸۷)، س ۱۳ تا ۱۶: فلمّا وجدنا النفس الجزئیّة في الانسان تستفید من نفس جزئیّة أُخری موجودة في شخص آخر، علمنا أنّهما جزآنِ: المفید والمستفید فاذا ثبتت الجزئیّة فیهما، صحّ أنّ لهما کُلًّا منه تنبعث هذه الجزئیّات. فقد صحّ أنّ <لهما> نفسًا کلّیّةً منها انبعاث الجزئیّات، فاعرفه.

صف سی و سِیُّم[۱]

سخن اندر آن کی[۲] حرکات فلك مخالف نیست مر اختیار نفس کلّی را[۳]

[§۳۳:۱] اندر اثرهای حکمت، کی پیدا است اندر نهاد عالم، پیدا است کی بر نفس کلّی پوشیده نبوده است حرکات و افعال فلك از آغاز عالم تا به انجام او.

[§۳۳:۲] و نفس کلّ حاجتمند نیست کی بگرداند مر چیزی را از حرکات فلك و حالهای آن از بهر آنك نهاد این بغایت حکمت بوده است.

[§۳۳:۳] و نیست هیچ چیز کز حرکات فلك و کواکب همی پیدا شود جز برمراد نفس کلّی.

[§۳۳:۴] و یافته نشود اندر قوّتهای فلك باطل شدن قوّتی کی بدان باطل شدن نوعی باشد از انواعهای موالید، تا روا باشد کی چیزی پیدا شود بخلاف آنچه هست.

[§۳۳:۵] وگر از حرکات فلك چیزی بودی بر خلاف مراد نفس کلّی لازم آمدی که بدان حرکتِ بی‌مراد چیزی حاصل آمدی که اندر زایش عالم آن نبوده بودی.

[§۳۳:۶] و چون هیچ چیز پیدا نمی‌شود اندر عالم جز آنك بوده است دانستیم کی کمّیت فلك برمراد نفس کلّ است.

[§۳۳:۷] معارضه اگر کسی گوید[۴] که حادثهای بزرگ که اندر عالم همی‌افتد از زلزله و صاعقه و قحط و افراط آب و آتش و طاعون و جز آن که آفرینش حیوان

---

۱ ایا: سوم.

۲ ایا: آنك.

۳ قس: کتاب الینابیع، الینبوع العشرون (۲۰): في کیفیة حرکات الفلك علی مراد النفس واختیارها مع وجود الجبر فیه، ص ۴۹ تا ۵۱.

۴ |⟵برگ [اس:۶۲-الف].

بدان تباه می‌شود نشان آن است کی [کمیّت فلك][5] نه ‹به مراد›[6] نفس[7] کلّی است چون صنعتهای او را تباه می‌کند. جواب او را گوییم که[8] چنین شناعتها به نفس‌کلّی آن کس بازبندد که از[9] آفرینش عالم مقصود نفس‌کلّی مر این حیوان را داند که همی‌خورند و همی‌خسبند، و نه چنان است.

[§۸:۳۳] و بباید دانستن که اختیار نفس‌کلّی به بودن عالم اختیار زمانی نبوده است؛ و اختیاری که به زمان بباشد زمان اندر او نقصان تواند آوردن.

[§۹:۳۳] امّا نفس اندر فلك حرکتی نهاده است ازبهر تباه شدن شخصها را از پس یکدیگر تا بدان سبب بیرون آمدن نفس باشد از حد قوّت به حدّ فعل.

[§۱۰:۳۳] و وبا و بلا که اندر عالم ظاهر شود از قحط و غرق و جز آن بسبب دو چیز باشد: تباه کردن[10] آلتی[11] را باشد و یا[12] پیدا کردن قصدی را.

[§۱۱:۳۳] اعنی که فلك همیشه زایشها همی بیرون آرد و عالم را تهی نکنند و بعضی از آنك بیرون آرد آلت باشند مر پیدا شدن مقصودی را و بعضی خود مقصود باشند.

[§۱۲:۳۳] و چون عالم پر شود از آلت که مقصود ازو بحاصل شود، یا مقصود آشکارا شود اندر میان شخصها که بطبع مانندهٔ مقصود باشند، و قوّتهای سعادت

۵ تصحیح قیاسی.
۶ اس: بمراد؛ ایا: بر مراد.
۷ اس: [«نفس» کمرنگ شده است].
۸ ¦⟵برگ [ایا:۵۰-الف].
۹ اس: [«از» با جوهر شنگرف بالای سطر نوشته شده است].
۱۰ اس، ایا: + یا.
۱۱ اس، ایا: قصدی. || تصحیح قیاسی. نك: کتاب الینابیع، الینبوع العشرون (۲۰)، ص ۵۰، بند (۹۹)، س ۱۶ تا ۱۸: وربّما کان ظهور ما في العالم سببًا لشیئین: لافساد واظهار، افساد لآلة واظهار لقصد، یعنی انّ الفلك دائمًا یخرج الموالید الفوج بعد الفوج من غیر فترة؛ فمنهم آلة ظهور المقصود، ومنهم غیر آلة.
۱۲ اس، ایا: - یا.

فلکی روی سوی مقصود نهد، و آن آلتها که بدوماننده باشند بی‌نصیب مانند از سعادت.

[§۱۳:۳۳] تا آن وبا و بلا اندر ایشان بسبب گسسته شدن سعادت از ایشان پدید آید، و ایشان که آلت بودند به پیداآمدن مقصود باطل شوند.

[§۱۴:۳۳] برمثال درودگری که بسیار چوب گوناگون که اندر جوهر همچون چوب آن در باشد که همی‌سازد فرازآرد خرد و بزرگ تا به فرازآوردن آن همه چوبها آن در که همی‌خواهد ساختن بسازد. و چون مقصود او حاصل آمد آن تراشها و چوب‌ریزها بسوزد و بیندازد و آن در را از میان برگیرد.

[§۱۵:۳۳] پس هر که بپسندد مر خویشتن را که از آن شخصها باشد که ایشان اندر وقت پیدا[۱۳] شدن مقصود، آلت باشند مر مقصود را، به خوردن طعام و شراب و طرب و جستن شهوتها مشغول شود و روی[۱۴] به صنعتهایی دارد[۱۵] که فایدهٔ آن به جسم بازگردد تا زیانکار ازین جهان بیرون شود و اندر رنجها و بدی[۱۶] افتد.

[§۱۶:۳۳] و هر که بسندکار[۱۷] باشد ازین جهان بدان قدر که او را بسنده باشد و پرداخته شود مر طلب کردن فایده‌های عقلی و علمهای آلهی[۱۸] را و این عالم طبیعت را آلت خویش گیرد تا آراسته و نیك بخت ازین عالم بیرون شود و بهمسایگی آن کس که مقصود نفس کلّ او است برسد و لذّت پذیرد از عالم عقل و نفس و برسد به چیزهائی که «هیچ چشم چنان ندیده است و نه هیچ گوش صفت او شنیده است و نه بر دل هیچ مردم آن گذشته است».[۱۹]

۱۳ ایا: + پیدا [کلمه «پیدا» دوبار نوشته شده است].

۱۴ ¦⟵برگ [ایا:۵۰-ب].

۱۵ ¦⟵برگ [اس:۶۲-ب].

۱۶ ایا: رنجهای جاویدی.

۱۷ ایا: پسندکار. || نك: دهخدا: بسندکار. [بَ سَ] (صفت مرکب) راضی و خشنود.... قانع. صبور. خرسند به بهرهٔ خویش.

۱۸ اس: الهی.

۱۹ در اینجا مؤلف تنها ترجمهٔ فارسی بخشی از حدیث پیامبر (ص) را آورده است. || نك:

[§۳۳:۱۷] و هرکه عالم مر او را آلت خویشِ سازد اندر بیرون آوردن مقصود زیانکار شود بدان جهان. ایزد تعالی ما را از آن گروه کناد که عالم را آلت خویش گیریم اندر کسب کردنِ فایده‌های عقلی و ما را از آن کسان دور داراد که عالم مر ایشان را آلت خویش گرفت اندر بیرون آوردن مقصود آفریدگار خویش.

البخاری، محمد بن اسماعیل، صحیح البخاری (دمشق-بیروت: دار ابن‌کثیر، ۱۴۲۳ق/۲۰۰۲م)، (۶۵) کتاب التفسیر، (سورة السجدة-۳۲)، باب ۱: ﴿قَوْلِهِ: فَلاَ تَعْلَمُ نَفْسٌ مَا أُخْفِيَ لَهُمْ من قُرَّةِ أَعْيُنٍ﴾، حدیث ۴۷۸۰، ص ۱۲۰۰ تا ۱۲۰۱: حَدَّثَنِي إِسْحَاقُ بْنُ نَصْرٍ، حَدَّثَنَا أَبُو أُسَامَةَ، عَنِ الأَعْمَشِ، حَدَّثَنَا أَبُو صَالِحٍ، عَنْ أَبِي هُرَيْرَةَ رضى اللّٰهُ عنه عَنِ النَّبِيِّ صلى الله عليه وسلم «يَقُولُ اللّٰهُ تَعَالَى أَعْدَدْتُ لِعِبَادِي الصَّالِحِينَ مَا لاَ عَيْنٌ رَأَتْ، وَلاَ أُذُنٌ سَمِعَتْ، وَلاَ خَطَرَ عَلَى قَلْبِ بَشَرٍ، ذُخْرًا، بَلْهَ مَا أُطْلِعْتُمْ عَلَيْهِ». ثُمَّ قَرَأَ: ﴿فَلاَ تَعْلَمُ نَفْسٌ مَا أُخْفِيَ لَهُمْ مِنْ قُرَّةِ أَعْيُنٍ جَزَاءً بِمَا كَانُوا يَعْمَلُونَ﴾ [سورة السجدة (۳۲)، آیت ۱۷]، (انظر الحدیث: ۳۲۴۴، ۴۷۷۹).

صف سی و چهارم

سخن اندر آنك خدای را[1] سود و زیان نیست

[§۱:۳۴] سود مر آن را تواند بودن و مر آن را شاید بودن که او را زیان تواند بودن، ازبهر آنك این هردو مخالفان‌اند[2] و پذیرندهٔ مخالفان جوهر باشد، و ایزد تعالی از جوهر برتر است.

[§۲:۳۴] و توحید یکتا آن است که هرچه اندر آفریده‌ها بینی و دانی از صفتها و اضافت، آن از خدای تعالی همه دور کنی.

[§۳:۳۴] و چون مردم حاجتمند بود به کشیدن حاجتها بخویشتن و دور کردن مضرّتها از خویشتن، نشانی داد مردم که ‹[بر]تر ازو چیز است›[3] بدانچ منفعت پذیرفت و مضرّت را دور کرد.

[§۴:۳۴] ازبهر آنك پذیرفتن منفعت مر چیزی را از چیزی باشد که برتر ازو است و همچنین دور کردن مضرّت مر چیزی ضعیف را لازم آید که مضرّت‌پذیر باشد.

[§۵:۳۴] پس نه روا بود که کسی گوید که خدای تعالی عالم را بیافرید[4] یا مردم را پدید آورد ازبهر کشیدن منفعت یا دور کردن مضرّت.

[§۶:۳۴] و هرکه خدای را[5] زیان و سود اثبات کند ضعیفی و عاجزی بدو، جلّت

---

۱ ایا: + تعالی.

۲ اس، ایا: مخالفانند.

۳ اس: ترازوخراست؛ ایا: ترا زو خیرست. || اما، قرائن متن ازجمله بند ذیل همین بند، به اضافهٔ احتمال از قلم افتادن کلمهٔ «بر»، قرائتهای ذیل را نیز محتمَل می سازد: (۱): '[بر] تر ازو خیر است'؛ (۲): '[بر]تر ازو چیز است'. و مصحح در اینجا قرائت شماره (۲) را اصحّ میداند.

۴ ¦⟵برگ [ایا:۵۱-الف].

۵ ¦⟵برگ [اس:۶۳-الف].

قدرته، باز بسته بود! چنانك پیدا کردیم که پذیرفتن منفعت و دور کردن مضرّت مر چیزی ضعیف را لازم آید؛ تَعَالَی اللّٰهُ عَنْ ذٰلِكَ عُلُوًّا کَبِیراً.[۶]

[§۷:۳۴] و گوییم که عقل اوّل خود اندر دو حال بی‌نیاز است هم از[۷] پذیرفتن منفعت و هم از دور کردن مضرّت. امّا بی‌نیازی عقل کلّ از پذیرفتن منفعت بدان پیوست کزو برتر و شریفتر و تمامتر چیز نیست. و منفعت از چیزی توان پذیرفتن که برتر از تو باشد.

[§۸:۳۴] و هیچ چیز نیست که آن اندر ذات عقل کلّ نیست چنانك پیش ازین برهان آن نمودیم. و چون هیچ چیز نیست از لطیف و کثیف کز ذات او بیرون است که عقل است، ممکن نیست که عقل از چیزی منفعت پذیرد؛ چه منفعت پذیرفتن چیزی از چیزی دیگر باشد، و بیرون از عقل خود هیچ چیز ضر و نفع نیست.

[§۹:۳۴] و امّا ایمنی عقل از مضرّت و ناکوشیدن او به دفع مضرت کردن از ذات خویش بدان روی است که هیچ چیز ازو قویتر و تمامتر و شریفتر نیست و مضرت چیزی از چیزی باشد کزو قوی‌تر باشد.

[§۱۰:۳۴] پس به هر دو روی درست شد به برهان منطقی و بیان عقلی که نمودیم که عقل کلّ از کشیدن منفعت بخویشتن و دفع کردن مضرّت از خویشتن بی‌نیاز است. و چون عقل که آفریده است بدین منزلت باشد چگونه روا باشد که زیان و سود را کسی به خدای تعالی بازبندد.

[§۱۱:۳۴] معارضه اگر کسی گوید که چون منفعت و مضرت به خدای تعالی منسوب نیست چرا بنده بر نیکی که کند نیکی یابد و بر بدی که کند بدی یابد، و چون از کردار او چیزی به خدای بازنگشت؟ چرا مکافات او به نیکی نبود؟

---

۶ اشارت به سورة الإسراء (۱۷)، آیت ۴۳: سُبْحَانَهُ وَ تَعَالیٰ عَمَّا یَقُولُونَ عُلُوًّا کَبِیراً.

۷ ایا: اندر.

[§۱۲:۳۴] برمثال کسی[۸] که به کوه شود و سنگها را بشکند و به جَرّها[۹] اندر افتد؛ چون خداوند بنیاد درست را از آن سودی و زیانی نیست نه مر او را چیزی دهد و نه بیازاردش.

[§۱۳:۳۴] وگر مر او را کاری نیکو کند و اندر عمارت بنیاد او بیفزاید مکافات او به نیکی کند وگر از بنیاد او چیزی ویران کند مر او را بیازارد.

[§۱۴:۳۴] جواب او را گوییم که سؤال[۱۰] که کردی نیکو است و لکن مثال که آوردی نه راست است. و نگر تا بینی مردم چون به چشم روشنایی آفتاب نگرد به گونه گون کار راه برد که او را از آن فایده‌ها باشد و چون چشم فراز کند[۱۱] از گونه گون فایده و بسیار نوع لذّتها بازماند.

[§۱۵:۳۴] پس، از چشم فراز کردنِ او، زیان او را همی‌دارد نه آفتاب را و به پذیرفتن آن نور و راه بردن سوی کارها از گونه گون نفع و فایده‌ها سود مر او را باشد نه مر آفتاب را. وگر او چشم بازکرد آفتاب بدو عنایتی بیش از آن نکرد که به دیگران کرد؛ وگر چشم فراز کرد عنایت ازو بازنگرفت که او بدان سودی نیافت.

[§۱۶:۳۴] بل که او چون روی از فایدهٔ خویش بگردانید، فایده بدو نرسید از آفتاب، و آفتاب به حال خویش همی‌بود. و به فایده گرفتن آن کس از آفتاب منفعتها بدو رسید، و به چشم فراز کردن او از آفتاب فایده‌های او بریده شود.

[§۱۷:۳۴] و همچنین به پذیرفتن علم توحید منفعت مر موحّد را باشد نه مر توحید را؛ و به تقصیر کردن او اندر آن معنی مضرّت او را بود نه توحید را؛ و مضرّت و منفعت به بنده بازگردد نه به خدای.

---

۸ ¦⟵برگ [ایا:۵۱-ب].

۹ نك: دهخدا: جر. [جَ ر ر] ... بن کوه. ...|| مغاك و گودال در زمین.

۱۰ ¦⟵برگ [اس:۶۳-ب].

۱۱ نك: دهخدا: فراز کردن. [فَ كَ دَ] (مصدر مرکب) نزدیك کردن. پیش آوردن ...|| بستن.

[۱۸:۳۴§] و امّا جواب آنچ[۱۲] گفتی چون کسی به کوه شود و سنگ شکند خداوندِ بنا او را نیازارد و نه چیزی دهد، آن است کی چون این کس از خداوند بنا چیز نیافت بدانچ رنج خویش ضایع کرد مر او را آزردن نبود از خداوند بنا، و بدان روی که[۱۳] رنج خویش ضایع کرد عقوبت یافت به نایافتنِ فایده از آنچ کرد؛ و چون کار نگاه کرد و فایده بیافت آن نشان ثواب بود او را.

۱۲ ایا: آنچه.

۱۳ ¦←برگ [ایا:۵۲-الف].

صف سی و پنجم

سخن اندر قوّتهای نفسانی که اندر مردم است

[§۱:۳۵] در[۱] نفس مردم سه قوّت است: یکی قوّت غضبی که مردم بدان قوّت با حیوان سخن‌ناگوی برابر است و انباز است؛ و دیگر قوّت شهوانی که بدین قوّت مردم با نبات انباز است؛ و سدیگر قوّت ناطقه که مردم بدین قوّت از نبات و حیوان جدا است. و بدین سه قوّت مراد آفریدگار از آفرینش بحاصل آمد.[۲]

[§۲:۳۵] و آفرینش دو بود: یکی[۳] آفرینش عالم است به صورت جسد مردم که آن صورت زنده‌ای[۴] است سخنگوی میرنده، و عالم جسمانی بدان بایست تا این صورت مردم بحاصل آمد. و دیگر آفرینش صورت نفس مردم بود صورت زندهٔ سخنگوی دانای نامیرنده، و جسد مردم بدان بایست تا نفس دانا از مردم بحاصل آید.

[§۳:۳۵] پس گوییم که قوّت ناطقه مر صورت نفسانیِ باقی را به منزلت[۵] هیولی بود. از بهر آنك به سخن توانست پذیرفتن مر علم را؛ همچنانك چوب تواند پذیرفتن مر صورت کرسی را.

---

۱ ایا: - در.

۲ نك: جامع الحکمتین، فصل ۱۱: ‹اندر فرشته و پری و دیو›، ص ۱۴۳ تا ۱۴۴، بند (۱۴۵): و گوییم که نفس ناطقه اندر هر مردمی فرشتهٔ بقوّت است، و فرشتهٔ بقوّت پریست چنانك گفتیم. و نفس شهوانی و نفس غضبی اندر هرکسی دو دیو بقوّت است. هرکسی که ناطقهٔ او مر غضبی را و شهوانی را بطاعت خویش آرد، آنکس فرشته شود. و هرکس که شهوانی و غضبی او مر ناطقهٔ او را بطاعت خویش آرد، آنکس بفعل دیو شود...؛ نیز: فصل ۲۹: <اندر تأثیر کواکب سعد و نحس در نفس و جسد>، ص ۲۹۴ تا ۲۹۵، بند (۳۳۷): ...تا از دو حاسّت سعادت که آن چشم و گوش است، و از دو حاسّت شقاوت که آن دهان <و> فرجست، مر سه نفس را — از ناطقه و شهوانی و غضبی — نصیب آید.

۳ |⟵برگ [اس:۶۴-الف].

۴ اس، ایا: زنده‌ء.

۵ اس: [حرف «ب» در کلمهٔ «بمنزلت» کمرنگ است].

[§۴:۳۵] و قوّت شهوانی مر صورت جسدانی را به منزلت هیولی بود ازبهرآنك جز بقوّت شهوت[۶] جسد زیادت نپذیرد به کشیدن غذا.

[§۵:۳۵] و قوّت غضبی مر هردو را یاری‌گر بود تا هردو صورت بیاری قوّت غضبی بحاصل همی آید.

[§۶:۳۵] و امّا بقوّت غضبی، صورت نفسانی باقی مر قوّت ناطقه را بدان بحاصل آید که مر دشمنان را از خویشتن بقوّت غضبی دور کند تا به اکتساب فضایل و معرفتِ شکرِ مُنعمْ صورت باقی را بیابد.

[§۷:۳۵] و امّا به معرفت قوّت غضبی، صورت جسدانی مر قوّت شهوانی را بدان بحاصل شد کی دشمن خویش را[۷] بقوّت غضبی دفع توانست کردن و جفت جستن از جنس خویش و طلب کردن خورش و پوشش که صلاح جسد اندر آن بود.

[§۸:۳۵] این همه بقوّت غضبی بود مردم را. وگر قوّت غضبی قوّت ناطقه را یاری ندادی، قوّت ناطقه هرگز، به استفادت علم ورزیدن، عبادت و شکر منعم نتوانستی کردن؛ ازبهرآنك نفس شهوانی بر ناطقه چیره شدی و ناطقه را مقهور کردی و نفس ناطقه ضایع شدی.

[§۹:۳۵] و همچنین اگر یاری نبودی مر نفس شهوانی را از نفس غضبی، طلب ‹خوردنی و پوشیدنی›[۸] و جفت خویش نتوانستی کردن، و دشمن را از خویشتن دور نتوانستی داشتن، و مادّت حیوان گسسته شدی.

[§۱۰:۳۵] و نیز اگر نفس ناطقه مر قوّت غضبی را مَعونَت نکردی هیچ حیوان از دشمن نتوانستی پرهیز کردن و ندانستی که صلاح او در چیست.

[§۱۱:۳۵] وگر معونت شهوانی مر ناطقه را نبودی به نگاه‌داشت قوّت حیوانی،

---

۶ ایا: شهوانی.

۷ ¦←برگ [ایا:۵۲-ب].

۸ ایا: نوشیدنی و خوردنی.

به برون کشیدن خورش[۹] و آسایش، قوّت ناطقه پایداری[۱۰] نیافتی و از پرهیز هلاك شدی.

[§۱۲:۳۵] پس کردگار عالم، به جود باری سبحانه، این هر سه قوّت مختلف یاریگرانِ یکدیگر ساخت، تا زین روی که گفتیم دو مراد او اندر دو صورت جسمانی و روحانی مردم به دنیا و آخرت تمام شود.

[§۱۳:۳۵] و هریکی ازین سه قوّت برای نفس حیوانی شاید خواندن. وگر مر این قوّتها را قوّتهای نفس خوانی و همه بیك نفس کلّ منسوب کنی روا باشد. وگر مر هریکی را نفس خوانی اشارت برتر از ذات این قوّتها کرده باشی.

[§۱۴:۳۵] و حکماء[۱۱] اوایل هم قُویٰ[۱۲] خواندند مر این قوّتها را و هم نفسها خواندند. و مثالی بدهیم مر این هرسه قوّت را از روی طبایع تا به فهم شنونده نزدیکتر باشد.

[§۱۵:۳۵] و گوییم سبیل قوّت غضبی[۱۳] با قوّت شهوانی و قوّت ناطقه از روی طبیعت سبیل رطوبت است ایستاده میان حرارت و برودت. ‹اگر غلبه›[۱۴] مر حرارت را باشد رطوبت با او یار شود، وگر غلبه مر برودت را باشد رطوبت با او یار شود.

[§۱۶:۳۵] ازبهر آنك اگر رطوبت حرارت را پذیرد هوا گردد که گرم و تر است وگر رطوبت برودت را پذیرد آب گردد که سرد و تر است.

---

۹ ¦⟵برگ [اس:۶۴-ب].

۱۰ اس: پای داری.

۱۱ ایا: حکمای.

۱۲ نك: دهخدا: قوی. [قُ وا] ... جِ قوة. ... در فارسی گاه قوا نویسند بقیاس «اعلا» و «مولا».

۱۳ ¦⟵برگ [ایا:۵۳-الف].

۱۴ اس: [حرف «ر» در «اگر» مخدوش است؛ و کلمهٔ «غلبه»، که در متن مخدوش است، در حاشیهٔ برگ با جوهر پر رنگ واضح نوشته شده است].

[§۱۷:۳۵] همچنین قوّت غضبی را میل بدان قوّت افتد که غلبه او را باشد. اگر ناطقه غالب باشد یار ناطقه شود؛ وگر شهوانی غالب باشد یار شهوانی شود.

[§۱۸:۳۵] و مثالی دیگر از روی حیوانی، سبیل قوّت غضبی را و دو قوّت ناطقه و شهوانی، سبیل سگی شکاری است که هرچه اندر عالم است بتواند گرفتن به میان دو مرد صیّاد که همّت ایشان مختلف است بغایت اختلاف.

[§۱۹:۳۵] چنانك صید یك مرد بمثل شیر و پلنگ بود و صید دیگر مرد مار و موش باشد همّت یکی عالی و بزرگوار و همّت آن دیگر دون و خسیس؛ و آن سگ همیشه فرمان‌بردار آن کس باشد که او[۱۵] به همّت خویش هشیارتر و صید خویش را جویاتر باشد. و چون سگ سپس آن مرد صیّاد هشیار رود آن ناهشیار را ناچاره سپس ایشان باید رفتن. این است مثال[۱۶] قوّت غضبی با قوّت ناطقه و شهوانی راستا راست.[۱۷]

[§۲۰:۳۵] و ناطقه و شهوانی هردو جویندگان زندگانی‌اند و خوشی. ناطقه زندگانی و خوشی جاودانی جوید و شهوانی زندگی و خوشی این جهانی جوید.[۱۸] و این گروه را خدای تعالی فرمود کز ستور گُم‌بوده‌تر اند بدین آیت کی گفت، قوله: إِنْ هُمْ إِلاَّ كَالْأَنْعَامِ بَلْ هُمْ أَضَلُّ سَبِيلاً.[۱۹] گفت: «ایشان نیستند مگر چون ستور بل کی ایشان گمراه‌ترند».

[§۲۱:۳۵] پس گوییم چون آرزوی نفس ناطقه بیشتر باشد به طلب خوشی و زندگی باقی، طلب استفادت علم کند و میل به عمل شریعت و عبادت خدای

---

۱۵ ایا: - او.

۱۶ اس: [کلمهٔ «مثال» که در متن خوانا نیست، در حاشیهٔ برگ با جوهر پر رنگ واضح نوشته شده است].

۱۷ نك: دهخدا: راستا راست. (قید مرکب) برابر. مساوی ... || هم وزن. برابر در اندازه.

۱۸ ¦⟵برگ [اس:۶۵-الف].

۱۹ سورة الفرقان (۲۵)، آیت ۴۴: أَمْ تَحْسَبُ أَنَّ أَكْثَرَهُمْ يَسْمَعُونَ أَوْ يَعْقِلُونَ إِنْ هُمْ إِلاَّ كَالْأَنْعَامِ بَلْ هُمْ أَضَلُّ سَبِيلاً.

دارد، قوّت غضبی میل بدو[۲۰] کند، و چون میل غضبی به ناطقه اوفتد شهوانی سپس روِ ایشان گردد بضرورت و همه کارهای مردم موافق عقل آید بغایت نیکویی و راستی. و اگر آهنگ قوّت شهوانی بیشتر باشد به طلب لذّت جسد، میل غضبی سوی شهوانی افتد، و ناطقه متابع شهوانی و غضبی شود. همه کارهای مردم مخالف عقل اوفتد از دست پیش کردن به ناشایستها چون زنا و لواطه و دزدی[۲۱] و دروغ و بیدادی. این همه کارها زشت است و مخالف عقل است.

[§۲۲:۳۵] پس هر چه سوی عقل نیکو است اندر او راحت و قوّت ناطقه است و رنجِ قوّت شهوانی است. و هر چه سوی عقل زشت است اندر او راحت شهوانی است و رنج عاقله است.

[§۲۳:۳۵] و همه رسولان، علیهم السّلام، سیاست و مالش مر قوّت شهوانی را کردند تا فرمان‌بردار باشد مر ناطقه را به انواع عبادت از نماز و روزه و حجّ و زکاة و جهاد و پارسایی و خرسندی و راست‌گفتن و جُستن علم و خویشتن را زیردست دارا داشتن و اندر این همه کارها راحت و لذّت مر نفس ناطقه را است و قوّتِ او است و همه نیکو است بعقل و اندر این همه کارها رنج شهوانی است و ضعف او.

[§۲۴:۳۵] و همه حکماء پیشین که خدای‌شناس بودند همه متعلّمان را به آغاز تعلیم پرهیز فرمودندی، و مر نفس شهوانی را نپروردندی، بل گفتندی که علم آلهی را بیاموزید و نفس شهوانی را فروشکسته دارید. از بهر آنك با غلبه و قوّت شهوانی علم نتوان پذیرفتن. گفتیم اندر مراتب قوّتهای نفس آن مایه که خردمند را کفایت است.

۲۰ ¦⟵برگ [ایا:۵۳-ب].

۲۱ اس: [حروف «د» و «ز» در ابتدای کلمه «دزدی» محو شده است].

صف سی و ششم[۱]

سخن اندر پاکیزه کردن نفس از گناه

[§۱:۳۶] امّا اندریافتن گناه خویش و پاکیزه کردن نفس بدان است که هر کاری که آن سوی عقل زشت است نکنی.

[§۲:۳۶] وگر مؤمن را هوا و نفس شهوانی بدان کشد[۲] تا آن کار بکند آن گناه اندر نفس او ثابت شود و نگاری و نبشته‌ای[۳] گردد اندر نفس او، و نگار و نبشتهٔ گناه زشت است نزدیك عقل.

[§۳:۳۶] و شمار[۴] خلق سوی عقل است، آن عقل کی او کلّ است. و هر نفس که با نگاری پیش عقل کلّ شود، که مر آن را دشمن دارد، آن نفس جاودان اندر عقاب بماند و صورت نگار زشت که بر هیولی جای گرفت ازو جدا نشود مگر [به][۵] پدیدآمدنِ نگاری و صورتی نیکو هم بر آن هیولی که این هر دو از یکدیگر گریزانند و چون نیکویی بیاید زشتی کی دشمن او و خلاف او است بگریزد.

[§۴:۳۶] و گوهر نفس گوهری است که هم صورت نیکو پذیرد و هم صورت زشت، بی هیولی و بی طبیعتی[۶] و بی هیچ زمان. و بپای شدن صورت نیکو افتادن و تباه شدن صورت زشت است.

[§۵:۳۶] و چون مؤمن بر گناه خویش پشیمانی خورد و توبه کند بدان توبه مر نفس

---

۱ ←برگ [اس:۶۵-ب].

۲ ←برگ [ایا:۵۴-الف].

۳ اس، ایا: نبشته‌ء.

۴ نك: دهخدا: شمار. [شُ] ... حساب. ...: چون نکنم جان فدای آنکه به حشر/ آسان گردد بدو شمار مرا. (ناصرخسرو، [دیوان اشعار، ص ۱۲، س ۲۴، به‌اهتمام: نصرالله تقوی])؛ ... ای بارخدای خلق یکسر / با توست به روز حق شمارم. (ناصرخسرو، [دیوان اشعار، ص ۲۸۷، س ۱۴، به‌اهتمام: نصرالله تقوی])

۵ تصحیح قیاسی.

۶ اس: طسی؛ ایا: طبیبی.

او را سُستی باشد از آن صورت زشت. و چون پس از توبه کار نیکو کند، آنچ سوی عقل نیکو است، آن صورت نیکوی[۷] او بجای آن صورت زشت که پیش از توبه بود بایستد، چنانك خدای تعالی میفرماید[۸] قوله: إِلاَّ مَنْ تٰابَ وَ آمَنَ وَ عَمِلَ عَمَلاً صٰالِحاً فَأُوْلٰئِكَ يُبَدِّلُ اللّٰهُ سَيِّئٰاتِهِمْ حَسَنٰاتٍ وَ كٰانَ اللّٰهُ غَفُوراً رَحِيماً.[۹] گفت: «مگر آن کس که توبه کند و بگرود و کار نیکو کند پس ایشان آنند که بَدل کند خدای زشتیهای ایشان به نیکوییها و خدای پوشنده و مهربان است».

[§۶:۳۶] و توبهٔ نصوح آن باشد که، آنچ سوی عقل زشت است، دست از آن بازدارد، و آنچ سوی عقل نیکو است مر آن را کاربندد، و نیز از آن سپس بدان کار زشت کی کرده بود بازنگردد.

[§۷:۳۶] و خبر است از رسول، صلی[۱۰] اللّٰه علیه وآله، که گفت: المعترف بالذّنب کمن لاذنب له و المُصِرُّ علی الذنب کالمستهزی بربّه.[۱۱] گفت: «هر که[۱۲] خستو شود[۱۳] به گناه خویش همچون کسی است کی او را گناه نیست؛ و هر که بر گناه بایستد[۱۴] چون کسی باشد[۱۵] که بر پروردگار خویش افسوس کند».[۱۶]

---

۷ ایا: نیکوئی.

۸ اس: [«سی‌فرساید» خوانا نیست].

۹ سورة الفرقان (۲۵)، آیت ۷۰.

۱۰ اس: صل.

۱۱ نك: الکلینی، محمد بن یعقوب، الكافي، تصحیح: علی اکبر غفاری و محمد آخوندی (تهران، ۱۴۰۷ق)، ج ۲، (۱۹۲) بَابَ التَّوبَة، ص ۴۳۵: ۱۰ - عنه، عن أحمد بن محمد، عن علي بن النعمان، عن محمد بن سنان، عن یوسف [بن] أبي یعقوب بیاع الأرز، عن جابر، عن أبي جعفر (علیه السلام) قال: سمعته یقول: التائب من الذنب کمن لا ذنب له والمقیم علی الذنب وهو مستغفر منه کالمستهزئ.

۱۲ اس: - هر که.

۱۳ نك:دهخدا: خستو شدن. [خُ شُ دَ] (مصدر مرکب) معترف شدن. اقرار کردن. اذعان کردن.

۱۴ ¦⟵برگ [اس:۶۶-الف].

۱۵ ¦⟵برگ [ایا:۵۴-ب].

۱۶ نك: دهخدا: افسوس کنان. [اَ كُ] (نعت فاعلی مرکب، قید مرکب) در حال ریشخند کردن. قس: دهخدا: افسوس.

[§۸:۳۶] و دست از گناه بازداشتن پاك کردن صورت زشت است و نبشتهٔ زشت از نفس؛ و نیکویی کردن و دست اندر کاری زدن که سوی عقل پسندیده است، نگاشتن صورت نیکو است بجای صورت زشت.

[§۹:۳۶] و روا نیست خردمند را کز گناه به توبه بازنگردد و صورت زشت خویش را نیکو نکند که عفو و رحمت خدای تعالی بسیار است چنانك همی‌گوید، قوله: قُلْ يٰا عِبٰادِيَ الَّذِينَ أَسْرَفُوا عَلىٰ أَنْفُسِهِمْ لاٰ تَقْنَطُوا مِنْ رَحْمَةِ اللّٰهِ إِنَّ اللّٰهَ يَغْفِرُ الذُّنُوبَ جَمِيعاً.[۱۷] همی‌گوید کی: «بگوی با بندگان من آنك گناه بسیار کردید از رحمت خدای نومید نباشید که خدای بیامرزد همه گناهان را».

[§۱۰:۳۶] امّا اندر یافتن گناهی که آن از روی ستم کردن و خواسته بردن مردمان باشد آن است کی چون[۱۸] توبه[۱۹] کند اگر خواسته‌ای[۲۰] که آن ستده باشد همان خواسته برجای باشد به خداوندش بازدهد و[۲۱] حلالی کردن ازو بخواهد پس اگر آن خواسته برجای نباشد بدل آن خواسته به قیمت آن به خداوندش بازدهد اگر طاقت دارد.

[§۱۱:۳۶] و اگر طاقت ندارد نیّت چنان کند که اگر خواسته یابد عوض بازدهد وگر آن کس کی این مؤمن برو ستم کرده است زنده نباشد به فرزندان او برساند.

[§۱۲:۳۶] وگر آن کس را فرزند نباشد به بیت‌المال خداوند زمانهٔ خویش رساند بر دست حجّت جزیره تا آن صورت زشت او کزان ستم ثابت شده باشد از نفس او زایل شود.

[§۱۳:۳۶] پس اگر[۲۲] این مؤمن نیّت نیکو بکند و دستش نرسد که آن حق بازدهد،

---

۱۷ سورة الزمر (۳۹)، آیت ۵۳.

۱۸ اس: [حرف «ن» از «چون» مخدوش است].

۱۹ اس:[«توبه» کمرنگ شده است].

۲۰ اس، ایا: خواسته‌ء.

۲۱ اس: [«و» مخدوش است].

۲۲ اس: – اگر.

آن نیّت نیکوی او پیش نفس او از عقوبت سپری شود چنانك رسول مصطفی، صلی[۲۳] الله علیه وآله، گفت: النيّةُ الحسنةُ جُنَّةٌ حِصِينَةٌ. گفت: «نیّت نیکو سپری استوار است».[۲۴]

[§۳۶:۱۴] پس اگر طاقت بازدادن یابد و بازندهد، و زین جهان بیرون شود، گناه او یکی دو شود. از بهر آنك گناهش دوتای گشت یکی گناه پیشین که کرده بود[۲۵] دگر دروغزنی[۲۶] که کرد با خدای تعالی. ازیرا که توبه کرد و بدان وفا نکرد تا زشتی بر زشتی بیفزود.

[§۳۶:۱۵] همچنانك چون طاقت یابد و وفا کند[۲۷] و حق مردمان بازدهد مزد او دوتای شود یکی مزد بازدادن حق مردمان و دیگر مزد اثبات کردن صورت نیکو و پاك کردن صورت زشت که بدانچ با خدای تعالی عهد کرده بود وفا کرد.

[§۳۶:۱۶] و بیاساید از بیم نکال[۲۸] آن صورت زشت. و از درکات دوزخ به درجات بهشت رسد چنانك خدای تعالی همی گوید، قوله: إِلاَّ مَنْ آمَنَ وَ عَمِلَ صٰالِحاً فَأُولٰئِكَ لَهُمْ جَزٰاءُ الضِّعْفِ بِمٰا عَمِلُوا وَ هُمْ فِي الْغُرُفٰاتِ آمِنُونَ.[۲۹] همی گوید: «که مگر آن کس کی بگرود و کار نیکو کند ایشانند آنك ایشان را است مکافات دوتای بدانچ کردند و ایشان اندر مرغزارهای بهشت اند ایمن گشته».

---

۲۳ اس، ایا: صل.

۲۴ نك: ابو معاش، سعيد، فضائل اميرالمؤمنين الإمام علي بن ابي طالب (عليه السلام) في القرآن الكريم (قم: دارالمودة، ۱۴۳۲ق)، ج ۳، الفصل الخامس: «آيات الصراط المستقيم في القرآن»، الآية الاولى، حديث (۴۴): ص ۲۶۶ تا ۲۶۷.

۲۵ ¦⟵برگ [ایا:۵۵-الف].

۲۶ اس، ایا: دروغ زنی.

۲۷ ¦⟵برگ [اس:۶۶-ب].

۲۸ نك: دهخدا: نکال. [نَ] ... عقوبت. ... شکنجهٔ سخت. عذاب....: بر ظاهر امثال مرو کت نفزاید / نزد عقلا جز همه خواری و نکالی. (ناصرخسرو، [دیوان اشعار، ص ۴۱۱، س ۵، به اهتمام: نصرالله تقوی]).

۲۹ سورة سَبَأ (۳۴)، آیت ۳۷.

[§۳۶:۱۷] و هر که راست گوید و به عهد وفا کند اندر نفس خویش خوی و آرایشی یابد، و از مردمان ثنای نیکو شنود، و اندر نفس او آن وفا و راستی صورتی شود که شادی و خوشیِ آن جاودان بدو پیوسته باشد.

[§۳۶:۱۸] و امّا معاملت مؤمنان از حدود دین و با یکدیگر از دوستداری و نیکوکاری و نصیحت و معونت اندر حالهای دینی و دنیاوی، از یاری دادن به مال و علوم و گفتار و کردار، بغایتِ نیکویی باید کی باشد و مزد ایشان مضاعف باشد از بهر آنك نیکویی کردن با همه خلق نیکو است و لیکن با مؤمنان نیکوتر و فاضلتر است و مزد آن بیشتر است.

[§۳۶:۱۹] از بهر آنك مؤمن به مؤمن سزاوارتر است چون دیگر مردمان. و سبیل مؤمن با مؤمن، به روحانی، سبیل برادر با برادر و خواهر و مادر و پدر و عم و جدّ است به زایش نفسانی که دوم زایش است.

[§۳۶:۲۰] و سبیل مسلمان با مؤمن، به روحانی، سبیل همسایه با همسایه است. و حق برادر و پدر بیش از حق همسایه است. و نیکویی کردن با مؤمنان[۳۰] آراستن صورت روحانی است.

[§۳۶:۲۱] و همچنین ناشایست و زشتکاری با همه مردمان زشت است سوی عقل و گناه است، و لکن با مؤمنان زشت‌تر و فاحش‌تر؛ و درستیِ این سخن قول خدای است اندر مخاطبه با زنان پیغامبر، علیه‌السّلام، قوله: یٰا أَیُّهَا النَّبِیُّ قُلْ لِأَزْوٰاجِكَ إِنْ كُنْتُنَّ تُرِدْنَ الْحَیٰاةَ الدُّنْیٰا وَ زِینَتَهٰا[۳۱] فَتَعٰالَیْنَ أُمَتِّعْكُنَّ وَ أُسَرِّحْكُنَّ سَرٰاحاً جَمِیلاً * وَ إِنْ كُنْتُنَّ تُرِدْنَ اللّٰهَ وَ رَسُولَهُ وَ الدّٰارَ الْآخِرَةَ فَإِنَّ اللّٰهَ أَعَدَّ لِلْمُحْسِنٰاتِ مِنْكُنَّ أَجْراً عَظِیماً * یٰا نِسٰاءَ النَّبِیِّ مَنْ یَأْتِ مِنْكُنَّ بِفٰاحِشَةٍ مُبَیِّنَةٍ یُضٰاعَفْ لَهَا الْعَذٰابُ ضِعْفَیْنِ[۳۲] وَ كٰانَ ذٰلِكَ عَلَى اللّٰهِ یَسِیراً * وَ مَنْ یَقْنُتْ مِنْكُنَّ لِلّٰهِ وَ رَسُولِهِ وَ تَعْمَلْ صٰالِحاً نُؤْتِهٰا

۳۰ ¦⟵برگ [ایا:۵۵-ب].

۳۱ اس: + وَزِینَتَهَا. || ¦⟵برگ [اس:۶۷-الف].

۳۲ اس، ایا: - ضِعْفَیْنِ.

أَجْرَهٰا مَرَّتَيْنِ وَ أَعْتَدْنٰا لَهٰا رِزْقاً كَرِيماً.[۳۳] گفت: «ای پیغامبر بگوی مر جفتانت را کی اگر شما زندگانیِ این جهانی خواهید و آرایش او، بیایید تا شما را دست بازدارم[۳۴] بنیکویی. وگر خدای را خواهید و پیامبر او را و سرای بازپسین را خدای بسیج کرده است مر نیکوکاران را از شما مزدی بزرگ. ای زنان پیغامبر هر که از شما کاری ناشایست کند او را عذاب دوبار کنند و این کار بر خدای آسان است. و هر که از بهر خدای[۳۵] و پیامبر را نیکویی کند مزد او دوباره بدهیم و آراسته‌ایم مر او را روزی خوب».

[§۳۶:۲۲] و اندر تأویل مر این مخاطبه[۳۶] را سه روی است. یکی روی جسدانی است خاصّه، و روی دوم روحانی است خاصّه، و روی سدیگر روحانی است عامّه.

[§۳۶:۲۳] امّا روی جسدانیِ خاصّه پند است مر زنان جسدانی پیغامبر را تا کاری ناشایست نکنند و زشتکاری پیشه نگیرند که زشتیِ ایشان از آن سپس که زنان پیغامبر گشتند زشت‌تر از زشتیِ دیگر بندگان باشد.

[§۳۶:۲۴] و امّا مخاطبهٔ روحانیِ خاصّه آن است که این آیات پند است مر دوازده یار پیغامبر را، علیه السّلام، که ایشان اندر روحانی او را برابر زنان‌اند اندر جسدانی و زنان روحانی مستفیدان علم‌اند[۳۷] قرارگاه زایش روحانی‌اند چنانك زنان جسدانی قرارگاه زایش جسدانی‌اند.

[§۳۶:۲۵] پس زشتکاریِ یاران رسول زشت‌تر است از زشتکاریِ دیگر مسلمانان و مضرّت زشتکاریِ ایشان بر خلق بیشتر است و زیان آن بزرگتر است به دین و دنیا.

[§۳۶:۲۶] و علم خدای محیط بود به عصیان زشت‌کاری بهری از زنان جسدانی

۳۳ سورة الأحزاب (۳۳)، آیات ۲۸ تا ۳۱.

۳۴ نك: دهخدا: دست بازداشتن. [دَ تَ] ... رها کردن.

۳۵ اس: [حروف «د»، «ا» و «ی» در کلمه «خدای» مخدوش اند].

۳۶ اس: [کلمه «مخاطبه» مخدوش است].

۳۷ ¦⟵برگ [ایا:۵۶-الف]. || پسوند «اند» در ابتدای برگ [ایا:۵۶-الف] تکرار شده است.

پیغامبر و بهری از روحانیِ او، علیه‌السّلام، از بهر آن بود کی حجّت بدین آیت بر ایشان لازم کرد به وعدهٔ نیکویی و زلیفن به زشتی.

[§۲۷:۳۶] و[۳۸] امّا مخاطبهٔ روحانیِ[۳۹] عامه اندر این آیت پند و اندرز است همه حدود دین را و مؤمنان را که ایشان گیرندهٔ علم‌اند از رسول، علیه‌السّلام، به میانجیان کز پس او بودند و باشند تا روز راستخیز که زشتکاریِ ایشان زشت‌تر است از زشتکاریِ دیگر مردمان که استفادت ایشان از راه راست نیست. و راه راست به راه[۴۰] عقل است به میانجیان و درجات.

[§۲۸:۳۶] و اهل حشو زشتکاری[۴۱] به جهل و حسد طلبند، و حدود دین و مؤمنان به بصیرت کنند. پس زشتکاریِ حدود دین[۴۲] و مؤمنان با یکدیگر به روحانی و جسمانی از گناهان بزرگتر است. و زشت‌کاری[۴۳] مؤمن با خدای از راه عصیان ایشان باشد مر میانجیان را که میان مؤمن و میان رسول و وصی و امام باشند به دست بازداشتن طاعت ایشان و نفاق کردن.

[§۲۹:۳۶] و آن گسسته کردن رسن خویش باشد مؤمن را با خدای و رسول مگر که توبه کند و به راه طاعت بازآید، چنانك خدای تعالی میفرماید، قوله: إِنَّ الْمُنٰافِقِينَ فِي الدَّرْكِ الْأَسْفَلِ مِنَ النّٰارِ وَ لَنْ تَجِدَ لَهُمْ نَصِيراً * إِلاَّ الَّذِينَ تٰابُوا وَ أَصْلَحُوا وَ اعْتَصَمُوا بِاللّٰهِ وَ أَخْلَصُوا دِينَهُمْ لِلّٰهِ فَأُولٰئِكَ مَعَ الْمُؤْمِنِينَ وَ سَوْفَ يُؤْتِ اللّٰهُ الْمُؤْمِنِينَ أَجْراً عَظِيماً.[۴۴] گفت: «منافقان به پایگاه فرودین اندراند از آتش و ایشان را یاری

۳۸ اس: [حرف «و» مخدوش است].
۳۹ |←برگ [اس:۶۷-ب].
۴۰ ایا: راه.
۴۱ اس: رستکاری؛ ایا: رشتکاری.
۴۲ اس: [کلمه «دین» بالای خط نوشته شده است].
۴۳ اس: رست کاری؛ ایا: رستکاری.
۴۴ سورة النساء (۴)، آیات ۱۴۵ تا ۱۴۶.

دهنده‌ای[۴۵] نیابی مگر آنها را که[۴۶] توبه کنند و کار نیک کنند و دست در ‹حَبْلِ اللّٰهِ الْمَتِین›[۴۷] زنند و دین خویش خدای را خالصه کنند پس ایشان با مؤمنان باشند و خدای مؤمنان را مزدی بزرگ بدهد».

[§۳۶:۳۰] آن مقدار که مؤمن هشیار را اندر آن بیداری افتد، و افزاید، یاد کرده شد، از باب اندریافتن گناهی که کرده باشد به توبه و نیکوکاری و بازناگشتن به بدی.

۴۵ اس، ایا: دهنده‌ء.

۴۶ ¦—←برگ [ایا:۵۶-ب].

۴۷ اشارت به: آیت ۱۰۳ از سورة آل عمران (۳): وَ اعْتَصِمُوا بِحَبْلِ اللّٰهِ جَمِيعاً وَ لاٰ تَفَرَّقُوا وَ اذْكُرُوا نِعْمَتَ اللّٰهِ عَلَيْكُمْ إِذْ كُنْتُمْ أَعْدٰاءً فَأَلَّفَ بَيْنَ قُلُوبِكُمْ فَأَصْبَحْتُمْ بِنِعْمَتِهِ إِخْوٰاناً وَ كُنْتُمْ عَلىٰ شَفٰا حُفْرَةٍ مِنَ النّٰارِ فَأَنْقَذَكُمْ مِنْهٰا كَذٰلِكَ يُبَيِّنُ اللّٰهُ لَكُمْ آيٰاتِهِ لَعَلَّكُمْ تَهْتَدُونَ؛ و آیت ۵۸ از سورة الذاريات (۵۱): إِنَّ اللّٰهَ هُوَ الرَّزّٰاقُ ذُو الْقُوَّةِ الْمَتِينُ. [مؤلف دو عبارت «حَبْلِ» و «الْمَتِينُ» را، که در این دو آیه ذکر شده اند، در ترجمه و تعبیر خود راجع به آیات ۱۴۵ تا ۱۴۶، از سورة النساء (۴)، استفاده کرده است].

صف سی و هفتم

سخن اندر آنك پدیدآرندهٔ طبایع نفس کلّ است

[§۱:۳۷] حکماء[۱] علم الّهی و شناسندگان افعال فلکی و خداوندان علم طبایع متفق‌اند بر آنك صفت نفس، آنك او بدان صفت از دیگر چیزها[۲] حَیِّز[۳] است، 'فعالةٌ بالطّبع علّامةٌ بالقوّة' است. گویند که نفس کارکن است بطبع خویش و آموزنده است اندر حدّ قوّت یعنی که اگر آموزگار یابد دانا شود.

[§۲:۳۷] و از نفسهای جزوی که اندر عالم است از نبات و حیوان و مردم دلیل بر درستی این قول یافته همی‌شود. و بدانچ روح نمو به نبات اندر است به هیچ وقت از کار نیاساید ازبهرآنك به زمستان همی مایه فراز کشد و به دیگر فصلها مر آن را بیرون آرد و پرورش همی‌کند. و نفسهای حیوان از طلب کردن غذا و بَرجَستنِ[۴] جفت خویش نیاساید و مردم به بیداری و خفتگی از کاربستن خویش فارغ نیست.[۵] پس درست شد که کارکردن همه مر نفس را است بجملگی.

[§۳:۳۷] و چون مر نفس مردم را ما از نفس کلّ جزو یافتیم، چنانك برهان آن اندر این کتاب بازنمودیم، و نفس مردم با جزویّتِ خویش چیزها همی بیرون آرد که

---

۱ ایا: حکمای.

۲ ¦←برگ [اس:۶۸-الف].

۳ اس: حیز؛ ایا: جدا. [«حَیِّز» به معنای «مُنْحاز» (بیرون از، و مسلط بر دیگر چیزها) است، که هم‌معنیِ «جدا» و «متمایز» است. نظر مؤلف بر تَفَوُّق و احاطهٔ نفس بر دیگر چیزهایِ طبیعی دلالت میکند و به همین واسطه نفس را قادر بر دخل و تصرف در طبیعت می‌داند]. || نك: دهخدا: حیز [حَ یْ یِ] ...(اصطلاح فلسفه) سطح باطن جسم حاوی که مماس با سطح ظاهری جسم محوی باشد. و آن در نظر ابن سینا و جمعی از فلاسفه اعم از مکان است، زیرا حیز شامل وضع هم می‌شود، چنانکه در فلک‌الافلاک که حیز دارد و مکان ندارد، بجهت آنکه ورای آن جسمی نیست که مماس آن باشد. || [و در اینجا بمثل، همان نسبت که فلک‌الافلاک با اجرام سماوی دارد، نفس با طبایع دارد].

۴ نك: دهخدا: برجستن. [بَ جَ تَ] ... جهیدن. برجهیدن. جستن....|| جهیدن ستوران و پرندگان نر بر ماده. ... || طپیدن و جنبیدن رگ.

۵ نك: جامع الحکمتین، فصل ۶: ‹اندر تعریف «من»›، ص ۱۰۱ تا ۱۰۲، بند (۹۶).

عالم با بزرگی خویش آن بیرون نیاورده است چون پدیدآوردن آبگینه از سنگ و نبات، و بیرون آوردن ابریشم از برگ درخت تود، به یاری کرم قژ، و بیرون آوردن نوعی حیوان از میان دو نوع چون استر از میان اسب و خر و جز آن.[۶]

[۴:۳۷§] و طبایع همه اشکال بود لونها و گوهرها، و اندرونشان صنعت و کار پیدا و روشن بود. دانستیم که نفس‌کلّی سزاوارتر است بدین صنعت کلی، و پدیدآوردن این طبایع کلّی، تا جزو او همی صنایع جزوی بتواند کردن. و این دلیلی ظاهر و روشن است خردمند را بر آنك نفس‌کلّی است ‹کی که›[۷] این جواهر و طبایع او پدید آورده است.

۶ ¦⟵برگ [ایا:۵۷-الف].

۷ ایا: که؛ اس: کی که [در اینجا، وقوع «که» پس از «کی» از روی عمد و جهت تأکید آمده است].

صف سی و هشتم

سخن اندر اثبات ثواب و عقاب[1]

[§۱:۳۸] اگر مردم را معاد نبودی که بازشدندی بدان ازبهر بیافتن مکافات ابدی، تا نیکوکار به ثواب و بدکردار به عقاب رسد، آفرینش عالم و آنچ اندر او است بازی بودی. ازبهر آنك هیچ چیز[2] باطل نشد از آن چیزها که عالم بیرون آورد به تدبیر صانع خویش.

[§۲:۳۸] و ضایع ناشدن چیزها که[3] اندر عالم پدید آمد همه بسبب بودش مردم بود. چنانك گوییم[4] اگر مردم نبودی گوهران گداختنی و ناگداختنی نبودی.

[§۳:۳۸] و آنچ از کانها پدید آمد از آن[5] باطل شدی و زو هیچ جانور را فایده نبودی و چیزهای خوشبوی چون مشك و عنبر و کافور و جز آن همه باطل گشتی، و چندین جامَه‌ها کز ابریشم و از پشم، مردم بحاصل کرد همه باطل بودی، و گوناگون فایده که مردم گرفت از نبات و از میوها و پوستها و دندان و استخوان و سُروهای[6] حیوان همه ضایع بودی.

[§۴:۳۸] و چون مردم بحاصل آمد و چندین فایده از آفرینش بگرفت دانستیم که آن همه چیزها آفریدگار ازبهر مردم آفریده بود و گوایی داد بر درستی این حال

---

۱ قس: کتاب الینابیع، الینبوع الثامن والثلاثون (۳۸): في أن للبشر عودا إلى ثواب أبدي، ص ۸۷ تا ۹۰.

۲ ایا: - چیز.

۳ اس: [حرف «که» کوچك و کمرنگتر بین دو کلمه «چیزها» و «اندر» نوشته شده است].

۴ ¦⟵برگ [اس:۶۸-ب].

۵ ایا: - از آن.

۶ اس، ایا: سُروهاء. || نك: دهخدا: سرو. [سُ] ... اوستا «سرو» (شاخ جانور)... مطلق شاخ را گویند خواه شاخ گاو باشد خواه شاخ گاومیش و شاخ گوسفند و امثال آن.

قول خدای تعالی که گفت، قوله:[۷] هُوَ الَّذِي خَلَقَ لَكُمْ مَا فِي الْأَرْضِ جَمِيعاً.[۸] گفت: «او آن است کی بیافرید از بهر شما هر چه اندر زمین است بجملگی».

[§۵:۳۸] و چون همه منافع عالم به مردم پدید آمد، و مردم برمثال دیگر حیوان بزیست، و به مردم[۹] اگر او را بازگشتن باردیگر[۱۰] نباشد، این فضل که مردم را بود بر جملگی آفرینش تا از همه چیزی فایده گرفت ضایع شود، یا بایستی که این شریفتر[۱۱] آفرینش، که مردم بود، ضایع شدی. پس لازم آمد که معادی باشد مردم را بی‌فنا.

[§۶:۳۸] و نیز گوییم که چون از آفرینش بر[۱۲] حکمت کز صانع حکیم پدید آمد چیز ضایع نشد واجب نیاید که این تفاوت عظیم که اندر میان دو مردم است یکی نیکوکار و دیگر بدکردار ضایع شود.

[§۷:۳۸] و ما همی بینیم بدکرداران را که اندر این عالم با عزّ و جاه و فرمان روایی اند، و نیکوکاران و ستم‌رسیدگان با خواری و اندوه و بیچارگی و دردااند. وگر مر این هر دو گروه را بازگشتی نباشد که هر کسی به جزای آنچ کرده است برسد، و با این تفاوت بزرگ که اندر زندگی دنیایی میان دو تن بود، و پس از مرگ هر دو برابر باشند به ناچیز شدن، از عدل کردگار لازم نیاید، و اندر صنعت حکیم به آفرینش عالم چنین نیست.

[§۸:۳۸] از بهر آنك طبایع که عالم ترکیبْ ازو یافته است عدلِ قایم است، و اندر

---

۷ اس: – قوله.

۸ سورة البقرة (۲)، آغاز آیت ۲۹.

۹ ایا: – و بمردم.

۱۰ ایا: – باردیگر؛ اس: [«باردیگر» مخدوش است. اما در حاشیهٔ متن این کلمه واضح نوشته شده است].

۱۱ |←برگ [ایا:۵۷-ب].

۱۲ اس، ایا: پر. || تصحیح قیاسی.

آفرینش جانوران و نبات، عدل پیدا است. و چون راستی از ترکیبی بشود آن ترکیب پای ندارد.

[§۹:۳۸] پس روا نباشد[۱۳] که اندر آفرینش مردم این تفاوت برود. پس لازم آید که مردم را بازگشتن باشد که هریکی از بدکردار و نیکوکار به جزای خویش برسد، چنانك خدای تعالی همی‌گوید، قوله: أَمْ حَسِبَ الَّذِينَ اجْتَرَحُوا السَّيِّئَاتِ أَنْ نَجْعَلَهُمْ كَالَّذِينَ آمَنُوا وَ عَمِلُوا الصَّالِحَاتِ سَوَاءً مَحْيَاهُمْ وَ[۱۴] مَمَاتُهُمْ سَاءَ مَا يَحْكُمُونَ.[۱۵] همی‌گوید: «یا چنان همی‌پندارند آنها که بدیها کردند که ما ایشان را چنان کسها کنیم که گرویدگان کی کارهای نیکو کردند برابر باشند زندگی و مردگی ایشان. بد حکمی است این کی همی‌کنند».

[§۱۰:۳۸] پس این آیت همی آواز دهد خردمندان را اندر خلق که پس از مرگ و جدا شدن نفسها از جسدها این تفاوت همی پدید خواهد آمدن چون امروز پدید نیامد. و زین تأخیر که همی افتد عجب نباید داشتن که بودنی همچون بوده است سوی خردمند پس سوی عقل بوده‌تر است.

[§۱۱:۳۸] و این اندك روزگار[۱۶] این جهانی سوی مردم ضعیف‌خِرَد بسیار نماید، کی او فانی است ازین زندگی و اندر بودنی دیدارش نیست. و سوی عقل کلّ آنچ[۱۷] خواهد بود سخت نزدیك است چنانك خدای تعالی همی‌گوید:[۱۸] إِنَّهُمْ يَرَوْنَهُ بَعِيداً * وَ نَرَاهُ قَرِيباً.[۱۹] گفت: «ایشان دور همی بینندش و ما نزدیك همی بینیمش».

[§۱۲:۳۸] و نیز گوییم که چون اندر مردم نفسی همی‌بینیم شریف‌تر از آنك اندر

---

۱۳ ¦←برگ [اس:۶۹-الف].

۱۴ ایا: او.

۱۵ سورة الجاثية (۴۵)، آیت ۲۱.

۱۶ ¦←برگ [ایا:۵۸-الف].

۱۷ ایا: آنچه.

۱۸ ایا: + قوله.

۱۹ سورة المعارج (۷۰)، آیات ۶ تا ۷.

حیوان است و آن نفس سخنگوی است که همی پیدا آید و علم پذیرد و بشنود و بشنواند و بداند و دیگری را دانا کند، و زین نفس مردم را اندر عالم افزونی نبود اندر زندگی او، و مر خویشتن را بدان نفس زیادتی بقا نتوانست الفغدن، و اندر همه نفسهای نباتی و حیوانی جستن بقا نهاده است، لازم آید که آن کس که این نفس سخنگوی اندر مردم نهاد، غرضی را نهاد.

[۱۳:۳۸§] و چون اندر این عالم از آن غرض چیزی پدید نیامد واجب آید که آن غرض آفریدگار مردم از نهادن نفس سخنگوی اندر مردم پس از جدا شدن روح او از جسد او[۲۰] پدید آید. و آنچ نیکوکردار اندر نعمت و لذّت[۲۱] و راحت باقی شود و بدکردار اندر رنج و شدّت و درد و بلا همیشه گردد.

[۱۴:۳۸§] پاکست حکمت ایزد سبحانه از آنك محال اندر آفرینش روا دارد. و هر نیکوکاری و بدکرداری را مکافات آنچ ایشان کرده باشند برساند.

۲۰ اس: [عبارت «از جسد او» دوبار نوشته شده، اما بار دوم روی آن خط کشیده شده است].
۲۱ ¦⟵برگ [اس:۶۹-ب].

صف سی و نهم

سخن اندر آنك او[1] به هر مکانی هست[2]

[§۱:۳۹] گروهی از مردمان گویند که ایزد تعالی به هر مکانی هست و هیچ جای ازو خالی نیست و مر هیچ جای ازو پوشیده نیست. و چنان همی دانند که این توحید است و نفی صفات ناستوده است از خدای.

[§۲:۳۹] و ما گوییم که آنچ به هر مکانی هست و هیچ جای ازو خالی نیست و هیچ جای ازو پوشیده نیست آن طبیعت است. و عبارت آن طبیعت به دو سخن کشد: یکی قوّت فاعله یعنی کارکن، و دیگر ابتدای[3] حرکت. و هر کدام ازین دو را بگیری هیچ مکان از ایشان خالی نیست.

[§۳:۳۹] از بهر آنك مکان و زمان که صورت از ایشان و اندر ایشان پدید آید بوقت صورت‌کردن چیز اندر نفس بقوّت عقل از قوّت فاعله و آغاز حرکت خالی نباشد.

[§۴:۳۹] و نفس و عقل خالی‌اند از مکان صورت کرده، و مکان خالی نیست از قوّت فاعله، اعنی کارکن، و آغاز جنبش. و[4] چون مکان ازین دو حال خالی نشاید بودن، چگونه روا باشد که مُبدِع حقّ به مکانِ حاجتمند بدین دو چیز، اندر باشد، سپس از آنك عقل و نفس کی آفریدگان خدای‌اند[5] از مکان و زمانی[6] بی‌نیازند.

[§۵:۳۹] و از بهر آن گفتیم که مکان از قوّت فاعله و آغاز جنبش خالی نیست که

---

۱ ایا: – او.

۲ قس: کتاب الینابیع، الینبوع الحادی والعشرون (۲۱): في القول بـ«أن الله بکلّ مکان» لایلیق بالخلق الأوّل فضلاً عن المُبدِع جل جلاله وتعالی، ص ۵۱ تا ۵۳.

۳ ¦⟵برگ [ایا:۵۸-ب].

۴ ایا: – و.

۵ اس، ایا: خدایند.

۶ ایا: زمان.

هر مکانی را حال گردنده است، به اختلاف و احوال، از گرما و سرما و تاریکی و روشنایی و تنگی و فراخی و جز آن.

[§۳۹:۶] و گشتن احوال از قوّت گردانندهٔ احوال پدید آید و آن قوّة فاعله باشد. و نیز از جنبش باشد گشتن احوال وگر جنبش نبودی گشتن احوال نبودی.

[§۳۹:۷] و چون حال مکان گردنده بود، از جنبش خالی نبود. و همچنین قوّت فاعله بدانچ پدید آرد اندر هر مکانی،[۷] از گشتن حالها و پدید آمدن جانوران، گوایی همی‌دهد که او به هر مکانی حاضر است.

[§۳۹:۸] و مثالی دهیم مر این سخن را چنانك گوییم که هرگاه که توهّم کنیم که بعضی از هوا مکان شد مر بخاری را کز آب برخاست و بر هوا رفت و جای گرفت و آن بخار متمکّن شد چاره‌ای[۸] نیست از صورت[۹] کردن قوّت فاعله اندر آن بخار مکان‌گیر از بهر آنك اگر بقوّت آفتاب آن بخار بگدازد بقوّت فاعله گدازد وگر حرکت کند بقوّت فاعله کند به برتر شدن یا به فروتر آمدن.

[§۳۹:۹] پس درست کردیم که طبیعت است آنچه او به همه مکانها حاضر است. و نفس و عقل از مکان برتر است، از بهر آنك نفس و عقل تمام‌اند و تمام را به مکان حاجت نباشد.

[§۳۹:۱۰] و طبیعت آنك نگاهبان[۱۰] مکان است[۱۱] چون آتش جوهر او و جوهر هوا

---

۷ ¦⟵برگ [اس:۷۰-الف]. || عبارت «اندر هر مکانی» در ابتداء برگ [اس:۷۰-الف] تکرار شده است.

۸ اس: چاره‌ء؛ ایا: چاره.

۹ اس: [حروف «ص» و «و» در کلمه «صورت» خوانا نیست، اما در حاشیه متن ابتدای کلمه یعنی «صور» دوباره نویسی شده است].

۱۰ اس: نگاه‌بان.

۱۱ ¦⟵برگ [ایا:۵۹-الف].

از مکان کناره را نگاه دارند، و جوهر آب و جوهر خاك میانهٔ مکان نگاه دارند، و جوهرهای ستارگان دایرها[۱۲] نگاه دارند.

[§۳۹:۱۱] وگر این گوهرها نگاه‌داشته نبودی به نگاهبانی[۱۳] طبیعت، آسمانها و زمین تباه شدندی و ایزد تعالی حکمت خویش باطل کرده بودی.

[§۳۹:۱۲] پس گوییم که طبیعت حدّی است از حدود عقل[۱۴] که او شریفتر آفریده است از آفریدگان ایزد تعالی. و او[۱۵] است که به هر مکانی هست. و ایزد تعالی بزرگوارتر از آن است که او را به منزلت طبیعت شاید گفتن. تَبٰارَكَ اسْمُهُ[۱۶] و تَعٰالیٰ جَدُّهُ.[۱۷]

---

۱۲ اس، ایا: وابرها [کذا]. || تصحیح قیاسی. قس: كتاب الينابيع، الينبوع الحادي والعشرون: في القول بـ«أن الله بكل مكان»، لا يليق بالخلق الأول، فضلاً عن المُبدِع جل جلاله تعالی. ص ۵۲، بند (۱۰۱): وكذلك أن الأفق يحفظ جوهر النار والهواء، وكذلك الوسط يحفظ جوهر الماء والأرض، والدوائر تحفظ جواهر الأفلاك والكواكب.

۱۳ اس: نگاه‌بانی.

۱۴ ضمیر «نا» در آیات ۱۶، ۱۷، ۷۹، و ۱۰۴، از سورة الأنبياء (۲۱)، اشاره به حدود عقل در این رابطه دارد: وَ مٰا خَلَقْنَا السَّمٰاءَ وَ الْأَرْضَ وَ مٰا بَيْنَهُمٰا لاٰعِبِينَ (۱۶)* لَوْ أَرَدْنٰا أَنْ نَتَّخِذَ لَهْواً لاَتَّخَذْنٰاهُ مِنْ لَدُنّٰا إِنْ كُنّٰا فٰاعِلِينَ (۱۷)* فَفَهَّمْنٰاهٰا سُلَيْمٰانَ وَ كُلاًّ آتَيْنٰا حُكْماً وَ عِلْماً وَ سَخَّرْنٰا مَعَ دٰاوُدَ الْجِبٰالَ يُسَبِّحْنَ وَ الطَّيْرَ وَ كُنّٰا فٰاعِلِينَ (۷۹)* يَوْمَ نَطْوِي السَّمٰاءَ كَطَيِّ السِّجِلِّ لِلْكُتُبِ كَمٰا بَدَأْنٰا أَوَّلَ خَلْقٍ نُعِيدُهُ وَعْداً عَلَيْنٰا إِنّٰا كُنّٰا فٰاعِلِينَ (۱۰۴). برای آیت ۱۶، نك: زادالمسافر، قول ۲۳، ص ۳۶۲، و زادالمسافرین، قول ۲۳، ص ۳۵۱؛ نیز برای آیت ۱۰۴، نك: زادالمسافر، قول ۲۲، ص ۳۳۰، و زادالمسافرین، قول ۲۲، ص ۳۲۱.

۱۵ یعنی طبیعت.

۱۶ اشارت است به سورة الرَّحْمٰن (۵۵)، آیت ۷۸: تَبٰارَكَ اسْمُ رَبِّكَ ذِي الْجَلاٰلِ وَ الْإِكْرٰامِ.

۱۷ اشارت است به سورة الجِنّ (۷۲)، آیت ۳: وَ أَنَّهُ تَعٰالیٰ جَدُّ رَبِّنٰا مَا اتَّخَذَ صٰاحِبَةً وَ لاٰ وَلَداً.

صف چهلم

سخن اندر عالم جسمانی که اندر آفاق نفس کلّ است[۱]

[§۴۰:۱] گوییم که چاره نیست از آنك مر جسم را نهایت باشد. از بهر آنك حقیقت جسم آن است که مر او را سه بُعد است، چون درازا و پهنا و ژرفا. و هر یکی ازین بعدها دو کناره دارد و میانه‌ای.[۲]

[§۴۰:۲] و چون بُعدهای جسم را نهایت باشد جسم را نهایت باشد. و چون جسم را نهایت درست شده باشد[۳] که از بیرون این فلك کلّ که عالم است نه زمان است و نه مکان و نه جرمی تهی است و نه هیچ چیز از چیزهای طبیعی، از بهر آنك همه طبیعیّات از اندرون فلك است و فلك محیط است به طبایع احاطتی طبیعی.

[§۴۰:۳] و ما دانیم[۴] که نفس جزوی که امروز اندر زمان است چون مر این جسد را بیوکند به وهم، و فراموش کندش، او به چیزی هیولانی و حسی نماند. و هیچ چیز با جوهر او نماند مگر علم محض.

[§۴۰:۴] و چون نفس جزوی که اندر مردم است برشود سوی بالا به طلب کردن آنچ[۵] از بیرون فلك است، بقوّت علم، و نفی کند جرم را و جسم را، چه از خالی و چه از پر، چیز نیابد مگر اثباتی محض بیرون این جرم گردنده که فلك است.

[§۴۰:۵] و چون طبیعیّات به کناره رسد چیز نباشد مگر سازندهٔ طبیعیّات و چون نفس جزوی بیرون این فلك چیز نیافت و زو بگذشت درست شد که آن[۶] برشدن

---

۱ قس: کتاب الینابیع، الینبوع التاسع عشر (۱۹): في أن الأفلاك بجمیع قواها ونجومها وحرکاتها في أُفق النفس، ص ۴۷ تا ۴۹.

۲ اس، ایا: میانهء.

۳ اس: + درست شده باشد [عبارت «درست شده باشد» تکرار شده است].

۴ ¦⟵برگ [اس:۷۰-ب].

۵ ایا: آنچه.

۶ ¦⟵برگ [ایا:۵۹-ب].

او به عالم لطیف از لطیفیِ خویش و هم‌گوشگی با نفس‌کلّی [است] تا ببیند[۷] آن سرور لذّات و عزّ و شرف روحانی که نفس او اندر آن غرقه شود.[۸]

[§۴۰:۶] وگر برشدن نفس جزوی به عالم لطیف از جهت علم ریاضی بِنا شد،[۹] که هندسه ازو است،[۱۰] پیدا شود مر او را جوهر نفس‌کلّ، که محیط است به جرم گردنده، احاطت علّت به معلولِ خویش و احاطت صانع به مصنوع خویش، نه چون محیط شدن جسم لطیف به جسم کثیف.

[§۴۰:۷] و محیط شدن نفس‌کلّی به عالم طبیعت محیط شدنی علمی است و احاطت علمی را از اندرون و بیرون هر دو یکسان باشد. پس درست شد که افلاک و عالم اندر افق نفس‌کلّی است.

[§۴۰:۸] و نیز گوییم که آن دلیل کی مردم بدو بتواند دانستن که افلاک به همه حرکات گردان است و متناهی است و اندر رسیدن او بدین علم به علمی باشد که پیش ازین بدانسته باشد، تا آن علم راه نماید مر او را سوی این علم.

[§۴۰:۹] و آن علم آن است که بداند که هر دایره[۱۱] را[۱۲] نهایت آن باشد که خطها

---

۷ ایا: به بیند.

۸ قس: کتاب الینابیع، الینبوع التاسع عشر (۱۹)، ص ۴۸، بند (۹۲)، س ۳ تا ۶: فاذا النفس الجزئیّة قد بلغت کلّیّتها حین لم تجد شیئًا من الطبیعیّات خارجاً عن الجرم المستدیر، ووجدت العلم هناك ثابتًا، فان كان سلوكها بتأييد لطيف من الفس الكلّيّة، رأت هناك من السرور واللّذّة والعزّ والشوق ما تستغرق نفسها فيه.

۹ اس: نبا شد، ایا: نباشد [کذا]. || تصحیح قیاسی. نك: کتاب الینابیع، الینبوع التاسع عشر (۱۹)، ص ۴۸، بند (۹۲)، س ۶ تا ۹: وان لم یکن سلوکها الّا من جهة الاستدلالات بالوقوف علی الریاضیات، ثبت عندها جوهریّة الكلّ المحيط بالجرم المستدير احاطة العلّة بالمعلول واحاطة الصانع بالمصنوع، لا كاحاطة الجسم الكبير بالجسم الصغير، ولا كاحاطة الجسم اللطيف بالجسم الكثيف.

۱۰ ایا: [حروف «س» و «ت» در کلمه «ازوست» بالای خط نوشته شده است].

۱۱ اس، ایا: دایرهٔ.

۱۲ ایا: – را.

کز مرکز او بیرون شود هریکی براندازهٔ دیگر باشد تا محیط دایره و نهایت دایره بر سر آن خطها باشد.

[§۴۰:۱۰] و یافتیم مر خطها را کز مرکز زمین همی بیرون آید که بنهایت همی رسد آنجا که فلكِ محیطْ سطح مَرُویَسْت کی همی‌گردد. پس آن سطحِ محیط منتهای عالم است. و این دانستن اندر غریزت نفس است.

[§۴۰:۱۱] پس بدین دانستن، کی نفس جزوی را حاصل آمد از راه تعلیم، درست گشت که این عالم اندر افق نفس کلّ است.[۱۳]

[§۴۰:۱۲] و نیز مردم حکم کند[۱۴] بر فلك تا فایده‌ها ازو بحاصل کند و خردمند بداند که فایده اندر فلك ازبهر نفس جزوی نهادند.

[§۴۰:۱۳] و چیزی کز بهر جزوی نهاده باشند ناچاره بهر[۱۵] کلّ آن جزو نهاده باشند. ازبهرآنك فایدهٔ جزو جز از کلّ خویش نشاید بود.

[§۴۰:۱۴] پس گوییم که چشم بیننده اندر مردم ازبهر بازداشتن مضرّتها است از خویشتن و کشیدن منفعتها بذات خویش و فلك را حاجت نیست به چیزی کی بدان[۱۶] مضرّت از خویشتن بازدارد یا بدان منفعت بخویشتن کشد.

[§۴۰:۱۵] و همچنین گوش شنوا مر مردم را ازبهر منفعت گرفتن او بایست از چیزی که او را اندر آن حاجت است و فلك را حاجت نیست به شنودن چیزها.

---

۱۳ قس: کتاب الینابیع، الینبوع التاسع عشر (۱۹)، ص ۴۸، بند (۹۳)، س ۱۲ تا ۱۶: وأیضًا فان الانسان اذا استدلّ على أنّ الأفلاك بجميع حركاتها مستديرة متناهية، أخذ من هذه المقدّمة، و هي أنّ كلّ دائرة لا نهاية لها، فانّ الخطوط التي تخرج من مركزها إلى المحيط غير متناهية. و قد وجدنا الخطوط التي تخرج من الأرض — و هي المركز — ‹إلى› المحيط متناهية. و هذه غريزة النفس، فانّ النفس هي المحيطة بالفلك و الفلك في أُفقها، فاعرفه.

۱۴ ¦←برگ [اس:۷۱-الف].

۱۵ اس: [کلمه «بهر» بالای خط ریز نوشته شده است].

۱۶ ¦←برگ [ایا:۶۰-الف].

[§۴۰:۱۶] و همچنین دیگر حواس نایافتن اندر فلکها و یافتن آن اندر مردم همی دلیل کند بر حاجتمندی مردم بدان و بی‌نیازی فلك از آن.

[§۴۰:۱۷] پس چون ما یافتیم مردم را که به نفس جزوی همی حکم کند بر منفعتهای فلکی و بیرون آرد فایده‌ها و حکمتهای او را، دانستیم که نفس کلّی، که این نفس مردم ازو جزوی است، مر این فایده‌ها را اندر فلك نهاد تا نفس جزوی را ممکن است بیرون آوردن آن ازو و بنهادن مر حکم را برو بواجبی.[۱۷]

[§۴۰:۱۸] وگر نفس کلّی اندر فلك این حکمتها ننهاده بودی نفس جزوی آن ازو بیرون نتوانستی آوردن.

[§۴۰:۱۹] پس درست کردیم که فلك با آنچ اندر او است اندر افق نفس کلّی است تا پیدا شد مر نفس جزوی را نظم و ترتیب آن.

۱۷ نك: دهخدا: - بِواجِبی؛ قید کیفیت و وصف، به معنی چنانکه باید، کاملا درست، بواجب (از روی وجوب): به لوازم این خدمت بواجبی قیام نتواند نمود.

صف چهل و یکم

سخن اندر سرما و گرمای قیامت

[§۴۱:۱] سرما و گرما دو کناره است مر اعتدال را، و راحت و لذّت اندر اعتدال است. و نفس بر اعتدال قرار گیرد و زین هر دو کناره بگریزد.

[§۴۱:۲] و همچنین هر حالی ستوده میانجی است به میان دو حال ناستوده. و قول حکماء[۱] علم آلهی اندر این معنی آن است که گویند: کل مدح هو عدل بین حاشیتین[۲] الجور.[۳] گویند: «هر ستایشی دادی است اندر میان دو کنارهٔ ستم». چنانك دلیری میانجی است به میان بزدلی[۴] و دیوانگی. و دلیری که میانجی است ستوده است[۵] و دو کنارهٔ او که دیوانگی و بزدلی[۶] است نکوهیده است. و همچنین جوانمردی کردن میانجی است میان زفتی و اسراف. و جوانمردی ستوده است و هر دو کناره‌اش هم زفتی و هم اسراف نکوهیده است.

[§۴۱:۳] چنانك خدای تعالی فرمود، قوله: وَ لاٰ تَجْعَلْ يَدَكَ مَغْلُولَةً إِلىٰ عُنُقِكَ وَ لاٰ تَبْسُطْهٰا كُلَّ الْبَسْطِ فَتَقْعُدَ مَلُوماً مَحْسُوراً.[۷] گفت: «مکن دست را با گردن بسته،[۸] یعنی از بخیلی، و نیز مگستر مر دست را همه گستردن تا بننشینی[۹] ملامت زده و پشیمان شده». و خردمند میانجی است میان بیهدگی و عاجزی از سخن و جز آن.

---

۱ ایا: حکمای.

۲ اس: حاشیی؛ ایا: حاشیتن.

۳ اس، ایا: جور.

۴ اس: بردلی؛ ایا: بددلی.

۵ ¦←برگ [اس:۷۱-ب].

۶ اس: بزدلی؛ ایا: بددلی.

۷ سورة الإسراء (۱۷)، آیت ۲۹.

۸ ¦←برگ [ایا:۶۰-ب].

۹ اس، ایا: بنه نشینی.

و دیگر خصلتهای[۱۰] ستوده همه میانجی است و ستوده است به میان دو کنارهٔ ناستودهٔ خویش.

[§۴:۴۱] پس گوییم که اعتدال از آن میانجیان ستوده است به میان دو کنارهٔ ناستوده که یکی ازو گرما است و دیگر سرما و این هر دو دشواری اندر دو کنارهٔ عالم اند. گرمی بغایتِ برتری است کی مرکز آتش است[۱۱] و سردی بغایتِ فروتری است. و بدین دو چیز نفس اندر این عالم رنجه شود و آن حال کی میان این دو حال است نفس ازو لذّت یابد.

[§۵:۴۱] پس ترسانیدن پیامبران، علیهم السّلام، مر امّت را به سرما و گرمای قیامت از ایشان بر سبیل مثل بود. و بدین گفتار معنی آن خواستند که هر که او توحید را بی میانجیِ اولیای خدای و بی عمل پذیرد مفرط شود، اعنی از حدّ اندرگذرد.

[§۶:۴۱] ازیراك بی میانجی اولیا و رسول و وصی و امام به ترتیب مر توحید را صفت نتوان کردن.

[§۷:۴۱] و اگر کسی بی این میانجیان توحید جوید مُعَطِّل[۱۲] شود اعنی که خدای را نیست گوید.

[§۸:۴۱] پس اگر بی میانجی اولیای خدای خواهد که نیست بگوید و بکوشد تا اثبات کند به تشبیه اندرافتد.

[§۹:۴۱] و این هر دو کنارهٔ توحید است. یکی تشبیه ماننده به سرمای[۱۳] زمهریر که او فرودین نقطهٔ عالم است.

---

۱۰ اس: خصلتها.

۱۱ ایا: [عبارت «که مرکز آتش است» در فاصله بین خطوط به شکل وارونه اما خوانا نوشته شده است].

۱۲ نك: دهخدا: معطل. [مُ عَ طْ طِ] ... آنکه صانع عزوجل را انکار کند و شرایع را باطل انگارد. ج، معطلون. ... و رجوع به معطله شود.

۱۳ اس: سرماء.

[§۴۱:۱۰] و مردم اندر تشبیه آن وقت افتد که با مثالهای کثیف و ظاهر شریعت توحید جوید.

[§۴۱:۱۱] و همچنین، چون بی‌ظاهر، بر مثل و شناختنِ تأویل آن مثلها توحید جوید، اندر تعطیل افتد که آن برترین حدّی است از عالم که آنجا آتش سوزان است.

[§۴۱:۱۲] و آنچ به میانجی میانجیان حق گفته شود و اعتقاد کرده شود[۱۴] بر اعتدال باشد و آن کس از سرما و گرمای قیامت رسته شود، چنانك خدای تعالی میگوید، قوله: لاٰ یَرَوْنَ فِیهاٰ شَمْساً وَ لاٰ زَمْهَرِیراً.[۱۵] همی‌گوید: «نبینند[۱۶] اندر بهشت نه گرما و نه سرما».

[§۴۱:۱۳] معنیش آن خواست که[۱۷] مؤمنان را توحید آلوده نشود نه به تشبیه و نه به تعطیل.

[§۴۱:۱۴] و هم این معنی بود کز رسول، صلی الله علیه وآله،[۱۸] پرسیدند از حال بهشت کی سرد است یا گرم. وی، علیه السّلام، جواب داد و گفت: هواءٌ سَجْسَجٌ،[۱۹] مثل بَرد السَّحَر.[۲۰] گفت: «هوای[۲۱] بهشت میانه است نه سرد است و نه گرم

۱۴ ¦⟵برگ [اس:۷۲-الف].

۱۵ سورة الإنسان (۷۶)، آیت ۱۳: مُتَّکِئِینَ فِیهاٰ عَلَی الْأَرٰائِكِ لاٰ یَرَوْنَ فِیهاٰ شَمْساً وَ لاٰ زَمْهَرِیراً.

۱۶ اس، ایا: نه بینند.

۱۷ ¦⟵برگ [ایا:۶۱-الف].

۱۸ ایا: + و سلّم.

۱۹ نك: دهخدا: سجسج. [سَ سَ] ... زمین هموار خوش نه دُرشت نه نرم. || مابین طلوع فجر تا طلوع آفتاب. ... || هوای خوش نه سرد و نه گرم. ... هوای معتدل نه گرم و نه سرد. ...: صفة الجنة وهوأها السجسج وکذا ظلل الجنة سجسج؛ ای معتدل لا حرّ ولا قر، ویوم سجسج؛ روز نه سرد و نه گرم. ... گویند: یوم سجسج؛ که نه گرم آزار دهنده باشد و نه سرد.

۲۰ اس: السجر [کذا].

۲۱ اس، ایا: هواء.

همچون خنکی سپیده دم».[۲۲] و گفتن او، صلی الله علیه و آله،[۲۳] کی «بهشت نه سرد است و نه گرم» نشانی بود از آنك[۲۴] اندر بهشت مرگ نیست از بهر آنك مرگ ازین دو حال مخالف است یا سرمای بی حد یا گرمای بی حد؛ و هر چیزی که آن به چهار درجه سرد است از داروها یا به چهار درجه گرم است آن چیز زهر کشنده است. و هر کجا سرما و گرما نباشد مرگ نباشد.

[§۴۱:۱۵] این بود معنی ترسانیدن پیامبران،[۲۵] علیهم السّلام، مر خلق را به سرما و گرمای[۲۶] قیامت؛ و چنان بباید دانستن مؤمن را که بقیامت نه سرما است و نه گرما.

[§۴۱:۱۶] و این مثلی بود رسولان زدند بل چنان باید صورت کردن که اگر همه سرماهای عالم جسمانی بر یك مردم جمله کنی تا همه قوّت خویش بدان یك تن رساند صد سال اندر آن یك تن از آن سرما آن رنج نبیند[۲۷] که بِیَك دَم‌زَدن از رنج سرمای قیامت بیند؛ و حال گرمای قیامت هم بر این جمله قیاس باید کردن.

[§۴۱:۱۷] و لکن ما خواستیم تا معنی رنج بدین عقوبت مر خلق را که پیامبران،[۲۸] علیهم السّلام، زلیفن کردند بازنمائیم نه آن خواستیم که عقوبت آخرت را نفی کنیم، نَعُوذُ بِاللّٰهِ مِن عَذٰابِ اللّٰهِ.

۲۲ نك: المیبدی، ابوالفضل رشیدالدین، کشف الأسرار و عدّة الأبرار: (معروف به تفسیر خواجه عبدالله انصاری)، به‌اهتمام: علی اصغر حکمت (تهران، ۱۳۸۲ش)، ج ۶، قوله تعالی: ۴-النوبة الثانیة: «جَنّٰاتِ عَدْنٍ [الَّتِي وَعَدَ الرَّحْمٰنُ عِبَادَهُ بِالْغَيْبِ (سورة مریم -۱۹، آیت ۶۱)]»، ص ۷۱.

۲۳ ایا: + و سلّم.

۲۴ ایا: ازان که.

۲۵ ایا: پیغامبران.

۲۶ اس: گرماء.

۲۷ اس، ایا: نه بیند.

۲۸ ایا: پیغامبران.

صف چهل و دوم

سخن اندر برزخ[۱]

[§۱:۴۲] [سخن اندر برزخ،] از قول گروهی از داناانِ[۲] خواجهٔ شهید بوالحسن نخشبی،[۳] رَضِيَ اللّٰهُ عَنْهُ، اندر این معنی آن است که از بَرِ فلك[۴] الأفلاك نوری لطیف است نه متحرّك و نه ساکن، که سر زبرین از آن نور باریك است و به نفس‌کلّ پیوسته است، و سر فرودینش کثیف و سطبر است اندر فلك[۵] پیوسته است.[۶]

[§۲:۴۲] و هر نفسی که علمی از علمها بیاموزد آن علم مر او را دست بازندارد که نیست شود بل که او را باقی کند. و اگر آن علم دینی بود، پرورده شده باشد به عمل شریعت و پرهیز، چون آن نفس از جسد جدا شود از فلك و اجرام بگذرد و بدان نور رسد که یك سر ازو به نفس‌کلّ پیوسته است و دیگر سرش به فلك پیوسته است، و بدان طرف باریك لطیف قرار گیرد، و به نفس‌کلّ پیوسته شود.

[§۳:۴۲] و هرچه نفس بدکرداران و معاقبان باشد بدین طرف قرار گیرد که به فلك پیوسته است.

[§۴:۴۲] و قول شهید اندر کتاب محصول آن است که عالم جسمانی فنا پذیرد به آخِرِ کار. و او، رَضِيَ اللّٰهُ عَنْهُ، به تناسخ و گشتن نفس از جسدی به دیگر جسدی [نـ]گوید.[۷]

---

۱ عنوان این صف (یعنی: «سخن اندر برزخ») را بایستی همراه جملهٔ اول قرائت کرد تا نحوهٔ خواندن جملهٔ آغازین درست آید.

۲ ایا: دانایان.

۳ محمد بن احمد النسفی (النخشبی).

۴ ایا: [«فلك» در فاصله بین خطوط نوشته شده است].

۵ ¦⟵برگ [اس:۷۲-ب].

۶ ¦⟵برگ [ایا:۶۱-ب].

۷ تصحیح قیاسی. || ویلفرد مادلونگ نیز می‌نویسد که «نگوید» درست است. نك: ویلفرد

[§۵:۴۲] و قول دهقان،[۸] که پسر شیخ شهید بود، و صاحب جزیرهٔ خراسان[۹] پس از [بو]یعقوب او بود، اندر برزخ آن است که گوید: برزخ نفس طبیعی است، و نفوس مردم تا به عالم طبیعی پیوسته باشند از برزخ رها[۱۰] نیابند، و آزیر[۱۱] طبایع بباشد.[۱۲]

[§۶:۴۲] و اشارت نکرد به چیزی مر برزخ را چنانک پدرش کرد. و دهقان بر بویعقوب طعن کرد اندر این معنی و گفت کی او تناسخی بود.

[§۷:۴۲] و قول بهری از فاضلان علم شریعت حقّ آن است کی برزخ علم ظاهر است و مثلها و رمزهای شریعت است.

[§۸:۴۲] و چنان گفتند این کسان که هر نفسی که علم ظاهر را به صورت خویش کند اندر این عالم باشد تا آن زمان که به علم عقل رسد و چون به علم عقل رسد آنگه از عالم طبیعت بیرون شود و به عالم عقل رسد.

[§۹:۴۲] و سوی این مردمان چنان است کی دوزخ عالم جسمانی است و فانی است و بهشت عالم روحانی است و باقی است. و چنین گفتند این مردمان که قایم قیامت که پیغامبر خلق را بدو خواند، هرکه مر او را بحقیقت دانست، و نفس خویش را بشناخت، او به کارکرد[۱۳] ازین عالم بدان عالم رسد و مر او را بازدارنده‌ای[۱۴] نماند.

مادلونگ، 'ابویعقوب السجستاني و تناسخ'، ایرانیکا واریا: مقالات در بزرگداشت پروفسور احسان یارشاطر (لیدن، ۱۹۹۰)، ص ۱۳۲ از متن، و ص ۱۴۲، یادداشت شماره ۸.

۸ دهقان پسر محمد بن احمد النسفی است.

۹ اس، ایا: خرلان [کذا]. || تصحیح قیاسی. این خطای کاتب است و درست آن «خراسان» است. || نك: مادلونگ، 'ابویعقوب السجستاني و تناسخ'، ص ۱۴۲، یادداشت شماره ۹.

۱۰ ایا: رهایی.

۱۱ اس: ازبر؛ ایا: ازبر. || تصحیح قیاسی. نیز نك: دهخدا: آزیر. ... مماله‌ٔ آزار: در جهان چندانکه خواهی بیشمار / نیستیّ و محنت و آزیر هست \ وز فلك چندانکه خواهی بی قیاس / نفرت آهو و خشم شیر هست. (انوری).

۱۲ اس: نباشد؛ ایا: نباشد. || تصحیح قیاسی.

۱۳ نك: دهخدا: کارکرد. [كَ / كِ] ... کار کردن و عمل. ... عمل و کار و کردار و فعل.

۱۴ اس، ایا: بازدارنده‌ء.

[۱۰:۴۲§] و قول گروهی از حکیمان اندر برزخ آن است که برزخ علم فکری است[۱۵] و علم فکری میانجی است میان علم شریعتی و میان علم عقلی. و این قول نزدیك است به قول شهید که گوید برزخ میانجی است از میان فلك و میان عالم نفس.

[۱۱:۴۲§] و قول گروهی اندر برزخ آن است[۱۶] که نفس تا هفت مرتبت برو نگذرد به عالم عقلی نرسد همچنانك جسد به هفتم مرتبت تمام شود و به نعمتهای جسمانی رسد. مر نفس را بدان هفت مرتبت بکار باید تا اندر عالم عقل بفعل آید و به نعمتهای ابدی و ثوابهای باقی رسد.

[۱۲:۴۲§] و امّا شرح این حال ما اندر کتاب مصباح گفته‌ایم به برهانهای عقلی نه بر طریق تناسخ و نه بر دعوی بی‌برهان.

[۱۳:۴۲§] و قول بویعقوب سجزی را اندر برزخ جای چنان است که برزخ مر شریعتهای پیامبران را خواهد و ایشان را، علیهم السّلام، خداوندان دور ستر خواند و قایم را، علیه السّلام، خداوند دور کشف خواند و خداوند کور عظیم نیز گویدش.

[۱۴:۴۲§] و از پیش آدم، علیه السّلام، سخن گوید وز پس قیامت بگوید که چنین خواهد بودن بی‌معنی و برهانی. و چنین گوید که نفسهای تعلیمی بقوّت تأیید انبیا، علیهم السّلام، اندر عالم جسمانی قرار گرفتند، و بقوّت خداوند کور بزرگ روحانی شوند. و نزدیك او برزخ شرایع انبیا است.

[۱۵:۴۲§] و جایی دیگر هم بویعقوب برزخ مر شخصهای مردم را گوید، و گوید که نفسها اندر شخصها همی‌گردند اندر این عالم تا آن وقت کی خداوند قیامت بیاید آنگه هر نفسی کی نیکوکار باشد به تأیید رسد و به عالم عقلی برشود و آن بهشت است، و هر نفسی که بدکردار باشد تأیید نپذیرد[۱۷] و اندر عالم جسمانی بماند و

۱۵ ¦⟵برگ [ایا:۶۲-الف] .

۱۶ ¦⟵برگ [اس:۷۳-الف].

۱۷ اس: نه پذیرد.

دوزخ این است. و بویعقوب را سخنان نیك و پسندیده بسیار است. امّا آنچ اندر اثبات تناسخ گفت خداوندان نپسندیدند.[۱۸]

[§۴۲:۱۶] و قول اهل ظاهر اندر برزخ آن است که برزخ گور است، این کنده‌ای[۱۹] که کالبد مردم اندر او نهند، و میان ایشان اندر این سخن خلافی نیست. اما اندر عذاب گور و صفت منکر و نکیر[۲۰] اختلاف[۲۱] است میان اهل ظاهر. این جمله که گفته شد گفتار اهل شریعت است اندر برزخ.

[§۴۲:۱۷] و امّا سخن طبایعیان و منطقیان و تناسخیان آن است که بگوییم ازین پس سخن بیشتر مردمان از اهل فلسفه و طبایع چنان است که برزخ نامی شریعی است که خداوند شریعت آورد. و ایشان مر خداوند شریعت را ناموس[۲۲] گویند.[۲۳]

[§۴۲:۱۸] و بعضی به نام و معنی برزخ منکر شدند، و بهری به معنی مقر آمدند و به نام منکر شدند.

---

۱۸ نك: زادالمسافر، قول ۲۶، ص ۴۴۱: و شیخ بویعقوب سجزی — رحمة الله — به وقتی که سوداش رنجه کرده بود، در این معنی سخن گفته است و متابعان خاندان حق را سوی این مذهب دعوت کرده است اندر کتابی که مر او را سوس‌البقا نام نهاده است و اندر کشف‌المحجوب و اندر رسالهٔ باهره و جز آن از تألیف‌های خویش، و چو خداوند زمان او بشنود که او [مر] این مذهب را تقویت کرد، از او نپسندید و گفت که «مر او را سودا غالب شده است»؛ و لیکن گروهی از شیعت بر قول او همی روند و آن خطاست. || نیز نك: زادالمسافرین، قول ۲۶، ص ۴۲۱ تا ۴۲۲.

۱۹ اس، ایا: کنده‌ء.

۲۰ ایا: نکر.

۲۱ ¦⟵برگ [ایا:۶۲-ب] .

۲۲ نك: دهخدا: ناموس. (معرب، اِسم) احکام الهی. ... شریعت. ... قانون و شریعت و احکام الهی. ... یکی روز بود که عیسی تعلیم میداد ... و او ناموس می آموزانید. ... یهودیان گفتند که ناموس داریم در ناموس ما مرگ بر وی واجب است که خود را فرزند خدا ساخت. ... مپندارید که آمدم تا ناموس و توریت باطل کنم، نه نیامدم که منسوخ کنم. (انجیل فارسی ص ۶۰ از حاشیهٔ برهان قاطع چ معین). || قاعده. دستور. ... قانون. آئین ... || وحی. ... || ملائکه.... ملائک. ... || (اِسم خاص) جبرئیل. ... نام جبرئیل علیه السلام... صاحب راز. آگاه بر نهانی امر. ...صاحب سِر که مطلع از باطن کار توست.

۲۳ ¦⟵برگ [اس:۷۳-ب].

[§۴۲:۱۹] و سخن آن کسان که به معنی اقرار دادند و آن آن مردمانند از فیلسوفان که دوزخ مر عالم جسمانی را گویند و بهشت مر عالم روحانی را نهند. و این مردمان بمذهب حقیقت میل کنند و خواهند که سخن فلسفی و شرعی را بهم فرازآرند، و مذهب ایشان آن است که برزخ این شخص مردم است.

[§۴۲:۲۰] و قول ایشان آن است که چون نفس مردم حقایق فلسفی و شریعی و عقل و معقول بشناسد او به عالم روحانی رسد و هیچ بازدارنده‌ای[۲۴] نماند او را از آن عالم، و اندر عالم عقلی با فریشتگان بماند اندر نعمتهای ابدی و قدرت جاودانی، و او صورتی گردد از علم و حکمت نگاشته بر نفسی بسیط علمی و عقلی و فکری.

[§۴۲:۲۱] و عقاب بزرگ این گروه جاودان ماندن است اندر دایرهٔ طبیعت. و طبیعت مر آن قوّت خواهند کی نفس کلّ بدان قوّت جنبانندهٔ فلك‌الأفلاك است. و فلك‌الأفلاك جنبانندهٔ همه فلکها است و آن قوّتِ[۲۵] فاعلهٔ برین است طبایع را و عالم جسمانی را.

[§۴۲:۲۲] و قول ابوالحسن عامری اندر کتاب مقالات چنان است که مهتران ثنویان ایدون[۲۶] گویند که معنی برزخ از اوّل موجود است مردم را از آغاز کون او، و لکن هرکسی به معنی دیگر گویند.

[§۴۲:۲۳] و نزدیك بزرگان ثنویان چنان است کی ظلمت را دو قوّت است هردو نکوهیده یکی شهوت و دیگر جهل. برزخ ظلمت است که روح اندر او بدین دو قوّت نکوهیده بیاویزد[۲۷] که هردو قوّت دیوان است. و دیوان[۲۸] آن کسانند که این دو قوّت نگاه دارند. و هر نفسی که بدین دو قوّت اندر مانده باشد اندر برزخ

---

۲۴ اس، ایا: بازدارنده‌ء.

۲۵ ایا: قوة.

۲۶ نك: دهخدا: ایدون. [ای/آ/اِ] ... اینچنین. ... اینچنین و بدین طریق. ... همچنین.

۲۷ ایا: نیاویزد.

۲۸ ¦⟵برگ [ایا:۶۳-الف] .

باشد همیشه و هرگز روح او به عالم نورانی نرسد. و آن وقت که[۲۹] نور از ظلمت جدا شود و نور بر ظلمت قادر شود، نفس این کسان اندر دایره ظلمت بماند جاودان.

[§۲۴:۴۲] و چنین گویند که نور را دو قوّت است هردو ستوده یکی پارسایی و دیگر علم و این هردو قوّتهای[۳۰] نورانی‌اند.[۳۱] و چنین گویند که روحی که پارسا شود و قوّت شهوانی را بشکند، آن وقت کی نور کلّی بر ظلمت قادر شود او بدان عالم نورانی رسد، و بدان عالم بماند جاودان با قدری تمام و نعمتی دایم.

[§۲۵:۴۲] و ما گوییم که جملهٔ سخنها اندر نفی برزخ و اثبات آن بر چهار قسمت است، قسمتهای عقلی، که هیچ عاقل از عقلآءِ مذاهب مر آن را باز نتوانند زدن:

[§۲۶:۴۲] یکی قول[۳۲] آن کسان است که برزخ همی محسوس گویند و هم موهوم. و محسوس شخصها را خواهند و موهوم مر آن نور را خواهند که زبر فلک‌الأفلاک است. خواجهٔ شهید یاد کند و این نیز قول آن مردمان است کز عبدان که صاحب جزیرهٔ عراق بود حکایت کنند.

[§۲۷:۴۲] و دیگر قول آن کسان است که برزخ را نه محسوس گویند و نه موهوم؛ و آن فلاسفه و دهریان و طبایعیان و فلکیان‌اند.

[§۲۸:۴۲] و سدیگر قول آن کسها است که برزخ را[۳۳] محسوس را گویند و موهوم نگویند[۳۴] و آن تناسخیان‌اند که[۳۵] به مذهب افلاطون دعوی کنند و آن هم طریق [بو]یعقوب سجزی است.

---

۲۹ یعنی تا آن زمان که «چنین» باشد... (پس) «چنان» خواهد بود.

۳۰ ایا: + پسندیده‌اند و.

۳۱ ¦⟵برگ [اس:۷۴-الف] .

۳۲ اس، ایا: قوت.

۳۳ ایا: - را.

۳۴ اس، ایا: نه گویند.

۳۵ ایا: - که.

[§۲۹:۴۲] و چهارم قول آن کسان است که برزخ موهوم گویند و محسوس نگویند و بدان مر آن نور را خواهند که زبر فلك است بر طریق خواجه شهید و پسرش،[۳۶] حسن مسعود، و آن احمد صالح که پیش از ایشان بود.

[§۳۰:۴۲] پس ما مر[۳۷] این سخنهای شریف را و سرّهای عظیم را جمله یاد کردیم ازبهر صلاح خداوندان عقل را تا کسانی که راه نمی[۳۸] دانند راه برند، و گمراهان مر بیچارگان را از راه نبرند، و سخن حقّ را از باطل بدانند و مُحَقِّقان را از مُبْطِلان جدا کنند.

[§۳۱:۴۲] و شنودیم که یکی از ضعیفان جوینده یکی را از عالمان پرسید از حال و حقیقت برزخ. آن دانا از آن ضعیف هزار درم خواست بهای آن سخن و این درم ازو بستد تا این سخن مر او را بگفت که آن سخن کفر است، و هر کسی مر روایىِ کار خویش را بی‌فرمان سخن همی‌گویند، و خویشتن را و خلق را بآتش همی‌برند. چنانك خدای تعالی می‌گوید، قوله: فَاتَّبَعُوا[۳۹] أَمْرَ فِرْعَوْنَ وَ مٰا أَمْرُ فِرْعَوْنَ بِرَشِيدٍ * يَقْدُمُ قَوْمَهُ يَوْمَ الْقِيٰامَةِ فَأَوْرَدَهُمُ النّٰارَ وَ بِئْسَ الْوِرْدُ الْمَوْرُودُ *[۴۰] وَ أُتْبِعُوا فِي هٰذِهِ لَعْنَةً وَ يَوْمَ الْقِيٰامَةِ بِئْسَ الرِّفْدُ الْمَرْفُودُ.[۴۱] همی‌گوید: «پس فرمان فرعون رفتند و فرمان فرعون نه راست بود؛ فرعون پیش قوم خویش می‌رود روز قیامت تا بیارد ایشان را به آتش؛ و آن بدآوردن[۴۲] حالی است وز پس ایشان است اندر این جهان لعنت، و به روز قیامت آن بد سود کردن است».

[§۳۲:۴۲] این است قول هر گروهی اندر برزخ که یاد کرده شد؛ و ما حقیقت برزخ

---

۳۶ حسن مسعود برادرِ دهقان، پسر محمد بن احمد النسفی، است.

۳۷ ایا: – مر.

۳۸ ¦⟵برگ [ایا:۶۳-ب].

۳۹ اس، ایا: وَ اتّبعُوا.

۴۰ ¦⟵برگ [اس:۷۴-ب].

۴۱ سورة هود (۱۱)، آیات ۹۷ تا ۹۹.

۴۲ نك: دهخدا: بد آوردن. [بَ وَ دَ] (مصدر مرکب) دچار مانع شدن. شکست خوردن. بدشانسی آوردن. ... پیش آمدهای بد برای کسی پیش آمدن.

بفرمان خداوند روزگار المستنصربالله، صلوات الله علیهِ و علی آبائِهِ[۴۳] الطّاهِرین و أبنائِهِ الأکرَمین، اندر کتاب مصباح[۴۴] یاد کرده‌ایم.

---

۴۳ ایا: آیاته.

۴۴ این کتاب مؤلف باقی نمانده است.

صف چهل و سِیُّم[1]

سخن اندر فرق میان نفس و روح

[§۱:۴۳] هر گروهی از اهل مذاهب را اندر نفس و روح اختلاف است.

[§۲:۴۳] و بیشتر مردم اهل ظاهر بر آن است که نفس این جسد کثیف است و مردم این هیکل ظاهر است.

[§۳:۴۳] مگر از مذهب معتزله و بهری از مردمان صابی[2] که گویند مردم این جسد کثیف است.

[§۴:۴۳] و قول اهل ظاهر آن است که روح عرضی است[3] لطیف، و آن زندگانی است که مردم بدان سخنگوی است و اندریابنده.

[§۵:۴۳] و مذهب بیشتر از فلاسفه آن است کی نفس گوهری بسیط است زنده و اندریابنده و سخنگوی.

[§۶:۴۳] و نزدیك حکماءِ شریعت روح شریفتر از نفس است؛ و نزدیك فلاسفه

---

۱ ایا: سوم.

۲ نك: دهخدا: صابی. ... مفردِ صابئین: [بِ] ... صابِئَه. نامی که به دو فرقهٔ کاملاً مشخص اطلاق میشود: ۱ - ماندائی ها یا صبه، فرقهٔ یهودی و مسیحی بین النهرین (مسیحیان پیرو یحیی معمد). ۲ - صابئین حران، فرقهٔ مشرك که مدتها در دورهٔ اسلام وجود داشتند. صابئین که در قرآن ذکر آنها آمده، فرقهٔ واسطهٔ بین یهودیان و مسیحیان اند و از اهل کتاب بشمار میروند، اینان بطور مسلم همان ماندائی ها میباشند و این کلمه باید مشتق از ریشهٔ «ص ب ع» [عبری] (فرورفتن در آب) باشد که عین آن ساقط شده و بمعنی «معمدون» است یعنی کسانی که تعمید را با تغسیل در آب اجرا میکنند. صابئین مشرك از این امر ابداً اطلاع ندارند و شاید این اسم را از جهت احتیاط به خود داده اند تا از اغماضی که قرآن دربارهٔ آن دسته از صابئین روا داشته بهره مند شوند. (دائرة المعارف اسلام، [ویرایش نخست]، ج ۴، ص ۲۲).

۳ |⟵برگ [ایا:۶۴-الف].

نفس شریفتر از روح.[۴] و هر گروهی را بر این دعوی خویش حجّتها است که آن را بیوکندیم از بیم گرانی و درازی کتاب را.

[§۷:۴۳] و اندر کتب افلاطون چنان است کی نفسهای مردم چون از کالبد جدا شود اندر حیوانات شود براندازهٔ آن خوها که آن مردمان گرفته باشند. آنك خوی شیران دارد نفس او اندر شیری شود، و آنك طبع خران و گاوان دارد نفسهای ایشان اندر آن خران و گاوان شوند.

[§۸:۴۳] و خردمندان از اهل شریعت دانند که این سخن ناخوب است. و گروهی از شاگردان افلاطون[۵] گفتند که حکیم فاضل بدین قول اثبات تناسخ نخواست[۶] و لکن این سخن براندازهٔ روزگار خویش گفت مر سیاست خلق را بر سبیل رمز و مثل.

[§۹:۴۳] و از فُرفُریوس[۷] حکایت کنند که اندر کتاب طبیعة الانسان از یونانیان گفت که ایشان گویند کی نفس بسیار گونها است چنانك شخص بسیار گونها است. و هر نوعی از نفسها اندر نوع جسد خویش شود. و آنِ مردم جز اندر جسدهای مردم نشود؛ و آنِ ستور جز اندر ستور نشود. و هم بر این مثال هر روانی اندر تنی شود که درخور او باشد.

[§۱۰:۴۳] و قول افلاطون نیز چنان هست[۸] که گوید روانهای بدان که از تنهای ایشان بیرون شود دیوان گردند. و دیو نزدیك او نفس بدکردار است کز جسد جدا شده باشد.

---

۴ ایا: + است.

۵ ¦⟵برگ [اس:۷۵-الف].

۶ اس، ایا: نه خواست.

۷ ایا: فرفورس. || نك: دهخدا: فرفریوس. [فُ فُ] ... نام حکیمی بوده جلیس اسکندر. ... پرفیر. فیلسوف اسکندرانی شاگرد پلوتن (متولد ۲۳۲ یا ۲۳۳ و متوفی ۳۰۴ م.) است. اسکندر مقدونی پنج قرن پیش از وی میزیسته اما در اسکندرنامهٔ نظامی او معاصر اسکندر شناخته شده است.

۸ ایا: چنانست.

[§۱۱:۴۳] و شاگردان افلاطون گفتند که آن تنها که افلاطون گفت نه این تنهای کثیف است و آن تنها که زین تنهای کثیف زاده باشند و به فعل آن[۹] نفس کی اندر او باشد باقی بماند، ابدالآبدین.

[§۱۲:۴۳] و امّا افلاطون اندر معاد ایدون گوید که روانهای بدان کز کالبدهای بدان جدا شود باز عالم نفسانی نتواند شدن، بل‌که[۱۰] او را این آلت جسدانی کار باید کردن تا لطیف و صافی شود.

[§۱۳:۴۳] و ثواب نزدیك او آن است که نفس جوهری گردد چون عقل؛ یعنی که نفس عقل است بقُوّت،[۱۱] و عقل گردد بفعل. آن وقت باز عالم آلهی بازشود نزدیکی علّت خویش، و جواهر روحانی را بیابد بنفس، چنانك بدین جسد مر جواهر محسوس را یافته است. امروز ثواب نزدیك افلاطون این است.

[§۱۴:۴۳] باز گروهی گفتند که بویعقوب سجزی مر نفس را بیرون این عالم کثیف قرارگاهی نگوید و این سخن اندر کتاب کشف المحجوب از گفتار او پیدا است.[۱۲]

---

۹ ¦⟵برگ [ایا:۶۴-ب].

۱۰ ایا: بلك.

۱۱ ایا: بقُوّة.

۱۲ نك: السجستاني، ابویعقوب اسحاق بن احمد، کشف المحجوب، رساله در آئین اسماعیلی از قرن چهارم هجری، تحقیق و مقدمه بزبان فرانسوی: هنری کربین، گنجینهٔ نوشته‌های ایرانی (۱) (تهران، ۱۳۲۷ش/۱۹۴۹م)، مقالت چهارم، جستار اول، ص ۴۰ تا ۴۱.
|| نکته کلیدی، اما سربسته، در این سخن، استفادهٔ ناصرخسرو از عبارت «قرارگاه» است؛ که دو وجه دارد: اول اینکه با تعریف سجستانی از «هستی» در جستار اول از مقالت دوم سازگار است؛ دوم اینکه با تعریف «نفس» در قول بیست و پنجم: «اندر آنکه مردم از کجا آمد و کجا همی شود؟» (ص ۳۸۵ تا ۴۳۱) از کتاب زادالمسافر، در پاسخ به این سؤال که: «نفس آدمی از کجا آمده است و به کجا میرود؟» منافاتی ندارد. زیرا، در زادالمسافر، ناصر خسرو توضیح میدهد که «نفس» نه از «جایی یا مکانی» آمده تا بخواهد به «جایی یا مکانی» بازگردد:

> گوییم: «کجا» — که مر آن را به تازی «أین» گویند — لفظی است که براوفتد بر جوهری اندر مکانی و بر آنچه او اندر مکان نیست نیوفتد. و هرچه آن اندر چیزی پدید آید، از چیزی دیگر پدید آید، چو پدید آمدن نور اندر عالم از قرص آفتاب و پدید آمدن تری اندر خاک از آب و جز آن از چیزهایی [که] پدید آیند اندر چیزهایی. و هرچه آن پدید آید از چیزی، به محلّ جزوی باشد از آن چیز؛ از [بهر] آنکه نام و لفظِ «از» — که مر

[§۱۵:۴۳] و گروهی از شاگردان بویعقوب که گفتند که ما سرّ مذهب او دانیم ایدون گفتند که مذهب بویعقوب آن است کی نفس چون صافی شود به عالم علوی بازگردد[۱۳] و جاودانه بماند.

[§۱۶:۴۳] و گروهی از صابیان چنین[۱۴] گویند کی روانهای بَدان نماند از پس تنهای ایشان، چنان نماید که ایشان را اندر تنهای ددگان کرده‌اند. بر آن مثال کی مردم اندر خواب ببینند چیزهائی کزان بترسند وزان غمگین شوند کی مر آن را حقیقتی نباشد و عقاب بدکرداران این است نزدیك صابیان.

[§۱۷:۴۳] و گروهی گفتند از ایشان که روانهای بدکرداران همه نیست شوند، وز آنها نمانند[۱۵] ماندنی مطلق بی‌غم. و ثواب و عقاب نزدیك ایشان این باشد. و این

آن را به تازی «مِنْ» گویند — دلیل است بر بعضی و جزوی از کلّی، چنان که گوییم: «فلک از جسم است» بدانچه جزوی است از او. و هر چه آن از چیزی پدید آید، نیز اندر چیزی پدید آید. و این قول بر عکس آن مقدّمه است؛ چنان که چو نور از آفتاب پدید آید، اندر زمین همی پدید آید و [اندر] چیزهایی که قابل آن است. و چو حال این است، واجب آید که آنچه نه از چیزی پدید آید، ناچاره نه اندر چیزی پدید آید؛ چو پدید آمدن جوهر عقل و نفس که مبدعات‌اند، نه از چیزی‌اند [و] نه اندر چیزی‌اند. (ص۳۸۵ تا ۳۸۶) ... و چو درست کردیم که صورت‌ها اندر جسم نه از ذات جسم آمده است، درست شد که از صانعی امده است به قصد گه ان صانع نه جسم است و لیکن جوهر است؛ از بهر آنکه جسم جوهر است و جوهر از عرض صورت نپذیرد. و چو آن صانع جوهر است و نه جسم است، نفس است که متصرّف اندر جسم اوست. ...پس درست کردیم که وجود جسم به وجود طبایع است و طبایع اندر جسم صورت‌هااند نه اعراض‌اند، و طبایع اندر جسم از نفس موجود شده است و نفس جوهر است و جز جسم است و به مکان حاجتمند نیست و افعال او اندر جسم پدیدآینده است. و بدین شرح ظاهر کردیم که نفس مردم اندر جسم نه از جسم آمده است، از بهر آنکه جسم متناهی است و چو جسم متناهی است و نفس اندر او آمده است، جز [از] او آمده است و جز از متناهی آمده است، بل از نه‌متناهی آمده است و نه‌متناهی نفس است. پس نفس مردم از جوهری نامتناهی اندر جسم متناهی آمده است و به ذات خویش نیامده است، بل[که] به قصد صانع عالم آمده است. (ص ۴۰۸ تا ۴۰۹)

۱۳ ¦⟵برگ [اس:۷۵-ب].

۱۴ ایا: - چنین.

۱۵ اس: بماند؛ ایا: بمانند [کذا].

مذهب را بهری از مردمان دعوی کنند از اهل حقایق و گفتند منزلت بر سه بهر است. ثواب است و عقاب است و تلاشی[۱۶] است یعنی نیست گشتن. و نیست گشتن مر آن نفسها را باشد که صورت علمی از علمها [نـ]پذیرفته[۱۷] باشد چون نفوس کودکان و دیوانگان.[۱۸]

۱۶ نک: دهخدا: تلاشی. [تَ] ... (از: «ل ش و») نیست و نابود شدن. منحوت است از لاشیء. ... پوسیدن جثه و پراکنده گشتن اجزای وی از هم.

۱۷ تصحیح قیاسی.

۱۸ ¦←برگ [ایا:۶۵-الف].

صف چهل و چهارم

سخن اندر شریعت که چرا بایست نهاد

[§۱:۴۴] عالم جسمانی بر آن است که هر رکنی از رکنهای طبایع هم‌پهلو شده است با رکنی دیگر کی میان ایشان هردو ماننده است به رویی از رویها؛ چنانک آب با خاك هم‌پهلو شده‌اند و با یکدیگر آمیخته‌اند، بدان مانندگی[۱] که با یکدیگر دارند[۲] اندر سردی.

[§۲:۴۴] همچنین باد و آب هم‌پهلواند بدانچ میان ایشان انبازی است اندر تری. و آتش از باد همی نیرو یابد بدان مانندگی[۳] که میان ایشان است اندر گرمی. و هریکی ازین طبایع با مانند خویش قرار گرفته‌اند، و صلاح از میان ایشان پدید آمده است. اگر آب از خاك جدا ماند از هردو جُداجُدا جز فساد چیز نیاید و نفع از هردو باطل شود.

[§۳:۴۴] و چون حال عالم برین[۴] جمله بود، تا صلاح اندر خلق بسبب ایشان پدید آید، انبیاء،[۵] علیهم السّلام، شریعت را تألیف کردند، برمثال صورت مردم، ظاهر او همه مخالف و پراکنده از عبارتهاء گوناگون و همه مخالف یکدیگر همچنانك حواس مردم از بینایی و شنوایی و بویایی و گویایی همه مخالف یکدیگرند.

[§۴:۴۴] و باطن شریعت[۶] همه یکی مقصود[۷] و اشارت بیك تن بود اندر عالم که راهنمای[۸] خلق او باشد، همچنانك باطن مردم یکی بود نفس که این حواس

۱ اس، ایا: مانندهء.
۲ اس، ایا: دانند. || تصحیح قیاسی.
۳ ایا: مانندهء.
۴ ایا: بدین.
۵ اس: [کلمه «ایشان» خط زده شده است و بالای سطر کلمه «انبیاء» نوشته شده است].
۶ ¦⟵برگ [اس:۷۶-الف]. || اس: [«باطن شریعت» مخدوش است].
۷ اس: [کلمه «بود» بعد از «مقصود» آمده، اما روی آن خط کشیده شده است].
۸ اس: راه‌نمای.

کارهای مخالف خویش همه پیش او همی برند براستی تا خردمندان[۹] بدانند که پیغامبران،[۱۰] علیهم السّلام، فرستادگان آفریدگار عالم‌اند که تألیف شریعت ایشان بمانند آفرینش خدای است. پس نخست حکمت اندر نهاد شریعت این بود.

[§۵:۴۴] و دیگر حکمت اندر تألیف شریعت، بظاهرهای مخالف، آن بود که چون پیغامبران، علیهم السّلام، مر این خلق را مخالف یافتند اندر طبایع ایشان، و نفوس مردمان فریشتگان بودند اندر حدّ قوّت، و بظاهر اندر[۱۱] فعل دیوان بودند، ایشان، علیهم السّلام، شریعت را همچنان نهادند بظاهر همه مخالف و مانند سخن بی‌هوشان، و بباطن راهنمای[۱۲] سوی فریشتگی؛ تا چون شریعت مانند خلق آمد آن مانندی که میان شرایع و میان خلق اوفتاد اندر این روی که گفتیم خلق بر آن قرار گرفت.

[§۶:۴۴] برمثال طلسمها که دانایان کرده‌اند اندر شهرها ازبهر زیان گزندگان از پشه و مار و کژدم و جز آن. و هر طلسمی که بکرده‌اند صورتی کرده‌اند از آهن یا از مس یا جز آن مانند مار یا پشه یا کژدم یا جز آن، و مر آن نوع گزنده را [راه][۱۳] بدان صورت کی اندر آن شهر نهاده‌اند بسته کرده‌اند، و آن گزندگان بر آن صورت آرامیده‌اند، و رنج ایشان از شهر برخاسته است، چنانک به شهر مرو پشه نباشد.

[§۷:۴۴] و وقتی از دیوار کهن در مرو برجی فرود آمد وزان برج خنبره‌ای[۱۴] بیرون آمد اندر او پشه‌ای[۱۵] رویین[۱۶] نهاده چون مر آن را بیرون کردند پشه به شهر

---

۹ اس: [«ان» در آخر «خردمندان» مخدوش است].

۱۰ ایا: پیغمران.

۱۱ ¦⟵برگ [ایا:۶۵-ب].

۱۲ اس، ایا: راه نمای.

۱۳ تصحیح قیاسی.

۱۴ اس، ایا: خنبرهء.

۱۵ اس، ایا: پشهء

۱۶ ایا: روبین.

اندرآمد و مردمان را رنجه کرد. ‹تا باز مر آن پشهٔ رویین را هم اندر آن خنبره کردند و جایی پنهان کردند و پشه از شهر بیرون شد›.[۱۷]

[۸:۴۴§] و به شام شهری است که آن را معرةالنعمان[۱۸] خوانند. و چون از حلب سوی طرابلیس روی آن شهر بر راه است. و چون از دروازهٔ شهر اندر شوی بر راه ستونی سنگین است برپای کرده بلند. بر سر آن ستون صورت کژدمی است بزرگ از سنگ تراشیده، و مر آن صورت را بر سر آن ستون استوار کرده، و من[۱۹] آن را دیدم گفتند مردمان آن شهر که این طلسمی است کز قدیم‌باز[۲۰] اینجا نهاده است، و بدین شهر کسی کژدم ندید است، و اگر از بیرون شهر کسی کژدمی بگیرد و به شهر[۲۱] اندرآرد و رها کند آن کژدم تا از شهر بیرون نشود نیارامد.

[۹:۴۴§] پس پیغامبران، علیهم السّلام، مر شریعت را برابر صورت مردم فسادکن ساختند تا فساد مفسدان را به شریعت از خلق بازداشتند و ایشان را بدان[۲۲] آرام

---

۱۷ ایا: – تا باز مران پشهٔ رویین را هم اندران خنبره کردند و جایی پنهان کردند و پشه از شهر بیرون شد.

۱۸ نك:دهخدا: معرةالنعمان. [مَ عَ رْ رَ تُنْ نُ] ... شهر بزرگ قدیمی و مشهوری است از اعمال حمص بین حلب و حماة. آب آن از باران و محصولش زیتون و انجیر است....یازدهم رجب از شهر حلب بیرون شدیم به سه فرسنگ دیهی بود چند قنسرین می گفتند و دیگر روز چون شش فرسنگ شدیم به شهر سرمین رسیدیم بارو نداشت. شش فرسنگ دیگر شدیم معرةالنعمان بود، بارهٔ سنگین داشت. شهری آبادان و بر در شهر اسطوانهٔ سنگین دیدم چیزی در آن نوشته بود به خطی دیگر از تازی ... بالای آن ستون ده ارش قیاس کردم. و بازارهای او بسیار معمور دیدم و مسجد آدینهٔ شهر بر بلندی نهاده است در میان شهر و کشاورزی ایشان همه گندم است و بسیار است و درخت انجیر و پسته و بادام و انگور فراوان است و آب شهر از باران و چاه باشد. در آن مردی بود که ابوالعلاء معری می گفتند، نابینا بود و رئیس شهر او بود... (سفرنامهٔ ناصرخسرو، چ برلین، ص ۱۴ و ۱۵).

۱۹ ایا: مر.

۲۰ ¦←برگ [اس:۷۶-ب].

۲۱ اس: [حرف «ب» در «بشهر» مخدوش است].

۲۲ ایا: بران.

دادند. وگر نه چنین کردندی جاهلان امّت مر داناان را تباه کردندی و فساد[۲۳] عالم بودی از آن. و این سیاستی نیکو بود از پیامبران، علیهم السّلام، مر امّت را.

[§۱۰:۴۴] و شریعت اندر میان خلق امروز برمثال آن صورت است که فساد بدان صورت از خلق بریده شده است. و دیگر آن است که اندر کاربستن شریعت مردم را راست کردن است بر صلاح و خیر.

[§۱۱:۴۴] و کاربستن شریعت مر آن قوّت را کز نفس نگاهبان[۲۴] و زنده دار جسد است هم بدان منزلت است که اقرار دادن به شهادت مر آن قوّت را است کز نفس بر زفان موکل است، و بجای دانش است مر آن قوّت را کز نفس قرارگاه او دل است. و بر هر قوّتی از قوّتهای نفس انسانی مر خدای را تعالی طاعتی است براندازهٔ توانایی آن قوّت[۲۵] از طاعت خدای تعالی که او را تواناییِء آن است، چنانك خدای تعالی می گوید، قوله: لاٰ يُكَلِّفُ اللّٰهُ نَفْساً إلاّٰ وُسْعَهٰا.[۲۶] گفت: «خدای نفرماید هیچ کس را جز آنك توانایی او آن است».

۲۳ ¦⟵برگ [ایا:۶۶-الف].

۲۴ اس: نگاه‌بان.

۲۵ اس، ایا: + و بر هیچ قوتی.

۲۶ سورة البقرة (۲)، آیت ۲۸۶.

صف چهل و پنجم

سخن اندر اثبات فنای جسد و بقای نفس

[§۱:۴۵] گروهی از مردمان ایدون گویند که بقای نفس اندر بقای[۱] جسد است و دعوی کنند کی چون جسد را فنا افتاد نفس را هستی نماند.

[§۲:۴۵] و این آن گروهند[۲] کز حکم علم آلهی و تقدیر کلّی خبر ندارند و خویشتن با ستور ‹همی برابر›[۳] کنند و نمی‌نگرند که هرچیزی که بظاهر مر دیگر چیز را مخالف است بباطن خویش مخالف[۴] است. و بسبب[۵] آن مخالفت که میان ایشان اندر ظاهر هست اندر باطن نیز[۶] ایشان[۷] [را][۸] تفاوتی عظیم است.

[§۳:۴۵] برمثال درخت خرما که مر درخت بید را بظاهر مخالف است، بدانچ هریکی را صورتی دیگر است، و چون درخت بید را ببُرّی دیگرباره بروید و درخت خرما چون[۹] ببُرّی بنروید.[۱۰]

[§۴:۴۵] پس بدین مخالفت کی میان این دو[۱۱] درخت اندر ظاهر است، بنگر ای برادر که چه مایه فرق است میان درخت خرما و درخت بید، که درخت خرما

۱ ایا: بقاء.
۲ اس: + که.
۳ ایا: برابر همی.
۴ اس: [حرف «ف» در «مخالف» مخدوش است].
۵ اس: [حرف «ب» در ابتدای «بسبب» مخدوش است].
۶ ایا: - نیز.
۷ اس: [«نیز ایشان» کمرنگ شده است].
۸ ¦←برگ [اس:۷۷-الف]. || تصحیح قیاسی.
۹ اس: [حروف «م» و «ا» در «خرما» و «چ» در «چون» مخدوش هستند].
۱۰ اس، ایا: بنه‌روید.
۱۱ ¦←برگ [ایا:۶۶-ب].

را می‌دیدیم که اندر زمین حجاز با بسیاری خرما که آنجا است هزار درم قیمت نهادند و درخت بید اگرچه بزرگ شود به ده درم نه‌ارزد.[۱۲]

[§۴۵:۵] پس گوییم که میان جسد کثیف فرمان‌بردارِ نادان و میان نفس[۱۳] لطیف فرمان‌فرمایِ دانا تفاوت بیش از آن است که میان درخت خرما و درخت بید است.

[§۴۵:۶] و بباید دانستن که چنان نیست که آن نادان همی‌گوید کی فعل نفس بی‌جسد پدید نیاید. بل‌کی فعل نفس به لطافت است و مر او را به دانستن علمی به جسد حاجت نیست.

[§۴۵:۷] بل‌کی[۱۴] حاجت مر آن کس را است به جسد کی خواهد که بداند کی اندر نفس انگشتری‌گر از صناعت چیست تا انگشتری‌گر مر آن صورت لطیف را که خود از بیرون آوردن آن بر سیم بی‌نیاز است بیرون آرد تا آن نادان ببیند.[۱۵]

[§۴۵:۸] پس درست شد که نفس از جسد بی‌نیاز است و جسد به نفس حاجتمند است که اگر نفس ازو جدا شود وی مرداری بماند. و دیگر که نفس بی‌جسد چیزها سازد به اندیشه و اندر خواب بی‌آلت جسدانی سخن گوید و بشنود و کارکند و جز آن.

[§۴۵:۹] و دیگر ان است کی نفس مر جسد مردار را که همی زنده و کارکن دارد واجب نیاید که چیزی که او مرده‌ای[۱۶] را زنده دارد خود بذات خویش زنده نباشد. و هر که این سخن گوید خردمندان ازو کناره گیرند. پس درست شد کی نفس از جسد بی‌نیاز است.

[§۴۵:۱۰] و گوییم که فنای صورت جسد لازم است اندر عقل از بهر آنك جسد خود

---

۱۲ یعنی: نمی‌ارزد، ارزش ندارد، نیرزد.

۱۳ اس: [کلمه «نفس» مخدوش است، اما در حاشیه متن دوباره واضح نوشته شده است].

۱۴ ایا: بلك.

۱۵ اس، ایا: به‌بیند.

۱۶ اس، ایا: مرده‌ء.

اندر ذات خویش جزوهای مخالف است چنانك مر او را زیر است و زبر و پیش و پس و چپ و راست. و آن[17] همه مخالف هستند[18] و چیز[19] مخالف باقی نباشد.

[§۱۱:۴۵] و از دیگر روی فنای جسد بر آن لازم آید[20] که جسد از طبایع چهارگانهٔ مختلف ترکیب و تألیف یافته است، و مخالفان بی‌میانجی فراز یکدیگر نیایند، و چون فرازآیند هر یکی از ایشان آرزومند باشند به بازگشتن سوی اصل خویش.

[§۱۲:۴۵] پس لازم آید که به آخر هر یکی سوی[21] اصل خویش بازگردند، و باقی نشوند. و به آخر میانجی از میان ایشان بیرون شود چون مقصود میانجی از فرازآوردن ایشان بحاصل شود.

[§۱۳:۴۵] و ما همی یابیم مر این نفس را که میانجی است میان این طبایع مخالف و ایشان را به صلح آورده است تا اندر یك کالبد جمله شدستند.

[§۱۴:۴۵] پس جمله کردن نفس مر این مخالفان را بدین فعل نیکو کی همی کنند[22] از مصلحت میان این دشمنان سخن همی‌گوید کی اندر این هیچ خلاف نیست.

[§۱۵:۴۵] و من از میانجی بی‌نیازم اندر ذات خویش؛ و چیزی که اندر او هیچ خلاف نباشد مر او را فنا لازم نیاید.

[§۱۶:۴۵] پس درست کردیم که نفس را فنا نیست و چون درست کردیم که جسد فانی است و آن مقدار بقا که او را است به میانجی نفس است هیچ گوایی نباید اندرآنك نفس اندر ذات خویش باقی است. از بهرآنك چیزی که به میانجی او مر فانی را بقا حاصل آید ناچاره ذات او باقی باشد.

---

۱۷ ایا: این.

۱۸ ایا: مخالفانند.

۱۹ ایا: چیزی.

۲۰ ¦⟵برگ [اس:۷۷-ب].

۲۱ ¦⟵برگ [ایا:۶۷-الف].

۲۲ ایا: کند.

[§۱۷:۴۵] و دلیل بر درستی این قول آن است که چون آتش گوهری است که روشنی و گرمی اندر او ذاتی است چون آهن که گوهرش سیاه و سرد است با آتش همسایگان شوند آنچ اندر آتش ذاتی است از نور و گرمی بحکم همسایگی همی به آهن دهد تا آهن از پس سیاهی و سردی گرم و روشن شود. و لکن آن گرمی و روشنی مر آهن را عرضی باشد و به آخر ازو بشود.

[§۱۸:۴۵] همچنین زندگی و حرکت اندر نفس ذاتی است.[۲۳] و چون نفس با جسد همسایگان شوند جسد از نفس زندگی و حرکت بپذیرد عرضی. و چون نفس ازو جدا شود زندگی و حرکت از جسد بشود.

[§۱۹:۴۵] پس درست شد که زندگی نفس ذاتی است و چیزی که زندگی مر او را ذاتی باشد او فنا نپذیرد. پس درست شد که به فنای جسد نفس فانی نشود.[۲۴]

[§۲۰:۴۵] و نیز گوییم که فنای جسد آن است که هر طبیعتی ازو بازشود به اصل خویش. و ما مر آن بازشدن ایشان را به اصلهای ایشان فنای جسد گفتیم.

[§۲۱:۴۵] و بازشدن طبایع هریکی به اصل خویش[۲۵] همی‌گوایی دهد کی نفس نیز به اصل خویش بازشود.[۲۶] و[۲۷] چون جسد نادان به اصلهای نادان بازگشت دانستیم که نفس دانا به اصل دانای خویش بازگشت.

[§۲۲:۴۵] و هرچیزی که به اصل خویش بازگردد قوی‌تر شود نه ضعیف‌تر. پس درست شد کی نفس بغایت قوّت خویش آن وقت رسد کز جسد جدا شود. پس درست کردیم که جسد فانی است و نفس باقی است.

---

۲۳ اس: + و جسد مردار شدست [«مردار» مخدوش است].

۲۴ ¦⟵برگ [اس:۷۸-الف]. || اس: نه شود.

۲۵ اس: [«خویش» مخدوش است].

۲۶ ¦⟵برگ [ایا:۶۷-ب].

۲۷ ایا: – و.

صف چهل و ششم

سخن اندر آنك صورتهای جسدانی را، اندر طبیعت، نفس کلّی نهاده است تا همی بیرون آید

[§۱:۴۶] گوییم کی اندر آفرینش چنان است که ظاهر چیزها بر باطن او دلیل است. چنانك بیشتر از درختان چنان است کی برگش به بارش ماننده است چنانك برگ درخت سیب همچون سیب گرد است. و برگ درخت انبرود هم شکل انبرود است و برگ درخت سنجد ماننده‌ٔ سنجد است.[۱]

[§۲:۴۶] و چون حال اندر نبات، کی آغاز به زایش او است، مر عالم را چنین یافتیم، گفتیم اندر مردم کی انجام زایش او است حال مانند این باشد.

[§۳:۴۶] پس یافتیم بار درخت مردم که مردم بدان از دیگر جانوران جدا است سخن گفتن [است]. و خداوندان سخن‌گویان مر پیامبران را، علیهم‌السّلام، یافتیم، که فرستادگان[۲] نفس‌کلّی بودند بسوی خلق به امر خدای سبحانه.

[§۴:۴۶] و ایشان، علیهم‌السّلام، مایهٔ صورتهای روحانی را که نفس مردم بدان باقی گردد اندر کتابهای خدای نهادند به زفان خویش تا مردمان معانی آن را همی بیرون آرند و یك‌بدیگر همی‌دهند تا آخرالدّهر.

[§۵:۴۶] و نادانانِ بی هیچ صورتْ، بدان مایهٔ صورتها که پیامبران، علیهم‌السّلام، اندر کتاب خدای تعالی و شریعت نهاده‌اند، صورت آخرتیِ نفسانی همی پذیرند، و همی بیرون شوند سوی عالم روحانی. و اصل آن پیامبران، علیهم‌السّلام، نهاده‌اند اندر کتاب.

[§۶:۴۶] و این حال دلیل کرد[۳] بر آنك صورتهای جسمانی را نفس‌کلّی همچنین

---

۱ قس: زادالمسافر، قول ۲۵، ص ۴۱۱ تا ۴۱۲.

۲ اس: فرستکان [در حاشیه متن «فرستادگان» نوشته شده است].

۳ |←برگ [اس:۷۸-ب].

مایه اندر[۴] طبایع نهاده است تا به روزگارها طبایع[۵] مر آن را همی بیرون آرد که این عالم کارکرد نفس کلّ است، و پیامبران، علیهم[۶] السّلام، گفتارهای نفس کلّی اند. و این دلیل کی گفتیم از آغاز نفس کلّی گرفتیم بر کردار او، و این دلیلی ظاهر است.

۴ ایا: اندرین.

۵ اس: [«طبایع» مخدوش است].

۶ ¦⟵برگ [ایا:۶۸-الف].

صف چهل و هفتم

سخن اندر آنك نفس از عقل کلّی فایده نه به زمان پذیرد

[§۱:۴۷] گوییم که چون جسم مرکب است و نفس بسیط است، و بسیط بر مرکب جاکول است، و حالهای جسمِ مرکب زیر زمان است.

[§۲:۴۷] و هر فایده کی جسم پذیرد از صورت و شکل و رنگ و بوی و جز آن به زمان تواند پذیرفتن، واجب آید از روی اضافت حال نفس به جسم که مر نفس را که بر جسم جاکول است به زمان حاجت نیست.

[§۳:۴۷] و مثل این چنان باشد کی هر عددی که آن جفت است به دو نیمه شود و اندر او کسر نیاید. و هر عددی که طاق است به دو نیمه نشود تا اندر او کسور[۱] نیاید. ازبهرآنك جفت مر طاق را مخالف است لاجرم خلاف ایشان[۲] به وقت به دو قسم کردن پدید آید.

[§۴:۴۷] و ازبهر آن است کی خلاف میان جفت و طاق بدان پدید آید کی هردو را به دو قسم کنی، که جفت اول دو است، و او[۳] مر همه عددها را ترازو است و بدو پدید آید طاق از جفت.

[§۵:۴۷] و این مثل مر متعلّم را فایده آن دهد که بداند کی چون جفت به دو نیمه شود بی‌کسر، پس بباید دانستن کی طاق مر جفت را مخالف است به دو نیمه نشود بی‌کسر.

[§۶:۴۷] همچنین بسیط که مرکّب را مخالف است حال او بخلاف حال مرکّب لازم آید. و چون معلوم است کی حالهای جسم مرکّب زیر زمان است بباید دانستن بحکم ضرورت که حالهای نفس بسیط زیر زمان نیست.

---

۱ ایا: کسر.

۲ ایا: انسان.

۳ ایا: + همه.

[§۷:۴۷] و دلیل بر درستی این قول آن است کی[۴] نفس مردم، تا دانا نشده است مر گرفتن علم را، زمان بکار بایدش تا بشنود و به شکل بیرون آرد و بازگوید تا آن علم اندر نفس او صورت بندد.

[§۸:۴۷] از بهر آنك علم بدو به میانجی[۵] دو جسم همی‌رسد یکی جسم آموزگار و دیگر جسم او خود که متعلم است.

[§۹:۴۷] و چون دانا شد، آنگاه هر چه فایده پذیرد[۶] از عقل خویش بی‌زمان پذیرد، نه به شنودن حاجت آیدش، نه به گفتن مر ذات خویش را. بسبب آنك[۷] نه از راه جسدی بدو همی‌رسد بل کز نفس مجرّد او میرسد آن همه علم.

[§۱۰:۴۷] باز چون مر[۸] کسی[۹] را ببایدش گفتن و آموختن آن علم را[۱۰] روزگار بایدش تا بگوید آن علم را و شکل بنماید مر آن کسی را که فرود او است، بسبب آنك جسم او و جسم شاگرد اندر میان دو نفس آیند و این بیانی روشن است.

۴ اس: [کلمه «اگر» نوشته شده اما روی آن خط کشیده شده است، و کلمه «کی» روی آن در بالای خط نوشته شده است].

۵ ایا: میانجی.

۶ ¦⟵برگ [اس:۷۹-الف].

۷ ¦⟵برگ [ایا:۶۸-ب].

۸ اس: [«مر» مخدوش است].

۹ اس: [حرف «ی» در کلمه «کسی» مخدوش است].

۱۰ ایا: – را.

صف چهل و هشتم

سخن اندر نفس مردم که جزو است نه اثر از نفس کلّی[1]

[§۱:۴۸] آگاه باشید که نفس مردم جزو است نه اثر از نفس کلّی. و دلیل بر درستی این قول آن است کی نفسهای مردم فعل کلّ خویش همی‌کند اندر پدیدآوردن شکلها و صورتها و صنعتهای عجیب کردن ازبهر کشیدن منفعت را بخویشتن و دور کردن مضرت از خویشتن و نیز از جهت کشیدن منفعت به جز از خویشتن، برمثال نگاشتن نفس کلّی مر طبیعت را و نهادن نوعها و شکلها و صورتها اندر او و پدید کردن قوّتهای طبیعی از جهت کشیدن منفعتها و دور کردن مضرّتها از انواع حیوان اندر وقتی دون وقتی. پس بدین سبب پیدا شد کی آنك اندر مردم است نفس جزوی است از نفس کلّی.

[§۲:۴۸] و دیگر دلیل بر آنك نفس مردم جزوی است از نفس کلّی نه اثر او است آن است کی اثر آهنگ نکند به بررسیدن بر علّت مؤثر خویش چنانك ‹مردم همی›[2] آهنگ کند به بررسیدن بر عقل کی علّت نفس کلّ است. و اثر را علم لازم نیاید و هرگز اندر مؤثر خویش نرسد چنانك دبیری اندر دبیر اثر است و هرگز دبیری از دبیر خویش خبر ندارد.

[§۳:۴۸] و چون یافتیم نفس جزوی را کی آهنگ کرد سوی اندررسیدن به عقل کلّ، کی او علّت نفس کلّ است، یقین شدیم که آن نفس کی اندر مردم است او جزو است از نفس کلّی بذات. و اثر از نفس گفتار است نه ذات او است. و گفتار بذات خویش نادان است و نفس دانا است و گفتار را علم و تمییز نیست.

---

۱ قس: کتاب الینابیع، الینبوع الثامن عشر (۱۸): في ان ما في البشر أجزاؤه من النفس الکلیة، ص ۴۶ تا ۴۷.

۲ ایا: همی مردم.

[§۴:۴۸] و دیگر[۳] آن است که اگر نفس مردم اثر بودی از نفس کلّی، و نفس کلّی[۴] به جزوی پیوسته است به خواندن مر او را به رسولان[5] سوی خویش و دادن نطق مر او را، و این همه از پیوند نفس کلّ است با نفس جزوی، آن وقت سزاوار با ناسزاوار پیوسته بودی.

[§۵:۴۸] و اندر حکمت چنین نشاید، و اثرپذیر از مؤثر اندر پذیرفتن اثر انباز و همراز باشند.

[§۶:۴۸] برمثال پذیرش چیزهای طبیعی اثر از آفتاب و اثر از اثر فاضلتر و شریفتر نباشد، و نفسها را یك بر دیگر شرف و فضل سخت بسیار است به پاکی و صلاح و پلیدی و فساد.

[§۷:۴۸] پس درست شد که نفس جزوی کی اندر مردم است نه اثر است از نفس کلّی بل کی[۶] جزو است ازو. وگر نفسها از نفس کلّ اثر بودی همه یکسان بودندی.

[§۸:۴۸] امّا اندر حال که علم نپذیرفته باشد نفس مردم از نفس کلّی اثر باشد. از بهر آنك اندر آغاز پیوستن نفس به جسد همه یکسان باشد، و چون علم پذیرفتند اجزای نفس کلّ شوند بر تفاوت، چنانك جزوی از جزوی بزرگ تر باشد و شریف تر.

[§۹:۴۸] و بدین قول کی گفتیم نفس مردم از نفس کلّ جزو است نه اثر، نه آن خواستیم کی جزو پاره‌ای[۷] ازو است کهتر و مهتر. و لکن آن خواستیم که پیدا کنیم کی جوهرِ نفس مردم جوهر نفس کلّ است و باقی است همچنو به پذیرفتن علم، و ناچیزشونده نیست چون اثر از مؤثر، کش به مؤثر خویش رسیدن نباشد.

---

۳ ¦⟵برگ [اس:۷۹-ب].

۴ ¦⟵برگ [ایا:۶۹-الف].

۵ اس: [«برسولان» مخدوش است].

۶ ایا: بلك.

۷ اس: فایده‌ء؛ ایا: پاره‌ء.

صف چهل و نهم

سخن اندر فریشتگان کی شمار بر ایشان نیوفتد[۱]

[۱:۴۹§] بباید دانستن کی هرچه شمار بر او افتد آن چیز زیادت و نقصان پذیرد. و هرچه بدین صفت باشد جسم باشد و فریشتگان[۲] جسم نیستند. پس درست شد کی شمار بر فریشتگان نیوفتد.

[۲:۴۹§] و اندر چیزهای[۳] جسمانی موجود است این شرط که شمرده را که چیزی برو برافزایی افزون شود، و اگر ازو چیزی نقصان کنی اندکی پذیرد، چنانك شش شماری است از شمردهای جسمانی گردآمده اندر دو و چهار که [میـ]ان[۴] پنج و هفت است.[۵]

[۳:۴۹§] ازبهرآنك[۶] چون از شش یکی کم کنی پنج ماند وگر یکی بر شش افزایی هفت شود. پس شش اندر حصار این دو شمار است کی یکی ازو بیش است و یکی کم است.

[۴:۴۹§] و امّا آن چیز کی اندك شود به افزونی[۷] شمرده،[۸] و بسیار شود به نقصان شمرده‌ای،[۹] آن چیز اندر حصار شمار نیاید. ازبهرآنك اندر روحانیات یکی را بجایگاه هزار بنهند و زیادت نگیرد، و هزار را بجایگاه یکی بنهند و نقصان نپذیرد.

---

۱ اس: بیوفتد. || قس: کتاب الینابیع، الینبوع الرابع والعشرون (۲۴): في أنّ الملائکة لایحصی لها عدد، ص ۵۹ تا ۶۱.

۲ ایا: فرشتگان.

۳ ایا: + که.

۴ اس: ان؛ ایا: آن.

۵ ¦⟵برگ [اس:۸۰-الف].

۶ ¦⟵برگ [ایا:۶۹-ب].

۷ اس: [«نی» در «بافزونی» مخدوش است].

۸ ایا: شمرد.

۹ اس، ایا: شمرده‌ء.

[§۴۹:۵] و مثال آن چنان است کی گویند[۱۰] ایزد تعالی با هر قطره باران یکی فریشته بفرستد کی مر آن را فرودآرد آنجا که خواهد. وگر خردمند اندر این فکر کند و حقیقت این را بداند بشناسد کی یك چیز از روحانی بسیار شود بی‌آنك زیادت پذیرد.

[§۴۹:۶] ازبهرآنك فرودآمدن باران یك چیز است از جهت روحانی و آن غرض بیرون آوردن نبات است، تا آن یك چیز کی باران است بسیار شود اندر قطره.

[§۴۹:۷] و براندازهٔ هر قطره‌ای[۱۱] عجایب بسیار است، تا بدان جای که ممکن باشد اندیشه کردن، کی عالم پرشود از زایش کزان قطرها بحاصل آید، بی‌آنك آن قوّت اوّل کی باران ازو بود هیچ بسیاری پذیرفت.

[§۴۹:۸] پس اگر مردم عمر خویش اندر اندیشه کند تا بجای آرد بسیاری آن چیزها را کز یك قطرهٔ باران بحاصل آمده است، اندیشهٔ او بغایت آن نرسد. و لکن آن شمردهای بسیار همه جسمانی باشد نه روحانی، و روحانی یکی باشد و آن باران است.

[§۴۹:۹] و آن چیزها کزان قطره پدید آید به یاری همه باران باشد، که آن یکی است، نه بذات آن قطره. و چون فعل باران یك فعل بود، بدانچ نبات پدید آورد، دانستیم کی آن روحانی کی آن چیز ازو بحاصل آمد یکی بود نه بسیار. چه اگر بسیار بودی، بایستی کی هریکی را فعل دیگر بودی.

[§۴۹:۱۰] پس اگر کسی گوید کی آن فریشتگان بسیارند و همه را فعل یکی است، گوییم که بسیار چیز که او را یك فعل باشد[۱۲] یکی باشد. چنانك آب را فعل آن است کی چیزها را سبز[۱۳] کند یکی است هرچند که جزوهاش بسیار است.

---

۱۰ ایا: + که.

۱۱ اس، ایا: قطره‌ء.

۱۲ |←برگ [ایا:۷۰-الف] .

۱۳ ایا: تر.

[§۱۱:۴۹] پس اگر گوید آب چگونه یکی است، یکی آب طلخ است،[۱۴] و یکی آب شور و یکی خوش؟ گوییم کی این عرضهایی است کی تو همی‌گویی و گوهر آب یکی است کی او سرد و تر است.[۱۵]

[§۱۲:۴۹] به نخستین[۱۶] صفت بازنمودیم کی یك جزو از روحانیون بسیار چگونه شود بی‌آنك اندر ذات خویش بسیاری پذیرد.

[§۱۳:۴۹] و مثل آن چیز که بسیار یکی شود از روحانیات آن است کی مردمان عامه با خاص بدان متفق‌اند کی کشیدن جانهای خلق به دست فریشته‌ای[۱۷] است کی او را ملك‌الموت خوانند، و سببهای مرگ اندر عالم بسیار است، و آشکار است پس بازگشت این سببهای بسیار کی هست مرگ را، به اتفاق دانا و نادان، بیك روحانی است.

[§۱۴:۴۹] وزین قیاس درست باشد کی چیزهای روحانی فراوان اندکی شود بی‌آنك نقصان پذیرد. و بدین دلیل کی نمودیم درست شد خردمند را که شمار مر جسمانیان را شُمرد و فریشتگان خدای را شمار نشمرد.[۱۸]

[§۱۵:۴۹] و دیگر گویند که ایزد تعالی بر هر چیزی فریشته‌ای[۱۹] موکّل کرده است، و هیچ چیز نیست، کی محتاج نیست کی فریشته‌ای[۲۰] برو موکل کنند، تا شمار او نگاه دارد اندر جنس و نوع آن هر شماری را بر حدّ آن، تا نیامیزد با شماری دیگر، و زیادت نگیرد و کم نشود از حدّ خویش، و حَرث و نسل یعنی رستن و زادن بجای خویش باشد.

---

۱۴ ¦⟵برگ [اس:۸۰-ب].

۱۵ ایا: ترست.

۱۶ اس: [«بنخستین» مخدوش است].

۱۷ اس، ایا: فریشتهء.

۱۸ ایا: نشمارد.

۱۹ اس، ایا: فریشتهء.

۲۰ اس، ایا: فریشتهء.

[§۴۹:۱۶] ازبهرآنك راستیِ عالم طبیعت به شمار است و خدای تعالی همی‌گوید، قوله: وَ أَحْصىٰ كُلَّ شَيْءٍ عَدَداً.[۲۱] گفت: «خدای بشمرد هرچیزی را به شماری». پس هرچیزی از اجناس و انواع ذات او خود موکلّ است کی او از آن موکل رهایی نیابد. و آن ذات مر او را روحانی است نه جسمانی.

[§۴۹:۱۷] ازبهرآنك اگر جسمانی بُدی تغیّر پذیرفتی.[۲۲] چنانك آن است آنچ روحانی است و آن راستی است از حال خویش نگردد. و لکن آنچ ازو جسمانی است و آن رنگ و بو است و خردی و بزرگی و قوّت و ضعف گردنده است.

[§۴۹:۱۸] و دیگر گوییم کی شمار آن کمّیت است، از قسم منفصل. و کمّیت چندی باشد، و چندی گوهرهای جسمانی را لازم آید.

[§۴۹:۱۹] پس اگر فریشتگان زیر شمار بودندی تا توانستی گفتن کی ایشان چندآند،[۲۳] خود جسم بودندی. وگر فریشتگان جسم بودندی، به نام فریشتگی سزاوار نبودندی.

[§۴۹:۲۰] ازبهرآنك این نام ملك سزاوار نیست مگر آن گوهر را کی ماننده نیست[۲۴] مر جسم را. و آنك به جسم ماند آن ملك نباشد که مملوك باشد.

[§۴۹:۲۱] و مَلَك ازبهر آن گفتند فریشته را کی فریشته پادشا است بدان روی که باقی است و نیستی نپذیرد، و توانا است بدانچ خواهد از خیر[۲۵] و صلاح.

---

۲۱ سورة الجن (۷۲)، آیت ۲۸.

۲۲ ¦←برگ [ایا:۷۰-ب].

۲۳ ایا: چندند.

۲۴ ¦←برگ [اس:۸۱-الف].

۲۵ اس: [حرف «ر» در «خیر» مخدوش است].

[۲۲:۴۹§] و این نام مثل است بر امام زمانه، علیه‌السّلام، و فرمان‌گزاران او، کی بفرمان خدای پادشا است بر بندگان. و مؤمنانِ او بفرمان او پادشائی دارند بر جانهای مؤمنان، تا ایشان را از حدّ قوّت به حدّ فعل آرند، وزین سرای فانی کثیف به سرای باقی لطیف رسانندشان،[۲۶] چنانك خدای تعالی میفرماید، قوله: وَ لَوْ نَشٰاءُ لَجَعَلْنٰا مِنْكُمْ مَلاٰئِكَةً فِي الْأَرْضِ يَخْلُفُونَ.[۲۷] گفت: «اگر خواهیم بکنیم از شما فریشتگان کی اندر زمین خلیفت باشند».

[۲۳:۴۹§] وگر ملك را شمار بشمردی مملوك بودی، و حکم کسی دیگر برو رونده بودی از جهت استحالت یا از جهت کون و فساد. پس چون مر فریشتگان را کون و فساد نیست درست شد که شمار بر فریشتگان نیوفتد.

۲۶ ایا: رسانند.

۲۷ سورة الزُّخْرُف (۴۳)، آیت ۶۰.

صف پنجاهم

سخن اندر آنك عقل را فنا نیست[۱]

[§۵۰:۱] گوییم کی معنی فنا آن است که چیزی کز چیزی پدید آمده باشد، وزو جدا شده باشد، هم بدان اصل خویش بازگردد. چنانك چیزی است از دو چیز، یکی لطیف و دیگر کثیف، چون نفس و جسد، چون هر یکی ازین دو با اصلهای خویش بازگردند، گویند مردم فانی شد.

[§۵۰:۲] و عقل از چیزی پدید نیامده است کزو جدا شده است. بل کی[۲] پدیدآمدن او نه[۳] از چیزی بوده است، بلکه[۴] به امر باری سبحانه، و امر باری به عقل پیوسته است. پس خود به اصل خویش بازگشته است و مر او را فنا لازم نیاید.

[§۵۰:۳] امّا هر چیزی که تباه شود تباه‌شدن او از دوگونه باشد: یا از جهت ذات آن چیز باشد یا از جهت ذاتی دیگر.

[§۵۰:۴] امّا آن چیز کی فنا و فساد او از جهت[۵] ذاتی دیگر باشد، آن ذات دیگر باید کی قاهر و قوی باشد، و ضد باشد مر این دیگر را، تا بقهر و قوّت و ضدّیِ خویش تباه کند مر ضدّ خویش را.

[§۵۰:۵] و آن چیز که فساد او از جهت ذات او باشد، آن طریق استحالت باشد[۶] کی مستحیل شود بسبب اختلافی[۷] که اندر ذات او باشد.

---

۱ ¦⟵برگ [ایا:۷۱-الف]. || قس: کتاب الینابیع، الینبوع السابع (۷): في أنّ العقل لايبيد، ص ۲۶ تا ۲۷.

۲ ایا: بلك.

۳ ایا: - نه.

۴ ایا: - بلکه.

۵ ایا: جهة.

۶ ¦⟵برگ [اس:۸۱-ب].

۷ ایا: اختلآء.

[§۶:۵۰] و ما اندر عقل چیزی نیافتیم جز از گوهر او،[۸] که[۹] مر او را مخالف گشتی. و عقل بسبب آن خلاف مستحیل نبودی اندر ذات خویش.

[§۷:۵۰] و نیز چیزی دیگر نیست که قوّت او ‹افزون از قوّت عقل است›،[۱۰] تا بدان قوّت مر عقل را قهر کند و فساد را اندر او آرد.

[§۸:۵۰] اگر کسی گوید کی ایزد تعالی کی پدیدآرندهٔ عقل است ازو قوی‌تر است و نه شاید کی مر عقل را قهر کند. جواب او را گوییم که ایزد، جلّ جلاله، برتر است از آنك او را قوّت گویند. بل‌کی او بخشد مر آفریدگان را قوّتهای شریف. و قوّتها مر ایزد را تعالی اندر امر او است نه اندر اویی او.

[§۹:۵۰] پس گر گوید قدرت و قوّت روا داریم ایزد را، از بهر آنك هر چه اندر امر او باشد اندر او باشد، گوییم که این عالم نیز بامر او بپای شده است، پس ازین قیاس روا باشد کی این عالم با این همه کثافت اندر ذات ایزد باشد، تَعٰالَی اللّٰهُ عَمّٰا[۱۱] یَقُولُ الظّٰالِمُونَ عُلُوًّا کَبِیراً.[۱۲]

[§۱۰:۵۰] و نیز گوییم امر ایزد سبحانَهُ کی بود، نه زیادت گرفت و نه نقصان پذیرفت، و نه امری دیگر پدید آمد بخلاف آن.

[§۱۱:۵۰] پارسیِ «کُنّ» آن باشد کی بباش. پس بدین فرمان ببود عقل تمام بی‌هیچ خلاف و نقصان. پس اگر روا باشد کی اندرآنچ به امر ایزد تعالی بود بی‌میانجی نقصان اندرآید، آن نقصان و فساد به امری دیگر باشد، و آن چنان باشد کی گویند لا تَکُنْ[۱۳] یعنی مباش.

---

۸ اس: [عبارت «گوهر او که» در متن مخدوش است؛ اما در حاشیه «گوهر او که» نوشته شده است].

۹ ایا: - که | + تا.

۱۰ ایا: از قوت عقل افزونست.

۱۱ ¦⟵برگ [ایا:۷۱-ب].

۱۲ اشارت به سورة الإسراء (۱۷)، آیت ۴۳: سُبْحٰانَهُ وَ تَعٰالیٰ عَمّٰا یَقُولُونَ عُلُوًّا کَبِیراً.

۱۳ اس: لایکن.

[§۵۰:۱۲] و ایزد تعالی برتر است از اندیشَهای ما، و منزّه است از باطل کردن حکمت. و امر خویش را ایزد تعالی برتر از آن یاد کرد کی آن دوباره روا باشد چنانك فرمود، قوله: وَ مٰا أَمْرُنٰا إِلاّٰ وٰاحِدَةٌ كَلَمْحٍ بِالْبَصَرِ.[۱۴] گفت: «نیست فرمان ما مگر یکی چون درفشدنی به چشم».

[§۵۰:۱۳] و نیز گوییم کی فسادْ گشتن چگونگی باشد، و چگونگی را به جوهرِ عقل دانند اندر چیزها، و گشتن چگونگی چیزی اندر چیزی دیگر باشد. چنانك چون مردم ازین کیفیّت کی دارد بگردد و چگونگی او اندر طبایع پیدا شود. ازبهرآنك خاکش باز خاك شود، و آبش باز آب شود، و گرمیش اندر آتش شود، و بادش اندر هوا شود تا او را فنا باشد، و چگونگی مردم اندر چگونگیهای دیگر شود.[۱۵]

[§۵۰:۱۴] پس اگر گوییم که عقل تباه شود، چه گوییم که اندر کدام جوهر پیدا شود کیفیّت آن فساد کی او را باشد.

[§۵۰:۱۵] پس اگر گوییم اندر عقل دیگر پیدا شود و عقل خود جز یکی نیست، چگونه چیزی اندر نیستی پیدا شود بوقت تباه شدن خویش.

[§۵۰:۱۶] و چون عقلی دیگر نیست، و فسادْ گشتن چگونگی باشد، و چگونگی را خود به جوهر عقل دانند، درست شد بدین برهان که نمودیم، که عقل را فساد نیست، چنانك خدای تعالی می‌گوید،[۱۶] قوله: كُلُّ شَيْءٍ هٰالِكٌ إِلاّٰ وَجْهَهُ.[۱۷] گفت: «هرچیزی تباه شود مگر روی خدای تعالی». و عقل روی خدای است، بدان سبب کی شناخت توحید به عقل است، همچنانك چیزها را به روی شناسند.

---

۱۴ سورة القمر (۵۴)، آیت ۵۰.

۱۵ ¦⟵برگ [اس:۸۲-الف].

۱۶ ایا: میفرماید.

۱۷ سورة القصص (۲۸)، آیت ۸۸.

[§۵۰:۱۷] دور است ایزد تعالی از همه اضافتها[۱۸] که آفریدگان خویش را داده است. و معنی وجه ایزد سبحانه چنان باید دانستن کی گویی چیزها را که بدانند به روی آن چیزها دانند و آن سبب کی چیزها را بدان بدانند روی آن چیز باشد.

[§۵۰:۱۸] و ما وحدت ایزد را تعالی که دور کردیم از بسیاریها به نور و شرف عقل توانستیم کردن. و اثبات کردن اندر محض مُبدِع حقّ را پاك از همه اثبات مبدعات، یعنی هستیها، به عقل اوّل توانستیم کردن، کی او رحمت مُبدِع حقّ است بر خلق. ازین قبل واجب آمد عقل اوّل[۱۹] را وجه ایزد تعالی خواندن.

[§۵۰:۱۹] و امّا از ضعف نفس نادان باشد این اندیشه کی گوید اگر ایزد تعالی مر عقل را قهر نکند او، جلّ ذکره، قادر و قاهر نباشد، و خدای تعالی مر عقل را لازم آید.

[§۵۰:۲۰] و اگر آن کس بداندی که اندر تباه کردن حکمت عجز ظاهر شود نه قدرت چنین سخن نگویندی.

[§۵۰:۲۱] ازبهرآنك مر استادی صانع قاهر جلد را روزگاری باید تا آسیابی یا دولابی بسازد، و نادانی عاجز بی‌تمییز آن را بیك ساعت تباه تواند کردن. و هرچند آن صانع استادتر باشد آن کارکرد او بیشتر پای دارد.

[§۵۰:۲۲] پس ازین حکم عقل کلّ کی او به اثر ایزد حق مخصوص است باید که ابدالآبدین باقی باشد، ‹نه که ایزد خلق او بل تباه کند›.[۲۰]

[§۵۰:۲۳] و اگر کسی خواهد که به قدرت مُبدِع حقّ بنگرد، و قهر او را بر آفریدگان ببیند،[۲۱] به چشم بصیرت بنگرد، تا ایشان بدان[۲۲] تباه کردنِ عقل شریف

---

۱۸ |⟵برگ [ایا:۷۲-الف].

۱۹ اس: [حرف «ل» در کلمه «اوّل» با جوهر شنگرف نوشته شده است].

۲۰ ایا: – نه که ایزد خلق او بل تباه کند.

۲۱ اس، ایا: به‌بیند.

۲۲ ایا: بران.

بزرگوار مر آن را ببینند،[۲۳] و آن قدرت آن است[۲۴] کی صفت عقل شریف،[۲۵] آنك او بدان از دیگر مبدعات و مخلوقات جدا است، آن است کی همه چیزها را بذات خویش[۲۶] بداند، و هیچ چیز را این اختصاص نیست.

[§۵۰:۲۴] پس عقل کلّی خود اندر این حصار کی یاد کرده شد بازداشته است و مقهور است، چه اگر او را این خاصیّت نباشد خود عقل نباشد.

[§۵۰:۲۵] و بدین روی دانسته شود که باری[۲۷] سبحانه که مر او را بدین خاصیت پدید آورد، نه از چیزی، برو قادر است، و [ا]مر باری سبحانه ازین صفتِ [عقل] منزّه است.[۲۸] و این فصل کی یاد کرده شد خردمند را اندر توحید چراغی روشن است.

۲۳ اس: به بینند؛ ایا: به بیند.

۲۴ ¦⟵برگ [اس:۸۲-ب].

۲۵ اس: [حرف «ش» در «شریف» محو شده است].

۲۶ اس: [حروف «ت، خ، و، ی» در «بذات خویش» مخدوش اند].

۲۷ ¦⟵برگ [ایا:۷۲-ب].

۲۸ تصحیح قیاسی. نك: همین کتاب، بند: [§۶۷:۲۹] نیز دانسته اند که هر موجودات کز عقل همی‌بودش پذیرد مر عقل را اندر آن جز فرمان برداری چیزی نیست. و فرمان باری سبحانه است که دور است از صفات عقل و آنچ فرود ازو است.

صف پنجاه و یکم

سخن اندر عقل کی او تمام است بفعل و قوّت[۱]

[§۵۱:۱] خردمند آن کس است کی از محسوس بر معقول دلیلی تواند گرفتن. و ما یافتیم مر چیزهای طبیعی را کی پیدا شد[۲] بفعل پس از آنك مر او را بقوّت یافته بودیم.

[§۵۱:۲] و هر چه یافتن آن به آغاز اندر حدّ قوّت نبود به انجام مر او را حدّ فعل یافته نشد. چون مردم که پیش از آن کی بفعل مردم شد اندر پشت پدر مردمی دیگر بود به حدّ قوّت، تا ممکن بود پیداشدن او بفعل. برمثال خرمابنی کی پیش ‹از آنك›[۳] خرمابن گشت بفعل یافتن او اندر دانۀ خرما بود بقوّت.

[§۵۱:۳] پس همچنین گوییم که امّهات پیش از آنك امّهات شدند بفعل، ناچاره اندر قوّت طبیعت امّهات بودند به حدّ قوّت. و دلیل بر درستی این قول آن است کی امروز امّهات به حدّ فعل‌اند و بودن ایشان امروز به حدّ فعل گوایی همی دهد که پیش از بیرون آمدن بفعل اندر حدّ قوّت بوده‌اند.

[§۵۱:۴] پس گوییم که چیزی که بفعل آید از قوّت و شرف باشد اندر حال فعل و باز به حال قوّت بازشود برمثال خرما دانه‌ای[۴] که او درخت خرما است بقوّت پس بفعل آید بدانچ درخت گردد و شریف باشد و باز آن درخت اندر دانۀ خرما شود بقوّت همچنانك از اوّل بود.

---

۱ قس: کتاب الینابیع، الینبوع التاسع (۹): في أنّ العقل تامّ بالفعل والقوّة، ص ۲۸ تا ۲۹.

۲ ایا: شدن.

۳ ایا: ازان که.

۴ اس، ایا: دانهء.

[§۵:۵۱] و آن چیز که بفعل آید و همچنان بماند و بقوّت بازنشود[۵] شریف‌تر باشد از آن چیز کی باز حال[۶] قوّت شود.

[§۶:۵۱] پس ازین حکم لازم آید کی عقل تمام بود و بفعل بود و باز حال قوّت نشد، بدانچ او اندر چیزی نبوده بود به حدّ قوّت تا بفعل آید، بل‌کی[۷] بودش او به امر بود نه از[۸] چیزی.[۹]

[§۷:۵۱] و چون لازم آمد بضرورت بودنِ[۱۰] چیزی نه از چیزی، و از عقل لازم آمد که آن چیز تمام بود بفعل، اعنی که اندر چیزی دیگر نبود تا به حدّ قوّت بودی. و نیز تمام بودی بقوّت،[۱۱] از بهر آنك چیزها بجملگی همه ازو پیدا آید، و آن عقل است.

[§۸:۵۱] پس درست کردیم که عقل تمام است بفعل و بقوّت، آن است که عقل شرف و قوّت از چیزی دیگر نپذیرد، چون گرفتن چیزهای طبیعی، کی قوّت و شرف بگیرد از دیگر چیزهای جسمانی و نورانی چون طبایع و افلاك و انجم.

[§۹:۵۱] و چون عقل از چیزی شرف نمی‌گیرد دلیل است کی او خود بفعل است، که اگر نه بفعل بودی کسب کردی از چیزی دیگر. و هر چیزی که از چیزی دیگر کسب کند اندر حال کسب‌کردن میان قوّت و فعل باشد. یك چند روزگار چون درخت خرما کز دانه بروید وزان حال که بروید نه دانهٔ خرما باشد و نه درخت.

[§۱۰:۵۱] چون عقل به میان قوّت و فعل نمی‌باشد، از بهر آنك نفس خود از عقل همی کسب کند، واجب آید کی عقل اندر حدّ قوّت نیست، تا بدان کسب بفعل بیرون آید چون چیزهای طبیعی.

۵ اس: [«نشود» مخدوش است].

۶ |⟵برگ [اس:۸۳-الف].

۷ ایا: بلك.

۸ ایا: – از.

۹ اس: [«چیزی» مخدوش است].

۱۰ |⟵برگ [ایا:۷۳-الف].

۱۱ ایا: بقوة.

[§۵۱:۱۱] و نیز گوییم که عقل را، از شمار، مرتبت یکی است، و یکی تمام است هم بقوّت و هم بفعل. و یکی اندر شمار نیست، چنانك هر شماری اندر شمار است، بل‌کی یکی علّت شمار است و همه شمارها اندر او است، همچنانك عقل علّت همه بودشهای[۱۲] او است، و همه بودها اندر او است.

[§۵۱:۱۲] و ممکن نیست کی شماری بر یکی پیشی کند تا آن شمار سبب باشد پیداشدن یکی را، چنانك یکی سبب است پیداشدن دو را، و دو سبب است مر پیداشدن سه را.

[§۵۱:۱۳] و دو اندر یکی به حدّ قوّت است چنانك سه اندر دو به حدّ قوّت است. و نشاید بودن که عددی بر یکی پیشی دارد تا آن عدد سبب باشد مر یکی را، و هم اندر او باشد به حدّ قوّت.

[§۵۱:۱۴] همچنین نشاید که عقل اندر چیزی باشد به حدّ قوّت[۱۳] تا ازو پیدا شود بفعل، کی اگر چنین[۱۴] بودی علّتها را نهایت نبودی وگر علّتها را نهایت نبودی[۱۵] معلولات پیدا نیامدی. و چون معلولات پیدا است دلیل است کی علّتها[۱۶] را نهایت است.

[§۵۱:۱۵] و نهایت علّتها[۱۷] عقل است و او را علّت نیست. و چیزی کی او را علّت نباشد او به حدّ قوّت[۱۸] نبوده باشد. پس درست شد که عقل تمام است هم بفعل و هم بقوّت.[۱۹]

---

۱۲ ایا: بودشها.

۱۳ ایا: قوة.

۱۴ اس: [عبارت «اگر چنین» مخدوش است].

۱۵ ¦⟵برگ [اس:۸۳-ب].

۱۶ ¦⟵برگ [ایا:۷۳-ب].

۱۷ اس: [«علّتها» مخدوش است].

۱۸ ایا: قوة.

۱۹ ایا: بقوة.

صف پنچاه و دوم

سخن اندر علّت زمان

[§۵۲:۱] زمان علّت است مر تمام شدن چیزهای طبیعی را. و چیزهای طبیعی باشنده است[۱] به جنبش طبایع. و طبایع جنبنده به گردش افلاك. و افلاك گردان است به حرکت نفس کلّی از حرکت شوقی کی آن را آرام نیست مگر به تمام شدن نفس و رسیدن او به مرتبت عقل کلّی.

[§۵۲:۲] پس گوییم کی زمان را علّت جنبش افلاك است کی جنبنده است به شوق نفس کلّی. پس علّت زمان شوق نفس کلّی است.

[§۵۲:۳] و زمان، که بر نفس لازم آید پدیدآوردن، بسبب بیرون آوردن او بود مر چیزها را از حدّ قوّت[۲] به حدّ فعل.

[§۵۲:۴] و نفس دانست کی آنچ[۳] فرود ازو باشد نتوانند[۴] مادّتهای او را پذیرفتن مگر به زمان. پس زمان واجب آمد مر فرودینان را از نفس، همچنانك رفتن قلم بکار آید مر پدید آوردن خط را از زیر قلم.

[§۵۲:۵] و حاجت آید فکرت مردم را به آلت و به قلم تا بیرون آرد حکمتها را از[۵] عقل. و همچنین همه آلتها که بدو عمل کنند از بهر آن فایده‌ها باید که فرود از آلتِ عمل پدید آید، نه از بهر حکمت آن عمل را، کز نفس[۶] بیرون آرند.

[§۵۲:۶] برمثال خط که نفس همی داند نبشتن. پس قلم و حِبْر[۷] و کاغذ و دست

---

۱ اس: [«است» ناخوانا است].

۲ ایا: قوة.

۳ ایا: آنچه.

۴ ایا: نتواند.

۵ اس: [حرف «از» خوانا نیست؛ اما بالای آن با جوهر شنگرف «ار» (از) نوشته شده است].

۶ اس: [«نفس» مخدوش است].

۷ نك: دهخدا: حبر. [حِ] ... زگاب. سیاهی. دوده. دودهٔ مرکب. مرکب. مداد. نقس. زگالاب.

و جنبش و جای و روزگار بباید تا آن نبشتن ازو پدید آید. و آن نبشتن از بهر آن همی باید تا کسی مر آن را ببیند[8] کزو فایده گیرد نه از بهر آن باید تا آنچ همی بایست بر کاغذ بنگارد.

[§۵۲:۷] پس درست شد کی آلت همه از بهر آن فایده را باید که فرود از عمل باشد و زمان آلتی است مر عمل عالم را. پس دانستیم که زمان از بهر پذیرندگان را بایست کی زیر عمل عالم اندر بودند.

[§۵۲:۸] و لکن چون نفس کلّی مر این آلت عظیم کلّی را پدید[9] آورد که زمان است چنان[10] آوردش از بایستگی کی اوهام[11] اندر او نمی‌توانند رسیدن به برگرفتن[12] مر او را. و این از تمامی حکمت بود که آلتی پدید آورد بدین شریفی و بایستگی.

[§۵۲:۹] اندر باید یافتن مر این فصل را که روشن[13] است و بسیار بزرگان را[14] اندر این شبهت‌اند.

سیاهی دوات: ... گر نباشد یاری حبر و قلم / کی فتد بر روی کاغذها رقم. (مولوی). قلقشندی گوید: سومین آلت کتابت مداد و حبر است و آنچه مانند آن باشد، و دربارهٔ آن به چهار مورد بحث می‌کنیم: مورد اول، در نام و ریشهٔ کلمهٔ مداد و حبر. مداد را از آن مداد گفته اند که به خامه مدد رساند... و ریشهٔ حبر به معنی رنگ است...

۸ اس، ایا: به بیند.

۹ ¦⟵برگ [ایا:۷۴-الف].

۱۰ ¦⟵برگ [اس:۸۴-الف].

۱۱ اس: [«اوهام» مخدوش است].

۱۲ نك: دهخدا: برگرفتن. [بَ گِ رِ تَ] برداشتن چیزی... || برداشت کردن. اخذ کردن. جدا کردن قسمتی از چیزی... || متصرف شدن. ضبط کردن... || بدست آوردن. حاصل کردن... || بردن. گنجایش داشتن.

۱۳ اس: [«روشن» مخدوش است].

۱۴ ایا: - را.

صف پنجاه و سوم

سخن اندر چه چیزی عالم بسیط

[§۱:۵۳] عالم نامی است گرفته از علم. و گردآرنده است این نام مر فایده‌دهنده و فایده‌پذیر را. از بهر آنك جملگی عالم جسمانی خود این دو چیز است. یا عالم نورانی است چون افلاك و کواکب یا سفلانی است چون طبایع.

[§۲:۵۳] و آن نورانی فایده‌دهنده است و این سفلانی فایده‌پذیر است. و هر چه اندر این دو میان از زایشها است همه مادّت‌پذیر است از طبایع.

[§۳:۵۳] و همچنین هر فایده‌دهنده‌ای[۱] و فایده‌پذیریِ عالم باشد از مردم، از بهر آنك غرض آفریدگار از عالم مردم است، از بهر فایده پذیرفتن او به علم.

[§۴:۵۳] نبینی[۲] کی رسول مصطفی، صلی الله علیه وآله، فرمود: النَّاسُ عَالِمٌ أو[۳] مُتَعَلِّمٌ (أو مُسْتَمِعٌ)[۴] وَ سَائِرُ النَّاسِ هَمَجٌ.[۵] گفت: «مردمان بجملگی دانش‌دهنده‌ای[۶] است و دانش‌پذیری و دیگر مردم خُرسان[۷] است».

---

۱ اس، ایا: فایده دهنده‌ء.

۲ اس، ایا: نه بینی.

۳ اس: [حرف «ا» (أ) در «أو» با جوهر شنگرف کمرنگ اضافه شده است].

۴ اس: [کلمه «مستمع» در حاشیه متن با جوهر شنگرف نوشته شده است].. || ایا: [«او مستمع» در فاصله میان خطوط با خط نازکتر نوشته شده است]. || اینجا، «أومستمع» در واقع معنی «أومتعلم» است، و حالت سومی را بیان نمیکند.

۵ ابن بابویه، الخصال، ج ۱، باب الإثْنَیْن، اَلنَّاسُ اِثْنَانِ عَالِمٌ وَ مُتَعَلِّمٌ، ص ۳۹.

۶ اس، ایا: دانش دهندهٔ.

۷ اس: حرسان؛ ایا: حرسات. || نك: دهخدا: خرس. [خُ] ... جِ اَخْرَس و خَرْساء. رجوع به اخرس و خرساء شود: آخر از استاد باقی را بپرس/ یا حریصان جمله کورانند و خُرس. (مولوی). اخرس. [اَرَ] ... گنگ. ... کندزبان. بی آواز. لال. مؤنث: خَرْساء. ج، خُرس، خُرسان: عاشقی بر خور و بر شهوتِ خود راست چو خِرس/ نفس گویای تو در حکمت ازآنست اخرس. (سنائی).
|| قس: وجه دین، گفتار ۴۶، ص ۳۲۶، س ۱۵ تا ۲۰: و چون آن مرد گفت ندارم مرورا بدیو بازخواند از بهر آنکه رسول علیه السّلام مرین دو تن را مردم بخواند بدین خبر که گفت: اَلنَّاسُ اثْنَانِ عَالِمٌ و مُتَعَلِّمٌ و سائِرُهُمْ کالهَمَج، گفت: مردم دو تن اند یکی عالم یعنی دانا و یکی

[§۵۳:۵] و چون گوییم جسمانی مرکب، گفته شود که آنچ او را درازا و بالا و پهنا است، آنچ از بر یکدیگر نِشاختَه[۸] است، چون جزوهای این عالم که بر یکدیگر نشسته[۹] است تا ازو عالم آمده است. این است معنی عالم جسمانی مرکب.

[§۵۳:۶] و چون گوییم عالم روحانی بسیط، گفته شود کی آن فایده‌پذیر و فایده‌دهنده، کی جزوها نیست مر او را، و کران نیست، و فراهم آورده نیست، و نه برنشاخته.[۱۰]

[§۵۳:۷] ‹وز نامها›[۱۱] نام هست کی چون آن نام بگویی بدان یك نام بسیار چیزها گفته شود جز آن، چنانك چون[۱۲] گویی روی مردم. این نامی باشد که گرد کند مر بسیار نامها را که اندر او است[۱۳] چون پیشانی و ابروها و چشمها و گوشها و بینی

متعلّم یعنی علم آموزنده و دیگران همه حشراتند؛ پس هر که بنفس خویش علم همی پذیرد از آنکه برتر ازوست و همیآموزد مر آنرا که فروتر ازوست، او از برادران فرشتگانست.
|| نیز قس: زادالمسافر، قول ۱۵، ص ۱۶۴ تا ۱۶۵: پس درست کردیم به قول خدای و بیان عقلی که این گروه از علم حق غافل‌اند <و دل ایشان تباهی گرفته است و به آن تباهی> بر خدای و رسول دروغ همی گویند. <و> خدای <تعالی> بر ایشان لعنت کرده است <بدین آیت> که همی گوید <،قوله>: قُتِلَ الْخَرَّاصُونَ*الَّذِينَ هُمْ فِي غَمْرَةٍ سَاهُونَ. (الذّاریات -۵۱: آیات ۱۰، ۱۱) این گروه‌اند که خود ندانند و چون مر ایشان را چیزی از آفریش خدای تعالی بنمایند، مر آن را نبینند و چو سخنی عقلی مر ایشان را شنوانند، گوش بدان ندارند و از ستوران گمراه‌ترند و غافلان امّت‌اند...
|| نك: دهخدا: خرص. [خَ] ... دروغ گفتن. || به تخمین و گمان سخن گفتن. || خرصان. [خُ] (عربی اِسم) جمع ِ: خِرص و خُرص.

۸ اس: نشاحته؛ ایا: ساخته. || نك: دهخدا: نشاختن. [ن ِ تَ] ... نشاندن. ... نشانیدن.... چو دیدش جهاندار بنواختش / بر تخت پیروزه بنشاختش. (فردوسی). || نشاندن. نصب کردن. تعبیه کردن. کار گذاشتن. رجوع به نشاندن شود. - اندرنشاختن؛ نصب کردن. به کار بردن. کار گذاشتن...- برنشاختن؛ نشاندن .نشانیدن.

۹ اس:نسسه؛ ایا: بسته.

۱۰ اس: برنشاحته؛ ایا: ساخته.

۱۱ ایا:– وز نامها | + و زمانها.

۱۲ ایا: - چون.

۱۳ ¦⟵برگ [ایا:۷۴-ب].

و مژه و بناگوش و رخ و زنخ و دهان. پس چون این همه نامها بیك جای گرد آیند همه را بجملگی روی باشد. و روی نامی است گردآرندهٔ این چیزهای نامدار.[۱۴]

[§۸:۵۳] و همچنین عالم نامی است گردآرندهٔ فایده‌دهنده و فایده‌پذیر.[۱۵] و عالم بسیط نامی است گردآرنده مر[۱۶] نفس و عقل را، و مر مادّت دادن عقل نفس را، و پذیرفتن نفس مر آن زیادت[۱۷] را از عقل کلّی بی زمان و مکانی.

۱۴ ¦⟵برگ [اس:۸۴-ب].

۱۵ ایا: فایده‌پذیرنده.

۱۶ اس: [«آرنده مر» مخدوش است]؛ ایا: +مر.

۱۷ ایا: مادّت.

صف پنجاه و چهارم

سخن اندر چگونگی عبادت عقل کلّی[۱]

[§۵۴:۱] چون علّت جسمانی و روحانی عقل بود، و بازپسین همه معلولات مردم بود، به نخستین علّت خویش بازگشت از راه پذیرفتن فایده ازو.

[§۵۴:۲] و عبادت آفریدگار بر معلول بازپسین لازم آمد واجب آید، کی علّت اول مر آفریدگار را پرستنده است.

[§۵۴:۳] و چون عبادت از مردم، ایزد تعالی بر بنیاد شهادت خواست، و آن چهار سخن و هفت فصل و دوازده حرف است، لازم آید که عبادت عقل مر باری سبحانه را هم بدین شهادت است.

[§۵۴:۴] و تخم شهادت اندر هویّت عقل ثابت است. و هیچ چیز نیست آشکارا شده اندر عالم کی تخم آن اندر عقل نیست. و ما دوست داریم که ما را آشکارا شود بر پرستش کردن[۲] عقل مر باری را سبحانه.

[§۵۴:۵] پس گوییم که تخم این چهار سخن اندر عقل تسبیح است اعنی پاکیزه کردن؛ و اضافت است اعنی بازبستن؛ و ابتهال است اعنی گردن نهادن؛ و تعظیم است اعنی بزرگ داشتن مر مُبدِع حقّ را سبحانه.

[§۵۴:۶] امّا تسبیح از آن به منزلت کلمه [لا][۳] باشد از شهادت. و عقل تسبیح کرد ایزد را، اعنی پاك کردن مر او را از هر چه یافت اندر هویت خویش و نفی کرد ازو تشبیه به همه[۴] رویها.

---

۱ قس: کتاب الینابیع، الینبوع الثالث والعشرون (۲۳): في کیفیة عبادة المُبدَع - وهو السابق — للمُبدِع، ص ۵۶ تا ۵۹.

۲ اس: [«کردن» مخدوش است].

۳ تصحیح قیاسی.

۴ اس: [«بهمه» مخدوش است]؛ ایا: - بهمه.

[§۷:۵۴] و امّا اضافت از آن به منزلت کلمه الٰه است از شهادت، اعنی که عقل پس از آن [که][۵] نفی کرد از مُبدِع حقّ همه[۶] تشبیهات را، مقرّ[۷] شد کی عقل و همه آفریده‌ها بازبسته‌اند به مُبدِع حقّ کی همه مر او را آند.

[§۸:۵۴] ابتهال، اعنی گردن نهادن از عقل، به منزلت کلمه الّا باشد از شهادت، اعنی کی، عقل از پس نفی صفات و اقرار به اضافت، تضرّع کند به ایزد تا بشناسد مُبدِع حقّ را مجرّد از صفتهای خلق.

[§۹:۵۴] و امّا تعظیم اعنی بزرگ داشتن از عقل به منزلت کلمه اللّٰه باشد از شهادت، اعنی عقل[۸] آنگاه که تضرّع کرد به ایزد تعالی، و بدید[۹] مر عقاب او را، توانایی نداشت کی بر آن واقف شدی، پس بزرگوار کرد مُبدِع حقّ را از همه هستی و نیستی.

[§۱۰:۵۴] امّا تخم هفت فصل شهادت اندر عقل چنان است که کلمه لا يك فصل است، و عقل تسبیح کرد[۱۰] مُبدِع حقّ را از جهت[۱۱] کلمه او که آن واحد محض است.

[§۱۱:۵۴] و کلمه الٰه[۱۲] دو فصل است همچنانك اضافت کی مانند او است دوگونه است. اضافت روحانیات و اضافت جسمانیات از جهت[۱۳] پرستش، اعنی کی جسمانی و روحانی هر دو آفریدگان خدای‌اند.

---

۵ تصحیح قیاسی.

۶ ¦⟵برگ [ایا:۷۵-الف].

۷ ایا: مقرّر.

۸ اس: [«عقل» مخدوش است].

۹ ¦⟵برگ [اس:۸۵-الف].

۱۰ اس: [«تسبیح کرد» مخدوش است].

۱۱ اس: جهة.

۱۲ اس، ایا: آله.

۱۳ اس، ایا: جهة.

[§۱۲:۵۴] و کلمه الّا دو فصل است و گردن نهادن بر دوگونه باشد، [اعنی عقل گردن نهد به نفی و گردن نهد به اثبات. و کلمه اللّٰه دو فصل است.] همچنین بزرگ داشتن بر دوگونه است. یکی بزرگ داشتن از هستی و دیگر از نیستی.[۱۴]

[§۱۳:۵۴] و امّا تخم دوازده حرف شهادت اندر عقل آن است که کلمه لا دو حرف است اعنی که غایت تسبیح ایزد تعالی از دو وجه است از جهت عقل و از جهت نفس. و کلمه اله سه حرف است، ‹اعنی کی عقل اضافت کند مر روحانی را و اضافت کند مر جسمانی را و اضافت کند مر علّت هردو را به باری سبحانه›.[۱۵] و کلمه الّا سه حرف است، ‹اعنی که گردن نهد عقل به نفی و گردن نهد به اثبات و گردن نهد به عجز که آن نه نفی است و نه اثبات›.[۱۶]

[§۱۴:۵۴] و کلمه اللّٰه چهار حرف است همچنان بزرگ داشتن بر چهار مرتبت است اعنی کی عقل بزرگ دارد مر ایزد را سبحانه از هَلیَّت[۱۷] اعنی از هستی، و از

۱۴ تصحیح قیاسی. قس: كتاب الينابيع، الينبوع الثالث والعشرون (۲۳)، ص ۵۷ تا ۵۸، بند (۱۱۱)، س ۱۸ تا ۱۹، و ۱: وكلمة «إلا» فصلان: كذلك الابتهال ابتهالان: يعني أن السابق يبتهل إليه بالنفي، ويبتهل إليه بالإثبات. وكلمة «اللّٰه» فصلان: كذلك التعظيم تعظيمان: تعظيم عن أيس، وتعظيم عن ليس.

۱۵ اس، ایا: اعنی که گردن نهد عقل بنفی و گردن نهد باثبات و گردن نهد بعجز که آن نه نفی است و نه اثبات. || تصحیح قیاسی. قس: كتاب الينابيع، الينبوع الثالث والعشرون (۲۳)، ص ۵۸، بند (۱۱۲)، س ۴ تا ۶: وكلمة «اله» ثلاثة أحرف، وكذالك الإضافة على ثلاث مراتب، يعنى انّ السابق يضيف اليه الروحانىّ ويضيف اليه الجسمانىّ، وهى كلمته جلّ وعزّ.

۱۶ اس، ایا: اعنی که عقل اضافت کند مر روحانی را و اضافت کند مر جسمانی را و اضافت کند مر علّت هردو را بباری سبحانه. || تصحیح قیاسی. قس: كتاب الينابيع، الينبوع الثالث والعشرون (۲۳)، ص ۵۸، بند (۱۱۲)، س ۶ تا ۸: وكلمة «الّا» ثلاثة أحرف، وكذالك الابتهال على ثلاث مراتب، يعنى انّ السابق يبتهل اليه بالنفى والاثبات وبالعجز الذى لا هو نفى ولا اثبات.

۱۷ هَلیَّت (هَ یِّ) فارسی (ریشه شناسی: عربی) مصدر صناعی است مرکب از هل و ئیت یعنی پرسش کردن از مطلب «هل» و سؤال از مطلب هل یعنی سؤال از اصل وجود شیء یا سؤال از وجود صفتی برای شیء. (فرهنگ فارسی معین، ج ۲، ص ۲۱۰۶)

لمّیَّت[18] اعنی چرایی، و از مائیّت[19] اعنی چه‌چیزی، و از کیفیّت اعنی[20] چگونگی. این است تخم شهادت اندر جوهر عقل کی بدان عبادت کند مُبدِع حقّ را.[21]

[§۵۴:۱۵] و همچنین قرار عالم[22] بر چهار امّهات است چون آتش و هوا و آب و زمین، و بر هفت ستارهٔ رونده است چون زحل و مشتری و مریخ و شمس و زهره و عطارد و قمر، و بر دوازده برج است چون حمل و ثور و جوزا و سرطان و اسد و سنبله و میزان و عقرب و قوس و جدی و دلو و حوت.

[§۵۴:۱۶] و قرار جسم مردم کی او راست‌تر از همه جسمها است بر چهار طبع است چون سودا و بلغم و خون و صفرا، و بر هفت اندام اندرونی است چون مغز و دل و شش و جگر و سپرز و زَهرَه و گُردَه،[23] و برابر دوازده برج دوازده اندام آشکار است چون سر و روی و گردن و سینه و شکم و پشت و دو دست و دو ران و دو پای.

[§۵۴:۱۷] و صورت کردیم بر دایره‌ای[24] کی بهم آورد این قسمتها از شهادت و از عالم و از بدن مردم و از عبادت عقل؛ و پدید کردیم هر قسمتی را با یکدیگر که[25] درخور است از چهار و هفت و دوازده و مرکز این همه عقل است.[26]

---

۱۸ لك: الوری، حسن، فرهنگ بزرگ سخن، ج ۷، ص ۶۴۴۲: لِمّیَّت (لِ مْ مِ یْ یَ) [عربی لِمِّیَّة] ... چرایی.... || نیز نك: دهخدا: لمائیة. [لِ ئی یَ] (عربی مصدر جعلی، اِسم مصدر) چرائی.

۱۹ نك:دهخدا: مائیت. [ئی یَ] ... ماهیت. ... سؤال از حقیقت شئ. ... رجوع به ماهیت شود.

۲۰ ¦⟵برگ [ایا:۷۵-ب].

۲۱ قس: کتاب الینابیع، الینبوع الثالث والعشرون (۲۳)، ص ۵۸، بند (۱۱۲)، س ۸ تا ۱۰: وکلمة «الله» أربعة أحرف، کذالك التعظیم علی أربع مراتب: تعظیمه عن اللمیة، وتعظیمه عن المائیّة، وتعظیمه عن الکیفیّة، وتعظیمه عن الکمیّة. فهذا بزر الشهادة في جوهر السابق الذی یعبد المبدع.

۲۲ اس: [کلمه «عالم» مخدوش است].

۲۳ ¦⟵برگ [اس:۸۵-ب].

۲۴ اس، ایا: دایرهء.

۲۵ اس: – که.

۲۶ ¦⟵برگ [ایا:۷۶-الف].

[§۱۸:۵۴] این است صورت پرستش عقل مر باری را سبحانه و تعالی برابر با حرفها و فصلها و کلمه‌های شهادت و برابر با آفرینش عالم و آفرینش مردم، بشناس، وَ اللّٰهُ أَعْلَمُ وَ أَحْكَمُ.[۲۷]

[نمودار ۲: صورت پرستش عقل مر باری را سبحانه و تعالی]

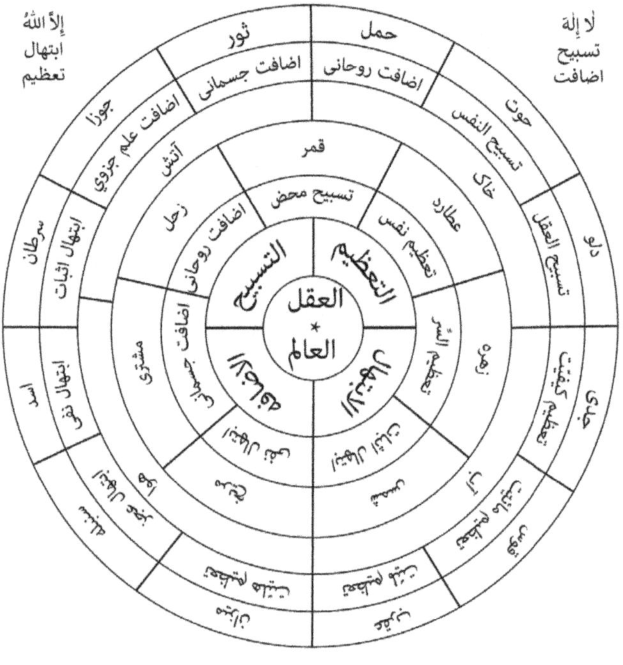

۲۷ ¦⟵برگ [اس:۸۶-الف]. || عبارت برگرفته از آیات قرآنی است، از جمله، نک: آل عمران، ۳۶؛ النِّسَاء، ۲۵؛ الأَنْعَام، ۱۲۴؛ هُود، ۴۵؛ العَنْكَبُوت، ۱۰؛ التِّين، ۸.

صف پنجاه و پنجم

سخن اندر آنك ثواب[۱] و عقاب علمی است نه حسّی[۲]

[§۵۵:۱] مقصود از لفظ ثواب یافتن خوشی است.[۳] و مقصود از لفظ عقاب یافتن دشواری است. و لذّت[۴] حسّی را بریدن است: چه از بی‌نیاز شدن طبایع که اندر کالبد مردم است، از حاجتمندی کی او را افتاده باشد، و آن را همی گرسنه و تشنه خوانند؛ و چه از سُترَه[۵] شدن حواس از شنیدن مر محسوسات را.

[§۵۵:۲] و واجب آمد کی آن لذّت کی نیك‌بختان یابند همیشگی باشد و مر آن را بریدن نباشد.

[§۵۵:۳] و نیست لذّتی کی آن دایم بر حال خویش است مگر لذّت علم کی چون چیزی را معلوم کردی هرچند او را بیشتر جویی و نزدیك‌تر گردانی خوشتر شود.

[§۵۵:۴] پس پیدا شد کی لذّت نیك‌بختان بدان عالم لذّتی علمی است از آن است کی همیشه است. چنانك ایزد تعالی همی‌گوید، قوله: مَثَلُ الْجَنَّةِ الَّتِي وُعِدَ الْمُتَّقُونَ تَجْرِي مِنْ تَحْتِهَا الْأَنْهٰارُ أُكُلُهٰا دٰائِمٌ وَ ظِلُّهٰا تِلْكَ عُقْبَى الَّذِينَ اتَّقَوْا وَ عُقْبَى الْكٰافِرِينَ النّٰارُ.[۶] همی‌گوید: «مثل آن بهشت کی امید دارند پرهیزگاران بدو همی‌رود زیر او جویها و بار درختان او همیشه است. آن عاقبت کار آن کسان است کی پرهیزگاری کردند و عاقبت کار کافران آتش است».

[§۵۵:۵] و دیگر آن است کی لذّتهای حسّی از یك راه نتوان یافتن بل‌کی[۷] از چند

---

۱ اس: + بواب.

۲ قس: کتاب الینابیع، الینبوع السابع والعشرون (۲۷): في أن الثواب هو العلم، ص ۶۵ تا ۶۷.

۳ اس: [«خوشی است» مخدوش است].

۴ اس: لذتی.

۵ نك: دهخدا: سترة. [سُ رَ] ... پوشش و آنچه بدان خود را از چیزی بپوشند.

۶ سورة الرعد (۱۳)، آیت ۳۵.

۷ ایا: بلك.

جای توان یافتن. و چون جایگاه آن لذّت تباه شود نیز لذّت یافتن نباشد. چنانك اگر چشم نباشد نیز آن لذّت را که به چشم توان یافتن از هیچ حاسّهٔ دیگر نتوان یافتن. و حکم اندر هر لذّتی همین است.

[§۵۵:۶] و سبیل نفس اندر باب یافتن مر معلومات را[۸] یك سبیل است. و نفس چون مر معلوم[۹] را بخویشتن کشد ازو لذت بی‌ملالت یابد، از بهر آنك آن لذّت روحانی است.

[§۵۵:۷] و هرچند کی لذّت روحانی بسیار گونها است نفس مر آن گونها را همه از یك سبیل پذیرد، و آن دانستن نفس است مر آن علمها را. و آن سبیل به بقای نفس باقی است. و تباه نشود آن سبیل تا به تباه شدن آن تباه شدن لذتها باشد، چنانك اندر لذّات جسمانی است کی به تباه شدن[۱۰] حواس تباه شدن لذّات است.

[§۵۵:۸] پس نفس کی دانا است باقی است، و علم که[۱۱] ذات او است به بقای نفس باقی است، و معلومات[۱۲] روحانی باقی است.

[§۵۵:۹] و چون معلوم و علم و عالم هرسه باقی باشد، آن لذّت کز میان سه باقی پدید آید بریده نشود.

[§۵۵:۱۰] پس درست کردیم کی لذّات نفسانی که باقی است علمی است، و نیز علم تباه نشود. و چون بحاصل شد قوی‌تر و بیشتر شود. و حس به کار فرمودن تباه شود.

[§۵۵:۱۱] و دلیل بر آنك لذّت علم باقی است آن است کی چون اندکی از چیزی بدانی ازو نیز آرزو شود و هرچند بیشتر دانی آرزوی دانستن بیشتر آید.

---

۸ ¦⟵برگ [ایا:۷۶-ب].

۹ اس، ایا: معلول [کذا].

۱۰ ¦⟵برگ [اس:۸۶-ب].

۱۱ اس: [«که» بالای خط با جوهر کمرنگ نوشته شده است].

۱۲ اس: [«معلومات» مخدوش است].

[§۵۵:۱۲] و لذّات حسّی بخلاف این است. ازبهرآنك چون مقداری از طعام بخوری، آن قوّت لذّت کی همی‌یابی کمتر شود، و هرچند بیشتر خوری لذّت کمتر شود، تا بدان جای رسد کی اگر ستم کنی تا آن کس يك لقمه افزونی بخورد بیمار گردد و هلاك شود آن خورنده.

[§۵۵:۱۳] و نیز لذّت علمی کی غذای روح است هرچند بیشتر مر آن را کاربندی خوشتر از آن آید کی اوّل کاربسته باشی، ازبهرآنك اوّل نادانسته باشد، و نیك معلوم نشود، و چون از پسِ آنك دانسته باشی بگویی یا بنمایی یا ازو براندیشی، لذّت تمام ازو آن وقت یابی.

[§۵۵:۱۴] و این بخلاف لذّت حسّی است که لقمهٔ بازپسین به ناخوشی و دشواری خورده شود، و لقمهٔ پیشین به آرزو و آسانی، ‹تا بدان جای›[۱۳] رسد به آخر که خورنده بوی آن طعام نتواند بردن.[۱۴]

[§۵۵:۱۵] پس درست شد که ثواب علمی است نه حسّی. و این برهان ظاهر است خردمند را.

۱۳ ایا: تا بجایی.

۱۴ ¦⟵برگ [ایا:۷۷-الف].

صف پنجاه و ششم

سخن اندر صفت بهشت و دوزخ[۱]

[§۱:۵۶] معنی بهشت جای اهل ثواب است و معنی دوزخ جای اهل عقاب است. و خدای تعالی مر بهشت را به تازی چند جای یاد کرد بجنّة[۲] و دوزخ را نار خواند. و جنّت بوستانی باشد آراسته به درختان بارور و اسپرغم‌های[۳] خوش و آب روان و جایهای با راحت و پاکیزه چنانك حس را اندر آن راحت باشد.

[§۲:۵۶] پس گوییم، کی چون درست کردیم ازین پیش کی ثواب علمی است نه حسّی، بباید دانستن کی فایده‌های عقلی که آن شناخت لطایف است — که جملگی[۴] آرایش و راحت و لذّت کی اندر این عالم همی‌آید ازآنجا[۵] همی‌آید — بوستانِ نفسِ سخنگوی است، کی[۶] مر آن را به گفتار و اندیشه بتوان[۷] یافتن. و آن آراسته است [به][۸] پیش‌روان دین کی ایشان درختان آن بوستان‌اند.[۹]

[§۳:۵۶] و بگشتن اندر آن بوستان و نگرستن به چشم بصیرت اندر آن مر نفس ناطقه را لذّت به راحت و شادی و آسانی باشد.

---

۱ قس: کتاب الینابیع، الینبوع الثامن والعشرون (۲۸): في معنی الجنة والنار، ص ۶۷ تا ۶۹.

۲ اس: [«بجنة» بالای خط نوشته شده است].

۳ اس: در حاشیه متن معنی اسپرغم توضیح داده شده است: «اسپرغم اسم خاص ریحان است. بعد از آن بطریق عمومی‌تر نوعی از خوشبوی است». || نك: دهخدا: اسپرغم. [اَ / اِ پَ غَ / اِ پَ رَ] ... گلها و ریاحین. ... گلها و ریاحین باشد مطلقاً و ریحانی را نیز گویند که آنرا شاه اسپرم خوانند. ... رستنیی است خوشبوی که بتازیش ریحان گویند.

۴ |←برگ [اس:۸۷-الف].

۵ اس: ازنجا.

۶ اس: [«کی» روی «است» بالای خط نوشته شده است].

۷ اس: نتوان؛ ایا: نتوان [کذا].

۸ تصحیح قیاسی.

۹ اس:[«درختان آن بوستان» مخدوش است].

[§۴:۵۶] و لکن علم آلهی اندر این عالم به لفظها و مثلها بسته باشد و جدا نشود از آن تا بدان وقت کی ایزد تعالی مر آن را تقدیر کرده است.

[§۵:۵۶] و چون وقت آن فراز آید آن حکمتها از میان مثلها و رمزها بیرون آید بر نیکوتر آرایشی کی چشم چنان ندیده است و نه هیچ گوش صفت آن بشنوده است و نه بر دل هیچ مردم آن گذشته است. و آن وقت نیز دل از آن سیر نشود و یابندهٔ آن از آن ملول نشود و از نگاه داشتن آن پرداخته نشود.

[§۶:۵۶] و پیش از آن همی ملول گشت چون اندر پوست مثلها و رمزها بود. و همی نگاه بایست داشتن مر آن را نبشتن و درس کردن بدان سبب کی اندر تیرگی لفظها و مثلها بود.

[§۷:۵۶] همی بدان مثال کی غذاها که مر جسم را شاید و قوام زندگی جسم بدان است چون اندر بوستان باشد به آغاز پوست و خاشاك و خار باشد.[۱۰] و پیش از وقت رسیدن پنهان باشد اندر میان برگ و شاخ و کشتهای خویش چون[۱۱] وقت آن باشد کی جسد زو همی زندگی خواهد پذیرفتن آن کثافتها را بیوکند و تلخی و ترشی را به شیرینی و خوشی بدل کند، و بیرون آید بر نیکوتر آرایشی به دیدار و خوشتر وجهی از مزه و با راحت تر جایی از بوی، و از میان کشتنی[۱۲] و برگ و شاخ بیرون آرندش و نیز جسد از چشیدن او رنجه نشود و از بوی او به راحت رسد. و نگاهبان[۱۳] او از نگاه داشتن او رسته شود.

[§۸:۵۶] این مثل بهشت است که مر او را خدای تعالی بوستان خواند که فواید او برابر کرده شد اندر باب نفسانی با فواید بوستان اندر باب جسمانی یك یك.

---

۱۰ ¦⟵برگ [ایا:۷۷-ب].

۱۱ اس: [«چون» بالای خط نوشته شده است].

۱۲ ایا: کشتن.

۱۳ اس: نگاه‌بان.

[§۵۶:۹] و امّا آتش کی آن جای گناهکاران[۱۴] است مثل دوزخ بدان ازبهر آن است که آتش بکار آید اندر صلاح جسد ازبهر پختن چیزهای خام را و نیز آتش تباه کند مر صورتهای جسدانی طبیعی را، چنانك صورت آن چیز[۱۵] ناپیدا کند و مجهول گرداندش.

[§۵۶:۱۰] همچنین شریعتهای پیامبران مثل است بر آتش کی آشکارا شدن آن بکار است[۱۶] صلاح ظاهر عالم را، و قوام خلق جسمانی بدان باشد.

[§۵۶:۱۱] مگر آن باشد کی مشغول بودن بدان تباه کند صورتهای لطیف را اندر شبهت و بماند اندر پوشش مثلها و رمزها. و صورت لطیف چون اندر ظاهر محض اوفتد خویشتن را اندر غایت بدبختی رساند.

[§۵۶:۱۲] و بجملةالامر آتش شریعتی مر صورتهای لطیف نفسانی را همچنان زیان دارد کی آتش طبیعی مر صورتهای کثیف جسدانی را زیان دارد.

[§۵۶:۱۳] و مثل ظاهر شریعت اندر زیان و سود او با صورت لطیف چنان است چون مثل زهر قاتل کی طبایع مر او را بیرون داده است اندر عالم ازبهر صلاح خلق را به وقتی کی بدان حاجتمند شوند مر شکستن بیماریهای صعب را. امّا[۱۷] کسی کی درست باشد گر ازو بخورد در وقت بمیرد.

[§۵۶:۱۴] همچنین کسی که مثلهای شریعتی را صورت بندد بی‌حقیقت تأویل[۱۸] زندگانی نفسانی او تباه شود، و بازماند از لذّتهای آن عالم، برمثال بازماندن آن کس، کی زهر بخورد، از زندگانی و لذّتهای این عالم.

[§۵۶:۱۵] و نیز آتش طبیعی موجود است به هر جایی و بوستان نه موجود است

۱۴ اس، ایا: گناه کاران.
۱۵ ¦⟵برگ [اس:۸۷-ب].
۱۶ اس: [«بکار است» مخدوش است].
۱۷ اس، ایا: + اگر.
۱۸ ¦⟵برگ [ایا:۷۸-الف].

به هر جایی. و هرکجا بوستان است برو موکل است که بی‌دستوریِ خداوندش اندر نتوان شدن.

[§۵۶:۱۶] و معنی آتش آن است کی شریعتهای بی‌تأویل، که صلاح خلق اندر این عالم بدان است، چون آتش به هر جایی موجود است، و بوستان کی مثل آن به علم تأویل است و برو موکل است به هر جایی نیست. و علم الٓهی را خزانه‌داران و موکلان‌اند کی بی‌دستوری اندر آن نتوان شد.

[§۵۶:۱۷] این است[۱۹] سبب ماننده کردن جای نیك‌بخت به بوستان و جای بدبخت به آتش. امّا از روی حقیقت آن راحت را که اندر بهشت است اندر عالم جسمانی مانندهای[۲۰] نیست و نه مر آن دشواری را که اندر دوزخ است مانندهای[۲۱] هست از دشواری جسدانی، خدای ما را از آن دور کناد، بمنّه و جوده، والسّلام.

۱۹ اس: [«اینست» مخدوش است اما در حاشیه با جوهر شنگرف صحیح آن نوشته شده است].

۲۰ اس، ایا: ماننده‌ء.

۲۱ اس، ایا: ماننده‌ء.

صف پنجاه و هفتم

سخن اندر آنك صورت عالم پیش از آفرینش نزدیك باری نبود[۱]

[§۵۷:۱] گروهی از مردمان چنین گویند[۲] کی ایزد تعالی پیش از آنك[۳] عالم[۴] را بیافرید چگونگی عالم مر او را معلوم بود. و حجّت آرند بر آنچ گویند اگر[۵] صورت عالم معلوم ایزد سبحانه نبودی، پس چنان باشد این سخن که ایزد تعالی بیافرید آن چیز[۶] کی ندانست مر آن را.

[§۵۷:۲] و خطا گفت آن کس کی چنین گفت، از بهر آنك صورتها که معلوم است نزدیك پیشه‌وران، پیش از آنك مر آن را پیدا آرند، از عاجزیِ ایشان است کی نتوانند چیزی جز آن که دانند و آموخته‌اند پیدا آرند، همچنان کی[۷] نتوانند چیزی کردن جز آن چیزی دیگر.

[§۵۷:۳] و آنچ ایشان آموخته باشند از صنعتها آن جز اندر نفسهای ایشان جای دیگر موجود باشد، و هیولیها کی ایشان مر آن صورتهای صنیعتی را بر آن پدیدار آرند نیز موجود باشد، تا ایشان مر آن صورتها را بر آن هیولیها پدید آرند.

[§۵۷:۴] امّا ایزد سبحانه، که چیز آفرید نه از چیز، حاجتمند[۸] نبود بدانچ آفرید به چیزی پیش از آفرینش. از بهر آنك چیزی نبود موجود کی صورتها را اندر آن بقا

۱ قس: کتاب الینابیع، الینبوع الثالث والثلاثون (۳۳): في أن العالم لا صورة له عند المُبدِع قبل الإبداع، ص ۷۶ تا ۷۹.

۲ ¦⟵برگ [اس:۸۸-الف].

۳ ایا: ازان که.

۴ اس: ادم؛ ایا: آدم. || تصحیح قیاسی.

۵ اس: [«اگر» مخدوش است].

۶ اس: [«بیافرید آن چیز» مخدوش است].

۷ ایا: همچنانك.

۸ ¦⟵برگ [ایا:۷۸-ب].

بودی، مگر علم باری سبحانه. بدان گفتیم کی آفریدگار عالم را بیافرید، و پیش از آفریدن، صورت عالم نزدیك او تَعٰالیٰ جَدُّهُ[۹] معلوم نبود.

[§۵:۵۷] وگر صورت عالم با باری سبحانه بودی پیش از آفریدن، چاره نبودی از آنك آن صورت یا چیزی بودی کز ناچیز بودی؛ اگر ناچیز بود ناچیز را چگونه صورت کرد ازبهر چیزی دگر را. یا پیش از آن چیزی دیگر نبود کی آن صورت را برگرفتی.

[§۶:۵۷] پس اگر چیز بود، صورت عالم چاره نبود، یا ازلی بود با[۱۰] مُبدِع حقّ یا نه ازلی بود.

[§۷:۵۷] اگر ازلی بود با او، چرا نگاه داشت مر عالم را تا وقت آفریدن او که عالم است. وگر ازلی نبود آن صورت با مُبدِع حقّ، و بیافرید مر آن صورت را پیش از آنك مر عالم را آفرید و صورت عالم را، پس خود چرا نگوییم کی مُبدِع حقّ مر عالم را بیافرید[۱۱] با صورت او بهم همان زمان کی عالم آفرید.

[§۸:۵۷] و صواب آن است کی گوییم صورت عالم با آفریدن عالم بیك جای بود، تا زمان گفته نباشد اندر میان صورت عالم و عالم، و صورت عالم معلوم نباشد با مُبدِع حقّ، تا این سخن درست شود کی مُبدِع حقّ عالم را نه از چیز آفرید. این است سخن حقّ آشکارا اندر عقل.

[§۹:۵۷] و[۱۲] دیگر کسب کردن[۱۳] اندر مطبوعات از ناتوانیِ صانعان است که نتوانند کردن پیش از دانستن آن چیز.

[§۱۰:۵۷] امّا مُبدِع حقّ کی امر او[۱۴] ابداع است حاجتمند نیست بدانچ صورتِ

۹ اشارت است به سورة الجنّ (۷۲)، آیت ۳: وَ أَنَّهُ تَعٰالیٰ جَدُّ رَبِّنٰا مَا اتَّخَذَ صٰاحِبَةً وَ لاٰ وَلَداً.
۱۰ ایا: یا.
۱۱ اس: بیافربد؛ ایا: ںںافرںد.
۱۲ اس: [«و» محو شده است].
۱۳ ¦⟵برگ [اس:۸۸-ب].
۱۴ اس: [«امر او» مخدوش است].

آنچ آفرید از نخست معلوم او باشد، تا واجب کند کی حکمت و قدرت او بغایت تمامی باشد.

[§۱۱:۵۷] و مثل این حال چنان است کی یکی باشد که او شعر نتواند گفتن. اگر خواهد که کسی ازو شعری بشنود نخست باید کی شعری را حفظ کند آن وقت بخواند؛ و جز آنك حفظ کرده باشد چیزی نتواند گفتن.

[§۱۲:۵۷] و دیگری باشد کی او شعر گفتن بر بدیهه گوید مر او را حاجت نیاید به حفظ کردن شعری گفته، بل کی بر بخت خویش بگوید چنانك خواهد[۱۵] اگر بیشتر خواهد بیشتر وگر کمتر خواهد کمتر.

[§۱۳:۵۷] پس آن کس که شعر از قوّت طبع خویش بتواند گفتن، یاد نگرفته، قادرتر باشد بر آنچ گوید از آن عاجز کی او شعر راست کرده یاد گرفته است، و جز بر آن مقدار کی داند و نزدیك او معلوم شده باشد توانایی[۱۶] ندارد.[۱۷]

[§۱۴:۵۷] و آن کس که او گوید صورت این عالم پیش از آفریدن او نزدیك باری سبحانه بود چنان دعوی همی کند که جز برین[۱۸] مقدار که این عالم است باری را سبحانه قدرت نیست.

[§۱۵:۵۷] از بهر آنك دعوی او چنان است که چرا [بیش از] این مقدار معلوم او، جلّت قدرته، نبود؛ که اگر بیش ازین بودی بیش ازین پیدا آوردی. و اندر این دعوی کی بکرد قدرت را به عجز منسوب کرد و ستایش نادان نکوهش باشد.

[§۱۶:۵۷] و بباید نگریستن اندر طبیعت کلّی کی او فرود مبدعات است کی چگونه همی پدید کند چیزهای طبیعی را بدان قوّت که مُبدِع حقّ مر او را داده

۱۵ ¦⟵برگ [ایا:۷۹-الف].

۱۶ اس: ندانی [کذا] [این خطا اصلاح شده و در حاشیه با جوهر شنگرف «توانایی» نوشته شده است].

۱۷ ایا: [«توانایی ندارد» بالای «باشد» در فاصله بین سطور نوشته شده است].

۱۸ ایا: بدین.

است اندر علّت او، بی‌آنك از نخست مر آن را صورت کند، بل بدان قوّت عظیم کی دارد هر چیزی را اندر صورتها بجایگاه خویش همی‌نهد.

[§۱۷:۵۷] همچنین گوییم که مُبدِع حقّ که با او چیز نیست و امر او ابداع محض است همه علم و حکمت بیافرید مر عالم را با همه صورتهای او بی‌آنك چگونگیِ آن معلوم بود نزدیك او، سبحانه، پیش از آفرینش آن.

[§۱۸:۵۷] نیز گوییم کی اگر صورت[۱۹] آن مرد موجود نبودی نزدیك مُبدِع حقّ و ناممکن بودی آفریدن چیزی نادانستن، اگر بدانندی کی چه می‌گویند بازگردندی از آن، از بهر آنك از یك روی همی روا ندارد آفریدن عالم به صورتی نادانسته و از دیگر روی همی روا دارند[۲۰] آفریدن عالم نه از چیزی، و مر ابداع ایزد را به آفریدن چیز نه از چیز مقر آمدستند کی این عظیم‌تر از همه تواناییها است. و منکر شدستند آن چیزی را کی فرود از آن است و آن صورت کردن[۲۱] عالم است بی‌آنك صورت نزدیك او معلوم بود.

[§۱۹:۵۷] و هرآنچ همی گویند صورت عالم پیش از ابداع عالم نزدیك مُبدِع حقّ موجود بود، مر صورت[۲۲] هر دو عالم[۲۳] را فضل همی نهند بر هر دو عالم، از بهر آنك روا همی‌دارند که خدای تعالی هر دو عالم را بیافرید نه از چیزی و روا نمی‌دارند که صورت عالم نزدیك او نبود پیش از آفرینش؛ و چون چنین همی‌گویند صورت عالم را بر عالم فضل می‌نهند. و فایده اندر دو عالم است نه اندر صورتهای آن. و خدای تعالی برتر است از آنك نزدیك او فاضلتر آن چیز باشد کی درو فایده نبود.

---

۱۹ ایا: صورة.

۲۰ ¦⟵برگ [اس:۸۹-الف].

۲۱ اس: [«کردن» مخدوش است].

۲۲ ¦⟵برگ [ایا:۷۹-ب].

۲۳ اس، ایا: علم [کذا]. تصحیح مفهومی.

صف پنجاه و هشتم

سخن اندر چیزهای طبیعی و صنیعی

[§۵۸:۱] طبیعی مر کردار نفس کلّ را گویند. و صنیعی مر کردار نفس جزوی را گویند.

[§۵۸:۲] و نفس کلّ مایه است مر طبیعت را، و بجنباند مر پدیدآورده‌های خویش را، و از کردارهای خویش بعضی را نُمُو داد اعنی افزودن چون رستنیها و بعضی را حس داد اعنی شناختن چون جانوران. و مر فعل او را بدین کی کرد طبع خواندند. و آنچ نفس جزوی کرد مر آن را صنع خواندند.

[§۵۸:۳] و طبع عاجز نیست از پدید آوردن چیزهای عظیم، بعلّتِ بزرگی، چون جانوران عظیم از پیل و مار و ماهی، و از پدید آوردن این قبّهٔ فلك که آورده است، و از هیکلهای بزرگ چون کوهها. و نیز عاجز نیست از پدید آوردن چیزهای سخت خرد، از جانوران، چون پشه و مور و جز آن، که اندر خردی خویش با صورتهای ‹تمام‌اند›،[1] و از رویانیدن چیزهای خرد چون کنجد و ارزن و تخم کوکنار[2] و سپندان و جز آن کی اندر آن تصرف کند بغایت لطافت.

[§۵۸:۴] و مر صنعت را تصرّف اندر میان چیزهای عظیم و میان چیزهای خرد است. و بکند نفس جزوی چیزهائی که مانند باشد مر طبیعی را، جز که میان طبیعی و صنیعی فرق آن است که صنیعی صورت طبیعی بنگارد، و لکن آن معنی که اندر طبیعی باشد اندر صنیعی نباشد.[3]

[§۵۸:۵] چنانك مردم نتواند کی از چوب دانهٔ خرما تراشد چنانك هم بدان صورت

---

۱ اس: تمام اندرو.

۲ نك: دهخدا: کوکنار. ... غلاف خشخاش باشد. ... غلاف غوزهٔ خشخاش باشد و به عربی رمان السعال گویند.

۳ ¦←برگ [اس:۸۹-ب].

باشد کی دانهٔ خرما است و هم بدان رنگ و هم بدان وزن باشد تا بدان جای[۴] که گر خردمندی را بنمایی بدیدار نشناسد مر آن طبیعی را از آن صنیعی. و لکن چون اندر زمین بنشانی مر آن صنیعی بنروید[۵] چنانك طبیعی روید.

[§۵۸:۶] و نیز اگر دانهٔ او از یکدیگر جدا شود یعنی کی شکسته شود دانهٔ خرما[۶] ‹و باد اندر او›[۷] راه یابد نروید. و مردم را اندر صنعت خویش این توانایی نیست کی مر آن دانهٔ بشکسته را همچنان اندام دهد کی طبیعت اندام داده بود تا آن دانه زپس آن شکستگی بروید.

[§۵۸:۷] اگر پرسد کسی کی چرا اگر مردم کی خداوند هر سه نفس نامیه و حسّیه و ناطقه است بهتر از همه جانوران است و از معادن و نبات چیزها همی‌سازد که آوازهای الوان آرد چنانك او خواهد چون آواز بوق و نای و از آلات رودها چون بربط و طنبور و جز آن و آن آلات کی سازد هم بر آن گونه کی خود بگوید آواز بیرون آرد؛ و [نـ]تواند[۸] نمود او حس را اندر صنعتی که بکند آوردن چنانك اگر از چیزی مرغی کند آن مرغ نجنبد[۹] و نپرّد[۱۰] و گر دانه‌ای[۱۱] تراشد چنانك گفتیم آن دانه نروید.

[§۵۸:۸] جواب او را گوییم ازبهر آن چنین است کی رستنی و جانور اندر بودش زایش عالم پیش از زایش مردم بوده است چنانك شرح اندر کتاب مفتاح گفته‌ایم. پس مردم را[۱۲] بر آنچ او بر بودش مردم پیشی دارد توانایی نیامد. امّا سخن گفتن

۴ |⟵برگ [ایا:۸۰-الف].
۵ اس، ایا: بنه‌روید.
۶ اس: + اندرو.
۷ ایا: و اندرو باد.
۸ اس، ایا: تواند. || تصحیح قیاسی.
۹ اس: نحنبده.
۱۰ اس، ایا: نه‌پرّد.
۱۱ اس، ایا: دانهء.
۱۲ اس: [«را» با جوهر شنگرف بالای خط اضافه شده است].

کی مردم بدان مخصوص است و پیش ازو آن مر هیچ چیز را نیست لاجرم مردم بر آن قادر است کی چیزها کی خود سازد آوازها را به حروفِ شمرده و[۱۳] راست کرده بیرون آرد چنانك از رودها همی بیرون آرد کی ساخته است.

[§۹:۵۸] و بدین روی همی پیدا شود کی نفس کلّی مر پدیدآرندهٔ این هر سه نفس است و نفس جزوی ازو بهری است بدانچ صنعت کلّیِ او بر آوازها پادشا است و بر نمو و حس قدرت ندارد و این برهان روشن است.

---

۱۳ ایا: – و.

صف پنجاه و نهم

اندر آن کی[1] نفس تأییدی تواند که شرف خویشتن بنماید مر آن نفس را که فرود او است

[§۵۹:۱] گوییم[2] به جود ولیِ[3] خدای تعالی[4] که نفس تأییدی عاجز نیست از نمودن شرف خویش بدانك فرود ازو است. و لکن آنك فرود ازو است [عاجز است][5] از دیدن مر شرف او را، مگر آنگاه کی خویشتن را به غذای علم پرورش کند از معدن علم،[6] تا[7] ز پس از آن پرورش بتواند از آن شرف پذیرفتن. و آن پذیرفتن دیدار او باشد مر شرف نفس تأییدی را.

[§۵۹:۲] همچنانك آفتاب کی صورت چیزهای جسمانی بنماید به خداوندان چشمهای درست، تقصیر نمی‌کند بنمودنِ صورتها مر آن کسها را کی چشمهای ایشان ضعیف است، و لکن آن چشمها طاقت نمیدارند به نگرستن سوی روشناییِ او. پس ایشان چشمهای خویش را معالجت کنند تا درست شود و توانایی یابد بر نگرستن اندر نور آفتاب. آن وقت بداند که عیب آن نادیدن مر چشم او را بود نه آفتاب را.

[§۵۹:۳] و دلیل بر درستی این قول آن است کی کسی کی او صناعتی داند بتواند آموختن مر آن کس را که دست‌افزار آن صناعت دارد. و لکن چون کسی دست‌افزار ندارد صناعت نتواند آموختن. و عیب آن ناآموختن ازو باشد از بی‌دست‌افزاری نه از اوستاد صناعت.

---

۱ ایا: آنك.

۲ ایا: – گوییم.

۳ ¦⟵برگ [اس:۹۰-الف].

۴ ¦⟵برگ [ایا:۸۰-ب]. || ایا: + گوییم.

۵ تصحیح قیاسی.

۶ اس: [«از معدن» مخدوش است].

۷ اس: [«تا» مخدوش است].

[§۴:۵۹] وگر کسی گوید کی استاد آن صناعت مر آن یکی را کی دست‌افزار داشت بیاموخت و مر آن را که دست‌افزار نداشت نتوانست آموختن محال گفته باشد، و عاجزی آن شاگرد به استاد حوالت کرده باشد.

[§۵:۵۹] این مثل بدان زدیم کی علمهای فرودین برمثال دست‌افزار است مر علمهای[۸] برین را. وگر علمهای فرودین نباشد آن علمهای برین به دست نیاید. و بدان نباید نگریستن کی علم فرودین حقیر است چه آن خطیر را بدان حقیر شاید یافتن.

[§۶:۵۹] چنانك مردی نویسنده بیك پارهٔ كلك كز وی قلمی تراشد چیزی نویسد کی به هزار دِرَم بخرند. وگر آن كلك‌پاره نایافته شود آن فایده مر او را به دست نیاید.

[§۷:۵۹] همچنین ستور بیچاره است از بررسیدن شرف مردم بدانچ دست[۹] ندارد از سخن گفتن و خرد و تمییز. مردم بیچاره نیست کی مر ستور را بیاموزد آنچ همی مردمی دیگر را آموزد. و لکن بیچاره ستور است کی همی‌نتواند مر آن شرف را که اندر مردم است[۱۰] پذیرفتن.

---

۸ اس: علمها.

۹ |← برگ [ایا:۸۱-الف].

۱۰ اس: – است.

صف شستم[۱]

سخن اندر هستها کی با عقل پدید آمد[۲]

[§۶۰:۱] هستها همه بیك دفعه با عقل پدید آمده است، و زو جدا توهّم[۳] نتوان کرد مر آن را. و آن همه هستها بر هفت بخشش است. برمثال عینِ جسمی کی مر او را شش جهت گرد گرفته است.

[§۶۰:۲] یکی ازو دهر،[۴] و دیگر حقّ، و سدیگر خرّمی، و چهارم برهان، و پنجم زندگانی، و ششم کمال، و هفتم بی‌نیازی. و اکنون دلیل آنك این هفت قسمت هستی با عقل کلّ بهم پدید آمده است بنماییم.

[§۶۰:۳] گوییم دلیل بر آنك دهر[۵] با عقل کلّ کَشَندَه است وز عقل جدا نشود، و دهر[۶] همیشه بگوا است، آن است که عقلهای جزوی کی الفغده است چون اندر رسند به معقولات همیشه گردد آن دانستن او مر آن معقول را از آن وقت کی آن چیز دانسته شود مر آن عقل جزوی را و نیز جدا نشود.

[§۶۰:۴] پس بدین دلیل دانستیم کی دهرِ[۷] مطلق کشنده است با عقل کلّی اندر آغاز آفرینش تا ابدالآبدین.

[§۶۰:۵] و دلیل بر آنك حقّ کشنده است با عقل کلّی و زو جدا نشود آن است کی چون عقل الفغدهٔ جزوی مر حقّ را بحقیقت بشناسد باطل آن ازو دور شود که خلاف حقّ است و آن حقّ با او بماند کزو جدا نشود.

---

۱ ¦⟵برگ [اس:۹۰-ب].

۲ قس: کتاب الينابيع، الينبوع السادس عشر (۱۶): في أنّ إبداع العقل إبداع قوی کثیرة، ص ۴۱ تا ۴۳. || نیز قس: جامع الحکمتین، ص ۲۰، و ۱۱۲ تا ۱۲۲.

۳ اس: [«جدا توهم» مخدوش است].

۴ اس: دهن؛ ایا: ذهن.

۵ اس: دهن؛ ایا: ذهن.

۶ اس: ذهن؛ ایا: ذهن.

۷ اس: ذهن؛ ایا: ذهن.

[§۶۰:۶] پس ازین جهت دانسته شد کی حقِّ مطلق آفریده شد با عقل کلّی و کشیده شد با جوهر او.

[§۶۰:۷] و دلیل بر آنك شادی کشیده شده است با عقل کلّی و زو جدا نشود آن است کی شادی به عقل الفغدهٔ جزوی پیوسته شود آنگه محیط شود بر حقیقت چیزی و دانستن عقل را شبهت اندر نیابد، و غم اندر شبهت، و شادی اندر حقیقت است. پس شادی از عقل کلّی جدا نشود.

[§۶۰:۸] و بدین دلیل دانسته شد که خرّمی مطلق کشیده شده است با عقل کلّی اندر حال پدیدآمدن او.[۸]

[§۶۰:۹] و دلیل بر آنك برهان کشیده شده است با عقل کلّی و زو جدا نشود آن است کی چون عقل الفغدهٔ جزوی مر معقول را بیابد به برهان یابد و چون برهان یافت با او بیارامد.

[§۶۰:۱۰] پس بدین روی درست شد کی برهانِ مطلق کشیده شده است اندر آفرینش با عقل کلّی.

[§۶۰:۱۱] و دلیل[۹] بر آنك زندگانی با عقل کلّی موجود شده است و زو جدا نشود آن است که عقل الفغدهٔ[۱۰] جزوی[۱۱] تا نادان بود اندر رسیدن به چیزی برمثال[۱۲] مرده‌ای[۱۳] باشد از آن نادانستنی و چون مر او را دانست مر آن چیز را که شناخت به منزلت زنده گشت.

---

۸ ¦⟵برگ [ایا:۸۱-ب].

۹ اس: [عبارت «و دلیل» ریز بالای خط نوشته شده است].

۱۰ اس: [اینجا، در کلمهٔ «الفغدهٔ» زیر حرف «ف» با جوهر شنگرف حرکت کسره گذاشته شده است، اما حرکت درست آن باید که فتحه باشد].

۱۱ اس: – جزوی.

۱۲ ¦⟵برگ [اس:۹۱-الف].

۱۳ اس، ایا: مرده‌ء.

[§۶۰:۱۲] پس ازین جهت دانسته شد کی زندگانیِ مطلق کشیده شده است با عقل کلّی به آغاز آفرینش.[۱۴]

[§۶۰:۱۳] و دلیل بر آنك کمال اندر پدید آوردن عقل کلّی با آن کشیده شده است و زو جدا نشود آن است کی کمال به جوهر عقل الفغدهٔ جزوی پیوسته شود چون محیط شود بر معلومات[۱۵] و توهّم نکند که کامل با ناقص برابر است بل کی داند که تمام برتر و بهتر است. پس ازین جهت معلوم شد که کمالِ مطلق کشنده است با جوهر عقل کلّی به آفریدن او.

[§۶۰:۱۴] و دلیل بر آنك بی‌نیازی کشیده شده است با آفرینش عقل کلّی و زو جدا نشود آن است کز بی‌نیازی برتر و شریفتر هیچ چیز نیست. و چون عقل کلّی از بی‌نیازیِ خویش مر نفس را بهره کند آن کس بغایت شرف رسد اندر خلق. و عقل الفغدهٔ جزوی[۱۶] کی قوّت گیرد به دانستن معقولات بی‌نیازی پذیرد.

[§۶۰:۱۵] پس ازین روی دلیل شد کی بی‌نیازیِ مطلق کشیده شده است با عقل کلّی اندر آفرینش و مر عقل را عظیم‌تر قوّتی بی‌نیازی است، و کمتر قوّتی دهر[۱۷] است مر او را، هرچند کی دهر[۱۸] نزدیك طبیعت اندر غایت شرف است از بهر دایمی را و از بهر آنك ایزد تعالی مر دهر[۱۹] را خزانهٔ حرکات زمانی کرده است.

[§۶۰:۱۶] و زیر این قوّتها که یاد کرده شد سرهای بسیار است. و قوّتهای عقل بیش از آن است کی مردم به گفتار اندر آن تواند رسیدن، از بهر آنك چیزهائی است کی عقل بدان[۲۰] یکتا است.

---

۱۴ اس: [«آفرینش» مخدوش است].

۱۵ اس: معلولات.

۱۶ اس: – جزوی.

۱۷ اس: دهن؛ ایا: ذهن.

۱۸ اس: دهن؛ ایا: ذهن.

۱۹ اس: ذهن؛ ایا: ذهن.

۲۰ ¦⟵برگ [ایا:۸۲-الف].

[§۶۰:۱۷] و بدانید کی یکی فروریزد مر آن را کمتر لحظتی بر معلول خویش را تا معلول او توانایی عبارت کردن آن یابد. و اکنون آن همه قوّتها گرد کرده است اندر نقطهٔ عقل که آن مرکز هردو جهان است.

[§۶۰:۱۸] پاك است آن خدایی که پیدا آورد جوهری شریف و کامل و بی‌نیاز چون عقل و ایزد برتر است از صفاتِ آفریدگان و دور است از گفتار ستمکاران. پاکا، بزرگوارا، خدایا، علمهای تو اندر خزاین تو است. بدان رسد کی تو مر او را به ارزانی داری، بزرگواری و عظمت و کبریایی و جلالت و وحدانیت ‹ترا است›. [۲۱]

[§۶۰:۱۹] بنگاشتم این قوتها کی عقل بدان یکتا است.[۲۲]

[نمودار ۳: قوتها کی عقل بدان یکتا است][۲۳]

۲۱ اس: تراست؛ ایا: توست.

۲۲ ¦⟵برگ [اس:۹۱-ب].

۲۳ در نسخهٔ اس، کلمهٔ «خرّمی» را بشکل «خورمی» نوشته است؛ بعلاوه، در هردو نسخهٔ اس و ایا «دهر» بغلط «ذهن» نوشته شده است. || نك: دهخدا: خورمی. [خوَرْ/ خُرْ، رَ] ... شادی. خرمی... رجوع به خرمی شود.

صف شست و یکم

سخن اندر شش جهت عالم[1]

[§۱:۶۱] ایزد تعالی مر عالم مرکّب را به شش جهت او تمام کرد چون زیر و زبر و چپ و راست و پس و پیش.

[§۲:۶۱] و هفتم آن خود عالم بود تا نشانی باشد مر بینندگان را به چشم بصیرت کی دین خدای هم به شش جهات[2] او تمام شود که هفتم برازندهٔ آن شش باشد.

[§۳:۶۱] و ازبهر آن دین خدای مانندهٔ عالم بایست که حاصل از عالم مردم بود کی بازپسین زایش عالم بود.

[§۴:۶۱] و به شناختِ آفریدگارِ عالم جز مردم چیزی نرسید. و دیندار[3] مردم بود و مردم ازبهر دین بایست همچنانك عالم ازبهر مردم بایست.

[§۵:۶۱] پس درست شد که عالم ازبهر دین بایست؛ و مردم ازبهر سبب دین، بمانند عالم آمد، کی دین علّتی بود از علّتهای عالم و عالم معلول دین بود، و علّت به معلول مانده باشد به رویی از رویها.

[§۶:۶۱] و عالم به شش جهت ازبهر آن مخصوص گشت که عدد خود نُه آمد از نهاد ایزدی و ده به یکی بازگشت به عَقد همچنانك بیست بدو بازگشت.[4] و سی بسه بازگشت.

[§۷:۶۱] و نُه عرض است که یك جوهر برازندهٔ آن است چنان است که شرح آن اندر کتاب مفتاح گفته ایم.

---

۱ قس: كتاب الينابيع، الينبوع الرابع والثلاثون (٣٤): في أنّ الزوج المركّب الذي يتلو الأربعة هو الستّة، ص ۷۹ تا ۸۱.

۲ ایا: جهت.

۳ اس، ایا: دین دار.

۴ |←برگ [ایا:۸۲-ب].

[§۶۱:۸] پس یك جوهر جسمی بردارنده است مر شش جانب را، و یك جوهر نیز بردارنده است مر نه عرض را.

[§۶۱:۹] و میان یکی که علّت شمار است، و میان نه کی تمامی اصل شمار است از آحاد، شش عددی تمام است.

[§۶۱:۱۰] ازبهر آنك جزوهای او برو زیادت نگیرد و کم زو نیاید، چنانك نیمهٔ شش سه است، و سیك او دو است، و ششیك او یك است، و چون مر این جزوها را جمله کنی شش آید نه کم و نه بیش.

[§۶۱:۱۱] و او راهنمای[۵] است بر شش صاحب شریعت از آدم تا محمّد مصطفیٰ، علیهم السّلام، کی ایشان هریکی اندر زمانهٔ خویش ازبهر راست کردن صورتهای روحانی آمدند اندر خلق آن زمانه.

[§۶۱:۱۲] و تمامیِ دعوت ایشان و راستیِ مقصود ایشان به هفتم ایشان باشد که خداوند قیامت است، سلام اللّٰه علی ذکره، کی بردارندهٔ همه قوّتهای پیامبران او است.

[§۶۱:۱۳] و معنیِ آنك جزوهای شش زیادت نکرد بر شش آن است که عدد امامان هر دوری که ایشان جزوهای صاحب شریعتان‌اند زیادت نگیرد بر عدد صاحب شریعتان و کم از ایشان نباشد.[۶]

[§۶۱:۱۴] بل‌کی اندر هر دوری که شش امام بگذرد هفتم را منزلتی باشد کی آن شش گذشته را آن نباشد. همچنین باشد[۷] تا دورهای شریعتان[۸] بسرآید.

---

۵ اس، ایا: راه‌نمای.

۶ ¦⟵برگ [اس:۹۲-الف].

۷ اس: [«باشد» مخدوش است].

۸ ایا: شریعت آن.

[§۶۱:۱۵] و ایزد تعالی مر این شش را، علیهم‌السّلام، یاد کرد بر سبیل رمز و مثل[۹] بر شش روز و فرمود عالم را اندر شش روز آفریدم، قوله: اللّٰهُ الَّذِي خَلَقَ السَّمٰاوٰاتِ وَ الْأَرْضَ وَ مٰا بَيْنَهُمٰا فِي سِتَّةِ أَيّٰامٍ ثُمَّ اسْتَوىٰ عَلَى الْعَرْشِ.[۱۰] گفت: «کی خدای آن است کی بیافرید آسمانها و زمین را و آنچ اندر این دو میان است اندر شش روز پس راست شد بر عرش».

[§۶۱:۱۶] و تأویل این شش روز صاحب شریعتان‌اند کی ایشان هریکی روزی بودند مر خلق را تا خلق بدیشان بدیدند به چشم دل مر عالم روحانی را همچنانك ببینند[۱۱] به چشم سر به روشنایی روز عالم جسمانی را.[۱۲]

[§۶۱:۱۷] و به آسمانها مر منزلهای پیامبران را خواست و به زمین مرتبت وصایت را خواست.

[§۶۱:۱۸] و بدانچ مر آسمانها را بسیار یاد کرد آن خواست کی ظاهرهای شریعت بسیار بود و مخالف بود. و بر آنچ مر زمین را یکی یاد کرد آن خواست کی تأویل همه شریعتها یکی بود.

[§۶۱:۱۹] و بدانچ گفت: «پس راست باستاد بر عرش» آن خواست کی دین به آخر راست باستد بر قایم کی او عرش خدای است بدانچ عرش قرارگاه باشد و قرار به امر باری اندر آفرینشِ عالم بر قایم باشد.[۱۳]

---

۹ اس: [«رمز و مثل» مخدوش است].

۱۰ سورة السجدة (۳۲)، آیت ۴. قس: سورة الأعراف (۷)، آیت ۵۴؛ سورة یونس (۱۰)، آیت ۳؛ سورة الفرقان (۲۵)، آیت ۵۹؛ سورة الحدید (۵۷)، آیت ۴.

۱۱ اس، ایا: به‌بینند.

۱۲ ¦⟵برگ [ایا:۸۳-الف].

۱۳ قس: همین کتاب، بند [§۶۷:۱۲]: و مر قایم را، علیه افضل‌السّلام، بذاتْ، او خبر خواند. ازبهر آنك او خبر است از امر باری سبحانه چنانك فرمود قوله: عَمَّ يَتَسٰاءَلُونَ * عَنِ النَّبَإِ الْعَظِيمِ * الَّذِي هُمْ فِيهِ مُخْتَلِفُونَ. گفت: «از چه پرسند؟ از آن خبر بزرگ کی ایشان اندر او مختلف‌اند» (سورة النَّبَأ (۷۸)، آیات ۱ تا ۳).

[§۶۱:۲۰] و این آیت دلیل همی[۱۴] کند که این همه خلافها به پدیدآمدنِ[۱۵] قایم راست شود و اکنون نه راست است.

[§۶۱:۲۱] و به دیگر روی هر خداوند زمانه‌ای[۱۶] عرش است بدانچ هر که به علم او برسد قرار یابد و دین او راست شود و اختلاف و شبهت از آن کس برخیزد.

[§۶۱:۲۲] و دلیل دیگر بر تمامی چیزها به شش حال آن است که[۱۷] جایی[۱۸] خالی[۱۹] نیابی از شش چیز چون هیولی و صورت و حرکت و سکون و زمان و مکان.

[§۶۱:۲۳] و به دیگر روی تأویل این شش چیز که یاد کرده شد آن شش روز است کی عالم اندر او آفریده شده است.

[§۶۱:۲۴] از بهر آنك روز مر آن مقدار را گویند که آفتاب از افق مشرق بگذرد تا به افق مغرب و این مقدار از عالم بدین گشتن آفتاب روشن شود.

[§۶۱:۲۵] و عالم را مقدار او آن است که طبیعت اندر آن اثر کند از قوّتهای خویش و طبیعت را شش قوّت است چون حرکت و سکون و هیولی و صورت و زمان و مکان.[۲۰] و هر چه اندر این شش قوّت است او زیر طبیعت است.

[§۶۱:۲۶] پس گوییم کی ظاهر معنیِ روز روشن کردن آفتاب است[۲۱] مر عالم را از مشرق تا مغرب، و باطن روز آن است کی طبیعت مر عالم را روشن کرد به حرکت و این نخستین روز است از آن شش روز که خدای تعالی عالم را اندر او آفرید.

---

۱۴ ایا: همی دلیل.

۱۵ ایا: بپدید آمدن. || اس: [«به» با جوهر شنگرف بالای خط نوشته شده است].

۱۶ اس، ایا: زمانهء.

۱۷ اس: - که.

۱۸ ایا: - جایی.

۱۹ اس: - خالی.

۲۰ ¦⟵برگ [اس:۹۲-ب].

۲۱ اس: - است.

[§۶۱:۲۷] و باز طبیعت مر عالم را روشن کرد به سکون و آن روز دوم است. و باز طبیعت مر عالم را روشن کرد به هیولی و آن روز سیم[۲۲] است و باز طبیعت روشن کرد مر عالم را به صورت و آن روز چهارم[۲۳] است. و باز طبیعت روشن کرد مر عالم را به زمان و آن روز پنجم است. و باز طبیعت روشن کرد عالم را به مکان و آن روز ششم است.

[§۶۱:۲۸] و بِماندَ آثارِ این قوّتهای طبیعت اندر عالم؛ و هر چیزی کی هست اندر عالم جسمانی ازین شش قوّت اندر او اثر است.

[§۶۱:۲۹] همچنین بگرد هر جسمانی شش جهت را گشتن است چون زیر و زبر و پس و پیش وچپ و راست کی هر شش بازبسته است بیك شخص کی بردارندهٔ آن شش جهت است بحکمت عظیم از صانع حکیم.

[§۶۱:۳۰] پس همچنین این شش صاحبان شریعت داعیان خداوند قیامت بودند. و این شش تن کی خلق را بدان هفتم خویش خواندند مانند بودند مر شش جهت را که هریکی دلیل همی‌کنند بر هفتم کی آن جسم است.

[§۶۱:۳۱] و عالم کی مر او را شش جهت بود سبب بود مر بیرون آوردن صورت جسمیِ مردم را.

[§۶۱:۳۲] و قایم قیامت، سلام الله علی ذکره، که مر او را این شش جهت بزرگوار بُوَد که هریکی خلق عالم را بدو دعوت کردند سبب بُوَد مر بیرون آوردن صورت لطیف از مردم.

[§۶۱:۳۳] و جزوهای شش را چون جمله‌کنی بیست و یك آید. چون یکی[۲۴] و دو

---

۲۲ ایا: سؤم.
نك: دهخدا: سیم. [س ِ یُ / س ِیْ یُ] (عدد ترتیبی، صفت نسبی) چیزی که در مرتبهٔ سوم واقع شود. ... ثالث. ثلاث. سوم. سِیوم. سِه اُم.
۲۳ ¦⟵برگ [ایا:۸۳-ب].
۲۴ ایا: یك.

و سه و چهار و پنج و شش دلیل است این جزوها[۲۵] بر آنك هر صاحب شریعتی را كه داعی بود مر خلق را چون اصلهای روحانی وصی بود و هفت امام و دوازده حجّت و این نیز بیست و یك باشد.

[§۶۱:۳۴] و عدد شش به سه قسمت شود چون نیمه و سِیَكْ و شِشْیَكْ دلیل است بر آنك هر صاحب شریعتی را سه منزلت است یكی منزلت رسالت و دیگر وصایت و سدیگر امامت.[۲۶]

[§۶۱:۳۵] نیمه دلیل است بر حدّ صاحب شریعت كی او نیمهٔ جسمانی از روحانی بیاورد به علم.

[§۶۱:۳۶] و سِیَكْ دلیل است بر وصی كی او سِیُّم[۲۷] است مر منزلت علم را كی از روحانی به دوّم منزلت به رسول رسید و به سیم منزلت بدو رسید كی وصی است.

[§۶۱:۳۷] و شِشْیَكْ دلیل است بر امام كی او یكی باشد از شش همه گویندگان خویش اندر هر دوری از دورها و این صورت دایره این[۲۸] صفت است.[۲۹]

---

۲۵ اس: حروفها.

۲۶ ¦⟵برگ [اس:۹۳-الف].

۲۷ ایا: سیؤم.

۲۸ ایا: بدین.

۲۹ ایا: + كه نموده ایم. || ¦⟵برگ [ایا:۸۴-الف]. || نیز قس: الملیجی، المجالس المستَنصِریَّة، المجلس الثالث: قائم القیامة — تأویل 'بِسْمِ اللَّهِ الرَّحْمَٰنِ الرَّحِیمِ'، الحدود الروحانیّة والجسمانیّة، ص ۳۱ تا ۳۶.

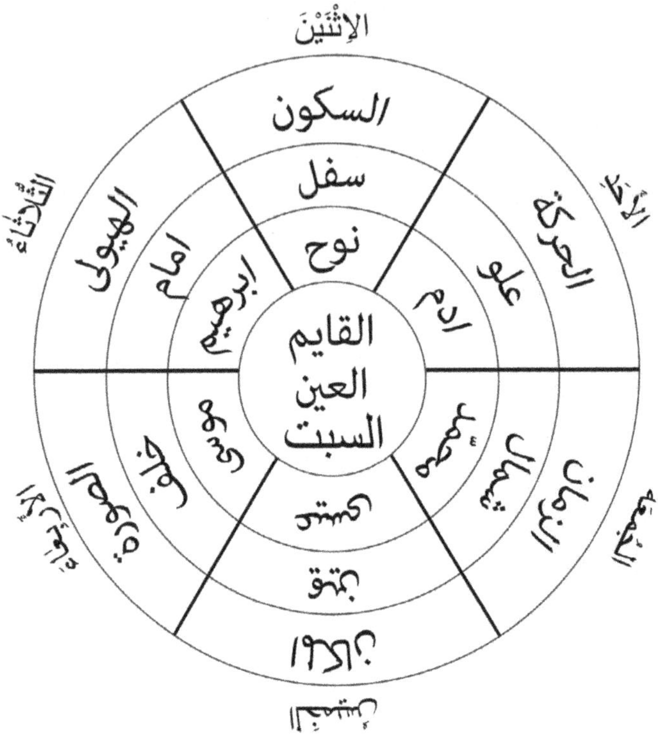

[نمودار ۴: قایم قیامت، سلام الله علی ذکره][۳۰]

۳۰ اس: البلثا؛ ایا: الثلثا. [رسم الخط «الثُّلاثاءُ» در نسخه‌های اس و ایا چنین است].
|| نك: دهخدا: شمال. [شَ/ شِ] ... بادی که از جانب دیار ثمود وزد، او ما استقبلک عن یمینک و انت مستقبل القبلة، یا آنکه مابین مطلع شمس و بنات نعش وزد و این صحیح است یا آنکه از مطلع بنات نعش تا جای سقوط نسر طائر. و شمال هم اسم باشد و هم صفت و به شب کمتر وزد و در آن لغات است. ج، شمالات و شمائل ... بادی که از طرف قطب و بنات النعش وزد. آن جهتی که چون شخص رو به مشرق بایستد در دست چپ وی واقع میشود. ... جانب قطب و بنات النعش را نیز مجازاً شمال گویند، چرا که دراصل لغت شمال بمعنی دست چپ است و این جانبی است که به طرف چپ کعبه منسوب است چه عرب کعبه را شخصی قرار داده اند که روی به مشرق است و پشت او به مغرب و به همین سبب دبور را از دبر بمعنی پشت کعبه مسمی کرده اند و همچنین شام را از مشأمه گرفته اند که دست چپ کعبه باشد. ... طرف دست چپ کسی که رو به مشرق ایستاده باشد. جانب رو به روی کسی که مشرق در جانب راست او قرار گیرد. مقابل جنوب. یکی از جهات اربعه.

صف شست و دوم

سخن اندر آنك بدی را در آفرینش مایه نیست[۱]

[§۶۲:۱] خویشتن بینان و بزرگی جویان از آموختن ننگ داشتند و از پس خداوندان دین نرفتند تا اندر خلاف ظاهرهای هلاک کننده هلاک شدند و بدی را با نیکی اندر آفرینش اثبات کردند.

[§۶۲:۲] و بهری از ایشان به نور و ظلمت گفتند و ایشان ثنویان اند. و بهری[۲] به یزدان و اهرمن گویند و ایشان مغانند از متابعان به آفرید.

[§۶۲:۳] و اندر عقل زشت است[۳] مر بدی را به خردمندی بازبستن؛ پس چگونه روا باشد مر بدی را به مُبدِع حقّ بازبستن.

[§۶۲:۴] و آن گروه، کی بدی[۴] را با نیکی ازلی دیدند، گفتند کی خداوند نیکی به آخر هلاک کند مر خداوند بدی را به وقت تمام شدنِ خویش.

[§۶۲:۵] و بدین قول، باطل همی کنند مذهب خویش را از بهر آنك اگر خداوند[۵] بدی[۶] ازلی است روا نباشد کی چیزی ازلی هلاک شود.

[§۶۲:۶] و ما اندر این باب سخن گوییم به حجّت عقلی و پدید کنیم کی[۷] بدی را اندر ابداع مُبدِع حقّ اصل نیست، بل کی به ابداع که امر خدای است همه نیکی است.

---

۱ قس: کتاب الینابیع، الینبوع الخامس والعشرون (۲۵): في أنّ الشر لا أصل له في الإبداع، ص ۶۱ تا ۶۳.

۲ اس: [«و بهری» مخدوش است].

۳ ¦⟵برگ [اس:۹۳-ب].

۴ اس: [«بدی» مخدوش است].

۵ ایا: خداوندی.

۶ ایا: - بدی.

۷ ¦⟵برگ [ایا:۸۴-ب].

[§۶۲:۷] نخست گوییم کی دلیل بر آنك بدی را اصل نیست آن است کی بدی را آنگاه نام برند کی بازخوانندش به چیزی ازو بهتر. پس نخست آن چیز باید کی بدو بازخوانند.

[§۶۲:۸] پس درست شد که ابتدا نیکی است، و بدی و بد ازبهر آن است کی بازمانده است از رسیدن به مرتبت نیکی.

[§۶۲:۹] معارضه اگر کسی گوید که این دلیلی نیست بر اثبات نیکی و نفی بدی ازبهرآنك همچنانك بدی را به نیکی بازبندند و گویند این بد کمتر از آن نیك است و گویند کی این نیك بهتر از آن بد است، و همه چیزهای مضاف را قیاس همین است چنانك چیز خرد کهتر از چیز بزرگ باشد و چیز بزرگ مهتر از چیز خرد باشد.

[§۶۲:۱۰] جواب او را گوییم کی حقیقت از چیزها به گوایی عقل پیدا آید و اندر عقل یافته آن است کی همی باید کی بدیها نیك شود و نمی‌باید کی نیکیها[۸] بد شود. و معلوم است کی بازگشت هرچیزی بدان باشد کزو پیدا شود. پس پیدا شد کی نهایت بدیها نیك است و از نیك مر او را گذر نیست؛ و نهایت نیکیها[۹] بد نیست چه نیك خود نهایت است و نهایت را نهایت نیست.

[§۶۲:۱۱] و چون معلوم شد کی نهایت بدها نیك است معلوم شد کی آغاز بودش همه بودها نیك است تا نهایت همه بودها به نیکی باشد. ازبهرآنك بازگشت هرچیزی بدان باشد کی آغازش ازو بوده است.

[§۶۲:۱۲] و توحید محض آن است کی گوییم مُبدِع حقّ پاك است از نیکی و بدی، و بیافرید مر عقل را، و همه نیکی را اندر ذات او حاصل کرد به امر خویش بی‌واسطه ای.

۸ ایا: نیکها.

۹ ایا: نیکها.

[§۶۲:۱۳] و چون امر یکی بود لازم آید کی آنچ[۱۰] ازو بود یکی بود و آن یکی نیك محض بود بی‌هیچ بدی.

[§۶۲:۱۴] و نظر عقل، کی پدید آمد بفرمان مُبدِع حقّ، نفس بود کی بپذیرفت فایده‌های عقلی را بی‌مکان و بی‌زمان و بی‌هنگامی. و از[۱۱] نفس‌کلّی همه نیکی است بذاتِ خویش.[۱۲]

[§۶۲:۱۵] و او را دو علم است یکی تمام و دیگر ناتمام. آنك تمام است از جهت ذات نفس است کی او تمام است اندر[۱۳] باب پذیرفتن فایده‌های عقلی و آنچ نه‌تمام است از جهت معلول او است و آن هیولی است[۱۴] کی عاجز است از پذیرفتن قوّت نفس‌کلّی بتمامی.

[§۶۲:۱۶] و دلیل بر درستیِ این دعوی آن است که هر صانعی را از مردم همچنین دو علم است یکی تمام و یکی ناتمام. آنچ تمام است مقصود صانع است چون کرسی کی او مقصود درودگر است و تمام است. و آنچ ناتمام است از عاجزیِ دست‌افزار است و آن تراشها و سربارهای چوب است.

[§۶۲:۱۷] و عمل نفس آنك تمام است آغاز حرکت وهمی است تا هیولی کزو پدید آمد عاجز آمد. و عاجزی هیولی آن است کی او مر ذات خویش را پدید نتواند آوردن مگر به یاری صورت که آن از طبیعت است.

[§۶۲:۱۸] و چیزی کز پدید آوردن ذات خویش بی‌یاریِ چیزی دیگر عاجز باشد نه چون چیزی باشد کی او بی‌نیاز باشد از یاری کردن چیزی دیگر مر پدید آوردن

---

۱۰ ایا: آنچه.

۱۱ ¦⟵برگ [ایا:۸۵-الف].

۱۲ اس: [«خویش» مخدوش است]. ||¦⟵برگ [اس:۹۴-الف].

۱۳ اس: [«اندر» مخدوش است].

۱۴ اس: [«است» مخدوش است].

ذات خویش را. و آن نفس است کی بی‌نیاز است از چیزی دیگر بنظر عقل کی بدو رسیده است.

[§۶۲:۱۹] پس اندر ابداعِ مُبدِعِ حقّ چیزی نیست از بدی. و نیز اندر نفی کردن بدی از جوهر عقل اثبات ذات عقل است. و اندر اثبات کردن بدی اندر جوهر عقل نفی کردن ذات عقل است. و نیست اندر جوهر عقل آنك نفی کند مر ذات او را.

[§۶۲:۲۰] پس اندر جوهر عقل چیزی نیست از بدی کی اثبات شود بل کز جهت نفی توان گفتن اندر عقل مر بدی را چنانك گویی بدی اندر عقل نیست. و اگر اندر جوهر عقل چیزی از بدی ثابت بودی – و جوهر او اصل همه نیکیها[۱۵] است – اختلاف اندر جوهر او موجود بودی. و چیزی کی اندر جوهر او اختلاف باشد مر او را تباه شدن لازم آید؛ و چیزی که او تباه‌شونده باشد برو ایمنی نباشد و بدو میل نکند خرد جزوی.

[§۶۲:۲۱] و نفسهای خردیافته میل کند[۱۶] به فایده گرفتن از عقل ‹و به واقف›[۱۷] بودن بر اثبات جوهر عقل و دور کردن مر او را از تباه شدن.

[§۶۲:۲۲] پس درست شد به گواییِ عقل[۱۸] جزوی[۱۹] که جوهر عقل[۲۰] کلّی از

۱۵ ایا: نیکها.

۱۶ ¦←برگ [ایا:۸۵-ب].

۱۷ ایا: و توافق؛ اس: و بوافف. || تصحیح قیاسی. قس: کتاب الینابیع، الینبوع الخامس والعشرون (۲۵)، ص ۶۳، بند (۱۲۳)، س ۱۰ تا ۱۲: وقد ترکن النفس إلی فوائد العقل لوقوفها علی إثبات جوهریّته وبعده من الاستحالة، وإنّما بعدَ جوهریّتهُ من الاستحالة لعدم التضادّ فیه.

۱۸ اس: [کلمه «عقل» محو شده است].

۱۹ اس: [کلمه «جزوی» مخدوش است].

۲۰ اس: عقلی.

استحالت دور است و نیکیها[۲۱] اندر او موجود است و هر چه[۲۲] نیکیها[۲۳] اندر جوهر او موجود باشد بدیها از جوهر او دور باشد.

[§۶۲:۲۳] و نیز جای بازگشتن نفسها[۲۴] آنک پیامبران،[۲۵] علیهم‌السّلام، خلق را بدان امید دادند بهشت است و بدی را از آنجای نفی کردند و گفتند کی اندر او مرگ نباشد. چنانك خدای تعالی گفت، قوله:[۲۶] لاٰ یَذُوقُونَ[۲۷] فِیهَا الْمَوْتَ إِلاَّ الْمَوْتَةَ الْأُولیٰ وَ وَقٰاهُمْ عَذٰابَ الْجَحِیمِ.[۲۸] گفت: «نچشند اندر بهشت مرگ مگر آن مرگ نخستین و نگاه‌داشت ایشان را خدای از عذاب دوزخ». و گفتند: «کز شراب بهشت دردسر نباشد و ‹نه سَیْری شود›[۲۹]»، چنانك گفت، قوله:[۳۰] لاٰ یُصَدَّعُونَ عَنْهٰا وَ لاٰ یُنْزِفُونَ.[۳۱]

[§۶۲:۲۴] پس چون جای ثواب بدین منزلت است از بی‌خلافی و آن از افاضت عقل است مر نفس‌کلّی را که بهشت او است.

---

۲۱ ایا: نیکها.

۲۲ ¦⟵برگ [اس:۹۴-ب].

۲۳ ایا: نیکها.

۲۴ اس: [«نفسها» مخدوش است].

۲۵ ایا: پیغامبران.

۲۶ ایا: + تعالی.

۲۷ اس: لایدون [کذا] [در حاشیه با جوهر شنگرف به «لایذوقون» تصحیح شده است].

۲۸ سورة الدخان (۴۴)، آیت ۵۶.

۲۹ اس: نه سیری شود؛ ایا: نه سپری شود. || «سَیْری شدن» به معنای شیدا شدن است. چون هوشِ انسانِ مست زایل و سرگردان میشود. و این همان معنی کلمهٔ «یُنزِفُونَ» است که ناصرخسرو آن را به فارسی ترجمه کرده است. || نك: دهخدا: سیری. [سَ / سِ] (صفت نسبی) سَیرکننده. به مجاز، نظارگی. ...: تا سحر سیری مهتاب جمالش بودم/ جامهٔ صَبر کتان بود نمی‌دانستم. (محمدسعید اشرف).

۳۰ ایا: + تعالی.

۳۱ سورة الواقعة (۵۶)، آیت ۱۹.

[§۶۲:۲۵] و[۳۲] بدین جوهر، عقل — کی به وحدتْ باری، تعالی و تقدّس،[۳۳] آفریده است — دور است از همه بدیها.

۳۲ ایا: – و.

۳۳ اس: – تعالی و تقدّس.

صف شست و سِیُّم[۱]

سخن اندر فضل اهل ثواب بر یکدیگر[۲]

[§۶۳:۱] تفاوت میان اهل ثواب اندر عالمِ[۳] عُلوی نه بر این گونه است کی اندر این عالم است.

[§۶۳:۲] ازبهر آنك نعمت جسمانی آشکار است و حسد آید خداوندان نعمت اندك را از خداوندان نعمت بسیار ازیرا که حقیر نماید ایشان را نعمت اندك، و الم و رنج پذیرند از بسیاری نعمت کسی دیگر.

[§۶۳:۳] و ثواب آن جهانی علمی است و پنهان است و حسد نیاید خداوندان ثواب اندك را از خداوندان ثواب بسیار. و چنان پندارند کی ثواب ایشان خود بغایت است وزان افزون‌تر کی ایشان را است کسی را ثواب نیست. و خداوندان ثواب اندك اندر لذّت باشند و خداوندان[۴] ثواب بسیار همچنان اندر لذّت باشند همیشه.

[§۶۳:۴] و مثال آن اندر این عالم یافته است. میان اهل علم تفاوت بسیار است. و گروهی از ایشان به اندکی علم رسیده‌اند و گروهی بسیاری علم یافته‌اند. و خداوندان علمِ اندك مُعجَب باشند به علم خویش و پندارند که[۵] به علم و حکمت ایشان خود کسی نیست. چنانك خدای تعالی همی گوید، قوله: كُلُّ حِزْبٍ بِمٰا لَدَيْهِمْ فَرِحُونَ.[۶] همی‌گوید: «هر گروهی بدانچ نزدیك ایشان است شادمانه‌اند».

---

۱ ایا: سوم.

۲ قس: کتاب الینابیع، الینبوع التاسع و العشرون (۲۹): في كيفيّة التفاضل بين المثابين، ص ۶۹ تا ۷۰.

۳ اس، ایا: علم.

۴ ¦⟵برگ [ایا:۸۶-الف].

۵ ایا: – که.

۶ سورة المؤمنون (۲۳)، آیت ۵۳؛ سورة الروم (۳۰)، آیت ۳۲.

[§۵:۶۳] اندك علمان آگاه نباشند از آنچ دانایان بزرگ دانند. و چون آگاه نباشند[۷] حسد نیایدشان رنجه نشوند.

[§۶:۶۳] وگر حسد عذابی[۸] بزرگ نبودی، خدای تعالی مر رسول مصطفی را، صلی اللّٰه علیه وآله، نفرمودی ازو پرهیزیدن سوی پروردگار خویش. چنانك گفت، قوله:[۹] وَ مِنْ شَرِّ حٰاسِدٍ إِذٰا حَسَدَ.[۱۰] گفت: «بگوی که من به خدای پرهیزم از شرّ حاسدی کی حسد کند».

[§۷:۶۳] وز شرّ حاسدانِ وصی بود که چندان هزار خلق در آتش می‌شوند.

[§۸:۶۳] و خداوند علم بسیار و ثواب بی‌شمار محیط باشد مر او را که[۱۱] علم و ثواب اندکی باشد. و فضل علم خویش همی بیند بر علم آنك فرود ازو باشد. و منّت و رحمت خدای را شناسد.

[§۹:۶۳] ونیز تفاوت اهل ثواب بر دیگر روی آن است کی رسیدن ثواب به هر نفسی براندازهٔ آرزوی او باشد به علم، و نفس [را] آرزو به علم بر مقدار لطافت و پاکیزگی گوهر او باشد.

[§۱۰:۶۳] هر که نفس او لطیف‌تر و صافی‌تر باشد آرزوی او به بررسیدن بر چیزها بیشتر باشد و به تمامیِ خویش آهنگ بیشتر کند و ثواب او عظیم‌تر باشد.

[§۱۱:۶۳] و هر که گوهر نفس او تاریك و کثیف باشد آرزوی او به بررسیدن بر چیزها کمتر باشد و تمامیِ خویش را کمتر جوید و ثواب او کمتر باشد. این است تفاوت میان اهل ثواب.

---

۷ اس: ¦⟵برگ [اس:۹۵-ب]. || [حروف «ش» و «ن» در «نباشند» محو شده‌اند].

۸ ایا: غذای.

۹ اس: [«قوله» مخدوش است].

۱۰ سورة الفلق (۱۱۳)، آیت ۵.

۱۱ اس: [«که» بالای خط نوشته شده است].

صف شست و چهارم

سخن اندر آنك نفس به مرتبت عقل نرسد[۱]

[§۱:۶۴] بباید دانستن کی شرف و بها و تمامی و بی‌نیازی مر عقل کلّ را بدان است که او مُبْدَع است و هیچ چیز برو پیشی ندارد، اندر یافتن هستی میان او و میان ابداع هیچ میانجی نیست.

[§۲:۶۴] و چون حال چنین است روا نیست هیچ چیز کی ازو فرود است بدین مرتبت رسد. و همه چیزها فرود ازو است از نفس و جز نفس.

[§۳:۶۴] وگر نفس به مرتبت عقل رسد آنگاه لازم آید کی مُبْدَعْ جوهری دیگر باشد، نه این باشد کی نفس همچنو شد، و نیز مادّتْ نفس از ابداع محض یابد[۲] بی‌میانجیِ عقل، باید کی نفس[۳] همان فضیلت بیابد که[۴] عقل یافته است.

[§۴:۶۴] بررسیدن نفس به مرتبت عقل محال است. و نیز عقل اندر آفرینش برابر[۵] ذوات است و نفس برابر[۶] همّتها است. و همّتها را رسیدن نیست اندر منزلت ذوات. از بهر آنك ذات[۷] اندر سه زمان[۸] ثابت باشد. اندر[۹] زمان گذشته و زمان وقت و زمان آینده و همّت جز اندر زمان وقت نباشد.

۱ ¦⟵برگ [ایا:۸۶-ب]. || اس: نه‌رسد. || قس: کتاب الینابیع، الینبوع الخامس والثلاثون(۳۵): في أنّ أحداً لا یبلغ مرتبة العقل، ص ۸۱ تا ۸۲.

۲ ایا: باید.

۳ اس: [یك کلمه بعد از «نفس» محو شده است].

۴ اس: [«که» واضح نیست].

۵ ¦⟵برگ [اس:۹۵-ب].

۶ اس: [«برابر» مخدوش است].

۷ اس: [«ذات» مخدوش است].

۸ اس: [«سه زمان» مخدوش است].

۹ اس: [حرف «ر» در کلمه «اندر» از قلم افتاده است].

[§۵:۶۴] پس نفس کی مانندهٔ همّت است نرسد[۱۰] به مرتبت عقل کی مانند ذات است. و چون نفس کی او جفت عقل است به مرتبت عقل نرسد، آنچ فرود از نفس است کمتر رسد به مرتبت[۱۱] عقل.

[§۶:۶۴] و نیز عقل برابر هَلیَّت است، اعنی هستی؛ و نفس برابر ماهیّت است، اعنی چه‌چیزی. و چه‌چیزی گرفتار است به بند جنسها و نوعها، و طبیعت بر ماهیّت محیط است.

[§۷:۶۴] و هَلیَّت بیرون است از طبیعت و آنچ بیرون طبیعت باشد شریفتر از آن باشد کی آنچ از اندرون طبیعت باشد.

[§۸:۶۴] پس نفس نرسد به مرتبت عقل که نفس به منزلت ماهیّت است و عقل به منزلت هَلیَّت و هر کجا ماهیّت باشد آنجا هَلیَّت باشد و هر کجا هَلیَّت باشد آنجا ماهیّت نباشد.

[§۹:۶۴] و نیز آن است کی نفس مر عقل را است و عقل مر نفس را نیست. و چیزی کز جهت ذات خویش به چیزی دیگر بازبسته باشد به منزلت آن چیز کی بدو بازبسته باشد نتواند رسیدن.

[§۱۰:۶۴] پس نفس به منزلت عقل نرسد کی عقل متّحد است به کلمه مُبدِع حقّ، و مُبدِع حقّ کلمه خویش را دور کرده است از کرانه شدن. چنانك گفت،[۱۲] قوله: قُلْ لَوْ كٰانَ الْبَحْرُ مِدٰاداً لِكَلِمٰاتِ رَبِّي لَنَفِدَ الْبَحْرُ قَبْلَ أَنْ تَنْفَدَ كَلِمٰاتُ رَبِّي وَ لَوْ جِئْنٰا بِمِثْلِهِ مَدَداً.[۱۳] گفت: «بگو کی اگر دریا مداد باشد مر سخنهای پروردگار مرا، اسپَری شود دریا، پیش از آنك اسپَری شود سخنهای پروردگار من. وگر دریایی مانندهٔ آن مدد فرستادیمی مر او را».

---

۱۰ اس: نه‌رسد.

۱۱ اس: منزلت.

۱۲ |⟵برگ [ایا:۸۷-الف].

۱۳ سورة الكهف (۱۸)، آیت ۱۰۹.

[§۱۱:۶۴] و چیزی که او را کناره نباشد رسیدن بدو ناممکن باشد. از بهر آنک رسیدن بدو کناره شدن او بود. و ایزد تعالی نفی کرد کناره شدن او. پس هیچ چیز به مرتبت عقل نرسد.

صف شست و پنجم

سخن اندر چگونگی بسیاری عالم از یك امر[۱]

[§۶۵:۱] ایزد تعالی مر عالم جسمانی را بر شمار آفرید و یکی را علّت شمار پدید آورد تا ازو بسیاری پدید آمد.

[§۶۵:۲] و مر یکی را چون اندر یکی زنی[۲] جز یکی نیاید، پس این همان یکی باشد او و خود علّت خویش باشد. و ازین[۳] قول پیدا شود که مر یکی را علّت نیست. و چون او را علّت نیست پس او خود نیز معلول نباشد.[۴]

[§۶۵:۳] و چون یکی[۵] به هستی هست و همه هستها یا علّت است یا معلول، و چون درست شد که مر یکی را علّت نیست، درست شده باشد کی یکی معلول نیست. و چون معلول نیست ناچاره علّت[۶] است. پس یکی علّت است مر بسیاری را.

[§۶۵:۴] و نیز گوییم کی اگر یکی علّت بسیاری نیست، پس بسیاری خود علّت بسیاری است. و چون بسیاری را علّت بسیاری گویی، چنان گفته شود کی بسیاری را خود بسیاری پیدا آورد، و ما حال بخلاف این همی بینیم. ازبهرآنك هر بسیاری اندربسته شده است به عددی که آن عدد به یکی، کی علّت[۷] عدد است، نزدیکتر ازو است.

---

۱ قس: کتاب الینابیع، الینبوع السابع والثلاثون (۳۷): في توهّم الکثرة من علة واحدة وهی أمر الله، ص ۸۶ تا ۸۷.

۲ ¦←برگ [اس:۹۶-الف].

۳ اس: [«از این» مخدوش است].

۴ اس: [«نباشد» مخدوش است].

۵ اس: [«چون یکی» مخدوش است].

۶ اس، ایا: عقل [کذا]. || تصحیح قیاسی.

۷ ایا: + آن.

[§۵:۶۵] پس پیدا شد کی بسیاری، یکی پدید آورد، و دیگر کی میان بسیاریها انبازی است از جهت ماندگیِ ایشان به یکدیگر.

[§۶:۶۵] چنانك بمثل نُه بسیار است و پانزده نیز بسیاری دیگر. و هر یکی ازین دو عدد به سه قسمت شود. پس میان ایشان به سه انبازی است.[۸]

[§۷:۶۵] و از دیگر روی مر هزار را هزار دیگر ماننده است کی جز به برهان قوی و نگاه داشتن تمام مر ایشان را از یکدیگر نتوان شناخت.

[§۸:۶۵] و مر هیچ عدد را با یکی انبازی و ماندگی نیست از آنچ یکی هیچ قسمت نپذیرد.

[§۹:۶۵] و هیچ عدد را یکی نزدیکتر از دو نیست، و مشکل بشود[۹] کسی را کی گوید یکی همچند دو است یا دو همچند یکی است.

[§۱۰:۶۵] و بر این دلیلهای بسیار است کی بسیاری از وحدت پدید آمدن است. چنان‌کی[۱۰] گوییم که آسمانها و ستارگان بازبسته‌اند به جنبش نفس کلّ و همه را بدین روی یك طبیعت است کی جنبنده‌اند.

[§۱۱:۶۵] و از جهتِ حرکاتِ کواکب، همی‌زاید زایشهای عالم از معادن و نبات و حیوان کی مختلف‌اند اندر طبایع خویش.

[§۱۲:۶۵] و همچنین تخم درخت یك چیز است به دیدار بیننده، و صورت درخت ازو همی‌زاید، کی او را شاخها و برگها و میوهای بسیار است. و همچنین نطفهٔ حیوان یك چیز است کزو شخص پدید آید[۱۱] با اندامهای[۱۲] مخالف و طبایع متضادّ.

---

۸ ¦⟵برگ [ایا:۸۷-ب].

۹ اس، ایا: بشود.

۱۰ ایا: چنانك.

۱۱ ¦⟵برگ [اس:۹۶-ب].

۱۲ اس: اندامها.

[§۶۵:۱۳] پس درست شد کی هر بسیاری که هست بازشدن او به وحدت است.[۱۳] ازین روی گفتیم کی همه بودنیهای عالم را علّت امر باری است کی یکی است و بزرگوار است. و مُبدِع حقّ کی پدیدآرندهٔ او است دور است از همه بازبستهای جسمانی و روحانی.

۱۳ اس: [«است» مخدوش است].

صف شست و ششم

سخن اندر معنیِ نام کلمه مُبدِع حقّ سبحانه[۱]

[§۶۶:۱] سخن گوییم اندر نامِ امرِ باری‌سبحانه کی «کلمه» چرا است، تا مؤمن راهجوی[۲] را بیداری افزاید. گوییم کی کلمه چهار حرف است.

[§۶۶:۲] و معنیش آن است کی بردارندگانِ وحدت ایزد چهارند: دو روحانی و دو جسمانی.

[§۶۶:۳] ازو کاف دلیل است بر تأیید عقل. از بهر آنك اصل همه هستیها او است، و معدن همه گوهرهای عُلوی و سفلی است. و اندر عقل است تخم صورتهای روحانی و جسمانی.

[§۶۶:۴] چنانك اتفاق است میان دانایان کی همه بودنیها از «کن» پیدا شد، پیش از آنك کاف به نون[۳] رسید. و عقل کافی[۴] است مر هرچه را زیر او است. و زبرسوی عقل هیچ چیز نیست. و عقل کامل است یعنی تمام است، کی اندر او نقصان نیست.

[§۶۶:۵] و عقل کَیْلِ[۵] مُبْدِع است، کی بدو بنموده شود بر خلق نصیب ایشان از وحدت، بر مقدار مرتبت ایشان. و عقل[۶] کلامِ خدای است بحقیقت، و آن کی

---

۱ قس: کتاب الینابیع، الینبوع التاسع والثلاثون (۳۹): في معنی الکلمة للمُبدِع، ص ۹۰ تا ۹۴.

۲ اس، ایا: راه‌جوی.

۳ ¦⟵برگ [ایا:۸۷-الف].

۴ ایا: کانی. || قس: کتاب الینابیع، الینبوع التاسع والثلاثون (۳۹)، ص ۹۰-۹۱، بند (۱۷۸)، س ۵ تا ۶: وهو الکفایة لمن دونه، ولیس وراءه شیء، بل هو الکافی والکامل والتامّ الذی لا نقصان فیه، .....

۵ اس، ایا: کل [کذا]. || نك: دهخدا: کیل. [کَ] ... پیمانه... ج، اکیال. || تصحیح قیاسی. قس: کتاب الینابیع، الینبوع التاسع والثلاثون (۳۹)، ص ۹۰ تا ۹۱، بند (۱۷۸)، س ۶ تا ۷: وهو کیلُ الله الذی به یکیل الخلائق حظّهم من وحدته علی مقدار مراتبهم. وهو کلام الله بالحقیقة.

۶ ایا: + کل.

گفتند، «کی قرآن[۷] کلامِ ایزد است»[۸] آن است، معنیش آن بود کی اساس پیوسته است به عقل.

[§۶۶:۶] و لام مانند شد به نفس کلّ ازبهرآنك به نفس لازم آمد لمّیَّت، کی آن اصل خطابها است. و به نفس لامع باشد اعنی بدرفشید نور عقل اندر عالم جسمانی از شخصهای جزوی. و او را لازم آمد لَوم، اعنی ملامت اگر مخالف شود مر عقل را، چنانك ایزد تعالی گفت، قوله:[۹] وَ لاٰ أُقْسِمُ بِالنَّفْسِ اللَّوّٰامَةِ.[۱۰] گفت: «سوگند بخورم بنفس ملامت کننده». و نفس لوح ایزد است کی بیابند اندر نفسها بر مقدار درجات ایشان.

[§۶۶:۷] و میم از حرف «کلمه» مانند شد به ناطق. ازبهرآنك ناطق مَلِكِ عالمِ جسمانی است. همی‌دارد آن را چنانك خواهد و تدبیر همی‌کند اندر کار بندگان ایزد به وحی چنانك بیند. چنانك خدای تعالی همی‌گوید، قوله: فَقَدْ آتَیْنٰا آلَ إِبْرٰاهِیمَ الْكِتٰابَ[۱۱] وَ الْحِكْمَةَ وَ آتَیْنٰاهُمْ مُلْكاً عَظِیماً[۱۲] همی‌گوید: «بدادیم فرزندان ابراهیم را کتاب و حکمت و بدادیمشان پادشائی بزرگ».

---

۷ اس: کی قران؛ ایا: که قران. || نك: كتاب الينابيع، الينبوع التاسع والثلاثون (۳۹)، ص ۹۰ تا ۹۱، بند (۱۷۸)، س ۷ تا ۹: وهو الذی قیل فی القرآن «كلام الله» عنى بذالك أنّ الأساس هو الذی اتّحد بالسابق من جهة التأويل.

۸ نك: سورة البقرة (۲)، آیت ۷۵؛ سورة التوبة (۹)، آیات ۶، ۴۰؛ و سورة الفتح (۴۸)، آیت ۱۵.

۹ ایا: + تعالی.

۱۰ سورة القيامة (۷۵)، آیت ۲.

۱۱ |⟵برگ [اس:۹۷-الف].

۱۲ سورة النساء (۴)، آیت ۵۴. || اس: [«عظیماً» مخدوش است].

[§۶۶:۸] و معرفت ایزد به ناطق باشد مر خلق را. و مِهْدیٰ[۱۳] باشد ناطق، و «مسجدِ أقصیٰ»[۱۴] باشد ناطق، اندر او پرستند مر خدای را.

[§۶۶:۹] و ها از «کلمه» مانند اساس است. ازبهر آنك او هادی است خلق را و هدیۀ ناطق است به امت.

[§۶۶:۱۰] و میم و ها اندربسته ‹شد[ند، و] کاف›[۱۵] و لام گشادگان‌اند، دلیلند بر آنك اصلین روحانی‌اند و اساسین جسمانی‌اند.

[§۶۶:۱۱] و لام و ها از «کلمه» موافق‌اند لام پسین را و ها را از «اللّٰه». ‹و کاف و میم›[۱۶] مختلف‌اند الف و لام را از «اللّٰه».

---

۱۳ نك: دهخدا: مِهدیٰ. [مِ دا] (عربی اسم) ... آنچه هدیه در وی آرند چون طبق و جزآن که با هدیه باشد. ... || (صفت) هدیه آورنده.
نیز نك: دهخدا: مُهدی. [مُ] (عربی صفت) هدیه کننده. اهداکننده.
|| در بند بعد، این ارتباط آشکار می‌شود، یعنی اینکه، ایزد مُهدي (هدیه کننده) است، و ناطق، که فرستاده و پیام آور ایزد است، مِهدیٰ (هدیه آورنده) است، و اساس که او هدیۀ ناطق به امت است هادی است. [اساس، یا امام زمان در هر روزگاری، مانند مسجد الحرام است که نزدیک مؤمنان است. و همانگونه که در لیلة أسری پیامبر (ص) از مسجد الحرام به مسجد الأقصی شتافت، مؤمن برای رسیدن به هدایت الهی بایستی از راه اساس و امام به ناطق رسد تا از او به ایزد هدایت یابد. و به این خاطر ناصرخسرو ناطق را مسجد الأقصی، أعنیٰ مسجدِ دور (برین)، نامیده است که، حدّ پیامبر (ص) در پرستش حق بالاترین حدّ است و رحمت او دربرگیرندۀ تمام عالمیان است — وَ مٰا أَرْسَلْنٰاكَ إِلاّٰ رَحْمَةً لِلْعٰالَمِينَ (سورة الأنبياء (۲۱)، آیت ۱۰۷)، و دوم اینکه راه به او از مسجدِ نزدیک، یعنی امام، روشن میشود، و امام مسجدِ نزدیک است چون او کعبۀ دل است که از خویشتن مؤمنان به ایشان نزدیکتر است].

۱۴ اشاره به سورة الإسراء (۱۷)، آیت ۱: سُبْحٰانَ الَّذِي أَسْرىٰ بِعَبْدِهِ لَيْلاً مِنَ الْمَسْجِدِ الْحَرٰامِ إِلَى الْمَسْجِدِ الْأَقْصَى الَّذِي بٰارَكْنٰا حَوْلَهُ لِنُرِيَهُ مِنْ آيٰاتِنٰا إِنَّهُ هُوَ السَّمِيعُ الْبَصِيرُ.

۱۵ اس: شدبکاف؛ ایا: شد بکاف [کذا]. || تصحیح قیاسی.

۱۶ اس، ایا: و ها و کاف. || تصحیح قیاسی. قس: کتاب الينابيع، الينبوع التاسع والثلاثون (۳۹)، ص ۹۲، بند (۱۸۱)، س ۴ تا ۶: وانّ اللام الثانی والهاء من کلمة اللّٰه متّفقان، والكاف والميم مختلفانِ على الألف واللام الأوّل من كلمة اللّٰه، على أنّ التركيب والتأويل لا اختلاف فيهما، والتأويل والتنزيل مختلفانِ من جهة النطقاء.

[§۶۶:۱۲] دلیل است بر آنك میان ‹ترکیب و تأویل›[۱۷] اختلاف نیست، و ‹تأویل با تألیف›[۱۸] مختلف اند[۱۹] از جهت ناطقان.

[§۶۶:۱۳] ازیرا کی هر ناطقی کی آیند بر مقدار صفاء خویش بردارد و شریعت بر مقدار زمان خویش نهد. و ترکیب اندر هر زمانی ترکیب است. همچنین، تألیفِ شرایع مختلف است و تأویل بر حال خویش است و اندر او اختلاف نیست.[۲۰]

[§۶۶:۱۴] و جمله حساب حروف «کلمه» نود و پنج است. دلیل است بر آنك آنچ ظاهر شد از کلمه ایزد پنج حروف[۲۱] روحانی است، چون اصلین و جدّ[۲۲] و فتح و خیال، و نُه سفلی است چون اساسین و هفت امام.[۲۳]

[§۶۶:۱۵] و همچنین [وجود][۲۴] یافتن همه چیزها اندر چهار معنی اوفتاد برابر

---

۱۷ اس، ایا: ترکیب و تألیف [کذا]. || تصحیح قیاسی. نك: یادداشت ۲۰ همین صف.

۱۸ اس، ایا: تأیید با تألیف [کذا]. || تصحیح قیاسی. نك: یادداشت ۲۰ همین صف.

۱۹ ¦⟵برگ [ایا:۸۷-ب].

۲۰ تصحیح قیاسی. قس: کتاب الینابیع، الینبوع التاسع والثلاثون (۳۹)، ص ۹۲، بند (۱۸۱)، س ۱ تا ۱۱: والـ«هاء» نظیر الأساس الذی هو الهدی، وهو هدیة الناطق الی أُمّته. وهذانِ الحرفانِ — أعنی المیم والهاء — مضمومانِ؛ والکاف واللام مفتوحانِ، علی أنّ السابق والتالی روحانیّان، والناطق والأساس جسمانیّانِ. وانّ اللام الثانی والهاء من کلمة اللّه متّفقان، والکاف والمیم مختلفانِ علی الألف واللام الأوّل من کلمة اللّه، علی أنّ الترکیب والتأویل لا اختلاف فیهما، والتأویل والتنزیل مختلفانِ من جهت النطقاء. فانّ کلّ ناطق یحمل التأیید علی قدر صفوته، ویؤلّف الشریعة علی مقدار زمانه ودوره. وأمّا الترکیب فانّه في کلّ وقت علی نسقٍ واحدٍ وترتیب واحد؛ کذالك التأویل. وانّما صنعة الأشیاء المؤلّفة بالتألیف الشرعیّ لاتختلف باختلاف الشرائع، بل هو علم محض لایشوبه الاختلاف والتنازع، وأنّما الاختلاف والتنازع في الظاهر وحده دون الخفیّ.

۲۱ ایا: - حروف. || اس: [کلمه «حروف» مخدوش است].

۲۲ اس، ایا: حد.

۲۳ قس: کتاب الینابیع، الینبوع التاسع والثلاثون (۳۹)، ص ۹۲، بند (۱۸۲)، س ۱۲ تا ۱۴: وانّ جملة حروف «کلمة اللّه» من جهة العدد خمسة وتسعون، علي أنّ الذین ظهروا من کلمة اللّه — جلّ جلاله — إنّما هي الخمسة العلویّة: الأصلان والجدّ والفتح والخیال؛ والتسعة السفلیّة من الأساسَین والأتمّاء السبعة.

۲۴ تصحیح قیاسی.

چهار حروف «کلمه» چون ذات و همّت و قول و کتاب، و مانند این چهار ‹تأیید و ترکیب›[۲۵] و تألیف و تأویل.

[§۶۶:۱۶] و تأیید برابر ذات است. از بهرآنك عقل ‹را[ه] نماید›[۲۶] به تأیید، و دلیلی کند بر هر چیزی کی او را ذات است. و تأیید از معدن عقل است. همچنین چیزهائی کی آن را معنی است همه آن است کی عقل بیرون داد.

[§۶۶:۱۷] امّا همّت برابر ترکیب است. از بهرآنك مرکّبِ صناعی جز به همّت نفس مرکّب نشود. و همّت و فکرت از معدن نفس است. همچنین همّتها را نفس بیرون داد تا صورت بست.

[§۶۶:۱۸] و قول برابر تألیف است. ازبهرآنك تألیف صورت سخن باشد و تألیف یاز[۲۷] ناطق است.

۲۵ ایا: ترکیب و تأیید.

۲۶ اس: را نماید؛ ایا: را نماید. || تصحیح قیاسی. قس: کتاب الینابیع، الینبوع التاسع والثلاثون (۳۹)، ص ۹۳، بند (۱۸۳)، س ۲ تا ۴: أمّا التأویل [کذا؛ نسخه تصحیح مصطفی غالب (ص ۱۶۹) و ترجمه انگلیسی پال واکر (ص ۱۰۸) هردو «التأیید» را صحیح میدانند] فانّه یوازی ذوات الأشیاء، إذ للمؤیّد في كلّ شيء ممّا له ذات، دلالة وإعمال لما یدرکه بالتأیید. وانّ التأیید من حيّز العقل؛ كذالك الأشياء ذوات المعاني ممّا قد أخرجه العقل.

۲۷ اس: تألیف نار؛ ایا: تألیف باز. || تصحیح قیاسی: «تألیف یاز» یعنی آنکس که ارادهٔ تألیف میکند که در اینجا مقصود ناطق است. || نك: دهخدا: یاز. ... نموکننده و بالنده، چه درختی که ببالد گویند «یازید» یعنی بالید... || دست به چیزی دراز کردن را نیز گفته اند... || قصد و اراده کننده...

|| نیز قس: کتاب الینابیع، الینبوع التاسع والثلاثون (۳۹)، ص ۹۳، بند (۱۸۴)، س ۶ تا ۷: وأمّا القول، فهو یوازی التألیف الذي ألّفه الناطق بقوّته، إذ یوازی التألیف الأصوات التي تكون بالقوّة، وهو حيّز الناطق — علیه السلام.

[§۶۶:۱۹] و کتاب برابر تأویل است، و [تأویل] برابر بیان؛[۲۸] و تأویلْ نقشِ[۲۹] صورتهای عقل است اندر دلهای جویندگان. و اندر عالم هیچ چیز نیست کی کتاب نپذیرد چون گل و نبات و معادن.

[§۶۶:۲۰] گوییم کی چون خردمند بنگرد[۳۰] اندر بقای نوع مردم بر حالِ خویش، و اجرام علوی را بر حالِ خویش یابد، باید کی شخصهای مختلف را همی‌بیرون آرد به عددی، راست اندر صورت، او بداند که مر این شخصها را حاصلی نیست جز این کی همی‌بیند، و حاصل چیز به بقا اندر است.

[§۶۶:۲۱] پس پیدا شودش کی بازگشت مردم به بقا است. وگر چنین نبودی، اندر پدید آوردن شخصها از پس یکدیگر چه فایده بودی؟

[§۶۶:۲۲] و خردمند، کی این کارکرد بدین[۳۱] دایمی همی بیند، داند که آن کارکن را، کی این کار همی‌کند، اندر این کار غرضی سخت بزرگ است، و نیز داند کی غرض او بحاصل همی‌آید تا این کار بدین پیوستگی میکند.

[§۶۶:۲۳] امّا کار جز از کشیدن منفعت را ازبهر بازداشتن مضرت لازم نیاید. وگر این دو معنی برگرفته شود، کار بازی باشد.

[§۶۶:۲۴] و اندر صنعتْ بَر حکمتِ عالم پیدا است کی بازی از آفریدگار دور است.

---

۲۸ اس: ساں؛ ایا: نبات [کذا]. || تصحیح قیاسی. قس: کتاب الینابیع، الینبوع التاسع والثلاثون (۳۹)، ص ۹۳، بند (۱۸۴)، س ۸ تا ۱۱: وأمّا الکتابة فانّها توازی التأویل، إذ التأویل انّما هو البیان ونقش الصور العقلیّة في قلوب المرتادین. ولیس في العالم شیء الّا وهو یقبل الکتابة — من الخشب والمدر والأنواع والمعادن والحیوان — علی أنّ التأویل یستخرج من کلّ شیء ویستدلّ بکلّ شیء.

۲۹ اس: بفس؛ ایا: نفس [کذا]. || تصحیح قیاسی. نك: یادداشت قبل.

۳۰ ¦⟵برگ [اس:۹۷-ب].

۳۱ ¦⟵برگ [اس:۸۹-الف].

[§۶۶:۲۵] و لکن چنان نباید دانستن که ایزد بی‌همتا را که برتر از صفات است، و از صفات‌پذیر و از صفات‌ناپذیر، کشیدنِ منفعت است یا دور کردن مضرّت.

[§۶۶:۲۶] و نیز بباید دانستن کی آن کار که منفعت بخویشتن کشد و مضرت از خویشتن دور کند آن آفریده‌ای[۳۲] باشد نه آفریدگار محض. و این سخن را ایزد تعالی بر سبیل رمز اندر قرآن یاد کرده است و اندر انجیل نیز یاد کرده است.

[§۶۶:۲۷] امّا آنچ در قرآن است، قوله تعالی: يٰا أَيُّهَا الَّذِينَ آمَنُوا إِنْ تَنْصُرُوا اللّٰهَ يَنْصُرْكُمْ وَ يُثَبِّتْ أَقْدٰامَكُمْ.[۳۳] همی گوید: «ای گروندگان اگر شما خدای را یاری دهید خدای شما را یاری دهد و پایهای شما برجای بدارد». و تأویل این آیت آن است کی اگر نفس‌کلّی را به پذیرفتن علم توحید فرمان برید، او مر شما را به تأیید یاری دهد و باقی شوید.

[§۶۶:۲۸] و دیگر جای همی‌گوید، قوله:[۳۴] وَ أَقْرِضُوا اللّٰهَ قَرْضاً حَسَناً.[۳۵] همی‌گوید: «و مر خدای را وام دهید وامی نیکو».

[§۶۶:۲۹] تأویلش آن است کی بطاعت مر فرستادگان او را پیش آیید تا او غرض خویش بحاصل کند اندر پدید آوردن خداوند قیامت و شما را به سرای جاویدی این وام بازدهد.

۳۲ اس، ایا: آفریده‌ء.

۳۳ سورة محمّد (۴۷)، آیت ۷.

۳۴ ایا: + تعالی.

۳۵ سورة المزمّل (۷۳)، آیت ۲۰: فَاقْرَؤُا مٰا تَيَسَّرَ مِنَ الْقُرْآنِ عَلِمَ أَنْ سَيَكُونُ مِنْكُمْ مَرْضىٰ وَ آخَرُونَ يَضْرِبُونَ فِي الْأَرْضِ يَبْتَغُونَ مِنْ فَضْلِ اللّٰهِ وَ آخَرُونَ يُقٰاتِلُونَ فِي سَبِيلِ اللّٰهِ فَاقْرَؤُا مٰا تَيَسَّرَ مِنْهُ وَ أَقِيمُوا الصَّلاٰةَ وَ آتُوا الزَّكٰاةَ وَ أَقْرِضُوا اللّٰهَ قَرْضاً حَسَناً وَ مٰا تُقَدِّمُوا لِأَنْفُسِكُمْ مِنْ خَيْرٍ تَجِدُوهُ عِنْدَ اللّٰهِ هُوَ خَيْراً وَ أَعْظَمَ أَجْراً وَ اسْتَغْفِرُوا اللّٰهَ إِنَّ اللّٰهَ غَفُورٌ رَحِيمٌ. قس: سورة الحدید (۵۷)، آیت ۱۸: إِنَّ الْمُصَّدِّقِينَ وَ الْمُصَّدِّقٰاتِ وَ أَقْرَضُوا اللّٰهَ قَرْضاً حَسَناً يُضٰاعَفُ لَهُمْ وَ لَهُمْ أَجْرٌ كَرِيمٌ.

[§۶۶:۳۰] چه وام آن باشد کی چیزی بستاند کسی کی دران وقت نباشدش[۳۶] و لکن سپس آن خواهدش بود آن[۳۷] چیز.

[§۶۶:۳۱] پس همچنین است حال نفس کلّ اندر رسیدن به مرتبتی کی همی جوید که امروز آن نیست او را و چون خداوند قیامت بیابد وی بدو بدان مرتبت رسد.[۳۸]

[§۶۶:۳۲] و امروز کارکردِ نیکان وام است بر خدای. مؤمنان را توفیق دهاد به وام دادن مر خدای را. و هم این سخن را در انجیل یاد کرده است و گفته است:[۳۹]

[§۶۶:۳۳] [۳۲] کی ایزد مر خلق را به قیامت گرد کند. نیکان و بدان را بیك جای [...] [۳۴] و مر نیکان را گوید که نیك کردید بجای من [...] [۳۵] گرسنه بودم مرا سیر کردید. [...] [۳۶] برهنه بودم مرا پوشیده کردید. بازداشته بودم مرا رها کردید.

[§۶۶:۳۴] [۳۷] جواب دهند نیکان مر او را، گویند: ربّنا تو کی گرسنه بودی تا ما ترا سیر کردیم، یا تشنه بودی تا ترا سیراب کردیم، [۳۸] [...] یا برهنه بودی تا ترا بپوشیدیم، [۳۹] [...] یا بازداشته بودی کی ما ترا رها کردیم؟

[§۶۶:۳۵] [۴۰] ایزد تعالی گوید ایشان را کی راست همی گویید و لکن هر چه به نفسهای خویش کردید بجای من کردید.

---

۳۶ ¦⟵برگ [اس:۹۸-الف].

۳۷ اس: [«آن» مخدوش است].

۳۸ ¦⟵برگ [ایا:۸۹-ب].

۳۹ قس: کتاب الینابیع، الینبوع الثامن والثلاثون (۳۸)، ص ۸۸ تا ۸۹، بند (۱۷۴): «إن الربّ یجمع الأبرار والفجار في موضع واحد، فیقول للأبرار: نعم ما فعلّتم وصنعتم بمکاني. کنت جائعاً فأطعمتموني، وکنتُ عطشانا فأسقیتموني، وکنتُ عریاناً فکسیتموني، وکنتُ محبوساً فأطلقتموني. فیجیبونه فیقولون: ربّنا! متی کنتَ جائعاً وعطشانا وعریاناً ومحبوساً، فأطعمناك وسقیناك وکسوناك وأطلقناك؟ فیقول الله لهم: صدقتم، ولکن کلّما صنعتم بأنفسکم فقد صنعتم بي. ثم یقول للفجار: بئس ما صنعتم بمکاني. کنتُ جائعاً، فلم تطعموني إلی آخره. فیقولون: ربّنا! متی کنتَ کذلك؟ فیقول: نعم صدقتم، ولکن کلّما لم تصنعوه بأنفسکم فکأنّکم لم تصنعوا بي».

[§۳۶:۶۶] [۴۱] پس بگوید[۴۰] مر بدکرداران را که بد کردید[۴۱] بجای من [...] [۴۲] گرسنه بودم مرا سیر نکردید، تشنه بودم مرا آب ندادید، [۴۳] [...] برهنه بودم مرا نپوشیدید، بازداشته بودم مرا رها نکردید.

[§۳۷:۶۶] [۴۴] جواب دهند بدکرداران و گویند ربّنا تو کی گرسنه بودی که ما ترا سیر نکردیم، و کی تشنه بودی که ترا آب ندادیم، و[۴۲] کی برهنه بودی که ترا نپوشیدیم، و کی بازداشته بودی که ترا رها نکردیم؟

[§۳۸:۶۶] [۴۵] ایزد تعالی مر ایشان را گوید راست همی‌گویید و لکن هرچه بجای نفس خویش کردید بجای من کردید.

[§۳۹:۶۶] تأویل این مخاطبه و سخنها و جوابها آن است کی این مخاطبه از نفس‌کلّی باشد با نفسهای جزوی.

[§۴۰:۶۶] ازبهرآنك نفس‌کلّی به مرتبت خویش نرسد مگر از راه کسب کردن نفسهای جزوی اندر عالم طبیعی و پذیرفتن فایده‌های عقلی به میانجی محسوسات.

[§۴۱:۶۶] ایزد تعالی آگاه کرد ما را از چگونگی برانگیختن نفسها اندر آن عالم

۴۰ اس: نکویید.

۴۱ اس: کردند [با جوهر شنگرف زیر حرف «ن» در «کردند» دونقطه گذاشته شده است].

۴۲ ایا: – و.

لطیف،[۴۳] قوله:[۴۴] وَ مِنْ آیاتِهِ أَنْ خَلَقَکُمْ مِنْ تُرابٍ ثُمَّ إِذا أَنْتُمْ بَشَرٌ تَنْتَشِرُونَ.[۴۵] گفت: «و از نشانهای خدای آن است کی بیافرید شما را از خاک. پس شما[۴۶] مردمی گشتید کز شما همی[۴۷] نطفه پراکنده شود».

[§۶۶:۴۲] و تأویل این آیت آن است که[۴۸] مستجیب برمثال خاک است که به باران زنده شود.[۴۹] همچنان مستجیب به علم داعی از نادانی دانا شود.

[§۶۶:۴۳] و باز به سخن خویش دیگری را زنده کند، همچنانك مردم ‹نبات را بخورد›[۵۰] و نطفه پدید آرد کزو زنده‌ای[۵۱] دیگر آید.

[§۶۶:۴۴] و میان نبات و میان حیاتِ حسّی انبازی نیست اندر ظاهر، تا آن زمان که پیدا شود صورت حسّاس از خاك به میانجی نبات، و اندر خاك نه زندگی است و نه روشنی البتّه.

---

۴۳ قس: کتاب الینابیع، الینبوع الثامن والثلاثون (۳۸)، ص ۸۹، بند (۱۷۵)، س ۷ تا ۱۷: ویشبه أن تکون هذه المخاطبة من النفس الکلّیّة مع الجزئیّات في هذا العالم، لأنّها لا تبلغ إلی شيء من مرتبتها إلا بما اکتسبت الجزئیّات في هذا العالم من الفوائد العقلیّة بوسائط المحسوسات. فقد أعلمنا اللّٰه کیفیّة بعث النفوس في دار المعاد بقوله «ومن آیاته أن خلقکم من ترابٍ ثمّ إذا أنتم بَشَرٌ تنتشرون». ولیس بین التراب والحسّیّة في الظاهر مناسبة ولا مشارکة یوقف علیها إلا أن تظهر صورة حساسة متنفّسة وفإذا أمکن الصورة الحسّاسة المتنفّسة کونها من التراب الیابس — الذي لا حیاة فیه ولا نور ولا ضیاء — فبعث الصور الخفّیة من العلم البارق اللامع في النفس الناطقة أولی وأحری، لما بین هذه الصور الخفیّة وبین العلم من المناسبة، والمشاکلة من جهة النور والضیاء والحیاة، إذ لا یشكّ أحد أنّ العلم هو الحیاة، وأنّ الحي یصیر میتاً بانقطاع العلم عنه.

۴۴ ایا: + تعالی.

۴۵ سورة الروم (۳۰)، آیت ۲۰.

۴۶ ¦⟵برگ [اس:۹۸-ب].

۴۷ ایا: - همی.

۴۸ اس: [«این آیت آن است که» مخدوش است].

۴۹ ¦⟵برگ [ایا:۹۰-الف].

۵۰ ایا: بخورد نبات را.

۵۱ اس، ایا: زنده‌ء.

[§۶۶:۴۵] و چون از خاكِ سیاهِ مرده صورتِ حسّاس زنده همی برانگیخته شود، ممکن باشد برانگیختن صورتهای روحانی کی پوشیده است اندر نفس ناطقه.

[§۶۶:۴۶] و این صورت روحانی سزاوارتر است به برانگیخته شدن، بدان نسبت کی میان علم و میان نفس ناطقه هست.

[§۶۶:۴۷] ازبهرآنك هیچ کس را از اهل علمِ حقیقت شك نیست اندرآنك علم زندگانی است و زنده‌ای[۵۲] که علم ازو جدا شود مرده گردد.

[§۶۶:۴۸] و هرچند کی علم ثواب است مر نفس را آن ثواب مر او را نه اندر عالم فانی است. ازبهرآنك این عالم نه معدن نفس است، چه او نه از گوهر این عالم است. و چون مردم را ثواب واجب است و ثواب اندر این عالم نیست، چاره نیست مر او را از بازشدن به عالم بقا و صفا.[۵۳]

[§۶۶:۴۹] و دلایل عقلی بر اثبات ثواب آن است کی هیچ چیز نیست اندر این عالم که مجموع‌تر است صلاح آن از اثبات ثواب و معاد.

[§۶۶:۵۰] وگر کسی معاد را باطل کند، ازو مفسدتر کسی نباشد. وگر همه خلق ثواب و معاد باطل بینند همه مر یکدیگر را هلاك کنند.

[§۶۶:۵۱] و ممکن نباشد کی چیزی که او را اثبات نباشد صلاحش بدین بزرگی باشد، کی صلاح ثواب و معاد است، و خلق چنین بر هستی او یك سخن شوند.

[§۶۶:۵۲] اگر کسی گوید[۵۴] چیست از صلاح اندر اثبات معاد، او را گوییم که اندر

---

۵۲ اس، ایا: زنده‌ء.

۵۳ قس: کتاب الینابیع، الینبوع الثامن والثلاثون (۳۸)، بند (۱۷۵)، ص ۸۹، س ۱۷ تا ۱۸، ص ۹۰، س ۱: واذا كان العلم هو الثواب في دار الفناء الذى هو ليس من معدنه ولا من سنخه، فهو — أعنى العلم — في عالمه ومعدنه أولى أن يكون ثواباً وجزاءً. فاذًا للبشر عود الى ثواب أبديّ أزليّ، فاعرفه.

۵۴ ایا: + که.

اثبات معاد آرام اهل عالم است، و بازشدن ایشان ‹یك ز دیگر›[۵۵] از جهت رغبت[۵۶] و ترس.

[§۶۶:۵۳] وگر مردم[۵۷] را ترس نباشد زایش خلق برخیزد بدانچ[۵۸] یکدیگر را هلاك کنند و ایمنی نماند خلق را از یکدیگر[۵۹] و به نشاط جفت گرفتن[۶۰] نپردازند.

[§۶۶:۵۴] معارضه اگر کسی گوید که ترسانیدن[۶۱] پیامبران، علیهم السّلام، مر خلق را به معاد سیاستی بود تا بر یکدیگر ستم نکنند و فساد اندر عالم نیز[۶۲] راه نیابد و لکن چیزی نبود از آنچ گفتند جز این نام، جواب مر او را گوییم که زلیفن بر دوگونه است. یکی جسمانی است و دیگر روحانی.

[§۶۶:۵۵] و زلیفن جسمانی از پادشاهان باشد و بر حسها باشد. و زلیفن روحانی از پیامبران باشد.

[§۶۶:۵۶] و ممکن نیست کی زلیفن جسمانی ثابت شود جز بدانك ظاهر شود مر جسم را از زخم و بازداشتن و کشتن. و نفس حسّی ازین زلیفن ترسد.

[§۶۶:۵۷] پس اگر پیامبران زلیفن کردند مر نفس ناطقه را کردند و نفس ناطقه نادان‌تر نبود از نفس حسّی. و لازم آمد که زلیفن ایشان باطن بود.

---

۵۵ ایا: از یك دیگر.

۵۶ اس، ایا: رهبت [کذا]. || تصحیح قیاسی. قس: کتاب الینابیع، الینبوع الثامن والثلاثون (۳۸)، بند (۱۷۶)، ص ۹۰، س ۴ تا ۶: فان قال قائل: وما في إثبات المعاد من جميع المصالح؟ يقال له: سكون أهل العالم ودفع بعضهم من بعض من جهة الرغبة والرهبة. فانّه لولا خوف المعاد، لهلك الحرث والنسل.

۵۷ اس: [«گر مردم» مخدوش است].

۵۸ ایا: + مر.

۵۹ ¦⟵برگ [ایا:۹۰-ب].

۶۰ ¦⟵برگ [اس:۹۹-الف].

۶۱ اس: [عبارت «اگر کسی گوید که ترسانیدن» مخدوش است].

۶۲ اس: [عبارت «فساد اندر عالم نیز» مخدوش است]. || ایا: - نیز.

[§۵۸:۶۶] و شناختن آن از راه تأویل بود. و تأویل نیست مگر بازبردن عاقبت چیزها به اوّل آن.

[§۵۹:۶۶] پس حقیقت آن زلیفن روحانی به عاقبت لازم آید نه بدین عالم جسمانی.

[§۶۰:۶۶] وگر نفسهای ناطقه مر حقیقت آن زلیفن را اندر جوهر نیافتی،[۶۳] همه خلق بر پذیرفتن آن جمله شدندی چنین که شده‌اند.

[§۶۱:۶۶] و قول را نیابند[۶۴] مگر اندر قایل، اعنی سخن مردم [را] معلوم نباشد مگر از رحمت او.

[§۶۲:۶۶] و اندر سخن هم راست باشد و هم دروغ. و این حال دلیل است بر آنك اندر حدّ پیامبری دو مرتبت باشد. یکی مرتبت ایمان و دیگر مرتبت نفاق. پس راست و دروغ مانندهاند با ایمان و نفاق.

[§۶۳:۶۶] و بر این چهار چیز، خلق به چهار نام نامزد شدند. و این چهار نام که پیامبران مر خلق را بدان نامها نام نهادند ملائکه است و شیطان و جن و انس.

[§۶۴:۶۶] امّا[۶۵] ملائکه دلیل است بر آن کسها کی تأیید از عقل بدیشان پیوسته است.

[§۶۵:۶۶] و امّا جن دلیل است بر فواید و قوّتهای نفسانی که پیوسته است از نفس کلّی پوشیده به گروهی از خلق کی حقّ ایشانند.

۶۳ اس، ایا: نه یافتی.

۶۴ ایا: نه یابند.

۶۵ اس: املا. || ایا: و امّا.

[§۶۶:۶۶] و امّا شیطان[۶۶] دلیل است بر آن کس کی قرار گرفت بر ظاهر بی‌بیان، و بی‌حقیقت و معنی[۶۷] و بیراه[۶۸] شد و گردن کشید از حدود خدای.

[§۶۶:۶۷] و امّا اِنس دلیل است بر اهل حقّ کی اُنس گرفتند، اعنی کی شادمانه شدند به تأویل و برستند از شکها و شبهتها، و تأویلْ حصارِ جانهای ایشان است از هلاك.

[§۶۶:۶۸] و از دلایل عقلی بر اثبات معاد آن است[۶۹] کی پیامبران، علیهم السّلام، خلق را به معاد ترسانیدند از بهر صلاح عالم را و صلاح خلق را تا[۷۰] عالم و خلق برجای بماند. و بدین سیاست عالم و خلق تباه نشود.[۷۱]

[§۶۶:۶۹] پس[۷۲] این خود دلیلی بزرگ است بر اثبات معاد بر آنك این سخن از آفریدگار عالم و خداوند خلق گفتند ایشان، علیهم السّلام.

[§۶۶:۷۰] از بهر آنك آفریدگار عالم بهتر داند کی صلاح عالم او اندر چیست.

[§۶۶:۷۱] و چون صلاح عالم از گفتار ایشان بحاصل آمد، دانستیم کی آن سخن آفریدگار بود کی گفتند، درست گشت کی راست گفتند.

[§۶۶:۷۲] و چون راست گفتنِ[۷۳] ایشان، علیهم السّلام، ثابت شد، معاد ثابت شد. و این برهانی است مر نفس خردمند را روشن تر از آفتاب.

---

۶۶ ¦⟵برگ [ایا:۹۱-الف].

۶۷ ایا: – و معنی.

۶۸ اس، ایا: بی راه.

۶۹ ¦⟵برگ[اس:۹۹-ب].

۷۰ اس: [«تا» مخدوش است].

۷۱ اس: [«نشود» مخدوش است].

۷۲ اس: [«پس» مخدوش است].

۷۳ ایا: گفتند.

صف شست و هفتم

سخن اندر اثبات[۱] سه فرع روحانی: جد و فتح و خیال[۲]

[§۶۷:۱] عالم[۳] روحانی را به دلایل عالم جسمانی توان شناختن، به دلیلی کردنِ حدودِ خدای تعالی.

[§۶۷:۲] پس گوییم بفرمان خداوندان حقّ،[۴] علیهم‌السّلام، مر جویندگان علم حقیقت را کی ما عالم جسمانی را دو اصل همی‌یابیم:

[§۶۷:۳] یکی ازو فایده‌دهنده چون عالم جرمانی که افلاك و انجم است، و دیگر ازو فایده‌پذیر چون طبایع چهارگانه کی زیر افلاك است.

[§۶۷:۴] و زایش از میان این نر و ماده سه گونه همی‌یابیم از معادن و نبات و حیوان.

[§۶۷:۵] و بجملگی عالم جسمانی بدین قسمت کی گفتیم به پنج بهره شد. دو ازو به منزلت پدر و مادر، و سه از ایشان به منزلت فرزندان.

[§۶۷:۶] پس این حال همی دلیل کند که عالم علوی همچنین به پنج بهر است: دو ازو به منزلت آسمان و زمین، و سه ازو به منزلت حاصل آمدگان از میان ایشان.

[§۶۷:۷] و گوایی دهد بر درستی این قول گفتار رسول، علیه[۵] السّلام: بَيْنِي و بَيْنَ رَبِّي خمس وسايط: جبرئيل و ميكائيل و اسرافيل و اللّوح و القلم. گفت: «میان

---

۱ اس: – اثبات.

۲ اس: – جد و فتح و خیال. || قس: کتاب الینابیع، الینبوع الثامن والثلاثون (۳۸): في أنّ للبشر عوداً الى ثواب أبديّ، ص ۸۷ تا ۹۰؛ نیز: الینبوع التاسع والثلاثون (۳۹): في معنى الكلمة للمُبدِع، ص ۹۰ تا ۹۴.

۳ ایا: – عالم.

۴ اس: [در کلمه «خداوندان» دو حرف آخر یعنی «ان» (جمع) بالای خط نوشته شده است].

۵ ¦⟵برگ [ایا:۹۱-ب].

من و میان[۶] پروردگار من پنج میانجی است: جبرئیل و میکائیل و اسرافیل و لوح و قلم».[۷]

[§۶۷:۸] تأویل این خبر آن است کی پروردگارْ خویشْ [۸] مر امر باری را خواست کی تمامیِ پدیدآمدنِ امر از راه قایم است، علیه افضل السّلام.

[§۶۷:۹] و پیغامبران، علیهم السّلام، بدان نصیب کز امر باری یافتند خلق را به آمدن قایم خبر دادند و ترسانیدند.

[§۶۷:۱۰] و ایشان را انبیا بدین سبب خواندند کی خلق را از آمدن قایم خبر دادند. و پارسی انبیا خبردهندگان باشند.

[§۶۷:۱۱] و خدای تعالی مر پیامبران را خبردهندگان خواند بدانچ ایشان خبر قایم به خلق رسانیدند و خلق را بدو دعوت کردند.

[§۶۷:۱۲] و مر قایم را، علیه افضل السّلام، بذاتْ، او خبر خواند. از بهر آنك او خبر است از امر باری سبحانه چنانك فرمود قوله: عَمَّ يَتَسَاءَلُونَ * عَنِ النَّبَإِ الْعَظِيمِ * الَّذِي هُمْ فِيهِ مُخْتَلِفُونَ.[۹] گفت: «از چه پرسند؟ از آن خبر بزرگ کی ایشان اندر او مختلف اند».

[§۶۷:۱۳] و بدین خبر قایم را، علیه افضل السّلام، همی خواهد کی مردمان اندر او مختلف اند.

---

۶ ایا: - میان.

۷ نك: النعمان بن محمّد، القاضي ابوحنیفه، اساس التأویل، ص ۷۰: قال رسول الله (صلّی الله علیه و سلم): انني آخذ الوحي عن جبريل، و جبريل يأخذه عن ميكائيل، و ميكائيل يأخذه عن اسرافيل، و اسرافيل يأخذه عن اللوح، و اللوح يأخذه عن القلم، فصار التأييد يتصل بالنطقاء من خمسة حدود علوية، و يتصل عنهم للمستجيبين بواسطة خمسة حدود سفلية، فالحدود العلوية هم الذين ذكرناهم، و الحدود السفلية هم الأُسُس و الائمة و الحجج و النقباء اصحاب الجزائر، و الاجنحة و هم الدعاة.

۸ ¦⟵برگ [اس:۱۰۰-الف]. || ایا: - خویش.

۹ سورة النَّبَأ (۷۸)، آیات ۱ تا ۳.

[§۱۴:۶۷] و بیشتر از مردمان همی گویند که روزی است زمانی که مدّت او پنجاه هزار سال است، آن روزی است کی اندر او[۱۰] خدای[۱۱] با خلق شمار کند.

[§۱۵:۶۷] و گروهی همی گویند که آن خبر مهدی است که بیاید و دین خدای آشکارا کند و کافران را همه مسلمانان کند.

[§۱۶:۶۷] و گروهی همی گویند که آن خبر خود وصیّ رسول، علیه السّلام، است.

[§۱۷:۶۷] و اهل حقیقت همی گویند که آن خبر آن کس است که بسبب خبردادن ازو مر پیامبران را، علیهم السّلام، نام خبردهندگان لازم آمد.[۱۲]

[§۱۸:۶۷] پس چون رسول مصطفی، علیه السّلام، بدین خبر که یاد کردیم، ما را بگفت کی «میان من و آن خدای پنج میانجی است»:

[§۱۹:۶۷] و نخست جبرئیل را یاد کرد که او فریشتهٔ مقرب است و سفیر است میان خدای و میان پیامبران وی.

[§۲۰:۶۷] و دیگر میکائیل را گفت کی جلال و عظمت او افزون است از جلال و عظمت جبرئیل.

[§۲۱:۶۷] و باز اسرافیل را یاد کرد که فرمانهای خدای تعالی از لوح او[۱۳] پذیرد، وزان پس لوح را گفت، و باز قلم را گفت برین[۱۴] ترتیب کی یاد کردیم.

[§۲۲:۶۷] کزین پنج میانجی عظیم‌تر و شریف‌تر آن است کی مر او را بازپس‌تر

۱۰ ایا: – اندر او.

۱۱ ایا: + تعالی اندرو.

۱۲ اس: + پس چون رسول مصطفی علهیم السلام نام خبردهندگان لازم آمد [عبارت «پس چون رسول مصطفی علهیم السلام نام خبردهندگان لازم آمد» در نسخه اس ابتدا نوشته شده و سپس روی آن خط کشیده شده است].

۱۳ ¦⟵برگ [ایا:۹۲-الف].

۱۴ ایا: بدین.

یاد کرد، و آن[15] بازپس‌ترین[16] به خدای تعالی نزدیکتر است نزدیکیِ علم نه نزدیکیِ مسافت.

[§۶۷:۲۳] و روا باشد کی جبرئیل کی پنجم حدّ است از خدای تعالی فریشته باشد و قلم کی نخستین حدّ است قلمی باشد بی‌جان و بی‌علم و لوح تخته‌ای[17] باشد بی‌جان از آنکه چیزی برو نویسند؟

[§۶۷:۲۴] پس گوییم که قلم از عالم روحانی به منزلت آسمان است از عالم جسمانی. و آن عقل کلّ است که او محیط است بر هر دو عالم؛ همچنانك آسمان محیط است بر عالم جسمانی.

[§۶۷:۲۵] و لوح از عالم روحانی به منزلت زمین است از عالم جسمانی. و آن نفس کلّ است که او پذیرندهٔ قوّتهای عقل کلّ است و پدیدآرندهٔ فایده‌های او است مر عمر جاویدی را. همچنانك زمین پذیرندهٔ فایده‌های آسمان است و پذیرندهٔ قوّتهای او است مر عمر فانی را.

[§۶۷:۲۶] و عقل را بر قلم بدان مثل زدند که خط نویسنده تا از قلم پدید نیاید دانسته نشود. و خط اندر قلم از نفس مردم آید که مر نفس مردم را به قلم هیچ مانندگی و پیوستگی نیست.

[§۶۷:۲۷] همچنانك، امر باری سبحانه به عقل پیوسته شد بی‌آنك عقل را به هویّت باری سبحانه هیچ مانندگی یا پیوستگی بود، جز آنك پدید آمدن مکوّنات از عقل یافته همی‌شود چنانك نبشته از قلم یافته همی‌شود.

[§۶۷:۲۸] همچنانك، خردمندان هرچند که نبشته از قلم همی پدید آید دانسته‌اند

---

۱۵ ایا: ازان.

۱۶ |⟵برگ [اس:۱۰۰-ب].

۱۷ اس، ایا: تخته‌ء.

کی مر قلم را اندر آنچ همی‌نویسد جز فرمان برداری چیزی نیست. و آن نوشته مایهٔ نفس دبیر است.

[§۶۷:۲۹] نیز دانسته‌اند که هر موجودات کز عقل همی‌بودش پذیرد مر عقل را اندر آن جز فرمان برداری چیزی نیست. و فرمان باری سبحانه است که دور است از صفات عقل و آنچ فرود ازو است.

[§۶۷:۳۰] و مر نفس را به لوح از آن مثل زدند که خط از قلم بر لوح پدید آید و تا لوح نباشد قوّتی کز نفس نویسنده به قلم رسد به صورت پیدا نشود.

[§۶۷:۳۱] همچنین فایده‌های عقل جز به پذیرفتن نفس مر آن را اندر دو عالم[۱۸] پیدا نشد.

[§۶۷:۳۲] و نفسهای جزوی از مردم بر درستی این حال گوایی همی دهد از بهر آنک عقل اندر عالم یافته نشود مگر به نفس مردمی که آن را پذیرفته باشد.

[§۶۷:۳۳] و سخنهای عقل[۱۹] از نفس سخنگوی یافته شود. و صنعتها که اثر عقل اندر آن پیدا باشد مردم تواند کردن که او نفس جزوی است.

[§۶۷:۳۴] پس درست شد که لوح نفس کلّی است. و پیدا شد که آسمان عالم علوی عقل است، و زمین عالم علوی نفس است.

[§۶۷:۳۵] پس از آن پنج حد که رسول، علیه السّلام، گفت: «ایشان میان من و میان خدای میانجی‌اند» دو حد را صفت گفته آمد برابر دو رکن از عالم جسمانی.

[§۶۷:۳۶] و سه حدّ از آن بماند برابر سه زایش کز عالم [روحانی][۲۰] بحاصل آمده

۱۸ |⟵برگ [ایا:۹۲-ب].

۱۹ |⟵برگ [اس:۱۰۱-الف].

۲۰ تصحیح قیاسی.

است. و آن اسرافیل است و میکائیل و جبرئیل برابر سه زایش عالم جسمانی که آن معادن است و نبات و حیوان.

[§۶۷:۳۷] پس گوییم که همچنانك از زایش عالم جسمانی نخست معادن بحاصل آمد و پس ازو نبات و پس او حیوان، لازم آید کزان دو اصل عظیم، نخست[۲۱] جدّ بوده است و پس او فتح و پس او خیال.

[§۶۷:۳۸] پس جدّ اندر عالم روحانی برابر است با معادن اندر عالم جسمانی. و فتح اندر عالم روحانی برابر است با نبات اندر عالم جسمانی. و خیال اندر عالم روحانی برابر است با حیوان اندر عالم جسمانی.

[§۶۷:۳۹] و هریکی ازین سه زایش عالم جسمانی بدو قسمت شود چنانك معادن بدو قسمت است یا گوهرهای گداختنی یا ناگداختنی. و نبات نیز بدو قسمت است یا بارور است یا بی‌برست. و حیوان نیز بدو قسمت است یا ناطق است یا غیر ناطق.

[§۶۷:۴۰] این حال دلیل است کی هریکی ازین سه حد روحانی را اندر دو عالم اثر است.

[§۶۷:۴۱] و عالم روحانیماننده است به گوهر ناگداختنی که همیشه بر حال خویش است. و عالم جسمانی ماننده است به گوهر گداختنی کی حال او گردنده است و بر یك حال نیست.

[§۶۷:۴۲] و عالم روحانی ماننده است به نبات بارور، از آنچ فایده‌های باقی اندر او حاصل همی آید. و عالم جسمانی ماننده است به نبات بی‌بر کزو[۲۲] هیچ فایده بحاصل نیاید.

---

۲۱ ایا: نخستین.

۲۲ ¦←برگ [ایا:۹۳-الف].

[§۴۳:۶۷] و عالم روحانیماننده است به جانور سخنگوی، از آنچ مایهٔ او امر خدای است بدانچ عبارت کنند ازو به کلمه و به کن!

[§۴۴:۶۷] و عالم جسمانی ماننده است به حیوان سخن‌ناگوی، بدانچ رغبت ستوران،[۲۳] و کسانی که به ستوران مانند، اندر او است.

[§۴۵:۶۷] و اثر هر حدّی ازین سه حدّ روحانی اندر عالم علوی آن است کی فایده بپذیرند از آن حد کی برتر ازو است. و اثر او اندر عالم جسمانی آن است کی آن فایده را برساند بدان حد کی فرود ازو است.

[§۴۶:۶۷] چنانك گوییم جدّ قوّت امر را بپذیرد از نفس و مر آن را به فرود از خویشتن برساند به فتح. و فتح مر آن را از جدّ بپذیرد و به فرود از خویشتن برساند به خیال. و خیال مر آن را از فتح بپذیرد و به فرود از خویشتن برساند به ناطق.

[§۴۷:۶۷] و ناطق اندر عالم جسمانی همان منزلت دارد کی عقل اندر عالم روحانی دارد. پس ناطق مر آن فایده را کز خیال بپذیرد کی برتر ازو است به وصی رساند که فرود ازو است. برمثال پذیرفتن عقل از امر و رسانیدن به نفس کلّی.

[§۴۸:۶۷] و مر وصی را اندر عالم علوی مرتبهٔ نفس[۲۴] است. پس وصی آن فایده را کز ناطق بپذیرد کی برتر ازو است به امام رساند کی فروتر ازو است برمثال پذیرفتن نفس از عقل و رسانیدن به جدّ.

[§۴۹:۶۷] و[۲۵] مر امام را اندر عالم جسمانی همان منزلت است کی جدّ را اندر عالم روحانی است. پس امام آن فایده را کز وصی پذیرفته است کی برتر ازو

۲۳ ¦⟵برگ [اس:۱۰۱-ب].

۲۴ اس: [عبارت «مرتبهٔ نفس» بالای خط نوشته شده است].

۲۵ ایا: [«و» مخدوش است].

است به باب خویش رساند کی فروتر ازو است برمثال پذیرفتن جدّ از نفس کلّی و رسانیدن به فتح.

[§۶۷:۵۰] و مر باب امام را اندر عالم جسمانی همان منزلت است کی مر فتح را اندر عالم علوی است. پس باب مر آن فایده را کز امام بپذیرد که برتر ازو است به حجّت رساند کی فروتر ازو است برمثال پذیرفتن فتح از جدّ و رسانیدن به خیال.

[§۶۷:۵۱] پس حجّت را[۲۶] اندر عالم جسمانی همان منزلت است کی مر خیال را اندر عالم روحانی است.

[§۶۷:۵۲] و مر تأیید را از حجّت گذر نیست و فرود ازو[۲۷] پذیرندگان مر فرمان را بشرح توانند پذیرفتن نه برمز.

[§۶۷:۵۳] و رسول مصطفی، صلی الله علیه وآله، مر این حدود جسمانی را بپای کرد برابر حدود روحانی تا خردمندان به دلالت حدود جسمانی مر حدود روحانی را بشناسند و هر کسی بر حدّ خویش باستند.

[§۶۷:۵۴] و گوایی دهد بر درستی این دعوی گفتار رسول مصطفی، صلی الله علیه وآله، کی گفت: أخذت من الخمس وأعطیت الی الخمس. گفت: «بستدم از پنج[۲۸] و بدادم به پنج».

[§۶۷:۵۵] و عالم جسمانی یك چشم‌زخم[۲۹] خالی نیست[۳۰] و نبوده است از یك تن کی تأیید از عالم علوی بدو پیوسته باشد تا خلق و عالم بدان تأیید پایندگی یابد. و آن کس یا پیامبر باشد اندر زمان خویش یا وصیّ او باشد اندر عصر خویش یا امام باشد از فرزندان او اندر روزگار خویش.

۲۶ اس: [«را» بالای خط نوشته شده است].

۲۷ ¦⟵برگ [ایا:۹۳-ب].

۲۸ ¦⟵برگ [اس:۱۰۲-الف].

۲۹ چشم زخم، در اینجا، یعنی: به اندازهٔ آسیبی اندك و شکستی کوچك.

۳۰ اس: [عبارت «خالی نیست» تکرار شده است].

[§۶۷:۵۶] و رسانندهٔ تأیید از امر باری سبحانه به پیغامبرِ دور جدّ است؛ و رسانندهٔ تأیید به وصیِّ رسول اندر عصر او فتح است؛ و رسانندهٔ تأیید به امام زمانه اندر روزگار او خیال است.

[§۶۷:۵۷] و جز این سه تن اندر عالم جسمانی کسی از عالم علوی تأیید نپذیرد.

[§۶۷:۵۸] و گوا بر درستی این دعوی از عالم آن است کی روشنایی اندر عالم از سه اصل است:

[§۶۷:۵۹] یکی از آفتاب کی او هم گرم است و هم روشن و هم باقی. و او برمثال جدّ است کی فایده از نفس کلّی پذیرد کی اصل است نه فرع، و چون بگذارد[۳۱] مر آن را به فتح گذارد کی فرع است نه اصل.

[§۶۷:۶۰] و دیگر روشنایی اندر عالم از ماه و ستارگان است که ایشان را روشنایی هست و بقا هست و گرمی نیست. و آن برمثال فتح است کی فایده از فرع[۳۲] پذیرد و آن جدّ است و چون بگذارد به فرع گذارد که خیال است.

[§۶۷:۶۱] و سدیگر روشنایی اندر عالم از آتش است که او را روشنی و گرمی هست و بقا نیست. و او برمثال خیال است کی فایده از فرع روحانی پذیرد و چون بگذارد به اصل جسمانی گذارد کی ناطق است.

[§۶۷:۶۲] پس همچنانك روشنی اندر عالم جسمانی ازین سه خداوند نور است: یکی آفتاب و دیگر ماه و ستارگان و سدیگر آتش، و مر هر یك را حالی دیگر است،[۳۳] روشنایی اندر عالم دین ازین سه خداوند نور روحانی است: یکی جدّ و دیگر فتح و سدیگر خیال. و هریکی را حالی دیگر است اندر پذیرفتن امر و گذاردن آن چنانك شرح آن گفتیم.

---

۳۱ ایا: بگزارد [در این صف از نسخهٔ ایا همه جا فعل «گذاردن» سهواً با «ز» نوشته شده، لذا همه جا بدون اشاره تصحیح شده است].

۳۲ اس، ایا: فتح [کذا]. || تصحیح قیاسی.

۳۳ |← برگ [ایا:۹۴-الف].

[§۶۷:۶۳] و گوا از نفس مردم، که او تمامتر زایش عالم جسمانی است، آن است بر اثبات این سه فرع روحانی، که نفس مردم که با عقل جفت است، و فعلهای ایشان ازین جسد پیدا همی‌آید،[۳۴] سه قوّت دارد کی هریکی از آن ایستاده‌اند به تمام شدن دو صورت مردم یکی صورت جسمانی و دیگر صورت روحانی.

[§۶۷:۶۴] و آن سه قوّت کی مر نفس مردم را است یکی از قوّت تأیید است کی برابر جدّ است، و دیگر ازو قوّت شهوانی است کی برابر فتح است، و سدیگر قوّت ناطقه است کی برابر خیال است.

[§۶۷:۶۵] مقابله کردیم مر عالم کهین را کی مردم است با عالم روحانی.

[§۶۷:۶۶] و چون مر عالم دین را با نفسها برابر کنیم گوییم کی ناطق برابر است با نفس نامیه از مردم، و اساس او برابر است با نفس[۳۵] شهوانی از مردم، و امام برابر است با نفس ناطقه از مردم.

[§۶۷:۶۷] از بهر آنك نفس نامیه آغاز است از بودش جسد مردم کز حد نطفگی[۳۶] همی‌بالد، برمثال نبات، همچنانك به ناطق آغاز عالم دین است و زو پدید آید بالشِ[۳۷] دینی.[۳۸]

[§۶۷:۶۸] و نفس شهوانی میانه است مر بودش مردم را که طعام و شراب را جستن گیرد و بهتر از آن گزیدن گیرد، همچنانك اساسْ تأویلِ حقّ مر نفس خردمندان را

۳۴ ¦⟵برگ [اس:۱۰۲-ب].

۳۵ اس: + او برابر است با نفس [عبارت «او برابر است» خط زده شده است، اما «با نفس» خط نخورده و تکرار شده است].

۳۶ ایا: بطفلی [کذا].

۳۷ نك: دهخدا: بالش. [لِ] اسم مصدر از بالیدن... اسم از بالیدگی. نمو. بالیدگی. افزایش. ... رشد... نمو کردن.

۳۸ ایا: دین.

حریص گرداند برجستن غذای نفسانی و مردمان بدو حریص شوند بر[۳۹] جدا کردن حقّ از باطل.

[§۶۷:۶۹] و نفس ناطقه آخر است[۴۰] از مردم، کی چون او پدید آمد، مردم تمام شد اندر بودش و عمارت[۴۱] به دینِ[۴۲] نفس، چیزی را که خود داند.

[§۶۷:۷۰] همچنانك امام آخر مؤیّدان است و او است کی مردم ازو از فنا به بقا رسد. و مر مثلها و رمزهای[۴۳] ناطق را، به حقّ عبارت تواند کردن، به شناختِ امام.

[§۶۷:۷۱] و همچنانك نفس ناطقه از همه نفسها شریفتر است امام را منزلت از همه منزلتها برتر است.

[§۶۷:۷۲] و گوا بر درستی این قول آن است که[۴۴] منزلت امام منزلت خداوند[۴۵] قیامت است، علیهم السّلام، که همه ناطقان خلق را دعوت سوی او کردند.

[§۶۷:۷۳] و از شرف و منزلت امامت بود کی خدای تعالی فرمود روز قیامت هر گروهی را به امام ایشان خوانیم، قوله؛[۴۶] يَوْمَ نَدْعُوا كُلَّ أُنَاسٍ بِإِمَامِهِمْ فَمَنْ.[۴۷] گفت: «آن روز که بخوانیم هر گروهی را به امام ایشان» و نگفت کی بخوانیم به رسول ایشان.[۴۸]

[§۶۷:۷۴] شرح کردیم سخن را اندر اثبات سه فرع روحانی کی بقای عالم جسمانی

۳۹ ایا: مر.
۴۰ ایا: + آخرست [تکرار شده است].
۴۱ اس، ایا: عبارت [کذا]. || تصحیح قیاسی. نك: همین صف، بند آخر: [§۶۷:۷۴].
۴۲ اس: بدىن؛ ایا: بدین.
۴۳ ایا: زمرهای.
۴۴ ¦⟵برگ [ایا:۹۴-ب].
۴۵ اس: [کلمه «خداوند» بالای خط نوشته شده است].
۴۶ ایا: + تعالی.
۴۷ سورة الإسراء (۱۷)، آیت ۷۱.
۴۸ ¦⟵برگ [اس:۱۰۳-الف].

و عمارت عالم دین به میانجی ایشان است بدان اندازه که مستجیب راه‌دان را بدان بیداری افزاید.

صف شست و هشتم

سخن اندر آنچ ازو توهّم نتوان کردن

[§۶۸:۱] امر باری سبحانه اندر توهّم نیاید و اندیشه اندر او نرسد به هیچ روی از رویها.[۱]

[§۶۸:۲] و مر امر را وحدت گفتند. و وحدت یکی باشد و احد از وحدت واحد شود.

[§۶۸:۳] چنانك گوییم یکی بباید تا یکی ازو یکی باشد. همی‌دانیم کی یکی از یکی پدید آمد و یکی هست و لکن مر او را جز اندر یکی اثبات نیست.[۲]

[§۶۸:۴] همچنانك همی دانیم کی چشمهٔ آفتاب، از نور او جهان روشن شده است، و نور اندر او قرار دارد؛ و لکن نور را ندانیم که آن حال کی دارد از چه دارد.

[§۶۸:۵] وگر گوییم کی نور چون از چشمهٔ آفتاب جدا شود چگونه باشد؟[۳] وهم آن را نتواند[۴] پذیرفتن.

[§۶۸:۶] از بهر آنك اگر اندیشه کند کی نور چون از آفتاب جدا شود چیزی باشد کمتر از چشمهٔ آفتاب یا بزرگتر ازو، و آن خود هم چشمهٔ آفتاب باشد و نه مجرّد نور باشد.

[§۶۸:۷] و نور مجرّد را وهم نپذیرد؛ و نیز چشمهٔ آفتاب را بی‌نور وهم نپذیرد.

---

۱ نك: جامع الحکمتین، ص ۱۲، بند (۱۵)، س ۳ تا ۵: و رسول علیه السّلام گفت: اندر آفرینش اندیشه کنید و اندر آفریدگار اندیشه مکنید بدین خبر «تفکّروا في الخلق ولا تفکّروا في الخالق.»

۲ نك: جامع الحکمتین، فصل ۱۲: ‹اندر شرح «یکی»›، ص ۱۴۵ تا ۱۵۱.

۳ ایا: [«با» در «باشد» مخدوش است].

۴ اس، ایا: بتواند. || تصحیح قیاسی-مفهومی.

[§۶۸:۸] وگر کسی گوید کی چشمهٔ آفتاب چون نور ازو جدا شود سیاه باشد این نه روا باشد. از بهر آنك روا نباشد که نور امروز اندر تاریکی قرار گرفته باشد.

[§۶۸:۹] وگر چشمهٔ آفتاب تاريك بودی بی‌نور، پس نور اندر ضدّ خویش قرار گرفته بودی و این محال بودی.

[§۶۸:۱۰] پس درست شد کی نور را بی‌چشمهٔ آفتاب اثبات نیست. و هم[۵] چنان مر چشمهٔ آفتاب را بی‌نور اثبات نیست.

[§۶۸:۱۱] و همچنین گوییم کی امر باری را سبحانه که به عقل متّحد شده است، چون متّحد شدن نور به آفتابْ‌چشمه، به مجرّد وهم اندرنیاید.

[§۶۸:۱۲] معارضه اگر کسی گوید که چشمهٔ آفتاب، بی‌نور، چنان باشد[۶] کی[۷] ما همی‌بینیم شمس به وقت کسوف، اعنی به وقت گرفتن آفتاب همی‌بینیمش چون نور ازو جدا شود، جرم او سیاه نماید.

[§۶۸:۱۳] جواب او را گوییم آنك تو همی‌بینی به وقت آفتاب گرفتن آن قرص سیاه آن نه جرم آفتاب است بی‌نور بل‌کی[۸] آن جرم ماه است کی برابر شده است با قرص آفتاب و بازداشته است مر روشنایی آفتاب را از زمین.

[§۶۸:۱۴] و آفتاب چشمه ازو دور است کی او به آسمان چهارم است و قرص ماه به آسمان نخستین است. و آفتاب بدان وقت که ما مر او را همی[۹] گرفته بینیم به حال خویش روشن است بر فلك خویش.

---

۵ ¦←برگ [ایا:۹۵-الف].

۶ ¦←برگ [اس:۱۰۳-ب].

۷ اس: [کلمه «کی» محو شده است].

۸ ایا: بلك.

۹ ایا: – همی.

[§۱۵:۶۸] و آن تیره که همی‌بینیم جرم ماه است و جرم ماه شفّاف نیست، اعنی کی روشنی ازو بیرون نگذرد.

[§۱۶:۶۸] بل‌کی[۱۰] چون آیینه‌ای[۱۱] است کز آهن باشد کی چون آفتاب به روی آیینه اندر تابد عکس ازو روشن بازجهَد و چون بر پشت آینه تابد روشنیِ آفتاب سوی روی آیینه بیرون نتابد.

[§۱۷:۶۸] وگر جرم ماه شفاف بودی، چنانك نور ازو بگذشتی، ماه هرگز نقصان نپذیرفتی.

[§۱۸:۶۸] وگر جرم ماه بنور زیادت و نقصان نپذیرفتی، حال عالم گردنده نبودی. و هیچ چیز خام از میوها پخته نشدی، و هیچ نارسیده نرسیدی، و آفتاب را کسوف نبودی، و بسیار حکمت که اندر زیادت و نقصان نور ماه بسته است باطل شدی.

[§۱۹:۶۸] و لکن چون جرم ماه چنان نیست که نور ازو بگذرد چون آفتاب ازو بر گوشهٔ بتابد آن گوشه ازو نور پذیرد و ما به زمین مر آن گوشه را ببینیم[۱۲] برمثال پاره‌ای[۱۳] از دایره‌ای.[۱۴]

[§۲۰:۶۸] و هرچند آفتاب روباروی‌تر شود روشنی او ما بیشتر بینیم، تا به مقابله برسد که همه قرص ماه به روشنیِ آفتاب از جانب به نور آراسته شود.

[§۲۱:۶۸] امّا بباید دانستن کی همیشه یك روی ماه[۱۵] از[۱۶] آفتاب تمام روشن است

۱۰ ایا: بلك.

۱۱ اس، ایا: آیینهء

۱۲ اس، ایا: به‌بینیم.

۱۳ اس، ایا: پارهء.

۱۴ اس، ایا: دایرهء.

۱۵ ¦⟵برگ [ایا:۹۵-ب].

۱۶ اس: [عبارت «ماه از» بالای خط نوشته شده است].

و لکن تابش آن روشنی به همه وقت سوی زمین نیست، و کسانی که درین علم[۱۷] دست دارند بدانند حقیقت.

[§۶۸:۲۲] آنچ ما دانستیم گفتیم درین معنی و اندر این شرح که بکردیم جواب بوالهیثم گورگانی[۱۸] گفته شد که او اندر قصیدهٔ سوالات[۱۹] خویش این سئوال بکند.

[§۶۸:۲۳] و اکنون بشرح سخن خویش بازشویم گوییم که مر امر باری را سبحانه بحقیقت عقل کلّی شناسد که بدو پیوسته است پیوستن نور به آفتاب.

[§۶۸:۲۴] و وهمها را سوی امر که او چیزی نیست راهی نیست.

[§۶۸:۲۵] و عقل کی نخست چیز است مایهٔ وهمها است، و زو به نفسهای جزوی اثر پیوسته است.

[§۶۸:۲۶] و ما نیز هویّت عقل را بدان تأثیر دانیم کزو به ما پیوسته است به رهنمایی[۲۰] نایبان او که پیامبران اند، علیهم السّلام.

[§۶۸:۲۷] و نشاید کی گوییم: ‹عقل را ما اندریافته ایم›؛[۲۱] که اگر چنین گوییم، گفته باشیم که ما بر عقل محیطیم.

[§۶۸:۲۸] بل کی گوییم عقل اندر ما مانندهٔ ما است ذات خویش را[۲۲] و دیگر چیزها را.

[§۶۸:۲۹] چنانک خدای تعالی همی گوید، قوله: لَا تُدْرِكُهُ الْأَبْصَارُ وَ هُوَ يُدْرِكُ

۱۷ اس، ایا: عالم [کذا]. || تصحیح مفهومی.
۱۸ خواجه ابو الهیثم احمد بن حسن جرجانی.
۱۹ ¦←برگ [اس:۱۰۴-الف]. || نك: جامع الحکمتین، فصل ۱۸: ‹اندر خواص ماه›، ص ۱۹۱ تا ۲۰۳.
۲۰ اس، ایا: ره نمایی.
۲۱ ایا: ما عقل را اندر یافته ایم.
۲۲ ایا: – را.

الْأَبْصٰارَ وَ هُوَ اللَّطِيفُ الْخَبِيرُ.[۲۳] فرمود: «کی اندرنیابد مر او را دیدارها و او اندریابد مر دیدارها را و او جزوها ندارد و خبر یافته است».

[§۶۸:۳۰] پس گوییم که عقل اندر ما اثر کرد تا بدان اثر کزو یافتیم مر او را بشناختیم.

[§۶۸:۳۱] و شناختن ما مر او را دلیل است بر اثر کردن او در ما. از بهر آنك چون ما مر او را بدانستیم حال ما دیگر شد از آنچ بود.

[§۶۸:۳۲] ازیرا کی نادان که دانا شود چنان باشد کی مرده زنده شود. و بزرگ حال گشتنی باشد مرده زنده شدن!

[§۶۸:۳۳] و عقل کلّی، ‹به اندریافتن›[۲۴] ما مر او را، دیگر حالی نپذیرفت بل کی[۲۵] او بر حال خویش بود.

[§۶۸:۳۴] و دلیل این اندر محسوسات موجود است چون ما اندر چیزی دیدنی بنگریم، صورت آن چیز اندر چشم ما اثر کند، تا نفس ما مر آن را از پس آن پرده نیك اندر ببیند.[۲۶]

[§۶۸:۳۵] پس آن چیز دیدنی بر حال خویش باشد و اثر او اندر چشم ما افتد تا حال چشم ما دیگر شود، بدانچ اندر او صورتی[۲۷] پیدا آید کی پیش از آن صورت اندر او نبود.

[§۶۸:۳۶] پس درست شد کی محسوس همی اندر حس اثر کند نه حس اندر محسوس.

---

۲۳ سورة الأنعام (۶)، آیت ۱۰۳.

۲۴ ایا: تا بدریافتن.

۲۵ ایا: بلك.

۲۶ اس، ایا: به بیند.

۲۷ ¦⟵برگ [ایا:۹۶-الف].

[§۶۸:۳۷] چه محسوس بر حال خویش است و حاسّ را همی حال بگردد به دیدن چیزی کی ندیده است.[۲۸]

[§۶۸:۳۸] پس گوییم کی عقل جزوی اندر ما اثر است از عقل کلّی، و نطق، اعنی سخن گفتن، اندر ما اثر است از نفس کلّی.

[§۶۸:۳۹] و ما به اثر نفس کی به ما رسید مر او را بشناختیم، و اندر نتوانستیمش یافتن چنانك او است.

[§۶۸:۴۰] و دلیل بر آنك تمییز ما اثر است از عقل و نطق ما اثر است از نفس آن است کی نخست ما مر چیزی را به عقل بیابیم آن وقت ‹مر آن را›[۲۹] به نطق بیرون توانیم دادن.

[§۶۸:۴۱] پس گوییم که وهم ما کالبد است مر علم الّهی را و عِلمْ روحِ آن کالبد است.

[§۶۸:۴۲] و خیالْ بستنِ ما مر معنی را از معنیها کالبد است مر وهم ما را.

[§۶۸:۴۳] و باز اندیشهٔ ما کالبد است مر آن خیال را؛ و باز حفظ ما، یعنی یادگرفتن، کالبد است مر اندیشه را؛ و باز تمییز، اعنی جدا کردن بد از نیك، کالبد است مر حفظ را.

[§۶۸:۴۴] و باز نطق، اعنی گفتار، کالبد است مر تمییز را؛ و باز حس کالبد است مر نطق را؛ و باز طبع کالبد است مر حس را.

[§۶۸:۴۵] و جملگی این همه کالبدها دوش[۳۰] شده است اندر این هیکل افزاینده که جسد است.

۲۸ ¦⟵برگ [اس:۱۰۴-ب].

۲۹ ایا: مرو را.

۳۰ ایا: روشن [کذا].

[§۴۶:۶۸] و همچنین عقل کلّی کالبد است مر امر باری را؛ و امر باری روح عقل است.

[§۴۷:۶۸] و دیگر حدود علوی و سفلی هر یکی کالبد است مر آن حد را کزو برتر است، و همه جمله نور یافته‌اند به کلمه باری سبحانه.

[§۴۸:۶۸] و حال اندر ترکیب عالم همین است: از آنچ هوا گرد گرفته است مر زمین را و آب را؛ و آتش گرد گرفته است مر هوا را؛ و فلك نخستین گرد گرفته است مر آتش را؛ و دیگر فلکها مر یکدیگر را جسمها گشته‌اند.

[§۴۹:۶۸] و نفس کلّی گرد گرفته است مر عالم را با آنچ اندر او است به گرد گرفتن قدرت، نه جسمی؛ و بیرون ازین جسم کلّی چیز نیست.

صف شست و نهم

سخن اندر شرح «کن» کی امر خدای است[۱]

[§۶۹:۱] معنی آنك خدای تعالی امر خویش را به دو حرف بازبست[۲] و مر آن را «کن» خواند به دو قسمت شود:

[§۶۹:۲] یکی ازو آن است کی ممکن نیست پدید آمدن چیزی از موجودات روحانی و جسمانی مگر از میان جفتی یا لطیف یا کثیف. و بودشِ همه جفت را علّت امر باری است.[۳]

[§۶۹:۳] پس عبارت کردند امر باری را به دو حرف تا بدانند کزان علّت[۴] پدید آمدْ جفتها همه. و مر آن علّت را نشاید عبارت کردن مگر از جهت این دو حرف کی جفتی اندر این دو حرف[۵] پیدا است.

[§۶۹:۴] و هیچ چیز نیست از موجودات که نه جفتی اندر او پیدا است. از بهر آنك امر علّت همه چیزها است.

[§۶۹:۵] و چون حال چنین بود این دو حرف کز امر بدو عبارت کردند گوایی داد به جفتیِ خویش، کی همه آفریدگان جفت‌اند همچنانك کاف با نون جمع است، و پای‌دارِ[۶] همه جفتها به امر خدای است.

---

۱ قس: کتاب الینابیع، الینبوع الثالث (۳): في معنی إضافة أمر الله الی هذَین الحرفَین وهما الکاف والنون، ص ۱۷ تا ۱۹.

۲ ¦⟵برگ [ایا:۹۶-ب].

۳ ایا: + سبحانه.

۴ ¦⟵برگ [اس:۱۰۵-الف].

۵ اس: [کلمه «حرف» مخدوش است].

۶ قس: کتاب الینابیع، الینبوع الثالث (۳)، ص ۱۷، بند (۲۶)، س ۱۵ تا ۱۷: فکان هذانِ الحرفانِ المزدوجانِ في هذه الکلمة — التی کونها عن أمر — شهادة من جمیع المخلوقین المزدوج کلّ واحد منهما مع صاحبه — کازدواج الکاف مع النون — بأنّ قیامهم جمیعاً بأمر تعالی.

[§۶۹:۶] و دیگر معنی آن است اندر «کن» که کاف به حساب جمل بیست بود و نون پنجاه باشد. و جملهٔ هر دو هفتاد باشد، و هفتاد هفت‌بار ده باشد.

[§۶۹:۷] و معنیش آن است که امر مُبدِع حقّ که آن را ارادت[۷] خوانند، اعنی خواست خدای، آن بود که پیدا شود هفت حرف علوی، که بدان پدید آمد صورتهای روحانی. و خواست که پیدا شود هفت ستارهٔ جرمانی که بدیشان پدید آید صورتهای جسمانی.

[§۶۹:۸] و خواست کی پیدا شود اندر عالم قوایم پیغامبران هفتگانه از بهر سیاست ناموسی مر هر دو صورت جسمانی و روحانی را اندر این بدن مردم.

[§۶۹:۹] و میان کاف و نون از حروف معجم دو حرف است و آن لام است و میم. و چون مر این دو حرف را بهم آری «لم»[۸] باشد. و آن «چرا» باشد. و «چرا» بازجُستِش[۹] باشد، یعنی کی آنچ ازو باز توان جستن میان کاف و نون است، که او امر ایزد است.

[§۶۹:۱۰] و نیز روا بود کی گوییم کاف و نون که اول پدید آید مثل است بر دو اصل لطیف. و لام و میم کز میان ایشان[۱۰] پدید آید مثل است بر دو اصل کثیف.

[§۶۹:۱۱] و نیز پیش از کاف، از حروف معجم، یا بود؛ و از پس نون سین بود. و این دو نیز هفتاد باشد.

---

۷ اس: ارادات.

۸ نك: دهخدا: لم. [لِ مَ] (عربی قید مرکب) ... بهر چه. برای چه. چرا. از چه.

۹ اس: بازحسش؛ ایا: بازجستن. || بازجُستِش اسمی است که از اسم (مصدر) بازجست (بازجستن) ساخته شده است. مانند: مالش از مال (مالیدن)، خارش از خار (خاریدن).

۱۰ اس: [حرف «الف» در ابتدای «ایشان» به دندانهٔ اول حرف «ن» از کلمهٔ قبل آن یعنی «میان» وصل شده است].

[§۱۲:۶۹] دلیل است بر هفت امام که سیاست و قوام[۱۱] دعوت حقّ بدیشان است و به چهار اصل که یاد کردیم.

[§۱۳:۶۹] و اشارت قول ایزد بدیشان است کی همی‌گوید، قوله: یس* وَالْقُرْآنِ الْحَكِيمِ.[۱۲] «سوگند است از خدای تعالی بدین دو حرف (که دلیل است بر هفت امام) و به قرآن پر حکمت» که دلیل است بر خداوندان تأویل قرآن.

[§۱۴:۶۹] و از جهت نهاد حروف[۱۳] «ا، ب، ت، ث» پیش از کاف قاف است و پس از نون واو است و قاف[۱۴] صد[۱۵] باشد و واو شش و[۱۶] این هردو بر يك عِقْد[۱۷] باشد.

[§۱۵:۶۹] و این حال دلیل است بر آنك از پس امامان[۱۸] هفتگانه، خلیفتان قایم کی نفخ صور روحانی بدیشان باشد نیز هفت باشد.

[§۱۶:۶۹] پس ازین دو حرف کن کاف متحرك است و نون ساکن دلیل است بر آنك نهایت ابداع مُبدِع حقّ از جهت دو اصل روحانی به هیولی و صورت رسد، که یکی ازو متحرك است و دیگر ساکن.

[§۱۷:۶۹] وز جهت شخصهای طبیعی اندر عالم جسمانی به اساسین رسد کی یکی خداوند تألیف است[۱۹] چون متحرك کی گفتار او گوناگون است و آن ناطق است و دیگر خداوند تأویل است چون ساکن کی معنی او یکی است و آن اساس است.

---

۱۱ ¦⟵برگ [ایا:۹۷-الف].

۱۲ سورهٔ یس (۳۶)، آیات ۱ تا ۲.

۱۳ ¦⟵برگ [اس:۱۰۵-ب].

۱۴ اس: [«و قاف» مخدوش است].

۱۵ اس: ضد [کذا] [بالای خط اصلاح شده و «صد» نوشته شده است].

۱۶ اس: [«و» مخدوش است].

۱۷ بر قاعدهٔ حساب جمل، ارزش قاف یک صد است، و جمع یک با شش برابر هفت است؛ در حالی که، کاف (۲۰) و نون (۵۰) جمعشان هفتاد است که خود مضربی از هفت است. || نك: دهخدا: عقد. [ع ِ]...- هم عقد؛ هم سلک. هم رشته...

۱۸ اس: [«امامان» مخدوش است].

۱۹ ایا: – است.

[§۶۹:۱۸] و حروف کاف سه است: کاف و الف و فا؛ و حروف نون سه است: نون و واو و نون؛ جمله شش باشد. یعنی کی کارهای روحانیان و جسمانیان بر شش حد رونده است چون دو اصل روحانی و دو اصل جسمانی و دو فرع ایشان امام و حجّت.

صف هفتادم

سخن اندر علّت بقای عالم

[§۱:۷۰] اگر کسی پرسد کی پایداری عالم به چیست؟ جواب او آن است کی گویی پایداری چیزها به علّت باشد. و علّتِ چیز آن باشد که چون او را برگیری، معلول او برخیزد. چنانك آفتاب علّت روز است اگر آفتاب را برگیری، روز برخیزد.

[§۲:۷۰] پس گوییم که پایداری عالم به حرکت و سکون است، اعنی که جنبش و آرام. از[1] بهر آنك از عالم آسمانها جنبان است و زمین آرامیده است، و زایش عالم همه ازین دو چیز پدید آمده است کی صفت یکی متحرك است و صفت دیگر ساکن.

[§۳:۷۰] وگر حرکت و سکون را به وهم برگیری عالم به برخاستن ایشان برخیزد. ازبهر آنك متحرّك و ساکن پذیرا باشند مر حرکت و سکون را، و پذیرای این دو صفت آسمان است و زمین و آنچ اندر این دو میان است.

[§۴:۷۰] و چون صفت نباشد، کی آن حرکت و سکون است،[2] صفت پذیر نباشد کی آن[3] متحرّك و ساکن است. و چون به برخاستن حرکت و سکون همی عالم برخیزد، درست شد که پایداری عالم به حرکت و سکون است.

[§۵:۷۰] و نیز مردم را عالم صغیر خوانند یعنی جهان کهین. و مردم به اندامهای خویش همی اندرین دو حال بسته شده است. چنانك از اندامهای مردم بهری جنبان است چون دستها و پایها و چشمها و رگها، و بهری آرمیده است چون میانهٔ سر و گوش و بینی و جز آن.

[§۶:۷۰] و پایندگیِ مردم از راه طبیعت اندر این عالم بدین اندامها است که بر

---

۱ ¦←برگ [ایا:۹۷-ب].

۲ ¦←برگ [اس:۱۰۶-الف].

۳ اس: [«کی آن» مخدوش است].

حرکت و سکون است. و چون پایداری مردم که عالم صغیر است به حرکت و سکون است، پایداری عالم کبیر هم بدین باشد.

[§۷:۷۰] و حال اندر دیگر زایشهای عالم چون نبات و حیوان و جز آن همین است که یاد کرده شد.

صف هفتاد و یکم

سخن اندر آنك عقل را جنبش نیست[1]

[§۷۱:۱] هر جنبنده‌ای[2] را جنبش است. و اندر آغاز عقلها ثابت است کی جنبش پیش از جنبنده باشد. وگر عقل متحرّك بودی، حرکت پیش ازو بودی. وگر پیش از عقل چیزی بودی ورا نام سابقی واجب نیامدی. پس درست شد کی عقل متحرك نیست بل‌که ساکن است.

[§۷۱:۲] و نیز هر متحرکی را حرکت ازبهر چیزی دیگر باشد که آن چیز ساکن باشد، و بر آن متحرك پیشی دارد، تا آن متحرك به افزونیِ[3] رسیدن به آرامِ آن ساکن بجنبد. و بر عقل چیزی پیشی ندارد نه وهمی و نه حسّی کی اندر جوهر عقل حرکت آمدی به آرزوی سکون آن چیز کی[4] پیش ازو بود.

[§۷۱:۳] پس درست شد که عقل متحرك نیست و ساکن است، و به سکون عقل اندریابید[5] هر متحرّکی طبیعی و روحانی.

[§۷۱:۴] و دیگر حرکت مر چیزها را بدو سبب باشد: یا ازبهر جستن چیزی را باشد کی آن مر او را نیست؛ یا ازبهر جستن جایگاه خویش باشد کی او از آن جایگاه بیفتاده باشد.

[§۷۱:۵] و عقل حاجتمند نیست کی حرکت کند ازبهر چیزی را از چیزها که او را

---

۱ قس: کتاب الینابیع، الینبوع الثامن (۸): في أنّ العقل ساکن، ص ۲۷ تا ۲۸.

۲ اس، ایا: جنبنده‌ء.

۳ ایا: افروفی.

۴ ¦←برگ [ایا:۹۸-الف].

۵ اس: اندربابید؛ ایا: اندر تأئید [کذا]. || تصحیح قیاسی. قس: کتاب الینابیع، الینبوع الثامن (۸)، ص ۲۷، بند (۴۷)، س ۸ تا ۱۱: انّ کلّ شیء متحرّك انّما تظهر حرکته من أجل شيء ساکن. ولا یسبق العقل شيء، فیتوهّم في جوهره حرکة بسکون الشيء الذی سبقه. ولمّا لم یسبق العقل شيء، کان العقل ساکنًا غیر متحرّك، لیدرك سکونه حرکة کلّ متحرّك طبیعيّ وروحانيّ.

نیست که همه چیزی خود او است.[۶] و آن است کی خدای تعالی میگوید، قوله: وَ هُوَ عَلىٰ كُلِّ شَيْءٍ قَدِيرٌ.[۷] همی گوید: «کی او بر همه چیزی پادشا است».

[§۷۱:۶] و نیز مر عقل را زوال نیست از منزلت خویش تا از بهر بازیافتن[۸] خویش بجنبد، از بهر آنك همه مکانها و منزلتها مر عقل را است.

[§۷۱:۷] و مثل او به همه جایها راست باشد توهّم کردن، کی او مکانی را همی طلب کند محال است.

[§۷۱:۸] و نیز حرکت متحرك به دو سبب باشد: یا طلب تمامی را باشد که او را نباشد؛ یا از بهر نگاه داشتن تمامی خویش را باشد کی ترسد کزو بشود.

[§۷۱:۹] و این هردو حال از عقل دور است، ازیرا که عقل بغایت تمام است، و افزونیِ او از تمامیِ او تمامی نیست.

[§۷۱:۱۰] و ایزد تعالی او را ایمن کرده است از آنك شرف ازو بستاند. پس عقل متحرك نیست و ساکن است.

[§۷۱:۱۱] معارضه اگر کسی گوید کی عقل را حرکت از بهر آن است تا مبدع خویش را سبحانه اندر یابد، و حاجتمند است سوی اندررسیدنِ مُبدِع حقّ و محیط شدن بر جلال او. و چون پیدا شد کی او حاجتمند است پیدا شد کی او متحرك است.

[§۷۱:۱۲] جواب او را گوییم اگر عقل کلّی توهّم کردی به اندریافتن مر مُبدِع حقّ را، و آن ناممکن است، خود نه عقل بودی.

۶ |⟵برگ [اس:۶-۱۰۶-ب].

۷ در مجموع این عبارت قرآنی در هفت آیت آمده است: سورة المائدة (۵)، آیت ۱۲۰؛ سورة هود (۱۱)، آیت ۴؛ سورة الروم (۳۰)، آیت ۵۰؛ سورة الشوری (۴۲)، آیت ۹؛ سورة الحدید (۵۷)، آیت ۲؛ سورة التغابن (۶۴)، آیت ۱؛ سورة المُلك (۶۷)، آیت ۱.

۸ اس: [«باز» در «بازیافتن» مخدوش است].

[§۱۳:۷۱] از بهر آنك عقل واجب گرداند بر عاقل کوتاه کردن طمع از رسیدن اندر مُبدِع حقّ.

[§۱۴:۷۱] از بهر آنك امر باری سبحانه اثر است از باری سبحانه و اثر را اندر رسیدن نیست به موثّر خویش. و این قضیّت اندر عقل ثابت است و عقل مخالف نشود مر چیزی را که اندر جوهر او ثابت است.

[§۱۵:۷۱] پس عقل توهّم نکند محیط شدن بر آنكْ عقل را به اثر خویش آفرید.[۹]

۹ ایا: آفریدست. || ¦⟵برگ [ایا:۹۸-ب].

صف هفتاد و دوم

سخن اندر اثبات جان نفس ناطقه

[§۷۲:۱] زندگانی نفس ناطقه اندر شناخت توحید است بی‌تشبیه و تعطیل. و صورت او[۱] بر گونهٔ صورت عالم علوی است.

[§۷۲:۲] و نفس ناطقه چون به صورت همچون عالم علوی شود و هم گوهر آن عالم گردد، و آن شناختن حروف علوی و حدود[۲] جسمانی باشد، و متابع شدن مر ایشان را، و ولایت داشتن مر هریکی را براندازهٔ حقوقمندیِ او و نه بیشتر و نه کمتر.

[§۷۲:۳] و دلیل بر درستی این دعوی از عَیّارِ[۳] عالَم آن است کی افلاک گردان است بر نطفهای خلق، کی هریکی از آن مردمی است اندر حدّ قوّت، تا بدان گشتن قوّتهای خویش را بدان نطفها رسانند، و صورت ازو پدید آرد و بجنبانَدَش تا بیرون آرَدَش بر صورت خویش.

[§۷۲:۴] همچنین تأیید از حدود علوی و تعلیم از حدود سفلی بگذرد بر نفسهای ناطقه کی آن فریشتگانند، اندر حدّ قوّت، تا بدان تأیید و تعلیم مر آن نفسها را بجنبانند، جنباندنی علمی تا بیرون آرند حس بر صورت خویش.

[§۷۲:۵] و چون نفس ناطقه به صورت روحانیان گشت، به نعیم آخرتی رسید؛ همچنانك نطفه به صورت این عالم گشت، به نعیم دنیاوی رسید.

---

۱ اس: – او. || ایا: [کلمه «او» در بالای حرف «ت» از کلمه «صورت» در فاصله بین دو خط نوشته شده است].

۲ ¦⟵برگ [اس:۱۰۷-الف].

۳ نك: دهخدا: عیار. [ع َیْ یا] ... بسیار آمدوشدکننده و گریزنده و مرد تیزخاطر. ... بسیارگشت و بهر سو رونده در چراگاه. ... بسیار گشت کننده... تردست و زیرك و چالاك. ...: گرچه طراری و عیارِ جهان، از تو / عالم الغیب کجا خواهد طراری؟ (ناصرخسرو، [دیوان اشعار، ص ۴۱۷، س ۲۲، به اهتمام: نصرالله تقوی]).

[§۶:۷۲] و عادت افلاك اندر نطفهای جسمانی آن است کی او را به صورت خویش بیرون آرد، و جنبنده گرداند؛ و باز چندان بگرد او بگردد تا پس از آن جنبش به مرگی بیارامد.

[§۷:۷۲] پس همچنین است عادت حدود خدای اندر نفسهای ناطقه که آن نطفهای روحانی است کی بگرد او بگردد تا زنده کندش به معرفت توحید و مرده گرداندش از شهوات.

صف هفتاد و سِیُّم[۱]

سخن اندر اثبات عقل مجرّد[۲]

[§۱:۷۳] بباید شناختن کی هرچیزی کی او بذات خویش تمام باشد شریف‌تر از آن چیز باشد کی ایستادن او به چیزی دیگر باشد.

[§۲:۷۳] پس اگر کسی گمان برد کی اثبات عقل بدین شخصها است اعنی کالبدهای مردم کی[۳] فعل عقل ازو همی پیدا شود پس آن کس گمان برده باشد کی شخص مردم فاضلتر از عقل است.

[§۳:۷۳] و چون شناختن نیك از بد به عقل است، نه به جسد، درست شد کی عقل بی‌جسد ایستاده است بذات خویش.

[§۴:۷۳] وگر[۴] نه چنین بودی و عقل با جسد انباز بودی اندر محیط شدن بر چیزها بایستی کی جسد بر ذات خویش محیط شدی چنانك عقل برو محیط شده است.

[§۵:۷۳] وگر عقل را آمیزش بودی با جسد، بایستی کی جسد را با عقل هم‌جنسی بودی.[۵]

[§۶:۷۳] و چون جسد فاسد است و عقل باقی است و جسد محاط است و عقل محیط است، روا نباشد کی با این مخالفت کی میان ایشان است با یکدیگر بیامیزند.

---

۱ ایا: سوم.

۲ قس: کتاب الینابیع،الینبوع العاشر (۱۰): في إثبات عقل مجرد، ص ۳۰ تا ۳۲.

۳ ¦←برگ [ایا:۹۹-الف].

۴ ایا: و اگر.

۵ ¦←برگ [اس:۱۰۷-ب].

[§۷:۷۳] و چون پیدا[۶] شد کی عقل را با جسد آمیزش واجب نیست، پیدا شد کی عقل مجرّد ثابت است.

[§۸:۷۳] و چگونه آمیزد عقل با جسد؟ و اندر هر چیزی از جزوهای جسد عقل را پادشاهی است کی مر او را صورت کند و شکل او را از بر خویش دارد و اندر او مثال[۷] و اشارت و[۸] توهّم کند. و مر شخص را عقل از آن حال کی باشد بجایی دیگر تصور بتواند[۹] کردن.[۱۰]

[§۹:۷۳] و نیز آن چیز که با چیزی[۱۱] بیامیزد او میان قوّت و فعل باشد. و فعل او بر آن گونه باشد کی تواند که دیگر بار بیامیزد.

[§۱۰:۷۳] و از عقل چیزها بفعل باشد نه بقوّت، چه او گهر نخست است کی ازو پدید آمد اوایل عقلی. وگر در عقل قوّتی بودی جز از فعل، بفعل بازنیافتندی آن چیزها را که اندر قوّت است و باطل شدی برهانها و قیاسها. از بهر آنك آنچ اندر

---

۶ اس: [«پیدا» مخدوش است].

۷ نك: دهخدا: مثال. [مِ] (عربی اسم) فرسان. ... حکم. ... حکم و فرمان. ج، اَمثِلَه و مُثل و مُثُل. ... فرمان پادشاهی و مطلق حکم. (غیاث) (آنندراج): بباید دانست که خواجه خلیفت ماست در هر چه به مصلحت بازگردد و مثال و اشارهٔ وی روان است. (تاریخ بیهقی چ ادیب ص ۱۵۰). شاگردان و یاران هستند، همگان بر مثال تو کار میکنند تا کارها بر نظام قرار گیرد. (تاریخ بیهقی چ ادیب ص ۱۴۷).

۸ ایا: – و.

۹ اس، ایا: نتواند. || تصحیح مفهومی.

۱۰ قس: کتاب الینابیع، الینبوع العاشر (۱۰)، ص ۳۱، بند (۵۴)، س ۳ تا ۹: وکیف یشوب العقل الجسد وفی کلّ جزء من اجزاء الجسد له تصویر وتشکیل وتمثیل واشارة وتوهّم واحالة الی حالة أُخری؟ فلو کان العقل مشوباً بالجسد، کان العقل یتوهّم احالة ذاته عند احالة الجزء المشوب به من الجسد. واذا توهّم احالة ذاته، امتنع علیه التصویر والتشکیل. ولیس یمتنع علیه التصویر والتشکیل في وقت من الاوقات. فلیس العقل اذًا یشوب شیئًا من أجزاء البدن. فاذا العقل مجرّد غیر مشوب بشیء من الجسد.

۱۱ ایا: + دیگر.

حدّ قوّت باشد گردنده باشد از حال به حال. و آنچ[۱۲] از حال به حال گردنده باشد مر او را به چیزی یابند کز حال به حال نگردد.

[§۷۳:۱۱] و آنچ گردنده را بدو یابند عقل است کی او از حال به حال گردنده نیست. و چیزی کز حال به حال نگردد او بفعل باشد نه بقوّت. پس درست شد کی عقل با جسد آمیزش ندارد از بهر آنك او بفعل است نه بقوّت.

[§۷۳:۱۲] و چگونه آمیزش کند عقل به جسد مرکّب از چهار طبع، وگر عقل با جسد بیامیختی ممکن بودی که با یکی ازین طبایع نیز بیامیختی؟[۱۳] و واجب آمدی که اثر عقل اندر طبایع پیدا شدی، و البته اثر عقل اندر طبایع پیدا[۱۴] و یافته نیست.

[§۷۳:۱۳] پس دانستیم که عقل را آمیزش نیست با چیزی که آن مرکّب است و جسد از مرکّبات است. پس عقل را آمیزش نیست با جسد و دور است از آمیختن با مرکّبات و مجرَّد است بذات خویش.

۱۲ ایا: آنچه.

۱۳ ¦⟵برگ [ایا:۹۹-ب].

۱۴ اس: [بعد از کلمه «پیدا» کلمه «شدی» نوشته شده، اما خط زده شده است].

صف هفتاد و چهارم

سخن اندر آنك عالم را دانش نیست

[§۷۴:۱] گروهی از طبایعیان چنین گفتند که ستارگان و افلاك[۱] دانایان و گویندگانند.

[§۷۴:۲] و حجّت آوردند بر آن، آنچ گفتند که جانوران و سخنگویان را عالم همی بیرون آرد و روا نباشد کی بیرون آوردهٔ عالم را فضیلتی باشد که مر عالم را، کی بیرون آورندهٔ[۲] او است، آن نباشد.

[§۷۴:۳] و ما پیدا کنیم مر خردمندان را، که عالم را و آنچ اندر او است، از ستارگان و افلاك و طبایع، حیات نیست و نه دانش.

[§۷۴:۴] و گوییم که دانایان مردم را عالم کهین گفتند. و مردم رنج و راحت را شناسنده است از زیر پای خویش تا به تارك سر.

[§۷۴:۵] و چون عالم مردم مهین است، ازین قیاس آسمان سر عالم باشد و زمین پای او.

[§۷۴:۶] وگر دست مردم از آسمان دور است پایش به زمین نزدیك است و به زمین قرار دارد، و مر او را همی‌گرداند چنانك خواهد از حالی به حالی.

[§۷۴:۷] و همی بیند که مر زمین را که او انباز آسمان است اندر بیرون آوردن زایشها، حس و زندگی نیست. و مر زمین را چنانك حس نیست نطق نیست و نداند که بدو چه همی‌کنند و نه از گردانیدن و شکستن دردی و آسانی همی‌یابد.

[§۷۴:۸] و چون زمین را که ما بدو پیوسته بودیم بی‌خبر یافتیم از آنچ همی‌کند

---

۱ |←برگ [اس:۱۰۸-الف].

۲ اس، ایا: بیرون آوردهٔ [کذا]. || تصحیح قیاسی.

وز آنچ بدو همی کنند، حکم کردیم بر آب که انباز او است و بر هوا که انباز آب است و بر آتش کی انباز باد است به نادانی و هر چهار را نادان یافتیم.

[§۹:۷۴] و این چهارگانه کارپذیران بودند و انبازان بودند با فلك و ستارگان اندر پدیدآوردن[۳] نبات و حیوان. و چون این انبازان بی‌جان و نادان بودند دانستیم که آسمان و ستارگان که دست ما بدیشان نمی‌رسد همچنین‌اند[۴] بی‌جان و نادان که این دیگران انبازان ایشان‌اند.

---

۳ ¦⟵برگ [ایا:۱۰۰-الف].

۴ ایا: – اند.

صف هفتاد و پنجم

سخن اندر خطاب عقل با نفس[1]

[§۷۵:۱] حکما را اندر این معنی سخن است بدانچ بازجستند تا بدانند کی نخست عقل فایده‌های خویش فروریخت بر نفس، یا نخست نفس طلب کرد فایده را از عقل.

[§۷۵:۲] و گفتند اگر گوییم که نخست عقل فایدهٔ خویش فروریخت بر نفس، [پیش از] طلب کردن نفس مر آن را، مر عقل را[2] مُسرف خوانده باشیم. و خدای تعالی همی‌گوید: «که مسرفان را دوست ندارم» بدین آیت، قوله:[3] وَ لاٰ تُسْرِفُوا إِنَّهُ لاٰ يُحِبُّ الْمُسْرِفِينَ.[4] گفت: «مدهید جز به حد که خدای دوست ندارد مر دهندگان بی‌حد را».

[§۷۵:۳] وگر گوییم نخست نفس طلب کرد از عقل مر فایدهٔ خویش را، و تا نخواست از عقل چیز نیافت، مر عقل را به بخیلی منسوب کرده باشیم.

[§۷۵:۴] و خدای تعالی همی‌گوید: «هرکه بخیلی کند با خویشتن کند». یعنی کی چون کار نکند مزد نیابد، و چون چیز ندهد چیز ندهندش. قوله: مَنْ يَبْخَلُ وَ مَنْ يَبْخَلْ فَإِنَّمٰا يَبْخَلُ عَنْ نَفْسِهِ.[5]

[§۷۵:۵] و ما گوییم که آن خطاب که عقل را با نفس است زمان لازم نیاید.

[§۷۵:۶] از بهر آنك علّت زمان حرکت است و حرکت از فعل نفس پدید آمده است. و نفس و عقل برتر از زمانند.

---

۱ ایا: نفس با عقل. || قس: كتاب الينابيع، الينبوع الحادي عشر (۱۱): في كيفيّة مخاطبة العقل للنفس، ص ۳۲ تا ۳۴.

۲ ¦⟵برگ [اس:۱۰۸-ب].

۳ ایا: – قوله.

۴ سورة الأنعام (۶)، آیت ۱۴۱.

۵ سورة محمّد (۴۷)، آیت ۳۸.

[§۷:۷۵] و چون ثابت شد کی این دو اصل عظیم از زمان برترند، پیشی و پسی از میان ایشان برخاست.

[§۸:۷۵] و چون این قاعده دانسته شد، گوییم که عقل را با نفس دو خطاب است یکی ازو علوی و دیگر سفلی.

[§۹:۷۵] و خطاب علوی و سفلی از عقل مر نفس را تایید او است، ازبهر پدیدآوردن صورتهای طبیعی را به حکمت، و آن خطاب پدید آید در عالم جسمانی بر صورتهای طبیعی.

[§۱۰:۷۵] و بداند خردمند که اگر نه تأثیر عقل بودی اندر نفس هیچ صورت براستی ترکیب نپذیرفتی.[۶] و دلیل بر درستی این قول آن است که هر نفسی به کار کردن جاکول است و لکن از کار دانستن عاجز است.

[§۱۱:۷۵] و نفس را کار کردن غریزی است. و معنی غریزی آن باشد که آن را نباید کسب کردن بل کی آن خود اندر آفرینش باشد.

[§۱۲:۷۵] چنین که حرکت و نیروی را نباید همی کسب کردن هیچ کس را، که آن خود حاصل است اندر هر نفسی.

[§۱۳:۷۵] و چون آثار حکمت اندر صورت نبات و حیوان بدیدیم، بدانستیم کی آن حکمت از خطاب عقل است با نفس.

[§۱۴:۷۵] و نخست از خطاب عقل کی با نفس کرد هیولی و صورت موجود شد.

[§۱۵:۷۵] و [ز] آن خطاب مر طبیعت را، که آن فعل نفس است، این که اندر عالم

---

۶ |⟵برگ [ایا:۱۰۰-ب].

خویش هر چیزی را بسزای او صورت و قوّت همی‌دهد، نصیب آمد. تا بدان نصیب طبیعت از عالم خویش اندرآویخت.[۷] همچنانك نفس از عقل اندرآویخته[۸] است.

[§۷۵:۱۶] وگر عقل او را با نفس کلّی خطاب جسمانی نبودی، ممکن نبودی که نفسهای جزوی اندر این عالم از عقل عقلانی نصیب گرفتی و راه یافتی سوی فایده‌های عقلانی.

[§۷۵:۱۷] چون اندر عالم فایدهٔ نفس جزوی از عاقلان و حکیمان بدیدیم، دانستیم کی این ترتیب اندر عالم نفس کلّی نهاد از آن خطاب که عقل کلّی با او کرد اندر معنی عالم جسمانی.

[§۷۵:۱۸] و مر عقل را با نفس خطابی دیگر است هم جسمانی. و بدان خطاب، عقل مر نفس را آگاه کند از حقیریِ چیزهای طبیعی و بازنمایدش از حقیریِ او بدانچ اندر او است از اختلاف و ضدّی.

[§۷۵:۱۹] تا بداند کی آن فایده‌ها که او همی‌یابد از جهت عالم روحانی شریفتر است از آنچ وی اندر آن آویخته است از چیزهای جسمانی طبیعی مختلف.

[§۷۵:۲۰] تا بدان آگاه کردن از عقل مر نفس را، نصیبی از نفس اندر این عالم آید، و رغبت کنند نفسهای جزوی اندر عالم علوی. و خوار و حقیرتر شود به چشم ایشان این عالم و آنچ اندر او است.

[§۷۵:۲۱] و نفس کلّی و جزویّات او بدین خطاب[۹] از بند طبیعت رسته شوند و راحت و نعمت جاویدی یابند.

[§۷۵:۲۲] امّا آن خطاب کی عقل با نفس کرد از جهت روحانی آغاز آن شوقی دایم

---

۷ ¦⟵برگ [اس:۱۰۹-الف].

۸ اس: [«آویخته» مخدوش است].

۹ ¦⟵برگ [ایا:۱۰۱-الف].

است کی عقل بر نفس افاضت کرد، اعنی برو ریخت، تا همیشه آرزومند باشد به علّت خویش، و آهنگ همی‌کند همیشه سوی عقل بدان شوق.

[§۲۳:۷۵] و مر خویشتن را شادمانه بیند و فراموش کند اندرآویختن خویش را به طبیعت، تا پندارد که او تهی شد از پوشش طبیعت. و همی الفنجد بدان شوق مر افاضتهای عقلی را براندازهٔ محیط شدن خویش.

[§۲۴:۷۵] و چون آن افاضتها بپذیرد و به عالم طبیعی نگرد، اثر آن پذیرفتن اندر نفسهای جزوی کار کند، تا بدان آرزومند شوند نفسهای نیکان و متابعان امامان سوی عالم علوی و دست بازدارند از[10] اندرآویختن بدین عالم.

[§۲۵:۷۵] و مر عقل را با نفس خطابی دیگر هست هم روحانی. و آن فروریختن عقل است مر عجز را بر نفس.

[§۲۶:۷۵] تا بدین هردو فایده مر نفس را میان شوق و عجز اندرآورده است، تا همی الفنجد فایده‌ها از عقل[11] بدان افاضت شوقی که عقل برو کرده است و بازایستد از کسب از جهت آن افاضت عجز. ازبهرآنك فزون از آن نتواند پذیرفتن کی مقدار او است.

[§۲۷:۷۵] وگر افاضت از عقل بر نفس شوقی بودی، بی‌افاضت عجزی، ذات نفس باطل شدی اندر طلب کردن آنچ او را طاقت آن نبود. پس چون نفس محیط شود به هرچه خواهد، بداند که آن علّت او بر وی عجز باریده است و خرسند شود و بیاساید از طلب.

[§۲۸:۷۵] و بدان عاجزیِ او اندر عالم جسمانی پیدا آید کم شدن دانایان[12] و رغبت ناکردن نفسهای جزوی اندر علم.

---

۱۰ اس، ایا: – از.

۱۱ |⟵برگ [اس:۱۰۹-ب].

۱۲ اس: داناان.

[§۲۹:۷۵] و همچنین اگر افاضت از عقل بر نفس از عجز بودی، بی‌افاضت شوقی، نفس ناقص بماندی، و فایده نگرفتی چون ندانستی کی شوق از علّت او بر او باریده است.

[§۳۰:۷۵] پس گوییم کی عقل بر نفس شوق و عجز را فروریخت، از بهر آنك بر ذات خویش اندر توحید نفی و اثبات[۱۳] را لازم کرده بود. و نفی چون عجز است و اثبات چون شوق.

[§۳۱:۷۵] از بهر آنك عقل چون خواست که اثبات کند مُبدِع حقّ را، بازداشت مر او را نفی از صورت کردن مر مُبدِع حقّ را به چگونگی و اشارت کردن بدو. و چون خواست کی نفی کند مر مُبدِع حقّ را به تعطیل، بازداشت مر او را اثبات از تعطیل و انکار.

[§۳۲:۷۵] و همچنین بر نفس حرکت و سکون پدید آمد. حرکت چون شوق و سکون چون عجز. و پدید آمد از حرکت و سکون هیولی و صورت، هیولی چون شوق و صورت چون عجز.

[§۳۳:۷۵] از بهر آنك هیولی همیشه آرزومند است به پذیرفتن فایدهٔ نفس از راه صورت پس یکدیگر، و صورت عاجز است از پذیرفتن صورتی دیگر با خویشتن. چنانك هیولی با صورت جسمی صورتی دیگر نتواند پذیرفتن.

[§۳۴:۷۵] این است خطاب عقل با نفس.

---

۱۳ ¦⟵برگ [ایا:۱۰۱-ب].

صف هفتاد و ششم

سخن اندر چگونگی پیوستن فایدهٔ عقل به نفس[1]

[§۷۶:۱] گوییم، همچنانك، صورت بر دو نوع است[2] یکی جسمانیِ کثیف و یکی روحانیِ لطیف.

[§۷۶:۲] فایده‌های طبیعی از افلاك و کواکب به زایشهای عالم پیوسته است کی قرارگاه آن مرکز زمین است. و آن فایده‌ها به حرکت دایم پیوسته است تا صورتهای طبیعیِ شخصی بدان پدید آمده است.

[§۷۶:۳] و فایده‌های عقل به نفس به سکون دایم است، کی نفس از عقل همی‌پذیرد، تا پدیدآید بدان صورتهای روحانی دایم.

[§۷۶:۴] و آن فایده کی نفس[3] از[4] عقل به سکون دایم پذیرفت بیشتر از آن فایده‌ها بود که مر آن را آمیخته پذیرفت به چیزهای طبیعی که آن را زوال و پراکندن است.

[§۷۶:۵] و آن فایده‌ها، کی آمیخته بود به چیزهای طبیعی، نفس را بر بقاء آن ایمنی نبود، از بهرآنك مر آن را حرکت بود و چیز متحرك پایدار نباشد.

[§۷۶:۶] و زین سبب افتاد اختلاف بسیار اندر رایهای[5] خردمندان که علمها[6] بیرون آوردند به نفسی کی آن به طبیعت پیوسته بود و با او آمیخته.

---

۱ قس: کتاب الینابیع، الینبوع الثاني عشر (۱۲): في کیفیّة توهّم إتّصال فوائد العقل بالنفس، ص ۳۵ تا ۳۶.

۲ ¦⟵برگ [اس:۱۱۰-الف].

۳ ایا: – کی نفس.

۴ ایا: کز.

۵ اس: رایهاء؛ ایا: راههاء.

۶ اس، ایا: علما. || تصحیح قیاسی-مفهومی.

[§۷۶:۷] و مر نفس را قوّت[۷] اندر بیرون آوردن علم بر مقدار سکون او باشد با عقل و بر مقدار جدا شدن او از چیزهای طبیعی.

[§۷۶:۸] و هر نفسی کی دانش پاکیزه‌تر پذیرد از آلایش طبیعت، مر عقل او را ثبات بیش باشد و زوال کمتر پذیرد.

[§۷۶:۹] و هر نفسی کی سکون از عقل کمتر پذیرد و به چیزهای طبیعی متحرك پیوسته باشد فایدهٔ او به اثبات کمتر باشد و زوال زودتر پذیرد.

[§۷۶:۱۰] و هر نفسی کی سکون عقلی تمام پذیرد، فایده‌های عقلی را بپذیرد پذیرفتنی بی‌زوال و ایشان مؤیّدان باشند از بندگان ایزد سبحانه.

[§۷۶:۱۱] و حکما گفته‌اند کی میل کردن به چیزهای طبیعی دور شدن است مر او را از فایده‌های عقلی. و میل کردن نفس به طبیعت سبب بدبختی است مر او را و بار آوردن عقوبت جاویدی.

[§۷۶:۱۲] و میل کردن نفس به عقل دور شدن است مر او را از نقصان طبیعت و نزدیك بودن به علّت خویش کی آن عالم ابداع است. و میل کردن نفس به عقل سبب تمامی نفس باشد و حاصل شدن راحت ابدی و سرور عقلی و ثواب آلهی مر او را.

[§۷۶:۱۳] ایزد تعالی ما را رغبت دهاد اندر طلب کردن مر عالم عقلی را و پرهیز دهاد ما را از طبیعتِ[۸] هلاك‌کننده و آلایشهای پلید او.

---

۷ ¦⟵برگ [ایا:۱۰۲-الف].

۸ ¦⟵برگ [اس:۱۱۰-ب].

صف هفتاد و هفتم

سخن اندر راحت و رنج نفس مجرّد

[§۷۷:۱] رنج و راحت مر نفس را امروز کی به طبیعت پیوسته است بسبب موافقت او رسد کی بیفتد مر او را با چیزی یا بسبب مخالفتی کی مر او را باشد با چیزی.

[§۷۷:۲] چنانك نفس را با عقل موافقت است و با جهل مخالفت دارد. لاجرم از دانستن شادمانه شود و به راحت برسد و از نادانستن غمگین شود و رنجه گردد.

[§۷۷:۳] و بجملگی راحتها مر نفس مردم را اندر این عالم از دانش است؛ و همه رنجها مر او را از نادانی است.

[§۷۷:۴] ازبهرآنك چون بیمار شود رنجه شود. اگر بداند کی رهایش او از آن بیماری اندر[۱] چیست و آن چیز چگونه به دست آید، همان ساعت به راحت رسد و آن رنجش به راحت بدل شود. وگر نداند که چه باید کردن اندر آن رنج بماند.

[§۷۷:۵] و هر حالی کی آن نه بر راستی باشد نفس اندر این عالم از آن رنجه شود. چون از سرمایی کز حد بیرون باشد و چون از گرمای سخت و چون از آوازهای بی‌نظام کز حدّ اعتدال بیرون باشد چون آواز رعد و خران[۲] و چون دیدن صورتهای زشت کی مر نفس را آن ناپسند است اندر حال حاضر.

[§۷۷:۶] ازبهرآنك او را ازبهر نیکوتر صورتی آفریده‌اند و آن صورت به عالم روحانی است. و راحتهای نفس اندر این عالم از دیدن صورتهای نیکو است و از شنودن آوازهای راست و به نظم و خوردن چیزهای معتدل و بودن اندر هواهایی کی نه سرد است و نه گرم.

---

۱ ¦⟵برگ [ایا:۱۰۲-ب].

۲ اس: خران؛ ایا: حران.

[§۷:۷۷] پس مر نفس را خوشی اندر عالم روحانی بدان بهره باشد که اندر این عالم بدو رسیده باشد از کلمه باری سبحانه. تا چون بدان وقت کز طبیعت جدا شود و بدان اصل خویش بازرسد موافق باشد مر آن اصل را و به راحت رسد بسبب موافقت خویش با آنچ بدو بازگردد.

[§۸:۷۷] وگر اندر این عالم به علم و عمل مر جای خویش را عمارت نکرده[۳] باشد، اندر آن چیزها که او را فرموده باشند اندر این عالم، و آن فرمان را خوار داشته باشد،[۴] اصل او مر او را مخالف باشد. بدانچ اصل او کی نفس کلّ است مطیع است مر مُبدِع حقّ را، و چون این نفس جزوی عاصی باشد، مخالف باشد مر اصل خویش را.

[§۹:۷۷] و عاصیِ جزوی از مطیع کلّی رنجه شود بحکم مخالفت کی او دارد. رنجه شدنی که هیچ گوینده صفت آن رنج نتواند گفتن وزان اندر عذاب جاویدی رسد.

[§۱۰:۷۷] وگر با اصل خویش موافق باشد به طاعت مُبدِع حقّ اندر ثواب ابدی رسد.[۵]

۳ اس: [برای رفع ابهام، بالای «نکر» در کلمه «نکرده»، با جوهر کمرنگتر «نه کر» نوشته شده است].

۴ ¦⟵برگ [اس:۱۱۱-الف].

۵ ایا: + والسّلام.

صف هفتاد و هشتم

سخن اندر فرق میان معرفت و علم[۱]

[§۷۸:۱] معرفت شناخت باشد و علم دانش باشد.[۲]

[§۷۸:۲] و معرفت اندر مردم و حیوان سرشته[۳] باشد و کسب کردنی نیست، و علم سرشتنی نیست بل کسب کردنی است.

[§۷۸:۳] جان مردم، که لطیف است، شناختنی است نه دانستی. از بهر آنك اندر هر نفسی سرشته است دانستن کی اندر این کالبد چیزی است که او را جان خوانند و کالبد بدان چیز زنده است؛ و لکن چگونگی و چه‌چیزی و کجایی و چراییِ او را نداند پس او را معرفت خوانند.

[§۷۸:۴] و تن دانستنی است و بباید آموختن دانستن او را تا بدانی کی علّت تن غذای[۴] است، و کثیف است اعنی از جزوهای بسیار ترکیب یافته است.

[§۷۸:۵] و اندر او چهار طبع است: یکی صفرا که گرم و خشك است برابر آتش از عالم. و دیگر خون که گرم و تر است برابر هوا از عالم. و سدیگر بلغم است کی سرد و تر است برابر آب از عالم. و چهارم سودا است که سرد و خشك است برابر خاك از عالم.

[§۷۸:۶] و بِدان کی کالبد مردم فرزند این عالم است کی اندر او چهار طبع است چنانك اندر این عالم چهار امّهات است.

[§۷۸:۷] و حکایت کنند از ارسطاطالیس حکیم کی شاگردی ازو پرسید از فرق میان

---

۱ ¦⟵برگ [ایا:۱۰۳-الف].

۲ قس: جامع الحکمتین: ص ۲۴۸، بند (۲۷۸)، س ۶ تا ۱۳: و فیلسوف ایرانی فرق کرده است میان معرفت و علم ... .

۳ اس: [در حاشیه متن عبارت «سرشته یعنی در خمیر آب و گل» نوشته شده است].

۴ ایا: غذا.

معرفت و علم. وی جواب داد کی: «به فلان شهر بودی»؟ شاگرد[۵] گفت: «بودم». گفت: «چه دیدی اندر این راه»؟ گفت: «دِه‌ها[۶] دیدم و آبهای روان. و پاره‌ای[۷] بیابان و رودی بود بر راه تا بدان شهر رسیدم. و آن شهر را آبادان دیدم[۸] صفت او چنین و چنین».

[§۸:۷۸] حکیم مر او را گفت: «این همه که گفتی علم است و از دانسته گفتی»؛ آن وقت گفت: «از آن شهر و آن سو نیز زمین و شهرها است»؟ شاگرد گفت: «هست». گفت: «چگونه است صفت آن بگوی». شاگرد گفت: «ندانم کی چگونه است، و لکن دانم که هست». حکیم گفت: «این یکی[۹] که گفتی از معرفت گفتی. و این را معرفت گویند کی هستش بدانی و چگونگی‌اش ندانی».

[§۹:۷۸] پس گوییم که عالم علوی روحانی شناختنی است و دانستنی نیست. و عالم جسمانی دانستنی است و آفریدگار[۱۰] عالم از حصار شناختن و دانستن بیرون است، تَعَالَی[۱۱] اللّٰهُ عَنْ ذٰلِكَ عُلُوًّا كَبِيرًا.[۱۲]

۵ ایا: – شاگرد.

۶ ایا: دیهها.

۷ اس، ایا: پاره‌ء.

۸ ¦⟵برگ [اس:۱۱۱-ب].

۹ ایا: – یکی.

۱۰ ¦⟵برگ [ایا:۱۰۳-ب].

۱۱ اس، ایا: تعال.

۱۲ اشارت به سورة الإسراء (۱۷)، آیت ۴۳: سُبْحَانَهُ وَ تَعَالَىٰ عَمَّا يَقُولُونَ عُلُوًّا كَبِيراً.

صف هفتاد و نهم

سخن اندر آنك هست نیست نشود[1]

[§۷۹:۱] بباید شناختن که[2] هستها نه از هست به جود باری سبحانه بود. و آن جودی تمام بود که آفریدگار بدان رادی کرد[3] بر هستها تا هر چیزی نصیب خویش از آفرینش بیافت. چنانك خدای تعالی همی‌گوید از جواب موسی، علیه السّلام، کی مر فرعون را، لعنة الله، داد، قوله:[4] قٰالَ رَبُّنَا الَّذِي أَعْطىٰ كُلَّ شَيْءٍ خَلْقَهُ ثُمَّ هَدىٰ.[5] گفت: «ای فرعون خدای ما آن است کی هر چیزی را آفرینش او بداد پس راه راست بنمود».

[§۷۹:۲] و چون این قاعده دانسته باشی، بدانی کی از[6] نیست شدن هستها بخل باری سبحانه ظاهر شود؛ همچنانك به جود او، تعالی جدّه، هست شدن هستها بود از نیست. و نقصان اندر جود مُبدِع حقّ روا نیست.

[§۷۹:۳] و خردمند داند که چون به هست شدن نیست باری سبحانه [را][7] نام رادی لازم آمد، و این صفتی ستوده بود، به نیست شدن هستها مر او را سبحانه نام بخیلی لازم آید که آن صفتی نکوهیده است.

[§۷۹:۴] و خدای را تعالی نامهای نیکو است و نامهای زشت نیست. چنانك گفت، قوله:[8] قُلِ ادْعُوا اللّٰهَ أَوِ ادْعُوا الرَّحْمٰنَ أَيًّا مٰا تَدْعُوا فَلَهُ الْأَسْمٰاءُ الْحُسْنىٰ.[9] گفت:

---

۱ قس: کتاب الینابیع، الینبوع الثالث عشر (۱۳): في أنّ الآیس لا یصیر لیساً، ص ۳۷ تا ۳۸.

۲ اس: – که.

۳ نك: دهخدا: راد. ... صاحب همت و سخاوت.

۴ ایا: + تعالی.

۵ سورة طه (۲۰)، آیت ۵۰.

۶ اس: [کلمه «از» بالای خط نوشته شده است].

۷ تصحیح قیاسی.

۸ ایا: + تعالی.

۹ سورة الإسراء (۱۷)، آیت ۱۱۰.

«بگو ای محمّد که بخوانید الله را یا بخوانید رحمان را هرکدام خوانید مر او را است[۱۰] نامهای نیکو».

[§۵:۷۹] پس این آیت همی دلیل کند که خدای را نام زشت نیست و بخل از نامهای زشت است. وز نیست کردن هست نام زشت بحاصل آید.

[§۶:۷۹] پس درست شد کی نیست شدن هست روا نیست، چنانك هست شدن هست روا است.

[§۷:۷۹] وگر ما گوییم که هستها نیست شود و نیست خود علّت پیدا شدن هستها بود، پس گفته باشیم علّت شود مر پیدا شدن نیست را.

[§۸:۷۹] آن وقت چنان باشد کی گوییم معلول علّت باشد مر پیدا شدن علّت خویش را. و این نه ممکن[۱۱] است. بل کی[۱۲] ناروا است.

[§۹:۷۹] پس هست نیست نشود چنانك نیست هست شد.

[§۱۰:۷۹] و نیز اندر هست شدن هستها از نیست پیدا شدن عقل و نفس است، و وجود طبایع و مطبوعات است، و زایش عالم از معادن و نبات و حیوان و مردم و ثواب وعقاب و بهشت و دوزخ و شناسندگانِ توحیدِ مُبدِعِ حقّ کی بزرگتر است از همه فضیلتها، و انواع حکمت و عجایب تدبیر را که اندر آن است که نهایت نیست.

[§۱۱:۷۹] و اندر نیست شدن هستها باطل شدن عقل و نفس[۱۳] است، و نایافته شدن طبایع و مطبوعات و زایش آن، و نیستیِ شناسندگان توحید و ثواب و عقاب.

---

۱۰ ¦⟵برگ [اس:۱۱۲-الف].
۱۱ ¦⟵برگ [ایا:۱۰۴-الف].
۱۲ ایا: بلك.
۱۳ ایا: نفس و عقل.

[§۱۲:۷۹] و ایزد تعالی دور است از باطل کردن حکمتهای خویش و روا نباشد از جود و جلال او.

[§۱۳:۷۹] پس هست نیست نشود چنانك نیست هست شد. و نیز مر نیست را کرانه نیست. و بی‌نهایت است آنچ پیش از هست شدن هستها بود.

[§۱۴:۷۹] و چون گوییم هستها نیست شود و مر هستها را نهایت است ازبهر آنك يك كنارهٔ هست ازآنجای است کز نیستی به هستی[۱۴] آمده است و دیگر کناره‌اش[۱۵] این باشد کز هستی به نیستی شود، پس ازین قیاس گفته باشیم کی چیزها را نهایت علّت شود مر پیدا شدن چیز بی‌نهایت را و بی‌کناره،[۱۶] اعنی که متناهی علّت باشد چیز نامتناهی را، و نامتناهی علّت است مر متناهی را، پس این محال باشد.

[§۱۵:۷۹] و درست شد کی روا نباشد نیست شدن[۱۷] هستها. و این برهانی روشن است مر خردمند را.[۱۸]

---

۱۴ ایا: هست.

۱۵ اس: کناره‌ش.

۱۶ ایا: بی کرانه.

۱۷ ¦⟵برگ [اس:۱۱۲-ب].

۱۸ ایا: + واللّه أعلم و أحکم.

صف هشتادم

سخن اندر آنك چرا همه نفسهای حیوان اندر نعمت عالم علوی رغبت نکنند و بدان نرسند؟

[§۸۰:۱] نفسهای جزوی اندر این عالم آرزومندند بدان نعمتها که آراسته شده است ایشان را اندر آن عالم.

[§۸۰:۲] و آرزو کردن نفس مردم مر آن نعمتها را بدان است که این نفسهای مردمی نزدیك شده است به نفس کلّی که نعمتهای آخرتی همه ازو است.

[§۸۰:۳] و مر نفس جزوی را درجتی نمانده است[۱] که آن را بجوید تا از راه آن درجت بدان نعمت رسد. چنانك مر نبات را مانده است درجت حسّی و مر ستور را[۲] مانده است درجت سخن گفتن.

[§۸۰:۴] و دلیل بر درستیِ این قول آن است کی کودك خرد چون حس بیابد حریص شود بر کشیدن غذا بخویش و هرچه بیابد بدهن اندر نهد.

[§۸۰:۵] ازبهر آنك[۳] از راه حس مر او را با غذا نزدیکی افتاده است، و اندر میان حس کی حیوان است و نبات کی غذا است درجتی نمانده است که کودك را اندر آن حاجت است تا از راه آن درجت حس را بخویش کشد.

[§۸۰:۶] همچنین چون میان نفس جزویِ مردم و میان نفس کلّی که خداوند نعمتهای باقی است درجتی نمانده است مگر درجت آموختن و طاعت داشتن، جز نفس مردم آرزومند نیست بدان نعمت.

[§۸۰:۷] و دگر حیوان و نبات را همی درجات بباید گذاشتن تا بدین درجت رسند.

---

۱ ¦⟵برگ [ایا:۱۰۴-ب].

۲ اس: [عبارت «ماندست چنانك مر نبات را»، پس از «مر ستور را» نوشته شده، اما با جوهر شنگرف خط زده شده است].

۳ ایا: + از بهر آنك.

[§۸:۸۰] و چون نبات و حیوان از نعیم آن جهان دور است، نعیم این جهانی را ایزد تعالی اندر طبایع به حدّ قوّت نهاده است تا به روزگار بفعل همی آید و به هر نوعی از حیوان از آنچ ایشان را شایسته است همی‌رسد.

[§۹:۸۰] تا به وقت رسیدن[۴] قوّتهای عالم سفلی همه بجملگی از راه نفس مردم به عالم علوی، و یافتن ایشان مر آن نعمتها را کی آنجاست، [دررسند].[۵] ذَٰلِكَ تَقْدِيرُ الْعَزِيزِ الْعَلِيمِ.[۶]

---

۴ ایا: + تا بوقت رسیدن.

۵ اس، ایا: - دررسند. || تصحیح مفهومی. نک: دهخدا: دررسیدن. [دَرْ، رَ/رِ دَ] (مصدر مرکب) رسیدن. اندر رسیدن. فرا رسیدن. درپیوستن. در عقب آمدن. ملحق شدن. پیوستن. ...: پشتم قوی به فضل خدایست و طاعتش / تا دررسم مگر به رسول و شفاعتش. (ناصرخسرو، [دیوان اشعار، ص ۲۱۴، س ۷، به اهتمام: نصرالله تقوی]).

۶ سورة الأنعام (۶)، آیت ۹۶؛ سورة یس (۳۶)، آیت ۳۸؛ سورة فصلت (۴۱)، آیت ۱۲.

صف هشتاد و یکم[۱]

سخن اندر چگونگی رفتن اثر نفس کلّی اندر پذیرندگان

[§۸۱:۱] [رفتن اثر نفس کلّی اندر پذیرندگان] ازو بر دو گونه است یکی ازو عامّ است و دیگر خاص.

[§۸۱:۲] آنچ[۲] عام است ازو آن است کی گسترده است و زو باریده بر جملگیِ عالم، بر چیزهائی کی اندر او است از نفس نامیه و حسّیّه و ناطقه، و بویها و رنگها اندر شکوفها، و مزها دادن اندر میوها، و جز آن.

[§۸۱:۳] و این همه یك قوّت است کز نفس کلّی وز عالم جسمانی برو بارنده[۳] است هموار.

[§۸۱:۴] و لکن بسبب تفاوت صورتها و قوّتها[ء] چیزها به برتری و فروتری، که نتوانستند مر آن اثر را بر یك حال فراپذیرفتن،[۴] آنچ از نفس کلّی برو بارید متفاوت نیامد.[۵]

[§۸۱:۵] و چون هر[۶] چیزی از آن قوّت براندازهٔ لطافت و شکل و صورت و جایگاه و روزگار خویش نصیبی پذیرفت، هریکی نامی دیگر یافت چون سخن و حسّ و رستن و رنگها و بویها و مزّها.

[§۸۱:۶] و امّا آن قوّت کز نفس کلّی پذیرفتن آن خاصّ است آن است کی پیوسته

---

۱ ¦⟵برگ [اس:۱۱۳-الف].

۲ ایا: آنچه

۳ اس: باربده.

۴ نك: دهخدا: فراپذیرفتن. [فَ پَ رُ تَ] (مصدر مرکب) پذیرفتن: فروتنی کردن و فرمان بردن و هرچه گوید فراپذیرفتن.

۵ اس: نه امد؛ ایا: نه آمد.

۶ ¦⟵برگ [ایا:۱۰۵-الف].

شد به کسانی که آهنگ کردند بدان و مر آن را بهره‌ای[۷] به اختیار خویش طلب کردند و بپذیرفتند و آن پیامبران،[۸] علیهم السّلام، بودند.

[§۷:۸۱] و گروهی را آن قوّت خاص از نفس کلّی اندریافت به تفضل، و منّت او بر ایشان برگردانید از درجات ایشان از درجات اهل عالم، و آن ‹پیامبران، علیهم السّلام، بودند›.[۹]

۷ اس، ایا: بهره‌ء.

۸ ایا: پیمبران.

۹ ایا: پیمبران بودند علیهم السلام.

صف هشتاد و دوم

سخن اندر آنک بررسیدن از چراییِ عالم محال است[۱]

[§۸۲:۱] و از جستن، آن چیز نخستین به هستی باشد، و پس از آن از مائیّت[۲] گویند و آن چه‌چیزی باشد، و پس از آن بررسیدن از چگونگی باشد. و چون بازجستن درست آمد، آن وقت جستن از چرایی باشد که آن را لمّیّت گویند.

[§۸۲:۲] و چون چگونگی چیزی درست نشده[۳] باشد از چرایی او بررسیدن محال باشد.

[§۸۲:۳] و مثال این چنان است کی کسی واقف شده باشد و از چگونگی بودش نبات از طبایع به یاری جنبشهای افلاک و کواکب، آن وقت روا باشد کی چرایی کون نبات بجوید.[۴]

[§۸۲:۴] و اتفاق است میان حکما کی هیچ کس واقف نشد بر چگونگی بودش عالم از آفریدگار.

[§۸۲:۵] و گفتند کی پدیدآمدن از آفریدگار به امر بود، و نتواستند چگونگی پدیدآمدن عالم را از امر به هیچ روی دانستن، و بر این قول بایستادند بضرورت.

[§۸۲:۶] پس چون رایهای حکیمان متفق شد بر آنک اندررسیدن به چگونگی بودش عالم محال است، طلب کردن چرایی کون عالم محال‌تر از جهت پوشیده بودن چگونگی آن.

---

۱ قس: کتاب الینابیع، الینبوع الخامس عشر (۱۵): في أنّ السؤال، «لِمَ خلق الله العالم؟» محال ممتنع، ص ۴۰ تا ۴۱.

۲ اس، ایا: مادت [کذا]. || تصحیح قیاسی.

۳ اس، ایا: نه شده.

۴ ¦←برگ [اس:۱۱۳-ب].

[§۷:۸۲] وگر کسی گوید: «چراییِ عالم بشاید دانستن [بی][5] چگونگی آن»، چنان گفته باشد که: «من ندانم کی قرآن چگونه است و لکن دانم کز بهر چیست»، و این محال سخنی است.

[§۸:۸۲] و مثل این حال چون نردبانی است[6] به چهار پایه کی نخست پایه ازو هَلیَّت است اعنی هستی، و دیگر پایه ازو مائیَّت است اعنی چه‌چیزی، و سدیگر پایه ازو کیفیَّت است اعنی چگونگی، و چهارم پایه ازو لمیَّت است اعنی چرایی.

[§۹:۸۲] و چون مردم تختی خواهد کردن از پایهٔ نخستین بایدش گرفتن.

[§۱۰:۸۲] وز هستیِ چیز هلیّت[7] بجویی، وزان چه‌چیزی [مائیّت][8] جویی، و از چگونگی جویی وزان کیفیّت، چرایی جویی[9] وزان چرایی [لمیّت][10] جویی.

[§۱۱:۸۲] و صورت این نردبان حکمت بکردم تا مُستَرشِد[11] را بدان هدایت افزاید:

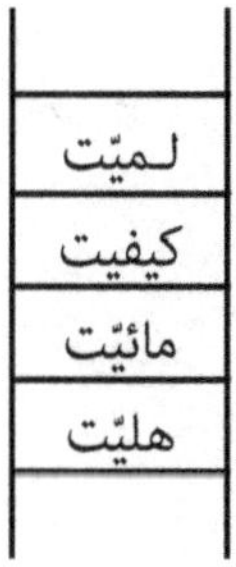

[نمودار ۵: نردبان حکمت]

۵ تصحیح قیاسی.
۶ ¦←برگ [ایا:۱۰۵-ب].
۷ اس، ایا: + لمیّت [کذا]. || تصحیح قیاسی.
۸ تصحیح قیاسی.
۹ اس، ایا: + ماهیّت.
۱۰ تصحیح قیاسی.
۱۱ نك: دهخدا: مسترشد. [مُ تَ شِ] (عربی صفت) نعت فاعلی از استرشاد. راست روی خواهنده و رهنمایی طلب کننده. ... طلب کنندهٔ رشد و راه راست. ... || مرید. ...مقابل مرشد.

[§۸۲:۱۲] پس اگر کسی گوید که «من از چرائی[۱۲] عالم بررسم بی‌آنك از چگونگیِ او بررسیده باشم و دانسته»، چنان گفته باشد کی «من به چهارم پایهٔ نردبان برشوم بی‌آنك از سیوم پایهٔ نردبان بگذرم». و این جستنی نایافتنی باشد.

[§۸۲:۱۳] و نیز آن قوّت واجوینده کی برانگیزد مردم را تا بررسد بر[۱۳] چراییِ آفرینشِ عالم ازین عالم پدید آمده است.

[§۸۲:۱۴] و چیزی کز چیزی پدید آید، جزوی باشد ازو، و چگونه توان واقف شدن بر چراییِ چیزی به بهری از آن چیز.

[§۸۲:۱۵] و چنان بایستی کی این قوّت واجوینده بیرون از عالم بودی تا بدو بر عالم واقف شایستی شدن، کی جزو بیرون نشود از کلّ خویش.

[§۸۲:۱۶] و چون نفس جوینده[۱۴] جزو[۱۵] عالم است، بدانچ ازو پدید آمده است، محال است ازو کی بازجوید از چرایی عالم. این قول حکما است و رئیسانِ دانایان پیشین.

[§۸۲:۱۷] و امّا حکماء[۱۶] دیانت گفتند کی چراییِ چیزها بباید شناختن. چه از دین و چه از دنیا که تمامیِ مردم اندر این است.

[§۸۲:۱۸] و چون اندر آفرینش آثار حکمت همی‌بینیم، دانیم کی آفرینش عالم حقّ است از آفریدگار، و حقِّ وی حقیقت است، چنانك رسول مصطفی، صلّی[۱۷] اللّٰه علیه وآله، فرمود: لِکُلِّ حَقٍّ حَقیقَةٌ.[۱۸] گفت: «هر حقّی را حقیقتی است».

---

۱۲ اس، ایا: خدای [کذا]. || تصحیح قیاسی.

۱۳ اس، ایا: و [کذا]. || تصحیح قیاسی.

۱۴ |←برگ [اس:۱۱۴-الف].

۱۵ ایا: [«جزو» مخدوش است].

۱۶ اس: حکما.

۱۷ اس، ایا: صل.

۱۸ نك: الفتّال النیسابوري، محمد بن احمد، روضة الواعظین و بصیرة المُتَّعِظین (قم: انتشارات رضی، ۱۳۷۵ش)، ج ۲، ص ۴۱۴؛ قس: ابن عساکر، علی بن الحسن، تاریخ مدینة الدمشق،

[§۸۲:۱۹] و حقّ چون آفتاب است، و حقیقت چون روشنایی است؛ و حقّ چون چشم است، و حقیقت چون[۱۹] بینایی.

[§۸۲:۲۰] و حقّ و حقیقت چنان است کی بصر و بصیرت، و خدای تعالی همی‌گوید، قوله:[۲۰] وَ مٰا خَلَقْنَا السَّمٰاوٰاتِ[۲۱] وَ الْأَرْضَ وَ مٰا بَيْنَهُمٰا لاٰعِبِينَ * مٰا خَلَقْنٰاهُمٰا إِلاّٰ بِالْحَقِّ وَ لٰكِنَّ أَكْثَرَهُمْ لاٰ يَعْلَمُونَ.[۲۲] گفت: «نیافرید[یـ]م[۲۳] آسمانها و زمین را و آنچ اندر این دو میان است به بازی. و نیافرید[یـ]مشان[۲۴] مگر بحق؛ و لکن بیشتر از ایشان ندانند».

[§۸۲:۲۱] پس این گفتار کی همی گوید کی بیشتر از ایشان ندانند[۲۵] همی دلیل کند که آن کسان کی بدانند کی آسمان و زمین را ایزد تعالی از بهر چه آفرید، آن رسول باشد و آن کس کی بجای او ایستاده باشد اندر هر زمانی یك تن از عالم.

[§۸۲:۲۲] پس درست شد که دانستن چرایِیِ عالم واجب است و ممکن است از روی دین و قول خدای تعالی و خبر رسول مصطفی، علیه السّلام.

[§۸۲:۲۳] وزان روی کی سخن منطقیان است درست کردیم کی بررسیدن از چرایِیِ عالم محال است.

به اهتمام: عمر بن غرامة العمروي (بیروت: دار الفکر، ۱۴۱۶ق/۱۹۹۶م)، ج ۳۸، ص ۲۷۴.

۱۹ |←برگ [ایا:۶-۱۰-الف].

۲۰ ایا: تعالی.

۲۱ اس: السما؛ ایا: السمآء.

۲۲ سورة الدخان (۴۴)، آیات ۳۸ تا ۳۹. قس: سورة الأنبياء (۲۱)، آیت ۱۶: وَ مٰا خَلَقْنَا السَّمٰاءَ وَ الْأَرْضَ وَ مٰا بَيْنَهُمٰا لاٰعِبِينَ. در این آیت کلمه «السماء» مفرد است اما در آیت ۳۸، از سورة الدخان (۴۴)، السَّمٰاوَاتِ آمده است.

۲۳ اس، ایا: نیافریدم [کذا].

۲۴ اس، ایا: نیافریدمشان [کذا].

۲۵ ایا: – پس این گفتار که همی گوید که بیشتر ازیشان ندانند.

[§۲۴:۸۲] تا راهجوی[۲۶] را اندر عالم دین میدان فراخ شود.[۲۷]

۲۶ اس، ایا: راه جوی.

۲۷ ایا: فراخ باشد [روی «باشد»، در بین خطوط، کلمه «شود» نوشته شده است]. || ایا: + واللّٰه أعلم وأحکم.

صف هشتاد و سِيُّم[۱]

سخن اندر آنك صورت عالم پیش از پدید آمدن او[۲] اندر نفس کلّی بود

[§۸۳:۱] آن کسان کی گفتند صورت عالم پیش از آن که آشکارا شد نزدیك مُبدِع بود، ایشان خالق از مخلوق نشناختند، و مُبدَع را از مُبدِع بازندانستند.[۳]

[§۸۳:۲] و ما گوییم، به جود خداوند زمانه،[۴] کی این صورتها کز طبیعت بر این جسدها پدید آمده است همه اندر لوح محفوظ، کی آن نفس کلّ است، نقش است.

[§۸۳:۳] و هیچ چیز اندر عالم صورتی نپذیرفته است از جزویّات و کلیّات کی اصل آن اندر نفس موجود و معلوم نبوده است.

[§۸۳:۴] و دلیل بر درستی این دعوی آن است کی مردم صناعتی تواند کردن کی داند، و چیزی کی ندانسته است نتوان کردن، و صورتی که ندیده است حکایت آن نتواند کردن.

[§۸۳:۵] و هر صنعتی کی صانعی از نفسهای جزوی بکند از نخست مر آن صنعت را برجای خویش نقش کرده باشد پیش از آنك بیرون آردش بر هیولی.

[§۸۳:۶] پس چون اندر جزویّات[۵] چنین یافتیم کی مر صنعت را نفس ناطق نخست اندر ذات خویش نقش کند به معاونت اوستادی کی آن استاد از کسی دیگر یاری نخواهد، دانستیم کی این صنعت کلّی که عالم است از نخست نفس کلّی، کی

۱ ایا: سوم.
۲ ایا: – او.
۳ قس: زادالمسافر، قول ۱۹: اندر علّت بودش عالم جسم، ص ۲۶۱ تا ۲۸۴.
۴ ¦⟵برگ [اس:۱۱۴-ب].
۵ ¦⟵برگ [ایا:۱۰۶-ب].

نفوس مردم جزویّات او-آند،[۶] به معاونت عقل کلّی، کی او از یاریِ کسی بیزار است، اندر ذات خویش نقش کرد.

[§۷:۸۳] آن وقت مر آن نقش را بر هیولی نخستین بیرون آورد چنین کی امروز آشکار است.

[§۸:۸۳] و بدین صنعت که ما یاد کردیم نفس کلّ است کی او بندهٔ خاضع است خدای را تعالی.

[§۹:۸۳] و ایزد سبحانه از مانند بودن به آفریدگانِ لطیف و کثیف خویش دور است.

۶ ایا: اویند.

صف هشتاد و چهارم

سخن اندر پادشائیِ قوّت روحانی بر قوّت طبیعی[۱]

[۱:۸۴§] مرد هشیار چون اندر قوّت روحانیِ خویش نگرد، که آن را تمییز خوانند، و آن یابد مر او را محیط شده بر همه قوّتهای طبیعی.

[۲:۸۴§] و بنهد هر یکی را از آن قوّتها بجایگاه خویش، و قوّت تمییز فرق کند میان چیزها بحقیقت، و حکم کند بر طبیعیّات.[۲]

[۳:۸۴§] ازبهر آنك قوّتهای طبیعی اندر چگونگیها توانند رسیدن، چنانك چشم را قوّت طبیعت است کی اندر رنگ و شکل[۳] و جنبش و آرام رسید، و اندر آنچ ازین قوّت بیننده است و این همه چگونگی است.

[۴:۸۴§] و همچنین مر گوش را قوّت طبیعت است کی اندر چگونگی شنیدنیها رسد. و قوّت چشندگی که[۴] او را ذایقه خوانند اندررسد به چگونگیِ مزها از شیرین و طلخ و ترش و جز آن.

[۵:۸۴§] و قوّت تمییز اندر چراییِ چیزها رسد که مردم به قوّت ممیّزه داند که شکر چرا شیرین است و حنظل چرا طلخ است.

[۶:۸۴§] و دانستن چرایی برتر است از دانستن چگونگی چنانك پیش ازین شرح آن گفتیم اندر این[۵] کتاب.

---

۱ قس: کتاب الینابیع، الینبوع السادس والعشرون (۲۶): في أنّ القوی الطبیعیة لا قدر لها عند القوی الروحانیّة، ص ۶۴ تا ۶۵.

۲ ایا: طبیعتها.

۳ ¦⟵برگ [اس:۱۱۵-الف].

۴ اس: [کلمه «که» بالای خط ریز نوشت شده است].

۵ اس: [بالای کلمه «اندر» با جوهر همرنگی که برای نوشتن کلمه «این» در حاشیه بکار رفته، علامت ضربدر گذاشته شده است].

[§۷:۸۴] پس آن قوّت او بر چراییِ چیزها پادشا باشد. پس درست شد کی این[۶] قوّت روحانی پادشا است بر قوّت طبیعی.

[§۸:۸۴] و نیز قوّت روحانیِ تمییزی پادشا است بر قوّت طبیعی، به اندیشه بدل کند[۷] مر آن چیزها را کزین قوّتهای طبیعت است.

[§۹:۸۴] چنانك گرم را سرد اندیشد، و سرد را گرم، و خشك را تر اندیشد، و تر را خشك، و سپید را سیاه، و شیرین را طلخ.

[§۱۰:۸۴] و این همه مخالفان را به اندیشه، کی مر او را اندر آن پادشائی است، بدل کند.

[§۱۱:۸۴] و قوّت طبیعی مر چیزی را از آنچ باشد بدل نتواند کردن، مگر همچنان تواندش یافتن کی هست. اگر سرد است سرد یابدش وگر خشك است خشك یابدش.

[§۱۲:۸۴] و چون رنگها و بویها و مزها و جز آن اندر قوّتهای طبیعت است، و قوّت ممیّزه بر طبیعت پادشا است، خوار آید نزدیك او این قوّتها و بدل تواندش کردن سوی ذات خویش به فکرت.

[§۱۳:۸۴] وگر قوّت ممیزه بر قوّتهای طبیعی پادشا نبودی، عاجز بودی از اندیشه کردن بر مخالفت قوّتهای طبیعی. پس درست شد کی قوّت روحانی پادشا است بر قوّتهای طبیعی.

[§۱۴:۸۴] معارضه اگر کسی گوید که قوّت ممیّزه نتواند کی مر طلخ را شیرین داند و ترش را شور یا زشت را نیکو بیند، جواب او را گوییم قوّت ممیّزه چیز را بر مخالفت او چنان بدل کند بحقیقت کی انگور ناپخته را چنان بدان ترشی و سختی

۶ اس: [«این» در حاشیه متن نوشته شده است].

۷ ¦⟵برگ [ایا:۱۰۷-الف].

و سبزی همی‌یابد و همی بدل کند او را کی این انگوری شیرین سیاه نرم و خوش است[8] بحکم آنك چنان خواهد بودن.

[§۱۵:۸۴] یا مر سرکهٔ ترش رونده را گوید این چیزی شیرین بوده است اندر خوشهٔ آویخته از درختی کزین صفتها امروز چنین‌اند و هیچ چیز نیابد.

[§۱۶:۸۴] یا مر صورت کودکی خرد را که تمییز کند گوید این صورتی خوب خواهد شدن، و قوّت طبیعی اندر آن کودك است صورت زشت همی‌یابد.

[§۱۷:۸۴] و نیز قوّت تمییز که روحانی است خدمت خویش فرماید مر قوّتهای طبیعی را، مر هریکی را بر مقدار او، چنانك مر چشم را دیدن فرماید، و مر گوش را شنیدن فرماید، و مر بینی را بوییدن فرماید، و کام را چشیدن و دست را بسودن.

[§۱۸:۸۴] و این هرپنج قوّت برمثال بندگان فرمان‌برداران هرچه یابند[9] از چیزها هریکی براستی پیش قوّت ممیّزه برد و عرضه کند؛ و قوّت ممیّزه چنانك خواهد مر آن سخن را عبارت کند.

[§۱۹:۸۴] اگر خواهد مر طلخ را شیرین گوید و سپید را سیاه کند و دیگر چیزها را کی این قوّتها سوی او برده باشند چنانك مراد او باشد بگوید، و قوّتهای طبیعی خدمت نتواند فرمودن مر قوّت روحانی را.

[§۲۰:۸۴] پس اگر قوّت طبیعی را نزدیك قوّت روحانی خطری بودی همچنان ایشان مر او را خدمت خویش فرمودندی.

[§۲۱:۸۴] و چون خدمت فرمای مر قوّت روحانی را یافتیم و خدمتکار مر قوّت طبیعی را یافتیم، دانستیم که مر قوّت روحانی را پادشاهی است بر قوّت طبیعی.[10]

---

۸ ¦⟵برگ [اس:۱۱۵-ب].

۹ ¦⟵برگ [ایا:۱۰۷-ب].

۱۰ ایا: + و السّلام.

صف هشتاد و پنجم

سخن اندر آنك آفریده به آفریننده نماند

[§۸۵:۱] اگر هیچ چیز از آفریده بآفریننده مانستی، واجب آمدی کی آن چیز، نه از چیز، چیزی توانستی کردن چنانك ایزد تعالی.

[§۸۵:۲] و چیزی کی مر او را به چیزی دیگر ماننده نباشد، فروماند از کردن فعلی مانند فعل آن چیز کزو برتر است، ای مانند بدو.

[§۸۵:۳] و دلیل بر درستی این قول آن است کی نفسِ ستور را مانندی نیست به نفس مردم، از آنچ نفس مردم سخنگوی است و نفس ستور سخنگوی نیست.

[§۸۵:۴] لاجرم مرد صناعتها کند گوناگون کی ستور از آن فرومانده است،[1] و هیچ روی از رویها بنتواند[2] همی گرد صنعت گشتن و نه بر آن محیط شدن، بدان سبب کی نفس مردم را به نفس ستور ماننده نیست.

[§۸۵:۵] پس اگر هیچ آفریده را به آفریدگار حقّ ماننده بودی، بتوانستی[3] نه از چیزی چیزی کردن و پدید آوردن.

[§۸۵:۶] و چون هیچ چیز نمی‌یابیم از لطیف و کثیف کی او نه از چیزی چیزی توانست پدید آوردن، و نیز هیچ کس واقف نتوانست شدن بر چگونگی پدید آوردن چیزی نه از چیز، دانستیم که هیچ چیز از لطیف و کثیف ماننده نیست به مُبدِع حقّ به هیچ رویی[4] از رویها. [فَـ]تَعٰالَی اللّٰهُ الْمَلِكُ الْحَقُّ[5] الْمُبِینُ.[6]

---

۱ ¦⟵برگ [اس:۱۱۶-الف].

۲ اس: [«بسواند» مخدوش است]؛ ایا: نتواند. || تصحیح قیاسی.

۳ اس، ایا: نتوانستی.

۴ ایا: روی.

۵ سورة طه (۲۰)، آیت ۱۱۴؛ و سورة المؤمنون (۲۳)، آیت ۱۱۶.

۶ نیز نك:سورة النُّور (۲۴)، آیت ۲۵: یَوْمَئِذٍ یُوَفِّیهِمُ اللّٰهُ دِینَهُمُ الْحَقَّ وَ یَعْلَمُونَ أَنَّ اللّٰهَ هُوَ الْحَقُّ الْمُبِینُ. || ¦⟵برگ [ایا:۱۰۸-الف].

صف هشتاد و ششم

سخن اندر سبب تأیید پیوستن به مؤیّدان

[§۸۶:۱] تأیید به نفس مردم پیوسته نشود مگر به عمل و علم. و هرگاه کی مردم عمل شریعت نکند و علم را از راه عمل اندرنپذیرد، بازماند از پذیرفتن تأیید و از رسیدن به درجهٔ مؤیّدان. مردم به عمل بیرون آید از حد قوّت به حدّ فعل.

[§۸۶:۲] برمثال بیرون آمدن چیزهای طبیعی از حدّ قوّت به حدّ فعل، به دو چیز، کی آن هردو مانندهاند به عمل و علم، چنانك سیبی کی بر درخت خویش از حدّ قوّت بفعل بیرون خواهد آمدن مادّت بایدش پذیرفتن از طبایع از راه درختِ خویش. و هر روز به پذیرفتن آن مادّت شکل او و رنگ او همی‌گردد.

[§۸۶:۳] و آن پذیرفتن مادّت مر او را از طبایع، به میانجیِ درخت، مانَنده است به عملی کی مردم کند از شریعت به میانجی خداوندان شریعت. و چون آن سیب از عمل همی پذیرد وزان بازنایستد[۱] چون عمل به آخر رسید مر آن سیب را بوی خوش و رنگ نیکو و مزهٔ شیرین یابد که آن بوی و رنگ و[۲] مزه مر او را مانَنده است به علمی کی مردم آن را بیابد، به میانجیِ آن عمل کی کند.

[§۸۶:۴] پس آن سیب بدین دو حال کی یکی مانندهٔ عمل است و دیگر مانندهٔ علم است از حدّ قوّت به حدّ فعل رسد. اگر اندر میانه کی آن سیب از طبایع مادّت همی‌پذیرد که آن مر او را عمل است،[۳] از پذیرفتن مادّت و از ماندنِ[۴] سببی از اسباب[۵] تباه شود و از درخت خویش بیوفتد، و به رنگ و بوی و مزه نرسد، که آن

---

۱ اس، ایا: بازنه ایستد.

۲ اس: – و.

۳ ¦⟵برگ [اس:۱۱۶-ب].

۴ ایا: – و از ماندن | + به: [...از پذیرفتن مادّت به سببی از اسباب بازماند تباه شود و از درخت خویش بیوفتد...].

۵ ایا: + بازماند.

مر او را به مرتبت[۶] علم است. پس همچنین کسی کی او از عمل شریعت بازایستد به علم آن نرسد از تأیید دور ماند.

[§۵:۸۶] و دلیلی گوییم دیگر بر حال پیوستن تأیید را به مؤیّدان و گوییم کی روشنایی چشم نکند جز اندر چشم درست کی آن از عیب و درد و بیماری پاك باشد. همچنین تأیید کی او مانند روشنایِیِ چشم است نپیوندد[۷] جز به کسی کی عمل او و علم پاکیزه باشد.[۸] و نفس او شسته باشد به آب عمل و علم از آلایشهای طبیعی. و این بیانی شافی است[۹] خردمندان را.[۱۰]

۶ ایا: بمنزلت.

۷ اس، ایا: نه پیوندد.

۸ ¦←برگ [ایا:۱۰۸-ب].

۹ ایا: + مر.

۱۰ ایا: + و السّلام.

صف هشتاد و هفتم

سخن اندر آنك شهادتِ لاٰ إِلٰهَ إِلاَّ اللّٰهُ کلید بهشت است[1]

[§۱:۸۷] آگاه باشید ای برادران که ایزد تعالی مر همه آفریدگان را به کلمه خویش آفرید. و کلمه مُبدِع حقّ از یافتن پنهان است و اندر صفتی از صفتها نیاید.

[§۲:۸۷] ازبهرآنك وی آفرینش محض است، و آن چیز کردنِ چیز باشد نه از چیز. و این فضیلت اندر چیزی از چیزها نه یابند تا مر خلق را کلمه مُبدِع حقّ حاصل شدی، کی آن بهشت است بحقیقت.

[§۳:۸۷] و چهار حرف کلمه شهادت بجملگی کلید بهشت است. و آن دلیل است بر چهار اصل روحانی و جسمانی که پایداری دو عالم علوی و سفلی بدیشان است.

[§۴:۸۷] پس گوییم که نخست عقل کلید است مر همه هستهای روحانی و جسمانی را.

[§۵:۸۷] ازبهرآنك عقل با کلمه مبدع یك چیز است و همه هستها را هستی از کلمه مُبدِع حقّ است.

[§۶:۸۷] و نفس کلّ کلید است مر همه چیزهای ترکیبی را به مقدارِ بهر خویش از کلمه.

[§۷:۸۷] ازبهرآنك چیزها را که مر او را نظم و تألیف است زیر وهم نشاید آوردن مگر به صورت کردن مر آن را اندر نفس لطیف.

۱ قس: کتاب الینابیع، الینبوع الثلاثون (۳۰): في معنی الشهادة، ص ۷۰ تا ۷۳. || نیز قس: الملیجی، المجالس المستَنصِریَّة، المجلس الرابع: تأویل 'لاٰ إِلٰهَ إِلاَّ اللّٰهُ'، تأویل جزء من سورة الحمد، ص۳۶ تا ۴۰.

[§۸:۸۷] پس پیدا آمد کی نخست چیزهای ترکیبی و تألیفی اندر نفس‌کلّی بوده است[۲] پیش از پدید آمدن.

[§۹:۸۷] و نفس‌کلّی بگشاید مر همه چیزهای ترکیبی را تا پدید آمد به گشایش او. پس او کلید مرکبات است.

[§۱۰:۸۷] و سخن کی پیغامبران، علیهم‌السّلام، بر آن پادشا بودند کلید همه سیاستها است.

[§۱۱:۸۷] نبینی[۳] مردم، کی سخن گفتن عام مر او را بود، پاسبان و سالار همه جانوران گشت.

[§۱۲:۸۷] و پیغامبران، علیهم‌السّلام، کی سخن گفتن خاص کی آن کلام الٓهی بود مر ایشان را بود، ایشان پاسبان و سالار خلق گشتند.

[§۱۳:۸۷] پس درست شد کی سخن کلید سیاستها است، و سخن پیامبران کلید است مر همه الفاظ منطقی را کی بدان عبارت کردند فضیلتهای[۴] عقلانی و نفسانی را، و بدان خبر دادند از صورت هر دو عالم و از بودنیهای فلکی. و به ناطق گشاده شد دَرِ نگاه‌داشت خلق از راه شریعت کی بقوّت کلمه مُبدِع حقّ[۵] مر آن را بنهاد.

[§۱۴:۸۷] و وصیّ کلید بود مر همه معنیهای پوشیده را، که بدو گشاده و آراسته شده بود از علم لطیف اندر مثالهای[۶] کثیف.

[§۱۵:۸۷] و ترکیب نفس به عقل از راه تأویل اساس پدید آمد.

[§۱۶:۸۷] پس اساس کلید بود مر حقیقتهای ترکیب نفس را و تألیف ناطق را.

---

۲ ¦⟵برگ [اس:۱۱۷-الف].

۳ اس، ایا: نه بینی.

۴ ¦⟵برگ [ایا:۱۰۹-الف].

۵ ایا: – حق.

۶ ایا: مثلهای.

[§۸۷:۱۷] ازبهر آنك حاصل آن ترکیب نفس کلّی مر جسم مردم را تمام شدن نفس سخنگوی بود.

[§۸۷:۱۸] و تمامیِ نفس سخنگوی اندر تأویل بود و خداوند تأویل اساس بود.

[§۸۷:۱۹] و حاصل آن تأویل ناطق مر شریعت و کتاب را معنیهای آن بود تا به نفسهای جزوی رسد.

[§۸۷:۲۰] و آن معنیها از راه تأویل اساس همی‌رسد به نفسهای جزوی.

[§۸۷:۲۱] پس درست شد کی اساس کلید بود مر حقیقت ترکیبی و تألیفی را.

[§۸۷:۲۲] و گوییم کی لا از شهادت چون دندانهٔ کلید بهشت است، و دندانهٔ فکر و تمییز است، و فکر اندیشه باشد، و تمییز جدا کردن چیز باشد از چیز.

[§۸۷:۲۳] و لا دو حرف است نیمهٔ حَرف اللّٰه کی آن دندانهٔ عقل است مر کلید بهشت را.

[§۸۷:۲۴] ازبهر آنك اللّٰه چهار حرف است و لا کلمه نفی است و اللّٰه کلمه اثبات است دلیل است مر نفس ممیّزه [را].[۷]

[§۸۷:۲۵] و بدو نیم کرد مر آن عالم را کز عقل به ناطق پیوسته شد، و جدا کرد مر نیمهٔ ظاهر را از نیمهٔ باطن و تنزیل را از تأویل جدا کرد.

[§۸۷:۲۶] و ‹قوّت مفکّره›[۸] حاجتمند شد به نفی کردن تشبیه از توحید ناطق.

[§۸۷:۲۷] و عقل بدو نیم نکرد مر آن را که مُبدِع حقّ اندر او بنهاد. بل کی[۹] مر آن را[۱۰] بغایت تمامی بیرون داد به چهار حرف اللّٰه.

---

۷ تصحیح قیاسی.

۸ ایا: قوة مفکّره [حرف «ک» در «مفکّره» مخدوش است].

۹ ایا: بلك.

۱۰ ¦⟵برگ [اس:۱۱۷-ب].

[§۸۷:۲۸] و چهار تمامی شمار است ازبهرآنك شمار از چهار مرتبت نگذرد چون آحاد و عشرات و مائین و الوف.

[§۸۷:۲۹] و عقل اثبات کرد صانع حقّ را چون مقرّ شد به مُبدعی او، راست، کی کلمه اللّٰه از اثبات است.

[§۸۷:۳۰] و اله دندانهٔ ناطق[۱۱] است ازبهرآنك ناطق اندر عالم خلیفه[۱۲] عقل است بدانچ گفتار ناطق مخالف[۱۳] عقل نیست.

[§۸۷:۳۱] و کلمه اله بیك حرف از کلمه اللّٰه کمتر است و آن لام است و معنیش[۱۴] آن است کی ناطق[۱۵] نیافت مر آن تمامی را کی عقل یافت.

[§۸۷:۳۲] و ناطق[۱۶] خداوند سه مرتبت است چون رسالت و وصایت و امامت.

[§۸۷:۳۳] و الّا دندانهٔ نفس است. و کلمه استثنا است اعنی دوتای کردن سخن و دلیل است بر آنك نفس [(التالی)] [مانند] [الـ]سابق [(عقل)] است. اعنی پیش دست است اندر باب پیدا کردن هستهای جسمانی [نه اندر باب هستهای] روحانی.[۱۷]

---

۱۱ اس، ایا: نطق [كذا]. || تصحیح قیاسی. نك: یادداشت (۱۳) ذیل.
۱۲ اس، ایا: خلاف [كذا]. || تصحیح قیاسی. نك: یادداشت (۱۳) ذیل.
۱۳ اس، ایا: بظاهر موافق [كذا]. || تصحیح قیاسی. نك: کتاب الینابیع، ص۷۲، بند (۱۴۱)، س ۷ تا ۱۰: و(إله) شطرية الناطق، إذ هو خليفة السابق في العالم الجسماني. وفي (إله) نقصان حرف واحد من (اللّٰه) وهو (لام). على أن الناطق لم ينل التمامية كما نالها السابق، وهو صاحب المراتب الثلاث من الرسالة والوصاية والإمامة.
۱۴ ¦←برگ [ایا:۱۰۹-ب].
۱۵ اس، ایا: نطق [كذا]. || تصحیح قیاسی. نك: یادداشت (۱۳) فوق.
۱۶ اس، ایا: نطق [كذا]. || تصحیح قیاسی. نك: یادداشت (۱۳) فوق.
۱۷ تصحیح قیاسی. قس: کتاب الینابیع، الينبوع الثلاثون (۳۰)، ص۷۲، بند (۱۴۱)، س ۱۰ تا ۱۲: و(إلّا) شطرية التالي، وهي كلمة الاستثناء، على أن التالي مثل السابق في إظهار الأيسيات الجسمانية، لا في باب الأيسيات الروحانية.

[§۳۴:۸۷] و این چهار کلمه رهنمای‌اند[۱۸] بر چهار اصل کی چون مر آن را بهم فرازآری همه درهای کلمه ایزد گشاده شود.

[§۳۵:۸۷] و نیز کلید مر در بسته را بذات خویش نگشاید، مگر به گشایندهٔ فهم، کی هیچ کس جاکول نتواند شدن به مرتبت چهار اصل، کی ایشان کلید و کلمه مُبدِع حقّ‌اند، مگر به میانجی حدّی چون امام یا حجّت یا داعی.

[§۳۶:۸۷] و بر کلید دندانه‌ای[۱۹] نباشد کی بدو در گشاده شود تا همه دندانه‌ها بهم نباشد.

[§۳۷:۸۷] همچنین اگر دلیل منکر شود بیك مرتبت ازین چهار مرتبت، چون اصلین و اساسین، ممکن نباشد کی جوینده را چیزی گشاده شود از کار دین.

[§۳۸:۸۷] و هرچند جهد کند به گشادن در، جز رنج مر او را چیزی بحاصل نیاید. همچنانك چون از کلید دندانه‌ای[۲۰] کم باشد جهد گشاینده سود ندارد.

[§۳۹:۸۷] وگر بی دندانه بسیار بجنباند بنای کلیدان از جای ببرد و مراد او برنیاید.

[§۴۰:۸۷] پس، ازین معنی گفتند کی لَا إِلٰهَ إِلاَّ اللّٰهُ کلید بهشت است. و این بیانی شافی و برهانی روشن است مر مؤمن مخلص را.[۲۱]

---

۱۸ اس: ره‌نمای‌اند.

۱۹ اس، ایا: دندانهء.

۲۰ اس، ایا: دندانهء.

۲۱ ایا: + و السّلام.

صف هشتاد و هشتم

سخن اندر پاداش نیکی و بدی

[§۸۸:۱] گوییم به رحمت خداوند حقّ کو بر ما فروباریده است، کی پاداش معیّن است[۱] مر جزای کاری کی کسی بکند اگر نیك، نیك و اگر[۲] بد، بد.

[§۸۸:۲] و چون امروز اندر این عالم پاداش آنچ مردم بکند از نیك و بد همی بدو نرسد،[۳] دلیل همی‌باشد بر آنك مر وعده را همی مانْد رسیدنِ پاداش به هر کسی، چنانك خدای تعالی همی‌گوید، قوله:[۴] قُلْ لَکُمْ مِیعٰادُ یَوْمٍ لاٰ تَسْتَأْخِرُونَ[۵] عَنْهُ سٰاعَةً وَ لاٰ تَسْتَقْدِمُونَ.[۶] همی‌گوید: «مر شما[۷] را وعده است به روزی کی شما را از آن زپستر نتوانید شدن و نه پیشتر».

[§۸۸:۳] و چون این حال بدانستیم کی پاداش نیك و بد مر وعدهٔ خدای را مانده است، گوییم کی بازماندن کاری کردنی از وقتی تا به وقتی دیگر جز به علّتی نباشد.

[§۸۸:۴] و علّت بازماندن کارِ کردنی جز نقصان لازم نیاید. ازبهر آنك بازماندن و نقصان هر دو شکل یکدیگرند.

[§۸۸:۵] و روا نباشد کی علّت بازپس ماندنِ کارِ کردنی تمامی باشد کی آن متناقض باشد.

---

۱ ¦⟵برگ [اس:۱۱۸-الف].
۲ ایا: و گر.
۳ ایا: برسد.
۴ ایا: + تعالی.
۵ اس: ىستاخِرونَ؛ ایا: یَستأخرون.
۶ اس: ىستَقدِمُونَ؛ ایا: یَستَقدِمُون. || سورة سَبَأ (۳۴)، آیت ۳۰.
۷ ¦⟵برگ [ایا:۱۱۰-الف].

[§۸۸:۶] و چون حال معلوم گشت بدانستیم کی این پاداش از خدای نخواهد بُدَن مر خلق را، که اندر او نقصان روا باشد.

[§۸۸:۷] و آن پاداش نه از عقل باشد که او را غایت کمال باشد.

[§۸۸:۸] و چون پاداش جز مر نفس مردم را نبود، دانستیم کی آن جز از نفس کلّی نیست کی همی پاداش خواهد دادن.

[§۸۸:۹] و چون مر نفس مردم را از آغاز پیدا شدن اندر این عالم ناقص یافتیم و او آثار نفس کلّی بود، دانستیم کی این نقصان اندر اصل مردم بوده است کی آن نفس کلّی است تا اندر آثار او کی نفوس جزوی است چنین نقصان رونده گشت.

[§۸۸:۱۰] و چون نقصان اندر نفس کلّی ازین روی ظاهر گشت گوا آمد ازین حال بر آن قول کی گفتیم اندر این فصل کی بازماندن کاری کردنی را علّت نقصانی باشد.

[§۸۸:۱۱] پس آن نقصان اندر نفس کلّی است کی پاداش ازو به خلق به وقت تمام شدن آن نقصان رسد.

[§۸۸:۱۲] و تمامیِ او اندر بحاصل شدن خداوند قیامت است علیه افضل التحیّة و السّلام.

[§۸۸:۱۳] و چون علّت تأخیر پاداش بازگفتیم و خداوند پاداش را دانستیم، گوییم کی پاداش مر نیکوکاران را بر سه گونه باشد.[۸]

[§۸۸:۱۴] براندازهٔ کار او باشد راستا راست ‹نه بیش و نه کم›.[۹] چنانك خدای تعالی

---

۸ ¦⟵برگ [اس:۱۱۸-ب].

۹ ایا: نه کم و نه بیش.

میگوید، قوله:[۱۰] هَلْ جَزٰاءُ الْإِحْسٰانِ إِلاّٰ الْإِحْسٰانُ.[۱۱] همی‌گوید، بر سبیل سؤال: «کی مکافات نیکویی نیست جز نیکویی؟».

[§۸۸:۱۵] و نمی‌گوید کی زیادتی دهم بر نیکویی. و این از خدای تعالی عدل است.

[§۸۸:۱۶] و یا بیش از آن باشد کی نیکوکار سزاوار آن باشد. چنانك خدای تعالی همی‌گوید، قوله: مَنْ جٰاءَ بِالْحَسَنَةِ فَلَهُ عَشْرُ أَمْثٰالِهٰا.[۱۲] همی‌گوید: «هرکه بیارد نیکویی مر او را است[۱۳] ده‌چندان».

[§۸۸:۱۷] و دیگر جای گفت، قوله:[۱۴] لَنَجْزِيَنَّهُمْ أَجْرَهُمْ بِأَحْسَنِ مٰا كٰانُوا يَعْمَلُونَ.[۱۵] همی گوید: «ما جزا دهیم مزد کار[۱۶] نیکوکاری که ایشان کرده باشند». و جزا دادن کارها بر حکم نیکوکاری کی مکافات راستا راست است، بل‌کی[۱۷] آن فضل از خدای تعالی باشد.

[§۸۸:۱۸] و سدیگر پاداش آن باشد کی آن نه بر قیاس نیکویی باشد کی همی چنان مر او را بدهند یا از آن بیشتر. بل‌کی[۱۸] مر آن مکافات را بر آن کردار قیاسی [ذ]باشد،[۱۹] چنانك خدای تعالی میفرماید، قوله:[۲۰] فَأُولٰئِكَ يَدْخُلُونَ الْجَنَّةَ يُرْزَقُونَ

۱۰ ایا: + تعالی.
۱۱ سورة الرحمٰن (۵۵)، آیت ۶۰.
۱۲ سورة الأنعام (۶)، آیت ۱۶۰.
۱۳ ¦⟵برگ [ایا:۱۱۰-ب].
۱۴ ایا: + تعالی.
۱۵ سورة النحل (۱۶)، آیت ۹۷.
۱۶ ایا: – کار.
۱۷ ایا: بلك.
۱۸ ایا: بلك.
۱۹ اس، ایا: باشد. || تصحیح قیاسی.
۲۰ ایا: + تعالی.

فِيهٰا بِغَيْرِ حِسٰابٍ.[۲۱] همی‌گوید: «آن گروه را به بهشت اندر آرند[۲۲] روزی دهندشان اندر او بی‌شمار». و این از خدای تعالی بر خلق منّت باشد.

[§۸۸:۱۹] و مر بدکرداران را هم بدین مرتبه‌ها پاداش وعده کرد.

[§۸۸:۲۰] گروهی را به بدی وعده کرد راستا راست؛ چنانك فرمود، قوله:[۲۳] وَ جَزٰاءُ سَيِّئَةٍ سَيِّئَةٌ مِثْلُهٰا.[۲۴] گفت: «مکافات بدی بدی است همچنان».

[§۸۸:۲۱] مر گروهی را گفت:[۲۵] فَلَنُذِيقَنَّ الَّذِينَ كَفَرُوا عَذٰاباً شَدِيداً وَ لَنَجْزِيَنَّهُمْ أَسْوَأَ الَّذِي كٰانُوا يَعْمَلُونَ.[۲۶] گفت: «بچشانـ[یـ]م[۲۷] مر کافران را عذابی سخت و جزا دهیمشان به بدتر کاری کی ایشان کرده باشند».

[§۸۸:۲۲] و گروهی را گفت، قوله: أُولٰئِكَ الَّذِينَ لَعَنَهُمُ اللّٰهُ وَ مَنْ يَلْعَنِ اللّٰهُ فَلَنْ تَجِدَ لَهُ نَصِيراً.[۲۸] گفت: «آن گروه آنند کی خدای مر ایشان را لعنت کرد و هر کی خدای مر او را لعنت کند تو مر او را یاریگری[۲۹] نیابی».

[§۸۸:۲۳] و دلیل بر این مراتب میان عالم و متعلم بتوانی یافتن[۳۰] کی متعلم از عالم چیزی بپرسد، عالم مر او را جواب دهد. و این جزای راستا راست[۳۱] باشد.[۳۲]

[§۸۸:۲۴] و چون بر جواب این سؤال چیزی دیگر بگوید، کی او را بدان رهنمون

۲۱ سورة غافر (۴۰)، آیت ۴۰.
۲۲ ایا: + و.
۲۳ ایا: + تعالی.
۲۴ سورة الشوری (۴۲)، آیت ۴۰.
۲۵ ایا: + قوله تعالی.
۲۶ سورة فُصِّلَت (۴۱)، آیت ۲۷.
۲۷ اس: بچشانم.
۲۸ سورة النساء (۴)، آیت ۵۲.
۲۹ اس، ایا: یاری گری.
۳۰ ایا: یافت.
۳۱ ¦⟵برگ [اس:۱۱۹-الف].
۳۲ ایا: است.

باشد بر چیزی دیگر،[۳۳] و آن از عالم فضل باشد بر متعلم کی او را طاقت به رسیدن آن نباشد، آن منّت باشد از عالم بر متعلم.

[§۸۸:۲۵] چنانك خدای تعالی گفت اندر قصّهٔ سلیمان، علیه‌السّلام، که او امام زمانه بود. مر او را گفت، قوله: هٰذٰا عَطٰاؤُنٰا فَامْنُنْ أَوْ أَمْسِكْ بِغَیْرِ حِسٰابٍ.[۳۴] گفت: «این عطای ما است»، و بدان مر تأیید را خواست، کی به امام پیوسته باشد، پس گفت: «منّت نهْ، اگر بازدارْ، بی‌شماری».

[§۸۸:۲۶] و آنك او پادشا شود بر منّت نهادن، و آن گرفتن علم امام باشد، ازبهرآنك این دو کناره است مر علم را: یك کناره‌اش[۳۵] آن است کی ناپرسیده بگوید و ناخواسته بدهد.

[§۸۸:۲۷] و دیگر کناره‌اش[۳۶] آن است کی اگر بپرسد نگوید[۳۷] وگر بخواهد ندهد،[۳۸] و بازدارد از آن کس کی سزاوار آن نباشد.

[§۸۸:۲۸] و میانهٔ این دو طرف آن است کی چون پرسند بگوید و این مراتب جز مر امام حقّ را نباشد.

[§۸۸:۲۹] و پیوستن تأیید پیامبران، علیهم‌السّلام، از خدای تعالی منّت است.

[§۸۸:۳۰] ازبهرآنك هیچ کس را طاقت طلب کردن پیامبری نباشد چه آن مراتب را به جهد نتوان یافتن و آن منّت خدای باشد.

[§۸۸:۳۱] چنانك ایزد تعالی همی حکایت کند از گروهی از پیامبران که در بنی‌اسرائیل بُدَند، قوله: قٰالَتْ لَهُمْ رُسُلُهُمْ إِنْ نَحْنُ إِلاّٰ بَشَرٌ مِثْلُکُمْ وَ لٰکِنَّ اللّٰهَ یَمُنُّ

---

۳۳ اس: + بکوید کی او را.

۳۴ سورة ص (۳۸)، آیت ۳۹. || ←|برگ [ایا:۱۱۱-الف].

۳۵ اس: کناره‌ش.

۳۶ اس: کناره‌ش.

۳۷ اس، ایا: بگوید [کذا]. || تصحیح قیاسی.

۳۸ اس، ایا: بدهد [کذا]. || تصحیح قیاسی.

عَلیٰ مَنْ یَشٰاءُ مِنْ عِبٰادِهِ.[۳۹] گفت: «مر این بنی‌اسرائیل را پیامبران گفتند ما هستیم مگر مردی همچون شما و لیکن خدای منت نهد بر هرکه خواهد از بندگان خویش».

[§۳۲:۸۸] این است مرتبه‌های پاداش کی یاد کرده آمد نیك را نیك و بد را بد.

[§۳۳:۸۸] ایزد تعالی ما را نیکی دهاد تا سزاوار مکافات نیکی شویم.

۳۹ سورة ابراهیم (۱۴)، آیت ۱۱.

صف هشتاد و نهم

سخن اندر فرق میان ازل و ازلیّت و ازلی

[§۸۹:۱] بباید دانستن کی ازلی مر چیزی را گویند[۱] کی او را آغاز نباشد و ابدی مر چیزی را گویند کی او را انجام نباشد.

[§۸۹:۲] و چون گویی ازل[۲] و ازلیّت و ازلی مثال آن به نزدیك گردانیدن و همچنان باید کی گویی آتش و آتشی و آتشین.

[§۸۹:۳] و آتش آن است کی او از عالم کنارهٔ زبرین گرفته است و صفت او گرم و خشك است از طبایع.[۳]

[§۸۹:۴] و آتشی آن است کی آتش بدان معنی از دیگر چیزها جداست بر آن روی کی آن معنی جز آتش را نیست، و مر آن را از آتش جدا [نـ]یابند.[۴] و آن معنی را فصل خوانند اندر حدود منطق.

[§۸۹:۵] و آن برمثال وحدت است کی آن جز مر واحد را نیست، مر او را از واحد جدا نیابند. واحد به وحدت از اِثنَین[۵] و اِثْنَتَین[۶] جدا است.

[§۸۹:۶] و آتشین چیزی را گویند کی او را از آتش کرده باشند. و آن صورتی باشد از آتش محض کرده چنانك صورتی کنند از چوب و مر او را چوبین گویند.

---

۱ ¦⟵برگ [اس:۱۱۹-ب].

۲ اس، ایا: ازلی [کذا]. || تصحیح قیاسی.

۳ قس: جامع الحمکتین، فصل ۱۷: اندر ازل و دیمومت و خلود و ابد، ص ۱۸۷ تا ۱۹۱؛ رساله در جواب ۹۱ فقره اسئله، ص ۵۷۹ تا ۵۸۱.

۴ اس، ایا: یابند [کذا]. || تصحیح قیاسی. ||¦⟵برگ [ایا:۱۱۱-ب].

۵ اس: اثس \ اثمس [در نسخهٔ اس دستخط کاتب بسیار مُغلَق است]؛ ایا: آتش. || تصحیح قیاسی.

۶ اس: اثسں؛ ایا: آتشین. || تصحیح قیاسی.

[§۷:۸۹] و اکنون چون مثال نمودیم از محسوسات اندر معنی ازل و ازلیّت و ازلی گوییم.

[§۸:۸۹] که ازل ابداع است محض کی از مُبدِع حقّ پدید آمد بی هیچ علّتی، و مر او را آغاز نبود ازبهر آنك آغازِ چیز علّت او باشد. و چون ابداع علّتِ همه علّتها بود خود او آغاز بود، مر آغاز را آغاز لازم نیاید. و مر او را امر خوانند[۷] و کلمه خوانند.[۸] و این نام مر او را لازم آمد از بهرِ وی آغازیِ او.

[§۹:۸۹] و ازلیّت مر آن بهره را باید دانستن کی عقل اوّل از کلمه باری سبحانه[۹] بود.[۱۰] آن بهر، بهر بزرگ است، و هویّت عقل بدان بهره اشارت پذیرفت، وز آنچ فرود ازو پدید آمد ازبهر جدا شد. پس آن بهرۀ ازلیّت است.

[§۱۰:۸۹] امّا ازلی خود عقل است کی ازل بی‌میانجی بدو پیوسته است. و هیچ چیز دیگر را این خاصگی نبود و نخواهد بودن به امر باری کی مر عقل را است.

---

۷ اس: خوانید.

۸ اس: خوانید.

۹ ایا: – سبحانه.

۱۰ اس: بد.

صف نودم

سخن اندر اثبات قیامت[1]

[§۹۰:۱] خردمند کی اندر تدبیر طبیعت بنگردی، بیندی بیرون آوردن اشخاص را که ایشان نَه جزواند از عالم، چون معادن و نبات و حیوان از امّهات.[2]

[§۹۰:۲] از پیوستن نفس به امّهات، بداند کی آنچ ازین زایشها همی پدید آید، نه بقوّت عالم است، و از ذات او است.

[§۹۰:۳] ازبهرآنك نیابد اندر امّهات، که ایشان اصلهای عالم‌اند چون آتش و باد و آب و خاك، آن چیزها کی اندر زایشها یابد، کی ایشان شاخهای عالم‌اند، چون گوشت و استخوان و رگ و پی و جز آن.

[§۹۰:۴] پس بداند که این چیزها به یارىِ چیزی دیگر بحاصل آید اندر این زایشها که آن اندر اصلها نبود.

[§۹۰:۵] و معلوم او شد کی نفس کلّی قادرتر از هیولی[3] و صورت است، و از بیرون آوردن طبیعت، کی آن علّت گرمی و خشکی و سردی و تری است.

[§۹۰:۶] ازبهرآنك مر طبایع چهارگانه را اندر هیولی و صورت یابد نهاده و همه جمله یك جسم گشته.

[§۹۰:۷] پس هیولی و صورت به فرازآوردن این طبیعت اندر خویشتن سزاوارتر از آن نیست کی[4] گوید طبایع چهارگانه مر هیولی و صورت فرازآورد و بخویشتن کشید.

---

۱ قس: کتاب الینابیع، الینبوع السادس والثلاثون (۳۶): في رتبة صاحب القیامة، ص۸۲ تا ۸۵.

۲ ¦←برگ [اس:۱۲۰-الف].

۳ ¦←برگ [ایا:۱۱۲-الف].

۴ اس: [کلمه «کی» بالای خط نوشته شده است].

[§۸:۹۰] و چون این شش چیز یکی سزاوارتر از دیگری نیست بجمله کردنِ این پنج چیز، ناچاره قاهری باید که ایشان همه فرازآورده و مقهور او باشند. و آن فرازآورنده و قاهر نفس کلّ است کی ایزد تعالی این قدرت بدو بخشیده است.

[§۹:۹۰] و این حجّتی است از حجّتهای ایزد تعالی کی لازم آید بر خردمندان از اقرار دادن به یگانگی ایزد بی همتا.

[§۱۰:۹۰] ازبهر آنك چون از اصلی نشد[۵] به فرعی پدیدآمده[۶] و اندر فرع چیزی یابند کی اندر اصل او مر آن را نیابند، بدانند کی آن چیز را اندر آن فرع، آن کس پدید آورده بود.

[§۱۱:۹۰] پس گوییم که تمامی آشکارا شدن کلمه باری سبحانه به خداوند قیامت باید و هرچیزی را پیش از هست شدن و یافتن، هست به رویی از رویها.

[§۱۲:۹۰] و لکن مر عقل اوّل را، پیش از ابداع،[۷] کو نیستی است، یافتن نیست.

[§۱۳:۹۰] و همچنین بدین منزلت پیدا شود منزلت پیامبران، علیهم السّلام، و شرف ایشان ازبهر آنك ایشان به هستی آوردند مر سخنان گردندهٔ شایسته را — کی آن به میان سخنگویان شناخته بود[۸] — به گزید،[۹] کزو[۱۰] سخن مردمان از آن حکمتها خالی بود.

[§۱۴:۹۰] پس ایشان، علیهم السّلام، فرازآوردند مر آن سخنان را به توفیق نفس کلّی،

---

۵ اس: بسد؛ ایا: نشد.

۶ ایا: آمد.

۷ اس: بداع.

۸ ¦⟵برگ [اس:۱۲۰-ب].

۹ اس: بکرید؛ ایا: بکربدند. || تصحیح قیاسی. نك: دهخدا: گزیدن. [گُ دَ] ... (از «گز» + «یدن» = پسوند مصدری) پهلوی، ویچیتن (انتخاب کردن، تعیین کردن).

۱۰ ایا: - کزو | + و.

و الهام نفس مر ایشان را، تا محیط شد آن سخنان کی ایشان، علیهم‌السّلام، تألیف کردند بر همه سخنان دیگر کز نفس‌کلّی اندر آن سخنان اثر نبود.

[§۹۰:۱۵] همچنان محیط شدنی کی مردم محیط شود بر عالم به یاریِ نفس‌کلّی، کی مر عالم را از نفس آن یاری نبود.

[§۹۰:۱۶] و پیامبران، علیهم‌السّلام، بدان سخنان از دو عالم، عالم روحانی و عالم جسمانی، حکایت کردند، و هر دو عالم بر درستیِ آن گوایی داد.

[§۹۰:۱۷] و پدید آوردند بخشها و حدها مر خلق را[11] اندر پایگه‌ها که پیش از آن اندر میان خلق آن نبود.

[§۹۰:۱۸] پس گوییم کی چون از پیامبران، علیهم‌السّلام، میان خلق[12] خبرها پیدا آمد از عدل و راستی، و حکمهای دنیاوی، وز خبرهای[13] عالم علوی، کی آن پیش از پیامبران، علیهم‌السّلام، اندر میان خلق موجود نبود. دانستیم کی آن چیزها مر پیامبران را، علیهم‌السّلام، آفرینندهٔ خلق آموخت؛ چنانك خدای تعالی گفت، قوله: وَ عَلَّمَكَ مٰا لَمْ تَكُنْ تَعْلَمُ وَ كٰانَ فَضْلُ اللّٰهِ عَلَيْكَ عَظِيماً.[14] گفت: «بیاموخت ترا آنچ ندانستی و فضل خدای بر تو بزرگ بود».

[§۹۰:۱۹] پس چون درست شد که آنچ اندر میان خلق نبود از پیامبران، علیهم‌السّلام، کی ایشان هم مردمان بودند، به یاریِ آفریدگار خلق پدید آمد، درست شد هستیِ قیامت آنك پیامبران، علیهم‌السّلام، خلق را دعوت بدو کردند.

[§۹۰:۲۰] و آن، آن روز بزرگ است کی اندر او برانگیخته شود نفسهای لطیف و صورتهای باطن آشکارا شود به آشکارا شدن خداوند قیامت، علی ذکره‌السّلام.

---

۱۱ ؛⟵برگ [ایا:۱۱۲-ب].
۱۲ ایا: – میان خلق.
۱۳ ایا: جیزهای.
۱۴ سورة النساء (۴)، آیت ۱۱۳.

[§۹۰:۲۱] از بهر آنك پیامبران که پیش از خداوند قیامت بیامدند شریعتها نهادند و پدید آوردند چیزی که بدان برانگیخته شد نفسهای جزوی از مرگّبی نادانی.

[§۹۰:۲۲] و پیش از ایشان نبود مر نفسها را آن انگیزش. چون کار بغایت رسید بدان ثواب بزرگ کی خدای تعالی وعده کرده بود، و صورتهای لطیف توانا شوند بر پذیرفتن فایده‌های عقلی[15] بی‌تألیف.

[§۹۰:۲۳] و لکن امروز مردم غافل است از آنچ مر او را اندر پیش است، از بزرگیِ آن روز و بلندیِ درجت آن حد، چنانك خدای تعالی همی گوید، قوله:[16] وَ مٰا أَرْسَلْنٰاكَ إِلاّٰ كَافَّةً لِلنّٰاسِ بَشِيراً وَ نَذِيراً وَ لٰكِنَّ أَكْثَرَ النّٰاسِ لاٰ يَعْلَمُونَ.[17] همی گوید: «و نفرستاد[یـ]م[18] ترا ای محمّد جز همه مردمان را مژده‌دهنده و بیم‌کننده و لکن بیشتر مردمان ندانند».

[§۹۰:۲۴] و اگر بنگرد مردم اندر حالها کی برو رفته شد از اوّل بودش او تا به آخر، به یقین شود کی او همی برانگیخته خواهد شدن، چنانك او از آن خبر ندارد امروز.

[§۹۰:۲۵] چنانك خدای تعالی همی‌گوید، قوله:[19] وَ نُنْشِئَكُمْ فِي مٰا لاٰ تَعْلَمُونَ * وَ لَقَدْ عَلِمْتُمُ النَّشْأَةَ الْأُولىٰ فَلَوْ لاٰ تَذَكَّرُونَ.[20] همی‌گوید: «شما را بیافریدیم اندر آنچ شما ندانید و دانستید آفرینش[21] نخستین را چرا یاد نکنید»؟ یعنی کی شما را چنان از حالی به حالی بردند کی خبر نداشتید.

---

۱۵ ¦⟵برگ [اس:۱۲۱-الف].
۱۶ ایا: + تعالی.
۱۷ سورة سَبَأ (۳۴)، آیت ۲۸.
۱۸ اس، ایا: نفرستادم.
۱۹ ایا: + تعالی.
۲۰ سورة الواقعة (۵۶)، آیات ۶۱ تا ۶۲.
۲۱ ¦⟵برگ [ایا:۱۱۳-الف].

[§۲۶:۹۰] و مردم از آغاز پدید آمدن تا به آخِر کار خویش همی گردد از حالی به حالی شریفتر تا بغایت خویش رسد.

[§۲۷:۹۰] از بهر آنك مردم از اوّل بودش خویش نطفه بود اندر پشت پدر خویش، و قوّت نامیه، یعنی زیادت شونده، بپذیرفت از بر آن حال.

[§۲۸:۹۰] و لکن آن قوّت موهوم بود مر کسی دیگر را که همی دانست که آن[۲۲] نطفه چه همی‌خواهد شدن اندر حال دیگر که اندر آن رحِم مادر افتد از آن حال کی هست.

[§۲۹:۹۰] و چون اندر رحِم مادر زیادت پذیرفت و اندامهاش راست شد مر پذیرفتن زندگانیِ طبیعی را، تا بدان شایسته شود مر پذیرفتن حس را، بی‌آنك اندر شکم مادر از حس خبر[۲۳] بود، یا ممکن بود مر او را واجب شدن بر چگونگی پیوستن حسّ بدو.

[§۳۰:۹۰] و هرچند کی او را از حس خبر نبود، پذیرفتن حس و رسیدن قوّت حس بدو[۲۴] موهوم بود نزدیك آن کس کی محیط بود بر حال او اندر حالی دیگر و وقتی دیگر.

[§۳۱:۹۰] و چون از شکم مادر بیرون آمد و به شکم این فلك رسید حس بدو پیوست همچنان‌کی[۲۵] آن دانا توهّم کرده بود.

[§۳۲:۹۰] و آن کودك کار بَستْ مر حواس خویش را اندر یافتن چیزهای محسوس[۲۶]

---

۲۲ ایا: از.

۲۳ ایا: حیز.

۲۴ ایا: – بدو.

۲۵ ایا: همچنانك.

۲۶ |⟵برگ [اس:۱۲۱-ب].

و گفتن مر آن یافته‌ها را به زفان با آن کسی کی اندررسیده بود حواس او بدان از دیدنیها و شنودنیها و بوییدنیها و[۲۷] چشیدنیها[۲۸] و بسودنیها.[۲۹]

[§۳۳:۹۰] و بدین چیزها کی اندریافت یاری یافت اندر یافتن و واقف شدن بر چیزهای حقیقی، و توهّم[۳۰] ازین عالم طبیعی به عالم علوی رسید.

[§۳۴:۹۰] پس چون ازین عالم نفس او بدان عالم روحانی رسید، پیوسته شد پادشاهیِ دایم و ثواب آلهی ابدی، و توانا گردد بر پذیرفتن فایده‌های آن عالم و غذا پذیرد از نعیم ابدی و راحت جاودانی.

[§۳۵:۹۰] جز کی دیدن او بحقیقت مر عالم روحانی را امروز کی نفس او به جسد پیوسته است نه ممکن است.

[§۳۶:۹۰] و لکن قبول او مر آن فایده‌ها را و دیدن او مر آن عالم روحانی را به وقت جدا شدن روح او از جسد او موهوم است و گمان برده است نزدیك آنك برو محیط است، محیط بودن آن خردمند بر آن کودك خرد و دانستن او کی چون[۳۱] کودك از شکم بیرون آید حس پذیرد بی‌آنك کودك را از آن خبر بود.

[§۳۷:۹۰] چون آن حال همچنان آمد کی آن خردمند اندیشیده بود و آن کودك حس[۳۲] بیافت، دانستیم گی آن حال همچنان خواهد بُدَنْ کی خداوندان شریعت گفتند، و نفس مردم مر عالم روحانی را پس از جدا شدن او از جسد بخواهد دیدن ناگاه، و نفس مردم از حال زندگانیِ طبیعی به زندگانی ابدی رسد بی‌هیچ زمان.

---

۲۷ ایا: [«و» مخدوش است].

۲۸ اس:چشدها؛ ایا: جشیدنیها.

۲۹ اس: بسودنیها؛ ایا: پسودنیها. || نك: دهخدا: پسودن. [پَ دَ] ... دست مالیدن. لمس کردن. دست زدن. ... ببسودن. ببساویدن. مَس. نیز نك: دهخدا: بسودن. [بِ دَ] ... پسودن. دست زدن و لمس کردن.

۳۰ ایا: و توهم.

۳۱ ¦⟵برگ [ایا:۱۱۳-ب].

۳۲ ایا: – حس.

[§۳۸:۹۰] برمثال کسی کز خواب به بیداری رسد بی هیچ درنگی. و فرقی عظیم است میان خواب و بیداری چنانك فرقی عظیم است میان زندگی[۳۳] طبیعی و میان زندگانیِ روحانی.

[§۳۹:۹۰] وگر تقصیر کرده باشد اندر کارهای آن جهانی خویشتن را پشیمانی یابد. چنانك خدای تعالی فرمود، قوله:[۳۴] وَ أَسَرُّوا النَّدٰامَةَ لَمّٰا رَأَوُا الْعَذٰابَ وَ جَعَلْنَا الْأَغْلاٰلَ فِي أَعْنٰاقِ الَّذِينَ كَفَرُوا هَلْ يُجْزَوْنَ إِلاّٰ مٰا كٰانُوا يَعْمَلُونَ.[۳۵] گفت: «و پنهان دارند مر پشیمانی را چون دیدند مر عذاب را و کردیم غلها اندر گردن آن کسها کی کافر شدند و جزا نیابند جز بدان که کرده باشند».

[§۴۰:۹۰] و دلیل بر آنك مردم ازین عالم طبیعی بدان عالم نفسانی شود، آن است که مردم را بینی که چیزی نداند پس مر او را[۳۶] از جهت تعلیم دانستن آن چیز نادانسته گشاده شود تا پنداری کز[۳۷] ‹جایی به جایی›[۳۸] دیگر شد.

[§۴۱:۹۰] پس بِچه شرف باشد آن وقت کی تأیید از خداوند قیامت بدو پیوسته شود، آنك همه پیامبران، علیهم السّلام، خلق را دعوت بدو کردند؟

[§۴۲:۹۰] خلق را آن روز به دو گروه بینی: گروهی آن باشد کی بدو بگرویدند و او را حقّ دانستند و به آشکارا شدن او امیدوار بودند.

[§۴۳:۹۰] و ایشان آن روز نور کلمه بپذیرند به میانجی او، علیه افضل السّلام و[۳۹] التحیّة، و اندر نعیم جاویدان مخلّد گردند.

---

۳۳ اس: رندکی؛ ایا: زندگانی.

۳۴ ایا: + تعالی.

۳۵ سورة سَبَأ (۳۴)، آیت ۳۳.

۳۶ ¦⟵برگ [اس:۱۲۲-الف].

۳۷ اس: [سرکشِ حرف «ک» در «کز» کمرنگ شده است].

۳۸ اس: حالی بحالی؛ ایا: جابی بجایی. || تصحیح مفهومی.

۳۹ ایا: + اکمل.

[§۹۰:۴۴] و گروهی آن باشد کی ازو اندر شك بودند و غافل بودند از فرمان خدای. ایشان بدان نور سوخته شوند و اندر عقوبت جاویدان مانند. چنانك خدای تعالی فرمود، قوله: وُجُوهٌ يَوْمَئِذٍ نٰاضِرَةٌ[۴۰] * إِلىٰ رَبِّهٰا نٰاظِرَةٌ * وَ وُجُوهٌ يَوْمَئِذٍ بٰاسِرَةٌ * تَظُنُّ أَنْ يُفْعَلَ بِهٰا فٰاقِرَةٌ.[۴۱] همی گوید:[۴۲] «رویهایی[۴۳] آن روز تازه[۴۴] باشد؛ و سوی پروردگار خویش نگرنده باشد؛ و رویهایی آن روز ترش گشته باشد؛ تا گمان بری که پشتشان همی بشکند».

[§۹۰:۴۵] ایزد ما را از آن گروه کناد که آگاهی دارند از[۴۵] آشکارا شدن خداوند قیامت، علیه افضل السّلام؛[۴۶] وزان گروه مکناد کی غافل باشیم از آنچ بر ما واجب است بر حدّ خویش.[۴۷]

---

۴۰ اس: ناظِره؛ ایا: ناظِرَهٌ. [کذا].

۴۱ سورة القیامة (۷۵)، آیات ۲۲ تا ۲۵.

۴۲ ایا: – همی گوید.

۴۳ اس: دیدهایی.

۴۴ |⟵برگ [ایا:۱۱۴-الف].

۴۵ ایا: – از.

۴۶ ایا: + والتحیّة.

۴۷ ایا: + آمین یا رب العالمین.

صف نود و یکم

سخن اندر پیوست تأیید به مؤیّد[۱]

[§۹۱:۱] گوییم کی پیوستن تأیید به مؤیّد از عالم علوی شریفتر است از پیوستن قوّتهای ستارگان آسمان به زایشهای طبیعی.

[§۹۱:۲] و لکن نزدیك گردانیدن وهم را، این دو حال یك به دیگر نزدیك اند.

[§۹۱:۳] و مردم همی یابد مر قوّتها را اندر زایشهای عالم کز افلاك و انجم بدیشان پیوسته است.

[§۹۱:۴] و همی داند مردم کی مر نبات را و حیوان را و بیشتر مردم را از چگونگی پیوستن آن قوّتها خبر نیست.

[§۹۱:۵] و همی یابد هر شخصی از زایشها از آثار قوّتها و حرکتهای کواکب بر قدر[۲] آن اثر که اندر او است،[۳] از لطافت و کثافت، تا هر یکی از آن پدید کند[۴] از صورت خویش آنچ اندر او موجود است از قوّتها و خاصیّتهای طبیعی.

[§۹۱:۶] پس همچنین تأیید اندریافت از عالم روحانی مر گوهرهای روحانی را کی پیوسته شد به شخصهای مردم.

[§۹۱:۷] همچنانك نیافتیم چیزی از زایشهای عالم سفلی کی او را قوّتی بود که بدان قوّت مر این عالم را خدمت توانست فرمودن و منفعتها که صانع اندر او تقدیر کرده است مر آن را توانست آوردن، جز این شخص مردم کی او مر طبایع

۱ قس: کتاب الینابیع، الینبوع الأربعون (۴۰): في کیفیة اتصال التأیید بالمؤیّدین في العالم الجسدانی، ص ۹۴ تا ۹۷.

۲ اس: بر قدر؛ ایا: بقدر.

۳ اس: کاندروست؛ ایا: کندروست.

۴ ←برگ [اس:۱۲۲-ب].

را هریکی را جداجدا کار بَستْ. چون آتش را در پختن چیزهای خام و ساختنِ[5] رنگها و گداختن گوهرها و جز آن. و چون مر باد را کار بَستْ که بر آبهای عظیم بگذشت، و کشتیهای گران را اندر دریا بدو راند، و برو آسیاها ساخت و جز آن. و چون مر خاك را کزو چندین بناهای عجیب ساخت و گوهرهای پرفایده ازو بیرون آوردند، همه منافع و عجایب عالم به آشکارا شدن مردم آشکارا شد.

[§۸:۹۱] همچنین نیافتیم از هیچ شخصی از شخصهای مردم کسی کی او را ممکن بود خدمت فرمودن[6] و کار بستن مر عالم روحانی را، و بیرون آوردن منفعتها را که صانع اندر او تقدیر کرده است، مگر پیمبران را، علیهم السّلام، کی ایشان به سخن منطقی کی بیاوردند هرچیزی را ازین عالم بجایگاه خویش بنهادند.

[§۹:۹۱] و پدید آوردند سیاستهای عجب و حکمتهایی که اندر آن است کمال عالم روحانی. و پیدا کردن آن منفعتها از ایشان، علیهم السّلام، بود و بَس.

[§۱۰:۹۱] و آغاز پیوستن تأیید به مؤیّدان زفان[7] باشد کی او توانا همی‌باشد بر بیرون آوردن چیزهای پوشیده نه از راه حواس، چنانك به حس دلیل کند بر چیزهای پوشیده.

[§۱۱:۹۱] بل‌کی[8] مؤیّد به تأیید آنگه رسد کی نفس او محسوسات را فراموش کند و از حس جدا ماند به وقت بیرون آوردن آنچ بدو پیوسته شود از عالم علوی و رغبت کند اندر معقولات، آن معقولات کی آن[9] اندر آویخته نباشد به چیزهای هیولانی.

[§۱۲:۹۱] چنانك معروف است میان علماء دینی که چون رسول مصطفی، صلی

---

۵ اس: ساحس؛ ایا: شناختن.

۶ ¦⟵برگ [ایا:۱۱۴-ب].

۷ اس: [کلمه «زفان» بالای خط نوشته شده است].

۸ ایا: بلك.

۹ ¦⟵برگ [اس:۱۲۳-الف].

اللّٰه علیه وآله، برو وحی آمدی گونهٔ روی او بگشتی و به حالی شدی میان خفتگی و بیداری و عرق از اندامهای او بگشادی و بهیچ چیز ننگریستی تا باز به هوش آمدی آن وقت آنچ به وحی بدو رسیده بدی به زفان عبارت کردی.

[§۱۳:۹۱] پس آن حال[۱۰] ازو، علیه السّلام، دلیل بود بدانچ گفت بدان[۱۱] از محسوسات بر معقولات دلیل گرفت.

[§۱۴:۹۱] و فرق میان دانایان مؤیّد و دانای[۱۲] نامؤیّد آن است کی دانای نامؤیّد اندرمانده است به نگاه داشتن علمها و حکمتهای خویش به دلیل گرفتن از محسوسات.

[§۱۵:۹۱] و دانای مؤیّد آن را[۱۳] حاجت نیست اندر ذات خویش بیرون آوردن حکمتهای معقول، بر آنچ از برتر از آن دلیل گیرد، تا از محسوس بر معقول یاری خواهد.

[§۱۶:۹۱] و لکن باشد کی اندر نفس مؤیّد چیزی روحانی پدید آید ازبهر بیان کردن حکمتی را یا تمامت کردن چیزی را، کی از مؤید چاره نیابد از عبارت آن به چیزی محسوس، کی اگر آن عبارت نه از طریق محسوسات کند، مردمان زمانه ندانند. و صورت نبندد[۱۴] اندر نفسهای ایشان آنچ مر آن مؤیّد را صورت بسته است مگر آن وقت کی مر آن را مانند کند به محسوسی.

[§۱۷:۹۱] و تا ایشان آن چیز را بخلاف آن نبینند،[۱۵] [که][۱۶] مؤیّد مر ایشان را خبر دهد، عیان خویش نهلند و خبر او نپذیرند.

---

۱۰ ایا: – حال.

۱۱ ایا: – بدان.

۱۲ اس: دانا؛ ایا: [حرف «ی» در «دانای» مخدوش است].

۱۳ اس: موبدان را؛ ایا: مؤیّد را آن.

۱۴ اس: سندد. || ایا: + بندد. || ¦⟵برگ [ایا:۱۱۵-الف].

۱۵ اس، ایا: نه بینند.

۱۶ تصحیح قیاسی.

[§۹۱:۱۸] وگر پیوستن تأیید به مؤیّد از جهت حواس بودی خبرهای[۱۷] ایشان را فضیلت نبودی که بر ‹[علم] عیان [حسی] خلق›[۱۸] گذشتی.

[§۹۱:۱۹] پس پیوستن تأیید به مؤیّدان از جهت غیر[۱۹] حواس است و آن منطق محض است کی پیامبران، علیهم‌السّلام، بدان مقهور کردند خلق را.

[§۹۱:۲۰] و مردمان بدان منطق محض را از ایشان، علیهم[۲۰] السّلام، نتوانستند پذیرفتن مگر به سخن تألیفی کی ایشان مر آن را به حروف بگزارند.

[§۹۱:۲۱] و نیز پیوستن تأیید به مؤیّد نگاه کردن ایشان باشد اندر شخصهای عالم از نبات و حیوان و مردم، کزان نگاه کردن مؤیّد بگشاید[۲۱] از علم غیب چیزهائی کی آفرینش آن چیز ازبهر آن علم بوده است، کو[۲۲] نامور و جاکول شود بدان نگرستن از سرهای بسیار.

[§۹۱:۲۲] و نیز باشد کی مؤیّد سخنی بشنود از کسی کی آن کس خود معنی آن نداند؛ و مؤیّد را بگشاید از آن سخن چیزی عجیب، وزان در او گشاده شود اصلی کی واجب شود وز خلق کار بستن آن اندر دوران مؤیّد.

---

۱۷ اس: حیزهای.

۱۸ اس، ایا: عیان خلق. || تصحیح قیاسی. نك: کتاب الینابیع، الینبوع الأربعون (۴۰)، ص ۹۶، بند (۱۸۸)، س ۱ تا ۲: فلو کان اتصال التأیید بهم من جهة الحواس، لما صار لأخبارهم هذه الفضیلة التي تفوق علم العیان الحسّيّ.

۱۹ اس، ایا: علّت [کذا]. || تصحیح قیاسی. نك: کتاب الینابیع، الینبوع الأربعون (۴۰)، ص ۹۶، بند (۱۸۹)، س ۳ تا ۹: وقد قیل: لیس الخبر کالمعاینة، لکن لما کان اتصال التأیید بهم من غیر جهة الحواس - وهو النطق المحض الذي لا یشوبه شيء من الحروف والتألیفات - قهروا الخلق بما عاینوه بحواسهم وأدرکوه بمنطقهم المؤلفة ذات الحروف.

۲۰ اس: علیه.

۲۱ ¦⟵برگ [اس:۱۲۳-ب].

۲۲ اس: کوه.

[§۹۱:۲۳] و زینگونه[۲۳] باشد شناختن چگونگی پیوستن تأیید به مؤیّد اندر عالم جسمانی.

۲۳ اس، ایا: وزین گونه. || نک: دهخدا: زینگونه. [گو نَ/ نِ] (قید مرکب) مخفف از اینگونه. ازاینسان. بدین طرز.

صف نود و دوم

سخن اندر فرق میان قرآن و میان خبر رسول

[§۹۲:۱] از جویندگان علمِ حقیقت، گروهی کی فرق نتوانند کردن میان سخن خدای و سخن رسول، علیه السّلام، گویند: 'هم آیات قرآن و هم اخبار از یاران رسول، علیه السّلام، به ما رسید و ما هر دو سخن را همی بزرگ باید داشتن و فرمان برداری باید کردن'.

[§۹۲:۲] پس چه علّت بود کی رسول، صلی اللّٰه علیه وآله، یك سخن را ایدون گفت کی 'این خدای همی‌گوید'، و یك سخن را گفت کی 'این من همی‌گویم'.

[§۹۲:۳] و ما خواهیم کی فرق میان سخن خدای کی قرآن است[۱] و میان خبر رسول بازنماییم، و پیدا کنیم که حال چنان بود که رسول مصطفی، صلّی[۲] اللّٰه علیه وآله، گفت، و گفتار او راست بود به برکت خداوند حقّ و دستوریِ او.

[§۹۲:۴] گوییم کی چون صلاح عالم اندر آن سخن یافتیم کی رسول مصطفی، صلی[۳] اللّٰه علیه وآله، به ما بگزارد، و ما را گفت کی این گفتار خدای است، ما را درست شد که او، علیه السّلام، راست گفت.

[§۹۲:۵] ازبهرآنك اگر آن سخن آفریدگار عالم نبودی، کار عالم بدان راست نشدی. و به سخن هیچ خلق احوال عالم نظام نگیرد مگر به سخن خداوند خلق.

[§۹۲:۶] و چون ازین روی معلوم شد که قرآن سخن خدای است، گوییم کی فرق میان قرآن و میان خبر رسول آن است کی گفتار خدای را کی آفرینش عالم و آفرینش مردم است، چنانك خدای تعالی گوید، قوله: سَنُرِيهِمْ آيَاتِنَا فِي الْآفَاقِ وَ فِي

۱ ¦←برگ [ایا:۱۱۵-الف].

۲ اس، ایا: صل.

۳ اس، ایا: صل.

أَنْفُسِهِمْ حَتّٰى يَتَبَيَّنَ لَهُمْ أَنَّهُ الْحَقُّ.[۴] همی گوید: «سرانجام[۵] بنماییمشان نشانهای ما اندر کنارهای عالم و اندر نفسهای ایشان تا پیدا شود مر ایشان را کی آن حقّ است».

[§۷:۹۲] و مر خبر رسول را، علیه السّلام، گواه آیت قرآن است. چنانك رسول مصطفی، صلی[۶] اللّٰه علیه وآله، فرمود: سَيُكْذَبُ علىَّ [ك]ما كُذِبَ على الأنبياءِ من قبلی. فماجاءكم مني ما يخالف كتاب اللّٰه لم اقدرْ و كيف أخالف كتاب اللّٰه و به اهتدَيتُ. گفت: «سرانجام بر من دروغ گویند همچنانك دروغ گفتند بر پیمبران که پیش از من بودند. پس آنچ[۷] بیاید به شما از خبر من کی مر کتاب خدای را مخالف باشد آن نه من گفته‌ام و چگونه مخالف شوم مر کتاب خدای را و راه راست بدان یافتم».[۸]

[§۸:۹۲] و گوایی مر قول خدای را آفرینش عالم و ترکیب جسد مردم کی چنان گوایی میدهد کی خدای تعالی همی‌گوید، قوله: وَ السَّمٰاءَ بَنَيْنٰاهٰا[۹] بِأَيْدٍ وَ إِنّٰا لَمُوسِعُونَ * وَ الْأَرْضَ فَرَشْنٰاهٰا فَنِعْمَ الْمٰاهِدُونَ * وَ مِنْ كُلِّ شَيْءٍ خَلَقْنٰا زَوْجَيْنِ لَعَلَّكُمْ تَذَكَّرُونَ.[۱۰] همی‌گوید: «ما آسمان را برآوردیم به نیروها و ما توانایيم؛ و زمین را بگستریدیم[۱۱] و ما نیك جاسازندگانیم؛ و از هرچیزی ما بیافریدیم دو جفت مگر ایشان یاد کنند».

---

۴ سورة فُصِّلت (۴۱)، آیت ۵۳.

۵ ¦⟵برگ [اس:۱۲۴-الف].

۶ اس، ایا: صل.

۷ ایا: آنچه.

۸ قس: المجلسی، محمّد باقر، بحار الأنوار، ج ۲، باب ۹۲: علل اختلاف الاخبار وکیفیة الجمع بینها والعمل بها ووجوه الاستنباط، ص ۲۲۷.

۹ اس: بنیها.

۱۰ سورة الذاريات (۵۱)، آیات ۴۷ تا ۴۹.

۱۱ ایا: بگستردیم.

[§۹۲:۹] و اندر حدّ تأویل، «آسمان» ناطق را می‌خواهد کی او برتر از همه خلق است به مرتبت، چنانك آسمان برتر از همه جسمها است.[۱۲]

[§۹۲:۱۰] و بدانچ همی‌گوید «بناکردیمش به نیروها»، بدان نیروها عقل و نفس را خواهد و حدود روحانی را کی پیامبری به قوّت ایشان رسد به مردم.

[§۹۲:۱۱] و بدانچ گفت «ما توانگرانیم»، اشارت بعقل و نفس کرد کی تأیید و ترکیب از ایشان است و این هردو مایهٔ پادشایی است.

[§۹۲:۱۲] و بدانچ گفت «کی زمین را بگسترانیدیم»، بدان مر اساس را خواست کی او مر فایده‌های عقلی را کز راه ناطق بر عالم جسمانی بارد به منزلت زمین است مر فایده‌های آسمان را کی بر طبایع بارد.

[§۹۲:۱۳] و بدانچ گفت «ما نیك جاسازندگانیم»، آن خواست کی، همچنانك زمین قرارگاه است مر جسمها را، اساس قرارگاه است مر نفسها را.

[§۹۲:۱۴] پس سخت بزرگ نعمتی بود بپای کردن اساس کی بدو نفسها از شبهت مثل و رمز رسته شده‌اند[۱۳] و قرار یافتند از افتادن گهی بدین مثل[۱۴] و گهی بر آن رمز اندر ظاهر شریعت کی مر یکدیگر را مخالف است.

[§۹۲:۱۵] پس گفت «از هرچیزی دو جفت آفریدم»؛ یعنی کی پیامبری از آن چیزها است کی او با وصایت جفت است.

[§۹۲:۱۶] مگر ایشان یاد کنند و بدانند کی چون همه چیزها جفت است، پیامبری[۱۵] نیز جفت است و تنزیل با تأویل جفت است. بر ظاهر بی‌معنی نایستند.[۱۶]

---

۱۲ ¦⟵برگ [ایا:۱۱۶-الف].

۱۳ ایا: شدند.

۱۴ ¦⟵برگ [اس:۱۲۴-ب].

۱۵ ایا: پیمبری.

۱۶ اس، ایا: نه‌ایستند.

[§۱۷:۹۲] پس مر این قول را آفرینش عالم گوایی میدهد کی آسمان برگرفته است به بلندتر مکانی، و فایده‌های او از مردم دور است و ممکن نیست رسیدن دست مردم بدو.

[§۱۸:۹۲] و همچنانك منزلت رسول بلند است و کسی را رسیدن بدانچ او گوید بمثل و رمز تواند اندریافتن مر آن را.

[§۱۹:۹۲] و زمین زیر آسمان قرار گرفته است و همی‌پذیرد مر قوّتهای آسمان را و مر آن قوّتها را بصورت همی بیرون آرد از گونه‌گونه غذاها تا خلق بدان به جسم فایده گیرند.

[§۲۰:۹۲] همچنانك اساس مر آن مثلها را کی رسول بگذارد پذیرفته است، و معنیهای آنچ امروز آورده است تا نفسهای خلق بدان غذا یابند.

[§۲۱:۹۲] و هرکی بر ظاهر محض بایستد همچنان است کی خاك بخورد به امید آنك بدان زندگانی یابد، همچنان، از ظاهر، زندگانی ابدی حاصل نیاید.

[§۲۲:۹۲] وز آفرینش مر این آیت را گواه است کی عقل مثل است بر آسمان و نفس مثل است بر زمین.

[§۲۳:۹۲] و کسی را[۱۷] به اندریافتن نفس، دسترسی[۱۸] نیست مگر به میانجی زمین کی او جسم است.

[§۲۴:۹۲] و به میانجی جسم از نفس چندین فایده‌های عجیب پدید همی‌آید از صناعتهای گوناگون و پذیرفتن فایده‌های عقلی کی بدان نفس عمر جاویدی یابد.

[§۲۵:۹۲] و نیك جایگاهی ساخته است صانع حکیم مر نفس را این جسم، جفت گردانیده است ایشان را با یکدیگر.

---

۱۷ |⟵برگ [ایا:۱۱۶-ب].

۱۸ اس، ایا: دست‌رسی.

[§۲۶:۹۲] و قول رسول کی مر او را این آیت گوایی دهد آن است کی وی، علیه السّلام، گفت مر امیرالمؤمنین علی را، علیه السّلام: أنا و أنتَ یا علي أبوا هذه الأُمّة لَعَنَ اللّٰه مَن عَقَّ والِدَیهُ. گفت: «من و تو یا علی پدر و مادر این امّتیم دور کناد خدای آن را کی بیازارد پدر[۱۹] و مادر خویش را».[۲۰]

[§۲۷:۹۲] و این همان سخن است کی خدای گفت: [وَ السَّمٰاءَ بَنَیْنٰاهٰا بِأَیْدٍ وَ إِنّٰا لَمُوسِعُونَ. همی گوید:] «آسمان را بناکردیم به نیروها * و زمین را بگستردیم»،[۲۱] ازبهرآنك مر پدر را از فرزند محل آسمان باشد و مادر را محل زمین باشد.[۲۲]

---

۱۹ ¦⟵برگ [اس:۱۲۵-الف].

۲۰ نك: جامع الحمکتین، بند ۲۲۶، ص ۲۰۹ تا ۲۱۰: پس چنانك جسد ما را مادر پرورد بقوّت پدر، نفس ما را نیز مادر و پدرست. پدر نفسانی خلق رسول خدای است، که آموزگار خلق اوست بفرمان خدای. چنانك گفت: قوله «وَ یُعَلِّمُهُمُ الْکِتٰابَ وَ الْحِکْمَةَ وَ إِنْ کٰانُوا مِنْ قَبْلُ لَفِي ضَلٰالٍ مُبِینٍ.» [سورة آل عمران (۳)، آیت ۱۶۴] و مادر نفسانی ما وصیّ رسول است، چنانك رسول گفت مر وصیّ خویش را که من و تو ای علی! پدر و مادر این امّتیم، لعنت خدای بر آن پسران باد که مادر و پدر خویش را بیازارد بدین خبر «أنا و أنت یا عليّ! أبوا هذه الأمّة، لعن اللّٰه من اعنیٰ والدیه» و چنانك فرزند از مادر بر آید، طعامی که پدرش بیارد مر آن فرزندان را نشاید ازو خوردن، بل نخست مادرش آن را بخورد، و اندر ترکیب خویش مر آن را شیر نرم و خوش گوارنده گرداند، آنگه مر آن را بفرزند دهد، نیز آنچ رسول بگوید از تنزیل مر امّت نو عهد را که ضعیف است نشاید، تا نخست وصیّ آن را از آن مثلها و رمزها بتأویل جدا کند، و چنان سازدش بعبارت‌هاء لطیف که آن ضعیف نو عهد مر آن را بتواند شنودن و پذیرفتن، همچنانك مر آن کودك را ببندند نیز مر مستجیب را عهد گیرند و برو وثیقت‌ها کنند بسبب آنچ مر او را بشنوانند، و گوش مر نفس ناطقه را هم بدان منزلت است که دهان مر نفس بهیمی راست، و تنزیل و تأویل مر نفس ناطقه را بمنزلت طعام و شراب است مر جسد را. || قس: االنعمان بن محمّد، القاضي ابوحنیفه، اساس التأویل، ص ۶۴.

۲۱ سورة الذاریات (۵۱)، آیت ۴۷.

۲۲ نك: وجه دین، گفتار ۳۶، اندر واجبی اطاعت امام زمان و بیان آن، ص ۲۷۷ تا ۲۷۸: و چون جسم را تمامی اندر آن بود که به خوشیهای این جهانی برسد از لذّات جسمانی به میانجی پدر و مادر، گفتیم که تمامی نفس نیز باید اندر آن باشد که او بلذّات عالم روحانی برسد به میانجی پدر و مادر نفسانی. پس بحکم ضرورت اثبات شد مر نفس مردم را از پدری و مادری همچنانکه جسم مردم را از پدر و مادر چاره نیست. و چون پدر جسمانی مردم را فایده دهنده بود و مادرش فایده پذیرنده بود گفتیم که پدر روحانی نیز فایده دهنده باشد و مادر نفسانی فایده پذیرنده باشد. پس گفتیم که آن پدر دینی که او مر نفس مؤمن را به محّل پدر است رسولست صلّی اللّه علیه و آله و سلّم و آن مادر دینی او مر نفس مؤمن را بمحلّ مادر

[§۲۸:۹۲] ازیراك[۲۳] از پدر اندر فرزند جز آن کی آبی نبود که به ابتدا مر آن آب به رحِم مادر آید چنانك آسمان جز آن نیست کی آب فرو فرستد و مادرِ فرزند آن آب را نگه دارد، و تعهّد کند، و صورت پیدا آید.

[§۲۹:۹۲] و مر او را بصورت راست زنده بیرون آرد جمله شده، همچنانك زمین مر آن قوّت را که اندر آب است نگه دارد و از خویشتن مر او را مدد کند و صورتی گرداندش با رنگ و بوی و مزه و شکل و جمله شده بیرون آردش.

[§۳۰:۹۲] همچنین آبش[۲۴] اندر زمینِ[۲۵] مؤمن از ناطق جز آن نیست کی مر او را به کلمه شهادت خواند، و مر آن را به گردن او اندرکرد، و گفت رستگاریِ تو اندر این است.[۲۶]

[§۳۱:۹۲] و مر او را به وصیِ خویش سپرد — مثل سپردن پدر مر آن آب را به مادر — تا وصی معنیِ آن به مؤمن رساند.

[§۳۲:۹۲] اگر ازو طاعت یابد، بیرون آردش از حدّ دیوی به حدّ فریشتگی و به زندگی جاویدی رساندش و از هلاك ایمن کندش، همچنان‌کی[۲۷] مادر آن آب

است مر وصیّ اوست، و تنزیل ناطق مر صورت نفسانی مؤمن را بمنزلت نطفهٔ پدر است مر جسم را، و تأویل وصیّ مر آنصورت نفسانی را بمرتبت نطفهٔ مادر است مر جسم را. و بفراز آمدن هر دو نطفهٔ روحانی صورتی پدید آید آراسته مر عالم روحانی را هم‌چنان که بفراز آمدن دو نطفهٔ جسمانی بر آراسته صورتی پدید آید مر عالم جسمانی را. || نیز قس: المؤیَّد في الدین الشیرازی، المجالس المؤیَّدیَّة، تحقیق و تقدیم: مصطفی غالب (بیروت، ۱۹۷۴)، المجلس السادس من المِائة الأُولی، ص ۲۴ تا ۲۸.

۲۳ ایا: ازیرا که.

۲۴ اس: اںش؛ ایا: آتش [کذا] [حروف «ا» و «ت» در «آتش» اندکی مخدوش است].

۲۵ ایا: + اندر زمین [عبارت تکرار شده است].

۲۶ برای تأویل «گردن» نك: وجه دین، گفتار ۳۵، ص ۲۶۹ تا ۲۷۰ (در تأویل آیت ۴ از سورة محمّد (۴۷): فَإِذٰا لَقِيتُمُ الَّذِينَ كَفَرُوا فَضَرْبَ الرِّقٰابِ حَتّٰى إِذٰا أَثْخَنْتُمُوهُمْ فَشُدُّوا الْوَثٰاقَ فَإِمّٰا مَنًّا بَعْدُ وَ إِمّٰا فِدٰاءً حَتّٰى تَضَعَ الْحَرْبُ أَوْزٰارَهٰا).

۲۷ ایا: همچنانك.

نطفه را به نگاه‌داشتِ خویش از تباه شدن نگاه داشت و به زندگانی و به حس رسانیدش.

[۳۳:۹۲§] پس ناطق مر نفس مؤمن را به منزلت آسمان است مر نبات را و به منزلت پدر است مر فرزند را، و اساس مر نفس مؤمن را به منزلت زمین است[۲۸] مر نبات را و به منزلت مادر است مر فرزند را.

[۳۴:۹۲§] پس مر این خبر را [که] یاد کردیم، از آیات کی پیش ازین اندر این صفت مر آن را تفسیر و تأویل گفتیم، گوا است. و مر آن آیت را آفرینش عالم و ترکیب جسد مردم است گوا.

[۳۵:۹۲§] و نیز گوییم کی نفس قدسی چون به کسی پیوسته شود آن کس پیامبر گردد؛ و نفس قدسی مر پیامبر[۲۹] را هم بدان منزلت است کی نفس ناطق مر مردم را است.[۳۰]

[۳۶:۹۲§] نبینی[۳۱] کی خداوند نفس قدسی مر خداوند نفس ناطقه را مسخّر خویش کند، همچنانك خداوندان نفس ناطقه مر خداوندان نفس حسّی را کی جانوران‌اند مسخر کرده‌اند. چنانك خدای تعالی همی‌گوید، قوله: وَ رَفَعْنَا بَعْضَهُمْ فَوْقَ بَعْضٍ دَرَجَاتٍ لِيَتَّخِذَ بَعْضُهُمْ بَعْضاً سُخْرِيًّا.[۳۲] گفت: «برگرفتیم گروهی را از بر گروهی تا مر گروهی را مسخّر کرد».

[۳۷:۹۲§] پس گوییم کی غایت نفس ناطقه آن است کی تا سخنی بگوید معنی‌دار

۲۸ ¦⟵برگ [ایا:۱۱۷-الف].

۲۹ ایا: پیمبر.

۳۰ قس: جامع الحکمتین، فصل ۱: اندر ذکر سبب تصنیف کتاب، بند (۱۵)، ص ۱۲، س ۹ تا ۱۰: سخنی که از نفس قدسی نبوی رود و از خاطری پدید آید که منزل روح الامین باشد چنین درست و قوی و برهانی باشد.

۳۱ اس، ایا: نه بینی.

۳۲ سورة الزُّخْرُف (۴۳)، آیت ۳۲. || ¦⟵برگ [اس:۱۲۵-ب].

به لفظی مهذّب بی‌حشو، یا مسجّع چون خطبَهای عرب، یا مقفّا و موزون چنانك شعر است کی به ترازوی عقل سخته[۳۳] است.

[§۳۸:۹۲] و هر بیتی را به آخر او سخنی مانند آنك به آخر آن دیگر بیت است آورده است. و هر یکی را معنی دیگر است، و دیگر خداوندان نفس ناطقه از گفتن همچنانی عاجزند، و مر آن کس را همه مسخّر او و هم چنان مقفا و موزون نیست.

[§۳۹:۹۲] بل‌کی[۳۴] وقتی سخن خویش را بغایت رساند، و بنهایت آن قوّت است کی چیزی بگوید، و بدان وقت کی آن خواهد گفتن، نخواهد کی سخن کسی بشنود کی خاطر او از آن فروماند.

[§۴۰:۹۲] پس بدان شرف کی سخن منظوم را است بر سخن منثور، خداوند[۳۵] سخن منظوم همی جدایی[۳۶] جوید از گویندگان سخن منثور و با[۳۷] فرود از خویشتن اندر یك زمان قرار نیابد.

[§۴۱:۹۲] و آن کس همه سخن خویش شعرِ معنی‌دار بتواند گفتن از بهر آنك شعر مر نفس ناطقه را به منزلت بار است مر درخت میوه‌دار را.

[§۴۲:۹۲] و هر چه از درخت میوه بیرون آید همه میوهٔ شیرین خوشبوی نیك رنگ نباشد. بل بر درخت مر یکی بار را صد برگ باشد کی شکل مانند بار دارد و لکن به مزه و بوی چون بار نباشد.[۳۸]

[§۴۳:۹۲] پس گوییم کی چون نفس قدسی به بنده‌ای[۳۹] از بندگان[۴۰] خدای پیوسته

---

۳۳ ایا: سنجیده.
۳۴ ایا: بلك.
۳۵ ایا: خداوندان.
۳۶ اس: حذابی؛ ایا: خدایی. || تصحیح قیاسی.
۳۷ اس، ایا: یا.
۳۸ قس: زادالمسافر، قول ۲۵، ص ۴۱۱ تا ۴۱۳.
۳۹ اس، ایا: ببندهء.
۴۰ |←برگ [ایا:۱۱۷-ب].

شود، آن بنده بدان نفس مر سخن روحانیان را بتواند پذیرفتن بی‌آواز و بی‌حروف و کلمات.

[§۴۴:۹۲] و بدان وقت کی سخن روحانیان بدو خواهد پیوستن وی از همه محسوسات بریده شود و حواس او از کار بماند؛ سبب مخالفت که معقول را با محسوس هست، تا بدان نفس شریف مر آن اشارت روحانی را بیابد.

[§۴۵:۹۲] آن وقت آن اشارت را، ازبهر عاجزی خلق را از پذیرفتن آن، به حروف آواز[۴۱] مرکب کند و بر محسوسات[۴۲] مثل گرداند و به خلق برساند.

[§۴۶:۹۲] و همه سخن آن مؤیَّد کی[۴۳] به نفس قدسی پیوندد وزان روی نباشد، ازبهرآنك هرچیزی را غایتی هست و آن غایت و نهایت نفسی[۴۴] قدسی است که کلام روحانیان را بیابد.

[§۴۷:۹۲] و هیچ چیز اندر عالم جسمانی که او گردنده است همیشه نهایت خویش نتواند بودن.

[§۴۸:۹۲] پس سخن خدای تعالی[۴۵] از نفس پیامبر،[۴۶] علیه السّلام، به منزلت شعر است از نفس ناطقه بمثل.

[§۴۹:۹۲] و خبر از نفس ناطق، علیه السّلام، به منزلت دیگر سخنها است از نفس ناطقه بمثل.

[§۵۰:۹۲] و سخن خدای تعالی از نفس رسول، علیه السّلام، به منزلت بار است از درخت بارور که برگ به شکل میوه باشد و لکن به بوی و مزهٔ او نباشد.

---

۴۱ اس: اواز؛ ایا: او از.

۴۲ اس: + را [«را» با جوهر خیلی کمرنگ نوشته شده است].

۴۳ ایا: – کی.

۴۴ ایا: نفس.

۴۵ ¦⟵برگ [اس:۱۲۶-الف].

۴۶ ایا: پیمبر.

[§۵۱:۹۲] و همچنین خبر رسول، و آن به معنی باشد که سخن خدای است. و اگر نفسهای خلق بر نگاه‌داشت خبر آن رغبت نکند کی بر نگاه‌داشت سخن خدای کند.

[§۵۲:۹۲] و سخن خدای از نفس قدسی به منزلت سخن معنی‌دار است گزارده به حروف و کلمات از نفس ناطقه.

[§۵۳:۹۲] و خبر رسول از نفس قدسی به منزلت آواز مردم است از نفس ناطقه.

[§۵۴:۹۲] و اندر سخن آواز است و لکن اندر آواز سخن نیست.

[§۵۵:۹۲] پس گوییم کی خداوندان تأیید چون اساس و امام و باب و حجّت مر سخن خدای را بحقّ برگرفتند، و بشناخت اندر آن فرمانها برفتند بر حقیقت نه بر ظاهر الفاظ.

[§۵۶:۹۲] هم بر آن مثال کی خداوندان نفس ناطقه مر سخن را چون بشنوند و براندازهٔ آن معنی برگیرند که اندر آن سخن باشد وز پس مراد گوینده روند و نگرند کی آن گوینده مر آن سخن را به آواز نرم گفت یا به آواز بلند. از بهر آنك شنوندگان خداوندان نفس ناطقه بودند.

[§۵۷:۹۲] و آن خداوندان نفس حسّی از جانوران کی مر ایشان را آواز وی نطق است مر زفان مردم[۴۷] و آگهی نداد به معنیِ آنچ مردم گوید نرسید.[۴۸]

[§۵۸:۹۲] چنانك اگر کسی بانگی بر ستوری زند به سخنی کی چنین کن یا مکن آن ستور از آن آواز بترسد و متحیّر شود و بازاستد[۴۹] از آنچ اندر آن باشد از حرکات خویش.

۴۷ |⟵برگ [ایا:۱۱۸-الف].

۴۸ اس: نه‌رسید.

۴۹ ایا: بازایستد.

[§۵۹:۹۲] و همچنین گر کسی مر[۵۰] آهویی را آواز دهد کی بیا یا برو آهو مر آن گفتار را به آواز برگیرد نه به نطق از بهر آنك آهو خداوند[۵۱] نطق نیست.

[§۶۰:۹۲] پس این ایستادن از آن سخن منطقیِ محض کی رسول، علیه السّلام، مر آن را به آواز و به نطق بگزارد بدان منزلت برگرفتند کی ایشان خود اندر آن بودند از سخن گفتن جسمانیان بر جسمها.

[§۶۱:۹۲] و لکن ترسنده شدند از آواز ناطق دور خویش بی‌آنك به معنیِ آن سخنان کی او گفت[۵۲] بریسیدند برمثال ترسیدن ستور و وحش از آواز مردم.

[§۶۲:۹۲] و بازاستادن[۵۳] مردم نادان از آنچ ناطق دور مر ایشان را از آن بازداشت نه بدان سبب کی[۵۴] بدانسته‌اند کی چنان باید کردن بحقیقت، بل کی بدان سبب است کی نفس ناطق دور را بر نفس امّت آن فضیلت است کی نفس مردم را بر نفس ستور است.

[§۶۳:۹۲] و همچنان چون ستوری طعامی ازآنِ مردم بخورد، اگر مردم بانگ برزند ستور از آن طعام دور شود، بدان زیادت قوّت که مر نفس ناطقه را بر نفس حسّی است، نه بدانك ستور بداند که او آن آواز از بهر آن زد که آن مر او را نباید خوردن، چه آن خورش مردم است و مر نفس ناطقه را قُوَّت است.

[§۶۴:۹۲] پس هم بر این مثال نفوس نادان بازایستادند ازآنچ مر ایشان را از آن بازداشتند.

---

۵۰ ایا: – مر.
۵۱ اس: + و خداوند [«خداوند» دوم خط زده شده است].
۵۲ |⟵برگ [اس:۱۲۶-ب].
۵۳ نك: دهخدا: بازاستادن. [اِ دَ] (مصدر مرکب) باز استادن از. عقب ماندن. توقف کردن. دست کشیدن. ترك کردن. بازداشته شدن. منع کرده شدن. برطرف کردن.
۵۴ اس: [کلمه «کی» بالای خط نوشته شده است].

[§۹۲:۶۵] و ظاهر امر و نهی خدای برمثال آواز است از سخن و باطن امر و نهی خدای برمثال معنی است از سخن.

[§۹۲:۶۶] پس مردم بحقیقت آن است کی فرمان خدای را به بصیرت پذیرد و پس‌رو هر آوازی نباشد. و بنگرد قول خدای را که بدین معنی همی‌گوید، قوله: أُولٰئِكَ كَالْأَنْعٰامِ بَلْ هُمْ أَضَلُّ.[۵۵] همی‌گوید: «ایشان چون ستوراننند بل‌کی[۵۶] راه گم‌کرده‌تر اند».

[§۹۲:۶۷] این است فرق میان آیت و خبر به نزدیك گردانیدن علم به وهم مستجیب.

۵۵ سورة الأعراف (۷)، آیت ۱۷۹.

۵۶ ایا: بلك.

صف نود و سِیُّم[۱]

سخن اندر آنك چیزها بدان دانسته شود[۲]

[§۱:۹۳] گوییم به جود خداوند حقّ کی عالم جسمانی دانستنی است و عالم روحانی شناختنی.

[§۲:۹۳] و مر عالم جسمانی را شش جانب او گرد گرفته است تا او کی هفتم است به گوایی آن شش جانب دانستنی شده است چون زیر و زبر و راست و چپ و پس و پیش.

[§۳:۹۳] همچنین[۳] گوییم که مر هر دانستنی را از معقولات که آن را به حس نتوان یافتن به شش چیز بتوان شناختن[۴] تا آن چیز معقول، کی این هفتمِ آن شش است، به گوایی آن شش چیز دانسته شود پس از آنك شناخته بود.

[§۴:۹۳] وزان شش چیز یکی خبر است.

[§۵:۹۳] و دیگر مثال است و آن ماننده است.

[§۶:۹۳] و سدیگر خُلْف[۵] است و آن نامانده باشد.

[§۷:۹۳] و چهارم ترتیب است و آن سپس یکدیگر کردن باشد.

[§۸:۹۳] و پنجم فصل است[۶] و آن جدا کردن باشد.

[§۹:۹۳] و ششم برهان است و آن حجّت باشد.

---

۱ ایا: سوم.

۲ ایا: شودد. || ¦⟵برگ [ایا:۱۱۸-ب].

۳ اس، ایا: هم چنین.

۴ ایا: + شناختن [کلمه «شناختن» تکرار شده، هرچند بعداً با جوهر شنگرف خط زده شده است].

۵ اس: خلف؛ ایا: خلق [کذا]. || تصحیح قیاسی.

۶ اس: [«فصل است» مخدوش است]. || ¦⟵برگ [اس:۱۲۷-الف].

[§۹۳:۱۰] و هفتم تمام است و آن[۷] واقف بودن داننده است بر دانستنی.

[§۹۳:۱۱] و مثال این چنان باشد که گوینده گوید: «آفریدگار این چیز باشد، ازو که پیش دست[۸] شود»، بی حقیقتی.

[§۹۳:۱۲] آن وقت مثال بنماید از درگری که در همی کند، و گویند: «این عالم را بنگر که آفریدگار مر او را از حال به حال همی گرداند، همچنان کی[۹] این درگر[۱۰] مر این در را کوتاه تر و درازتر و گران تر میکند».

[§۹۳:۱۳] آن وقت خُلْف آرد، گوید: «نه چنان سَبُك[۱۱] است که او را اندر این در که کرد هیچ صنعتی نیست»؛ تا گوید: «عالم نه چنین سَبُك[۱۲] است که اثر صانع، بل که چون دَرَسْتْ بر آثار صانع».

[§۹۳:۱۴] آن وقت ترتیب دارد، گوید: «چنانك این عالم صنعت از صانع همی پذیرد و بفرمان او کار می کند،[۱۳] برمثال پذیرفتن در آثارِ صنعت از درگر». مردم را که مصنوع است فرمان بردار باید بودن[۱۴] و از صانع خویش علم بباید پذیرفتن برمثال پذیرفتن در درگری را از درگر. و ما را کار باید کردن به علم، چنانك آفریدگار ما کار کرد به دانش، تا اندر حدّ بزرگی مانند شویم مر صانع خویش را.

---

۷ ایا: [کلمات «و آن» روی خط نوشته شده اند].

۸ دهخدا: پیش دست. [دَ] (صفت مرکب) سابق. ... سبقت گیر. متبادر. مقدم. بادی. سابق در پیشدستی کردن و غالب شدن.

۹ ایا: همجنانك.

۱۰ اس، ایا: درکر [در نسخه اس حرف «ر» در آخر «درکر» قدری گرد شده و ظاهرا شبیه «درکه» دیده میشود].

۱۱ دهخدا: سبك. [سَ بُ] ... خفیف. کم وزن. در مقابل سنگین. ... ضد گران. ... || بمجاز، سهل و آسان: چنین گفت بهرام با مهتران / که کاریست این هم سبك هم گران. (فردوسی)

۱۲ ایا: [حرف «ك» در کلمه «سبك» مخدوش است].

۱۳ ایا: همی کند.

۱۴ ایا: بود.

[§۹۳:۱۵] آن وقت فصل آرد و آن جدا کردن[۱۵] خبر ممکن باشد از خبر ناممکن. پس گوید کی: «این خبر که من گفتم ممکن است، و آن را 'شاید بود' گویند، و 'ناشاید بود' ناممکن باشد». و گویند عالم[۱۶] بذات خویش به شکلهای مخالف است، از افلاك چون گنبدها و از کواکب چون گویها و از آب رونده وز خاك ایستاده و از باد بزیده[۱۷] و جز آن. پس اگر مر این عالم را آفریدگار نبودی که این خلافها به خواست او بوده شده است، ممکن نبودی که چندین خلاف اندر عالم بوده شدی از ذات یك چیز کی عالم است. و از کوه بی‌صنعت سیم پاره‌ای[۱۸] بیرون آید بی‌شکل، و لکن ممکن نباشد کی انگشتری کرده بیرون آید به شکل و صورتش. این فصل باشد ازبهرآنك ممکن است کی مر عالم را آفریدگار است و ممکن نیست کی نیست.

[§۹۳:۱۶] آن وقت برهان گوید و آن حجّت باشد که گوید حال مردم از اوّل بودش و[۱۹] تا به آخر بودنش[۲۰] هیچ برمراد او نباشد. ازبهرآنك از شکم مادر بیرون آورد به وقتی بی‌خواست[۲۱] او، بدان دلیل کی چون بیرون آوردندش بخروشید و آن خروش از کودك نشان ناکامی او بود به آمدن اندر این عالم. و چون بزرگ شد[۲۲] خواست کی همچنان جوان بماند، نتوانست همچنان ماندن. و چون پیر گشت خواهد کی درین عالم بماند و نتواند ماندن. و چون آمدن و رفتن مردم به مراد او نبود،

---

۱۵ اس: حذاکردن.

۱۶ ¦⟵برگ [ایا:۱۱۹-الف].

۱۷ اس: بزنده؛ ایا: پرنده. || نك: دهخدا: بزیدن. [بَ دَ] ... وزیدن. ...: ای نقش مهر برهمه دلها نشسته‌ای/ وی باد لطف بر همه تنها بزیده‌ای. (اثیرالدین اخسیکتی).

۱۸ اس، ایا: سیم پاره‌ء.

۱۹ ایا: – و.

۲۰ اس: [حرف «ب» در «بودنش» مخدوش است]، ایا: بودش.

۲۱ ایا: بیخواست؛ اس: [«بی» واضح نیست]. || ¦⟵برگ [اس:۱۲۷-ب].

۲۲ اس: [کلمه «کی» بعد از «شد» نوشته شده اما ظاهرا خط زده شده است].

ناچاره به مراد آفریدگار او بود. ازبهرآنك چاره نیست کی یا او[۲۳] خود آفریدگار خویشتن[۲۴] است یا دیگری آفریدگار او است.

[§۱۷:۹۳] پس این برهان باشد بر حقیقت کردن خبر کی اول گفت. آفریدگار آن وقت مر داننده را بدین شش چیز که شرح آن گفته شد آفریدگار دانسته شود، و آن هفتمِ این شش است، و آن را تمام گویند.[۲۵]

۲۳ ایا: او یا.

۲۴ ایا: خویش.

۲۵ ایا: + الْحَمْدُ لِلّٰهِ رَبِّ الْعالَمِينَ.

صف نود و چهارم

سخن اندر فرق میان معجز پیامبران و میان سحر

[§۱:۹۴] گوییم که فرق میان معجز پیامبران[۱] و میان سحر ساحر بیش از آن است که تفاوت میان یاقوت سرخ و میان سفال.

[§۲:۹۴] هرچند پیدا کردن سوی نادان هردو کاری است کی دیگر مردمان از آن عاجز آیند.

[§۳:۹۴] امّا معنی معجز، رفتن قوّت آفریدگار است از راه[۲] پیامبر[۳] اندر چیزهای طبیعی، که چون قوّت آلهی بر نفس پیامبر گذرد و برو بر چیزهای طبیعی عیشی کند بَرمُرادِ پیامبران، آن وقت اندر آن چیز طبیعی اثر کند.

[§۴:۹۴] چنانك معروف است کی رسول مصطفی، صلی[۴] اللّٰه علیه وآله، مر درخت خرما را سوی خویش خواند آن درخت همچنان اندر زمین برفت تا پیش او، علیه السّلام، و باز بفرمان او بازگشت از پیش او.

[§۵:۹۴] و خردمند را ازین شگفتی نباید داشتن ازبهرآنك تا جملهٔ قوّت آفرینش اندر يك جسم جمع نشود آن کس پیامبر[۵] نشود.

---

۱ ایا: پیغامبران.

۲ |←برگ [ایا:۱۱۹-ب].

۳ ایا: پیمبر.

۴ اس، ایا: صل.

۵ ایا: پیمبر.

[§۶:۹۴] و مثال این حال اندر مطبوعات پیدا است چنانك اگر صد سال آفتاب بر چوبی همی تابد آن چوب سوخته نشود بقوّت آفتاب؛ و لکن چون آفتاب اندر بلور گذرد یا[۶] از آیینه[۷] ژرف رویی بازافتد در وقت آن چوب کی برابر آن باشد آتش گیرد.

[§۷:۹۴] و چون در[۸] اجسام مؤلّف چیزی یافتیم که فروغ آفتاب به میانجیِ او چنین فعل که هرگز از ذات او بی آن میانجی آن فعل نیامده بود پدید آورد، که روا باشد که آفریدگار عالم اندر عالم، به میانجی آن نفس شریف، که او را مر صلاح این صنعت عظیم خویش پدید آورده بود، چیزی کرد کی بی آن میانجی نکرده بود.

[§۸:۹۴] همچنین نیز اندر طلسمات یافته است مثال این که مردم به میانجیِ صورتی که بکند برمثال گزنده‌ای[۹] یا چرنده‌ای[۱۰] از پشه و مور و کژدم و جز آن، به وقتی معلوم همی ضرر و رنج آن گزنده از اهل آن زمین باز تواند داشتن، کی آن کس بی آن میانجی هرگز رنج آن جانور از نفس خویش باز نتواند داشتن.

[§۹:۹۴] و بدانچ ایزد سبحانه مر رسول را، علیه السّلام، پدید آورد تا، به میانجی او، صانع اندر عالمْ خلقِ عالم پدید آورد، ازو جلّت قدرته رحمتی عظیم بود بر خلق.

[§۱۰:۹۴] و نگوییم کی قدرت صانع حکیم عاجز بود از نگاه‌داشت خلق را از فساد.

[§۱۱:۹۴] و لکن گوییم که چون صلاح اندر خلق به رسول خویش پدید آورد دانیم که حکمت اندر این بود.

---

۶ اس: تا؛ ایا: تا [کذا]. || تصحیح قیاسی.

۷ اس، ایا: ادینه [کذا] [در نسخ اس و ایا، به ترتیب، در تحت و فوق کلمهٔ «ادینه»، با جوهر شنگرف، صحیح آن «آیینه» نوشته شده است].

۸ ¦⟵برگ [اس:۱۲۸-الف].

۹ اس، ایا: گزندهء.

۱۰ اس، ایا: چرندهء.

[§۱۲:۹۴] پس چه شگفت باید داشتن، اگر به میانجیِ نفس شریف پیامبر،[۱۱] آفریدگار عالم، ازبهر صلاح، خلق را چیزی پدید آورد که پیش از آن بی میانجیِ او آن چیز[۱۲] پدید نیاورده بود.

[§۱۳:۹۴] و امّا فرق میان معجز و سحر ساحر آن است که آنچ پیامبر کند هیچ کس آن نتواند کرد.[۱۳]

[§۱۴:۹۴] ازبهرآنك اندر هیچ نفسی آن خاصیّت نیست از روح‌القدس کی اندر نفس پیامبر باشد. و هیچ کس به جهد و آموختن مر آن معجز را نتواند پذیرفتن.

[§۱۵:۹۴] و نه پیغامبر معجز مر کسی را تواند آموختن.

[§۱۶:۹۴] برمثال صنعتی که مردم کند اندر آهنگری و درگری و جز آن، کی ممکن نیست که هیچ جانور که اندر او نفس ناطقه نیست آن صنعت از مردم بیاموزد،[۱۴] یا مردم بتواند که مر خرس را یا بوزینه را درگری بیاموزد، بسبب دورماندن خرس از نفس ناطقه.

[§۱۷:۹۴] پس همچنین هرکسی که اندر او از روح‌القدس بهره نباشد معجز از پیامبر[۱۵] نتواند آموختن، همچنانك آفتاب اندر سنگ تابد، از عَلس[۱۶] سنگ آتش پدید نتواند آوردن.

[§۱۸:۹۴] و سحر ساحر آن است[۱۷] کی چون آن سحر کسی دیگر بداند کردن

۱۱ ایا: پیمبر.
۱۲ ¦⟵برگ [ایا:۱۲۰-الف].
۱۳ ایا: کردن.
۱۴ اس: ناموزد؛ ایا: نیاموزد.
۱۵ ایا: پیغامبر.
۱۶ اس: عکس [کذا]؛ ایا: علًس. || نك: دهخدا: علس. [عَ] ... آشامیدن. ...|| سیاهی شب.
۱۷ ¦⟵برگ [اس:۱۲۸-ب].

و کسی کی رنج برد اندر ساحری ازو بتواند[۱۸] آموختن. و ساحر بتواند کی آن سبك‌دستی و ساختن خاصیّت چیزها مر کسی دیگر را بیاموزد.

[§۱۹:۹۴] ازبهرآنك میان نفس ساحر و میان نفسهای دیگر مُجانِسَت است.

[§۲۰:۹۴] و اندر سحر ساحر چیزی ‹دیگر نیست›[۱۹] کی اندر ‹دیگر مردمان›[۲۰] نیست.

[§۲۱:۹۴] و نیز که ساحر آن ساحری بیاموخته است از دیگری. و هرچیزی که مردمی آن بیاموزد ناچاره مردمی ازو بتواند آموختن.

[§۲۲:۹۴] و پیامبری که مردمی نتوان گرفتن، کسی از پیامبر، پیامبری نتواند آموختن کی آن ایزدی است.

[§۲۳:۹۴] و نیز معجز پیامبران[۲۱] بر هر چه او خواهد رونده باشد، ازبهرآنك [به][۲۲] قوّت آفریدگار همه چیزها ازو همی بعکس با آید. پس هر چه خواهد بتواند کردن اندر هر چه خواهد.

[§۲۴:۹۴] و فعل مشعبد جز اندر چیزهائی که طبع آن ساخته باشد نرود، بر اختیار کسی دیگر مشعبدی نتواند کردن، بل‌کی[۲۳] چیزهائی کند کی آن را ساخته است[۲۴] و بر آن گستاخ گشته.

[§۲۵:۹۴] پس فعل مشعبد محدود و متناهی است.

۱۸ اس، ایا: نتواند.
۱۹ ایا: نیست دیکر.
۲۰ ایا: مردمان دیکر.
۲۱ ایا: پیغامبران.
۲۲ تصحیح قیاسی.
۲۳ ایا: بلك.
۲۴ اس: ساختست؛ ایا: ساخت است.

[§۲۶:۹۴] و معجز پیامبران[۲۵] نامحدود و نامتناهی است.

[§۲۷:۹۴] و فرقی عظیم است اندر این دو میان.[۲۶]

۲۵ ایا: پیغامبران.

۲۶ ایا: + والسّلام. || ¦⟵برگ [ایا:۱۲۰-ب].

صف نود و پنجم

سخن اندر گزیدن خدای بنده‌ای[۱] را به پیامبری[۲]

[§۹۵:۱] خزانه‌های شرف و حکمت کز کلمه باری سبحانه بر عقل اول گشاده[۳] شده است بی‌اندازه است.

[§۹۵:۲] و لکن آنچ عقل اول از آن شرف کی یافت بر نفس کلّی ببارید بی‌نهایت نیست.

[§۹۵:۳] بل عقل بر نفس افاضتی کرد از جود باری بدان قدر کی نفس بدان توانا گشت، وَرا[۴] است نهادنِ عالم طبیعی، تا بدان بیرون آرد[۵] مر این شخصهای بُوَنْدَه[۶] و تباه شونده را؛ و بازداشت از نفس مر آن حکمت را کی بدان پیوسته شود عالم طبیعی به عالم روحانی.

[§۹۵:۴] و آن آن حکمت است کی مر آن را نفس خداوند قیامت، علیه افضل السّلام، بریزد، چنانك خدای تعالی میگوید، قوله: وَ إِنْ مِنْ شَيْءٍ إِلاّٰ عِنْدَنٰا خَزٰائِنُهُ وَ مٰا نُنَزِّلُهُ إِلاّٰ بِقَدَرٍ مَعْلُومٍ.[۷] همی‌گوید: «نیست هیچ چیز جز آنك نزدیك ما است خزینه‌های آن. و فرو نفرستیمش مگر به اندازهٔ[۸] دانسته».

[§۹۵:۵] و فروفرستادن مثل است بر فایده دادن حدّی برتر حدّی فروتر را، یعنی

---

۱ اس، ایا: بندهء.

۲ قس: السجستاني، ابویعقوب اسحاق، إثبات النّبوات، «في کیفیة قبول الرسالة من المُرسِل» ص ۲۲۷ تا ۲۳۲؛ نیز نك: همان، «في کیفیة کلام اللّٰه تعالی»، ص ۲۳۲ تا ۲۳۸، به‌اهتمام: ویلفرد مادلونگ، و پال واکر (تهران: مك‌گیل و کتاب رایزن، ۱۳۹۵ش/۲۰۱۶م).

۳ اس: [«گشاده» مخدوش است].

۴ «وَرا» یعنی: او را، برای او، از آنِ او.

۵ ایا: آورد.

۶ اس: لونده؛ ایا: کونده [کذا]. || تصحیح قیاسی.

۷ سورة الحِجْر (۱۵)، آیت ۲۱.

۸ ¦⟵برگ [اس:۱۲۹-الف].

کی آنچ نزدیك عقل است بی‌کناره است و آنچ او به نفس داده است به اندازه است.

[§۹۵:۶] و نفس کلّی آرزومند است بدانچ ازو بازداشته است از نصیب حکمت[۹] و شرف، و بدان اندر هردو عالم بقا یافته است.

[§۹۵:۷] و نفس مر آن شرف را کز[۱۰] عقل اوّل بدو پیوسته است و برو تابنده است و بر معلول خویش که آن طبیعت است تا از طبیعت کی آن فعل کلّ است آن شرف اندر نفسهای جزوی مردم اثر همی‌کند براندازۀ روشنی و تیرگیِ نفسها.

[§۹۵:۸] و هر نفسی که آن روشن‌تر است و مزاج طبایع اندر جسد او به راستی نزدیك‌تر است از آن شرف و حکمت نصیب بیشتر یابد.

[§۹۵:۹] و هر نفسی که آن تیره‌تر است و مزاج طبایع اندر جسد او ناراست و مخالف است از آن شرف بازماند.

[§۹۵:۱۰] و چون نفسی قرار گیرد اندر جسدی راست‌مزاج، دور از تیرگی و اختلاف طبیعت، پذیرا شد مر آثار نفس کلّی را کی بر طبیعت برو باریده است، پذیرفتن اصلی جوهری.

[§۹۵:۱۱] و او رسول از نفس کلّی شود[۱۱] از میان دیگر نفسها سوی آن نفسها کز پذیرفتن آن آثار بازپس ماندند.

[§۹۵:۱۲] و رسالت نام آن پذیرفتن است کی نفس پیامبر پذیرفت از آثار نفس کلّی و رسول گشت، از پذیرفتن، سوی دیگر مردمان بدو سبب:

[§۹۵:۱۳] یکی از آن آن است کی آن کسها کز پذیرفتن آثار نفس کلّی بازماند،[۱۲]

---

۹ ایا: + ها [«حکمت ها» بالای خط بر روی «نصیب» نوشته شده است].

۱۰ ایا: که.

۱۱ |←برگ [ایا:۱۲۱-الف].

۱۲ اس، ایا: بازماند [استفاده از فعل مفرد بجای جمع سبکی از این نثر است].

بسبب تیرگیِ نفسهای ایشان، هم از جنس او رسول‌اند و همبازی است میان رسول و میان ایشان بدین صورت مردمی. و جدایی است میانشان بسبب پذیرفتن آثار و فواید نفس کلّی.

[§۹۵:۱۴] و مثال انبازی و جدایی کی میان توانگر و درویش است کی درویش انباز است با توانگر اندر حاصل کردن توانگری با توانگر، بدان روی 'کی توانگریِ توانگر'[۱۳] 'به درویشیِ درویش' همی پدید آید.

[§۹۵:۱۵] و قیمت کرد[۱۴] هم درویش و هم توانگر همی پدید آرند.

[§۹۵:۱۶] شرف توانگری ایشان هر دو از توانگری انباز باشد، و خواست توانگر از درویش، بدانچ توانگر را چیزی است کی درویش را آن نیست.

[§۹۵:۱۷] پس رسول[۱۵] را به حکمت و شرف[۱۶] کز نفس کلّی پذیرفته است توانگر است، و خلق بدان حکمت و شرف درویشانند. چنانك خدای تعالی میگوید، قوله:[۱۷] يَا أَيُّهَا النَّاسُ أَنْتُمُ الْفُقَرَاءُ إِلَى اللهِ وَ اللهُ هُوَ الْغَنِيُّ الْحَمِيدُ.[۱۸] همی گوید: «ای مردمان شما درویشانید سوی خدای و خدای توانگر و ستوده است».

[§۹۵:۱۸] پس واجب گشت بر رسول از آن توانگری کی یافت حقّ همبازان و هم‌شکاران خویش بیرون کردن. و خدای تعالی بستود مر آن گروه را که «ایشان اندر مال خویش نصیب کردند خواهندگان را و بازماندگان را». چنانك گفت، قوله:[۱۹] وَ الَّذِينَ فِي أَمْوَالِهِمْ حَقٌّ مَعْلُومٌ * لِلسَّائِلِ وَ الْمَحْرُومِ.[۲۰]

---

۱۳ اس: کی توانگرتر آنك.

۱۴ [«قیمت کرد» به معنی قیمت گذاری و تعیین قیمت است].

۱۵ اس: [حرف «و» در کلمه «رسول» مخدوش است].

۱۶ ⟵برگ [اس:۱۲۹-ب].

۱۷ ایا: تعالی.

۱۸ سورة فاطر (۳۵)، آیت ۱۵.

۱۹ ایا: تعالی.

۲۰ سورة المعارج (۷۰)، آیات ۲۴ تا ۲۵.

[§۱۹:۹۵] و بدین کسان مر پیامبران را خواست اندر زمان خویش، و اساسان را خواست اندر عصر خویش، و امامان را خواست اندر زمانهٔ او، کی این علم خویش مر آن کسان را، کزان شرف و فضل — کی زندگی ابدی و نعمت همیشه اندر او است — وازماندند،[۲۱] نصیب کردند.

[§۲۰:۹۵] و دیگر سبب پیامبریِ[۲۲] پیامبران آن بود که آن نفسها کز پذیرفتن فواید نفس‌کلّی به نفس خویش[۲۳] بازماندند بی‌میانجی، عاجز نبودند از پذیرفتن آن فواید به وقت شنودن از رسول.

[§۲۱:۹۵] پس بدین سبب او رسول گشت از نفس‌کلّی به امر باری تا بشنواند مر خلق را آنچ ایشان را به دل طاقت پذیرفتن آن نبود، تا عدل خدای تعالی به خلق برسد و آن قوّت کی خلق را است اندر شنودن ضایع نشود.

[§۲۲:۹۵] و چون صانع حکیم دانست که ایشان طاقت نداشتند که مر آن افاضت روحانی را به دلهای خویش بپذیرفتندی[۲۴] بر ایشان خشم گرفت به بازداشتن پیغام جسدانی از ایشان که آن تکلیف بود[۲۵] و گفت، قوله: لٰا یُکَلِّفُ اللّٰهُ نَفْساً إِلاّٰ مٰا آتٰاهٰا.[۲۶] گفت: «خدای نفرماید[۲۷] نفسی را مگر آنچ او را طاقت آن داده است».

[§۲۳:۹۵] و نیز گوییم کی خدای تعالی بگزید از میان بندگان خویش رسولی را و مر او را بسوی دیگران فرستاد به پیغام ازبهر آنك از نخست مر عقل غریزی را بدیشان فرستاده بود که بدان عقل پیغام جسمانی نتوانستند[۲۸] پذیرفتن.

۲۱ وازماندن به معنی بازماندن است.
۲۲ اس، ایا: پیامبر و [کذا]. || تصحیح قیاسی.
۲۳ ¦←برگ [ایا:۱۲۱-ب].
۲۴ ایا: پذیرفتندی.
۲۵ [یعنی: بازداشتنِ پیغام جسدانی از (مَنهیّات)، که تکلیف بود، داده شد].
۲۶ سورة الطلاق (۶۵)، آیت ۷.
۲۷ ایا: نفرماید خدای.
۲۸ اس: نتوانستند؛ ایا: نتوانستند. || تصحیح قیاسی. || ¦←برگ [اس:۱۳۰-الف].

[§۲۴:۹۵] و نیز ازبهر آن بود فرستادن رسول به خلق که آن چیزی کی اندر گمان مردمان آید سوی بعضی از مردمان درست نشود مگر آنگه کی آن گمانی را محسوس بینند و بیابند.

[§۲۵:۹۵] و چون اندر دوری رسولی بیاید و مردمان را بترساند به چیزی کی اندر گمانهای ایشان آینده باشد، [از][۲۹] آن ترسانیدن گمان ایشان به یقین شود.

[§۲۶:۹۵] و مثال این چنان باشد کی اندر گمانهای ما ثابت است که چون آتش به هیزم فراداری هیزم را بسوزد.

[§۲۷:۹۵] وگر کسی بیاید و ما را گوید دیدم که آتش بهیزم دراوفتاد و بسوخت[۳۰] هیزم را مر گمان را بدان گفتار استواری افزاید.

[§۲۸:۹۵] و دلیل بر واجب گشتن فرستادن رسول از خدای به خلق این عالم طبیعی ثابت کنیم.

[§۲۹:۹۵] و گوییم کی پیدا شدن زایشهای عالم از معادن و نبات و حیوان از جهت حرکتهای کواکب و افلاك است به بودش هر نوعی از انواع زایشها.

[§۳۰:۹۵] سبب آن است هر بودش آن نوع را که به فضل پیش‌رو او است، تا برسد زایش عالم به مردم که بودش او ازبهر خویش است نه ازبهر چیزی دیگر.

[§۳۱:۹۵] چنانك گوییم که بودش نبات بسبب بودش ستور بود که[۳۱] اگر نبات نبودی ستور نبودی.

---

۲۹ اس، ایا: – از.

۳۰ اس، ایا: نسوخت. || تصحیح قیاسی.

۳۱ |← برگ [ایا:۱۲۲-الف].

[§۳۲:۹۵] و دلیل بر درستیِ این قول آن است که اگر نبات از ستور بازگیری ستور بمیرد.

[§۳۳:۹۵] و بودش ستور بسبب بودش ددگان گوشت‌خوار بود، چه اگر ستور گیاه‌خوار نبودی دده گوشت‌خوار نبودی.

[§۳۴:۹۵] و دلیل بر درستیِ این قول آن است که اگر گوشت‌خوار را از گیاه‌خوار بازداری بمیرد.

[§۳۵:۹۵] و بودش جانور سبب بود مر بودش مردم را. و اگر جانور نبودی مردم نبودی.

[§۳۶:۹۵] و دلیل بر درستیِ این قول آن است که اگر جانور از عالم برگیری مردم برگرفته شود.

[§۳۷:۹۵] و مردم سبب نبود مر بودن چیزی دیگر را بل‌کی[۳۲] بودش مردم خود از بهر ذات مردم بود.

[§۳۸:۹۵] و مردم از همه چیزها کی بودش ایشان پیش ازو بود شریفتر بود.

[§۳۹:۹۵] پس مر او را نگاه‌داشت واجب آمد بیك تن هم از مردم.

[§۴۰:۹۵] پس شرف آن نگاهبان[۳۳] مردم برتر آمد از شرف همه مردم.[۳۴]

[§۴۱:۹۵] و نیز مردم را دو حرکت است:

[§۴۲:۹۵] یکی حرکت عقل است کی بدان مر ذات خویش را نگاه دارد از آفتها و تدبیر جسم و روح خویش بدان حرکت کند.

---

۳۲ ایا: بلك.
۳۳ اس: نگاه‌بان.
۳۴ |←برگ [اس:۱۳۰-ب].

[§۴۳:۹۵] و دیگر حرکت آن است که اندر افعال مر آن را کار بندد بر نیك و بد.

[§۴۴:۹۵] و آن حرکت که مردم را عقلی است مر آن را گاه‌گاه کار بندد، و همیشه از مردم حرکت عقلی نیاید[۳۵] مگر به وقت کشیدن منفعتی یا به دفع کردن مضرّتی.

[§۴۵:۹۵] و این حرکتهای فرومایه[۳۶] از خوردن و رفتن و گفتن سخنهای نابکار و جز آن هروقتی باشد و همیشه.

[§۴۶:۹۵] پس ازین حکم همی واجب آید کی حرکات ستارگان و افلاك و آنچ ازبهر پدید آوردن این شخصهای تیرهٔ فرومایه باشد همیشه موجود باشد.

[§۴۷:۹۵] و آن حرکت کز بهر پدید آمدن شخص باشد کی اندر او نگاه‌داشت دیگر شخصها باشد کی گاه‌گاه باشد.

[§۴۸:۹۵] و چون حرکات ستارگان و افلاك و آن حرکت کی بدو سیاست خلق و صلاح عالم بحاصل آید متفق شوند، شخصی معتدل پدید آید کی آن شخص هم حرکت بودش خویش[۳۷] پذیرد و هم حرکت سیاستِ خلق.[۳۸]

[§۴۹:۹۵] و او رسول شود سوی دیگر مردمان کی شخصهای[۳۹] ایشان جز حرکت بودش نپذیرفته‌اند.

[§۵۰:۹۵] این است سبب گزیدن صانع مر یك مردم را به رسالت سوی دیگر مردمان.

[§۵۱:۹۵] و نیز گوییم کی ما فرومانده‌ایم از اندریافتن چیزی کی از آفرینش ما غرض آفریدگار ما آن است.

---

۳۵ اس: نماید؛ ایا: نیاید.

۳۶ ایا: [حرف «ف» در «فرومایه» مخدوش است].

۳۷ ایا: – خویش.

۳۸ یعنی: حرکت تشریعی.

۳۹ ¦⟵برگ [ایا:۱۲۲-ب].

[§۵۲:۹۵] پس واجب آید بر صانع حکیم فرستادن کسی از ما بسوی ما فروماندگان تا آگاهی دهد از آنچ رضاء او از ما در آن است.

[§۵۳:۹۵] و آنچ پیدا است چون آفتاب فایده‌های شریعی اندر خلق از پاکیزه داشتن مر نفس خویش را از فعل ستوران، و از طاعت داشتن مر آفریدگار خویش را به نماز، و از مُواسا[۴۰] کردن با درویشان به زکات، و جز آن.

[§۵۴:۹۵] وگر صانع حکیم ما را به مراد ما دست بازداشتی[۴۱] هرکسی راهی دیگر گرفتی و همیشه هرکسی اندر گمان افتادی از طریقت خویش که مگر حقّ جز آن است که او دارد.

[§۵۵:۹۵] و چون رسول خدای بیاید اندر دوری و خلق را از سوی حقّ خواند و خلق زیر یك فرمان جمله شوند و شك از میان خلق برخیزد و صلاح و آرام[۴۲] در[۴۳] میان خلق پدید[۴۴] آید.

[§۵۶:۹۵] بدین سبب بُوَد کی ایزد تعالی یك تن را از خلق به پیامبری[۴۵] اختیار کرد.

[§۵۷:۹۵] پس گوییم کی راستی و روشنی و پاکیزگی اندر شخص رسول خدای به نهایت و غایت باشد.

[§۵۸:۹۵] و اندر شخصهایِ راست‌گویْ دارندگانْ مر او را، و پذیرندگان مر فرمان خدای را بر زفان او، به مقدار باشد.

---

۴۰ نك: دهخدا: مواسا. [مُ] (از عربی، اِسم مصدر) مواساة. مواسات. آسایش و راحت و نیکخواهی و خیراندیشی و نیکویی و احسان و غمخواری و شفقت و مهربانی و همدمی و رفاقت و موافقت.

۴۱ نك: دهخدا: دست بازداشتن. [دَ تَ] (مصدر مرکب) رها کردن. ترك گفتن. دست کشیدن. ترك کردن. گذاشتن. یله کردن. هشتن.

۴۲ |⟵برگ [اس:۱۳۱-الف].

۴۳ ایا: – در.

۴۴ ایا: پیدا.

۴۵ ایا: پیغامبری.

[§۹۵:۵۹] و بمثل شخص رسول کمال راستیها و صلاح و زهد و پارسائی باشد. و همه شخصهای مؤمنان از خلق جزو باشند مر آن کل را.

[§۹۵:۶۰] و دلیل بر راستیِ آفرینش رسول و پاکیزگی و پارسائی و شرف و صلاح نفس او است که دانا و نادان بر سخن و فرمان آرمیده‌اند.

[§۹۵:۶۱] و نشان راستی و صلاح آن است که مردم بگوید و بدو فرازآید.

[§۹۵:۶۲] پس بازآمدن نفسهای خلق بر سخن پیامبر گوایی همی‌دهد بر اعتدال او و بر صلاح نفس او، علیه السّلام.

[§۹۵:۶۳] و نیست هیچ کس اندر عالم، و نبوده است کسی، کی خلق بر سخن آن کس قرار گرفته است چنین کی بر سخن پیامبران[۴۶] قرار[۴۷] گرفته‌اند.

[§۹۵:۶۴] و بباید دانستن خردمند را که قرار خلق بر سخن پیامبران،[۴۸] علیهم السّلام، بدان اوفتاد کی علّت بودش عالم امر خدای بود که مر آن را کلمه گفتند.

[§۹۵:۶۵] و کلمه سخنی باشد. و چون علّت عالم از باری سبحانه سخنی[۴۹] بود، عالم اندر آنچ بزاد بر مردم قرار گرفت که او زنده‌ای[۵۰] است سخنگوی.

[§۹۵:۶۶] و غایت و نهایت عالم او بود. و غایت و نهایتِ کارِ معلولْ آن باشد کی به علّت خویش مانند شود به رویی از رویها.

[§۹۵:۶۷] و چون عالم بذات خویش چون علّت خویش نتوانست شدن به

---

۴۶ ایا: پیغامبران.

۴۷ ¦⟵برگ [ایا:۱۲۳-الف].

۴۸ ایا: پیمبران.

۴۹ ایا: سخن.

۵۰ اس، ایا: زنده‌ء.

سخن گفتن، زایشها پدید آورد پس یکدیگر نیز[۵۱] تا برسانند مر زایش خویش را[۵۲] به مردم سخنگوی مانند عقل کی کلمه بدو پیوسته بود.

[§۹۵:۶۸] پس هر کی از مردم بدان اوّل پدیدآمده پیوسته شود، که کلمه باری با او است، رسول باشد گزیده از صانع حکیم تا بترساند مردم را بدانچ روح‌الامین اندر دل او افکنده باشد به زفان قوم خویش.

[§۹۵:۶۹] و بماند آن سخن به میان مردمان روزگار دراز. و آن سخن سبب باشد مر راستیی کارهای ایشان را و صلاح ایشان را، همچنانك آن سخن نخستین از باری سبحانه سبب بود[۵۳] مر راست شدن این عالم را.

[§۹۵:۷۰] و اگر گزیدن از خلق به رسولی مر[۵۴] یکی را از ایشان، سوی خلق نیست، بل کی سوی خدای است، چنانك همی گوید، قوله:[۵۵] وَ رَبُّكَ یَخْلُقُ مٰا یَشٰاءُ وَ یَخْتٰارُ مٰا کٰانَ لَهُمُ الْخِیَرَةُ سُبْحٰانَ اللّٰهِ وَ تَعٰالیٰ عَمّٰا یُشْرِکُونَ.[۵۶] گفت: «و پروردگار تو بیافریند آنچ خواهد و بگزیند»، یعنی از بندگان مر رسالت و وصایت و امامت را «و نیست گزیدن مر ایشان را»، یعنی که ایشان واقف نیستند بر روحانیان و پیوستن ایشان به خلق. «پاك است خدای و بلند است از آنك بگزینند مر آن را که ایشان مر او را انباز گیرند» اندر امامت.

[§۹۵:۷۱] ایزد تعالی ما را دور دارد از پس رفتنِ هوا[۵۷] و انباز گرفتن با کسی کی خدای تعالی او را بگزیده است.

---

۵۱ اس، ایا: ند [کذا]. || تصحیح مفهومی.

۵۲ ایا: – را.

۵۳ ¦⟵برگ [اس:۱۳۱-ب].

۵۴ ایا: مکر.

۵۵ ایا: + تعالی.

۵۶ سورة القصص (۲۸)، آیت ۶۸.

۵۷ ایا: – هوا.

صف نود و ششم

سخن اندر آنك چرا دو رسول اندر يكزمان روا نبود[1]

[§۱:۹۶] كسی كی گويد چرا اندر عالم دو رسول نبود چنان باشد كی گويد چرا در آسمان دو آفتاب چشمه نبود.

[§۲:۹۶] وگر آن كس انديشه كند بداند كه گر[2] اين آفتاب گردنده نيستی ميان دو قطب جنوبی و شمالی يك جای از زمين همه بسوختی از گرما و ديگر جا از سرما همه سنگ گشتی.

[§۳:۹۶] و چون يك آفتاب است و همی‌گردد از شمال به جنوب و از جنوب به شمال جايی از زمين به وقتی نبات همی بيرون آرد و جايی همی آسايد مر بيرون آوردن نبات را به وقتی ديگر. و اندر اين حكمتی عظيم است.

[§۴:۹۶] پس اگر گوييم دو پيامبر[3] يا دو امام بودی، هردو موافق بودندی اندر دعوت و شريعت، يا مخالف بودندی ايشان را با يكديگر جنگ افتادی و ناچاره يكی از ايشان مبطل بودی. و چون درست شد كی يكی از ايشان مبطل بودی، درست شدی[4] كه پيامبر زيشان خود يكی بيش نبودی همچنين كی امروز است.

[§۵:۹۶] پس اگر موافق يكديگر بودندی اندر دعوت بی هيچ خلاف پس خود همچنين بودی كه امروز است كه همه مسلمانان مر كافران را به محمّد مصطفیٰ،[5] عليه السّلام، می‌خوانند[6] بی هيچ خلافی و كسی به پيامبری هيچ دعوی نمی‌كند چون با او موافق‌اند و اين بيانی سخت روشن است.

---

۱ ←|برگ [ايا:۱۲۳-ب].

۲ اس: [كلمه «گر» بالای خط نوشته شده است].

۳ ايا: پيمبر.

۴ ايا: شد.

۵ ايا: مصطفا.

۶ ←|برگ [اس:۱۳۲-الف].

[§۶:۹۶] و نیز از طریق آفرینش گوییم که قوّتهای همه ستارگان و حرکتهای ایشان، از حرکتهایی که از نگاه‌داشت عالم حاصل شود، جمله باید شدن تا یك تن از حرکات و قوّتها بدان جای رسد که خلق را سیاست تواند کردن.

[§۷:۹۶] وگر آن قوّتها که[۷] از کسی بحاصل شود[۸] که خلق را سیاست کند، بدو قسمت شود و نگاهبان[۹] اندر هر دو ناتمام.

[§۸:۹۶] همچنانك همی دانیم کی قوّتهای همه طبایع و افلاك و انجم جمله شده است تا اثر زایشهاء عالم پدید آمده است.

[§۹:۹۶] وگر،[۱۰] جز این که پدید آمده است، عالم خواهد که چیزی پدید آرد، آن وقت کزین قوّتها جدا کند، ازین زایشها نقصان شود و آن زایش که نو پدید آید تمام نیاید.

[§۱۰:۹۶] پس یکی تمام، به حکمت نزدیکتر از آن باشد، که دو باشد هر دو ناقص.

[§۱۱:۹۶] پس گوییم[۱۱] که پدید آوردن یك شریعت تمام حکمتی عظیم بود از صانع حکیم تا همه خلق روی بدان آوردند.

[§۱۲:۹۶] برمثال همه اندام مردم که سالارِي یك دل همی تمام نگاه‌داشته باشد.

[§۱۳:۹۶] و اگر اندر این مردم دو دل بودی، هر دو ناقص بودی بدان دلیل که این قوّت که بدین یك[۱۲] دل پیوسته است بدو دل پیوستی.

---

۷ اس: [«که» محو شده است]؛ ایا: – که.

۸ ایا: نشود.

۹ اس، ایا: نگاه‌بان.

۱۰ اس: [«وگر» مخدوش است]؛ ایا: و کز [کذا].

۱۱ ¦⟵برگ [ایا:۱۲۴-الف].

۱۲ ایا: – یك.

[§۱۴:۹۶] و چنین کی یکی تمام است به دو قسمت شدی ناچاره هردو ناقص بودی.

[§۱۵:۹۶] و به ناقص بودن دل شکست اندر جسد راه یافتی. ازبهر این بود که خدای تعالی گفت، قوله: مٰا جَعَلَ اللّٰهُ لِرَجُلٍ مِنْ قَلْبَيْنِ فِي جَوْفِهِ.[۱۳] گفت: «خدای نکرد مردی را دُودِل از اندرون او».

[§۱۶:۹۶] همچنین روا نباشد که اندر زمانه‌ای[۱۴] دو صاحب شریعت باشد، یا اندر يك زمانه دو امام باشد، که شریعت بدان مُهمَل و باخَلَل[۱۵] شود.[۱۶]

[§۱۷:۹۶] همچنین که امروز چندین اختلاف هلاك‌کننده اندر دین افتاده است بسبب رفتن مردمان از پس امامان ناحق به هوای خویش.

---

۱۳ سورة الأَحزاب (۳۳)، آیت ۴.

۱۴ اس، ایا: زمانهء.

۱۵ نك: دهخدا: خلل. [خَ لَ] ... گشادگی میان دو چیز. رخنه. ... || پراکندگی در رأی. ... || عیب. ... - باخلل: بانقصان.

۱۶ ایا: بود.

صف نود و هفتم

سخن اندر آنك چون نفس از جسد جدا شود توانا شود[۱]

[§۱:۹۷] گوییم[۲] به توفیق خدای تعالی[۳] و جود ولیّش که نفس اندر مردم به سه مرتبت است: نامِیَه، و حسّیَّه و ناطِقَه، همچنانك زایش عالم به سه مرتبت است: معادن، و نبات و حیوان.

[§۲:۹۷] و نفس نامیه عاجز است اندر تخم از رستن و از کار بستن قوّت [که در][۴] او است.

[§۳:۹۷] و نفس حسّیه[۵] عاجز نیست از کار بستن قوّت خویش به یافتن مر محسوسات را.

[§۴:۹۷] و چون قوّت نفس انسانی اندر نطفه باشد، برمثال تخمی باشد، که اندر او درختی باشد با همه آلتهای درخت و عاجز باشد از پذیرفتن زیادت.

[§۵:۹۷] و چون اندر رحِم ماده اوفتد، توانایی یابد و قوّت کار بستن خویش به پذیرفتن زیادت. برمثال تخم کی اندر خاك افتد[۶] و آب و هوا و آتش مر او را یاری دهند.

[§۶:۹۷] و اندر آن حال کی اندر رحِم ماده باشد آن نطفه مر او را اندر حال خویش اختیار نباشد بل‌کی مجبور باشد. برمثال تخم که اندر خاك، آب و هوا و آتش بیابد[۷] نتواند که نروید.

۱ اس: [«شود» مخدوش است]، ایا: شودد.

۲ اس: [«گوییم» مخدوش است].

۳ ¦⟵برگ [اس:۱۳۲-ب].

۴ تصحیح قیاسی.

۵ اس، ایا: عاجزی [کذا]. || تصحیح قیاسی.

۶ ایا: اوفتاد.

۷ اس: ىىابد.

[§۷:۹۷] پس نطفه[۸] که اندر پشت مرد بود فعلی نبود او را نه به جبر و نه به اختیار. و چون اندر رحِمِ اوفتاد[۹] کارکن گشت به جبر که از آن نتوانست بازاستاد.

[§۸:۹۷] و تا بدان وقت که حس بدو نپیوست با شناختن بد و نیك، و دانستنِ دوست از دشمن، او مجبور بود.

[§۹:۹۷] و چون حس بیافت مختار گشت اندر فعلهای خویش و خواست بگفت و خواست خاموش بود، خواست برفت و خواست بنشست، و از درجهٔ جبر به درجهٔ اختیار افتاد.

[§۱۰:۹۷] و خداوند[ان] علم حقیقت مر مختار را ناتمام و ضعیف شناختند، و خود همچنین است ازبهرآنك مختار آن باشد کی خواهد بکند کاری و خواهد نکند.

[§۱۱:۹۷] و خواستن او مر چیزی را و از ناخواستن او همان چیز[۱۰] را از ضعیفی و عاجزی و ناتمامیِ او باشد.

[§۱۲:۹۷] چه اگر تمام بودی چیزی کردی که او را از آن باز نبایستی گشتن.

[§۱۳:۹۷] پس گوییم که مردم، اندر جبرِ یافتنِ حس[۱۱] و نطق، مختار است.

[§۱۴:۹۷] و مختار شریفتر از مجبور[۱۲] است؛ و لکن توانا نیست، که اگر توانا بودی، مختار نبودی، بل کی از اختیار بی‌نیاز بودی.

[§۱۵:۹۷] و چون مردم کز درجهٔ[۱۳] نفس نامیه[۱۴] به درجهٔ حسّی آمد از جبر به

---

۸ ¦⟵برگ [ایا:۱۲۴-ب].

۹ ایا: افتد.

۱۰ ایا: حبز.

۱۱ اس: حسی.

۱۲ اس: [«مجبور» مخدوش است].

۱۳ اس: [«مردم کز درجهٔ» مخدوش است].

۱۴ اس: [«نامیه» مخدوش است].

اختیار رسید،[15] لازم آید از حکم قیاس که چون از درجهٔ حس به درجهٔ عقل رسد قادر مطلق گردد.

[§۹۷:۱۶] و این آن وقت باشد که اندر کار بستن نفس ناطقه و پرورش او بر حقّ و کار بستن عمل و شناختن علم تقصیری نیوفتد تا از درجهٔ اختیار به درجهٔ قدرت رسد.

[§۹۷:۱۷] و این برهانی روشن است و راهی ستوده که نموده شد خردمند را.

۱۵ ¦—←برگ [اس:۱۳۳-الف].

صف نود و هشتم

سخن اندر آنك از پس توبه، از[1] گناه اثر[2] نماند

[§۹۸:۱] گوییم که مر بدی را اندر آفرینش اصل نیست چنانك پیش ازین اندر [این][3] کتاب دلایل آن نمودیم.[4]

[§۹۸:۲] و نیکی را اصل است چنانك روشنایی را که او مانند خیر است، چشمهٔ آفتاب اصل است، که نور ازو بر عالم فروباریده است.

[§۹۸:۳] و تاریکی را که او مانند شرّ است چشمه‌ای[5] پیدا نیست،[6] که تاریکی ازو همی اندر چیزی اثر کند.

[§۹۸:۴] معارضه اگر کسی گوید که زمین چشمهٔ تاریك است بدانچ تاریکی از سایهٔ او موجود است، و آن شب است کی کلّ ظلمت ‹ازو است›.[7] جواب مر او را گوییم که زمین را تاریکی نه ذاتی است چنانك مر چشمهٔ آفتاب را روشنایی ذاتی است.

[§۹۸:۵] وگر[8] زمین را تاریکی صفتی ذاتی بودی تاریکی ازو اندر اجرام آسمان اثر کردی همچنانك نور اجرام که آن مر اجرام را صفتی ذاتی است همی اندر زمین اثر کند به روشن کردن مر او را.

---

۱ ایا: – از.

۲ ایا: – اثر.

۳ تصحیح قیاسی.

۴ نك: همین کتاب، صف ۶۲: سخن اندر آنك بدی را در آفرینش مایه نیست؛ نیز قس: کتاب الینابیع، الینبوع الخامس والعشرون (۲۵): في أنّ الشّر لا أصل له في الإبداع، ص ۶۱ تا ۶۳.

۵ اس، ایا: چشمه‌ء.

۶ ¦←برگ [ایا:۱۲۵-الف].

۷ اس: ازوست؛ ایا: دروست.

۸ اس [«و» در «وگر» مخدوش است].

[§۹۸:۶] و لکن تاریك است تا رسیدن نور آفتاب بر جملگیِ شخص زمین بیك دفعه هموار.

[§۹۸:۷] و چون معلوم کردیم که مر بدی را اصل نیست اندر آفرینش، گوییم که مر نفس بدی را نیکی و خیر اصلی است، برمثال اندامها مر جسم را، و بدی و شر مر او را برمثال ریش و جراحت است و آبله.

[§۹۸:۸] وگر مر جسم[۹] را و اندامها را از آفرینش اصل و مادّت است، و ریش و جراحت را اصل نیست که باقی شود، بل‌که علّت که دارو مر او را بپزد.

[§۹۸:۹] و توبه براستی مر گناه را مانند مرهم نرم است مر جراحت را.

[§۹۸:۱۰] و همچنانك، چون مرهم به جراحت برنهی، قوّت کواکب مر آن جراحت را، به میانجیِ آن مرهم مادّت فرستد، و ریش را به میانجیِ[۱۰] دارو بگدازد اندر این عالم[۱۱] تا جسم از آن پاکیزه شود.

[§۹۸:۱۱] همچنان توبهٔ نصوح بر نفس گناهکار[۱۲] مرهم گردد و نور کلمه اندر آن عالم مر گناه او را به میانجیِ توبه بسوزد و نفس را پاکیزه کند. چنانك خدای تعالی میفرماید، قوله: وَ یَمْحُ[۱۳] اللّٰهُ الْبٰاطِلَ وَ یُحِقُّ الْحَقَّ بِکَلِمٰاتِهِ إِنَّـهُ عَلِیمٌ بِذٰاتِ الصُّدُورِ.[۱۴] همی‌گوید: «خدای پاك کند مر باطل را و اثبات کند حق را به سخنان خویش که او دانا است بدانچ در دلها است».

[§۹۸:۱۲] و نیکی برمثال اندام است اندر جسد که به پرورش قوّت گیرد و منافع به مردم پیوسته شود.

---

۹ اس [«جشم» سه نقطه بالای کلمه با جوهر کمرنگ‌تر نوشته شده است].

۱۰ اس: [«را بمیانجی» مخدوش است].

۱۱ ¦⟵برگ [اس:۱۳۳-ب].

۱۲ اس، ایا: گناه کار.

۱۳ اس، ایا: یمحوا.

۱۴ سورة الشوری (۴۲)، آیت ۲۴.

[§۹۸:۱۳] و پدید آمدن بدی از نفس بسبب بازماندن او است از نیکی، برمثال تاریکی بر زمین کی نارسیدنِ نِگَرِشِ[۱۵] آفتاب است بدان جایگاه.

[§۹۸:۱۴] و چون نور بر آن جایگاه افتد از تاریکی هیچ اثر نماند و کس نداند کی کجا رفت.[۱۶]

[§۹۸:۱۵] همچنین اندر نطفهٔ مردم که به رحِم افتد مر اندامهای اندرونی و بیرونی را اصل است، و لکن مر جراحت و گر[۱۷] و دنبل را اندر نطفه اصل نیست.

[§۹۸:۱۶] امّا اگر خوردنی و پوشیدنی که بقاء جسم بدان است نه موافق یابد بدان سبب ریشها و علّتها پدید آید بر جسد مردم، و لکن اندامی دیگر نروید،[۱۸] و آن علّت بی‌اصل به دارو بشود و چنان شود آن علّت که خود نبود.

[§۹۸:۱۷] همچنین به توبه نفس از گناه پاك شود چنانك برابر شود با بیگناه. چنانك رسول مصطفی، صلّی الله علیه وآله، فرمود: التَّائِبُ مِن الذَّنْبِ کَمَنْ لَا ذَنْبَ لَهُ.[۱۹] گفت: «بازگردنده از گناه چون آن کس است کی او را هیچ گناه نیست».

---

۱۵ نك: دهخدا: نگرش. [نِ گَ رِ] (اسم مصدر) نگاه کردن . دیدن. ... نگرستن... بینش. نظر. نگاه. ملاحظه . مشاهده. ... || (اصطلاح نجوم) نظر و اتصال در کواکب.

۱۶ ¦⟵برگ [ایا:۱۲۵-ب].

۱۷ نك: دهخدا: گر. [گَ] ... نام جوشی است مشهور که به عربی جرب گویند. ... در استعمال قدما به معنی بیماری مشهور است و در تداول امروزی، بمعنی مبتلای بدان بیماری است بجای گرگن و گرگین. مرضی است که مویها را بریزاند و بدن خاصه انگشتان خارش کند و مجروح شود و آن را به عربی جرب گویند و سرایت کننده است به دیگری. ... گریست این جهان بمثل زیرا / بس ناخوش است و خوش بخارد گر. (ناصرخسرو، [دیوان اشعار، ص ۱۴۸، س ۱، به اهتمام: نصرالله تقوی]).

۱۸ اس، ایا: نه روید.

۱۹ نك: الکلینی، محمد بن یعقوب، الكافي، تصحیح: علی اکبر غفاری و محمد آخوندی (تهران، ۱۴۰۷ق)، ج ۲، (۱۹۲) بَابَ التَّوبَة، ص ۴۳۵: ۱۰ - عنه، عن أحمد بن محمد، عن علي بن النعمان، عن محمد بن سنان، عن یوسف [بن] أبي یعقوب بیاع الأرز، عن جابر، عن أبي جعفر (علیه السلام) قال: سمعته یقول: التائب من الذنب کمن لا ذنب له والمقیم علی الذنب وهو مستغفر منه کالمستهزئ.

صف نود و نهم

سخن اندر برگرفتن شریعت به زمان خداوند قیامت

[§۹۹:۱] سخن اندر پرورش نفس و معالجت مر او را برابر باید با پرورش جسد و معالجت مر او را.

[§۹۹:۲] از بهر آنك جسد کالبد است مر نفس را، و کالبد مانند[۱] باشد مر آن جسد را که اندر او باشد.

[§۹۹:۳] پس گوییم که چون جسد مردم از راستی بشود، و طبایع اندر او[۲] میل کند از اعتدال، درستی و قوّت ازو بشود، تا بر طبیب حکیم واجب شود بازداشتن مر بیمار را از آنچ مر او را آرزو شود[۳] به[۴] تکلیف کردن مر او را از خوردن داروهای طلخ و ناخوش، آنچ او مر او را[۵] نخواهد، تا بدین دو روی بیماری را ازو دور کند و مر او را به تندرستی بازرساند.[۶]

[§۹۹:۴] و پس فرمان آن طبیب و بازداشتن او مر آن بیمار را از آنچ او خواهد برمثال غلّی باشد بر دست او، و قیدی باشد بر پای او، اندر وقت بیماری، و چون درست گشت و به حال خویش[۷] بازآمد طبیب آن غلّ و بند ازو برگیرد، و دست او بدانچ مر او را آرزو شود از طعام و شراب گشاده کند و خوردن داروهای ناخوش مر او را عفو کند.

[§۹۹:۵] پس همچنین است حال نفسها که بدین جسدها پیوسته‌اند که چون اندر

---

۱ ایا: ماننده.

۲ اس: اندو؛ ایا: اندرو.

۳ ایا: + و.

۴ ایا: - به.

۵ اس: [عبارت «از خوردن داروها» نوشته شده اما خط زده شده است].

۶ ¦⟵برگ [اس:۱۳۴-الف].

۷ اس، ایا: خوش. || [حال خویش= حال اوّلیّه].

زمانی مر عالمِ خویش را نفسها فراموش کنند بر عالم طبیعت عاشق شوند و بدو میل کنند، پرستش از ایشان مَر[۸] مُبدِع حقّ را فروماند.

[§۹۹:۶] و مر او را به آفریدگان برابر کنند اندر صفات، چنانك امروز همی‌کنند بیشتر ازین امت، که خداوند را تعالی صفت مخلوقات همی‌دهند، و همی‌پندارند کی ایشان موحّدان‌اند از عاشقی که بر این عالم شده‌اند.

[§۹۹:۷] و مردم چون چیزی را دوست دارد آن چیز به چشم سخت نیکو نماید.

[§۹۹:۸] پس صفت کردن امّت نادان مر ایزد را تعالی به صفت خلق از قادر و عالِم و حقّ و جز از[۹] آن گوایی همی‌دهد بر فتنه شدن ایشان بر این عالم که این‌همه صفت زایشهای او است.

[§۹۹:۹] تا واجب شد بر[۱۰] فرستادن طبیب سوی نفسهای خلق از پیامبران حقّ، علیهم‌السّلام، تا بازدارند مر ایشان را از بعضی از چیزهائی که آن را جوینده‌اند، و شاخ[۱۱] گشتن ایشان را از طاعت آنچ مر آن را دشوار دارند.

[§۹۹:۱۰] و اندر هر زمانی رسولی مر ایشان را ریاضت همی‌کند تا نفسها را بدان ریاضت پاك شدن باشد از بیماریِ نادانی و میل او سوی عالم طبیعی.

[§۹۹:۱۱] و چون زمانی که اندر او آفات تشبیه و تعطیل بر نفوس خلق[۱۲] اوفتاده است بگذرد، و نفسها به توحید و تقدیس ایزد تعالی رسد، این بندها و غلها از دُبُر[۱۳] برگیرد.

---

۸ ¦⟵برگ [ایا:۱۲۶-الف].

۹ ایا: – از.

۱۰ اس: ر؛ ایا: بر.

۱۱ اس: ساح؛ ایا: مباح [کذا]. || تصحیح قیاسی. شاخ گشتن یعنی اجباری شدن. با توجه به مضمون «ریاضت» در بندهای [§۹۹:۳]، [§۹۹:۴]، [§۹۹:۱۰] همین صف.

۱۲ ایا: – خلق.

۱۳ اس: دبر؛ ایا: دیو [کذا]. || تصحیح قیاسی. نك: دهخدا: دبر. [دُ] ... سپس پشت. .... || سپس و آخر هرچیز. ج، ادبار. ... و نیز رجوع به دُبُر شود.

[§۹۹:۱۲] و زیشان عبادات به اندیشهٔ پاك و خاطر روشن بسنده کنند، وز جسد بر آن اندیشه اشارت و مثال نخواهند.

[§۹۹:۱۳] چنانك خدای تعالی همی‌گوید اندر فضل مصطفی، صلی[۱۴] الله علیه وآله،[۱۵] که این غلها از خلق برگیرد، و مر آن شریعتهای گذشته را همی اغلال و اِصران[۱۶] خواند، قوله: وَ یَضَعُ عَنْهُمْ إِصْرَهُمْ وَ الْأَغْلٰالَ الَّتِي کٰانَتْ عَلَيْهِمْ.[۱۷] گفت: «(رسول، علیه السّلام،) فرونهد غلها کی بر ایشان بود».

[§۹۹:۱۴] و آن فروگرفتن بند و غل از امّت او، صلی[۱۸] الله علیه وآله، پیدا آمد بر آنچ توحید اندر طریق حقّ بغایت رسد اندر برج شهادت، که اندر او مجموع[۱۹] نفی و اثبات است، و آن تشبیه و تعطیل باشد.

[§۹۹:۱۵] و چون توحید ازین دو آلایش پاك بود شهادت به اخلاص آن است.

[§۹۹:۱۶] و هر که حقّ را از خاندان نبوّت نپذیرفت بدین دو دریا غرق شدند.

[§۹۹:۱۷] و هر که اندر کشتی نوحِ[۲۰] دور خویش آمد ازین هر دو غرقه شدن رسته گشت.

[§۹۹:۱۸] و چون کار به زمان خداوند قیامت، علی ذکره السّلام، رسد، و تشبیه و

---

۱۴ اس: صل؛ ایا: صلّ.

۱۵ ¦⟵برگ [اس:۱۳۴-ب].

۱۶ اس، ایا: اصرار [کذا]. || تصحیح قیاسی. || نك: دهخدا: اصر. [اَ] اِصْر. اُصْر... بار گران: وَ لٰا تَحْمِلْ عَلَيْنٰا إِصْراً. (قرآن ۲/۲۸۶)؛ و بار مکن بر ما بار گرانی را... ذنب. و اصل آن ثقیل است... ج، آصار، اِصران.

۱۷ سورة الأعراف (۷)، آیت ۱۵۷: الَّذِينَ يَتَّبِعُونَ الرَّسُولَ النَّبِيَّ الْأُمِّيَّ الَّذِي يَجِدُونَهُ مَكْتُوباً عِنْدَهُمْ فِي التَّوْرٰاةِ وَ الْإِنْجِيلِ يَأْمُرُهُمْ بِالْمَعْرُوفِ وَ يَنْهٰاهُمْ عَنِ الْمُنْكَرِ وَ يُحِلُّ لَهُمُ الطَّيِّبٰاتِ وَ يُحَرِّمُ عَلَيْهِمُ الْخَبٰائِثَ وَ يَضَعُ عَنْهُمْ إِصْرَهُمْ وَ الْأَغْلٰالَ الَّتِي كٰانَتْ عَلَيْهِمْ فَالَّذِينَ آمَنُوا بِهِ وَ عَزَّرُوهُ وَ نَصَرُوهُ وَ اتَّبَعُوا النُّورَ الَّذِي أُنْزِلَ مَعَهُ أُولٰئِكَ هُمُ الْمُفْلِحُونَ.

۱۸ اس، ایا: صل.

۱۹ اس: + و.

۲۰ ¦⟵برگ [ایا:۱۲۶-ب].

تعطیل کی بسبب سخن اندر شهادت آمده است برخیزد، و چون کار بر اندیشه افتد وی[۲۱] باقی بندها و غلها از امت برگیرد؛ و خلق را نگه دارد به سیاست ربّانی و قوّت نفس قدسی.

[۱۹:۹۹§] و چون مر شریعت را به دو حال یافتیم از محکم و متشابه، و محکم آن بود که عالم را بی آن صلاح نیست، و متشابه آن بود که اگر آن نباشد روا باشد که ظاهر عالم را فسادی نیوفتد.

[۲۰:۹۹§] خواستیم که بدین جای میان محکم و متشابه شریعت فرق کنیم؛ و پیدا کنیم که کدام برگرفته شود از خلق بدان زمان که نفوس خلق عالم مر علم توحید را به اخلاص پذیرا شوند. و بگوییم که آنچ برگیرند از شریعت چرا برگیرد.

[۲۱:۹۹§] پس گوییم که شریعت بعضی عقلی است و بعضی وضعی.

[۲۲:۹۹§] عقلی چون حرام کردن کشتن مردم باشد و ستدن مال مردمان به ناحق، و بستن نکاح میان مردان و زنان که بستها[۲۲] بدان درست است و چون فروختن چیزها از زمین و جامه و جز آن.

[۲۳:۹۹§] و این چیزهائی است که عالم را بی این نظام و راستی نیست وگر آن چیزها برگرفته شود نظام و راستی از عالم[۲۳] بشود.[۲۴] و این چیزها اندر زیر امر و نهی است اعنی کن و مکن.

[۲۴:۹۹§] و وضعی چون آب‌دست و نماز و زکوة و حجّ و جز از آن که این چیزهائی است نهاده از بهر آن چیزها کی پوشیده است در زیر آن.

---

۲۱ ایا: و.
۲۲ اس: [«بستها» مخدوش است].
۲۳ اس: [«وگر آن چیزها برگرفته شود نظام و راستی از عالم» مخدوش است]. || ¦⟵برگ [اس:۱۳۵-الف].
۲۴ ایا: − بشود | + برگرفته شود.

[§۹۹:۲۵] و حجّ خدای به خانهٔ خدای به مکّه است. همچنانك حجّ جهودان به بیت‌المقدّس است.

[§۹۹:۲۶] و هر یکی ازین دو خانه آن است مر گروهی را که مر آن خانه را مانندی نیست. و همچنین آتش‌خانه‌ها[۲۵] مر مغان[۲۶] را حجّ است.

[§۹۹:۲۷] و سبب این خانه‌ها، که پرستشگاه[۲۷] خلق گشت، آن بود که پیامبران دانستند که امّت پس از ایشان به فریب دیوان فریفته شوند و از پس ایشان روند.

[§۹۹:۲۸] تا هر پیامبری[۲۸] مر خانه‌ای[۲۹] را خدای نام کرد و خلق را بفرمود رای[۳۰] بدان کردن تا بدان مر ایشان را دلیل باشد بر آنك امام حقّ[۳۱] یکی است و نشاید هرکسی را امام خواندن مگر آن یك تن کی رسول بیان کند.

[§۹۹:۲۹] همچنان‌کی[۳۲] روی اندر پرستش خدای سوی هر خانه‌ای[۳۳] نشاید کردن مگر بدان یك خانه که رسول مر آن را خانهٔ خدای خواند.

[§۹۹:۳۰] تا خلق بدانند کی امام از خاندان رسول باشد و او خانهٔ علم خدای باشد.

[§۹۹:۳۱] و چون خلق عالم چنان شوند کی پادشائی دیوان از ایشان برخیزد، و

---

۲۵ اس، ایا: آتش‌خانها.

۲۶ نك:دهخدا: مغان. [مُ] (ا) جِ مغ. رجوع به مغ شود. || مغان در اصل قبیله ای از قوم ماد بودند که مقام روحانیت منحصراً به آنان تعلق داشت . آنگاه که آیین زرتشت بر نواحی غرب و جنوب ایران یعنی ماد و پارس مستولی شد مغان پیشوایان دیانت جدید شدند. در کتاب اوستا نام طبقهٔ روحانی را به همان عنوان قدیمی که داشته اند یعنی آترون می بینیم اما در عهد اشکانیان و ساسانیان معمولاً این طایفه را مغان می خوانده اند.

۲۷ اس، ایا: پرستش‌گاه.

۲۸ ایا: پیمبری.

۲۹ اس، ایا: خانهء.

۳۰ نك: دهخدا: رای. ...- رای آن کردن؛ عزیمت آن کردن.

۳۱ ¦⟵برگ [ایا:۱۲۷-الف].

۳۲ ایا: همچنانك.

۳۳ اس، ایا: خانهء.

امام زمانه حاجتمند نشود به نهان بودن از دشمنان، و خلق مر او را گردن نهند و زیر فرمان او آیند، آن وقت واجب شود خانهٔ جسمی برگرفتن که آن مثل است بر امام.

[§۹۹:۳۲] و همچنین روزه بر مسلمانان و جهودان و ترسایان و آتش‌پرستان و زمرهٔ[۳۴] مغان نشان است بر پوشیده داشتن حقّ از نادانان، و خاموش از آن علم کی سوی مردمان اندر آن زمان مر آن را روائی نیست، تا مؤمنان بدان سبب بردستِ دشمنان هلاك نشوند.

[§۹۹:۳۳] چنانك خدای تعالی همی‌گوید برمز اندر این معنی، قوله:[۳۵] يٰا أَيُّهَا النَّبِيُّ قُلْ لِأَزْوٰاجِكَ وَ بَنٰاتِكَ وَ نِسٰاءِ الْمُؤْمِنِينَ يُدْنِينَ عَلَيْهِنَّ مِنْ جَلاَبِيبِهِنَّ [۳۶] ذٰلِكَ أَدْنىٰ أَنْ يُعْرَفْنَ فَلاٰ يُؤْذَيْنَ.[۳۷] گفت: «ای پیامبر[۳۸] بگوی مر زنان خویشتن را (یعنی مر نقیبان دین را اندر وقت خویش) و دخترانت را (یعنی لاحقان[۳۹] امامان را) و زنان مؤمنان را (یعنی مر داعیان را) تا چادرهایشان بخویشتن نزدیك کنند (یعنی کی پوشیده باشند از دشمنان) کی آن نزدیکتر است بدانك بشناسندشان (یعنی تا آن ظاهریّان ندانند) پس رنجه ندارندشان».[۴۰]

[§۹۹:۳۴] و چون مر حقّ را نصرت پیدا آید به پیدا[۴۱] آمدنِ خداوند قیامت، و

---

۳۴ نك: دهخدا: زمره. [زُ رَ / رِ] گروه. جماعت.

۳۵ ایا: + تعالی.

۳۶ |←برگ [اس:۱۳۵-ب].

۳۷ سورة الأحزاب (۳۳)، آیت ۵۹. || اس: [کلمات «وَ بَنٰاتِكَ»، «وَ نِسٰاءِ» و «يُدْنِينَ» در این اینجا مخدوش اند].

۳۸ ایا: پیمبر.

۳۹ اس، ایا: لاحقتان.

۴۰ قس: السجستاني، ابویعقوب اسحاق، إثبات النّبوات، «في كيفيّت رفع الشرائع ولماذا ترفع»، ص ۲۷۶ تا ۲۸۲، به‌اهتمام: ویلفرد مادلونگ، و پال واکر (تهران: مك‌گیل و کتاب رایزن ۱۳۹۵ش/۲۰۱۶م).

۴۱ اس: بپیدا؛ ایا: پیدا.

مؤمنان بتوانند کی حقّ را آشکارا کنند و از دشمنان نترسند، بدین سبب برخاستن این موضع باشد که او مثل است بر خاموش بودن.

[§۹۹:۳۵] همچنان تن شستن از جنابت فریضه است، وزان وضعها است و مثل است بر دور داشتن و پاك کردن مر خویشتن را — و وقتِ پرداختن،[۴۲] از آنك بِکَوی[۴۳] از علم حقیقت کی بدان زایش[۴۴] نفسانی بحاصل آید — از دعوی کردن آن مرتبت مر خویشتن را [با] بازبستن مر آن را با امامان حقّ هفتگانه به فروریختن آب بر هفت اندام خویش.

[§۹۹:۳۶] یعنی که علم حقیقت که آب پاك است، بر آن مثل است، [و] مر امامان حقّ را است، تا برمثال مدّعیان حقّ نباشد که امت دعوی کردند و گمان بردند که مر امام حقّ را اندر آن نصیب نیست.

[§۹۹:۳۷] و چون قایم حقّ آشکارا شود و وقت ابلیسان[۴۵] دور بدو شکسته شود، جز بفرمان او کسی دعوت نکند، روا باشد کی این نشانی که برو مثل است برخیزد.

[§۹۹:۳۸] فامّا[۴۶] آب‌دست و نماز و زکوة هرچند کز وضعیّات است[۴۷] ماننده است به عقلیّات.

---

۴۲ نك: دهخدا: پرداختن. [پَ تَ] (مصدر) اداء. ادا کردن. تفریغ حساب. گزاردن حقی و دینی و جز آن. توختن وامی. تأدیه. کارسازی کردن. دادن. واپس دادن: دین خود را پرداختن؛ وام خویش ادا کردن. || تهی کردن. خالی کردن. تخلیه. مخلی کردن. تخلیه کردن. پاک کردن. صافی کردن.

۴۳ اس: بکوی؛ ایا: بکوبی. || نك: دهخدا: کاویدن. [دَ] (مصدر) (از: کاو + یدن پسوند مصدری). (از حاشیهٔ برهان چ معین). جستجو کردن. ... کابیدن. کافتن.

۴۴ |⟵برگ [ایا:۱۲۷-ب].

۴۵ ایا: - ابلیسان | + آید آن.

۴۶ نك: دهخدا: فأما. [فَ أمْ ما] بمعنی اما به کار رود.

۴۷ اس: - است.

[§۹۹:۳۹] از بهر آنك اندر آب دست پاكيزگی است مر تن را[۴۸] از پليديها و اندر او پاكيزگی و پارسائی مر نفس را است.

[§۹۹:۴۰] و اندر زكوة دست گرفتنِ درماندگان است و پيدا كردن سخاوت.

[§۹۹:۴۱] و شايد بود كه اين وضعيّات برگرفته نشود و شايد بود كه بعضی ازو برگرفته شود.

[§۹۹:۴۲] امّا هيچ كس را طاقت برگرفتن اين مثالها[۴۹] نيست و نباشد مگر خداوند ثواب و عقاب را.[۵۰] و هر كه[۵۱] پيش از پديدآمدن او، عليه افضل السّلام، اندر اين چيزها تقصير كند اندر لعنت خدای[۵۲] و خشم او گرفتار شود.

[§۹۹:۴۳] اگر كسی پرسد كه اين برگرفتنيها را قايم، عليه افضل السّلام، بيكبار برگيرد، يا به اوقات، يكان يكان، مر آن را از امت همی افكند، او را گوييم كه مر اين چيزها را قايم، عليه افضل السّلام، به نفس خويش از خلق برنگيرد.

[§۹۹:۴۴] و لكن امت چون هنگام بيايد به افتادن آن از ايشان شناسا شوند تا به وقت پيدا شدن او، عليه افضل السّلام، آنچ برگرفتنی باشد[۵۳] برگرفته شده باشد.

[§۹۹:۴۵] و چون هنگام پديدآمدن آن شريف شريفان باشد، بندهای شريعت گشاده گردد و خلق مهمل شوند، و خون ريختن ميان خلق فاش گردد، و عدل[۵۴] و رحمت از ميان خلق بيرون شود، و شر و خيانت آشكارا شود، و دانايان و مؤمنان

---

۴۸ ايا: – را.
۴۹ ايا: نهادها.
۵۰ ¦⟵برگ [اس:۱۳۶-الف].
۵۱ ايا: + كه.
۵۲ ايا: – خدای.
۵۳ اس: + باشد [«باشد» تكرار شده است].
۵۴ ايا: + و عدل [«و عدل» تكرار شده است].

بیچاره و درمانده شوند، و نادانان[55] و منافقان بر ایشان غلبه گیرند، و دانایان از دانش به نام بسنده کنند.

[§۹۹:۴۶] آن وقت حقّ بر اثر آن حال آشکارا شود و فرمان اندر عالم یکی شود. چنانك خدای تعالی همی‌گوید، قوله: يَوْمَ لَا تَمْلِكُ نَفْسٌ لِنَفْسٍ شَيْئاً وَ الْأَمْرُ يَوْمَئِذٍ لِلّٰهِ.[56] همی‌گوید: «روزی باشد که هیچ نفسی را بر هیچ نفسی پادشائی نباشد و فرمان آن روز خدای را باشد».

[§۹۹:۴۷] و دعوت به باطن محض باشد. و هر کس کز علم حقیقت خبر ندارد نتواند مر آن را پذیرفتن و نتواند مر آن را دفع کردن، و به دو جهان به بلا آویخته شوند.

[§۹۹:۴۸] و فساد از عالم به پدیدآمدن او، علیه افضل السّلام، از عالم برخیزد.

[§۹۹:۴۹] از بهر آنك نفس کلّی به پدیدآمدن او به عقل کلّی پیوسته شود.

[§۹۹:۵۰] و امروز شریعت به جهل برگرفته‌اند فردا[57] به عدل و حقّ برگیرند.

[§۹۹:۵۱] و خود چنین واجب آید از بهر آنك مردم میانجی است میان دیوی و فریشتگی و امروز جهان دیوان[58] دارند و فردا فریشتگان را باید داشتن.

---

۵۵ ¦⟵برگ [ایا:۱۲۸-الف].

۵۶ سورة الانفطار (۸۲)، آیت ۱۹.

۵۷ اس: [«فردا» مخدوش است].

۵۸ اس: [«دیوان» مخدوش است].

صف صدم[۱]

سخن اندر عقل کلّ کی او مُبدَع است نه مُبدِع[۲]

[§۱۰۰:۱] مُبدِع حقّ آن است کی چیز را نه از چیز او پدید آورد، و همه مُبدَعات ازین صنع عاجز آمدند.

[§۱۰۰:۲] و بدین سبب لازم آمد دانستن کی صانع عالمِ جسمانی نه مُبدِع حقّ است، بل کی[۳] [عالَمِ] روحانی است.

[§۱۰۰:۳] ازبهرآنك مر روحانی را اندر جسمانی متصرف یافتیم به بسیار رویها، چنانك همی‌بینیم که روح مردم مر جسم او را کار همی‌فرماید به گونه‌گونه علمها؛ و چون روح از جسد جدا شود جسد بی‌کار ماند.

[§۱۰۰:۴] و چون مر این عالم را جسم و نادان و بی‌کار یافتیم، دانستیم که کاربندِ او روحانی است کلّی عظیم و دانا.

[§۱۰۰:۵] و نیز مُبْدَعْ آن باشد که او چیزی نه از چیزی باشد، و مخلوق چیزی باشد از چیزی.

[§۱۰۰:۶] پس مُبدِع حقّ آن است، که او را از جهت اویی نام نیست، و از جهت ما، که پدیدآوردگانیم، نام او مُبدِع حقّ است، اعنی پدیدآورندهٔ چیز نه از چیز.[۴]

---

۱ ¦⟵برگ [اس:۱۳۶-ب].

۲ قس: کتاب الینابیع، الینبوع الخامس (۵): في أن العقل الأول أوّل مُبدَع، ص ۲۲ تا ۲۴.

۳ ایا: بلك.

۴ اس: [در حاشیهٔ راست صفحه نوشته شده: «ای هو سبحانه وتعالی خالق الشیء من غیر شئ وهو علی کل شئ قدیر»].

[§۱۰۰:۷] و مُبْدَعْ که او عقل است چیزی پدید[۵] آورده نه از چیزی [است].[۶] و او محیط است بر جملگی هرچه او را هستی است.

[§۱۰۰:۸] و مخلوق اوّل نفس کلّی است کی او نخستین چیز[۷] است پدیدآمده از چیزی، اعنی کی پدیدآمدن او به میانجی عقل است از امر باری سبحانه.

[§۱۰۰:۹] معارضه اگر کسی گوید: «چون همی‌گویی کی عقل آن است کی محیط است بر هرچه او را هستی است، پس چه ماند از خدایی که تو به عقل اثبات نکردی؟ پس به دعوی تو خود عقل خدای است».

[§۱۰۰:۱۰] جواب مر او را گوییم که نزدیك خاص و عام معروف است که بودش عالم را با آنچ اندر او است سبب کن بود از باری تعالی.

[§۱۰۰:۱۱] و چاره نیست مر این دو حرف را از فرازآرنده‌ای[۸] که [گر][۹] او مر آن را فرازنیاوردی،[۱۰] این کلمه ازین دو حرف حاصل نشدی، و چون این کلمه نبودی جهان نبودی.

[§۱۰۰:۱۲] و فرازآرندهٔ دو چیز لازم آید که جز آن دو چیز باشد و پوشیده‌تر و نایافته‌تر از ایشان باشد.

[§۱۰۰:۱۳] و چون بودش بدین [دو][۱۱] حرف نظام یافت، فرازآرندهٔ این دو حرف برتر باشد از باشانیدن، از بهر آنك باشانندهٔ[۱۲] عالمْ کن بود، اعنی بباش.

---

۵ ¦⟵برگ [ایا:۱۲۸-ب].

۶ تصحیح قیاسی.

۷ ایا: چیزی.

۸ اس، ایا: فرازآرندهء.

۹ تصحیح قیاسی.

۱۰ اس: ںاوردی؛ ایا: بیاوردی [کذا]. || تصحیح مفهومی.

۱۱ تصحیح قیاسی.

۱۲ اس: [«باشانندهٔ» مخدوش است].

[§۱۰۰:۱۴] پس نخست بر ما واجب شد[۱۳] دانستنِ کمترین دو حرف را، که آن دو اصل است مر دو جهان [را، و آندو را][۱۴] فرازآرنده‌ای[۱۵] هست، و جز این دو حرف هست.

[§۱۰۰:۱۵] و نیز لازم آید که فرازآرنده بِهمْ درخوردِ آن چیز باشد، کی اگر او را با ایشان درخوری نبودی ایشان به میانجیِ او فراز نیامدندی.

[§۱۰۰:۱۶] پس درست شد کی فرازآرندهٔ این دو حرف، [که][۱۶] دو اصل‌اند مر دو جهان را، باری سبحانه نیست. چه او، جلّ جلاله، اندرخورْبودنْ به آفریدگانِ خویش!

[§۱۰۰:۱۷] و مر او را نام نیست، و صفت نیست، و شمرده نیست، و بی‌نام و بی‌صفت [و] ناشمرده نیست. چه این همه که یاد کرده شد آفریدگان اویند.

[§۱۰۰:۱۸] پس گوییم کی هردو چیزی کی فراهم آید، فراهم آمدنِ ایشان سیم ایشان باشد، تا آن دو چیز بدو یك چیز شوند و نام پذیرند و صورت.

[§۱۰۰:۱۹] برمثال برخاستن شهوت از نفس مردم که آن فرازآرنده است مرد را با زن از روی طبیعت، و نکاح را از روی شریعت.[۱۷]

[§۱۰۰:۲۰] و آن است بهانه‌ای[۱۸] از برآمدن فرزند بحقیقت. و مر فرزند را به پدر و مادر بازخوانند، و بدان برخاستنِ شهوت بازنخوانند.

[§۱۰۰:۲۱] ازبهرآنك آن سبب نخستین است، و مر آن را یافتن نیست کند بقوّت ذهن و پاکی عقل.

---

۱۳ ¦⟵برگ [اس:۱۳۷-الف].

۱۴ تصحیح قیاسی.

۱۵ اس، ایا: فرازآرنده‌ء.

۱۶ تصحیح قیاسی.

۱۷ ¦⟵برگ [ایا:۱۲۹-الف].

۱۸ اس، ایا: بهانه‌ء.

[§۱۰۰:۲۲] و ما مر آتش را گرم و خشك یابیم. و گرمی کی اندر آتش است [اگر][۱۹] با تری یار شود هوا گردد، چنانك چون با خشکی یار شود [آتش گردد]؛[۲۰] و خشکی کی اندر آتش است اگر با سردی یار شود خاك شود، چنانك اگر[۲۱] با گرمی یار شود آتش گردد.

[§۱۰۰:۲۳] همچنین حال دیگر ارکان هم بر این جمله است.

[§۱۰۰:۲۴] و چون همی روا باشد گرمی را که اندر آتش است با خشکی یار است، با[۲۲] ضدّ تری کی خشکی است یار شدن خشکی را کند کی اندر آتش با گرمی یار است؛ با[۲۳] ضدّ گرمی کی سردی است یار شدن،[۲۴] دلیل همی‌کند کی آن علّت، که میان ایشان موافقت[۲۵] افکند، هست و موافق ایشان است،[۲۶] به رویی نامعلوم.

[§۱۰۰:۲۵] از بهر آنك نه سرد[۲۷] است آن علّت و نه گرم، نه تر است و نه خشك، که اگر آن علّت[۲۸] به یکی ازین[۲۹] صفات بودی،[۳۰] مر دیگری را مخالف بودی. و چون یکی را مخالف بودی نتوانستی میان ایشان موافقت افکندن، کی مخالفان بودند.

[§۱۰۰:۲۶] و مر آن علّت را کی گفتیم نام نیست و صفت نیست، و لکن چون

---

۱۹ تصحیح قیاسی.
۲۰ تصحیح قیاسی.
۲۱ اس: – اگر.
۲۲ اس، ایا: یا. || تصحیح قیاسی.
۲۳ اس: با؛ ایا: یا. || تصحیح قیاسی.
۲۴ اس: [«شدن» مخدوش است].
۲۵ ایا: + همی.
۲۶ اس: [«موافق ایشانست» مخدوش است].
۲۷ اس: [«سرد» مخدوش است].
۲۸ اس: [«آن علّت» مخدوش است].
۲۹ اس: [«ازین» مخدوش است].
۳۰ ¦⟵برگ [اس:۱۳۷-ب].

دیدیم فرازآمدن این[۳۱] مخالفان به یکی[۳۲] جای و هر یکی را از ایشان باز با مخالف یار خویش فرازآمده است، و دانستیم که روا باشد، برخاستنِ مخالفتْ ظاهر است از میان ایشان به موافقت هر یکی از ایشان با دیگری.

[§۱۰۰:۲۷] درست شد خرد را که مر[۳۳] هر دویی را از آن سیّمی هست کی او نگاهبان[۳۴] ایشان است اندر آن صورت کی هر یکی را هست از طبایع.

[§۱۰۰:۲۸] و چون همه چیز را اندر عالم جفت یافتیم و مر هر جفتی را از میانجی چاره نیست که مر ایشان را بهم فرازآرد.

[§۱۰۰:۲۹] همچنان کی[۳۵] آن میانجی جمع کرده است میان گرم و خشك تا صورت آتش ایشان بحاصل آمده است، و دیگر طبایع همچنان، و آن میانجی واجب آید که نه گرم است و نه سرد است نه تر است و نه خشك است.[۳۶]

[§۱۰۰:۳۰] لازم آید کی آنچ میان جوهر و عرض جفتی داده است نه جوهر است و نه عرض.

[§۱۰۰:۳۱] و چون چیزی بیرون نیست از آنك یا جوهر است یا عرض، معلوم کردیم که آن جفت‌کنندهٔ جوهر با عرض نه جوهر است و نه عرض، درست شد کی او چیزی نیست.

[§۱۰۰:۳۲] و چون آن علّت جفت‌کننده مر شیء را ردّ کرد نشاید که بیرون باشد از نه‌چیزی یا نه از نه‌چیزی، پس آن غایت کی گفتیم از دو بیرون نیست: یا نه‌چیز است یا نه نه‌چیز است.

---

۳۱ ایا: آن.

۳۲ ایا: بیك.

۳۳ ایا: – مر.

۳۴ اس: نگاه‌بان.

۳۵ ایا: همچنانك.

۳۶ ⟵ برگ [ایا:۱۲۹-ب].

[§۱۰۰:۳۳] پس ظاهر کردیم خردمند را که آنك[۳۷] نه، نه‌چیز است، و آنك نه‌چیز است نه خدای است، چه خدای تعالی[۳۸] برتر از آن است که مر او را ماننده باشد.

[§۱۰۰:۳۴] پس آن علّت جفت‌کننده مانند خدای نیست، که نه، نه، نه‌چیز است و نه، نه‌چیز است.

[§۱۰۰:۳۵] پس گوییم آن نیست که اثبات کردیم آن است کی خدای تعالی علّت دو عالم را ازو هست کرد، که او از نیست بود.

[§۱۰۰:۳۶] او معلول نخستین است که عقل است. و ایزدتعالی برتر است از علّت و معلول.

[§۱۰۰:۳۷] پس گوییم که عقل اوّل[۳۹] به علّت خویش معلول[۴۰] است و به رویِ معلولی با دیگر آفریدگان از چیزی[۴۱] دیگر ماننده است.

[§۱۰۰:۳۸] و لکن بدانچ علّت او معلول نیست از دیگر معلولات یگانه است.

[§۱۰۰:۳۹] و میان هر معلولی و میان علّت او جدایگی است بدانچ علّت او معلول علّتی دیگر است.

[§۱۰۰:۴۰] و نیز عقل کی دارا به علّت است هر مردمی را از عقل نصیب است و بی‌نیازند به او به دانستن، هرچند که دانش جزوی به دانش کلی نرسد.

[§۱۰۰:۴۱] زیرا کی دو تن باشند کی یکی از ایشان هزار درم دارد و دیگر یك درم دارد. اندر آن روی که هر دو تن را ملك است انبازان باشند.

---

۳۷ ایا: آن.

۳۸ ایا: – چه خدای تعالی.

۳۹ اس: [«اول» مخدوش است].

۴۰ اس: [«معلول» مخدوش است].

۴۱ ¦⟵برگ [اس:۱۳۸-الف].

[§۱۰۰:۴۲] پس آفریدگان به عقل مانندهاند و آنچ مر او را مانند‌ه باشد او نه خدای باشد. پس عقل نه خدای است.

[§۱۰۰:۴۳] و همچنین عقل زنده است کی هرگز نمیرد و همه زندگان هستند و فرود ازو، تا مردم بدید کی به زندگانی با او انبازند، هرچند که زندگانیِ او جاویدی است و دیگر چیزها زندگانی بدو یافته‌اند.

[§۱۰۰:۴۴] و حکم اندر زندگی جاویدی و زندگانیِ فانی همان است که مثال آن اندر انبازی میان دو خداوند ملك کی یاد[۴۲] کردیم.

[§۱۰۰:۴۵] پس همه زندگان مانند عقل‌اند و آنچ مر او را مانند باشد نه خدای باشد. پس عقل نه خدای است.

[§۱۰۰:۴۶] معارضه اگر کسی گوید که چون همی‌گویی که زندگی از عقل است، پس ازین شریف‌تر مرتبت چگونه باشد و صفت خدای همین است که خلق را جان او داده است.

[§۱۰۰:۴۷] جواب مر او را گوییم این صفت خدای نیست بر حقیقت که این صفت مطیع‌تر بنده‌ای[۴۳] است از بندگان خدای و آن عقل است.

[§۱۰۰:۴۸] و بباید دانستن که اثر آن مؤثر اندر چیزی براندازهٔ آن مرتبت باشد که اندر آن مؤثر موجود باشد.

[§۱۰۰:۴۹] و جز از آن نیاید از هرچیزی که ‹اندر او باشد›؛[۴۴] چنانك اندر میان عرب مثل است که گویند: مثل[۴۵] کلّ إناءٍ یترشّح بمافیه. گوید: «از هر آب‌جامی آن پالاید کی اندر او است».

---

۴۲ ¦⟵برگ [ایا:۱۳۰-الف].

۴۳ اس، ایا: بنده‌ء.

۴۴ ایا: باشد اندرو.

۴۵ اس: [«مثل» مخدوش است].

[§۱۰۰:۵۰] و چون مر عقل را زندگیِ جاوید صفت[۴۶] ذاتی بود، زندگان ازو بدان[۴۷] پیدا آمدند؛ وگر زندگان ازو پیدا نیامدندی، او زندهٔ جاویدی[۴۸] نبودی.

[§۱۰۰:۵۱] پس این حال ازو[۴۹] همی دلیل کند[۵۰] که او مجبور است از کردار خویش و این خاصیّت نتواند که ازو زندگانی و توانائی و دانش وز آنچ فرود ازو است فروبارنده نباشد.

[§۱۰۰:۵۲] و هر چه او مجبور باشد نه قاهری باشد، و آنچ برتر ازو قاهری باشد او نه خدای باشد، پس عقل نه خدای باشد.

[§۱۰۰:۵۳] و نیز عقل آن است که او مر ذات خویش را بذات بداند،[۵۱] و جز مر ذات خویش را نیز بداند. و او بدین صفت مخصوص است، و هیچ چیز را این صفت نیست، پس عقل اندر حصار این صفت است.

[§۱۰۰:۵۴] و آنچ او اندر حصار صفتی باشد چاره نیست مر او را از به حصار اندرکننده‌ای.[۵۲]

[§۱۰۰:۵۵] و آنچ مر او را دیگری به حصار اندرکرده باشد او نه خدای باشد. پس عقل نه خدای باشد. تَعٰالَی اللّٰهُ عَمّٰا یَقُولُ الظّٰالِمُونَ عُلُوًّا کَبِیراً.[۵۳]

[§۱۰۰:۵۶] سپاس مر خدای را که ما را از بهترین آفریدهٔ خویش اندر آفرینش بهره‌مند کرد بدانچ عقل را اندر آفرینش ما نهاد و بر زفان شریفتر سخنگوی با

۴۶ اس: [عبارت «جاوید صفت» مخدوش است].
۴۷ ایا: [«بدان» در میان دو سطر بالای «پیدا» نوشته شده است].
۴۸ ایا: جاوید.
۴۹ ایا: [«ازو» مخدوش است].
۵۰ ¦⟵برگ [اس:۱۳۸-ب].
۵۱ ایا: بداند بذات.
۵۲ اس، ایا: اندرکننده‌ء.
۵۳ اشارت به سورة الإسراء (۱۷)، آیت ۴۳: سُبْحٰانَهُ وَ تَعٰالیٰ عَمّٰا یَقُولُونَ عُلُوًّا کَبِیراً.

ما مخاطبه کرد محمّد خاتم‌النبیّین. و ما را به راهنمایان[۵۴] حقّ بازبرد از گروه شیاطین.

[§۱۰۰:۵۷] تمام کردیم مر این کتاب را و آراستیم مر این خوان[۵۵]...[۵۶] شریف را به صدگونه طعام و شراب گوارندهٔ پاکیزه؛ حلال باد اندر این شبنگاه روز آدینهٔ حقیقت و شبِ شنبهٔ حقّ آنچ ازین خوان بخورند روزه دارند به بصیرت.

[§۱۰۰:۵۸] و دور باد دست حرام‌خواران و میگساران و بی‌باکان و ناپاکان[۵۷] ازین صفهای خورشهای جان‌افزای به رحمت ایزد دادار دادفرمای بخشایندهٔ مهربان نیکوکار.

[§۱۰۰:۵۹] وَالصَّلاةُ عَلَى نَبِيِّهِ مُحَمَّدٍ وَآلِهِ الطَّيِّبِينَ الطَّاهِرِينَ.[۵۸]

---

۵۴ اس: راه نمایان.

۵۵ ¦⟵برگ [ایا:۱۳۰-ب]. ||.[برگ [ایا: ۱۳۰ب] خالی است].

۵۶ ¦⟵برگ [ایا:۱۴۹-ب]. || در فاصلهٔ برگهای [ایا:۱۳۱-الف] تا [ایا:۱۴۹-الف] نسخه منثور کتاب روشنائی نامه کتابت شده است.

۵۷ اس: باباکان.

۵۸ اس: + فُرِغَ مِنْ اِنْتِسَاخِهِ يَوْمَ الْأَرْبِعَاءِ السَّابِعِ وَالْعِشْرِينَ مِنْ صَفَرٍ. خُتِمَ بِالْخَيْرِ وَالظَّفَرِ سَنَةَ أَرْبَعٍ [وَ] سَبْعِينَ وَستِمائَةٍ وَهَذَا خَطُّ أَصْغَرِ عَبَادِ اللَّهِ تَعَالَى مُحَمَّدِ بْنِ أَبِي طَالِبٍ بْنِ أَبِي الْقَاسِمِ الْحُسَيْنِيِّ [اصل اعراب ندارد]. [در حاشیهٔ سمت راستِ پائین صفحه با جوهر کمرنگ یادداشتی نوشته شده است که ناخوانا است؛ در حاشیهٔ سمت چپ پائین همین صفحه، با همان جوهر کمرنگ، امضائی مشاهده میشود که باز ناخوانا است]. || ایا: + خُتِمَتْ هَذِهِ الرِّسَالَةُ الشَّرِيفَةُ اللَّطِيفَةُ المُوسُومَةُ بِخَوانِ الْإِخْوَانِ يَوْمَ الْجُمُعَةِ فِي التَّاسِعِ عَشَرَ مِنْ شَهْرِ ذِي الْقَعْدَةِ سَنَةَ اثْنَيْنِ وَسِتِّينَ وَثَمَانِمائَةَ اللَّهُمَّ اغْفِرْ لِكَاتِبِهَا وَلِصَاحِبِهَا وَلِقَارِئِهَا وَلِجَمِيعِ الْمُؤْمِنِينَ وَالْمُؤْمِنَاتِ وَالْمُسْلِمِينَ وَالْمُسْلِمَاتِ الْأَحْيَاءِ مِنْهُمْ وَالْأَمْوَاتِ. بِرَحْمَتِكَ يَا أَرْحَمَ الرَّاحِمِينَ وَبِحُرْمَةِ نَبِيِّكَ مُحَمَّدٍ وَآلِهِ أَجْمَعِينَ. خُتِمَتْ.[اصل اعراب ندارد].

فهرست آیات قرآنی

نام سورة	شماره سورة	آیت	بند	صف
البَقَرَة	۲	۲۰	[§۲۰:۱۰]	۲۰
	۲	۲۰ [1]	[§۲۹:۱۲]	۲۹
	۲	۲۹	[§۳۸:۴]	۳۸
	۲	۱۰۹	[§۲۹:۱۲]	۲۹
	۲	۱۴۸	[§۲۹:۱۲]	۲۹
	۲	۱۷۹	[§۱۷:۲۱]	۱۷
	۲	۲۵۷	[§۷:۲۱]	۷
	۲	۲۵۸ [2]	[§۱۰]	آغاز
	۲	۲۸۴ [3]	[§۹:۲]	۹

۱ «إِنَّ اللّٰهَ عَلىٰ كُلِّ شَيْءٍ قَدِيرٌ» در هفت آیت دیگر نیز آمده است: سورة البقرة (۲)، آیات ۱۰۹، و ۱۴۸؛ سورة آل عمران (۳)، آیت ۱۶۵؛ سورة النحل (۱۶)، آیت ۷۷؛ سورة النور (۲۴)، آیت ۴۵؛ سورة العنکبوت (۲۹)، آیت ۲۰؛ سورة فاطر (۳۵)، آیت ۱. || نیز قس: «إِنَّهُ عَلىٰ كُلِّ شَيْءٍ قَدِيرٌ» در سورة فُصِّلَت (۴۱)، آیت ۳۹، و سورة الأحقاف (۴۶)، آیت ۳۳؛ «وَ أَنَّـهُ عَلىٰ كُلِّ شَيْءٍ قَدِيرٌ» در سورة الحَجّ (۲۲)، آیت ۶؛ «فَهُوَ عَلىٰ كُلِّ شَيْءٍ قَدِيرٌ» در سورة الأنعام (۶)، آیت ۱۷؛ و «إِنَّكَ عَلىٰ كُلِّ شَيْءٍ قَدِيرٌ» در سورة آل عمران (۳)، آیت ۲۶، و سورة التحریم (۶۶)، آیت ۸.

۲ نیز نك: آیت ۸۶ از سورة آل عمران (۳)؛ آیات ۱۹ و ۱۰۹ از سورة التوبة (۹)؛ آیت ۷ از سورة الصف (۶۱)؛ و آیت ۵ از سورة الجمعة (۶۲). این آیت، یعنی: «وَ اللّٰهُ لاٰ يَهْدِي الْقَوْمَ الظّٰالِمِينَ»، شش بار در قرآن آمده است. همچنین آیت: «إِنَّ اللّٰهَ لاٰ يَهْدِي الْقَوْمَ الظّٰالِمِينَ» در چهار آیت دیگر آمده است: آیت ۵۱ از سورة الماعدة (۵)، آیت ۱۴۴ از سورة الأنعام (۶)، آیت ۵۰ از سورة القَصَص (۲۸)، و آیت ۱۰ از سورة الأحقاف (۴۶).

۳ «وَ اللّٰهُ عَلىٰ كُلِّ شَيْءٍ قَدِيرٌ» در هشت آیت دیگر نیز آمده است : سورة آل عمران (۳)، آیات ۲۹، ۱۸۹؛ سورة المائدة (۵)، آیات ۱۷، ۱۹، و ۴۰؛ سورة الأنفال (۸)، آیت ۴۱؛ سورة التوبة (۹)، آیت ۳۹؛ سورة الحشر (۵۹)، آیت ۶.

نام سورة	شماره سورة	آیت	بند	صف
البَقَرَة	۲	۲۸۶	[§۱۱:۴۴]	۴۴
آل عِمْرَان	۳	۲۹	[§۲:۹]	۹
	۳	۳۱	[§۲۰:۷]	۷
	۳	۱۰۳	[§۲۹:۳۶]	۳۶
	۳	۱۶۵	[§۱۲:۲۹]	۲۹
	۳	۱۸۹	[§۲:۹]	۹
النِّسَاء	۴	۲۶ [۴]	[§۲:۹]	۹
	۴	۴۸	[§۸:۲۰]	۲۰
	۴	۵۲	[§۲۲:۸۸]	۸۸
	۴	۵۴	[§۷:۶۶]	۶۶
	۴	۶۵	[§۱۶]	آغاز
	۴	۱۱۳	[§۱۸:۹۰]	۹۰
	۴	۱۱۶	[§۲۷:۷]	۷
	۴	۱۴۶-۱۴۵	[§۲۹:۳۶]	۳۶
المَائِدَة	۵	۱۷	[§۲:۹]	۹
	۵	۱۹	[§۲:۹]	۹
	۵	۳۲	[§۱۷:۱۷]	۱۷
	۵	۳۳	[§۳۴:۱۷]	۱۷

۴ «وَاللّٰهُ عَلِيمٌ حَكِيمٌ» در دوازده آیت دیگر نیز آمده است: سورة الأنفال (۸)، آیت ۷۱؛ سورة التوبة (۹)، آیات ۱۵، ۶۰، ۹۷، ۱۰۶، و ۱۱۰؛ سورة الحج (۲۲)، آیت ۵۲؛ سورة النور (۲۴)، آیات ۱۸، ۵۸، و ۵۹؛ سورة الحُجُرات (۴۹)، آیت ۴؛ سورة المُمْتَحَنَة (۶۰)، آیت ۱۰.

نام سورة	شماره سورة	آیت	بند	صف
المَائِدَة	۵	۳۸	[§۱۷:۳۳]	۱۷
	۵	۴۰	[§۹:۲]	۹
	۵	۴۵	[§۱۷:۳۲]	۱۷
	۵	۱۲۰ [5]	[§۷۱:۵]	۷۱
الأَنْعَام	۶	۱	[§۲۸:۳۰]	۲۸
	۶	۹۴	[§۳۰:۸]	۳۰
	۶	۹۶	[§۸۰:۹]	۸۰
	۶	۱۰۳	[§۶۸:۲۹]	۶۸
	۶	۱۴۱	[§۷۵:۲]	۷۵
	۶	۱۶۰	[§۸۸:۱۶]	۸۸
الأَعْرَاف	۷	۵۳	[§۸:۷]	۸
	۷	۵۴ [6]	[§۶۱:۱۵]	۶۱
	۷	۱۵۷	[§۹۹:۱۳]	۹۹
	۷	۱۷۹	[§۹۲:۶۶]	۹۲
الأَنْفَال	۸	۴۱	[§۹:۲]	۹
التَّوْبَة	۹	۱۵	[§۹:۲]	۹
	۹	۱۹	[§۱۰]	آغاز

۵ «وَهُوَ عَلَىٰ كُلِّ شَيْءٍ قَدِيرٌ» در مجموع در هفت آیت آمده است: سورة المائدة (۵)، آیت ۱۲۰؛ سورة هود (۱۱)، آیت ۴؛ سورة الروم (۳۰)، آیت ۵۰؛ سورة الشورى (۴۲)، آیت ۹؛ سورة الحديد (۵۷)، آیت ۲؛ سورة التغابن (۶۴)، آیت ۱؛ سورة المُلك (۶۷)، آیت ۱.

۶ قس: سورة الفرقان (۲۵)، آیت ۵۹.

نام سورة	شماره سورة	آیت	بند	صف
التَّوْبَة	۹	۳۹	[§۲:۹]	۹
	۹	۶۰	[§۲:۹]	۹
	۹	۷۳	[§۳۱:۱۷]	۱۷
	۹	۹۷	[§۲:۹]	۹
	۹	۱۰۶	[§۲:۹]	۹
	۹	۱۰۹	[§۱۰]	آغاز
	۹	۱۱۰	[§۲:۹]	۹
يُونُس	۱۰	۳ [۷]	[§۱۵:۶۱]	۶۱
	۱۰	۱۲	[§۷:۱۶]	۱۶
هُود	۱۱	۴	[§۵:۷۱]	۷۱
	۱۱	۹۷-۹۹	[§۳۱:۴۲]	۴۲
يُوسُف	۱۲	۵۳	[§۲:۱۷]	۱۷
الرَّعْد	۱۳	۳۵	[§۴:۵۵]	۵۵
إِبْرَاهِيم	۱۴	۴	[§۵۱:۹]	۹
	۱۴	۷	[§۲۵:۹]	۹
	۱۴	۱۱	[§۳۱:۸۸]	۸۸
الحِجْر	۱۵	۲۱	[§۴:۹۵]	۹۵
	۱۵	۳۹	[§۱۶:۱۷]	۱۷
النَّحْل	۱۶	۵	[§۹:۶]	۶

۷ قس: سورة الفرقان (۲۵)، آیت ۵۹.

نام سورة	شماره سورة	آیت	بند	صف
النَّحْل	۱۶	۴۳-۴۴	[§۱۳]	آغاز [۸]
	۱۶	۷۷	[§۱۲:۲۹]	۲۹
	۱۶	۹۷	[§۱۷:۸۸]	۸۸
الإِسْرَاء	۱۷	۱	[§۸:۶۶]	۶۶
	۱۷	۷	[§۴:۱۱]	۱۱
	۱۷	۲۹	[§۳:۴۱]	۴۱
	۱۷	۴۳	[§۱۰۱:۲۱]	۲۱
	۱۷	۴۳	[§۶:۲۳]	۲۳
	۱۷	۴۳	[§۱۳:۲۳]	۲۳
	۱۷	۴۳	[§۲۰:۲۸]	۲۸
	۱۷	۴۳	[§۶:۳۴]	۳۴
	۱۷	۴۳	[§۹:۵۰]	۵۰
	۱۷	۴۳	[§۹:۷۸]	۷۸
	۱۷	۴۳	[§۵۵:۱۰۰]	۱۰۰
	۱۷	۷۱	[§۱۷]	آغاز
	۱۷	۷۱	[§۷۳:۶۷]	۶۷
	۱۷	۱۱۰	[§۴:۷۹]	۷۹
الکَهْف	۱۸	۴۸	[§۱۴:۸]	۸

۸ آیت ۴۳ از آن، در آیت ۷ از سورة الأنبیاء (۲۱)، و آیت ۴۴ از آن، در آیت ۱۸۴ از سورة آل عمران (۳) نیز آمده اند.

نام سورة	شماره سورة	آیت	بند	صف
الكَهْف	۱۸	۱۰۹	[۱۰:۶۴§]	۶۴
مَرْيَم	۱۹	۳۸	[۱۲§]	آغاز
طٰهٰ	۲۰	۹-۱۰	[۱۱:۲۲§]	۲۲
	۲۰	۵۰	[۱:۷۹§]	۷۹
	۲۰	۷۴-۷۶	[۱۹:۱۹§]	۱۹
	۲۰	۱۱۴	[۶:۸۵§]	۸۵
الأَنْبِيَاء	۲۱	۹۵	[۸:۱۹§]	۱۹
الحَجّ	۲۲	۵۲	[۲:۹§]	۹
المُؤْمِنُون	۲۳	۱۲-۱۴	[۲:۷§]	۷
	۲۳	۵۳	[۴:۶۳§]	۶۳
	۲۳	۱۱۵	[۷:۹§]	۹
	۲۳	۱۱۶	[۶:۸۵§]	۸۵
النُّور	۲۴	۲	[۳۳:۱۷§]	۱۷
	۲۴	۱۸	[۲:۹§]	۹
	۲۴	۲۴	[۱۵:۱۹§]	۱۹
	۲۴	۲۵	[۶:۸۵§]	۸۵
	۲۴	۴۵	[۱۲:۲۹§]	۲۹
	۲۴	۵۸	[۲:۹§]	۹
	۲۴	۵۹	[۲:۹§]	۹
الفُرْقَان	۲۵	۴۴	[۲۰:۳۵§]	۳۵

نام سورة	شماره سورة	آیت	بند	صف
الفُرْقَان	۲۵	۷۰	[§۵:۳۶]	۳۶
الشُّعَرَاء	۲۶	۱۹۵-۱۹۳	[§۴۴:۹]	۹
القَصَص	۲۸	۶۸	[§۷۰:۹۵]	۹۵
	۲۸	۸۸	[§۱۵]	آغاز
	۲۸	۸۸	[§۱۶:۵۰]	۵۰
العَنْكَبُوت	۲۹	۲۰	[§۱۲:۹]	۹
	۲۹	۲۰	[§۱۶:۹]	۹
	۲۹	۲۰	[§۱۲:۲۹]	۲۹
الرُّوم	۳۰	۲۰	[§۴۱:۶۶]	۶۶
	۳۰	۳۲	[§۴:۶۳]	۶۳
	۳۰	۵۰	[§۵:۷۱]	۷۱
السَّجْدَة	۳۲	۴ [۹]	[§۱۵:۶۱]	۶۱
	۳۲	۱۷ [۱۰]	[§۱۶:۳۳]	۳۳
الأَحْزَاب	۳۳	۴	[§۱۵:۹۶]	۹۶
	۳۳	۳۶	[§۳۰:۷]	۷
	۳۳	۵۹	[§۳۳:۹۹]	۹۹
	۳۳	۳۱-۲۸	[§۲۱:۳۶]	۳۶
	۳۳	۴۶-۴۵	[§۴:۲۰]	۲۰

۹ قس: سورة الأعراف (۷)، آیت ۵۴؛ سورة یونس (۱۰)، آیت ۳؛ سورة الفرقان (۲۵)، آیت ۵۹؛ سورة الحدید (۵۷)، آیت ۴.

۱۰ این آیت در پانوشت ۱۹، ذیل همین بند، راجع به حدیث پیامبر (ص) آمده است.

نام سورة	شماره سورة	آیت	بند	صف
سَبَأ	۳۴	۲۸	[§۹۰:۲۳]	۹۰
	۳۴	۳۰	[§۸۸:۲]	۸۸
	۳۴	۳۳	[§۹۰:۳۹]	۹۰
	۳۴	۳۷	[§۳۶:۱۶]	۳۶
فَاطِر	۳۵	۱	[§۲۹:۱۲]	۲۹
	۳۵	۱۵	[§۹۵:۱۷]	۹۵
یٰسٓ	۳۶	۲-۱	[§۶۹:۱۳]	۶۹
	۳۶	۳۸	[§۸۰:۹]	۸۰
صٓ	۳۸	۳۹	[§۸۸:۲۵]	۸۸
الزُّمَر	۳۹	۵۳	[§۳۶:۹]	۳۶
غَافِر	۴۰	۴۰	[§۸۸:۱۸]	۸۸
	۴۰	۵۷	[§۱۳:۱۴]	۱۳
	۴۰	۶۷	[§۲۸:۲]	۲۸
	۴۰	۶۷	[§۲۸:۳۲]	۲۸
	۴۰	۸۰-۷۹	[§۳۱:۶]	۳۱
فُصِّلَتْ	۴۱	۱۲	[§۸۰:۹]	۸۰
	۴۱	۲۷	[§۸۸:۲۱]	۸۸
	۴۱	۴۶	[§۸:۱۵]	۸
	۴۱	۵۳	[§۹۲:۶]	۹۲
الشُّورىٰ	۴۲	۹	[§۷۱:۵]	۷۱

نام سورة	شماره سورة	آیت	بند	صف
الشُّورىٰ	۴۲	۲۴	[§۱۱:۹۸]	۹۸
	۴۲	۴۰	[§۲۰:۸۸]	۸۸
الزُّخْرُف	۴۳	۳۲	[§۳۶:۹۲]	۹۲
	۴۳	۶۰	[§۲۲:۴۹]	٤٩
	۴۳	۷۱	[§۱۴:۷]	۷
الدُّخَان	۴۴	۳۸-۳۹	[§۲۰:۸۲]	۸۲
	۴۴	۵۶	[§۲۳:۶۲]	٦٢
الجَاثِيَة	۴۵	۲۱	[§۱۸:۲۶]	۲۶
	۴۵	۲۱	[§۹:۳۸]	۳۸
الأَحْقَاف	۴۶	۱۹	[§۱۱:۷]	۷
مُحَمَّد	۴۷	۷	[§۲۷:۶۶]	۶۶
	۴۷	۲۸	[§۲۹:۷]	۷
	۴۷	۳۸	[§۴:۷۵]	۷۵
الحُجُرَات	۴۹	۸	[§۲:۹]	۹
الذَّارِيَات	۵۱	۴۷-۴۹	[§۸:۹۲]	۹۲
	۵۱	۵۸	[§۲۹:۳۶]	۳۶
القَمَر	۵۴	۵۰	[§۱۲:۵۰]	۵۰
الرَّحْمٰن	۵۵	۶۰	[§۱۴:۸۸]	۸۸
	۵۵	۷۸	[§۱۲:۳۹]	۳۹
الوَاقِعَة	۵۶	۱۹	[§۲۳:۶۲]	۶۲

نام سورة	شماره سورة	آیت	بند	صف
الوَاقِعَة	۵۶	۶۱-۶۲	[۲۵:۹۰§]	۹۰
الحَدِید	۵۷	۲	[۵:۷۱§]	۷۱
	۵۷	۴	[۱۵:۶۱§]	۶۱
	۵۷	۱۸ [۱۱]	[۲۸:۶۶§]	۶۶
الحَشْر	۵۹	۲	[۳:۳۰§]	۳۰
	۵۹	۶	[۲:۹§]	۹
المُمْتَحَنَة	۶۰	۱۰	[۲:۹§]	۹
الصَّفّ	۶۱	۷	[۱۰§]	آغاز
الجُمْعَة	۶۲	۵	[۱۰§]	آغاز
التَّغَابُن	۶۴	۱	[۵:۷۱§]	۷۱
الطَّلَاق	۶۵	۷	[۲۲:۹۵§]	۹۵
التَّحْرِیم	۶۶	۹	[۳۱:۱۷§]	۱۷
المُلْك	۶۷	۱	[۵:۷۱§]	۷۱
	۶۷	۳۰	[۱۲:۲۶§]	۲۶
المَعَارِج	۷۰	۶-۷	[۱۱:۳۸§]	۳۸
	۷۰	۲۴-۲۵	[۱۸:۹۵§]	۹۵
الجِنّ	۷۲	۳	[۱۲:۳۹§]	۳۹
	۷۲	۳	[۴:۵۷§]	۵۷
	۷۲	۲۸	[۱۶:۴۹§]	۴۹

۱۱ نك: پانوشت ۳۶ ذیل همین بند.

نام سورة	شماره سورة	آيت	بند	صف
المُزَّمِّل	٧٣	٢٠	[§٦٦:٢٨]	٦٦ [١٢]
المُدَّثِّر	٧۴	٢۶-٣١	[§٢۶:٩]	٢۶
القِيَامَة	٧۵	٢	[§۶۶:۶]	۶۶
	٧۵	٢٢-٢۵	[§٩٠:۴۴]	٩٠
الإِنْسَان	٧۶	١٣	[§۴١:١٢]	۴١
النَّبَأ	٧٨	١-٣	[§۶٧:١٢]	۶٧
الاِنْفِطَار	٨٢	١٩	[§٩٩:۴۶]	٩٩
الفَجْر	٨٩	٢٧-٣٠	[§١٩:٢٩]	١٩
الضُّحَىٰ	٩٣	۵	[§٧:١۶]	٧
التِّين	٩۵	٨	[§٢۶:١٨]	٢٦
الزَّلْزَلَة	٩٩	٧-٨	[§١٩:١٧]	١٩
القَارِعَة	١٠١	۶-٩	[§٣٠:۶]	٣٠
الهُمَزَة	١٠۴	۴-٧	[§٩:۴٢]	٩
الفَلَق	١١٣	۵	[§۶٣:۶]	۶٣

١٢ قس: سورة الحديد (۵٧)، آيت ١٨.

فهرست احادیث پیامبر[1]

بند	متن حدیث	بیانِ ناصرخسرو
[۸§]	[يَا عَلِيُّ إِنَّكَ قَسِيمُ النَّارِ وَ الْجَنَّةِ][2]	بخششْ کُنِ درکاتِ نیران و درجات جِنان، [علی مرتضی]
[۴:۷§]	أَخَذْتُ مِنَ الخَمْسِ و أَعْطَيْتُ إلى الخَمْسِ.	«بستدم حکمت آلهی را از پنج میانجی، و دادم به پنج میانجی».
[۱۹:۷§]	اَلْمَرْءُ مَعَ مَنْ أَحَبَّ.	«مرد با آن کس است کی او را دوست دارد».
[۹:۸§]	اَلسَّعِيدُ مَنْ سَعِدَ فِي بَطْنِ أُمِّهِ، وَ الشَّقِيُّ مَنْ شَقِيَ فِي بَطْنِ أُمِّهِ.	«نیک بخت آن است کی اندر شکم مادر نیک بخت است؛ و بدبخت آن است که اندر شکم مادر بدبخت شود».
[۱۹:۹§]	اَلدُّنْيَا قَنْطَرَةٌ فَاعْبُرُوهَا وَ لاَ تَعْمُرُوهَا.	«این جهان پلی است بگذرید برو، و آبادان مکنیدش».
[۳۳:۹§]	فَوَ الَّذِي نَفْسُ مُحَمَّدٍ بِيَدِهِ مَا بَعْدَ الْمَوْتِ غَيْرُ الْجَنَّةِ أَوِ النَّارِ.	«و سوگند خورد بدان کس که نفس محمد به دست او است که نیست پس از مرگ جز بهشت یا آتش».

۱ برای مآخذ احادیث پیامبر (ص)، نک: پانوشت‌های هر یک از بندها.

۲ نک: الصفّار، محمد بن الحسن، بصائر الدرجات في فضائل آل محمد (ص)، التحقيق والتصحيح: محسن کوچه باغي التبريزى (قم، مكتبة آية الله المرعشي النجفي، ۱۴۰۴ق)، الجزء الثامن، باب ۱۸: في اميرالمؤمنين (ع) أنّه قسيم الجنة والنار، ص ۴۱۴ تا ۴۱۸.

بند	متن حدیث	بیانِ ناصرخسرو
[۲:۱۱§]	مَنْ سَنَّ سُنَّةً حَسَنَةً فلَهُ أَجْرُهَا وَ أَجْرِ مَنْ عَمِلَ بِهَا إِلَىٰ يَوْمِ الْقِيَـٰمَةِ مِنْ غَيْرِ أَنْ يَنْقُصَ مِنْ أَجرِهِمْ شَيْئًا وَ مَنْ سَنَّ سُنَّةً سَيِّئَةً فلَهُ وِزْرُهَا وَ وِزْرِ مَنْ عَمِلَ بِهَا إِلَىٰ يَوْمِ الْقِيَـٰمَةِ مِنْ غَيْرِ أَنْ يَنْقُصَ مِنْ وِزْرِهِمْ شَيْءٌ.	«هرکه سنّتی نیکو بنهد او را باشد مزد آن و مزد آنك بدان سنّت کار کند تا روز قیامت، بی آنك از مزد آن کس‌ها چیزی کم شود. و هر که سنّتی بد نهد او را باشد بزه آن و بزه هر که بدان سنّت کار کند تا روز قیامت، بی آنك از بزه آن کس‌ها چیزی کم شود».
[۸:۱۷§]	لا تَزنُوا فتَزنُوا نساءكم.	«زنا مکنید کی با زنان خویش زنا کرده باشید».
[۵:۲۸§]	أَوَّلَ ما خَلَقَ اللّٰهُ تعالى اَلْعَقْلُ فَقَالَ لَهُ أَقْبِلْ فَأَقْبَلَ ثُمَّ قَالَ لَهُ أَدْبِرْ فَأَدْبَرَ فَقَالَ وَ عِزَّتِي وَ جَلَالِي مَا خَلَقْتُ خَلْقاً أعِزُّ عليَّ مِنْكَ بِكَ أُثِيبُ وَ بِكَ أُعَاقِبُ.	«نخستین چیزی که خدای بیافرید عقل بود. مر او را گفت پیش آی پیش آمد؛ پس گفت بازپس شو بازپس شد. پس خدای تعالی سوگند یاد کرد به عزّ و جلال خویش که چیزی نیافریدم گرامی‌تر بر من از تو. به تو ثواب دهم و به تو عقاب کنم».
[۱۶:۳۳§]	[(يَقُولُ اللّٰهُ تَعَالَى أَعْدَدْتُ لِعِبَادِي الصَّالِحِينَ) مَا لاَ عَيْنٌ رَأَتْ، وَلاَ أُذُنٌ سَمِعَتْ، وَ لاَ خَطَرَ عَلَى قَلْبِ بَشَرٍ.][۳]	«هیچ چشم چنان ندیده است و نه هیچ گوش صفت او شنیده است و نه بر دل هیچ مردم آن گذشته است».
[۷:۳۶§]	المعترف بالذّنب كمن لاذنب له و المُصِرُّ على الذنب كالمستهزى بربّه.	«هرکه خستو شود به گناه خویش همچون کسی است کی او را گناه نیست؛ و هر که بر گناه بایستد چون کسی باشد که بر پروردگار خویش افسوس کند».

۳ در اینجا مؤلف تنها ترجمهٔ فارسی بخشی از حدیث پیامبر (ص) را آورده است.

بند	متن حدیث	بیانِ ناصرخسرو
[۱۳:۳۶§]	النيّةُ الحسنةُ جُنّةٌ حِصِينَةٌ.	«نیّتِ نیکو سپری استوار است».
[۱۴:۴۱§]	هواءٌ سَجْسَجٌ، مثل بَرد السَّحَر.	«هوای بهشت میانه است نه سرد است و نه گرم همچون خنکی سپیده دم».
[۴:۵۳§]	النَّاسُ عَالِمٌ أو مُتَعَلِّمٌ (أو مُسْتَمِعٌ) وَ سَائِرُ النَّاسِ هَمَجٌ.	«مردمان بجملگی دانش دهنده‌ای است و دانش‌پذیری و دیگر مردم خُرسان است».
[۷:۶۷§]	بَيْنِي و بَيْنَ رَبِّي خمس وسايط: جبرئيل و ميكائيل و اسرافيل و اللّوح و القلم.	«میان من و میان پروردگار من پنج میانجی است: جبرئیل و میکائیل و اسرافیل و لوح و قلم».
[۱۸:۸۲§]	لِكُلِّ حَقٍّ حَقيقَةٌ.	«هر حقی را حقیقتی است».
[۷:۹۲§]	سَيُكْذَبُ عليَّ [كـ]ما كُذِبَ على الأنبياءِ من قبلى. فماجاءكم مني ما يخالف كتاب الله لم اقدرْ و كيف أخالف كتاب الله و به اهتدَيتُ.	«سرانجام بر من دروغ گویند همچنانک دروغ گفتند بر پیمبران که پیش از من بودند. پس آنچ بیاید به شما از خبر من کی مر کتاب خدای را مخالف باشد آن نه من گفته‌ام و چگونه مخالف شوم مر کتاب خدای را و راه راست بدان یافتم».
[۲۶:۹۲§]	أنا و أنتَ يا علي أبوا هذه الأُمّة لَعَنَ الله مَن عَقَّ والِدَيهُ.	«من و تو یا علی پدر و مادر این امّتیم دور کناد خدای آن را کی بیازارد پدر و مادر خویش را».
[۱۷:۹۸§]	التَّائِبُ مِن الذَّنْبِ كَمَنْ لَا ذَنْبَ لَهُ.	«بازگردنده از گناه چون آن کس است کی او را هیچ گناه نیست».

فهرست آیات کتاب مقدس: کتب عهد قدیم (توریت) و عهد جدید (انجیل)

بند	کتاب و شمارهٔ آیات	متن آیات
[§۱۱:۲۲]	توریت سِفْرِ خروج (۳): ۲ تا ۶	۲-و فرشتهٔ خداوند در شعلهٔ آتش از میان بوتهٔ بر وی ظاهر شد و چون او نگریست اینک آن بوته بآتش مشتعلست امّا سوخته نمیشود. ۳-و موسی گفت اکنون بدان طرف شوم و این امر غریب را به بینم که بوته چرا سوخته نمیشود. ۴-چون خداوند دید که برای دیدن مایل بدآنسو میشود خدا از میان بوته بوی ندا درداد و گفت ایموسی! ای موسی! گفت لبیّک. ۵-گفت بدین جا نزدیک میآ نعلین خود را از پایهایت بیرون کن زیرا مکانیکه در آن ایستادهٔ زمین مُقدَّس است. ۶-و گفت من هستم خدای پدرت خدای ابراهیم و خدای اسحاق و خدای یعقوب آنگاه موسی روی خود را پوشانید زیرا ترسید که بخدا بنگرد.[1]
[§۳۲:۱۷]	توریت سِفْرِ لاویان (۲۴): ۱۹ تا ۲۱	۱۹-و کسیکه همسایهٔ خود را عیب رسانیده باشد چنانکه او کرده باشد باو کرده خواهد شد. ۲۰-شکستگی عوض شکستگی چشم عوض چشم دندان عوض دندان چنانکه بآن شخص عیب رسانیده همچنان باو رسانیده شود. ۲۱-و کسیکه بهیمهٔ را کشت عوض آن را بدهد امّا کسیکه انسانرا کشت، کشته شود.[2]
[§۳۳:۶۶]	انجیلِ مَتّیٰ (۲۵): ۳۲ تا ۳۶	[۳۲] کی ایزد مر خلق را به قیامت گرد کند. نیکان و بدان را بیك جای [...] [۳۴] و مر نیکان را گوید که نیك کردید بجای من [...] [۳۵] گرسنه بودم مرا سیر کردید. [...] [۳۶] برهنه بودم مرا پوشیده کردید. بازداشته بودم مرا رها کردید.
[§۳۴:۶۶]	انجیلِ مَتّیٰ (۲۵): ۳۷ تا ۳۹	[۳۷] جواب دهند نیکان مر او را، گویند: ربّنا تو کی گرسنه بودی تا ما ترا سیر کردیم، یا تشنه بودی تا ترا سیراب کردیم، [۳۸] [...] یا برهنه بودی تا ترا بپوشیدیم، [۳۹] [...] یا بازداشته بودی کی ما ترا رها کردیم؟
[§۳۵:۶۶]	انجیلِ مَتّیٰ (۲۵): ۴۰	[۴۰] ایزد تعالی گوید ایشان را کی راست همی‌گویید و لکن هر چه به نفسهای خویش کردید بجای من کردید.

۱ مفهوم این آیات از کتاب مقدس در بند مذکور با اشاره قرآن به محتوای این آیات آمده است.

۲ همان.

بند	کتاب و شمارهٔ آیات	متن آیات
[§۶۶:۳۶]	انجیلِ مَتّیٰ (۲۵): ۴۱ تا ۴۳	[۴۱] پس بگوید مر بدکرداران را که بد کردید بجای من [...] [۴۲] گرسنه بودم مرا سیر نکردید، تشنه بودم مرا آب ندادید، [۴۳] [...] برهنه بودم مرا نپوشیدید، بازداشته بودم مرا رها نکردید.
[§۶۶:۳۷]	انجیلِ مَتّیٰ (۲۵): ۴۴	[۴۴] جواب دهند بدکرداران و گویند ربّنا تو کی گرسنه بودی که ما ترا سیر نکردیم، و کی تشنه بودی که ترا آب ندادیم، و کی برهنه بودی که ترا نپوشیدیم، و کی بازداشته بودی که ترا رها نکردیم؟
[§۶۶:۳۸]	انجیلِ مَتّیٰ (۲۵): ۴۵	[۴۵] ایزد تعالی مر ایشان را گوید راست همی‌گویید و لکن هر چه بجای نفس خویش کردید بجای من کردید.[۳]

۳ نک: کتاب مقدس: کتب عهد عتیق و عهد جدید، انجیلِ مَتّیٰ (باب ۲۵)، ص ۴۴ تا ۴۵، آیات ۳۱ تا ۴۶: ۳۱–امّا چون پسر انسان در جلال خود با جمیع ملائـکهٔ مُقدَّس خویش آید آنگاه بر کرسئ جلال خود خواهد نشست، ۳۲–و جمیع امّتها در حضور او جمع شوند و آنها را از همدیگر جدا میکند، بقسمیکه شبان میشها را از بزها جدا میکند. ۳۳–و میشها را بر دست راست و بزها را بر چپ خود قرار دهد. ۳۴–آنگاه پادشاه به اصحاب طرف راست گوید بیائید ای برکت یافتگان از پدر من و ملکوتی را که از ابتدای عالم برای شما آماده شده است بمیراث گیرید. ۳۵–زیرا چون گرسنه بودم مرا طعام دادید، تشنه بودم سیرآبم نمودید غریب بودم مرا جا دادید ۳۶–عریان بودم مرا پوشانیدید، مریض بودم عیادتم کردید، در حبس بودم دیدن من آمدید. ۳۷–آنگاه عادلان بپاسخ گویند، ای خداوند، کی گرسنه‌ات دیدیم تا طعامت دهیم یا تشنه‌ات یافتیم تا سیرآبت نمائیم ۳۸–یا کی ترا غریب یافتیم تا ترا جا دهیم یا عریان تا بپوشانیم ۳۹–و کی ترا مریض یا محبوس یافتیم تا عیادتت کنیم؟ ۴۰–پادشاه در جواب ایشان گوید هرآینه بشما میگویم آنچه بیکی از این برادران کوچک‌ترین من کردید، بمن کرده‌اید.
۴۱–پس اصحاب طرف چپ را گوید، ای ملعونان، از من دور شوید در آتش جاودانی که برای ابلیس و فرشتگان او مهیّا شده است. ۴۲–زیرا گرسنه بودم مرا خوراک ندادید، تشنه بودم مرا آب ندادید ۴۳–غریب بودم مرا جا ندادید، عریان بودم مرا نپوشانیدید، مریض و محبوس بودم عیادتم ننمودید. ۴۴–پس ایشان نیز بپاسخ گویند ایخداوند کی ترا گرسنه یا تشنه یا غریب یا برهنه یا مریض یا محبوس دیده خدمتت نکردیم؟ ۴۵–آنگاه در جواب ایشان گوید هرآینه به شما میگویم آنچه بیکی ازین کوچکان نکردید بمن نکرده‌اید. ۴۶–و ایشان در عذاب جاودانی خواهند رفت، امّا عادلان در حیات جاودانی.

فهرست مآخذ و منابع

ابن بابویه، محمد بن علی، **الخصال**، تصحیح: علی اکبر غفاری (قم، ۱۴۰۳ق/۱۳۶۲ش).

ابن سینا، حسین بن عبدالله، **الٰهیّات دانشنامهٔ علائی**، تصحیح: محمّد معین (همدان: دانشگاه بوعلی‌سینا، ۱۳۸۳ش).

———، **طبیعیّات دانشنامهٔ علائی**، تصحیح: سیّد محمّد مشکوة (همدان: دانشگاه بوعلی‌سینا، ۱۳۸۳ش).

———، **رسالهٔ منطق دانشنامهٔ علائی**، تصحیح: محمّد معین و سیّد محمّد مشکوة (همدان: دانشگاه بوعلی‌سینا، ۱۳۸۳ش).

ابن حنبل، احمد، **مسند الإمام احمد بن حنبل**، ۱۲ مجلد (قاهره: دار ابن‌الجوزی، ۱۴۳۷ق/۲۰۱۶م).

ابن عساکر، علی بن الحسن، **تاریخ مدینة الدمشق**، به‌اهتمام: عمر بن غرامة العمروي (بیروت: دار الفکر، ۱۴۱۶ق/۱۹۹۶م).

ابن عقدة الکوفي، احمد بن محمد، **فضائل امیرالمؤمنین (علیه السّلام)**، به‌اهتمام: عبدالرزاق محمد حسین حرزالدین (قم، ۱۴۲۴ق/۱۳۸۲ش).

ابو معاش، سعید، **فضائل امیرالمؤمنین الإمام علی بن ابی‌طالب (علیه السّلام) في القرآن الکریم** (قم: دارالمودة، ۱۴۳۲ق).

انوری، حسن، **فرهنگ بزرگ سخن**، ۸ مجلد (تهران: سخن، ۱۳۸۱ش).

البخاری، محمد بن اسماعیل، **صحیح البخاری** (دمشق-بیروت: دار ابن‌کثیر، ۱۴۲۳ق/۲۰۰۲م).

البرقي، احمد بن محمد، **المحاسن**، تصحیح: جلال الدین الحسینی المحدث (قم: دار الکتب الإسلامیة، ۱۳۷۱ق).

دهخدا، علی اکبر، **لغت‌نامهٔ دهخدا**، دورهٔ کامل در ۱۶ مجلد، مؤسسه لغت‌نامهٔ دهخدا، زیر نظر: دکتر محمّد معین و دکتر سیّد جعفر شهیدی (تا آذرماه ۱۳۴۵) (تهران: انتشارات دانشگاه تهران، ۱۳۷۷ش/۱۹۹۸م).

السجستاني، ابویعقوب اسحاق بن احمد، **إثبات النّبوات**، به‌اهتمام: ویلفرد مادلونگ، و پال واکر (تهران: مك‌گیل و کتاب رایزن، ۱۳۹۵ش/۲۰۱۶م).

———، **کتاب الإفتخار**، به‌اهتمام: اسماعیل ق. ح. پوناوالا (بیروت: دار الغرب الإسلامي، ۲۰۰۰م).

———، «**کتاب الینابیع**»، در **ایران و یمن - سه رسالهٔ اسماعیلی: ۱- کتاب الینابیع از ابو یعقوب سجستانی.- ۲- رسالة المبدأ والمعاد از سیدنا الحسین بن علی.- ۳- بعضی از تأویلات گلشن راز**، تصحیح و ترجمه و شرح فرانسوی: هنری کربین، گنجینهٔ نوشته‌های ایرانی (۹) (تهران: انستیتو ایران و فرانسه، ۱۳۴۰ش/۱۹۶۱م).

———، **کشف المحجوب**، رساله در آئین اسماعیلی از قرن چهارم هجری، تحقیق و مقدمه بزبان فرانسوی: هنری کربین، گنجینهٔ نوشته‌های ایرانی (۱) (تهران: انستیتو ایران و فرانسه، ۱۳۲۷ش/۱۹۴۹م).

الشیخ المفید، محمد بن محمد بن النعمان، **الأمالي**، تصحیح: علی اکبر غفاری (قم، ۱۴۰۳ق/۱۳۶۲ش).

الصفّار، محمد بن الحسن، **بصائر الدرجات في فضائل آل محمد (ص)**، تصحیح: محسن کوچه باغي التبریزی (قم، مکتبة آیة الله المرعشي النجفي، ۱۴۰۴ق).

الطوسی، نصیرالدین، **اخلاق محتشمی**، با سه رسالهٔ دیگر منسوب به او، با دیباچه و تصحیح محمّد تقی دانش‌پژوه، چاپ سوم (تهران: انتشارات و چاپ دانشگاه تهران، ۱۳۷۷ ش).

الفتّال النيسابوري، محمد بن احمد، **روضة الواعظين و بصيرة المُتَّعِظين** (قم: انتشارات رضی، ۱۳۷۵ش).

القمی، علی ابن ابراهیم، **تفسیر القمی**، تصحیح: السید طیب الموسوی الجزائری (قم، ۱۴۰۴ق).

کتاب مقدس: کتب عهد عتیق و عهد جدید، ترجمه از زبانهای اصلی عبرانی و کلدانی و یونانی، بریتش و فورِن بَیبَل سوسائیتیٔ (جماعت بریتانیایی و خارجی انجیل مقدّس) دار السّلطنهٔ لندن (لندن، ۱۸۹۵م).

الکلینی، محمد بن یعقوب، **الكافي**، تصحیح: علی اکبر غفاری و محمد آخوندی (تهران، ۱۴۰۷ق).

مادلونگ، ویلفرد، '**ابویعقوب السجستاني و تناسخ**'، **ایرانیکا واریا: مقالات در بزرگداشت پروفسور احسان یارشاطر** (لیدن، ۱۹۹۰)، ص ۱۳۱ تا ۱۴۳.[1]

المجلسی، محمّد باقر، **بِحار الأنوار**، تصحیح: س. ا. المیانجی و م. ب. البهبودی (بیروت: دار إحياء التراث العربي، ۱۴۰۳ق/۱۹۸۳م).

محقّق ترمذی، سیّد برهان الدین، **معارف: مجموعهٔ مواعظ و کلمات سیّد برهان الدّین محقّق ترمذی**، با تصحیحات و حواشی: بدیع‌الزّمان فروزانفر (تهران، ۱۳۳۹\ا چاپ دوم ۱۳۷۷).

مصباح الشريعة المنسوب للإمام الصادق (عليه السّلام) (بیروت: اعلمی، ۱۴۰۰ق).

معین، محمد، **فرهنگ فارسی معین**، دوره دو جلدی (تهران: آدانا: کتاب راه‌نو، ۱۳۸۱ش).

الملیجی، ابوالقاسم عبد الحاکم بن وهب، **المجالس المستَنصِريّة**، تحقیق: محمّد کامِل حسَین، سلسلة مخطوطات الفاطمیّین، ۱ (قاهرة: دارالفکر العربي، [۱۹۴۷]).

مولانا، جلال الدین محمّد بلخی، **مثنوی معنوی**، به‌اهتمام: رینولد آلّین نیکُلسون، دورهٔ کامل ۳ جلدی (حاوی شش دفتر) (لیدن: بریل، ۱۹۲۵م).

المؤیَّد في الدین الشیرازی، ابو نصر هبّة الله بن أبی عمران موسی، **المجالس المؤیّدیّة، المِائَة الأولی**، تحقیق و تقدیم: مصطفی غالب، سلسلة التراث الفاطمی (بیروت: دارالأندلس، ۱۹۷۴).

المیبدی، ابوالفضل رشیدالدین، **کشف الأسرار و عُدَّة الأبرار**: (معروف به **تفسیر خواجه عبدالله انصاری**)، به‌اهتمام: علی اصغر حکمت، ۱۰ مجلد (تهران، ۱۳۸۲ش)

ناصرخسرو، ابومعین حمید الدین، **دیوان اشعار حکیم ناصرخسرو قبادیانی**، به‌اهتمام: نصرالله تقوی (تهران: مطبعهٔ مجلس، ۱۳۰۷ش/۱۹۲۸م).

———، **جامع الحکمتین**، تصحیح و مقدمهٔ فارسی و فرانسوی: هنری کُربین و محمّد معین، گنجینهٔ نوشته‌های ایرانی (۳)، چاپ دوم (تهران: انستیتو ایران و فرانسه، ۱۳۶۳ش/۱۹۸۴م).

———، «**رساله در جواب ۹۱ فقره اسئله**»، در **دیوان اشعار حکیم ناصرخسرو قبادیانی**، به‌اهتمام: نصرالله تقوی (تهران: مطبعهٔ مجلس، ۱۳۰۷ش/۱۹۲۸م)، ص ۵۶۲ تا ۵۸۳.

———، **روشنائی نامه (شش فصل)**، تصحیح و ترجمه و مقدمهٔ انگلیسی ولادیمر ایوانف (لیدن: بریل، ۱۹۴۹م).

———، **زاد المسافر**، به‌اهتمام: اسماعیل عمادی حائری، ویراست ۲ (تهران: میراث مکتوب، ۱۳۹۳ش/۲۰۱۴م).

---

۱ نك:
Madelung, Wilferd, 'Abu Ya'qub al-Sijistani and Metempsychosis', *Iranica Varia: Papers in Honor of Professor Ehsan Yarshater* (Leiden, 1990), pp. 131-143.

———، **زادالمسافرین**، به‌اهتمام: محمّد بذل الرحمٰن (برلین: کاویانی، ۱۳۴۱ق/۱۹۲۳م).

———، **سفرنامه**، تصحیح و ترجمه انگلیسی: و.م. تاکستون[۲] (کوستا مِسا، کالیفورنیا: انتشارات مزدا، ۲۰۰۱م).

———، **گشایش و رهایش**، تصحیح و ترجمه و مقدمهٔ انگلیسی: فقیر محمّد هونزائی و پرویز مُرَوَّج (لندن، ۱۹۹۸م).

———، **وجه دین**، به‌اهتمام: غلامرضا اعوانی (تهران، ۱۳۹۸ق/۱۹۷۷م).

النعمان بن محمّد، القاضي ابوحنیفه، **اساس التأویل**، تصحیح: عارف تامر (بیروت، ۱۹۶۰م).

———، **شرح الأخبار في فضائل الأئمة الأطهار**، تحقیق: السیّد محمّد الحسینيّ الجلالي، ۳ مجلد (قم، ۱۴۳۱ق).

دی واکس، ب. کاررا،[۳] «**الصابِئَة**»، در **دائرة المعارف اسلام ویرایش نخست**، ۴ مجلد (لیدن: بریل، ۱۹۳۴م)، ج ۴، ص ۲۱ تا ۲۲.

۲ W. M. Thackston

۳ B. Carra de vaux

نمایهٔ اسامی، عبارات، و لغات و اصطلاحات